Relational Psychoanalysis
The Emergence of a Tradition

RELATIONAL PERSPECTIVES BOOK SERIES

Volume 14

RELATIONAL PERSPECTIVES BOOK SERIES

STEPHEN A. MITCHELL AND LEWIS ARON
Series Editors

In Preparation

Relational Psychoanalysis
The Emergence of a Tradition

edited by
Stephen A. Mitchell
Lewis Aron

THE ANALYTIC PRESS

1999   Hillsdale, NJ   London

Published by The Analytic Press, Inc.
101 West Street, Hillsdale, NJ 07642
www.analyticpress.com

Relational Psychoanalysis: The Emergence of a Tradition
edited by Stephen A. Mitchell and Lewis Aron
ISBN 0-88163-270-8

Text set in Adobe Sabon 10/12 by Compudesign, Rego Park, NY

Printed in the United State of America

10 9 8 7 6 5 4 3 2 1

*For our friends, students, and colleagues
in the relational community.
And with appreciation to the three institutions
in which this community has evolved:
The Division of Psychoanalysis (39) of the
American Psychological Association, Psychoanalytic Dialogues,
and the Relational Track of the New York University
Postdoctoral Program in Psychotherapy and Psychoanalysis.*

Contributors

Lewis Aron, Ph.D. (Editor)—Director, New York University Postdoctoral Program in Psychotherapy and Psychoanalysis; Coeditor, *Psychoanalytic Dialogues*; Past-President, Division of Psychoanalysis (39), American Psychological Association.

George E. Atwood, Ph.D.—Founding Faculty, Institute for the Psychoanalytic Study of Subjectivity, New York City; Professor of Psychology, Rutgers University.

Jessica Benjamin, Ph.D.—Faculty, New York University Postdoctoral Program in Psychotherapy and Psychoanalysis and the Psychoanalytic Studies Program of the New School for Social Research; editorial board, *Psychoanalytic Dialogues*; Associate Editor, *Studies in Gender and Sexuality*.

Philip M. Bromberg, Ph.D.—Training and Supervising Analyst and Faculty, William Alanson White Psychoanalytic Institute; Clinical Professor of Psychology, New York University Postdoctoral Program in Psychotherapy and Psychoanalysis; Associate Editor, *Psychoanalytic Dialogues*.

Nancy J. Chodorow, Ph.D.—Faculty, San Francisco Psychoanalytic Institute; Professor of Sociology, University of California, Berkeley; and member of editorial boards, *International Journal of Psycho-Analysis* and *Studies in Gender and Sexuality*.

Jody Messler Davies, Ph.D.—Supervising Analyst and Cochair, Relational Track, New York University Postdoctoral Program in Psychotherapy and Psychoanalysis; Faculty and Supervisor, National Institute for the Psychotherapies; Coeditor, *Psychoanalytic Dialogues*.

Michael Eigen, Ph.D.—Senior Faculty and Control/Training Analyst, National Psychological Association for Psychoanalysis; Faculty and Supervisor, New York University Postdoctoral Program in Psychotherapy and Psychoanalysis.

Mary Gail Frawley-O'Dea, Ph.D.—Clinical Professor and Supervisor, Derner Institute, Adelphi University; Faculty, Minnesota Institute for Contemporary Psychoanalysis; Continuing Education Faculty, National Psychological Association for Psychoanalysis.

Emmanuel Ghent, M.D.—Adjunct Professor of Psychology and Supervisor, New York University Postdoctoral Program in Psychotherapy and Psychoanalysis; Faculty and Supervising Analyst, William Alanson White Institute; Associate Editor, *Psychoanalytic Dialogues*.

Jay R. Greenberg, Ph.D.—Training and Supervising Analyst, William Alanson White Institute; Faculty and Supervising Analyst, New York University Postdoctoral Program in Psychotherapy and Psychoanalysis; Editor, *Contemporary Psychoanalysis*.

Adrienne Harris, Ph.D.—Faculty and Supervisor, New York University Postdoctoral Program in Psychotherapy and Psychoanalysis; Associate Editor, *Psychoanalytic Dialogues* and *Studies in Gender and Sexuality*.

Irwin Z. Hoffman, Ph.D.—Supervising Analyst and Faculty, Chicago Center for Psychoanalysis; Lecturer in Psychiatry, University of Illinois College of Medicine; editorial boards, *Psychoanalytic Dialogues* and *International Journal of Psycho-Analysis*.

Stephen A. Mitchell, Ph.D. (Editor)—Training and Supervising Analyst, William Alanson White Institute; Faculty, New York University Postdoctoral Program in Psychotherapy and Psychoanalysis; Coeditor, *Psychoanalytic Dialogues*.

Thomas H. Ogden, M.D.—Co-director, the Center for the Advanced Study of the Psychoses; Supervising and Training Analyst, Psychoanalytic Institute of Northern California; Faculty, San Francisco Psychoanalytic Institute.

Stuart A. Pizer, Ph.D.—Supervising Analyst and Faculty, Massachusetts Institute for Psychoanalysis; Faculty, Psychoanalytic Institute of Northern California, San Francisco; Clinical Instructor in Psychology, Harvard Medical School; Contributing Editor, *Psychoanalytic Dialogues*.

Owen Renik, M.D.—Training and Supervising Analyst, San Francisco Psychoanalytic Institute; Editor-in-Chief, *Psychoanalytic Quarterly*; Chairman, Program Committee, American Psychoanalytic Association.

Charles Spezzano, Ph.D.—Training and Supervising Analyst, Psychoanalytic Institute of Northern California; Contributing Editor, *Psychoanalytic Dialogues*.

Donnel B. Stern, Ph.D.—Supervising Analyst and Faculty, William Alanson White Institute, Manhattan Institute of Psychoanalysis, Institute for Contemporary Psychotherapy.

Robert D. Stolorow, Ph.D.—Faculty, Training and Supervising Analyst, Institute of Contemporary Psychoanalysis, Los Angeles; Faculty, Institute for the Psychoanalytic Study of Subjectivity; Clinical Professor of Psychiatry, UCLA School of Medicine.

Contents

Preface

Traditions cannot be founded or self-consciously created; they can only be retrospectively, self-reflectively discovered. Something works well or was exciting, or felt good, and you want to do it again. People become aware that they have been doing certain things the same way, planning activities, using concepts, over and over again. After a while, a sense of tradition accrues to events or approaches: an annual dinner; a form of celebration of a particular holiday; and certain concepts or ways of thinking, like evoking common heroes or heroines, retelling old stories, or sharing time-proven approaches to new problems. Traditions become meaningful when they add a richness and vitality to experience. Some repetitions are merely lifeless perseverations. But meaningful traditions become touchstones, adding a depth and sense of connectedness that helps generate fresh thoughts and feelings.

Traditions in Psychoanalysis

Psychoanalysis contains many multifaceted traditions, both clinical and conceptual. A psychoanalysis that does not draw on basic features of Freud's thought and practice would be virtually unrecognizable as psychoanalysis—thinking about mind in terms of unconscious processes; exploring the dialectic between present and past; grounding states of mind in bodily experiences; a careful, patient listening to the analysand's associations; a play in the dialectic between fantasy and reality; the focus on feelings about the analyst (transference) and psychical obstacles to uncomfortable thoughts and feelings (resistance).

In addition to this shared tradition, psychoanalysis has developed, over the course of its century-long history, an array of more circum-scribed traditions, sometimes emerging in the wake of the writings of a single individual (like Kleinian psychoanalysis and Melanie Klein, or self psychology and Kohut) and sometimes taking on a particular national/cultural cast (like French psychoanalysis in both its Lacanian and its more traditional Freudian forms, and American ego psychology, and British object relations theory). These variant forms of psychoanalysis are sometimes described as "schools," but they have actually emerged in a much less formal and systematic fashion than is suggested by that term. Literal schools are, in fact, founded; psychoanalytic "schools" have emerged as traditions within traditions. Sometimes they emerge around concepts of a particular author (e.g., Klein's notions of internal and part-objects; Kohut's concept of developmentally enhancing narcissism or empathy). Sometimes concepts have a particular saliency within one country and seem to catch a national sensibility (like Lacan's elusive abstractness and metaphysically oriented French intellectuality, or Hartmann's emphasis on adaptation, or Sullivan's vision of an interpersonal "field" and American pragmatism). These chords, once struck, slowly become both anchoring and inspirational for clinicians and subsequent writers who return to them again and again in their own thinking and writing. Thus are new psychoanalytic traditions born.

A Relational Tradition

Over the past two decades, a distinctly new tradition, generally associated with the term relational psychoanalysis has emerged within American psychoanalysis through a convergence of a number of important factors.

Interpersonal psychoanalysis had had a largely invisible presence on the American psychoanalytic scene for several decades. Its major theoretical founders, Harry Stack Sullivan, Erich Fromm, and Clara Thompson, made important contributions during the 1930s and 1940s. Their major concepts were loosely assembled into a multifaceted tradition by Thompson and institutionalized through the Washington School of Psychiatry and the William Alanson White Institute. But interpersonal theorists, in their dialectical swing away from classical intrapsychic theory, tended to deemphasize the internal world and internal psychic structures. This deemphasis made interpersonal psychoanalysis easy to dismiss by adherents of more traditional forms of psychoanalytic thought. Although interpersonal theory contained within it the seeds of an intrapsychic theorizing different from the Freudian structural model based on drive theory, those seeds had yet to germinate.

Object relations theory had begun to have a presence in the United States in the 1970s, with Guntrip's popularization of Fairbairn's contributions and the growing impact of Winnicott's work. Klein's theory was still stigmatized at the time, branded as anathema by American Freudian ego psychology; but some of Klein's major concepts were beginning to find an interested audience here. Bowlby's work had also begun to have an impact, spawning what was to become a remarkable, highly influential research tradition, but not within psychoanalysis proper. Object relations theory, then, seemed to be a cluster of largely unrelated theoretical innovations. As departures from traditional Freudian intrapsychic theorizing, they had implications for emphasizing actual relationships with significant others.

It was in the late 1970s that Kohut's (1977, 1984) work on narcissism broke off from the American ego psychology that had housed its beginnings and broadened into self psychology proper. Self psychology had a powerful presence within American psychoanalysis in two different respects: self psychology became a distinct school unto itself, with devoted adherents and a comprehensive theoretical and clinical framework, and self psychology operated as a more general sensibility that has influenced the thinking and clinical practice of analysts of virtually all other persuasions.

Finally, it was in the late 1970s and early 1980s that a distinctively American brand of psychoanalytic feminism began to make its presence felt. Because feminism, like psychoanalysis, has dealt centrally with issues of sex and gender, and because sex and gender are so closely related to social forces of various kinds, the brand of feminism that has developed in any locale tends—like the various traditions of psychoanalysis that have developed regionally—to reflect a strongly national/cultural cast. American psychoanalytic-feminism of the 1970s was very much influenced by the thinking of Dorothy Dinnerstein and Nancy Chodorow and the pathbreaking work of Carol Gilligan on moral development, and culminated in the distinctly American psychoanalytic feminism of Jessica Benjamin and her colleagues (especially the contributions of Virginia Goldner, Adrienne Harris, and Muriel Dimen). This group has led the way toward a distinctively American psychoanalytic feminism and feminist-psychoanalysis, jointly influenced by the relational traditions and a deep commitment to social criticism.

It was out of this rich mix of influences that relational psychoanalysis developed. Greenberg and Mitchell (1983) used the term relational pointedly to bridge the traditions of interpersonal *relations*, as developed within interpersonal psychoanalysis and object *relations*, as developed within contemporary British theorizing. But the term grew and began to accrue to itself many other influences and developments: later advances of self psychology, particularly intersubjecivity theory; social constructivism in its various forms; certain currents within contemporary psychoanalytic hermeneutics; more recent developments in gender theorizing: the important contributions of Merton Gill on the centrality of transference-countertransference interaction; and, with the English translation in 1988 of his *Clinical Diary*, the rediscovered legacy of Sándor Ferenczi. The growth of relational psychoanalysis was institutionally greatly enhanced by the emergence of Division 39 (Psychoanalysis) of the American Psychological Association as a national center of gravity and natural community for psychoanalysis outside the top-down control of the American Psychoanalytic Association; the "relational track" at New York University's Postdoctoral Program, in Psychotherapy and Psychoanalysis, the first specifically designed relational curriculum; and *Psychoanalytic Dialogues: A Journal of Relational Perspectives*, which has provided a forum for the development of comparative psychoanalysis in general and relational theorizing in particular.

Thus, since the mid-1990s, a relational tradition has emerged within American psychoanalysis with a particular set of concerns, concepts, approaches, and sensibilities. It operates as a shared subculture within the more general psychoanalytic culture, not by design, but because it has struck deep, common chords among current clinical practitioners and theorists in this country.

Looking Back

This book has two purposes, one retrospective, one prospective.

It seems appropriate at this time to look back and reflect on the emergence of the relational tradition within psychoanalysis. Where did we come from and how did we get here? What were some of the key ideas, the influential papers, the seminal perspectives that created the bridges that opened avenues for specifically relational theoretical and clinical innovation? Our hope is that these papers will be helpful to students who are becoming interested in psychoanalysis in the early years of the 21st century.

We chose authors whose work has been most frequently cited, generally approvingly, within relational circles but often disapprovingly by critics of relational positions. We tried to select early papers in the contributions of each author, papers that caught the emergence of new ideas that were later to undergo development and cross-fertilization with the work of other authors. We introduce each paper with a brief introduction, to set it in historical context and highlight its significance in the history of relational psychoanalytic ideas. (Aron's paper is introduced by Mitchell, and Mitchell's by Aron.) We also invited the authors to write brief afterwords to note important subsequent developments in their own thought.

The choices were, necessarily, brutally selective. Many of these authors have written numerous books. What we are after is not comprehensiveness, but the emergence and development of lines of thought that were to become influential and generative of subsequent work. Space allowing, many other authors could have, and should have, been included. The choices here, of course, reflect our own values and priorities. History writing and anthologizing, like everything else we do, draw on deeply subjective currents. Our regrets about authors and papers we were not able to include are somewhat assuaged by the anticipation of subsequent volumes that might track future developments in the relational psychoanalytic tradition.

As every psychoanalyst knows, understanding the past serves both retrospective and also prospective purposes. The exploration of history is often helpful in shedding light on current controversies and in generating ideas about where we need to go. Two of the most hotly debated issues in recent years concern the interface between relational psychoanalysis and classical psychoanalytic drive/defense theory on one hand, and contemporary social constructivism on the other. We have both written extensively on these questions (see, especially, Mitchell, 1988, chapters 1 and 2; 1993, chapters 3 and 4; 1997, chapters 7 and 8; Aron, 1996, chapters 1 and 2; and Aron's Introduction, Aron and Anderson, 1998). But because one's position on these issues has enormous importance in the way the "relational" tradition is defined, including the selection and contextualizing of key papers, we thought it best to note our own views on them up front.

Relational Psychoanalysis and Classical Theory

Greenberg and Mitchell (1983) originally identified a relational model in psychoanalysis as fundamentally *alternative* to classical drive theory. This position came under considerable criticism from some quarters and was the most controversial feature of that book. Why? The issue concerns ways of relating new ideas to preexisting theory, and there is a lot at stake. What is the relationship between the basic relational concepts that emerged in the mid-20th century in the seminal work of Sullivan and Fairbairn to the drive/defense model that preceded it and has continued alongside it into modern structural theory? There are several possibilities. One could regard the relational turn in psychoanalysis as simply an extension of the basic conceptual methodology established by Freud: internal and object relations are extensions of underlying drive processes, operating as "drive derivatives." One could regard the relational turn as generating new and alternative theories that are usefully held, alongside drive/defense theory, with different theories applying to different patients (e.g., Pine's mixed-models methodology).

Greenberg and Mitchell describe the synthetic and mixed-models approaches as "preservative" strategies. They are appealing in their inclusiveness; there is a lot to be said for them. What is lost? They miss what to us is, perhaps, the most significant feature of the emergence of the relational model: relational concepts do not provide understandings of different phenomena from those explored by the drive/defense model; relational concepts provide *alternative* understandings of the *same* phenomena. In the various preservative strategies, different areas of experience are assigned to the two traditions. The body, sexuality, pleasure, aggression, constitutionality, the patient's free associations are all assigned to the drive/defense model. And social and cultural processes, family systems dynamics, interpersonal relationships, the patient's relationship to the analyst—these are all assigned to the relational model.

But, alas, one cannot have everything. The inclusiveness of these preservative strategies is purchased at the price of delimiting the range of the two models. In its most radical form, each model actually *does* provide understandings of *all* the phenomena in question. Freud's "Totem and Taboo"(1913), and "Group Psychology and the Analysis of the Ego" (1921) were both bold attempts to offer new understandings of social and cultural phenomena in drive/defense terms. Conversely, the relational tradition has generated new understandings of precisely the phenomena that drive theorists have traditionally regarded as foundational: the body, sexuality, pleasure, aggression, constitutionality, the patient's free associations. In our view, positioning relational developments as additive rather than alternative misses the central point.

Relational Psychoanalysis and Constructivism

The first problem we encounter in exploring the interface between relational psychoanalysis and constructivism is that constructivism itself is not a simple concept or intellectual movement: there are many different types of constructivism (as there are many forms of its cousin, "postmodernism"), some more radical than others, and constructivism has become an important presence in virtually every contemporary intellectual discipline, but each in its own way.[1]

It is not surprising that relational thinking and some forms of constructivism have been closely entwined; they were both prefigured in

---

1. See Gill, 1994 (chapter 1) and Donnel Stern (1977, chapter 1) for excellent discussions of history and varieties of constructivism and its relationship to psychoanalysis.

Sullivan's formative contributions. Sullivan argued that mind occurs in what he called "me-you patterns," a precursor of later formulations of relational configurations. He also portrayed the analyst as a "participant-observer," a precursor of contemporary constructivist accounts of the analyst embedded in a transference–countertransference matrix. The basic underlying principle in both aspects of Sullivan's thought is the idea that mind always emerges and develops contextually, in interpersonal fields. Winnicott's (1960) powerful statement, "There is no such thing as an infant—only the infant-mother unit" (p. 39n), was a dramatic statement of what we might term "relationality" in developmental terms. But this understanding is also extendible to the analytic relationship as well, in which we might say, "There is no such thing as either the patient or the analyst—only the patient–analyst unit." The patient's experience of the analyst and the analyst's experience of the patient are constructed between the two of them. Thus, relationality shades quickly into constructivism, a particularly psychoanalytic form of constructivism.

Winnicott, of course, knew very well that there is also a separate mother and an individual baby. What he intended to convey was that there are also emergent properties of the dyad that transcend the individuality of the two participants. Similarly, relational analysts, in speaking of a "two-person psychology," have never intended to deny that there are two distinct individuals with their own minds, their own histories, and their own inner worlds, which come together in the analytic situation. Rather, the purpose of a "two-person psychology" is to emphasize the emergence of what Ogden calls "the intersubjective analytic third." These emergent properties of the dyad exist in dialectical relation to the individual subjectivities of the patient and the analyst.

What of the interface between relational psychoanalysis and the radical forms of constructivism that have created great ferment in the neighboring fields of political theory (e.g., Foucault) and gender studies (e.g., Butler)? Here the relationships seem to us to be more complex.

In political theory and gender studies, constructivism has been closely linked with social criticism and emancipatory struggles. Prior to constructivist critiques, various features of the status quo were defended as purely rational and enlightened (e.g., liberalism and humanism) or natural (e.g., heterosexuality). Constructivism in these areas has been a powerful conceptual tool in exposing the implicit power operations in these claims, the ways in which they mask values and privileged status. Thus, the enemy for constructivism in political and gender theory has been "essentialism" in its hydraheaded forms, concealing power under the banner of "nature."

There is clearly a close affinity between the relational critique of claims to the "natural" in classical psychoanalysis and the critique of essentialism in political and gender studies. But, from our point of view, constructivism in political and gender theory, in its dialectical swing away from essentialism, often becomes too airy and ungrounded, missing the ways in which the past, the inner world, developmental continuities, all have claims on our present experience. In their emancipatory zeal to shed social impositions, more political forms of constructivism seem not to appreciate that *we are what we have been,* and that we construct ourselves out of the materials at hand, including our bodies and their attributes.[2]

The two controversies we have been tracing (relational psychoanalysis and classical psychoanalysis: relational psychoanalysis and constructivism) converge on the question of what sort of constructivism might work best in relational psychoanalysis. Consider an analogy. Sculpture is constructed, we would all agree, completely constructed. But it is constructed out of materials, and the qualities and constraints of the materials are absolutely crucial. No one can make the same sculptures out of clay, marble, Lego blocks, and welded iron. That doesn't mean that sculpture is not constructed; it only means that it is not constructed out of thin air.

The reason these are controversies worth having is that they entail different views of the qualities and constraints of human bodies and their impact on the (relationally) contextual shaping of human experience. We favor a form of constructivism that grants some weight to the materiality of the body and its attributes, while at the same time we recognize that any ways in which those attributes are described are themselves social constructions.

Drive theories, even in their most contemporary forms, preserve attributes that are too fixed. By claiming to know in fixed terms what sexuality and aggression are, drive theories obscure important ways in which sexuality and aggression take on meanings in relational contexts. If the components are all Lego blocks, the possibilities are infinite but the constraints are powerfully delimiting.

More radical forms of constructivism in political and gender theory seem to regard any consideration of the attributes of human materiality as a back-sliding into essentialism. By depicting human sexuality and aggression purely as products of imagination and social power, radical constructivists obscure important ways in which constructions of sexuality and gender are constrained by our materiality and the weight imparted by

---

2. See Layton (1988) for an extremely thoughtful and lucid struggle to bridge the emancipatory constructivism of postmodernism with the psychodynamic concerns of relational psychoanalysis.

psychodynamic continuity. If construction is all, Michelangelo's *David* might just as well be fashioned out of iron or Lego blocks.

The Relational Tradition and Dialogue

Jay Greenberg (1998) recently clarified the distinction between the way the term relational was originally used by Greenberg and Mitchell (1983) and the way it has come to be used more recently. When Greenberg and Mitchell first used the term, they were distinguishing a set of theorists who had rejected drive theory and who instead placed relationships at the center of their theoretical systems. In particular, the American psychiatrist Harry Stack Sullivan and the Scottish analyst W. R. D. Fairbairn were viewed as the central theoretical axis of this fundamentally different model. Greenberg reminds us that when he and Mitchell categorized this group of theorists as relational they were doing so retrospectively, as scholars looking back on what was contemporaneously thought to be independent psychoanalytic developments. Sullivan and Fairbairn knew nothing of each other's work, and the various relational authors, as categorized by Greenberg and Mitchell, would not have recognized themselves as belonging to a common school. It was only retrospectively that they were being viewed as such.

In contrast, Greenberg pointed out that, in recent years, some analysts had been using the term relational as a designation for a contemporary school of psychoanalysis. The current claim is that there is a school of thought defined by common principles and shared tenets and that one might identify an analytic writer or clinician as a member of such a relational school, or not. Greenberg pointed to the danger of individuals feeling pressure to adhere to certain tenets as the price of belonging. Once a school is defined and organized, criteria for inclusion and exclusion are formulated, and thinking and practice become doctrinaire.

Greenberg's warning is surely worth heeding—the destructive impact of fundamentalism within psychoanalytic history is well known, and contemporary models are in no less danger than was classical theory of becoming degraded into a constrictive dogmatism. But once the common, basic presuppositions of the relational model were identified in the contributions of theorists like Sullivan and Fairbairn, Greenberg and Mitchell (1983), along with other authors, opened up a new conceptual space that many contemporary writers and clinicians found both hospitable and stimulating of new lines of theory building. Redefining the past often has an important impact on locating oneself in the present and orienting oneself toward the future.

Thus Charles Spezzano (1997) has suggested the term American Middle Group for relational theory that operates in the fertile tension between the intrapsychic and the interpersonal, which had been previously dichotomized in the classical and interpersonal traditions. Emmanuel Ghent (1992) has put it this way:

> Relational theorists have in common an interest in the intrapsychic as well as interpersonal, but the intrapsychic is seen as constituted largely by the internalization of interpersonal experience mediated by the constraints imposed by biologically organized templates and delimiters. Relational theorists tend also to share a view in which both reality and fantasy, both outer world and inner world, both the interpersonal and the intrapsychic, play immensely important and interactive roles in human life [p. xviii].

And Jessica Benjamin (1995) has suggested that "the relational perspective may best be characterized as an inquiry into questions of common concern that have come to the fore as a result of the adoption of the two-person model" (p. 3).

One of the themes that emerges repeatedly throughout these papers, and that we view as central to the relational project, is the "deconstruction" of misleading dichotomies and exaggerated polarization. Instead, the papers place an emphasis on maintaining the tension between the extremes, on ambiguity, dialogue, dialectic, and paradox.

As Ghent (1992) has argued,

> the more profound significance of the term relational is that it stresses relation not only between and among external people and things, but also between and among internal personifications and representations. It stresses process as against reified entities and the relations among processes all the way along the continuum from the physical and physiological, through the neurobiological, ultimately the psychological, and, for some, even the spiritual [p. xx].

Thus, by identifying past developments and a common underlying conceptual model, historical explications like those of Greenberg and Mitchell (1993) opened up what philosophers call a problematic—a matrix of issues and concerns that serve as a conceptual space within which new ideas develop.

Scholars, like analysts, are inevitably participants in the world they are studying. We are not simply observing the world or psychoanalytic ideas and uncovering structures and patterns in it, but, rather, we are bringing to it the fullness of our own subjectivity, our history, our biases, and our loyalties, all of which influence the ways in which we shape and construct that world. The psychoanalytic traditions that we present in this text is something that all the authors represented within have found themselves to be a part of and have, in turn, participated in shaping and influencing.

It should be apparent that the shared sensibility that we bring to the project of anthologizing key papers in the development of the relational tradition is a taste for controversy. We wanted to make our positions as explicit as possible and, at the same time, invite readers to engage these works in their own way, through their own interests and values. The vitality of any psychoanalytic tradition derives, most centrally, from its power to generate new ideas.

References

Aron, L. (1996), *A Meeting of Minds*. Hillsdale, NJ: The Analytic Press.
———— & Anderson, F.S., ed. (1998), *Relational Perspectives on the Body*. Hillsdale, NJ: The Analytic Press.
Benjamin, J. (1988), *The Bonds of Love*. New York: Pantheon.
Butler, J. (1990), *Gender Trouble: Feminism and the Subversion of Identity*. New York: Routledge.
———— (1993), *Bodies That Matter*. New York: Routledge.
Chodorow, N. (1978), *The Reproduction of Mothering*. Berkeley: University of California Press.
Dimen, M. (1993), Deconstructing difference: Gender, splitting, and transitional space. *Psychoanal. Dial.*, 1:335–352.
Dinnerstein, D. (1976), *The Mermaid and the Minotaur*. New York: Harper & Row.
Fairbairn, W. R. D. (1952), *An Object-Relations theory of the Personality*. New York: Basic Books.
Ferenczi, S. (1931), *The Clinical Diary of Sándor Ferenczi*, ed. J. Dupont. Cambridge, MA: Harvard University Press, 1988.
Freud, S. (1913), Totem and taboo. *Standard Edition*, 13; 1–161. London: Hogarth Press, 1965.
———— (1921), Group psychology and the analysis of the ego. *Standard Edition*, 18:69-143. London: Hogarth Press, 1955.
Ghent, E. (1992), Foreword. In: *Relational Perspectives in Psychoanalysis*, ed. N. J. Skolnick & S. C. Warshaw. Hillsdale, NJ: The Analytic Press.
Gill, M. (1994), *Psychoanalysis in Transition*. Hillsdale, NJ: The Analytic Press.
Gilligan, C. (1983), *In a Different Voice: Psychological Theory and Women's Development* .Cambridge, MA: Harvard University Press.
Goldner, V. (1991), Toward a critical relational theory of gender. *Psychoanal. Dial.*, 1:249–272.
Greenberg, J. (1998), Response to Adrienne Harris. Meeting of American Psychoanalytic Association, Toronto.
———— & Mitchell, S. (1983), *Object Relations in Psychoanalytic Theory*. Cambridge, MA: Harvard University Press.

Kernberg, O. (1976), *Object Relations Theory and Clinical Psychoanalysis*. New York: Aronson.

Kohut, H. (1977), *The Restoration of the Self*. New York: International Universities Press.

—— (1984), *How Does Analysis Cure?* ed. A Goldberg & P. E. Stepansky. Chicago: University of Chicago Press.

Layton, L. (1988), *Who's That Girl? Who's That Boy?* Northvale, NJ: Aronson.

Mitchell, S. (1988), *Relational Concepts in Psychoanalysis: An Integration*. Cambridge, MA: Harvard University Press.

Pine, F. (1991), *Drive, Ego, Object, Self*. New York: Basic Books.

Spezzano, C. (1997), The emergency of an American middle school of psychoanalysis. *Psychoanal. Dial.*, 7:603–618.

Stern, D. (1997), *Unformulated Experience: From Dissociation to Imagination in Psychoanalysis*. Hillsdale, NJ: The Analytic Press.

Winnicott, D. W. (1960), The theory of the parent-infant relationship. In: *The Maturational Processes and the Facilitating Environment*. New York: International Universities Press, 1965, pp. 37–55.

The Area of Faith in
Winnicott, Lacan and Bion

(1981)

Michael Eigen

▼　▼　▼　▼　▼

Editors' Introduction

Michael Eigen's evocative writing style and his complex clinical sensibility are unique in the literature and history of psychoanalysis. He falls neatly into no systematized school of thought, and it is not easy to place him in the context of psychoanalytic tradition. In this regard, Eigen has said of himself, "If I had to situate my writings, I think I see myself as part of a budding subculture of psychoanalytic mystics, more of whom may be coming out of the closet."

For many reasons, however, Eigen's contributions belong to the emerging relational tradition. "My style presupposes a taste for subjectivity," and Eigen's work is indeed an ongoing study of subjectivity, a passionate pursuit of the emotional intensity of the analytic encounter for both patient and analyst. His relational assumptions include an appreciation for the mutuality inherent in the early development of self and other and for the mutual openness to experience required by psychoanalysis. Human subjectivity, for Eigen, is constituted by the essential ambiguity of union and distinctness, the paradoxical recognition that subjectivity and objectivity constitute one another, as well as by the recognition that we are divided from ourselves by our acceptance of the dualism of mind and body, thought and affect. Eigen's relational sensibility may be most apparent to readers of his richly narrated case material, which always brings out the subtlety and complexity of intersubjective processes.

"The Area of Faith in Winnicott, Lacan, and Bion" is one of his most influential contributions and is a good point of entry to his extraordinarily romantic psychoanalytic world view. In the opening paragraph, Eigen defines the area of faith in terms of "a way of experiencing that is undertaken with one's whole being, all out," and here he quotes from Deuteronomy 6, "with all one's heart, with all one's soul, and with all one's might," a passage that in its original context was meant to describe the total and continuous commitment required in the love of God. Eigen's call is to live and experience life with passion in all of its fullness. Eigen was among the earliest to appreciate the profundity of Winnicott's contributions in highlighting that subjectivity becomes a possibility only with the object's survival of the subject's all out attacks. Whether focusing on "all-out" aggression and attacks on the object or on the "nuclear joy kernel" symbolized by the primary smile, Eigen's emphasis is consistently on living and experiencing with ardor; this is the area of faith held in common by Winnicott, Lacan, and Bion: the singular contribution of the psychoanalytic attitude, the evolution of openness to experience, all-out fervent confrontation with the emotional truth of one's subjectivity.

If one pole of the relational tradition is made up by those who emphasize the articulation of interpersonal experience, the social construction of knowledge, and the deconstruction of essentialist assumptions, then Eigen's work lies at the opposite pole, spiritual and even mystical, with his affirmation of true self and his call for unflinching confrontation with the emotional truth of one's own experience. Eigen's work is indeed a celebration of human subjectivity.

In *The Psychotic Core* (1986, Aronson) Eigen explored the phenomenology of madness. Not limiting himself to discussing the overtly psychotic, Eigen takes up the broad range of emotional states and mental disorders that constitute the mad dimensions of life. *The Electrified Tightrope* (1993, Aronson) is a carefully edited collection of Eigen's papers spanning the years 1973–1989, with an appreciative introduction by Adam Phillips and a moving aferward by Eigen that places his work in personal perspective. In the recent *The Psychoanalytic Mystic*, Eigen returns directly to the themes of the early essay included here. Drawing on Freud, Milner, Bion, Winnicott, and Lacan, Eigen explores the areas of overlap between psychoanalysis and mystical domains, the meditative and even the sacred dimensions of psychoanalytic work.

The Area of Faith in
Winnicott, Lacan and Bion*

▼ ▼ ▼ ▼ ▼

The basic concern of this paper is what I am calling the area of faith in the work of Winnicott, Lacan and Bion. By the area of faith I mean to point to a way of experiencing which is undertaken with one's whole being, all out, 'with all one's heart, with all one's soul, and with all one's might.' At the outset I wish to avoid quibbling over whether such experiencing is possible. My methodological strategy is to let what I mean by area of faith stay open and gradually grow richer as the paper unfolds.

Winnicott, Lacan and Bion have attempted sophisticated and intensive depth phenomenologies of faith in travail. For them, I believe, the vicissitudes of faith mark the central point around which psychic turmoil and conflict gather. In the hands of these authors, further, the area of faith tends to become a founding principle for the possibility of a fully human consciousness, an intrinsic condition of self-other awareness as such.

In Winnicott the area of faith is expressed in his descriptions of transitional experiencing (1953), and taken forward in his later work on object usage (1969). Since much work has already been published on transitional experiencing, my main concern will be with object usage.

In Lacan the area of faith is associated, at least in its developed form, mainly with the Symbolic order and his notion of the 'gap.' After discussing the underlying play of faith in these conceptions we will begin to see how Lacan and Winnicott heighten and extend each other's overlapping positions.

We will centre our discussion of faith in Bion on his work on O, his sign denoting ultimate reality. Bion's concepts clustering around O appear to provide the most flexible and general framework with which to understand Winnicott's and Lacan's basic concerns. Nevertheless, when these three authors are brought into relation with one another, the dimension of faith appears enriched by an interweaving of vistas which are not mutually reducible. Meta-perspectives on these views open still more vistas.

---

* Originally published in *International Journal of Psycho-Analysis*, 62:413–433. © 1981. Institute of Psycho-Analysis, London.

The Area of Faith in Transitional
Experiencing and Object Usage

The area of faith in Winnicott's transitional experiencing and object usage may be brought out more clearly by contrasting it, as Winnicott himself has done, with the Kleinian introjective-projective fantasy world. In Winnicott's scheme, transitional experiencing and object usage, respectively, point to a realm prior to and beyond Kleinian introjective-projective dramas. In the following discussion time sequence is less important than formal differences between phenomenological dimensions.

In transitional experiencing the infant lives through a faith that is prior to clear realization of self and other differences; in object usage the infant's faith takes this difference into account, in some sense is based on it. In contrast, the introjective-projective aspect of the self is involved in splitting and hiding processes, an inherently self-bound psychic web-spinning in which the possibility of faith is foreclosed. How these diverse experiential universes relate to one another is a complex problem which will be worked with only tangentially in the present paper. My immediate concern is the way object usage takes the life of faith in transitional experiencing forward, and the role introjective-projective processes play as a foil to this unfolding. In order to accomplish this, I must, in turn, discuss transitional experiencing, object relating (the introjective-projective world), and object usage. My aim is to show how faith evolves from transitional experiencing through object usage, in part by transcending (or undercutting) introjective-projective ordeals and barriers.

Transitional Experiencing

Winnicott situates transitional experiencing between the early emergence of consciousness and the infant's growing awareness of otherness outside himself.[1] In the transitional area self and other are neither one, nor two, but somehow together make up an interpenetrating field. The core of transitional experiencing has to do with an inherent fit between the infant's creativeness and the world. It is a fit that is lived and taken for granted, a faith that the infant lives out of without radically questioning its basis. In Winnicott's words,

---

1. I have elsewhere (Eigen, 1980a,b; Eigen & Robbins, 1980) discussed the weakness in Winnicott's starting point and will not take this problem up here. What is critical for the present discussion is the structural link between transitional experiencing and object usage that distinguishes these areas of experiencing from introjective-projective operations.

the essential feature in the concept of transitional objects and phenomena . . . is *the paradox:* the baby creates the object, but the object was
there waiting to be created and to become a cathected object . . . We will
never challenge the baby to elicit an answer to the question: did you create that or did you find it? (1953, in 1971, p. 89).

The infant here lives in an atmosphere of creativity, participates, as
it were, in a creativity bath. The question of where to locate the self and
object is slippery. The transitional object carries the meaning of that
which is, yet is not mother and that which is, and is not self. It, like
mother, mirrors the self and like the self, mirrors mother. Yet it cannot
be reduced to either. In so far as the transitional object is a first not-me,
it is so without any sharp sense of exteriority. It is perhaps an incipient
other, otherness in the process of being born, not yet wholly other. It is
expressive of a primary creative process at the origin of symbolic experience and is itself a vehicle for creative experiencing. As neither wholly
self nor other nor wholly outside these terms, it is itself symbolizing
experiencing emerging as such.

In an important sense, while the infant is living through creative
experiencing, he neither holds on to anything, nor withholds himself.
He may grip a teddy or blanket as a mother or self substitute for security, but this is not the heart of the transitional area. Transitional phenomena are not primarily tranquilizers. Objects held on to as
tranquilizers mark a rupture between the infant and the realm of creative experiencing, which he may seek to close by self-soothing practices. In the transitional dimension creative experiencing is open and
fluid, if also profoundly heightened. Apparent possessiveness and perseverations here, in part, provide an opportunity for intensifying the
feeling of creativeness, of digging deeper into the immersion process,
rather than simply reflecting compensatory needs. For Winnicott, in
contrast to Freud and Klein, creativity permeates psychic life and is
involved in the very birth of self and other, a process more fundamental than substitute strivings. Creativity is itself a primary term of human
experiencing. For Winnicott, the defensive use of creativity is a secondary development and not the home ground of the human self (Eigen,
1981b; Eigen & Robbins, 1980).

Object Relating: The Unit Self

Winnicott contrasts transitional experiencing (and object usage) with
object relating through projective-introjective operations by a unit self.
He describes this latter mode of relating in the following way:

> In object-relating the subject allows certain alterations in the self to take place, of a kind that has caused us to invent the term cathexis. The object has become meaningful. Projection mechanisms and identifications have been operating, and the subject is depleted to the extent that something of the subject is found in the object, though enriched by feeling. Accompanying these changes is some degree of physical involvement (however slight) towards excitement, in the direction of the functional climax of an orgasm . . . Object-relating is an experience of the subject that can be described in terms of the subject as an isolate (1971, p. 88).

Winnicott tends to situate this way of object relating as an intermediate phase between transitional experiencing and object usage. The object is meaningful but not yet experienced as wholly other. Rather, the subject continuously tends to bring any incipient sense of otherness into the circumference of its omnipotence. The self is an isolate here not because its sense of exteriority is over-developed, but because any promptings toward this sense collapse into the orbit of autarchic projective-introjective operations.

In the world of the unit self the subject grows through the continuous cycle of putting self in others and others in self. In projective-introjective identifications the self may disguise itself as another and another as oneself. The mind may capitalize on its invisibility and defensively play such crosscurrents off against each other. Through these operations the psyche can split itself, making secrecy and hiding possible, together with all the subtleties linked with self-deception.

Winnicott associates physical excitement with this area of the self, since introjective-projective identifications help mould erotic sensibility. Introjective-projective processes pave the way for structuralizing ego deformations associated with the erotization of mental functions. They make possible seductive and tantalizing expressive styles, which assault the true self feeling and intensify the life of bad faith.

The unit self, wherein unconscious lying becomes possible, stands in marked contrast with the rapt immersion of transitional experiencing and, we shall see, the clean air of object usage. For Winnicott the picture of a closed system perpetuated by a self-encapsulating network of projective-introjective operations, functions to help set off what life may be like when one feels free of this subjective bubble, when one is not closed in on oneself.

Object Usage

For Winnicott object usage occurs with the explosion of the introjection-projection circle and, reciprocally, occasions this explosion. The subject is reconstituted through a fresh realization that all is not self in disguise and, as in transitional experiencing, tastes a wholling innocence, although on a new plane. In transitional experience the unit self, the self as isolate, is as yet irrelevant, and in object usage it is undercut or transcended. In the former there is the freedom prior to a clearcut sense of sameness or difference, and in the latter the freedom brought about by news of difference.

In transitional experiencing the baby's sense of freedom was linked to a limitless feeling of wholeness, prior to raising the question of absolute limits. The new awakening in object usage involves the realization that the other is in some basic way outside one's boundaries, is 'wholly other'. And while this may precipitate disorganization and dismay, it culminates in quickening and enhancing the subject's sense of aliveness. It opens the way for a new kind of freedom, one *because* there is radical otherness, a new realness of self-feeling exactly because the other is now felt as real as well. The core sense of creativeness that permeates transitional experiencing is reborn on a new level, in so far as genuine not-me nutriment becomes available for personal use. The subject can *use* otherness for true growth purposes and, through the risk of difference as such, gains access to the genuinely new.

Winnicott links this new sense of otherness with the subject's realization that the object survives his destructive attacks. For Winnicott it is the subject's dawning awareness of the limitations of his all out destructive attacks (which once seemed boundless), that creates the experience of *externality* as such. In one of Winnicott's summaries, he describes this process in terms of the analytic situation in the following way:

> This destructive activity is the patient's attempt to place the analyst outside of omnipotent control, that is, out in the world. Without the experience of maximum destructiveness (object not protected) the subject never places the analyst outside and therefore can never do more than experience a kind of self-analysis, using the analyst as a projection of a part of the self (1969, in 1971, p. 91).

One cannot take Winnicott's description overliterally. One would have had to know the object had been there in order to appreciate its survival. Winnicott's description assumes and does not account for the original constitution of the object. What is at stake, however, is a fresh sense of what an object (and self) can be. The object that survives is *qualitatively* not the same object present at the attack's outset. The object that survives is one that could not be destroyed, whereas the object first attacked is one which the subject felt could or even should be. What is emerging is the sense of externality as imperishable living fact and principle. As living fact it is the Other as personal subject outside one's grasp. As principle it is a structural category which gives all beings, including oneself, the meaning: 'potentially other,' a being vulnerable to the transformations genuine difference can bring. It is this intersection of profound vulnerability and saving indestructibility that brings the paradox of faith to a new level.

Perhaps Winnicott's most memorable expression of the faith he points to is the following:

> This subject says to the object: 'I destroyed you', and the object is there to receive the communication. From now on the subject says: 'Hullo object!' 'I destroyed you.' 'I love you.' 'You have value for me because of your survival of my destruction of you.' 'While I am loving you I am all the time destroying you in (unconscious) *fantasy*.' (1971, p. 90).

What is happening is the 'continuous' destruction of the fantasy objects (the introjective–projective world) and the birth of the real object, the other subject outside all of one's psychic web-spinning. This 'real' is not quite Freud's 'reality'. Although it carries an urgency somewhat akin to necessity, it is not a reality one can adapt to in order to manipulate. It is a sense of the real that explodes all adaptive and manipulative attempts in principle. It is an all out, nothing held back, movement of the self-and-other feeling past representational barriers, past psychic films and shells, a floating freely in a *joyous shock of difference*. At this moment one is enlivened and quickened through the sense of difference. One is sustained sheerly through the unfolding sense of self-other presencing, a presencing no longer taken for granted but appreciated as *coming through*. This may be something akin to Job's and God's wrath turning into joyous appreciation of one another's mystery, a new found trust, wherein anything outside of the faith experience at that moment must seem unreal. The real here is self and other *feeling real* to one another, breaking past residues of depersonalization-derealization. In contrast, the Freudian reality basically requires some degree of depersonalization for adaptation and mastery to be possible. The category of mastery is irrelevant to the kind of self-other awareness at stake in the moment of faith, where all that exists of importance is the fact that we are real together, living in the amazing sense of becoming more and more real, where destructiveness makes love real, and love makes destructiveness creative.

Winnicott stresses that the destructiveness that creates the sense of externality is not essentially hostile (1971, pp. 90–3). This destructiveness, rather than reactive anger, seems to be an inherent part of developmental struggle. Winnicott recalls Greenacre's (e.g. 1952) examples of violence intrinsic to hatching processes, typical of a chick breaking out of an egg. In such instances one tries to move ahead with all one's might.

However, this general observation about the nature of developmental struggles does not appear to exhaust what Winnicott is trying to convey when he speaks of destructiveness creating externality. When Winnicott says that the object that survives the subject's destructive attacks is 'in process of becoming destroyed because real, becoming real because destroyed' (1971, p. 90), he means to suggest that these two facts, *the new sense of reality and the new sense of destruction, bring each other into being.* The texture of this argument is necessarily circular for what is involved is the emergence of a new experimental dimension in which each of the terms co-create each other. A quantum leap is in progress in which destruction creates the real at the same time that the real invites and sustains the subject's attempts to cancel it, a continuous process wherein self and other are freshly recreated through one another.

It is important that Winnicott takes this step beyond the simple notion that the creative destructiveness at stake is the pushing past the old by the new, a natural movement from one stage to another. For if the destruction began on the footing of the old order, the introjective-projective world, there could be no basis for affirming the all out wholling-in-differentiation experience that object usage implies. Destruction *within* the introjective-projective sphere tends to involve splitting and concealing processes. No all-out risk taking is possible within this system. The movement toward object usage, rather, involves the destruction *of* the introjective-projective order *and*, at the same time, contact with a sense of the real outside it: both these events are interwoven and produce each other.

Hence Winnicott's statement, 'the subject does not destroy the subjective object (projection material), destruction turns up and becomes a central feature so far as the object is objectively perceived, has autonomy, and belongs to "shared" reality' (1971, p. 91). It is the projective world that is 'continuously' destroyed at the same time that the real is 'continuously' born and vice versa, and both of these happenings are necessary for the real as such to be experienced. If there were no projective system, there would not be this fresh sense of the real, and the reverse holds as well. From this viewpoint, projective operations and the sense of the real require and feed each other, a type of figure-ground for one another. The object is being destroyed in fantasy and *as* fantasy and is felt as real because of this, at the same time its realness *makes fantasy* destructiveness possible. The realness *of* the object comes into being as a fantasy being destroyed at the same time it participates in an order beyond fantasy. The subject here, as in transitional experiencing, grows through paradoxical rather than dissociative awareness.

It is the survival of the object *qua* object, with its integrity intact, that is crucial. And by survival Winnicott stresses the importance of the object's not retaliating, for the latter would maintain the object within the subject's magical hold. As I noted earlier, the object that comes through the subject's attack is not, qualitatively, the same object that it was at the attack's outset. The object that comes through is outside the subject's grasp, whereas the object attacked is within it. In the moment that leads to object usage *both of these phases are maximized*. What is constituted is an experiential world which embraces both fully, one forever breaking through the other. In this complex system *an all out wholling feeling keeps breaking through diverse splits and compromises, neither term reducible to the other*.

We can deepen our sense of what Winnicott has achieved through his object usage formulation by realizing that Winnicott has expressed two different views concerning the importance of the other *qua* other, of which object usage was his most recent. His earlier account (1963) centred around the *capacity for concern* and reworked, but basically retained, the Kleinian guilt dynamics that characterize the depressive position. In contrast, Winnicott's object usage is a joy-base account of the growth of otherness. We will now allow the dynamics surrounding object usage and the capacity for concern to confront and heighten each other.

Object Usage and the Capacity for Concern: Joy and Guilt

It appears that Winnicott may have conflicting views concerning the subject's basic relation to the other *qua* other. We have studied Winnicott's account of the constitution of externality in which the object maintains itself outside the subject's destructive orbit. This culminates in a freeing feeling of subject and object difference, which ensures the category of the new. However, Winnicott (1963) following Klein, earlier rooted the subject's recognition of otherness (i.e., others as whole subjects) in guilt over hurting the loved other. This earlier account asserts that a genuine sense of otherness and guilt arise contemporaneously. The subject moves from anxiety to guilt and concern by being able to hold ambivalence and feel he can contribute something to the object in reparation.

In this earlier paper, 'object usage' is linked with the ruthless expression of instinctual drives, excitement states toward the object. The infant goes all out at the object and the latter must see to it that it survives.

Here the mother is object of the infant's instinctual desires, very much the Freudian and Kleinian libidinal object.

At the same time, the infant feels protective toward the aspect of mother that protects and cares for it, the holding environment mother. It is the coming together of these 'two mothers' in infantile perception that evokes the wish for reparation, the birth of concern. The infant tries to help the holding environment mother by modulating his libidinal-destructive attacks on the exciting mother, the two now perceived as the same person.

A quote from Winnicott will suffffice to show that his later object usage and earlier capacity for concern accounts contained many common elements, reworked in different ways.

> A sense of guilt is anxiety linked with the concept of ambivalence, and implies a degree of integration in the individual ego that allows for the *retention of a good object-imago along with the idea of a destruction* of it. Concern implies further integration, and further growth, and relates in a positive way to the individual's sense of responsibility, especially in respect of relationships into which the instinctual drives have entered (1963, in 1965, p. 73, my italics).

Winnicott's later account also involves a simultaneity of destruction, love and survival, but *without a need to make reparation*. The core affect of this later account is joy, not guilt. The infant feels grateful because he can destroy and love the object and the object survives. The feeling is that integrity is really possible without compromising self or other. The subject appreciates the other *qua* other for intrinsic reasons, without the self-splitting that guilt may occasion. In the kind of unity of destructiveness and love Winnicott depicts in his later object usage account, love is alive and strong enough to use destructiveness creatively, rendering guilt superfluous.

In the Kleinian guilt-based account, the primacy of joy could not truly be understood. It would be rationalized as a manic defence, part of the paranoid position, or associated with the joy that arises when one makes amends. It would have *no place in its own right, as an intrinsic part of self-other awareness as such*.

In the reparation account, I believe, a subtle form of megalomania, that undoes the possibility of otherness itself, is left undetected. If the infant needs to repair the mother because of the imaginary damage he has inflicted upon her, he remains caught in his own psychic web-spinning. *There can be no true otherness where the infant is concerned for mother because of a fantasy of destructiveness that he tries to undo.* It is precisely this fantasy that continuously is exploded in Winnicott's later object usage formulation, allowing otherness to emerge fully. The concern based on guilt is mired in fantasies of mastery and control, whereby even love functions in controlling ways, if only as a defence against hate. The need to be good in order to make up for being bad is a very different moment from the freedom of loving for its own sake. In the object usage formulation, joy is not defined by a background guilt, but is an intrinsically undefensive feeling.

In his object usage formulation, Winnicott appears to move beyond his earlier thought and provides a ground for human concern which is not anxiety-derived. The later account provides a basis for a non-defensive appreciation of otherness which may grow into concern. One might come to guard this otherness in order to protect the richness in living it offers. Both the 'I destroy you' and 'I love you' of object usage are valued as rock bottom given, primary inclinations of the human heart. They are spontaneous feelings toward others, not discharge mechanisms. This 'I love you' does not make up for 'I destroy you', but turns the latter to good use. Together they constitute a sustained reaching out, a hope, a joyous gambit. In saying this, however, I do not want to minimize the importance of guilt dynamics in actual living. A fuller working out of relationships between object usage and the capacity for concern dynamics is beyond our scope here. My wish is to point out a distinction which makes an important contribution to the way a subject feels about himself and others.

The object usage, and capacity for concern, accounts both draw on object relational possibilities inherent in Freud's theory of drive fusion. Both are ways love and hate are structured in relation to one another. In the object usage account, the primacy of love does not rely on any added notion of ego mastery or adaptive control in order to handle destructive wishes. Within the framework of the primacy of love, hate finds its own limits and adds to, because encompassed by, joyous creativeness. There is no such faith in the capacity for concern account, where one recoils at one's own evil, and remains fearful of what the monster within can do. Both are genuine and necessary human experiences. The latter may provide sobering self-restraint, but it is not the true freedom faith can bring.

The Area of Faith in Lacan

In order to begin to approach the ways Lacan and Winnicott differ, and from the perspective of their differences explore how they enrich each other, we must first say something of Lacan's three orders of unconscious mind and their relation to the phenomenon of the 'gap'. Lacan depicts three orders of unconscious mental events: the Real, Imaginary and Symbolic. Each will be taken up with an eye toward understanding them with reference to the faith dimension.

The Real, at least in one of its profiles, may be viewed as a repressed awareness of lived experience (Lemaire, 1977; Lowe, 1980). The originary world of spontaneously lived experience, the primordial inter-weaving of subject and object as, for example, described by Merleau-Ponty (1962, 1968), undergoes repression and becomes subject to increasing distortions through secondary revisions. This repressed awareness is a complex one, including both the originary subject-object interlocking *and* the latter's rupture, lived experiencing 'before' and 'after' the trauma of separation. We will leave open for now exactly what the nature and status of this separation is. Lacan points to our sense of incompleteness and dissatisfaction which he variously refers to in terms of separation from mother at birth or the break-up of an early, mute dual union of baby and mother through the advent of language (the latter associated with law, social order, father, the castration complex).

It is the spontaneously lived contrast between subject-object inter-locking *and* rupture that the Imaginary seeks to escape or undo. The Imaginary seeks to close all genuine gaps or fill them with 'mock' or 'parody' gaps, such as reactive withdrawal or oppositionalism, creating an illusion of self-sufficiency. Toward this end it employs mirroring or projective-introjective identificatory operations. Through these opera-tions the subject can create an exteriorized (mainly visual) image of him-self as an actor who masters anxiety by eliciting admiration/hostility from both his own self and world as audience. He becomes, as it were an imitation of himself (and others) by moulding his reactiveness in terms of image forms that aid his quasi-spurious sense of self-suffficiency. The subject supports his defensive use of mastery by seduction and power techniques which increasingly alienate him from his most pro-found feeling life. As he rivets himself to his exteriorized self-image, he more and more filters himself through its projections, and takes in those reactions of others most relevant to his self-mesmerization.

For Lacan it is the Symbolic that explodes the closed system of the subject's introjective-projective world. The Symbolic responds to the sub-ject-object interlocking and rupture inherent in the Real by trying to rep-resent this state of affairs, not annihilate or foreclose it. It builds on primordial experiencing and takes it forward, enriching it through the dimension of meaning. It does this not by simply returning to primor-dial experiencing (which, in any case, comes under the governance of primal repression), but by accepting the gap within the Real, and between the Real, Imaginary and the Symbolic. One requires a certain faith to tolerate and respect the gaps through which the life of authentic meaning unfolds.

Lacan associates the advent of the Symbolic with language and links the structure inherent in language with social structure, lawfulness (logos), the phallus, the father principle, the Other. The Imaginary tries to use or manipulate language so as to reinforce the subject's tyrannical illusion of mastery, his omnipotent self-encapsulation. The Symbolic provides a way out of self-enclosure through the subject's surrender to the life of meaning, the play of language, and the emergence of effective insights which outstrip his control. The gap between what is hidden and the pulsation of insight is respected and worked with, rather than delusively escaped or filled in. The subject is genuinely recreated through his participation in the movement of language, through his interaction with the Other, bearer of the Word (namely revelation).

The Symbolic and Imaginary orders intersect in complex ways, feeding and opposing each other. An important example of their irreducible co-presence, often used in Lacanian texts, is Freud's (1920) description of the child who throws a spool of string out of sight, and himself brings it back in view, the famous *Fort! Da!* anecdote in *Beyond the Pleasure Principle*. On the one hand the child tries to symbolize the lived fact of interlocking and rupture: his mother's absence and return. On the other hand he tries to subdue this fact by representing her as under his control: his demand can bring a representation of her to him. In this latter case he does not so much encompass the complex pressing issue so much as seek to undo it. He substitutes Imaginary victory over the persistent difficulty of presence-absence, instead of taking up the (perhaps impossible) challenge of symbolically sustaining both terms in non-controlling expectancy (a risk of faith). The bad faith in the subject's attempt at Imaginary triumph is his wish to turn the gap into something he can discount.

Lacan, Winnicott and Kleinians (namely, Segal, 1978; Meltzer, 1973) agree that human subjects cannot be fully constituted without access to the symbolic. It is through the subject's realization of the symbolic dimension that meaning can freely evolve. However, the Kleinian path to the symbolic is through the subject's capacity to value positive introjective identifications. For Lacan, as Winnicott, the symbolic function is rooted outside introjective processes. He situates the Kleinian introjective-projective fantasy realm in his Imaginary order, the megalomanic subject caught up in identificatory or mirroring processes.

His critique of American ego psychology rests on somewhat similar grounds, although is far more brutal. He rigorously attacks the idea of a cure based on a positive identification with the analyst, the line of development usually summed up as 'introjection-identification-internalization'. According to Lacan, good internalizations tend to function as psychic tranquilisers, benignly socialized versions of 'master-slave' dynamics. They help offset the personality's tendencies to paranoid-depressive anxieties by muting the risks a more profoundly grounded autonomy entails.

From Lacan's perspective, I believe, Kohut's (1971, 1977) presentation of his self psychology exhibits a similar problem. Kohut's picture of cure stresses the installation of a benign superego as an internal self-esteem regulating system. The transmuting internalization of the good analyst into a good superego (psychic structure) leaves the ego something of a child in relation to his good internal object, in effect subject to the 'tyranny of goodness'. The good superego may be counted on to make the ego feel better, even to guide it better and provide inspiration, but may seal off the possibility of a more profound regression, and a fiercer, more thorough search.

For Lacan, introjection-identification-internalization do not account for the Symbolic (the path toward 'cure'). Symbolization transcends them and makes them possible. They are limiting modes *of* symbolization and presuppose the more general creative activity they grow out of. They may help, but also often hinder the full play of meaning, one's search for emotional truth. They often fill in gaps within and between orders (the Real, Imaginary, Symbolic) with doses of premature goodness, foreclosing glimpses of what one must face. One must trust that through the gap between himself and the Other (the Unconscious, the Real, the Symbolic), creative play will save him. The subject's search for the truth about himself evolves by listening to a live play of meaning that always exceeds his grasp. Here faith is necessary. One cannot 'master' the real, or life of meaning in any fundamental way. One can only try to participate in one's own revisioning through impact and revelation, with all the openness and intensity of insight one can muster.

Comparisons Between Winnicott and Lacan

For Winnicott the symbolic begins at the level of lived experience, prior to language. Language itself grows out of the matrix of preverbal *symbolizing experiencing* and carries threads of the latter to new heights. In transitional experiencing primordial symbolization takes the form of an affective cognition in which self-other awareness creatively thrives. *Self-other awareness is itself the core of symbolizing experiencing* and perhaps remains humankind's most creative activity at various levels of developmental complexity. In terms of preverbal symbolizing experiencing, self and other are neither felt as identical nor experienced with any sharp division. Winnicott and Milner (1980) have at times expressed this phase of consciousness in terms of overlapping circles.

Winnicott's symbolic experiencing thus begins at the level of Lacan's Real. However, it does not exhaust the Real. For the latter includes the double 'fact' of subject-object interlocking *and* rupture. The events in Lacan's Real are more nearly encompassed by Winnicott's transitional experiencing *and* object usage. The latter deals with the realization of subject and object difference earlier than language.

A comparison like this raises difficulties and cannot be exact. For Lacan the unconscious—in the first instance, the primal repressed lived awareness of interlocking-rupture—is instituted by the advent of language. However, the Real also continuously eludes language. It is the reference to lived awareness that evocatively links Lacan's Real with Winnicott's transitional experiencing and object usage. For Winnicott, however, transitional experiencing and object usage are *not* essentially linked with repression. They are ways the subject lives all out through the feeling of wholeness (a paradoxical wholeness). Winnicott is saying that there are modes of experiencing which are both lived and symbolizing at a preverbal level, and which cannot be understood in terms of self-splitting processes. This is one of several differences between these authors which, we will see, cluster around deeper phenomenological commitments.

Another important divergence is that Winnicott's formulations do not imply the same sense of radical rupture that pervades the tenor of Lacan's account. Even in object usage, where externality is radically encountered as such, the feeling tone is one of basic goodness of 'news of difference' (Bateson's 1979 phrase), not catastrophe. In Winnicott the movement is one of dramatic unfolding rather than traumatic im- or propulsion. In his account a sense of basic harmony makes divergence revitalizing rather than essentially menacing. There is something seamless even about Winnicott's radical otherness. In Lacan the agonistic element is more emphatically stressed in the rupture of *juissance* and the latter's ironic reappearance in the life of meaning.

Winnicott expressed his alliance with the thread of connectedness, for example, in his work on the capacity for concern:

> We often discuss separation-anxiety, but here I am trying to describe what happens between mothers and their babies and between parents and their children when there is *no* separation, and when external continuity of child-care is *not* broken. I am trying to account for things that happen when separation is avoided (1965, p. 78).

This passage was written before Winnicott clearly distinguished the *use of the object* (1969) as personality nutriment from libidinal use of the object, as well as from the holding environment mother. However, his later account also retains a primacy of connectedness, wherein some form of subject-object togetherness persists in the midst of subject-object difference. In healthy development of object usage, the 'I destroy you' is encompassed by 'I love you'. The tension between these two terms generates useable rather than disruptive aliveness, a joyous quickening.

Lacan is more preoccupied with the rent in the heart of the real and the gap within and between orders of mental life instituted by language. The subject can turn this gap to good account by understanding it as the clearing where cultural creativity thrives. Nevertheless, the subject's main preoccupation is with this rupture and a considerable part of his striving for (and through) meaning involves seeing through ways he tries to avoid or foreclose the rifts that meaning brings. For Lacan the trick seems to be to catch on that we are continuously symbolizing some lack which our symbolizing activity itself both institutes and transcends.

Winnicott and Lacan agree that the Imaginary (e.g. introjective-projective dramas) marks the self's attempt to master trauma in a false way, usually through the subtle assertion of some mirage of self-suffficiency. The urge to exert control over what must not be merely 'controlled' cuts oneself off from one's most basic creative promptings. At some level the Imaginary occludes the sort of profound self-responsiveness that results in genuine personal evolution. One tries to control rather than open oneself to the transformation of dialogue, of interaction. For Winnicott, separation is part of the faith journey, an all out symbolizing experiencing at the preverbal level. For Lacan good faith is a matter of respecting the basic gap within lived awareness, as elaborated, enriched and transcended by verbal symbolizing capacity. In both these cases something other than control and identificatory dimensions (namely, the wish to stay on top or fuse) uplifts the self.

The Human Face

It is, I suspect, Lacan's basic distrust of the visual that, in part, leads to his situating the symbolic primarily in language. For Lacan vision is the site of seduction *par excellence*. In his account it is above all through the visual self-image that the Imaginary works. He uses, for example, the baby's self-recognition in a mirror (at roughly six months of age) as a paradigm of self-alienation. The perfect responsiveness and clearly-articulated boundaries of the mirror image provide a magical sense of control and cohesion that far outstrip the facts of everyday experience. The mirror or visual me, the actor for an audience, comes to be used as a defence against authentic body feelings, especially one's vulnerability and insufficiency.

The infant's relationship with his mother easily exploits this tendency. The infant's and mother's gaze capture each other. The infant grows by imitating but at the same time loses contact with his own subjective pulse. For Lacan it is through symbolic discourse, the living Word, that baby-mother seductiveness is purified. Here visual control is futile. What counts is emotional truth, self-disclosing meaning (Heidegger's full rather than empty speaking, Husserl's statements spoken with 'evidence'). The talking cure on the couch is a methodological strategy aimed at rendering visual control (the life of mimicry) futile and fostering awareness of one's basic situation. In this phenomenology, listening undercuts the power of seduction.

Winnicott, in contrast, emphasizes the positive (non-paranoid) aspect of the baby's visual experience. In optimal circumstances, baby and mother mutually mirror one another's *personal* qualities, so that one's sense of self is confirmed and evolves. An enhancing intermingling of self and other occur at the heart of self-experience.

For Winnicott, like Lacan, seduction is an alienating event. He has written (1971, pp. 98–9) that nothing is more treacherous for the developing self than tantalization, seduction to extreme. Seduction impinges on the infant's ongoing being, provoking the development of a False Self system. Vision may be misused to steal intrusively or to engulf, but is not necessarily or primarily employed this way. From Winnicott's viewpoint, Lacan's paranoid-seductive mirror me is a key way the self's use of sight may go wrong. It offers an excellent portrayal of an imaginary, false self which stains the human condition. Still, our seeing and seeing through also play a positive, nondefensive role in the texture of our lives. We can grow through a fundamentally fertile symbiosis between Word and vision, albeit one easily aborted or distorted. The human ego appears to have a mixture of paranoid and non-paranoid foundational experiences, the particular balance, in important part, dependent on the overall quality of responsiveness by the parental milieu (Weil, 1958; Winnicott, 1958, 1965, 1971; Kohut, 1971, 1977; Bion, 1977; Eigen, 1980a,b, 1981a; Eigen & Robbins, 1980).

Both Lacan and Winnicott in some way link the origin of the early self with the primordial experience of the face, although each present a different phenomenology of this basic experience. For Lacan it is paranoid-seductive, for Winnicott a matrix of true self-feeling. Spitz's (1965) work also links the early emergence of self-other awareness with the infant's response to the face or face mask. By roughly two or three months of age (perhaps earlier), the infant may spontaneously break out into a coherent, joyous smile to a face stimulus (eyes and nose must be represented). Like Lacan, Spitz reads a seductive or controlling (adaptive mastery) element into this smile. He feels this smile is primarily geared toward inducing maternal responsiveness. I find this smile more radically joyous, expressive of delight in recognizing personal presence. As Spitz also points out, it is part of a system of self-and-other mutual reverberation and resonance. To view this full and focused smile merely in terms of its value for ensuring survival says little of what kind of being survives *this* way, and scarcely does justice to its surplus of expressive meaning.

To live in and through a smile marks the advent of a radically new sort of consciousness, some extra x of subjective quality. In earlier papers (Eigen, 1980a,b,c, 1981c; also, see Elkin, 1972) I have suggested this smile is the home base of the human self, the felt criterion for what is most basically sensed as emotionally right or wrong. Soon enough the infant may smile when frightened or mad, signalling seductive intentionality or splits between thinking, feeling action (Lacan's Imaginary, Winnicott's False Self). However, the *primary smile* in question expresses all out, spontaneous living through faith (more basic than splitting), the primordial underpinning for the possibility of rebirth throughout a lifetime. This nuclear joy kernel, I believe, is inexhaustible. So, it seems, is suffering. Over and over, like Job, the true smile at the centre of human consciousness attempts to come through the struggles self-feeling must undergo.

The fact that the primordial human smile and the vision that evokes it support conflicting phenomenologies, both of which carry a ring of truth, dramatically brings out the challenge we face in discovering how thoroughly duality permeates us. In what way can we say that our sense of wholeness comes through our dual view? Can duality open out from or toward wholeness? Everywhere we look doubleness proliferates. Does our dual view keep our struggles for wholeness honest-cynical? The intrigue between our sense of wholeness and duality is intensified in Bion's formulations. Through his notation 'O' he takes on our need to engage ultimate reality, without compromising any conflicting experiential dimensions which may help or hinder us in this enterprise.

Bion: Faith in O

Bion uses the sign, 'O', to denote ultimate reality (namely, absolute truth, the godhead, the infinite, the thing-in-itself). For the psychoanalyst the O (ultimate reality) of psychoanalytical experience is what might be expressed as the emotional truth of a session. Strictly speaking, as psychoanalysts we live in the faith that emotional truth is possible, even necessary as a principle of wholesome psychic growth. In itself the emotional truth at stake may be unknown and unknowable, but nothing can be more important than learning to attend to it. This is paradoxical: an unknowable is to be the focus of our attention. Our faith in something important happening when we reach out toward the unknowable sustains the attention that clears a working space for truth. Our intention to attend to the evolution of emotional reality does make a difference in how we come to feel about ourselves as development proceeds. For better or worse, the individual who addresses this issue cannot be the same, in the long run, as one who does not.

Bion rigorously distinguishes the faith dimension, *the* locus of psychoanalytical experience, from all other events in human experience. Bion sees faith not only as a condition that makes psychoanalysis possible, but as the latter's *primary methodological principle*. In order to attempt to clarify this, he systematically distinguishes faith from knowledge and tries to work out the relationship between these two capacities. In this, we will see, he followed Kant, but with a shift of emphasis.

Bion grounds his thinking on the distinction between being and knowing and draws, from epistemological considerations, implications about the human condition. Being and knowing require each other. For us the being of knowing and knowing of being are inextricably intertwined. Our knowing I-feeling permeates the heart of our existence and makes it what it is. Nevertheless, the distinction between being and knowing is no mere intellectual exercise. We are not in the same qualitive space when we focus on knowing and when we focus on who we really are. In the former attitude we may gain knowledge about ourselves, but *knowing about* may or may not contribute much to genuine emotional change. If *we* are to develop as whole persons, the actual truth of our emotional realities must evolve. This state of affairs may be condensed in a paraphrase of one of Bion's cryptic orphisms: 'One cannot know O, one must *be* it' (1970, in 1977, p. 27).

The O of who we are may evolve to a point where we feel we know something about it. The evolution of O gives rise to formulations which aspire to express it. It is through discourse that we try to communicate about O. Without our knowing discourse the mere muteness of our being would cave in on itself. We hope, too, our formulations not only reflect O, but facilitate its evolution. If our formulations are good enough approximations of O, they may act as vehicles through which we become more at one with our own movement. However, for this to occur we must be aiming ourselves toward O, not mere knowledge.

It [O] stands for the absolute truth in and of any object; it is assumed that this cannot be known by any human being, it can be known about, its presence can be recognized and felt, but it cannot be known. It is possible to be at one with it. That it exists is an essential postulate of science but it cannot be scientifically discovered. No psycho-analytic discovery is possible without recognition of its existence, at-onement with it and evolution. (1977, p. 30).

Our formulations are couched in terms derived from sensuous experience, but the emotional truth we seek to express is not sensuous or spatial. It is not localizeable anywhere. When speaking about psychic reality spatial references are metaphorical or analogical. Emotional truth is inherently intangible, invisible or ineffable (i.e. consciousness sees and hears but can't be seen or heard). We use terms derived from sensuous experience to point to a realm beyond the latter. Our pointing is always an approximation, a guess, a conviction.

O does not fall in the domain of knowledge or learning save *incidentally*; it can 'become', but it cannot be 'known'. It is darkness and formlessness but it enters the domain K [knowledge] when it has evolved to a point where it can be known, through knowledge gained by experience, and formulated in terms derived from sensuous experience; its existence is conjectured phenomenologically (1977, p. 26; my italics).

We develop a phenomenology of intimations of emotional truth formulated with conviction and with the realization that we may be wrong. We aim in faith to connect with what is beyond our representations, as we use our representations to light up the mystery of who we are. We live parallel lives with ourselves in our being and knowing, and develop a critical trust in possible points of intersection, if intersection were possible. Communion with O is an imaginative adventure, not an acquired certainty to be taken for granted. This realization helps keep us honest, at the same time it provides fresh stimulus for inspired groping.

The fundamental distinction between Faith in O and all other attitudes is brought out most dramatically in Bion's discussions of the 'good therapist' and the container (e.g. 1970). The good therapist wants to help the patient and may learn all he can about the latter toward this end. However, the desire to help and know can get in the way rather than prove useful in a profound sense. Such activity may block the openness of mind necessary for inklings of the emotional truth of a session to form. Wanting to help and know can saturate the space in which O might evolve. The therapist who, even with the best intentions, is caught up in a subtle controlling or mastery stance toward the emotional reality of a session, is in danger of stunting perceptive listening and shutting out subtle currents of creative movement.

Bion's famous dictum, that the analytic attitude is one of freedom from memory and desire, must be understood in terms of the faith-mastery polarity, particularly with regard to his critique of the wish to know. He opts for a primacy of perception and attention over memory and knowledge as the analyst's most basic working orientation. In his view, the intention to attend and perceive rather than remember and know or impose a 'helpful' scenario, is the more fruitful attitude for creative unfolding. Knowledge, to be sure, spontaneously enters the process of freshly forming *gestalts* expressive of psychic reality. However, in the frame of mind designated by faith in O, one does not hold on to either what one knows or one's formulations, but is more deeply anchored (better, freely floating) in hopeful contact with the thing itself.

Even functioning as a 'good container' can present a danger for perceptive vision (1977, pp. 28–33). It is important to stress this because in analytic writings the positive aspects of the mind's containing function is usually emphasized (Green, 1975; Grotstein, 1979; Eigen, 1980b). In the latter instance, for example, thoughts or feelings the baby cannot process are evacuated into the mother, who contains and detoxifies them by her own mental functions (memory and reverie) and feeds the baby usable responses. More generally, the mind as container is more concerned with regulating the balance of pleasure and pain than with emotional truth. Ideally, the individual grows in his ability to contain and successfully represent his painful states along with his wish to feel good.

However, an orientation toward pleasure-pain regulation (here the containing function working through introjective-projective operations) tends to mitigate against intunement with movement of O. Attention to the emotional truth of situations must have a certain independence of pleasure-pain considerations. One cannot 'regulate' the movement of truth. Rather, one seeks to modulate oneself in relation to requirements that truth discloses. The containing function, at bottom, seeks to influence the movement of O in ego desirable directions, in fathomable and manipulable terms. It aims to cut one's ultimate reality to ego size. Ordinary good adaptations may make life manageable, but may diminish chances for profound psychic transformation. The natural attitude, however supportive and useful, is not the analytic attitude and can interfere with the most far-reaching kinds of therapeutic encounters. To try to control where truth will lead is to put oneself above truth, and so, in part, shut out the potentially reorienting effects of the latter. To maximize the possibility of contact with what is most important for becoming at one with oneself, the subject must relate to truth with faith.

Below are several quotes from Bion relevant to our primary concern in this section, the distinction of the faith dimension (*the* analytic attitude) from other inclinations.

for me 'faith' is a scientific state of mine and should be recognized as such. But it must be 'faith' unstained by any element of memory or desire (1977, p. 32).

The evocation of that which provided a container for possessions, and of the sensuous gratifications with which to fill it [e.g. the pleasure of helping or being helped], will differ from an evocation stimulated by at-one-ment (1977, p. 33).

It may be wondered what state of mind is welcome if desires and memories are not. A term that would express approximately what I need to express is 'faith'—faith that there is an ultimate reality and truth—the unknown, unknowable, 'formless infinite'. This must be believed of every object of which the personality can be aware: the evolution of ultimate reality (signified by O) has issued in objects of which the individual can be aware. The objects of awareness are aspects of the 'evolved' O and are such that the sensuously derived mental functions are adequate to apprehend them. For them faith is not required; for O it is (1977, p. 31).

In sum, the starting point for psychoanalytic work is the analyst's capacity to be at one with O. To paraphrase Bion, the more real the psycho-analyst is, the more he can be at one with the reality of the patient. The learnings and formulations that go into our acts of communication are necessarily derived from past sensuous experience and must be taken as analogies to be purified of the very terms employed. All formulations are, in part, signs of their own limitations. They are pointers, expressive vehicles of access, and undo themselves if they serve their purpose. The therapeutic *gestalt* that grows out of evolution of O is not a memory of past learning, but a present speculative seeing, a felt link with emotional truth that may be relevant for the latter's further evolution. If the analyst is able to sustain Faith in O and tolerate the development of formulations that reflect O, he may legitimately hope for a therapeutic outcome in which the analysand becomes more at one with himself, i.e. his own evolution.

Doubleness and Mystery: Beyond the Depressive Position

The tension between two or more orders of experience permeates the thought of Winnicott, Lacan and Bion. A basic tension in all of these writers is that between true and false turns of mind. Taken together, their approach is both Kantian and Biblical, yet distinctly psycho-analytic. The dynamic tension within and between different orders of mental life is a formal, as well as descriptive, characteristic of Freud's thought (Lowe, 1977, 1980; Bass, 1980, p. 40). The theme is ancient and restless, its turns unpredictable. The vicissitudes of faith involve the struggle not only to know but in some way be one's true self, to take up the journey with all that one is and may become, and to encounter through oneself the ground of one's being. This is undertaken with the knowledge that we are mediate beings, that certainty is beyond certain reach, but that anything short of this attempt portends disaster and is self-crippling. The undertaking itself involves one in continuous re-creation.

Although Winnicott, Lacan and Bion develop the theme of faith-through-doubleness in their own individual ways, there is a point at which they converge. The faith dimension is a common vertex through which they move along differing paths. In the present section I will try to situate some of their key differences in the light of their central crossing. My interest is not in 'reconciling' (reducing?) these theorists so much as seeing ways they help set each other in motion. My development draws on but is not limited to earlier sections. Some further summary and amplification of aspects of their thought is necessary in order to bring out the full flavour of how they fill out and challenge each other.

Winnicott

Winnicott assumes life is primarily creative and in infancy this creativity unfolds in phases with proper environmental help. For him a certain similarity, perhaps continuity, persists from biological to psychological spheres. However, this apparent monism quickly shifts keys. Human life, as it is lived, is shot through with antimonies. For example, he contrasts a basic True Self with a False Self, the latter a self-protective personality distortion. The true self feeling involves a sense of all-out personal aliveness, more than simple animal aliveness because it includes an awareness of being or feeling *real*. It thus requires a lived recognition of being the self one is, that this felt presence is one's true being. This connects with Bion's insistence that truth is necessary for wholeness and emotional growth. Falsity pollutes one's self-feeling, even if one has become used to it, or even takes it as the norm.

For Winnicott, the true self feeling is essentially undefensive. It may be defended and under pressure shrink or start to disappear (Eigen, 1973). But it is most basically unarmed and characterized by the feeling of genuine wholeness. In Winnicott's account the sense of wholeness evolves from a period of self-other harmonious mixup (to use Balint's

1968 phrase), through self-other distinction, and thrives on both these tendencies. At all points it (the sense of wholeness) is threatened by counter-tendencies toward disruption and perversion, especially tyrannical (False Self) introjective-projective fantasy operations whereby the self-feeling becomes demonized. With reference to the above account (pp. 2-18), Winnicott's False Self tends to correspond with what he termed the unit self, the self as an isolate, Lacan's Imaginary. He describes central aspects of the True Self's foundational journey in his accounts of transitional experiencing and object usage.

In the resulting dualistic clinical picture, truth and falsehood vie in the human soul. For Winnicott the essential battle is over one's sense of realness: does one feel real to oneself or merely a phantom or splinter self? The main problem that pervades his clinical writings is depersonalization and the profound self-splitting and self-anaesthesia that underwrite it. Both he and Bion link authentic wholling processes with trueness. This may be viewed as an assumption, a faith. From their viewpoint it is also profound description.

For Winnicott life requires violence (hatching processes). However, he believes that in human life, optimally, this occurs within a primacy of love. His object relations rewriting of the drive fusion theory opts for a primacy of unity-in-differentiation. For example, in his account of the use of the object we have seen that an 'I love you' spontaneously arises in the wake of the 'I destroy you', and this 'I love you' makes destructiveness creative. In this instance, the two together lead to a fuller, richer awareness of self and other, a revitalizing sense of otherness as such.

In sum, Winnicott's aim was to place the living sense of feeling true or false to oneself at the centre of human experience and thinking. He did this by raising the issue of how these two psychic tendencies meet the perennial vicissitudes of connexion and otherness. The particular psycho-analytic turn given to these issues involved a detailed account of the interaction of love and destructiveness within the context of subject-to-subject interactions at originary phases of the self's history.

Winnicott's True Self was apparently meant as a phenomenological expression, but it may also function as *a formal principle of personal growth*. Winnicott (1958, 1965, 1971; also, Eigen, 1973) believes that the True Self is in some sense absolutely private, incommunicado. However, not only is it inaccessible to everybody but oneself; it may be somewhat beyond the subject's reach as well. The subject both participates in true self feeling at the same time that he strives toward (more of) it, an inexhaustible paradox built into the very structure of self-feeling. The true self feeling may become defensively abused, so that true and false self mix-ups arise (evil seems good, and good evil). In such instances some overall skew or 'offness' in the personality will press for recognition, until the core subjective quality of what it feels like to be a person gets set right or is given up on ('Evil, be my good'). In this context, a 'Winnicottian' (given, as Khan [1979] says, that there's no such thing) therapy aims at working through the individual's profound depersonalization in a way that makes access to true self feeling possible. Nevertheless, even within the domain of true self feeling itself, mystery remains in fact and principle. More approach is always possible.

In both Lacan and Bion the subject's reaching after the true and real *explicitly* becomes a formal principle for full, personal evolution (in Bion, at least, it also is meant descriptively). The fundamental status of the need to generate meanings which reflect or bring the subject into accord with the truth about himself defines the tenor of these men's writings. This hunger for emotional truth is frequently at war with the ego as an adaptive mechanism (or system).

Lacan

Lacan (1977, 1978; Lemaire, 1977) seems to say that there is some primordial state of affairs that psychic life seeks to represent and deal with throughout its history. What this state of affairs is we cannot know. We can only create myths that function as markers for the unknown it is. The principal myths for Lacan involve the rupture of some fundamental union, i.e. the separation from mother's body at birth, the break-up of baby-mother dual union with the advent of language. These wounded unions leave the infant with a propensity to feel incomplete and insufficient, with a need or lack which becomes translated as desire. The human venture is the history of desire as it ceaselessly loses and rediscovers itself through the identificatory and symbolic registers. The imaginary order perpetrates endless misreadings, while the Symbolic makes as honest an attempt as possible to represent the basic situation beyond our grasp, the proposed wounded union.

The basic structure of Lacan's views, like Freud's, involves some basic state of affairs or fantasy, some basic x behind a ceaseless flow of transpositions which reflect or deal with it more falsely or truly. Lacan associates truth as such with the unknown state of affairs itself, the Real, from which we are barred from direct access by primal repression. The latter is instituted by our insertion into language, the basic medium of rupture. We may try to create a spurious image of wholeness, an Imaginary self-suffficiency. But we also strive to represent, as best we can, the *sense* of our division as it unfolds through the very gaps we are attempting to read. These three unconscious orders, The Real, Imaginary and Symbolic, are not reducible to one another. They express categories that form the basis of humankind's perennial date with conflict.

Bion, Lacan and Winnicott

For Bion (like Lacan, Freud, Kant), the ultimate reality of the self is beyond the reach of knowledge. However, for Bion, openness to the unknown is *the* formal and working principle by which psychoanalysis must proceed. Lacan also posits the unknowable. However, he tends to link it with a basic situation that has undergone repression, and reads psychic life in terms of its transforms. For Bion this would constitute one mode in which the unknowable can show itself. His position, I believe, is far more radical.

Bion's O has *no psychological locus at all*. Its status is not confined to any category one can possibly postulate concerning psychic life, yet it is assumed to be the ground of them all. No starting or ending point can be envisioned for O. It is always evolving. As we aim to express the emotional truth of a session, we cannot know ahead of time what this truth will look like. It may take the form (Lacan's, Freud's) of elemental situations travelling in disguise via condensations and displacements (Lacan's metaphor and metonymy). Or it may take as yet unperceived forms which require fresh methods of approach.

Lacan, too, stresses the importance of not oversimplifying the complexity of psychic life. The path of meaning is unpredictable, nor can one bottle the Real in one's representations. Both he and Bion stress the necessity of a doubleness of vision as an intrinsic part of one's working method. In this regard, Bion speaks of 'binocular vision', a metaperspective the subject continuously adopts on the interplay and barriers between conscious and unconscious processes. Lacan talks of the different languages employed by consciousness and unconscious mental orders. One reads unconscious meanings as one might a palimpsest or different sides of an obelisk. The emphasis in both writers is on what sort of attitude makes a 'simultaneous' reading of a plurality of dimensions possible. However, Bion leaves it open, in principle, as to what constitutive forms such a reading might look like. There are no working limits placed on the nature of O and its evolutions. One is not constrained to read emotional truth in terms of an unchanging situation. In Bion's view, what Lacan might call the basic situation (the x that is transposed, say, via metonymy), itself may be an evolved form capable of undergoing further evolution.

Lacan's entire panoply can be situated within a framework that, in Bion's vision, may be represented as evolutions of O or barriers against

this evolution. As a formal concept Lacan's Imaginary represents barriers against the evolution of O. His Symbolic expresses and possibly
facilitates this evolution. The status of the Real is more ambiguous. Is
it a lived dimension outside of meaning? Is it instituted by meaning? Is
it both inside and outside of meaning? In Lacan's writings it is all of
these in different contexts. As the primal repressed instituted by meaning, it eludes meaning and is expressed in disguised forms through
meaning.

Derrida (1978) also has challenged the structure of Lacan's thought
on the basis of this ambiguity. He, somewhat like Bion, questions the
need of postulating, even as a myth, a static basic x with which meaning is forever preoccupied. Like Lacan, however, he views the structure
of language as the defining dimension of human subjectivity and equates
meaning with languages. If, he argues, language is the privileged phenomenon that makes human subjectivity what it is, and psychic life is
the play of signifiers, there is no reason to look to a basic x outside of
language. Such a looking would be senseless and impossible. Meaning
feeds on meaning from its inception. If human psychic life *is* the life of
meaning, no situation extrinsic to the latter can be used to start it off.

Bion's position differs in important respects from both Lacan's and
Derrida's. As mentioned earlier, his O is not necessarily an ever recur-
rence of the same. It is, also, meaningful in a more profound sense than
language. For Bion, the subject seeks to express his emotional reality
through language. The latter may help feed the movement of his emotional truth but is not identical with it. In this regard, life may be richly
meaningful for the preverbal baby, as witnessed, for example, by the
radiant self-other awareness expressed in the smiling response.

If, given Bion's framework, the life of meaning goes deeper than language, language is one way (or series of ways) that meaning can be organized. The language operations charted by Lacan may be included by
and even reshape the unconscious but do not exhaust the latter. They
portray crucial ways a subject can be a subject, privileged ways meaning operates. For Bion emotional truth is not confined to language, nor
does it have a static basis. Its evolving quality spreads out in all temporal directions. We open ourselves to meet it. Our formulations try to
express what in faith we trust our gesture contacts.

In this context, Winnicott's transitional experiencing and use of the
object represent evolutions of O. They are formulations of preverbal
events alive with felt meaning, areas of lived truth linked with the
unfolding of self-other awareness. What is suggested is the emergence of
new experiential dimensions (new 'basic situations') rather than convo-
lutions of a repressed x. The formulations themselves are made in the

hope of helping the subject to discover and move in accord with his own meaningfully lived reality in an ongoing way.

All three authors, Winnicott, Bion and Lacan, express the subject's struggle to live faithfully, together with impediments to this endeavour. Their central concern is the subject's radically reorienting relations to lived truth as it moves through vicissitudes of meaning. This is a struggle that incorporates yet transcends identificatory/introjective-projective/internalization processes, and so goes beyond the depressive position, the path of symbol development in Kleinian thinking.

As discussed above, Winnicott's transitional experiencing and object usage constitute a world of experiencing at once symbolic and actual. The latter two orders permeate and support each other in a kind of seamless unity, giving rise to an unfolding of fresh experiential dimensions. In object usage the introjected other is ceaselessly destroyed in loving communion with a more radically freeing sense of otherness, an otherness intrinsically experienced with joy, not depressive guilt. Introjections form part of a larger psychic field which they may interfere with or subserve. In part, they are consolidating measures that are there to be transcended.

Lacan's style is more ironic. For him the distinction between self and other (correlatively, consciousness and the unconscious) is consititued through language. The life of meaning echoes the rupture of mute union, a rupture that meaning itself is. The subject is at war as to how he is to relate to his predicament. He may try identificatory (Imaginary) ways to fill in or escape the gaps he finds in himself and between himself and others. Or he may struggle to discover ways of representing the truth of his condition to himself, thereby achieving a modicum of transcendence. This latter acheivement in symbolic decentring may not exactly by joyous (although it involves the *juissance* of meaning), but it is not Kleinian introjective depression.

Introjective depression tends to save the subject from a more far-reaching and dizzying view of his meaning creating capacity. The subject's meaning creating capacity provides a meta-perspective on the category of introjection (and internalization). Indeed, introjection requires a perspective beyond itself. The subject moves between his identificatory capacity and his capacity to see through the latter. For Lacan, irony is the guardian of the subject's good faith. Through ironic consciousness the subject recognizes that he is too complicated to be wholehearted in any definitive sense, at the same time he moves from or toward whatever whole-heartedness is possible along a radically decentred path.

Bion's writings combine the most radical sincerity and irony. The subject who is attentive to evolutions of O is decentred from himself. He focuses on O. All aspects of his psychic life (in the strict sense, anything that implies possession: i.e. One's knowledge, desires, habits, pleasures) are distinguished from realizations that grow from the evolution of O. Even then, what the subject perceives may or may not express the prepotent truth about the emotional reality at hand. Nevertheless, he continues focusing on what he hopes is O and meets the turbulence that comes his way. His reward is not the certainty of being right or wrong at any given moment, but the profound change of quality and reorientation he finds himself undergoing as an experiencing subject.

Introjective-projective operations, from the present perspective, fall into the realm characterized by possessiveness. The subject tries to make something part of himself or the other. This involves controlling operations which may interfere with perception of emotional truth. When Bion does describe the evolution of O in a session as a movement from projective (fragmenting) to introjective (wholling) states, these latter terms depict a phasic unfolding that spontaneously occurs within an overarching openness toward O. Neither phase is courted or held onto. The subject directs himself with his whole being toward O. The projective-introjective movements that happen as a matter of course are not themselves the primary method or aim.

What is crucial is *how one relates to* whatever one may be relating to. In Bion's view, the basic analytic attitude or way of relating is to keep aiming toward O. If, for example, one's emotional reality or truth is despair, what is most important is not *that* one may be in despair, but one's attitudes *toward* one's despair. Through one's basic attentiveness one's despair can declare itself and tell its story. One enters profound dialogue with it. If one stays with this process, an evolution even in the quality of despair may begin to be perceived, since despair itself is never uniform.

What evolves in analysis is no mere knowledge about content, or pleasurable ways of interaction, or more successful adaptations. These may be involved but are not primary. The most precious gain is the evolution of openness toward experiencing, or, as Bion writes, 'experiencing experience', a process in which something more is always happening (or about to). The essential freedom analysis brings is the analytic attitude itself, the liberation of the capacity to focus on O.

Ideal Experiencing: God, Mother, Father

In sum, Winnicott, Lacan and Bion carry on Freud's theme of the self in conflict with the constituting dimensions through which it lives. My emphasis has been on a sense of wholeness which, nonetheless, continuously evolves through struggles which threaten to deform or occlude it. The paradoxical complexity of a wholling tendency that thrives on coming through tendencies toward depersonalization and dispersal, bears witness to the category of mystery as a basic dimension in which we live (Lowe, 1977).

In Winnicott's account, the sense of wholeness passes through phases in which the distance between self and other is taken for granted (transitional experiencing) and is acutely experienced (object usage). In Bion's work Faith in O represents a wholling attitude (linked with attention and creativity) which evolves, in part, by suffering through the divisions and disruptions psychic life is prone to. Whatever wholling principle exists in Lacan's thought ironically enters with the subject's realization of the impossibility of wholeness. Realization itself is a wholling as well as divisive act, even as it realizes its divisiveness.

The concerns of these authors converge on a central interest: creative experiencing, what makes it possible or hinders it (formally and descriptively). They chart detailed ways in which creative experiencing involves paradox, mystery or faith expressed through dialectical thinking. In effect, each tries to develop something of a phenomenology of creative experiencing. In so doing, these authors begin to sustain a radical encounter with what is the primary quality of experiencing as such: its intangibility or immateriality.

As mentioned earlier, experiencing as such is not spatially localizeable, yet it is that through which space awareness arises. An apparently unknowable, imperceptible dimension makes knowing and perception possible. Freud, of course, acknowledged the phenomenological immateriality of mind (at certain points he even tried to derive our primitive sense of space from the immaterial psyche's sense of its own 'depth'). However, by a sleight of hand he played down crucial aspects of this realization in the working out of his formal theory (Eigen, 1979, 1980a,b, 1981a). This is most readily seen in his treatment of 'ideal states', a basic form ideal experiencing can take.

Ideal states often refer to a sense of infinite perfection, whether beatific (divine) or horrific (demonic). Such ideal moments together with the images associated with them play a central role in the Freudian corpus. They are virtually omnipresent, complexly interacting with or against instincts and reality. Ideal qualities in one form or other appear as part of the object pole of instincts. In Freudian dramas, *instincts seek an ideal imago*. Desire is a noetic constant. The noematic nucleus of the shifting x desired carries an ideal glow. In Freudian dramas the ideal imago variously saturates one's own body, ego, mother, father, and so on to a wide range of possibilities (e.g. faeces, feet, science, nation, God).

In most Freudian literature the defensive and pathological uses of ideal images have been stressed, at best emphasizing their importance as compensations (Freud, 1914; Reich, 1953, 1954, 1960; Chasseguet-Smirgel, 1974). For Freud, ideal experiencing usually involved something in disguise (e.g. mother, father, sex, hostility, etc.). The capacity which produced ideal images tended not to be credited in its own right, but seen as a derived form of 'something else' (Eigen, 1979).

I believe the authors discussed in this paper, more than most psychoanalytic writers, systematically attempt to take up the problem of ideal experiencing in its own right, as a spontaneously unfolding human capacity related to existential concerns (for a discussion of where Kohut, 1971, 1977, falls short, see Eigen, 1979, pp. 294–6). Their critique of the identification-introjection-internalization track preserves what is valuable in the Freudian analysis of the defensive function of ideal images, but distinguishes this line from the inherently positive capacity it defensively deploys.

These authors attempt to differentiate the positive and negative aspects of ideal experiencing without reducing one to the other. Winnicott, for example, distinguishes the sense of wholeness (an ideal state) linked with True Self from perversions of ideal feelings linked with False Self (see Khan, 1979, for excellent descriptions of perverse ecstasies involving a demonized sense of wholeness). In the former instance, ideal moments of dual union may be regenerative and not primarily defensive (Eigen, 1980a,b,c, 1981a,c,d). Undefensive and defensive use of ideal states complexly intermingle in actual living. Neither term of this ongoing tension is absent for long, although either may dominate in any given instance.

In Lacan, both the Imaginary and Symbolic orders may function defensively. But the latter seeks to open out to Truth, while the former moves to foreclose the latter. Truth seeking requires a meta-perspective on defensiveness as such, and so, in principle, moves in contact with a more profound vision than the defensiveness it is caught in. In Bion, as indicated earlier, truth functions as an intrinsic principle of emotional growth and is not basically a defence against anxiety (although it may be so employed). Faith in O is an undefensive, open attentiveness to the emotional reality of a subject, his truth, and comes in fierce conflict with inclinations that fight against it (the latter includes introjective or projective tendencies toward 'premature wholeness').

All three authors maintain the critical importance of not confusing creative experiencing with introjection (or internalization) of mother and father images or functions. The sources of creative experiencing run deeper than internalization and go beyond it. If one reads these authors carefully, one discovers that *the primary object of creative experiencing*

*is not mother or father but the unknowable ground of creativeness as
such.* Winnicott, for example, emphasizes that what is at stake in transitional experiencing is not mainly a self or object (mother) substitute,
but the creation of a symbol, of symbolizing experiencing itself. The subject lives through and towards creative immersion (including phases of
chaos, unintegration, waiting). What he symbolizes and seeks more and
more of is the absorption of creative experiencing and the way this latter makes use of objects through successive waves of self-other awareness. Maternal or paternal object relations may subserve or thwart this
experiencing but must not be simply identified with it. A similar argument could be made for the subject's immersion in the life of meaning
as described by Lacan, or Bion's Faith in O.

By emphasizing the positive aspect of ideal experiencing as an irreducible term of human experience, these authors make it difficult to permit any facile 'mother' or 'father' reductionism. The latter, for example,
may be seen most dramatically in the tendency to equate God with father
(Freud) or mother (Klein). The primary ideal object cannot be reduced to
either. The mix-up between God, parents and self is a basic and perennial problem in human life, and psychoanalysis contributes much in chart-
ing this confusion. However, the terms of this dilemma can not be
collapsed into one another without deception. If parents and self are, in
part, gradually distinguished from idealizations, they cannot account for
the capacity to idealize. They are occasions which enable this capacity to
operate in developmentally sound or ill ways (Eigen, 1979; see Elkin,
1972, for a psychoanalytic account which tries to give ideal states their
due in an epistemologically-anthropologically sound context).

Winnicott's, Lacan's and Bion's emphasis on understanding the capacity to produce ideal images in its own right is no empty formalism. These
authors are wary of traditional idealist-empiricist bifurcations. As psychoanalysts, following Freud, they chart the vicissitudes of ideal experiencing *vis-à-vis* the hard facts of life, from early infancy on. However,
they do not obscure the irreducible co-presence of different orders of
experience, or try to explain one in terms of the other without reciprocity. I believe they explicitly bring out and heighten the problems at
stake in a psychic field wherein ideal experiencing and a spatial object
world permeate and withdraw from one another. It is the irreducible
(irreconcilable?) co-presence of immaterial and spatial dimensions of
lived experience (reflectively elaborated) that defines human consciousness. In systems language they are correlatives. They require each other
but cannot be equated in life as we know it so far.

I have tried to indicate ways in which three psychoanalytic writers
have begun to chart systematically the interplay of variant experiential

dimensions without compromising any of the basic terms involved. So far as I am aware, this is a radically new enterprise within psycho-analysis proper. It has been more usual for one of these terms to be made primary at the other's expense, or at least, in some way for primitive terms of experience to devalue each other. Whether or not the kind of project the approximations discussed point to can work, or will prove to be wishful thinking, remains to be seen.

The author's discussion made highly sophisticated attempts to artic-ulate the faith dimension, a 'critical faith' which functions both as a for-mal condition that makes psychoanalytical experience possible and, descriptively, as a specific state of mind (i.e. the psychoanalytic attitude). I wonder if the structure of their attempts does not connect in spirit, at least partly, with the Biblical injunction for a snake-smart brain and dovegentle heart. The wholling tendency expressed here is a differenti-ated one. It is not primarily based on mastery or control, although cir-cumspection comes into play. It grows most basically through a faith in a spontaneous play of experiencing and meaning which aims to express and unfold what is most real for the subject, his emotional truth or way of being a subject, who one is.

References

Balint, M. (1968). *The Basic Fault*. London: Tavistock.

Bass, A. (1980). The double game: Psychoanalysis and deconstruction. Unpublished paper given at the National Psychological Association for Psychoanalysis.

Bateson, G. (1979). *Mind and Nature. A Necessary Unity*. New York: E. P. Dutton.

Bion, W. R. (1970). *Attention and Interpretation*. London: Tavistock. (In *Seven Servants*.)

———— (1977). *Seven Servants*. New York: Jason Aronson.

Chasseguet-Smirgel, J. (1974). Perversion, idealization and sublimation. *International Journal of Psycho-analysis* 55:349–357.

Derrida, J. (1978). *Writing and Difference*. Chicago: University of Chicago Press.

Eigen, M. (1973). Abstinence and the schizoid ego. *International Journal of Psycho-Analysis* 54:493–498.

———— (1979). Ideal images, creativity, and the Freudian drama. *Psychocultural Review* 3:287–298.

———— (1980a). Instinctual fantasy and ideal images. *Contemporary Psycho-analysis* 16:119–137.

———— (1980b). On the significance of the face. *Psychoanal Review* 67:427–441.

———— (1980c). Expression and meaning: A case study. In *Expressive Therapy*, ed. A. Robbins. New York: Human Sciences.

———— (1981). Guntrip's analysis with Winnicott. *Contemporary Psychoanalysis* 17:103–117.

——— (1982). Creativity, instinctual fantasy and ideal images. *Psychoanalytic Review* 68:317–339.

——— (1983). A note on the structure of Freud's theory of creativity. *Psychoanalytic Review* 70:41–45.

——— (1984). On demonized aspects of the self. In *Evil: Self and Culture*, ed. M. C. Nelson & M. Eigen. pp. 91–123. New York: Human Sciences.

Eigen, M., & Robbins, A. (1980). Object relations and expressive symbolism. Some structures and functions of expressive therapy. In *Expressive Therapy*, ed. A. Robbins, pp. 73–94. New York: Human Sciences.

Elkin, H. (1972). On selfhood and the development of ego structures in infancy. *Psychoanalytic Review* 59:389–416.

Freud, S. (1914). On narcissism: An introduction. *Standard Edition* 14:73–102.

——— (1920). Beyond the pleasure principle. *Standard Edition* 18:7–64.

Green, A. (1975). The analyst, symbolization and absence in the analytic setting (on changes in analytic practice and analytic experience). *International Journal of Psycho-Analysis* 56:1–22.

Greenacre, P. (1952). *Trauma, Growth and Personality*. New York: International Universities Press.

Grotstein, J. S. (1979). Who is the dreamer who dreams the dream and who is the dreamer who understands it? *Contemporary Psychoanalysis* 15:110–169.

Khan, M. M. R. (1979). *Alienation in Perversions*. New York: International Universities Press.

Kohut, H. (1971). *Analysis of the Self*. New York: International Universities Press.

——— (1977). *The Restoration of the Self*. New York: International Universities Press.

Lacan, J. (1977). *Ecrits: A Selection*. New York: Norton.

——— (1978). *The Four Fundamental Concepts of Psychoanalysis*. New York: International Universities Press.

Lemaire, A. (1977). *Jacques Lacan*. London: Routledge & Kegan Paul.

Lowe, W. J. (1977). *Mystery and the Unconscious: A Study in Thought of Paul Ricoeur*. Metuchen, NJ: Scarecrow.

——— (1980). Evil and the unconscious: A Freudian exploration. *Soundings* 43:7–35.

Meltzer, D. (1973). *Sexual States of the Mind*. Strath Tay: Scotland: Clunie.

Merleau-Ponty, M. (1962). *Phenomenology of Perception*. London: Routledge & Kegan Paul.

——— (1968). *The Visible and the Invisible*. Evanston: Northwestern University Press.

——— (1977). Winnicott and overlapping circles. In *The Suppressed Madness of Sane Men*, pp. 279–286. London: Tavistock, 1987.

Reich, A. (1953). Narcissistic object choice in women. In *Psychoanalytic Contributions*. pp. 179–208. New York: International Universities Press, 1973.

——— (1954). Early identifications as archaic elements in the superego. In *Psychoanalytic Contributions*, pp. 209–235. New York: International Universities Press, 1973.

——— (1960). Pathologic forms of self-esteem. In *Psychoanalytic Contributions*, pp. 209–235. New York: International Universities Press, 1973.

Segal, H. (1978). On symbolism. *International Journal of Psycho-Analysis* 59:315–319.

Spitz, R. (1965). *The First Year of Life*. New York: International Universities Press.

Weil, E. (1958). The origin and vicissitudes of the self-image. *Psychoanalysis* 1:3–19.

Winnicott, D. W. (1953). Transitional objects and transitional phenomena. *International Journal of Psychoanalysis* 34:89–97.

———— (1958). *Collected Papers. Through Paediatrics to Psycho-Analysis*. London: Tavistock.

———— (1963). The development of the capacity for concern. *Bulletin of the Menninger Clinic* 27:167–176.

———— (1965). *The Maturational Processes and the Facilitating Environment*. New York: International Universities Press.

———— (1969). The use of the object and relating through identification. *International Journal of Psycho-Analysis* 50:711–716.

———— (1971). *Playing and Reality*. New York: Basic Books.

Afterword

After this paper was published, I received a letter from Clare Winnicott saying how pleased she was that someone had given Winnicott's "use of object" writings a reading he would be happy with. Apparently, she was bitter about the bad reception his paper had received in New York when he visited in 1968. She was, also, relieved that my paper did not try to conflate the contributions of three great men but instead amplified distinctive contributions.

The idea that we are always killing each other in unconscious fantasy and need each other to survive destruction, has never been more important. It may be that faith in the other's survival grows as a result of actual experience of this survival. But it often is true that some bit of faith enables awareness of what survives to be perceived.

All too often, one hears of cases in which actual murder pushes the object's ability to survive to the limit and destruction wins. The murderer, for moments, may succeed in living an objectless existence, or, more likely, may feel justified, since he has proven what everyone knows: the object is damaged, broken, incapable, not up to the task of survival. A kind of "faith" in destruction substitutes for generative faith.

Bion (1965) paints a picture of a negative universe, an antiworld, in which individuals are caught in a vortex of destruction. He evokes a force that goes on working after it destroys personality, time, space, existence. At the same time, he calls attention to a kind of faith, holding on to nothing, open to the impact of life. The very aliveness of life can be horribly threatening. We do what we can with what uplifts us and tears up apart. How much of ourselves and our aliveness can we use and manage to bear?

The themes I dealt with in my article—faith, doubleness, mystery—are basic today. So far, we have managed to survive the threat of nuclear disaster. But there are many other ways we may or may not be able to survive ourselves. As a group, we seem to flourish at our own expense—with many types of psychophysical toxins the price for success. We know very little about the forces we tinker with, although we like to think we can buy them off with a smile or a wink. The idea that faith is an attitude that can open crucial domains for further experiencing may turn out to be, at least, as important as technological skills. Faith may not only enable us to deepen awareness of subzero dimensions and destructive infinities but, also, invite us to be partners in its evolution—our own evolution.

I've amplified many of the themes in my "area of faith" paper in other works (see Eigen, 1996, 1998).

References

Bion, W. R. (1965) *Transformations*. London: William Heinemann.

Eigen, M. (1993), The area of faith in Winnicott, Lacan and Bion. In: *The Electrified Tightrope*, ed. A. Phillips. Northvale, NJ: Aronson, pp. 109–138.

———— (1996), *Psychic Deadness*. Northvale, NJ: Aronson.

———— (1998), *The Psychoanalytic Mystic*. Binghamton, NY: Esf.

The Patient as Interpreter of the Analyst's Experience

(1983)

Irwin Z. Hoffman

▼   ▼   ▼   ▼   ▼

Editors' Introduction

If the relational turn in psychoanalysis is thought of as a conceptual revolution, this early paper by Irwin Z. Hoffman surely constituted one of that revolution's first salvos. It seems an unlikely paper to have contributed to an upheaval in the history of ideas because, at first glance, its claims for itself seem quite modest. In the first line, Hoffman announces the presentation of a "point of view on the psychoanalytic situation" that will be accomplished, in part, "through a selective review of the literature."

Hoffman points to a long-standing genre within contemporary psychoanalysis of attacks on what he terms the "blank screen concept." In its most pristine form (and a proponent of such a form has become increasingly hard to find), the metaphor of the blank screen served as the centerpiece of a model of the analytic situation as thoroughly antiseptic, in which all the patient's experiences were generated within the mind of the patient, unprovoked, unstimulated, indeed unaffected by the analyst in any way at all. Critics of all stripes had been pounding away at this concept, in its starkest form, for years, creating the complacent impression that we are all surely immune from its falsities and misapprehensions. The brilliance of Hoffman's paper lies in his turning his critical focus from the dead horse that has been the object of these beatings, to its would-be assassins who, he discovers, are mounted on what turn out to be the deceased equine's close cousins.

By distinguishing between conservative and radical critiques of the blank screen concept, Hoffman framed the key question for contemporary psychoanalytic clinicians and theorists with a new clarity. We thought we were called on to choose between an anachronistic model of an antiseptic medium (a distorting patient and a cerebral, detached analyst) and newer models of the analytic situation that allowed the patient to experience the analyst, *in addition to* what arises from the transference, as an undistorted presence (as a partner in a "working alliance," a "real" object, an empathic listener, a provider of missing developmental functions). Hoffman demonstrated that the real choice for us is at once more subtle and stark.

What became most revolutionary about this early paper was Hoffman's demonstration that what he called the "social" paradigm (later to become Hoffman's "social constructivism" and later "dialectical constructivism") was not an additive to traditional concepts of transference as temporal displacements from the past, but a thoroughly alternative way of understanding the generation of experience within the analytic situation. Hoffman's perspective was both "relational" and "constructivist"—the analytic process was understood to center on the transformation of relational configurations between patient and analyst, and those configurations are cocreated in the interaction between the two participants.

Hoffman's major contributions of have been collected and integrated, along with several major new essays, in the recently published *Ritual and Spontaneity in the Psychoanalytic Process* (1998, The Analytic Press). Chapter 4 is an updated version of the original 1983 paper published here. Subsequent papers on closely related themes that also appear as chapters and are integrated into the book include: "Expressive Participation and Psychoanalytic Discipline" and "Dialectical Thinking and Therapeutic Action in the Psychoanalytic Process." A recent, extremely thoughtful consideration of the issues involved in the management of intense feelings in the countertransference is to be found in his commentary "Poetic Transformations of Erotic Experience" in *Psychoanalytic Dialogues* (1998, 8:791–804).

This paper presents a point of view on the psychoanalytic situation and on psychoanalytic technique through, in part, a selective review of the literature. An important underlying assumption of the paper is that existing theoretical models inevitably influence and reflect practice. This is often true even of models that practitioners claim they do not take seriously or literally. Such models may continue to affect practice adversely as long as their features are not fully appreciated and as long as alternative models are not recognized or integrated. An example of such a lingering model is the one in which the therapist is said to function like a blank screen in the psychoanalytic situation.

The Patient as Interpreter of the Analyst's Experience*

▼　　▼　　▼　　▼　　▼

The Resilience of the Blank Screen Concept

The psychoanalytic literature is replete with attacks on the blank screen concept, the idea that the analyst is not accurately perceived by the patient as a real person, but that he serves rather as a screen or mirror to whom various attitudes, feelings, and motives can be attributed depending upon the patient's particular neurosis and its transference expression. Critiques of this idea have come from within the ranks of classical Freudian analysts, as well as from Kleinians and Sullivanians. Even if one looks only at the classical literature, in one way or another, the blank screen concept seems to have been pronounced dead and laid to rest many times over the years. In 1950, Ida Macalpine, addressing only the implications for the patient's experience of classical psychoanalytic technique as she conceived of it (that is, not considering the analyst's personal contributions), said the following:

> It can *no longer be maintained* that the analysand's reactions in analysis occur spontaneously. His behavior is a response to the rigid infantile setting to which he is exposed. This poses many problems for further investigation. One of them is how does it react upon the patient? He must know it, consciously or unconsciously [p. 526, italics added].

Theresa Benedek said in 1953:

> As the history of psychoanalysis shows, the discussion of countertransference usually ended in a retreat to defensive positions. The argument to this end *used to be* (italics added) that the classical attitude affords the best guarantee that the *personality of the therapist* (author's italics)

---

* Originally published in *Contemporary Psychoanalysis*, 19:389–422, © 1983 W.A. White Institute.

would not enter the action-field of the therapeutic process. By that one assumes that as long as the analyst does not reveal himself as a person, does not answer questions regarding his own personality, he remains unknown as if without individuality, that the transference process may unfold and be motivated only by the patient's resistances. The patient—although he is a sensitive, neurotic individual—is not supposed to sense and discern the therapist as a person [p. 202].

In 1956 Lucia Tower wrote:

I have for a very long time speculated that in many—perhaps every—intensive analytic treatment there develops something in the nature of countertransference structures (perhaps even a "neurosis") which are essential and inevitable counterparts of the transference neurosis [p. 232].

In the 60's Loewald (1960), Stone (1961), and Greenson (1965) added their voices to the already large chorus of protest against this remarkably resilient concept. From varying theoretical perspectives, the critiques continued into the 70s and 80s as represented, for example, in the writings of Gill (1979; 1982a; 1982b; 1983; Gill and Hoffman, 1982a: 1982b), Sandler (1976; 1981) and Kohut (1977), among many others. In fact, the blank screen idea is probably not articulated as often or even as well by its proponents as it is by its opponents, a situation which leads inevitably to the suspicion that the proponents are straw men and that shooting them down has become a kind of popular psychoanalytic sport.[1]

I am persuaded, however, that the issue is a very important one and that it deserves repeated examination and discussion. The blank screen view in psychoanalysis is only one instance of a much broader phenomenon which might be termed *asocial conceptions of the patient's experience in psychotherapy*. According to these conceptions, there is a stream of experience going on in the patient which is divorced to a significant extent from the immediate impact of the therapist's personal presence. I say "personal presence" because generally certain theoretically prescribed facilitating aspects of the therapist's conduct are recognized fully as affecting the course of the patient's experience. But the paradigm is one in which proper or ideal conduct on the part of the therapist allows for a flow of experience which has an organic-like momentum of its own and which is free to follow a certain "natural" course. An intriguing example of this asocial paradigm *outside* of psy-

---

1. It is interesting that critics of the blank screen concept have frequently been concerned that others would think they were beating a dead horse (see, for example, Sterba, 1934, p. 117; Stone, 1961, pp. 18–19; and Kohut, 1977, pp. 253–255).

choanalysis can be found in client-centered therapy. Ideally, the classical client-centered therapist is so totally and literally self-effacing that his personality as such is effectively removed from the patient's purview. Carl Rogers stated in 1951:

> It is surprising how frequently the client uses the word "impersonal" in describing the therapeutic relationship after the conclusion of therapy. This is obviously not intended to mean that the relationship was cold or disinterested. It appears to be the client's attempt to describe this unique experience in which the person of the counselor—the counselor as an evaluating, reacting person with needs of his own—is so clearly absent. In this sense it is "im"-personal . . . the whole relationship is composed of the self of the client, the counselor being de-personalized for the purposes of therapy into being "the client's other self" [p. 208].

In psychoanalysis, the blank screen idea persists in more or less qualified and more or less openly acknowledged forms.[2] The counterpart of the notion that the analyst functions like a screen is the definition of transference as a distortion of current reality. As Szasz (1963) has pointed out, this definition of transference can serve a very important defensive function for the analyst, a function that may partly account for the persistence of the concept. I believe that another factor that has kept it alive has been the confusion of two issues. One has to do with the optimal level of spontaneity and personal involvement that the analyst should express in the analytic situation. The other has to do with the kind of credibility that is attributed to the patient's ideas about the analyst's experience. A theorist may repudiate the notion that the analyst should behave in an aloof, impersonal manner without addressing the question of the tenability of the patient's transference based speculations about the analyst's experience. To anticipate what follows, such speculations may touch upon aspects of the analyst's response to the patient which the analyst thinks are well-concealed or of which he himself is unaware. In general, recommendations pertaining to the analyst's personal conduct in the analytic situation may very well leave intact the basic model according to which the transference is understood and interpreted.

Standard Qualifications of the Blank Screen Concept

The notion that ideally the analyst functions like a screen is always qualified in the sense that it applies to only a part of the patient's total

---

2. Dewald's (1972) depiction of his conduct of an analysis exemplifies, as Lipton (1982) has shown, a relatively pure, if implicit, blank screen position.

experience of the therapist, the part that is conventionally regarded as neurotic transference. This is the aspect of the patient's experience which, allegedly, distorts reality because of the persisting influence of childhood events, wishes, conflicts, and adaptations. There are two kinds of experience that even the staunchest proponents of the screen or mirror function of the analyst recognize as likely to be responsive to something in the analyst's actual behavior rather than as expressions of pure fantasy. One is the patient's perception of the analyst as essentially trustworthy and competent, a part of the patient's experience which Freud (1912) subsumed under the rubric of the "unobjectionable" positive transference but which others, most notably Sterba (1934), Greenson (1965), and Zetzel (1956) have chosen to exclude from the realm of transference, designating it as the experience of the working or therapeutic alliance.[3] The second is the patient's recognition of, and response to, relatively blatant expressions of the therapist's neurotic and antitherapeutic countertransference. Both categories of experience lie outside the realm of transference proper which is where we find the patient's unfounded ideas, his neurotic, intrapsychically determined fantasies about the therapist. The point is well represented in the following statements (quoted here in reverse order) which are part of a classical definition of transference (Moore and Fine, 1968):

> [1] Transference should be carefully differentiated from the therapeutic alliance, a conscious aspect of the relationship between analyst and patient. In this, each implicitly agrees and understands their working together to help the analysand to mature through insight, progressive understanding, and control.

> [2] One of the important reasons for the relative anonymity of the analyst during the treatment process is the fact that a lack of information about his real attributes in personal life facilitates a transfer of the patient's revived early images on to his person. It also lessens the distortion of fantasies from the past by present perceptions. It must be recognized that there are situations or circumstances where the actual behavior or attitudes of the analyst cause reactions in the patient; these are not considered part of the transference reaction (See countertransference) [p. 93].

---

3. For discussions of the implications of Freud's position on this matter see Lipton (1977a) and Gill (1982, pp. 9–15).

Two Types of Paradigms and Critiques

In my view, critiques of the screen concept can be classified into two major categories: conservative critiques and radical critiques. Conservative critiques, in effect, always take the following form: they argue that one or both of the standard qualifications of the blank screen view noted above have been underemphasized or insufficiently elaborated in terms of their role in the analytic process. I call these critiques conservative because they retain the notion that a crucial aspect of the patient's experience of the therapist has little or no relation to the therapist's actual behavior or actual attitudes. The conservative critic reserves the term transference for this aspect of the patient's experience. At the same time he objects to a failure to recognize sufficiently the importance of another aspect of the patient's experience which is influenced by the "real" characteristics of the therapist, whether these real characteristics promote or interfere with an ideal analytic process. The dichotomy between realistic and unrealistic perception may be considered less sharp, but it is nevertheless retained. Although the realistic aspects of the patient's experience are now given more careful consideration and weight, in relation to transference proper the therapist is no less a blank screen than he was before. By not altering the standard paradigm for defining what is or is not realistic in the analytic situation, conservative critiques of the blank screen fallacy always end up perpetuating that very fallacy.

In contrast to conservative critiques, radical critiques reject the dichotomy between transference as distortion and non-transference as reality based. They argue instead that transference itself always has a significant plausible basis in the here-and-now. The radical critic of the blank screen model denies that there is any aspect of the patient's experience that pertains to the therapist's inner motives that can be unequivocally designated as distorting of reality. Similarly, he denies that there is any aspect of this experience that can be unequivocally designated as faithful to reality. The radical critic is a relativist. From his point of view the perspective that the patient brings to bear in interpreting the therapist's inner attitudes is regarded as one among many perspectives that are relevant, each of which highlights different facets of the analyst's involvement. This amounts to a different paradigm, not simply an elaboration of the standard paradigm which is what the conservative critics propose.

In rejecting the proposition that transference dominated experience and non-transference dominated experience can be differentiated on the grounds that the former is represented by fantasy which is divorced from reality whereas the latter is reality based, the radical critic does not imply that the two types of experience cannot be distinguished. Indeed, having rejected the criterion of distorted versus realistic perception, he is obliged to offer other criteria according to which this distinction can be made. For the radical critic the distinguishing features of the neurotic transference have to do with the fact that the patient is selectively attentive to certain facets of the therapist's behavior and personality; that he is compelled to choose one set of interpretations rather than others; that his emotional life and adaptation are unconsciously governed by and governing of the particular viewpoint he has adopted; and, perhaps most importantly, that he has behaved in such a way as to actually elicit overt and covert responses that are consistent with his viewpoint and expectations. The transference represents a way not only of construing but also of constructing or shaping interpersonal relations in general and the relationship with the analyst in particular. One could retain the term "distortion" only if it is defined in terms of the sense of necessity that the patient attaches to what he makes happen and to what he sees as happening between himself and the analyst.

The radical critiques are opposed not merely to the blank screen idea but to any model that suggests that the "objective" or "real" impact of the therapist is equivalent to what he intends or to what he thinks his overt behavior has conveyed or betrayed. What the radical critic refuses to do is to consign the patient's ideas about the analyst's hidden motives and attitudes to the realm of unfounded fantasy whenever those ideas depart from the analyst's judgment of his own intentions. In this respect, whether the analyst's manifest conduct is cold or warm or even self-disclosing is not the issue. What matters to the radical critic in determining whether a particular model is based on an asocial or truly social conception of the patient's experience is whether the patient is considered capable of understanding, if only preconsciously, that there is more to the therapist's experience than what meets the eye, even more than what meets the mind's eye of the therapist at any given moment. More than challenging the blank screen fallacy, the radical critic challenges what might be termed *the naive patient fallacy*, the notion that the patient, insofar as he is rational, takes the analyst's behavior at face value even while his own is continually scrutinized for the most subtle indications of unspoken or unconscious meanings.

Although we now have a broad range of literature that embraces some kind of interactive view of the psychoanalytic situation (Ehrenberg, 1982), emphasis upon interaction per se does not guarantee that any particular theoretical statement or position qualifies as one which views the transference in relativistic-social terms. Moreover, emphasis on interaction can obscure the fact that a particular theorist is holding fast, for the most part, to the traditional view of neurotic transference as a distortion of a given and ascertainable external reality.

Conservative Critiques: Transference in the Asocial Paradigm

Overview: Types of Conservative Critiques

Conservative critiques, as I said earlier, retain the dichotomy of transference and realistic perception, but argue that the standard qualifications of the screen function of the analyst require amplification. Some conservative critics like Strachey (1934) and Loewald (1960) offer reconceptualizations of the real, benign interpersonal influence of the analyst in the process without any recommendations for changes in prevailing practice. Others, like Stone (1961) and Kohut (1977), combine such reconceptualization with advocacy of less restraint and more friendly, spontaneous involvement than is customary. In this context, Freud is often cited as a practitioner who was extraordinarily free in his manner of relating to his patients.

Strachey, Loewald, Stone and Kohut have in common some kind of amplification of the realistically benign and facilitating aspects of the therapist's influence, although, to be sure, what is benign and facilitating in Stone and Kohut includes a certain optimal element of frustration or disappointment. The other major subdivision of conservative critiques are those which emphasize the importance and prevalence of objective perceptions of countertransference which, it is argued, fall outside the province of transference. Langs (1978) mounts the most systematic and thorough critique of this kind. Perhaps the clearest example of all the conservative critics is Greenson (1971) whose "real relationship" includes the patient's experience of both the working alliance and of countertransference and unequivocally excludes the experience of the transference.

Hans Loewald and James Strachey

A good example of a primarily conservative critique of the blank screen fallacy which advocates a greater emphasis on the benign facilitating aspects of the analyst as a real person (or object) without any suggestions for changes in technique is that of Loewald (1960). I say primarily conservative because there are ambiguous hints in Loewald's position of a more radical critique which would not dichotomize transference and reality, although I believe the overall thrust of his position is undeniably conservative. Loewald represents the classical position to which he objects as follows (and I quote it at some length because this is one of the clearest statements of the position):

> The theoretical bias is the view of the psychic apparatus as a closed system. Thus, the analyst is seen, not as a co-actor on the analytic stage on which the childhood development, culminating in the infantile neurosis, is restaged and reactivated in the development, crystallization and resolution of the transference neurosis, but as a reflecting mirror, albeit of the unconscious, and characterized by scrupulous neutrality.
>
> This neutrality of the analyst appears to be required (i) in the interest of scientific objectivity, in order to keep the field of observation from being contaminated by the analyst's own emotional intrusions; and (ii) to guarantee a tabula rasa for the patient's transferences . . . the analyst is supposed to function not only as an observer of certain processes, but as a mirror which actively reflects back to the patient the latter's conscious and partially his unconscious processes through verbal communication. A specific aspect of this neutrality is that the analyst must avoid falling into the role of the environmental figure (or of his opposite) the relationship to whom the patient is transferring to the analyst [p. 17].

While not discarding this position entirely, Loewald is concerned about the fact that it leaves something out or lends itself to a lack of sufficient attention to the influence of the analyst as a real object:

> [The analyst's] objectivity cannot mean the avoidance of being available to the patient as an object. The objectivity of the analyst has reference to the patient's transference distortions. Increasingly, through the objective analysis of them, the analyst becomes not only potentially but actually available as a new object, by eliminating step by step impediments, represented by these transferences, to a new object-relationship. There is a tendency to consider the analyst's availability as an object merely as a device on his part to attract transferences onto himself. His availability is seen in terms of his being a screen or mirror onto which the patient projects his transferences, and which reflect them back to him in the form of interpretations. . . .
>
> This is only a half truth. The analyst in actuality does not only reflect the transference distortions. In his interpretations he implies aspects of undistorted reality which the patient begins to grasp step by step as transferences are interpreted. This undistorted reality is mediated to the patient by the analyst, mostly by the process of chiseling away the transference distortions . . . [p. 18].

Here it is clear that Loewald is dichotomizing transference and non-transference experience along the lines of neurotic distortion, on the one hand, and a new appreciation of the real, presumably health-promoting aspects of the analyst, on the other. He goes on to elaborate on the therapeutic effects associated with the experience of collaboration with the real analyst in the process of self-discovery.

Loewald's position has a forerunner in Strachey (1934) in that Strachey too emphasized the new, real interpersonal influence of the analyst in the analytic situation. Loewald sees this new real influence in terms of patient's identification with the analyst's higher level of ego functioning, particularly with his rational perspective as it is brought to bear upon the patient's own neurotic tendencies. Strachey saw a new real influence more in terms of the patient's identification with the analyst's acceptance of the patient's hitherto repressed impulses, so that the modification that occurs involves a softening of the punitive tendencies of the patient's superego, rather than, as in Loewald, a strengthening of the reflective, integrative capacities of his ego.

Leo Stone and Heinz Kohut

Whereas Strachey and Loewald explicitly disclaim any intent to influence technique, Stone (1961), who also is interested in the patient's perceptions of the real, human qualities of the therapist, is concerned about the excessively impersonal, cold, stiff manner in which he believes many analysts approach their patients, and takes an unequivocal stance in favor of a more natural, friendly, and spontaneous manner. Stone takes issue with the implication that scrupulous neutrality and non-responsiveness will allow for the emergence of pure transference ideas uncontaminated by any interpersonal influence. Instead, certain kinds of frustrations associated with mechanically strict adherence to the so-called "rule of abstinence" will, Stone believes, amount to very powerful stimuli, inducing reactions, which, if anything, will be less readily understood in terms of their roots in the individual (see, for example, pp. 45–46).

Stone is clear in his rejection of the notion that transference fantasies will crop up spontaneously if the analyst manages to keep his personal, human qualities or reactions out of the patient's purview in keeping with what Stone believes is the prevailing understanding of proper analytic conduct. But what is Stone's view of the relationship between transference and reality when the analytic situation is modified in accord with his recommendations? In this respect, Stone (1961) is more ambiguous. At times he seems to be saying that the transference will, under those circumstances, include realistic perceptions of the analyst and that this is not only not regrettable but actually desirable:

For *all* patients, to the degree that they are removed from the psychotic, have an important investment in their real and objective perceptions; and the interplay between these and the transference requires
a certain minimal if variable *resemblance*, if the latter is to be effectively mobilized. When mobilized, it is, in operational fact of experience, always an integrated phenomenon, in which actual perceptions,
to varying degree, must participate [p. 41].

However, in certain of his remarks and despite many qualifications,
Stone seems to adhere to the standard dichotomy of transference and
reality. For this reason I believe I am justified in classifying him as a conservative critic of the screen function of the analyst. For example, consider this rather unequivocal stance:

I should like to state that clarity both in principle and in everyday communication, is best served by confining the unqualified term "transference" to that aspect or fraction of a relationship which is motivated by
persistent unmodified wishes (or other attitudes) toward an actual important personage of the past, which tend to invest a current individual in
a sort of misidentification with the unconscious image of the past personage [p. 66].

Stone is sympathetic to the views advanced by Tower, Racker, and
others which point to the usefulness of countertransference in understanding transference and which connote what Stone terms a "diminu-
tion of the rigid status barrier between analyst and analysand" (1961,
p. 80). However his preoccupation is decidedly with the question: how
should the analyst behave? It is very much less with the question: how
should the patient's experience of the analyst be understood? Whatever
the virtues of Stone's position, what is obscured by his emphasis on the
therapist's behavior is the patient's capability to understand that the analyst's manifest verbal and nonverbal behavior can conceal or carry a myriad of latent, more or less conscious attitudes and motives. I think Stone's
position exemplifies a particular variant of those conservative critiques
of the screen concept which stress the importance of the benign human
attributes of the analyst. Instead of arguing that in addition to transference, weight should be given to the patient's experience of the analyst's
real benign qualities, this variant argues that the analyst's humanness
draws out the transference, especially the positive transference. In a
sense, instead of the analyst functioning as a blank screen in relation to
the transference, he is seen as a kind of magnet for it, albeit a very
human one (pp. 108–109). Again, while the idea may not be wrong, it
is not the whole story, and the part of the story that it leaves out or
obscures is what lies at the core of the radical critiques, namely that the

therapist's outward behavior, however it is consciously intended, does not and cannot control the patient's perceptions and interpretations of the analyst's inner experience. As I said earlier, what the radical critic challenges is the view of the patient as *a naive observer of the analyst's behavior*. He argues against the expectation that, to the degree that the patient is rational, he will take the analyst's outward behavior and/or his conscious intent at face value. It is the taking of the analyst's outward behavior and/or his conscious intention and experience of himself as the basis for defining reality in the analytic situation that is truly the hallmark of the standard view of transference as distortion. And it is in this sense that Stone, with all his emphasis on what is appropriate outward behavior on the part of the analyst, leans towards the standard paradigm and can be categorized as a conservative critic of the notion that, ideally, the analyst should function like a screen.

I believe that Kohut's position on the screen function of the analyst, although it is, of course, embedded in a different theoretical context, can be classed with that of Stone as a special type of conservative critique. Kohut (1977) makes it clear that while it is particularly important in the case of disorders of the self it is also important in the case of the classical neuroses that the analyst not behave in an excessively cold and unfriendly manner. He believes that "analytic neutrality . . . should be defined as the responsiveness to be expected, on an average, from persons who have devoted their life to helping others with the aid of insights obtained via the empathic immersion into their inner life" (p. 252). But Kohut (1977), like Stone, conveys the impression that a friendly, naturally responsive attitude on the part of the analyst will promote the unfolding of the transference, whether classical or narcissistic, without specific reference to other aspects of the analyst's personality. For example, he writes:

> The essential transference (or the sequence of the essential transferences) is defined by pre-analytically established internal factors in the analysand's personality structure, and the analyst's influence on the course of the analysis is therefore important only insofar as he—through interpretations made on the basis of correct or incorrect emphatic closures—either promotes or impedes the patient's progress on his predetermined path [p. 217].

Especially in the case of the classical transference neurosis, Kohut is clear that the analyst does function as a screen for elaboration of transference ideas although he also facilitates change through emphatic responsiveness and interpretation. This model follows the line of conservative critics like Stone because the encouragement that is given to the analyst to express his humanness does nothing to alter the notion that the analyst as a real person is not implicated in the unfolding of the transference proper.

In the case of transferences associated with the disorders of the self, which Kohut increasingly viewed as the underlying disturbance even in the classical neuroses, the analyst as a real person is implicated more directly insofar as his empathy facilitates the self-selfobject tie that the patient's development requires. More precisely, the sequence of empathy, minor failures in empathy, and rectification of such failures promotes the "transmuting internalizations" which result in repair of the deficits in the development of the self which the patient brings to the analysis. However, it would seem that the whole complexity of the analyst's personal response to the patient is not something the patient would attend to in a way that was associated with any special psychological importance. To the extent that the patient is suffering from a disorder of the self, or a narcissistic disorder, he presumably does not experience the analyst as a separate person with needs, motives, defenses, and interests of his own. One might say that the patient is concerned about breaches in empathy and that he reacts strongly to them, but that he does not necessarily account for such failures or explain them to himself by attributing particular countertransference difficulties to the analyst which then become incorporated into the transference. In fact, to the degree that the patient is suffering from a disorder of the self, and therefore is experiencing the analyst as a selfobject, he is, by definition, a naive observer of the analyst as a separate, differentiated object. Thus, I believe I am justified in classifying Kohut as a conservative critic of the screen function of the analyst even taking into consideration his ideas about the narcissistic transferences.[4]

Robert Langs

Whereas Loewald, Strachey, Stone and Kohut are concerned with the fact that the screen concept lends itself to a deemphasis of the "real" therapeutic, interpersonal influence of the analyst, others have been concerned more with its tendency to obscure the importance and prevalence of real neurotogenic influences that the therapist exerts via his countertransference. Here again, the critique is conservative in form insofar as

---

4. The self psychology literature certainly includes discussion of likely countertransference reactions to particular kinds of narcissistic transferences (e.g., Kohut, 1971; Wolf, 1979), but these discussions omit consideration of the patient's specific ideas about the nature of the countertransference.

it merely expands upon one of the standard qualifications of the blank screen concept. A carefully elaborated critique of this kind is that of Robert Langs. No psychoanalytic theorist has written more extensively about the implications of the patient's ability to interpret the analyst's manifest behavior as betraying latent countertransference. In Langs's view, the patient is constantly monitoring the analyst's counter-transference attitudes and his associations can often be understood as "commentaries" on them (1978, p. 509).

However, despite his unusual interactional emphasis, Langs must be classified as a conservative critic of the blank screen fallacy because he is unequivocal about reserving the term transference for the *distorted perception* of the therapist, whereas accurate perceptions fall *outside* the realm of the transference. Thus, he writes, for example:

> Within the bipersonal field the patient's relationship with the analyst has both transference and nontransference components. The former are essentially distorted and based on pathological, intrapsychic unconscious fantasies, memories, and introjects, while the latter are essentially nondistorted and based on valid unconscious perceptions and introjections of the analyst, his conscious and unconscious psychic state and communications, and his mode of interacting [p. 506].

For Langs what is wrong with the classical position is that it overestimates the prevalence of relatively pure, uncontaminated transference. Because countertransference errors are relatively ubiquitous in prevailing practice and because the patient is preconsciously always on the lookout for them, what dominates most psychoanalytic transactions are unconscious attempts by the patient to adapt to this current reality and even to alter it by trying indirectly to "cure" the analyst of his interfering psychopathology. To be sure, even the patient's valid perceptions can be points of departure for "intrapsychic elaborations" which bear the stamp of the patient's psychopathology. Nevertheless, the main thrust of all of Langs's writings is that a certain environment can be established which will be relatively free of countertransference and in which the patient will therefore feel safe to engage in a very special kind of communication, one which can take place in this environment and nowhere else. This special kind of communication is, like dreams, a richly symbolic expression of deep unconscious wishes and fantasies that have little relation to the actual person of the analyst. These are the true transference wishes and fantasies. The patient is always on the verge of retreating from this kind of communication because he experiences it as potentially dangerous at a very primitive level to himself or to the analyst, and betrayals of countertransference

(whether seductive or attacking or whatever) invariably prevent, inter-
rupt, or severely limit this unique kind of communication.

Langs's position is based upon the same absolute view of reality
which is implicit in any position which retains the dichotomy between
distorted and undistorted perception of interpersonal events. Langs
believes, for example, that strict adherence to a prescribed set of rules
constituting what he calls the "basic frame" *will not* be interpreted—at
least not accurately—as any kind of expression of countertransference
which could endanger the kind of communication he wants to foster. By
the same token, violations of the frame *will* be perceived and responded
to in this way by virtually all patients.[5]

Langs appears to believe that there is a certain universal language
which always carries at least general unconscious meaning. He will not
claim to know *specifically* what it means to a particular patient that the
therapist allows him to use his phone, or that he changes his appointment time, or that he fails to charge for a cancelled appointment, or that
he tape records a session. But he does claim to know that all patients
are likely to see such behaviors correctly as reflecting some sort of deep,
unresolved, pathological conflict in the analyst. Conversely, he believes
it is possible for the analyst to behave in a way which will persuade the
patient that no such issues are active in the analyst to any significant
degree, that is, to a degree which, objectively speaking, would warrant
anxiety that the analyst's attitudes are dominated by countertransference.
Thus, the analyst, with help perhaps from a supervisor or from his own
analyst, can decide with some degree of confidence when the patient is
reading his unconscious motives correctly, which would represent a non-
transference response, and when he is merely fantasizing and distorting
because of the influence of the transference.

The conservatism of Langs's critique of the screen model in psychoanalysis is particularly ironic given the enthusiasm with which he cham-
pions the more radical positions of other theorists such as Searles
(1978–1979) and Racker (1968). Langs feels that these theorists (especially Searles) inspired many of his own ideas and he conveys the impression that in some sense he is taking up where they left off. However,
because Langs actually retreats to the standard dichotomy of transference and non-transference experience on the basis of distorting and non-

---

5. According to Langs, by maintaining the frame and intervening in an optimal manner, the therapist provides the patient with a secure holding environment. Langs's account of the nature and importance of this kind of environment
in the analytic process complements his account of the importance of countertransference errors, so that he, like Greenson, actually elaborates on both of the
standard qualifications of the screen concept.

distorting perceptions of the reality of the analyst's attitudes, I believe he actually takes a step back from his own sources of inspiration rather than a step forward.

Ralph Greenson

Perhaps the theorist who best exemplifies a conservative critique of the blank screen fallacy is Greenson (1965, 1971). Greenson's "real relationship" encompasses both the patient's accurate perceptions of the benign aspects of the analyst and his perceptions of the analyst's countertransference expressions, and Greenson's position is an emphatic objection to the tendency he sees to underestimate the inevitably important role of the real relationship in the analytic process. There is nothing in Greenson that alters in the slightest the standard understanding of transference as distortion and the standard dichotomy of transference and undistorted perception of the analyst. He writes (1971):

> The two outstanding characteristics of a transference reaction are: (1) It is an undiscriminating, non-selective repetition of the past, and (2) It is inappropriate, it ignores or distorts reality" [p. 217].

In contrast to the transference, Greenson states:

> The meaning of "real" in real relationship implies (1) the sense of being genuine and not synthetic or artificial and (2) it also means realistic and not inappropriate or fantastic [p. 218].

The extent to which Greenson is wedded to this dichotomy is betrayed by the fact that he cannot find his way out of it, even when it seems like he is trying to. Thus, for example, he says:

> I must add that in all transference reactions there is some germ of reality, and in all real relationships there is some element of transference [p. 218].

Here he seems to be saying that transference *itself* is not completely lacking in some sort of realistic basis, although the word "germ" suggests a very common kind of lip-service to this idea: the element of reality is considered to be so slight as to be hardly worth mentioning much less making an issue of in one's interpretive work. But even this concession is lost immediately in Greenson's very next sentence which he has in italics and which is clearly intended as a restatement or paraphrase of the first:

> *All object relations consist of different admixtures and blendings of real*
> *and transference components* [p. 218].

Now the idea that transference includes something real is superseded by the much blander notion that all relationships include something real as well as transference. In other words, the dichotomy of transference and realistic perception is retained.

Radical Critiques: Transference in the Social or Interpersonal Paradigm

Overview

Whereas conservative critics of the blank screen concept are relatively abundant, radical critics are relatively scarce, particularly among classical Freudian analysts. I would number among the foremost of them, Merton Gill (1979; 1982a; 1982b; 1983; Gill and Hoffman, 1982a; 1982b), certainly a leading exponent of this perspective coming out of a classical Freudian orientation; Joseph Sandler (1976), another classical Freudian who, however, conceptualizes the psychoanalytic situation in object-relations terms; Heinrich Racker (1968), who takes his cue from a landmark paper on countertransference by a fellow Kleinian, Paula Heimann (1950), but whose rich and detailed account of the inevitable reciprocity of transference and countertransference is unique in the literature. Another contributor to this stream of thought is Lucia Tower if only for her one remarkable paper on countertransference in 1956, the implications of which have never penetrated the mainstream of psychoanalytic thinking about the relationship between transference and reality. Levenson (1972; 1981), Issacharoff (1979), Feiner (1979; 1982), and Ehrenberg (1982) are among the neo-Sullivanians whose work leans heavily in this direction. Harold Searles (1978–1979) should certainly be included as a major exponent of the radical perspective. An important recent contribution is that of Paul Wachtel (1980), whose Piagetian conceptual framework for understanding transference I will be drawing on myself in what follows.

To digress for a moment, although I have counted Gill among the radical critics, within his later work there is actually a movement from a somewhat inconsistent but generally conservative position to a more consistently radical one. Thus, in his 1982 monograph, Gill (1982a) criticizes those, like Anna Freud and Greenson, who define transference in terms of distortion of reality (p. 12). However, his objection is tied specifically to what he describes as "a lack of recognition that Freud's inclusion of the conscious, unobjectionable positive transference in his concept of transference is not an unfortunate lapse but an integral aspect of the concept" (p. 12). Throughout his discussion of the distinction between the unobjectionable "facilitating" transferences and the "obstructing" transferences (pp. 9–15), it is only the former which is considered to have realistic features. There is nothing about realistic elements in the "obstructing" transferences, not to mention any question being raised about the dimension "realistic-unrealistic" itself. Overall, in the first six chapters of the monograph, Gill apparently had not yet extricated himself from the traditional asocial paradigm for understanding transference (that is, neurotic or obstructing transference) although he was struggling to do so. His transitional, but still essentially conservative stand is exemplified by the following:

> Analysts have largely followed Freud in taking it for granted that the analyst's behavior is such that the patient's appropriate reaction to it will be cooperation in the joint work. But there are significant interactions between the patient and the analyst which are *not transference* but to which the patient's appropriate response would not be cooperation. If the analyst has given the patient cause to be angry, for example, and the patient is angry, at least some aspect of the anger is neither a transference nor cooperation—unless the idea of cooperation is confusingly stretched to mean that any forthright appropriate reaction of the patient is cooperative since it is a necessary element in continuing an open and honest relationship. We do conceptualize inappropriate behavior on the analyst's part as countertransference, but what is our name for an analysand's realistic response to countertransference? [p. 94, italics added]

There is a noticeable shift in the book beginning with chapter 7 to a fully social and relativistic position (see, for example, p. 118). Moreover, in subsequent writing Gill became unequivocal in his adoption of the social paradigm for understanding all aspects of transference (Gill, 1982b; Gill, 1983; Gill and Hoffman, 1982a; 1982b).

I believe that the various proponents of the radical perspective may have more in common with each other than each of them has with what would generally be recognized as their particular school or tradition. In effect, I believe *there is a kind of informal "school" of thought which cuts across the standard lines of Freudian, Kleinian, and Sullivanian schools.* For example, what Gill (in his most recent work), Racker and Levenson have in common may be much more important than how they differ because what they have in common is a perspective on the fundamental nature of the psychoanalytic situation.

Radical critiques of the notion that the patient's neurotic transference experience is divorced from the actual nature of the analyst's participation, that is, that it distorts the actual nature of that participation, rest on two basic propositions, with one or the other or both emphasized depending upon the particular theorist. The two propositions, for which I am partly indebted to Wachtel (1980), are:

1. The patient senses that the analyst's interpersonal *conduct* in the analytic situation, like all interpersonal conduct, is always ambiguous as an indicator of the full nature of the analyst's experience and is always amenable to a variety of plausible interpretations.

2. The patient senses that the analyst's personal *experience* in the analytic situation is continuously affected by, and responsive to, the way in which the patient relates and participates in the process.

Implications of the Ambiguity of the Analyst's Conduct in the Analytic Situation

There is an underlying view of reality that the radical critiques of the screen concept share. This view is simply that reality is not a preestablished given or absolute. As Wachtel (1980) says, arguing from the perspective of Piaget's theory of cognitive development: "neither as children or as adult do we respond directly to stimuli per se. We are always constructing reality every bit as much as we are perceiving it" (p. 62). Moreover, the realm of interpersonal events is distinguished from that of physical events in that "such events are highly ambiguous, and consensus is much harder to obtain" (p. 69).

Keep in mind that we have as our principal concern one person's ideas (which may or may not be conscious themselves) about another person's experience. The other person's experience can only be inferred, it is never directly visible as such. Although we may believe we recognize signs of it in verbal and non-verbal behavior, the relationship between such signs and actual experience is always uncertain. When we think about patients, we know that there may well be discrepancies between what a patient says and what he consciously thinks as well as discrepancies between what he consciously thinks and what he vaguely senses but resists facing up to in himself. We know that the relation between what is manifest and what is latent may be extraordinarily complex. We know this of our patients and in a general way of ourselves. What we are prone to ignore or deny however is that this ambiguity and complexity applies to the way in which the therapist participates in the analytic process. As Racker (1968) says:

The first distortion of truth in "the myth of the analytic situation" is that analysis is an interaction between a sick person and a healthy one. The truth is that it is an interaction between two personalities, in both of which the ego is under pressure from the id, the superego, and the external world; each personality has its internal and external dependencies, anxieties, and pathological defenses; each is also a child with his internal parents; and each of these whole personalities—that of the analysand and that of the analyst—responds to every event in the analytic situation [p. 132].

And in another paper Racker (1968) says:

The analyst's relation to his patient is a libidinal one and is a constant emotional experience" [p. 31].

The safeguards of the analytic situation do not prevent the analyst from having this "constant emotional experience." What is more, every patient senses this, consciously or preconsciously. Also every patient brings to bear his own particular perspective in interpreting the meaning of the analyst's manifest behavior as it communicates, conveys, or inadvertently betrays something in the analyst's personal experience. The fact that a particular perspective may be charged with tremendous significance and importance for the patient does not nullify its plausibility. If anything the opposite may be the case. The patient's transference predisposition acts as a kind of geiger counter which picks up aspects of the analyst's personal response in the analytic situation which might otherwise remain hidden. As Benedek (1953) put it:

Rarely does one realize that the patient, under the pressure of his emotional needs—needs which may be motivated by the frustration of transference—may grope for the therapist as a real person, may sense his reactions and will sometimes almost read his mind . . . Yes, the patient . . . bores his way into the preconscious mind of the therapist and often emerges with surprising evidences of empathy—of preconscious awareness of the therapist's personality and even of his problems [p. 203].

What the patient's transference accounts for is not a distortion of reality but a selective attention to and sensitivity to certain facets of the analyst's highly ambiguous response to the patient in the analysis. What one patient notices about the analyst another ignores. What matters to one may not matter to another, or may matter in a different way. One could make a case for using the term "distortion" for just this kind of selective attention and sensitivity, but that is not usually the way the term is used and I do think it would be misleading. After all, it is not as though one could describe the "real analyst" or the true nature of the analyst's experience independent of any selective attention and sensitivity. As Wachtel (1980) says:

> To be sure, each patient's experience of the analyst is highly individual and shaped by personal needs and fantasies. But consider the enormous variation in perception of the analyst by those other than his patients— the differences in how he is experienced by his spouse, his children, his teachers, his students, his friends, his rivals. Which is the "undistorted" standard from which the transference distortion varies? [pp. 66–67].[6]

There is no perception free of some kind of pre-existing set or bias or expectation, or, to borrow from Piaget's framework, no perception independent of "assimilation" to some preexisting schema. Such assimilation does not twist an absolute external reality into something it is not. Rather it gives meaning or shape to something "out there" that has among its "objective" properties a kind of amenability to being assimilated in just this way. Moreover, the schema itself is flexible and tends to "accommodate" to what is in the environment even while it makes what is in the environment fit itself. Thus, turning to the clinical situation which concerns us, a patient who, for example, has a readiness to feel used, may detect and be selectively attentive and sensitive to whatever qualifies as a plausible indication of an exploitative motive on the part of the particular analyst he is seeing. With one analyst it might be his high fee, with another his use of a tape recorder for research purposes, with another his use of the therapy for his own training, with another his (allegedly) sadistic use of silence, with another his (allegedly) sadistic use of active interpretation.

The analytic situation is comprised of only two people, both of whom are *participating* in a charged interpersonal interaction which can result in either one of them resisting recognizing something in himself that the other discerns. From the perspective of the radical critic, it behooves the analyst to operate with this skepticism about what he knows of himself at a particular moment always in mind and to regard the patient as a potentially astute interpreter of his own (the analyst's own) resisted internal motives. In fact, in some cases a patient with a particular "transference predisposition" (a phrase that Racker uses that is comparable to the notion of schema) may guess something about the countertransference that most other independent judges would not have picked up. As Gill and I (1982b) have written:

---

6. In what seems to me to be a non-sequitur, Wachtel retreats from the implications of this position at the end of his paper (p. 74) and accepts the term distortion in a manner which contradicts the heart of his argument.

In some instances, a group of judges may agree that the therapist has behaved in a particular way, one which could be construed as seductive, or disapproving or whatever, only after some subtle aspect of his behavior is called to their attention by another single observer. This observer, might of course, be none other than the patient [p. 140].

Not despite the influence of the transference but because of it:

[The patient] may notice something about the therapist's behavior or suggest a possible interpretation of it that most judges would overlook. Nevertheless, once it is called to their attention, they may all agree that the patient's perceptions and inferences were quite plausible [p. 140].

Implications of the Responsiveness of the Analyst's Experience in the Analytic Situation

In what I have said so far I have deliberately contrived to deemphasize the second major consideration that addresses the implication of the analyst's personal presence for the transference. I have done this in order to take the argument associated with the ambiguous nature of the analyst's involvement as far as I could. But it is the second consideration, coupled with the first, that I think clinches the argument of the radical critic that the patient's plausible interpretations of the analyst's experience be considered part of the transference and that the transference not be defined in terms of perceptual distortion.

This second consideration is simply that the analyst in the analytic situation is continuously having some sort of personal affective reaction that is a response to the patient's manner of relating to him. What is more, every patient knows that he is influencing the analyst's experience and that the freedom the analyst has to resist this influence is limited. Patients create atmosphere in analysis—atmospheres which we sometimes actually speak of as though something were "in the air" between the participants. These atmospheres include the therapist's personal reaction to the patient, the patient guessing what the reaction is partly on the basis of what he thinks his own behavior is likely to have elicited, the analyst guessing what the patient is guessing, and so on.

Sandler (1976) puts it this way:

In the transference, in many subtle ways, the patient attempts to prod the analyst into behaving in a particular way and unconsciously scans and adapts to his perceptions of the analyst's reaction. The analyst may be able to "hold" his response to this "prodding" in his consciousness as a reaction *of his own* which he perceives, and I would make the link between certain countertransference responses and transference via the behavioral (verbal and non-verbal) *interaction* between the patient and the analyst [p. 44].

Sandler's emphasis on the analyst's behavior as a basis upon which the patient concludes (preconsciously) that he has elicited the response he is looking for underestimates the extent to which the patient's ideas about the countertransference can flow directly and plausibly from what he knows about the evocative nature of his own behavior. However the analyst believes he has behaved, if the patient thinks he, himself has been continually depreciating, or harshly critical, he has reason to believe that the analyst may feel somewhat hurt, or that he may experience a measure of irritation and a wish to retaliate. Such ideas do not require perceptual confirmation in order for the patient to believe, with reason, that they are plausible. The perceptual confirmation might follow in any number of ways. For example, if the analyst keeps his cool and shows not the slightest bit of irritation, the patient might well imagine that this is precisely the expression of the analyst's revenge, that is, that the analyst will not give the patient the satisfaction of thinking he can affect him in a personal way. And, undoubtedly, ostensible adherence to the more austere canons of "proper" analytic conduct can sometimes function as a disguised vehicle for the expression of intense countertransference attitudes on the part of the analyst. However, the perceptual confirmation may be secondary, since from the patient's point of view the die is cast and the outcome is highly likely given his own evocative behavior.

For a theorist like Racker the countertransference is inevitable and his discussion of it carries none of the opprobrium that comes across so heavily and oppressively in the work of Langs. Racker and Heimann take the same step forward with respect to countertransference that Freud took when he moved from thinking of the transference as an obstacle to thinking of transference as the principal vehicle of the analytic process. The countertransference in the social paradigm of the radical critics is likely to embody something resembling aspects of the patient's internal objects or aspects of the patient's self-representation. Heimann (1950) goes so far as to say:

> The analyst's counter-transference is not only part and parcel of the analytic relationship, but it is the patient's *creation*, it is part of the patient's personality [p. 83].

The element of hyperbole in Heimann's position illustrates an error that often appears in discussions of the mechanism of projective identification. Instead of being a blank screen, the analyst becomes an empty "container" (Bion, 1962) into which the patient deposits various parts of himself. Although the emphasis is on interaction, the metaphor of the container lends itself, ironically, to yet another asocial conception of the situation since somehow the analyst's personality has once again been extricated from the process (cf. Levenson, 1981, p. 492). Nevertheless, the concept of projective identification, with the hyperbolic metaphor removed, does help bridge the alleged gap between the intrapsychic and the interpersonal (Ogden, 1979). It should be evident that in this paper the terms "social" and "interpersonal" do not connote something superficial or readily observable from "outside" or something non-intrapsychic, the pejorative connotations that these terms have unfortunately acquired for many classical analysts. Experience that is conceptualized in the terms of the social paradigm is experience that is layered by reciprocal conscious, preconscious, and unconscious responses in each of the participants.[7] What is more, something can "unfold" in the course of the analysis which bears the stamp of the patient's transference predispositions. What is intrapsychic is realized in the patient's idea of the interaction of the transference and the countertransference which is likely to include a rough approximation of the quality if not the quantity of the actual countertransference. It is in this element of correspondence between the patient's idea of the countertransference and the actual countertransference that the elusive interface of the intrapsychic and interpersonal lies.

Implications of the Social Paradigm for Technique

The Impact of the Countertransference on the Fate of the Relationship

Because of the analyst is human, he is likely to have in his repertoire a blueprint for approximately the emotional response that the patient's transference dictates and that response is likely to be elicited, whether consciously or unconsciously (Searles, 1978–1979, pp. 172–173). Ideally this response serves as a key—perhaps the best key the analyst has—to the nature of the interpersonal scene that the patient is driven by transference to create. The patient as interpreter of the analyst's experience suspects that he has created something, the complement of the transference, in the

---

7. See Fourcher (1975) for a discussion of human experience as the expression of social reciprocity on multiple levels of psychological organization and consciousness.

analyst; that is, he suspects it at some level. What he does not know and what remains to be decided, is what role the countertransference experience of the analyst will have in determining the total nature of the analyst's response to the patient. In other words he does not know the extent to which the countertransference will combine with the transference to determine the destiny of the relationship. The extent to which the analyst's "objectivity," the tendency which is inclined towards understanding more than enacting, the extent to which this tendency will prevail and successfully resist the pull of the transference and the countertransference is unknown at any given moment not only to the patient but also to the analyst.

Within the transference itself, there is a kind of self-fulfilling prophecy, and with it, a kind of fatalism, a sense that the outcome is inevitable. The transference includes not just a sense of what has happened, or is happening, but also a prediction, a conviction even, about what will happen. The attempt to disprove this prediction is an active, ongoing, mutual effort, which is always accompanied by a real element of uncertainty. The analyst's uncertainty has as much if not more to do with his inability to know, in advance, how much his own countertransference will govern his response to his patient, as it has to do with his inability to measure, precisely, the patient's resistance and motivation for change. Moreover, the patient, as interpreter of the therapist's experience, has good reason to think and fear that the countertransference-evoking power of his transferences may be the decisive factor in determining the course of the relationship. Or, to say the same thing in another way, he has good reason to fear that the analyst's constant susceptibility to countertransference will doom the relationship to repeat, covertly if not overtly, the very patterns of interpersonal interaction which he came to analysis to change.

Pitted against the powerful alignment of transference and countertransference is the interest that the patient and the analyst share in making something happen that will be new for the patient and that will promote his ability to develop new kinds of interpersonal relationships. This is where the "objectivity" of the analyst enters and plays such an important role. It is not an objectivity that enables the analyst to demonstrate to the patient how his transference ideas and expectations distort reality. Instead it is an objectivity that enables the analyst to work to create another kind of interpersonal experience which diverges from the one towards which the transference-countertransference interaction pulls. In this other experience, the patient comes to know that the analyst is not so consumed or threatened by the countertransference that he is no longer able to interpret the transference. For to be able to interpret the transference fully means interpreting, and in some measure being receptive to, the patient's interpretations of the countertransference (Racker, 1968, p. 131). What ensues is a subtle kind of rectification. The patient is, in some measure, freed of an unconscious sense of obligation to resist interpreting the analyst's experience in order to accommodate a reciprocal resistance in the analyst. Ironically, the resistance in the patient sometimes takes the form of an apparently fervent belief that, objectively speaking, the analyst must be the very neutral screen that, according to the standard model he aspires to be (see Racker, 1968, p. 67). The patient takes the position, in effect, that his ideas about the analyst are nothing but fantasy, derived entirely from his childhood experiences, nothing but transference in the standard sense of the term. In such a case, the analyst must interpret this denial; he must combat this resistance not collude with it. To the extent that the analyst is objective, to the extent that he keeps himself from "drowning in the countertransference" (Racker, 1968, p. 132), which, of course, could take the form of repressing it, to that very extent is he able to actively elicit the patient's preconscious and resisted interpretations of the countertransference and take them in stride.

Interpretation as Rectification

Whether the therapist's response will be dominated by countertransference or not is a question that is raised again and again throughout the course of the therapy, probably in each hour with varying degrees of urgency. Also, it is a question that in many instances cannot begin to be resolved in a favorable direction unless or until a timely interpretation is offered by the therapist. At the very moment that he interprets, the analyst often extricates himself as much as he extricates the patient from transference–countertransference enactment. When the therapist who is experiencing the quality, if not the quantity, of the countertransference reaction that the patient is attributing to him says to the patient: "I think you think I am feeling vulnerable," or "I think you have the impression that I am hiding or denying my hostility towards you" or "my attraction to you," at that moment, at least, he manages to cast doubt on the transference-based expectation that the countertransference will be consuming and will result in defensive adaptations in the analyst complementary to those in the transference. The interpretation is "mutative" (Strachey, 1934) partly because it has a certain reflexive impact on the analyst himself which the patient senses. Because it is implicitly self-interpretive it modifies something in the analyst's own experience of the patient. By making it apparent that the countertransference experience that the patient has attributed to the analyst occupies only a part of his response to the patient, the analyst also makes it apparent that he is finding something more in the patient to respond to than the transference-driven provocateur. Not to be minimized as a significant part of this "something more" that the analyst now is implicitly showing a kind of appreciation for is the patient's capacity to understand, empathize with, and interpret the analyst's experience, especially his experience of the patient (cf. Searles, 1975).

As Gill (1979) has pointed out, the patient, through the analysis of the transference, has a new interpersonal experience which is inseparable from the collaborative development of insight into the transference itself. This new experience is most powerful when the insight into the transference includes a new understanding of what the patient has tried to evoke and what he has plausibly construed as actually having been evoked in the analyst. The rectification that I spoke of earlier of the patient's unconscious need to accommodate to a resistance that is attributed to the analyst is also more likely when the analyst is able to find the patient's interpretation of the countertransference in associations that are not manifestly about the psychoanalytic situation at all. When he does this, he demonstrates to the patient that, rather than being defensive about the patient's ideas about the countertransference, he actually has an appetite for them and is eager to seek them out.

Systematic use of the patient's associations as a guide to understanding the patient's resisted ideas about the countertransference is a critical element of the interpretive process in the social paradigm. Without it, there is a danger that the analyst will rely excessively on his own subjective experience in constructing interpretations. The analyst then risks making the error of automatically assuming that what he feels corresponds with what the patient attributes to him. In fact, Racker (1968), whom I have cited so liberally, seems to invite this criticism at times, although he also warns against regarding the experience of the countertransference as oracular (p. 170). It is true that in many cases the most powerful interpretations are constructed out of a convergence of something in the analyst's personal response and a theme in the patient's associations. However there are other instances when the associations suggest a latent interpretation of the analyst's experience which comes as a surprise to the analyst and which overrides what he might have guessed based upon his awareness of his internal state. Thus, continually reading the patient's associations for their allusions to the countertransference via the mechanisms of displacement and identification (Lipton, 1977b; Gill, 1979; 1982a; Gill and Hoffman, 1982a; 1982b) is a necessary complement to the analyst's countertransference experience in constructing interpretations and ensures that the patient's perspective, as reflected in the content of his communications, is not overshadowed by what the analyst is aware of in himself.

The Role of Enactment and Confession of Countertransference

The new experience that the patient has is something that the participants make happen and that they are frequently either on the verge of failing to make happen or actually failing to make happen. That is, they are frequently either on the verge of enacting transference-countertransference patterns or actually in the midst of enacting them, even if in muted or disguised ways. Where Gill, Racker, Searles, and Levenson among others differ from conservative critics like Langs is in their acceptance of a certain thread of transference-countertransference enactment throughout the analysis which stands in a kind of dialectic relationship with the process by which this enactment, as experienced by the patient, is analyzed.

I want to be clear that nothing I have said requires admission on the part of the analyst of actual countertransference experiences. On the contrary, I think the extra factor of "objectivity" that the analyst has to help combat the pull of the transference and the countertransference usually rests precisely on the fact that the nature of his participation in the interaction is different than that of the patient. This is what increases the likelihood that he will be able to subordinate his countertransference reactions to the purposes of the analysis. What Racker (1968) speaks of as "the myth of the analytic situation," namely that it is an interaction "between a sick person and a healthy one" (p. 132), is, ironically, perpetuated by those who argue that regular countertransference confessions should be incorporated as part of psychoanalytic technique.[8] Such regular self-disclosure is likely to pull the therapist's total personality into the exchange in the same manner that it would be involved in other intimate social relationships. To think that the analyst will have any special capability in such circumstances to resist neurotic forms of reciprocal reenactment would have to be based on an assumption that his mental health is vastly superior to that of the patient. Admissions of countertransference responses also tend to imply an overestimation of the therapist's conscious experience at the expense of what is resisted

---

8. Bollas (1983) has discussed and illustrated the usefulness of occasional judicious disclosures by the analyst of his countertransference predicament.

and is preconscious or unconscious. Similarly it implies an extraordinary ability on the part of the analyst to capture the essence of his experience of the patient in a few words whereas the patient may grope for hours in his free association before he reaches a verbalization that fully captures something in his experience of the analyst. Another way of saying this is to say that countertransference confessions encourage an illusion that the participants may share that the element of ambiguity that is associated with the analyst's conduct and that leaves it open to a variety of plausible interpretations has now been virtually eliminated. Once the analyst says what he feels there is likely to be an increment of investment on his part in being taken at his word. This is an increment of investment that the patient will sense and try to accommodate so that the reciprocal resistance to the patient's continuing interpretation of the therapist's inner experience can become very powerful.

Although countertransference confessions are usually ill-advised, there are times when a degree of personal, self-revealing expressiveness is not only inescapable but desirable (Ehrenberg, 1982; Bollas, 1983). In fact, there are times when the only choices available to the analyst are a variety of emotionally expressive responses. Neither attentive listening nor interpretation of any kind is necessarily a way out of this predicament because the patient may have created an atmosphere in which customary analytic distance is likely to be experienced by both participants as inordinately withholding, compulsive, or phony. As long as the ambiance is such that the patient and the analyst both know that whatever is going on more than likely has meaning that is not yet being spoken of or explored but eventually will be, openly expressive interpersonal interactions may do more good than harm and may continue for some time before it becomes possible to interpret them retrospectively in a spirit that holds any hope of benefit for the patient. In other words, it may be some time before the act of interpreting will become sufficiently free of destructive countertransference meaning so that the patient can hear and make use of the content of the intervention.

Again, it is not that instead of interpreting in such circumstances one should merely wait silently, but rather that a certain specific kind of spontaneous interpersonal interaction may be the least of the various evils that the participants have to choose from, or, more positively, the healthiest of the various transference-countertransference possibilities that are in the air at a certain time. It may be that such "healthier" types of interpersonal interaction actually do have something relatively new in them or maybe something with weak precursors in the patient's history that were not pathogenic but rather growth promoting. It is crucial that the therapist not assume this, however, and that he be guided by the patient's subsequent associations in determining how the patient experienced the interaction and what it repeated or continued from the past.

Exploration of History in the Social Paradigm

An important weapon that the patient and the therapist have against prolonged deleterious forms of transference-countertransference enactment, in addition to the analyst's relative distance, is an evolving understanding of the patient's history. This understanding locates the transference-countertransference themes that are enacted in the analysis in a broader context which touches on their origins. The historical context helps immeasurably to free the patient and the analyst from the sense of necessity and importance that can become attached to whatever is going on in the here-and-now. The therapist's distance and ability to reflect critically on the process is aided by the fact that he, unlike the patient, does not reveal his private associations. The patient's ability to reflect on the process relies much more heavily on being able to explain what is happening on the basis of what has happened in the past. Such explanation, because it demonstrates how the patient's way of shaping and perceiving the relationship comes out of his particular history, also adds considerably to the patient's sense of conviction that alternative ways of relating to people are open to him. Again, what is corrected is not a simple distortion of reality but the investment that the patient has in shaping and perceiving his interpersonal experience in particular ways. Moreover, the past too is not explored in a spirit either of finding out what really happened (as in the trauma theory) or in the spirit of finding out what the patient, for internal reasons only, imagined happened (the past understood as fantasy). The patient as a credible (not accurate necessarily, but credible) interpreter of the therapist's experience has as its precursor the child as a credible interpreter of his parents' experience and especially his parents' attitudes towards himself (see Hartmann and Kris, 1945, pp. 21–22; Schimek, 1975, p. 180; Levenson, 1981). The dichotomy of environmentally induced childhood trauma and internally motivated childhood fantasy in etiological theories has its exact parallel in the false dichotomy in the psychoanalytic situation between reactions to actual countertransference errors on the analyst's part and the unfolding of pure transference which has no basis or only a trivial basis in reality.

The Patient's Perception of Conflict in the Analyst

The therapist's analytic task, his tendency toward understanding, on the one hand, and his countertransference reactions, on the other, often create a sense of real conflict as part of his total experience of the relationship. I think this conflict is invariably a part of what the patient senses about the therapist's response. In fact one subtle type of asocial conception of the patient's experience in psychoanalysis is one which implies that from the patient's point of view the analyst's experience is simple rather than complex, and unidimensional rather than multifaceted. The analyst is considered to be simply objective, or critical, or seductive, or threatened, or nurturant, or empathic. Any truly social conception of the patient's experience in psychoanalysis grants that the patient can plausibly infer a variety of more or less harmonious or conflictual tendencies in the analyst, some of which the patient would imagine were conscious and some of which he would think were unconscious. In such a model, the patient as interpreter understands that, however different it is, the analyst's experience is no less complex than his own.

References

Benedek, T. (1953) Dynamics of the countertransference. *Bulletin of The Menninger Clinic*, 17:201–208.

Bion, W. (1962) *Learning from Experience*. New York: Basic Books.

Bollas, C. (1983) Expressive uses of the countertransference. *Contemporary Psychoanalysis*, 19:1–34.

Dewald, P. A. (1972) *The Psychoanalysis Process*. New York: Basic Books.

Ehrenberg, D. B. (1982) Psychoanalytic engagement. *Contemporary Psychoanalysis*, 18:535–555.

Feiner, A. H. (1979) Countertransference and the anxiety of influence. In: *Countertransference: The Therapist's Contribution to the Therapeutic Situation*, ed. L. Epstein & A. H. Feiner. New York: Aronson.

Feiner, A. H. (1982) Comments on the difficult patient. *Contemporary Psychoanalysis*, 18:397–411.

Fourcher, L. A. (1975) Psychological pathology and social reciprocity. *Human Development*, 18:405–429.

Freud, S. (1912) The dynamics of transference. *Standard Edition*, 12:99–108. London: Hogarth Press, 1958.

Gill, M. M. (1979) The analysis of the transference. *Journal of the American Psychoanalytic Association*, 27:263–288.

Gill, M. M. (1982a) *Analysis of Transference I: Theory and Technique*. New York: International Universities Press.

Gill, M. M. (1982b) Merton Gill: An interview. *Psychoanalytic Review*, 69:167–190.

Gill, M. M. (1983) The distinction between the interpersonal paradigm and the degree of the therapist's involvement. *Contemporary Psychoanalysis*, 19:200–237.

Gill, M. M. & Hoffman, I. Z. (1982a) *Analysis of Transference II: Studies of*

Nine Audio Recorded Psychoanalytic Sessions. New York: International Universities Press.

Gill, M. M. & Hoffman, I. Z. (1982b) A method for studying the analysis of aspects of the patient's experience of the relationship in psychoanalysis and psychotherapy. *Journal of the American Psychoanalytic Association,* 30:137–167.

Greenson, R. (1965) The working alliance and the transference neurosis. *The Psychoanalytic Quarterly,* 34:155–181.

Greenson, R. (1971) The real relationship between the patient and the psychoanalyst. In: *The Unconscious Today,* ed. M. Kanzer. New York: International Universities Press.

Hartmann, H. & Kris, E. (1945) The genetic approach to psychoanalysis. *The Psychoanalytic Study of the Child,* 1:11–30.

Heimann, P. (1950) On countertransference. *International Journal of Psycho-Analysis,* 31:81–84.

Issacharoff, A. (1979) Barriers to knowing. In: *Countertransference: The Therapist's Contributions to the Therapeutic Situation,* ed. L. Epstein & A. H. Feiner. New York: Aronson.

Kohut, H. (1971) *The Analysis of the Self.* New York: International Universities Press.

Kohut, H. (1977) *The Restoration of the Self.* New York: International Universities Press.

Langs, R. (1978) *Technique in Transition.* New York: Aronson.

Levenson, E. (1972) *The Fallacy of Understanding.* New York: Basic Books.

Levenson, E. (1981) Facts or fantasies: The nature of psychoanalytic data. *Contemporary Psychoanalysis,* 17:486–500.

Lipton, S. D. (1977a) The advantages of Freud's technique as shown in his analysis of the Rat Man. *International Journal of Psycho-Analysis,* 58:255–273.

Lipton, S. D. (1977b) Clinical observations on resistance to the transference. *International Journal of Psycho-Analysis,* 58:463–472.

Lipton, S. D. (1982) A critical review of Paul Dewald's "The Psychoanalytic Process." *Contemporary Psychoanalysis,* 18:349–365.

Loewald, H. (1960) On the therapeutic action of psychoanalysis. *International Journal of Psycho-Analysis,* 41:16–33.

Macalpine, I. (1950) The development of the transference. *The Psychoanalytic Quarterly,* 19:501–539.

Moore, B. E. & Fine, B. D. (1968) *A Glossary of Psychoanalytic Terms and Concepts.* New York: American Psychoanalytic Association.

Ogden, T. H. (1979) On projective identification. *International Journal of Psychoanalysis,* 60:357–373.

Racker, H. (1968) *Transference and Countertransference.* New York: International Universities Press.

Rogers, C. (1951) *Client-Centered Therapy.* Boston: Houghton Mifflin.

Sandler, J. (1976) Countertransference and role responsiveness. *International Review of Psychoanalysis,* 3:43–47.

Sandler, J. (1981) Character traits and object relationships. *The Psychoanalytic Quarterly,* 50:694–708.

Schimek, J. G. (1975) A critical re-examination of Freud's concept of unconscious mental representation. *International Review of Psycho-Analysis*, 2:171–187.

Searles, H. F. (1975) The patient as therapist to his analyst. In *Tactics and Techniques in Psychoanalytic Theory*, ed. P. Giovacchini, New York: Jason Aronson, Inc.

Searles, H. F. (1978–1979) Concerning transference and countertransference. *International Journal of Psychoanalytic Psychotherapy*, 7:165–188.

Sterba, R. (1934) The fate of the ego in analytic therapy. *International Journal of Psycho-Analysis*, 15:117–126.

Stone, L. (1961) *The Psychoanalytic Situation*, New York: International Universities Press.

Strachey, J. (1934) The nature of the therapeutic action of psychoanalysis. *International Journal of Psycho-Analysis*, 15:117–126.

Szasz, T. (1963) The concept of transference. *International Journal of Psycho-Analysis*, 44:432–443.

Tower, L. (1956) Countertransference. *Journal of the American Psychoanalytic Association*, 4:224–255.

Wachtel, P. L. (1980) Transference, schema and assimilation: The relevance of Piaget to the psychoanalytic theory of transference. *The Annual of Psychoanalysis*, 8:59–76.

Wolf, E. S. (1979) Countertransference in disorders of the self. In: *Countertransference: The Therapist's Contribution to the Therapeutic Situation*, ed. L. Epstein & A. H. Feiner. New York: Aronson.

Zetzel, E. R. (1956) Current concepts of transference. *International Journal of Psycho-Analysis*, 37:369–376.

Afterword *

In my zeal to debunk the fallacy of the blank screen in this paper, I failed to give due respect to the importance of the dialectic between the analyst's personal visibility and relative invisibility, a dialectic that has been explored in various contexts in subsequent papers. What is being fleshed out here, with perhaps something of the quality of an overcorrection to the myth of the blank screen, are the symmetrical or mutual aspects of the process. In emphasizing them, short shrift is

---

* This afterword is composed of excerpts from Hoffman's (1998) recent book. With the author's permission, the editors have adapted and woven together statements from the introduction to the book and from footnotes to Chapter 4, which is a later version of the essay that is republished here.

given to the element of wisdom associated with the idea of the analyst as more hidden than the patient, modified as that conception
must become when we make the transition from dichotomous to
dialectical thinking (p. xxi).

This article fails to give sufficient weight to the importance of the analyst's relative subordination of his or her own personal interest and
desire. In certain respects, the analyst *should* be less visible than the
patient. That asymmetry promotes both rational and irrational aspects
of the analyst's therapeutic authority. In general, the notion of a
dialectic between the patient's sense of the analyst as a person like
himself or herself and the patient's sense of the analyst as a person
with superior, even magical power is not recognized, much less developed in this essay. What *is* developed here is precisely one side of
that polarity, namely, the place of the patient's perception of the *symmetrical* aspects of the analyst's participation, rather than the asymmetrical aspects. Nevertheless, certain dialectical relationships *are* in
the foreground here, such as those between transference and countertransference, between the patient as interpreter and the analyst as
interpreter, and between interpretation and "association" in both parties (p. 101n).

The implication here that an independent current in the patient's
experience does not exist might be misleading. Clearly the patient
brings a myriad of internal structures (or schemas) to the encounter
with the analyst (innate dispositions, internal object relations, intrapsychic dynamics, patterns of selective attention and responsiveness). Yet
those structures emerge and are colored experientially in the context of
the interaction with the analyst who, in turn, brings his or her own
internal structures to the situation (p. 99n).

Another dialectic that is obscured in this paper is that between interpretive reflection on transference-countertransference enactments and
the fact of those enactments per se. Instead, there is an implication
of a dichotomous relationship between the two. It was only later that
I began to appreciate more fully the dialectical relationships between
enactment and interpretation and between repetition and new experience. Reflective interpretations are partly expressive of countertransference rather than fully transcending of it. And enactments may
be paradoxically integral to the emergence of new understanding and
of new ways of being in the analytic relationship and in the world.
On the one hand, by not giving sufficient weight to the dialectic of
the symmetrical and asymmetrical aspects of the relationship, in particular, by undervaluing the asymmetrical aspects, this paper probably

ends up moving too far from the traditional paradigm. On the other hand, because of the relative inattention to the dialectic of enactment and new experience, in particular because of its undervaluing of the paradoxically therapeutic potentials of enactments, it probably doesn't deviate from the traditional paradigm enough (Hoffman, 1998, pp. xxi–xxii).

The emphasis here on the tension between deleterious enactments, on the one hand, and interpretation of enactments, on the other, is somewhat misleading in that it fails to consider the subtle blending of old and new within virtually all interactions in the process, whether they are ostensibly interpretive, reflective, and exploratory, or noninterpretive and emotionally expressive. The paradoxical interplay of repetition and new experience, the way in which one can serve as necessary ground for the other, is obscured by the polarization here of regressive enactment and healthy understanding. My own sense of the complexity of the process, is conveyed, hopefully in later papers, developed more fully some years after this article was published in its original form (p. 124n).

In this paper I used the term "relativistic," which has encouraged the misunderstanding that my position is one of "radical relativism" or even solipsism (see, for example, Orange, 1992; Zucker, 1993). To say that experience is ambiguous and therefore open to a variety of interpretations does not mean that it is amorphous and that anything goes. I later used the term "perspectivist" which foreshadowed the emergence of a critical "constructivist" view of the psychoanalytic situation (p. 105n).

Over the years, my own views departed, in terms of emphasis, from those of Merton Gill, with whom I collaborated in the late 70s and early 80s. Perhaps most importantly, Gill's focus was generally upon the analysis of the transference in the context of appreciating the inevitability of the analyst's continuous interpersonal influence. My focus has been increasingly upon the dialectic of noninterpretive interpersonal interactions and interpretive interactions. Whereas for Gill, like Strachey, the heart of therapeutic action is in the moment of interpretation, for me it is in the dialectic of spontaneous, personal involvement and critical reflection on the process. In this perspective the analyst has the responsibility not only to interpret but also to contribute creatively to the development of the relationship in other ways, to wisely exercise his or her inescapable moral authority in the process, and to struggle through the paradox of participating in enactments while trying to understand and transcend them. An overemphasis on analysis of transference gravitates toward objectivism and "technical rationality" (p. 117n).

Bollas (1983) has discussed and illustrated the usefulness of *occasional* judicious disclosures by the analyst of his or her countertransference predicament. See also Burke (1992) for an attempt to spell out a rationale for disclosure. In my view, any approach that is overly specific in terms of technical principles threatens to rob disclosure of the elements of spontaneity and authenticity that are among its main benefits. The principal dialectic, as I see it, is between the inclination to reveal and the inclination to conceal aspects of one's personal experience in the analytic situation. Such an emphasis is less on discrete moments of choice as to whether to disclose or not to disclose and more on an ongoing dialectic between personally expressive and personally restrained behavior (p. 128n).

My views on this subject have been gradually changing away from the rather conservative position taken in this paper. Although restraint is called for in keeping with the asymmetrical arrangement, I now believe that it is often useful to be open with patients regarding one's personal reactions in the process. Such openness can facilitate identification and exploration of enactments as they occur; it can help the patient identify and take account of the analyst's biases as they affect his or her participation; and it offers the possibility for a level of spontaneous personal engagement which, in a dialectical relationship with psychoanalytic discipline, has great therapeutic potential. These considerations must be weighed against the reservations articulated in this essay (p. 129n).

References

Bollas, C. (1983), Expressive uses of the countertransference. *Contemp. Psychoanal.*, 19:1–34.

Burke, W. F. (1992), Countertransference disclosure and the asymmetry/mutuality dilemma. *Psychoanal. Dial.*, 2:241–271.

Hoffman, I. Z. (1998), *Ritual and Spontaneity in the Psychoanalytic Process: A Dialectical-Constructivist View.* Hillsdale, NJ: The Analytic Press.

Orange, D. M. (1992), Perspectival realism and social constructivism: Commentary on Irwin Hoffman's "Discussion: Toward a social-constructivist view of the psychoanalytic situation." *Psychoanal. Dial.*, 2:561–565.

Zucker, H. (1993), Reality: Can it be only yours or mine? *Contemp. Psychoanal.*, 29:479–486.

Unformulated Experience: From Familiar Chaos to Creative Disorder

(1983)

Donnel B. Stern

▼　▼　▼　▼　▼

Editors' Introduction

Ideas tend to come in clusters, and great ideas often burst forth in complex packages. Freud's extraordinary genius produced, in the 10 year span between 1895 and 1905, a package of remarkably generative notions: repression, unconscious conflicts, instinctual drive, infantile sexuality, the Oedipus complex, transference, resistance, and much, much more. Across the history of psychoanalysis, these ideas have been packaged together into what has been generally referred to as "classical psychoanalysis." Some of these ideas are necessarily conceptually entwined. For example, the Oedipus complex is unimaginable without infantile sexuality, or transference without resistance. But the linkage of some of these ideas is purely artefactual; they have become associated because they emerged together. They were connected to each other in the development of Freud's thought, but they are not necessarily conceptually joined. Sometimes it takes a while for that to become clear.

Over most of psychoanalytic history, until recently, the concept of the unconscious has been linked to Freud's theories of repression and instinctual drive, as if the three were different facets of the same phenomenon. Drives emerge from their source in the body and exert a pressure on the mind for discharge. Asocial and dangerous by their very nature, many derivatives of drives necessarily are turned back, repressed, at the frontier of awareness and thus become unconscious. The unconscious, in classical theory, is composed of the id's repressed drives and the parts of the superego and ego (including memories) that are drawn into conflicts generated by those unconscious drive impulses. Theorists who abandoned or eschewed drive theory were accused of lacking an awareness of both the unconscious and repression, as if the three were synonymous.

This early paper by Donnel Stern opened up new conceptual territory by introducing a way of theorizing about a distinctly psychoanalytic unconscious in non-drive theory terms. Stern took off from a tantalizing suggestion in one of Sullivan's lectures: "[one] . . . has information about one's experience only to the extent that one has tended to communicatè it to another or thought about it in the manner of commmunicative speech. Much of that which is ordinarily said to be *repressed* is merely unformulated." Because of his operationalist methodology, his warnings against theorizing about what cannot be felt and measured, Sullivan left this suggestion largely undeveloped. What is unformulated experience like? What are the processes and transformations through which it becomes formulated? These are the problems that were introduced by Stern in 1983, and these are the problems only recently brought into fuller development and linked with other advances in hermeneutics and constructivism in his book *Unformulated Experience: From Dissociation to Imagination in Psychoanalysis* (1997, The Analytic Press).

Early object relations theorists like Fairbairn theorized about nondrive unconscious structures, like internal objects, libidinal and antilibidinal egos. These operated something like Freud's unconscious drives: they had energy, and they were repressed. What is distinctive, and particularly contemporary, about Stern's notion of unformulated experience is that it is composed not of specific, repressed contents, but of vast domains of sensation, perception, and thought. And Stern moves far beyond Sullivan's suggestion to include, within the unformulated, not just material defended against, but rich sources of creativity.

The implications of the shift from the Freudian unconscious to the relationally unformulated are enormous and still being worked out. Stern's work anticipated and also helped bring about many later developments in relational theorizing: the shift from an emphasis on repression as the prototypic defense to dissociation; the importance of language in the construction of experience; the linkage between an interpersonal understanding of the contextual nature of mind and constructivism in cognitive psychology; the shift from a view of memory as the tapping of static, unchanged images (Stern's "warehouse") to a view of memory as perpetually transformed and reconstructed, as it is accessed and formulated in the present; and the centrality of uncertainty and curiosity in the analytic process.

Stern's *Unformulated Experience: From Dissociation to Imagination in Psychoanalysis* (1997, The Analytic Press) is a detailed and wide-ranging consideration of issues raised in this early paper. Part I explores various features of both formulated and unformulated experience in the context of contemporary hermeneutics and constructivism. Part II brings the concept of unformulated experience into juxtaposition with contemporary thinking about dissociation. And Part III provides clinical applications of Stern's approach. In addition, Stern has become one of the most lucid and influencial interpreters of the interpersonal tradition, most notably in his own contributions and editorial shepherding of *The Handbook of Interpersonal Psychoanalysis* (ed. M. Lionells, J. Fiscalini, C. Mann & D. Stern, 1995, The Analytic Press).

Unformulated Experience: From Familiar Chaos to Creative Disorder[1]*

▼   ▼   ▼   ▼   ▼

When a patient is finally able to think about a previously unaccepted part of life, seldom are fully formulated thoughts simply waiting to be discovered, ready for exposition. Instead, what is usually experienced is a kind of confusion—a confusion with newly appreciable possibilities, and perhaps an intriguing confusion, but a confusion or a puzzle nevertheless. Unconscious clarity rarely underlies defense. On the evidence of our obser-

* Originally published in *Contemporary Psychoanalysis*, 19(1):71–99 © 1983 W. A. White Institute.

1. An earlier version of this paper was presented at the Institute for Contemporary Psychotherapy, October 1981. I am grateful to Dr. Barry Protter for many productive discussions, to Dr. Allan Cooper for his criticism of earlier drafts, and to Mrs. Joann Kirtland for editorial assistance.

This paper won The Lawrence W. Kaufman Award for 1982.

vations of them as they emerge in awareness, the perceptions, ideas, and memories we prefer not to have, the observations we prefer not to make, are most often murky and poorly defined, different in kind than they will be when the process of completion has progressed to the level of words. "Unformulated experience" is the label I have chosen to refer to mentation characterized by lack of clarity and differentiation.[2]

Cognitions do not necessarily exist in the unformulated state, though, since the unformulated is a conglomeration not yet knowable in the separate and definable terms of language. As will be spelled out later, it is more accurate to say that unformulated material is composed of vague tendencies which, if allowed to develop to the point at which they could be shaped and articulated, would become this more lucid kind of experience.

The meaning in unformulated experience may take any one of the more precise forms toward which it moves. It is content without shape, "a beginning of insight, still unformulated, a kind of many-eyed cloud. . . . a humble and trembling inchoation, yet invaluable, tending toward an intelligible content to be grasped" (Maritain, 1953, p. 99). In William James's (1890) metaphor, each of us "sculpts" conscious experience from a block of the unformulated, which might have been carved in any number of different ways. Meaning becomes creation, not discovery. "Insight into an unconscious wish," says Fingarette (1963), "is like noticing a 'well-formed ship' in the cloud instead of a poorly formed 'rabbit.' On the other hand, insight is not like discovering an animal which has been hiding in the bushes" (p. 20).

1. Familiar chaos

The idea that thoughts can exist in an inchoate form was not available to Freud (1900, 1915), who based his theory on "the fundamental and

---

2. William James (1890) and Bergson (1903, 1907) have written about the emergence of thought from a less differentiated state. Their work has influenced the overall view of the paper. For James especially, the content of consciousness is a small selection of clearly articulated thoughts made from a vast array of vague and unformed possibilities. Language and focal attention formulate what is formless. Polanyi (1958) and Maritain (1963) have also been helpful in the development of the views presented here.

But for a general scheme, I am most indebted to Schachtel (1959, 1966), whose concept of embeddedness stimulated the idea of unformulated experience. The argument of the paper owes a great deal to his descriptions of curiosity and creativity, and to his dialectic of embeddedness vs. openness to one's world. I have cited Schachtel wherever I thought it was appropriate, but the reader may recognize the cast of his thought more frequently than I have been able to separate it from my own.

false assumption" that perception is a sensory given and immediately known to the subject (Eccles, 1970; cited by Basch, 1981. See also Schimek, 1975). This meant that any lack of clarity in a psychic element always had to be the consequence of later events, a product of the distorting effects of drive and defense. The contents of the Freudian unconscious and the materials of the primary process, which certainly seem to qualify as "inchoate," are not actually unformulated. It is true that the associations between elements and the form of the elements themselves are fluid, but cognitions in the Freudian scheme, even when they are disguised, are never anything less than fully realized. That is, they are carriers of meaning sufficiently well defined that the meaning could (if one would allow it) be put into words. "Thing-presentations" await only cathexis by the secondary process to become "word-presentations," and thus to gain access to the preconscious. But there is no true evolution in form here. The transformation of thing-presentation to word-presentation does not represent the growth of meaning into a more complete form—quite the contrary: Often the "real" meaning—the wish behind the idea—can exist only in the unconscious (or in later terminology, in the id). The word-presentation, in fact, is the paler form. In entering consciousness, a thing-presentation must become "less itself"; it must shed its primary process attributes and emerge tamed. In contrast, in order to enter consciousness, an unformulated thought must become "more itself."

Today, partially because of data and theory which have accrued since Freud wrote, it has become clear that experience, even at its most basic levels, is not a given: It is made, or constructed, and its construction proceeds in levels of progressive articulation. Experience may exist at any level of its construction, and thus the way is paved for a view of unformulated experience as a normal and natural phenomenon indicative neither of psychopathology nor conflict. It seems that we can be unaware of material not only because we refuse to acknowledge that we know it, but also because it has not yet attained a form in which consciousness can grasp it.

However, we also seem to have at least some influence over what parts of our own unformulated experience fail to attain a form assimilable by consciousness. Defensively motivated unformulated experience is a kind of "familiar chaos," to borrow a phrase from Paul Valery, a state of mind cultivated and perpetuated in the service of the wish not to think. The "chaos" refers to the natural form of undeveloped thought, and though we do not know exactly what it is, it does carry with it a comforting sense of familiarity. It may be banal and unquestioned, but it feels like our own. Familiarity is its camouflage. Defensively motivated unformulated experience is a lack of clarity and differentiation permitted or encouraged in cognitive material that, in more complete form, would be noxious.

Just as unformulated experience differs from thing-presentations, familiar chaos differs in its very nature from repressed experience or experience distorted by the other traditional defensive processes. Unformulated material is experience which has never been articulated clearly enough to allow application of the traditional defensive operations. One can forget or distort only those experiences which are formed with a certain degree of clarity in the first place. The unformulated has not yet reached the level of differentiation at which terms like memory and distortion are meaningful.

Most psychoanalysts seem to operate on the basis of the implicit hypothesis that people may resist the clarification of certain aspects of their experience, preferring vague, impressionistic formulations for which there genuinely are no words. We work as if the meaning in familiar chaos remains to be formed, as if there is not necessarily an underlying and pre-existing clarity in experience. Of course, the uncovering of veridical repressed memories has not been the central event in even the Freudian scheme of clinical psychoanalysis for many years (Freud, 1937; Kris, 1956). But even when Freud suggested that construction of the past was necessary, he still claimed that useful constructions presented purely historical truth, and that the unconscious was a storehouse of veridical memories. One might have to put up with the making of constructions as a practicality of the treatment, but theoretically speaking, "All of the essentials are preserved" (Freud, 1937, p. 260).

Harry Stack Sullivan made several references to lack of formulation as defense. Sullivan's work in this area was the earliest contribution, and it remains the most complete clinically derived description available.

Because the approach was a new one at the time, and not clearly differentiated from the classical theory of the defenses, it is not always obvious when Sullivan means repression (rejection or exclusion from consciousness of a fully formulated psychic element) and when he means lack of formulation. Nevertheless, the idea of defensively motivated lack of formulation is natural to Sullivan's theory, particularly to his notions of anxiety and the self-system.

The self-system includes all those experiences and ways of relating to others which have been found through experience to be safe and secure. Or from the other direction: The self-system rejects all experiences and modes of relating which are associated with anxiety. The predominant characteristic of the self-system is that it perpetuates itself. Once one finds for an interpersonal dilemma a solution which minimizes anxiety, or an apparent solution—a mode of perception, thought, feeling, or behavior—one may apply that solution indiscriminately from then on. New experiences come to be mistrusted simply because they are new. One does not know what they will bring, and so extracts from them only that which is already within the purview of the self-system. When this happens, the new disappears without ever having been noticed—or without being formulated. Anxiety leads us to search for the familiar and comfortable in experience, and throw out the rest.

Sullivan's clearest statement about lack of formulation is the following:

> . . . one has information about one's experience only to the extent that one has tended to communicate it to another or thought about it in the manner of communicative speech. Much of that which is ordinarily said to be *repressed* is merely unformulated (1940, p. 185).

That is, one keeps certain material unformulated in order not to "know" it. What is more, Sullivan seems to be suggesting that this is not material that has ever been formulated. Unlike repression, in which at least the original repression is a rejection from awareness, material affected by the process Sullivan describes here was never banished from consciousness—because it has never "been there."

This is a very different notion of defense, and Sullivan is only able to come to it because of his startlingly modern position (we will come across it later in a discussion of current cognitive theory) that lack of formulation as defense is merely a special use of processes that serve far more general cognitive functions. This position is never explicitly stated, but is implicit in Sullivan's (1953) concept of the three modes of experience.

The *prototaxic* mode appears chiefly in infancy and consists of a continuous present, a succession of momentary states without a "before" or "after." The *parataxic* mode is also non-rational. In it, experience is broken into parts for the first time, but different kinds of experience are not related to each other in a logical way. "They 'just happen' together or they do not, depending upon circumstances. . . . What is experienced is assumed to be the 'natural' way of such occurrences, without reflection and comparison" (Mullahy, 1947, pp. 287–288). This is the personal, subjective language of dreams and fantasies. The *syntaxic* mode is the realm of consensually validated meaning, meaning embodied in symbols which have the same significance to all of us. Language, as in Freud's secondary process, is the most important vehicle of the syntaxic mode, though words (again like Freud) can also be used in a parataxic— personal, autistic—way which makes one's meaning indecipherable. What Sullivan means in the passage about repression and lack of formulation is that if one keeps a meaning at the parataxic level, one prevents oneself from reflecting upon it. Reflection—thought—requires the symbolization of meaning. It requires that one either communicate a meaning to another person in a comprehensible linguistic form, or be able to. Because we mistrust the unfamiliar, being afraid that it will threaten our security, we may not symbolize it in communicable terms. It remains organized at the parataxic level, the fully formulated meaning never entering explicit awareness.

Thus, for Sullivan, one of the primary defenses is essentially "not thinking about it." This is accomplished by means of selective inattention, a process on which Sullivan (1953) lays heavy emphasis. What it means is that the control of focal attention, which helps separate the wheat from the chaff in everyday experiencing (again notice the adaptation of normal cognitive processes to defensive purposes), can also be used to keep something out of awareness. If one's focal attention is never trained on this "something," one is never aware of it; and if one is never aware of it, it remains parataxic—or unformulated. It is never elaborated into an experience in the syntaxic mode. In turn, this means one can never reflect on it. Anxiety is prevented, of course, but the strategy is equally effective in the prevention of learning. (It might be noted here that Freud [1900], too, proposed that attention was the final gateway into consciousness. But for Freud, this gateway was merely the entry into consciousness of material from the preconscious. Sullivan is proposing that the control of attention can result in something much more radical—in Freud's terms, something like keeping the material unconscious.)

Sullivan's concept of dissociation also employs the concept of unformulated experience. In the following passage, Sullivan suggests that unless an experience is reacted to, either positively or negatively, it does not become part of the self-system. It exists in dissociation, prototaxic (rarely) or parataxic (usually) in form, and is never known. It cannot develop, can never be elaborated. The concept is unique, since repression or dissociation is usually said to occur only as a result of, or in anticipation of, an unpleasant consequence.

> The facilitations and deprivations by the parents and significant others are the source of the material which is built into the self dynamism. Out of all that happens to the infant, only this "marked" experience is incorporated into the self. . . . For the expression of all things in the personality other than those which were approved and disapproved by the parent and other significant persons, the self refuses awareness, so to speak. It does not accord awareness, it does not notice; and these impulses, desires, and needs come to exist disassociated from the self, or *dissociated* (1940, pp. 21–22).

Sullivan suggests that dissociated material makes people anxious because they have never thought about it. One has built a whole self around these gaps in experience—sudden awareness of one of them would be devastating, disequilibrating, throwing off a whole system of anxiety avoidance. Thus, in consequence of the self-perpetuation of the self-system, dissociation, too, must be perpetuated. In the beginning of life, dissociation may simply be an "empty space" in the developing structure of experience, but as time passes and the self-system grows, the dissociation is no longer just "a place where something isn't," but an element of the self as vital to its continuing integrity as, say, the white space is to the visual structure of a painting. It thus becomes a matter of some delicacy to raise a patient's curiosity about this material without at the same time raising anxiety to unbearable intensity.

Sullivan's view is compatible with the observation that when resistance abates, disavowed thoughts do not suddenly pop up, fully formed, ready to take their place in the continuing unfolding of the treatment. Parataxic experience remains to be formed. However, I think Sullivan's position would be that the eventual syntaxic form of parataxically organized experience is predetermined by what has actually happened in the patient's life. Like Freud, Sullivan believed that the only truth that makes people free is historical truth. We shall later come across a different view.

Unformulated experience is for Sullivan merely the absence of mutuality and reason (see Klenbort, 1978, and Bromberg, 1979). Sullivan had great respect for the tenacity of the nonrational, but did not seem to share Freud's conviction that the nonrational was the source of the greatest contributions as well as the greatest suffering.

2. Constructions and associations

Like Sullivan, we might, entirely on the basis of clinical observations of its utility, accept the proposition that experience can exist in an unformulated state; or, like William James (1890), we might accept the idea on purely phenomenological grounds. However, today, unlike either James or Sullivan, we can turn to a body of scientific literature which adduces this same concept, unformulated experience, from the results of experimentation.

The theoretical view of thought from which the concept of unformulated experience is best understood might be called constructivism. The theories in this broad category, which includes most of present-day cognitive psychology, have in common an emphasis on experience as "made" or constructed, not merely received, as in the older associationist view. In associationist theories, such as Freud's, new experience is received, clear and fully formulated, and added to the store of memories as if it were an additional crate being stacked in a warehouse. Experience is a series of discrete mental entities, and concepts arise from various combinations, or associations, of these entities (Freud, 1900, 1925).[3] Memory is thus very much like that warehouse: Nothing need be changed by the addition of something new, and, like objects or entities, experiences are either present and fully formed or altogether absent. There is no place for the shadowy or unformed.

Many psychoanalysts who identify themselves as Freudian would undoubtedly accept without a second thought the idea that experience can exist in an unformulated mode. As long ago as 1939, Hartmann described a similar concept. In his view, though, unformulated experience was not the natural phenomenon we will see it to be from the constructivist vantage point, but an indirect result of the repression of earlier experiences which the ego would have needed to make a mature formulation. This view is not infrequently present in the work of contemporary theorists of drive and defense (e.g., Kernberg, 1980). However, there have been Freudian writers (Gill, 1963; Klein, 1976; Schafer, 1976) who have conceptualized the defensive process in ways not unsympathetic to defensive lack of formulation. The basic proposition that the fully formed experience exists unchanged in the unconscious memory trace (Freud, 1900, 1915; Lewy and Rapaport, 1944), though, has only infrequently been criticized from within the classical psychoanalytic tradition (Paul, 1967; Basch, 1981), and as recently as 1976, as eminent a theoretician as Loewald wrote that there was no reason to question the idea.

According to Freud, each experience is recorded and stored more or less permanently in the unconscious, much like a film or tape library. Conscious memories and other experience are the result of the distorting effects of drive and defense on the permanent unconscious record. This leads to the familiar psychoanalytic concept of self-deception: Deceiving ourselves means convincing ourselves that we do not know something when we actually do know it. The Freudian defensive processes are always processes of masking, or disguise, or outright expulsion and banishment of (fully formed) experience from consciousness. Again, the defenses take this form because all mental contents—conscious, preconscious, and unconscious—are conceptualized as fully

---

3. Outside psychoanalysis, there is probably no student of cognition today who holds an exclusively associationist theory, but there are constructivist theorists, both in psychoanalysis (Paul, 1967) and academic psychology (Claxton, 1980), who believe that an adequate theory of cognition will have to contain associationist elements.

formulated. The concept of unformulated experience makes no sense in an associationist theory. For Freud, experiences may be forgotten, transformed, masked or disguised, distorted, blended with other experiences until undetectable, defused by breaking all links to other experiences, or simply denied—but in all cases the experience still exists "in the psyche." Despite appearances to the contrary, the fully formulated experience is hidden somehow in the form of what we can see, like the prince in the frog. Fingarette (1963) calls this the "hidden reality" view; Neisser (1967) calls it the "reappearance hypothesis."

Argyris and Schön (1976) describe two kinds of theories people use in deciding what actions to take, "theories-in-use" and "espoused theories." Whatever we say about what we do (our espoused theories), we often base our actions on theories for which we have no words (our theories-in-use). We take many wise and correct actions for reasons we cannot specify. For many psychotherapists, lack of formulation as defense is just such a theory-in-use. In an associationist psychology, that is what it will have to remain, because the associationist language, and the habits of thought this language inculcates, cannot capture it.

From the constructivist point of view, however, the concept of unformulated experience makes sense as espoused theory as well. In this general view of thought, mental activity is seen as organic, continuous, and unitary. New experiences are not simply added on, like the crates stacked in the warehouse, but integrated with everything that has come before, in the way rain water becomes part of a lake, say, or the way salt dissolves in water. New experience often makes it necessary to attain a new cognitive equilibrium. One of the first theories available for description of this way of conceptualizing thought was Piaget's (1952), in which a mental organization adapts to the new by a dual process of assimilating it to pre-existing schemata and changing the schemata themselves, accommodating the form of the new experience. Arieti (1976), drawing on this general conceptual scheme, has given a description of thought consisting of levels of increasing differentiation. The most primitive level, but one which is still available to the adult, is imagery, by which Arieti means fleeting and uncontrollable mental representations. Of most interest for the present purpose is Arieti's intermediate level, amorphous cognition, "a kind of cognition that occurs without representation—that is, without being expressed in images, words, thoughts, or actions of any kind" (p. 54). To differentiate the functioning of amorphous cognition from other types of thought, Arieti calls its concept the "endocept," signifying its private, incommunicable nature.

The most pervasive language of progressive clarification is the language of information processing, which is derived from the workings of computers and has revolutionized academic psychology over the last fifteen years, replacing behaviorism as the dominant paradigm. The information processing metaphor refers to the forms through which information passes from the moment the stimulus hits the sense receptor, through perception, into consciousness and short-term memory, and eventually into long-term memory, where the information is used for a variety of purposes. Information at any stage in this process may feed back to an earlier stage, thereby influencing what comes after it.[4]

At each stage in this process, the form of the information changes, becoming more and more clearly articulated, and there are stages of processing occurring prior to the entry of the material into awareness. It is quite natural in this frame of reference for there to be forms of information which cannot be cognized within consciousness. This is not to say that the theorists in this area believe that motivation has anything to do with this lack of awareness. Generally, the view seems to be that consciousness is merely one stage through which information passes. For most cognitive psychologists, consciousness is merely a way station, no more and no less significant than any other station on the route.

However, there are some cognitive psychologists who doubt that cognition can be so neatly separated from affect and motivation (Broadbent, 1977; Erdelyi, 1974; Erdelyi and Goldberg, 1979; Neisser, 1967, 1976; Rosenblatt and Thickstun, 1977). These psychologists have proposed links between the information processing model of cognition and the psychoanalytic model of the defenses. Their accounts dovetail nicely with the idea of lack of formulation as defense. Bowlby (1980) has recently gone so far as to propose a comprehensive model of the defenses in which "the basic concept . . . is that of the exclusion from further processing of information of certain specific types for relatively long periods or even permanently" (p. 45).

Neisser (1967), the acknowledged father of cognitive psychology, was the first to use the information processing model to conceptualize the defenses. He spends most of his classic text discussing relatively immediate processes, i.e., those taking place within a very short time after the presence of a stimulus, such as attention, perception, immediate encoding, and short-term memory. In his last chapter, though, he speculates about long-term memory and thought, basing his ideas on the experi-

---

4. I will not attempt here to cover the data themselves, but will restrict consideration to those ideas growing out of the data which have relevance to the topic at hand. For reviews of the field, the reader is referred to the general texts which have appeared in recent years (e.g., Neisser, 1967; Posner, 1973; Lindsay and Norman, 1977).

mental work and theory he has presented on the more immediate processes. His work on defense, which includes some of the prefatory material, is worth presenting in some detail. The relationship of these ideas to Sullivan's will be obvious; what Neisser does here is to offer a look at the microscopic processes which might underlie Sullivan's broader scheme.

Neisser's basic point is that memories and thoughts are constructions, just as perceptions are, and that the processes of memory and thought go on in a way analogous to perception—especially analogous to visual perception. Neisser analyzes visual cognition as a two-stage process. In the first stage, incoming information is broken up into large and vague chunks or blocks of visual information, which might be organized, for example, as sky, building, street, movement (though of course not in these verbal terms). Neisser labels this primitive organizing function as the *preattentive processes.* The products of the preattentive processes are represented in *iconic storage.*[5] Iconic storage is a short-term system: If items in it do not become the object of focal attention in a very few moments, they disappear from storage—which means they are no longer represented in psychic life at all. Some sort of automatic selection process is necessary if we are not to be constantly overwhelmed by incoming stimuli, and thus the vast majority of the vague elements in iconic storage simply disappear without further processing. However, if these elements do become the object of focal attention, they are subject to further processing, which results in greater differentiation and detail. They enter consciousness and short-term memory at this point, and, depending on certain other factors, may enter long-term memory.

Thus I may focus my attention on a block of information organized as "movement," and I may note that there are many such movements, that they are automobiles, and that approximately half of them are taxis. In the meantime, the vague visual phenomenon representing "sky" has decayed in iconic storage, making it impossible for me ever to know whether during my concentration on the cars an airplane or a cloud passed overhead. This point in the processing of information—the point at which information must either be processed further in consciousness or allowed to decay (i.e., the area of the preattentive processes and iconic storage) is one probable locus for perceptual defense effects and perceptual vigilance effects.

---

5. Readers of earlier drafts have been confused by the usage of the term "iconic." In general usage, an "icon" is usually a static image. In cognitive psychology, "iconic" is a general reference to visual representation, including movement.

In Neisser's view, a memory or a thought is created analogously. Corresponding to the preattentive processes is what Neisser calls the primary process. This process is not identical to Freud's concept of the same name, but it bears certain similarities: irrational, uncontrollable, motivated, full of affect. It is a parallel form of information processing, everything going on at once, as opposed to the linear or serial or sequential secondary process (again, Neisser's version, not Freud's), which is the form of logical thought over which we have control—one element leads to another in orderly fashion.

Neisser, in a passage reminiscent of James, speculates that the primary process constantly casts up vague and unformed ideas and memories, analogous to the vague chunks or blocks into which the visual field is broken by the preattentive processes. And in the same way that focal attention continues the processing of only some of the preattentive material, leaving the rest of it to decay and disappear without ever having reached awareness (i.e., without ever having been "known"), the secondary process seizes upon and develops only some of the offerings of the primary process. Those offerings selected are then differentiated and formulated into complete thoughts or memories. But those primary process products not selected, and therefore not cognitively elaborated, just like the contents of ionic storage, either never enter consciousness at all, or like something on the tip of the tongue, disappear after only the briefest visitation, leaving a feeling that something was there, but we know not what. We may even know it was a dream, or a memory, or a thought of what to do after lunch; but even if its category and context can be identified, it is itself lost.

In Neisser's model, the point at which material is either attended to and elaborated by the secondary process or allowed to decay is open to emotional influence. He calls this *"deliberately avoiding construction in certain areas"* (p. 303; Neisser's italics). We are forcibly reminded of Sullivan's notions here, especially in the similarity between Neisser's transition from primary to secondary process and Sullivan's between parataxic and syntaxic modes. Neisser argues that any number of factors determine whether or not a particular cognition reaches an end point clearly enough defined to permit symbolization in language (consciousness), and he would agree with Sullivan that there is no reason that anxiety should not be among these factors. Here we have come full circle and discovered, from a contemporary experimental perspective, an idea quite similar to those Sullivan formulated entirely on the basis of clinical experience. Both writers agree that preventing material from reaching clarity is simply a special use of cognitive mechanisms which prevent us from being flooded with excess stimulation. Neisser, of course, would also agree with Sullivan that unformulated material cannot be reflected on.

However, Neisser takes a further step: In his model, unformulated experience is not available to memory. And therefore, we can add, historical truth is not necessarily available when the motivation not to know it has been analyzed. Instead, in Neisser's version, unformulated material has literally never been thought. It has decayed before it could ever be added to consciousness or memory. In psychoanalysis, from this point of view, when a patient has come to the point where he or she is willing to be curious about this experience, the cognitive representation must be at least partially created, not discovered. From other directions, both clinical and philosophical, this conclusion has been reached by a number of psychoanalytic writers (Blum, 1980; Fingarette, 1963, 1969; Issacharoff and Hunt, 1978; Loch, 1977; Loewald, 1960; Noy, 1978; Rosenberg and Medini, 1978; Spence, 1982; Viderman, 1980; Wolstein, 1982).

Summarizing: Lack of formulation as defense is difficult to conceptualize in an associationist psychology, but from a constructivist vantage point, such as Neisser's, it seems natural and perhaps even inevitable. In Freud's view, because all experience has been laid down, clear and fully formulated in the unconscious memory trace, defense always means finding a way not to know (consciously) something already known (unconsciously). In the view incorporating motivated lack of formulation, defense may also include purposefully never having known.

3. Resolving a paradox: James's "feelings of tendency"

The last statement highlights what may seem to be a problem for the whole concept of purposive lack of formulation: How can one tell oneself to refuse to formulate a thought without having first formulated it? How does one know what not to formulate? Erdelyi (1974), Neisser (1967), and Bowlby (1980) have each offered solutions to the problem from the information processing viewpoint. All three hold that the problem exists only as long as cognition is seen as an all-or-none phenomenon—i.e., as long as one either sees or does not see, hears or does not hear, remembers or does not remember. Cognition is all-or-none only if we restrict attention to what goes on in awareness. The problem disappears as soon as cognition is understood as a multistage phenomenon, only parts of which take place within awareness (as, for example, in Neisser's model). Processing can simply be stopped at any one of these stages. Erdelyi says, for example, that "the perceiver, on the basis of partial analysis of the information in ionic storage, may terminate further processing of remaining ionic materials" (p. 17). This particular process, as well as many others which might be imagined, would take place entirely outside awareness.

This solution to the paradox is viable if we assume something like Neisser's (1967) "executive" or Bowlby's (1980) subliminal perception. Bowlby has based his information processing model of the defenses on the proposition that we "perceive" more about our developing thoughts and feelings than we can be aware of. On the basis of this information (the "partial analysis of information in ionic storage," for example), we can either choose to continue the processing of the information, allowing it to enter awareness, or "terminate" processing before the information arrives. This model depends on the hypothesis that, on the basis of one's biases, long-term memory can feed back to the very beginning of the process of thought, extrapolate the eventual from the unformulated material would take if it entered consciousness, and on that basis select what material will be processed further and what material will be allowed to decay (Broadbent, 1958; Deutsch and Deutsch, 1963). Neisser's "executive" is an analogue of the "executive routine," a computer subprogram that can be written so that it tells all other subprograms when to operate. The executive itself does not have the capacity to carry out the work of the other subprograms; it is merely a carrier and applier of rules. Thus, it is possible in cognition to be the executive without having simultaneously to be the one who is told what to do. The model, Neisser concludes with relief, can run without homunculi.

However, it also seems reasonable to posit that we can turn away, or "terminate processing," on the basis of disturbing glimmers of meaning of which we are aware, at least for moments. It would seem that this, too, can occur without the complete formulation of an experience. An advantage of this alternative is that we do not have to take it on faith. As expressed (below) in the words of William James (1890), it is phenomenologically satisfying as well as scientifically plausible. And it is no small thing that conceptualizing the problem this way offers more hope that the process is amenable to psychoanalysis—for it is immensely difficult to understand in one's own personal terms a process, such as Bowlby's subliminal perception or Neisser's executive, which is by its very nature sealed off from consciousness.

James described these glimmers of meaning, or in his words, "feelings of tendency," in the following passages. If we add the wish to minimize anxiety to these descriptions of the kind of awareness we have of unformulated meanings, it becomes phenomenologically plausible that a thought or feeling can be discarded before it is formed.

But namelessness is compatible with existence. There are innumerable consciousnesses of emptiness, no one of which taken in itself has a name, but all different from each other. The ordinary way is to assume that they are all emptinesses of consciousness, and so the same state. But the feeling of an absence is *toto coelo* other than the absence of a feeling. It is an intense feeling (Volume 1, pp. 251–252).

The truth is that large tracts of human speech are nothing but *signs of direction* in thought, of which direction we nevertheless have an acutely discriminative sense, though no censorial image plays any part in it whatsoever. . . . One may admit that a good third of our psychic life consists in these rapid premonitory perspective views of schemes of thought not yet articulate (Volume 1, pp. 252–253).

Now what I contend for, and accumulate examples to show, is that "tendencies" are not only descriptions from without, but that they are among the *objects* of the stream, which is thus aware of them from within, and must be described as in very large measure constituted *of feelings of tendency*, often so vague that we are unable to name them. It is, in short, the reinstatement of the vague to its proper place in our mental life which I am so anxious to press on the attention (Volume 1, p. 254).

Great thinkers have vast premonitory glimpses of schemes of relation between terms, which hardly even as verbal images enter the mind, so rapid is the whole process. We all of us have this permanent consciousness of whither our thought is going. It is a feeling like any other, a feeling of what thoughts are next to arise, before they have arisen (Volume 1, pp. 255–256).

4. Creative disorder

Chaos, subjectivity, and disorder are more than the absence of communicability and mutuality—they are also the source of novelty. Piaget, emulating Bergson, was apparently fond of referring to the "creative disorder" of his office, presumably making reference to a comparable inner state. Isadora Duncan referred to "a state of complete suspense" as one of the stages in her invention of a dance. Brewster Ghiselin wrote, "In order to invent, one must yield to the indeterminate within him." Stephen Spender, when he came close to a new poem, said it was "something still vague, a dim cloud of an idea which I feel must be condensed into a shower of words." Alfred North Whitehead speaks of "the state of imaginative muddled confusion which precedes successful inductive generalization." (For the testimony of artists and philosophers, see Ghiselin, 1952. For scientists and mathematicians, see Hadamard, 1945, and Poincaré, 1908). The mathematician Marston Morse (1951) offers what could be a rejoinder to Sullivan's view of the nonrational:

> The first essential bond between mathematics and the arts is found in the fact that discovery in mathematics is not a matter of logic. It is rather the result of mysterious powers which no one understands, and in which the unconscious recognition of beauty must play an important part. Out of an infinity of designs a mathematician chooses one pattern for beauty's sake, and pulls it down to earth, no one knows how. Afterward the logic of words and of forms sets the pattern right. Only then can one tell someone else. The first pattern remains in the shadows of the mind (quoted by Maritain, 1953).

Sullivan never wrote about the roots of the creative process, and perhaps would have considered the topic outside the bounds of the operational psychiatry he wanted to found. For him, unformulated experience was always immature experience. It played no positive part in living. Furthermore, in Sullivan's view, and quite different from the view that comes to us from accounts of the creative process, unformulated experience, left to its own devices, could never coalesce or crystallize—could never formulate itself. Unless attention was directed to it, it never changed, developed, or cast up new thoughts. Unformulated experience, to use a word characteristic of Sullivan, was unfortunate—useless until it could be made communicable, syntaxic.

One can hardly disagree with the goal of formulating the unformulated. Obviously, formulation of some kind is always the aim. But to view all unformulated experience as parataxis, and thus immature, is to ignore the very means by which formulation is accomplished. Formulations derive from the unformulated.

Is an invention, a new idea, a poem—or, for that matter, a new thought about oneself—"immature" prior to the moment the thought can be captured in words? Is it not more accurate to say that the eventual product was in a state of possibility? If we value the eventual products, should we not also value the unformulated experience from which these products emerge?

The unformulated is possibility as well as parataxis, creative disorder as well as familiar chaos. And, however difficult we may acknowledge it to be to attend to unformulated material, attention by itself, contrary to Sullivan, just does not seem to be enough to bring the unformulated into reflective awareness. After all, if the unformulated is not assimilable by consciousness, what is it that attention can focus on? We know how uncommon it is for the ineffable to spring suddenly into the realm of the communicable as soon as resistance relaxes. It is not as if the unformulated is leaning against the door, just waiting for a chance to overcome resistance and tumble into the room.

The unformulated must organize itself first. It must begin to coalesce, perhaps by some process like that described by Neisser (1967). It must send up tendrils, or feelings of tendency. Then the function of attention can be focused and used to help a fully formed product emerge into awareness.[6]

As artists tell it, the unformulated often does coalesce without conscious intervention, but it must brew, and it takes its own time to do it. Mozart is one famous example: He could compose in a room full of noise and traffic, and could be interrupted at any point without being disturbed, because by the time he sat down to write, he was merely copying onto the page a piece of music which already existed in its entirety in his mind. About his ideas he wrote: "*Whence* and *how* they come I know not; nor can I force them" (Ghiselin, 1952, p. 44). Marina Tsvetaeva wrote that, if you are a poet (as she was), your hand belongs

---

6. Kris (1952) describes the creative process as an oscillation between purposeful intellectual activity and passive receptivity. This part of his view is consistent with the position taken in this paper, and has probably even influenced it. Kris is not cited in this discussion, though, for two reasons. First, since his view of cognition is based on Freud's, there is no place in it for the concept of unformulated experience. Second, the idea that the creative process depends on regression, even a controlled regression in the service of the ego, seems more true to the form of Freudian thought than to the phenomenon of creativity itself. Kris's position requires the assumption that the management of drive, not the formulation and emergence of meaning, is the primary work of cognition. In Schachtel's words,

> What distinguishes the creative process from regression to primary-process thought is that the freedom of the approach is due not to a drive discharge function, but to the openness in the encounter with the object of the creative labor (1959, p. 245).

Arieti (1976) avoids regression in his theory of creativity by postulating a "tertiary process" which integrates the secondary process and the primary process. Certain more classically oriented psychoanalytic writers (Kubie, 1958; Ehrenzweig, 1967; Noy, 1969, 1972; Roland, 1972) have stressed that the creative process and (under some circumstances) the primary process are integrative and generative in function, and that the concept of regression is therefore unnecessary as an explanatory principle in the field of creativity. Others (Winnicott, 1971; Pruyser, 1979) have removed the study of the creative process from the context of drive altogether, doing away with regression by substituting object relations for biology.

not to yourself, but to "that which wants to exist through you." In a letter to Pasternak she said, "We dream and write not when *we* please but when it pleases: a letter to be written, a dream to be seen" (Muchnic, 1980, p. 7). Burnshaw (1970) scatters through his text on artistic creation other testimony to the autonomous crystallization of the unformulated: The poet "does not know what he has to say until he has said it" (Keats); "It is not I who think but my ideas who think for me" (Lamartine); "Words rise up unaided and in ecstasy" (Mallarmé); "We get a new song when the words we want to use shoot up of themselves" (Orpingalik, an Eskimo poet); "It will come if it is there and you let it come" (Gertrude Stein); the thing to do is "to let each impression and each germ of feeling come to completion quite in itself . . . beyond the reach of one's own understanding" (Rilke).

We cannot force formulation. We can only prepare ourselves by immersion in our field of interest and then remain open to possibility, seizing it (attending to it) whenever it appears. It is not enough to "put our backs into" the forging of new formulations, though we must be willing to do this when the time comes and the vague outlines of something new begin to emerge. We must also work toward an acceptance of the uncertainty which is sometimes all that can be known of the content of the unformulated. This applies no less to the rest of us than it does to the artists who have captured the process in words.

Sullivan's goal, then, should be broadened to include not only formulation of the unformulated, but also acceptance of unformulated experience as creative disorder. In practice, this means that when the need for a particular piece of familiar chaos (i.e., defensively motivated unformulated experience) is successfully understood, what replaces it, and what makes new formulations eventually possible, is the acceptance of previously rejected uncertainty.

Now it is possible to specify the two uses of unformulated experience. In its use as creative disorder, its uncertainty is accepted, and feelings of tendency are encouraged, valued, and nurtured. One tries to capture in symbolic representation as many of them as possible, selecting and discarding only later. In familiar chaos, by contrast, there is little interest in what may emerge, and in fact, as Sullivan suggested, one is interested primarily in keeping the unformulated experience just as it is. What is defended against is not a thought, because no thought has been formed, but the process of thinking itself. When one prevents attention from focusing on feelings of tendency, the possibility and uncertainty of creative disorder are frozen into the autistic certainty of parataxis.

The link between chaos and creativity is reflected in Arieti's (1976) discussion of amorphous cognition, or "endoception," briefly cited above. Arieti's descriptions realize something of the nonrepresentational mental activity from which creative products emerge.

> In creative persons this endoceptual cognition is an indeterminate entity in search of a form, a groping for some definite structure. When a suitable form is found, this activity is transformed into creative work . . . (p. 62).

Arieti shares with Sullivan an emphasis on communicability, but he also sees in disorder the potential for growth:

> The endocept of the future creative work contains no more than possibilities of what can be actualized in different ways, according to what the author may choose to do (p. 64).

From this vantage point, we can return to Neisser's position that thought and memory are creation: A new thought about oneself or one's world, even a new memory, may be the same kind of phenomenon as the product of an artistic effort. Some of the experiences which emerge when resistance is resolved are no more predetermined than the daubs and streams of color in a Pollock painting. One may have only intimations of the mental activity that will take place when obstruction vanishes.

Gendlin (1964) takes just this position, bringing into the realm of psychotherapy the kind of observations that Arieti makes about the creative process, and that James and Neisser make about cognition in general.

> . . . a felt meaning can contain very many meanings and can be further and further elaborated. Thus, the felt meaning is not the same in kind as the precise symbolized explicit meaning. The reason the difference in kind is so important is because if we ignore it we assume that explicit meanings are (or were) already in the implicit felt meaning. We are led to make the felt, implicit meaning a kind of dark place in which countless explicit meanings are hidden. We then wrongly assume that these meanings are "implicit" and felt only in the sense that they are "hidden." I must emphasize that the "implicit" or "felt" datum of experiencing is a sensing of body life. As such it may have countless organized aspects, but this does not mean that they are conceptually formed, explicit, and hidden. Rather, we *complete* and form them when we explicate.
>
> Before symbolization, the "felt" meanings are *incomplete* (pp. 113–114).

Once seen, a new clarity may seem so inevitable that it is experienced as having "been there all the time," deceiving us into believing that it actually was (the "hidden reality" view). The previous lack of awareness is astonishing. The right words, once found, pull the figure out of a background that until a moment before was homogeneous. Alternatively, if the meaning remains implicit or felt, as in the case of many dreams, the moment may pass with only the awareness of the presence of a vague something. Yet enough is left that we recognize the thought if we have it again; and if someone else says it, or if the thought appears in print, we have a reaction of puzzlement and surprise that we ourselves have not thought of this very thing, something like, "I *knew* that."

Lack of formulation is lack of symbolization. Not to have a thought means not to translate unformulated experience into language. In the case of defense, it amounts to a refusal to make this leap into meaning, while in the case of the cultural blinders that rob us, as we grow up, of the vividness and intensity that experience seems to have for children, we are actually unable to make meanings (Schachtel, 1947). According to Schachtel's tragic view, because direct apperception and memory of true and raw experience would "explode the restrictive social order," society forces individual experience, which is all we really have, into banal, conventional schemata. Bergson (1903, 1907) and James (1890) conclude that language, although it formulates the formless and is therefore constitutive of experience, also seduces us into accepting a mythology of the world around us that is based—circularly—on the properties of language itself. In these ways, language and culture set the limits beyond which even creative disorder cannot spread.

5. Curiosity and acceptance of the familiar

There is always more than one meaningful interpretation of an event, of course, and we take it equally for granted how often people talk and act as if only the particular one they have selected could possibly be true. These constructions, defended so doggedly, may be the only visible evidence of lack of formulation being used defensively. One can stifle the uncertainty of creative disorder just as effectively by forcing an interpretation, usually a safe, conventional one, as by refusing to make one at all. Assumptions carried from one situation to the next, applied over and over again, are methods of structuring the world in such a way that one can avoid having to think about it. These assumptions and expectations are ways of keeping the process of attention reined in, fixed in a routine of illuminating only that which one already knows it will illuminate. If uncertainty cannot be made to disappear altogether, it can at least be dampened, made to die down. Everything often seems perfectly clear in this kind of world, though it may feel nearly unbearable. It is hard to conjure up the questions one might ask oneself. *In extremis*, this may be the world of psychosis, of the psychotically depressed person, for instance, who is absolutely sure of his or her failure and complete lack of worth. It is the world of the paranoid, peopled with beings who menace one terribly, but who always behave in predictable ways.

Every psychotherapist has worked with people who, when they begin to ask themselves questions, using their capacity to construct new interpretations, are surprised to find that they have never done it before. Looking back on it, they say, to paraphrase Mullahy's description of the parataxic mode, "That's just the way things were. It didn't require an explanation." The restriction of thought is a kind of stupidity in which everything smoothes out, and questions disappear into the familiar. (Even the "sharpening" attitide of the vigilant paranoid implies a "smoothing out"—there may be such attention to salient details that the person gives the illusion of perceptiveness, but the vastness of experience is actually left nearly untouched.) Unquestioning acceptance of the familiar ensures that there will be no inadvertent deployment of curiosity. The familiar swallows anything. It is bottomless. When experience fades into the familiar, it loses substance, it becomes a ghost. It may be gone forever, irretrievable in its original form. Bartlett's (1932) classic experiments on memory show that, as time passes, people remember a more and more conventional form of a story they have been told, even if the original form of the story deviated radically from conventionality. "The known," said Hegel, "just because it is the known, is the unknown." Unquestioning acceptance of the familiar is the attitude by which maintenance of unformulated experience as familiar chaos is accomplished.

If what is dreaded remains unformulated, it may be unclear what it is that one is afraid of, only that whatever is there is dreadful. And the solution is there for the taking: The solution is to restrict freedom of thought. The process is self-perpetuating, an aspect of the self-system. Like a totalitarian state, the heavily defended person has more to fear from freeing thought itself than from any particular construction thought might make. Open inquiry must be put to a stop. The capacity to see the familiar in the unfamiliar, one of the great achievements of infancy, becomes in adulthood an equally great impediment to thought's growth (Schachtel, 1959).

In the constructivist view, since each person is the author of his or her own experience, the only thing to be learned about oneself that can really be counted on to be the truth is that one is afraid to be curious. As a matter of fact, ever since Freud rejected the seduction theory, curiosity, not truth, has been the guiding value of psychoanalysis. The ideal patient is curious about everything. To be this curious requires the tolerance of enormous uncertainty almost constantly. It also requires the strength to anticipate being able to tolerate any and all thoughts and feelings one might have. It means allowing oneself, even encouraging oneself to the extent that it is possible, to complete all interpretations and constructions one finds undeveloped in oneself. Curiosity preserves the uncertainty in unformulated experience. Curiosity is the attitude by which unformulated experience is maintained as creative disorder. In these terms, psychoanalysis is the progressive awakening of curiosity, a movement from familiar chaos to creative disorder.

I have said that curiosity means allowing oneself to make constructions. "Allowing" may seem strange wording—or it may sound like some kind of conscious granting of permission to oneself to "go ahead and work on" thinking. To "work on" thinking is precisely the meaning not intended. Curiosity is an active attitude of openness (Schachtel, 1959), not a focused search, at least not to begin with. It means that rather than employing a focused beam of attention, a searchlight to look *for* things in experience, which in one way or another usually seems to result in conventionalizing, one allows the things that are there to impress themselves on one's consciousness. This involves taking one's hand off the tiller and letting what Schachtel (1973) called "global attention and perception" drift as it will. Then, when an interesting construction begins to form itself out of the preattentive material, one may stop and perform a more focused search on and around this construction to fill in the detail and give it the convincing quality Freud (1937) knew it had to have to be useful. Of course, it is no accident that this description of "allowing" is essentially a description of free association; but it is the ideal of free association.

In this view, then, psychoanalysis is not a search for the hidden truth about the patient and the patient's life. It is instead the emergence, through curiosity and the acceptance of uncertainty, of constructions which may never have been thought before. Furthermore, these constructions are not merely sensible stabs at history and description: As Sullivan was the first to see, they are part and parcel of the new world patient and analyst are creating between them. This fact permeates them and is at least as important as their degree of historical accuracy. As Rosenberg and Medini (1978) put it, "There is an emergent *process* of truth finding. . . . And it is developmental in the sense that it assumes continuities between past and present, although the past may become very changed as it is remembered" (p. 427).

In the same vein, Loewald (1960) proposes that change in psychoanalysis is the result of the reorganization of experience, not of the uncovering of fully formed truth.

Language, in its most specific function in analysis, as interpretation, is thus a creative act similar to that in poetry, where language is found for phenomena, contexts, experiences not previously known and speakable. New phenomena and new experiences are made available as a result of reorganization of material according to hitherto unknown principles, contexts, and connections (p. 242).

Issacharoff and Hunt (1978), arguing that scientific truth is not the object of psychoanalysis, and further, that each "new truth" in psychoanalysis is a product of the "shared experience and understanding" of this particular patient and analyst, agree than an interpretation is not only a way to rediscover lost experience.

It also does more, it defines, organizes, and expresses some previously inchoate, unstructured conglomerate of experience, perhaps something even too formless to be called "an experience." It creates a new experience and adds something new to the self of the experiencer (p. 293).

Wolstein (e.g., 1981), especially, has emphasized over the years the subjectivity of psychoanalytic truth and the dependence of the content of this truth on the unique, emergent qualities of the two participants' interaction. Even more recently, Wolstein (1982) has presented the view that this unique interaction leads to

transconscious psychic experience that becomes conscious as new actuality. It is transconscious in that it was never conscious before, and now becomes conscious for the first time (p. 415).

Fingarette (1963) writes, "Insight does not reveal a hidden past reality; it is a reorganization of the meaning of present experience, a present reorientation toward both future *and* past" (p. 20). Loch (1977), Viderman (1980), and Spence (1982)[7] make similar points about the nature of psychoanalytic truth and the interpersonal process by which it is created.

It is implicit in each of these papers (explicit in the cases of Loewald, and Issacharoff and Hunt) that the psychoanalytic process and the creative process have certain communalities. In both, the process is emergent, not predetermined. The outcome is unknowable, and a final outcome is unreachable. In both, an initial stage of receptivity is followed by inspiration, then by the application of directed, ordered thinking. In

---

7. By the time I read Spence's exciting work, it was too late to include it in the present paper. Some of Spence's views are similar to those taken here, although Spence arrives at them from a different direction.

both, constructions appear, are honed, and then themselves become springboards for the next generation of constructions. Each new construction, if it is useful, has something of the quality of "effective surprise," a term Bruner (1962) uses to describe the result of a truly creative act. Effective surprise, says Bruner,

> need not be rare or infrequent or bizarre and is often none of these things. Effective surprises . . . seem rather to have the quality of obviousness about them when they occur, producing a shock of recognition following which there is no longer astonishment (p. 18).

Effective surprise marks the symbolization of unformulated experience, the creation of explicit meaning. It provokes the feeling of recognition, the shock of recognition, because we have seen its vague outlines before—in parataxic, amorphous, felt form, in our feelings of tendency. It is as if we had been looking through poorly focused binoculars without realizing it. Somehow the adjustment is made, and suddenly and unexpectedly, the view leaps out at us in fine detail. In just this way, by creating between them a world of thought and curiosity, patient and analyst rescue unformulated experience from the oblivion of the familiar.

References

Argyris, C., and Schön, D. A. (1976) *Theory in Practice: Increasing Professional Effectiveness*. San Francisco: Jossey-Bass.

Arieti, S. (1976) *Creativity: The Magic Synthesis*. New York: Basic Books.

Bartlett, F. C. (1932) *Remembering: A Study in Experimental and Social Psychology*. Cambridge: Cambridge University Press.

Basch, M. F. (1981) Psychoanalytic interpretation and cognitive transformation. *International Journal of Psycho-Analysis*, 62:151–176.

Bergson, H. (1903) Introduction to metaphysics. In: *The Creative Mind*. New York: Philosophical Library, 1946, pp. 159–200.

Bergson, H. (1907) *Creative Evolution*. New York: Modern Library, 1944.

Blum, H. P. (1980) The curative and creative aspects of insight. In: *Psychoanalytic Explorations of Technique: Discourse on the Theory of Therapy*, Ed. H. P. Blum. New York: International Universities Press, pp. 41–70.

Bowlby, J. (1980) *Loss*. New York: Basic Books.

Broadbent, D. E. (1958) *Perception and Communication*. London: Pergamon Press.

Broadbent, D. E. (1977) The hidden preattentive processes. *American Psychologist*, 32:109–118.

Bromberg, P. M. (1979) Interpersonal psychoanalysis and regression. *Contemporary Psychoanalysis*, 16:647–655.

Bruner, J. (1962) The conditions of creativity. In: *On Knowing: Essays for the Left Hand*. Expanded edition. Cambridge, MA: Belknap Press of Harvard University Press, 1979.

Burnshaw, S. (1970) *The Seamless Web.* New York: Braziller.

Claxton, G. (1980) Remembering and understanding. In: *Cognitive Psychology: New Directions*, Ed. G. Claxton. London: Routledge and Kegan Paul, pp. 197–235.

Deutsch, J. A., and Deutsch, D. (1963) Attention: Some theoretical considerations. *Psychological Review*, 70:80–90.

Eccles, J. C. (1970) *Facing Reality: Philosophical Adventures by a Brain Scientist.* New York: Springer-Verlag.

Ehrenzweig, A. (1967) *The Hidden Order of Art.* Berkeley: University of California Press.

Erdelyi, M. H. (1974) A new look at the New Look: Perceptual defense and vigilance. *Psychological Review*, 81:1–25.

Erdelyi, M. H., and Goldberg, B. (1979) Let's not sweep repression under the rug: Toward a cognitive psychology of repression. In: *Functional Disorders of Memory*, Ed. J. F. Khilstrom and F. J. Evans. Hillsdale, NJ: Lawrence Erlbaum Associates, pp. 355–402.

Fingarette, H. (1963) *The Self in Transformation: Psychoanalysis, Philosophy, and the Life of the Spirit.* New York: Basic Books.

Fingarette, H. (1969) *Self-Deception.* London: Routledge and Kegan Paul.

Freud, S. (1900) The interpretation of dreams. *Standard Edition*, 4 and 5.

Freud, S. (1915) The unconscious. *Standard Edition*, 14:159–216.

Freud, S. (1925) A note upon the "mystic writing-pad." *Standard Edition*, 19:227–234.

Freud, S. (1937) Constructions in analysis. *Standard Edition*, 23:255–270.

Gendlin, E. (1964) A theory of personality change. In: *Personality Change*, Ed. P. Worchel and D. Byrne. New York: John Wiley, pp. 100–148.

Ghiselin, B. (1952) Introduction. In: *The Creative Process*, Ed. B. Ghiselin. Berkeley, CA: University of California Press, pp. 11–31.

Ghiselin, B. (Ed.) (1952) *The Creative Process.* Berkeley, CA: University of California Press.

Gill, M. M. (1963) Topography and systems in psychoanalytic theory. *Psychological Issues, Monograph 10.*

Hadamard, J. (1945) *The Psychology of Invention in the Mathematical Field.* New York: Dover, 1954.

Hartmann, H. (1939) *Ego Psychology and the Problem of Adaptation.* New York: International Universities Press, 1958.

Issacharoff, A., and Hunt, W. (1978) Beyond countertransference. *Contemporary Psychoanalysis*, 14:291–310.

James, W. (1890) *Principles of Psychology, Volumes I and II.* New York: Henry Holt and Co., 1899.

Kernberg, O. F. (1980) Some implications of object relations theory for psychoanalytic technique. In: *Psychoanalytic Explorations of Technique: Discourse on the Theory of Therapy*, Ed. H. P. Blum. New York: International Universities Press, pp. 207–240.

Klein, G. S. (1976) *Psychoanalytic Theory: An Exploration of Essentials.* New York: International Universities Press.

Klenbort, I. (1978) Another look at Sullivan's concept of individuality. *Contemporary Psychoanalysis*, 16:125–135.

Kris, E. (1952) *Psychoanalytic Explorations in Art*. New York: International Universities Press.

Kris, E. (1956) The recovery of childhood memories in psychoanalysis. In: *Selected Papers*. New Haven: Yale University Press, 1975, pp. 301–340.

Kubie, L. (1958) *Neurotic Distortion of the Creative Process*. New York: Noonday Press, 1977.

Lewy, E., and Rapaport, D. (1944) The psychoanalytic concept of memory and its relation to recent memory theories. In: *The Collected Papers of David Rapaport*, Ed. M. M. Gill. New York: Basic Books, 1967, pp. 136–159.

Lindsay, P. N., and Norman, D. A. (1977) *Human Information Processing, Second Edition*. New York: Academic Press.

Loch, W. (1977) Some comments on the subject of psychoanalysis and truth. In: *Thought, Consciousness, and Reality*, Ed. J. H. Smith. New Haven: Yale University Press, pp. 217–256.

Loewald, H. (1960) On the therapeutic action of psychoanalysis. In: *Papers on Psychoanalysis*. New Haven: Yale University Press, 1980, pp. 221–256.

Loewald, H. (1976) Perspectives on memory. In: *Papers on Psychoanalysis*. New Haven: Yale University Press, 1980, pp. 148–173.

Maritain, J. M. (1953) *Creative Intuition in Art and Poetry*. Princeton, NJ: Princeton University Press, 1977.

Morse, M. (1951) Mathematics and the arts. *The Yale Review*, Summer, 1951.

Muchnic, H. (1980) Chosen and used by art. *The New York Times Book Review*, October 12, pp. 7, 32–33.

Mullahy, P. (1948) *Oedipus: Myth and Complex*. New York: Grove Press.

Neisser, U. (1967) *Cognitive Psychology*. Englewood Cliffs, NJ: Prentice-Hall.

Neisser, U. (1976) *Cognition and Reality*. San Francisco: W. H. Freeman and Co.

Noy, P. (1969) A revision of the psychoanalytic theory of the primary process. *International Journal of Psycho-Analysis*, 50: 155–178.

Noy, P. (1972) About art and artistic talent. *International Journal of Psycho-Analysis*, 53:243–249.

Noy, P (1978) Insight and creativity. *Journal of the American Psychoanalytic Association*, 26:717–748.

Paul, I. H. (1967) The concept of schema in memory theory. In: Motives and thought: Psychoanalytic essays in honor of David Rapaport, Ed. R. R. Holt. *Psychological Issues Monograph* 18/19:219–258.

Piaget, J. (1952) *The Origins of Intelligence in Children*. New York: International Universities Press.

Poincaré, H. (1908) Mathematical creation. In: *The Creative Process*, Ed. B. Ghiselin. Berkeley, CA: University of California Press, 1952, pp. 33–42.

Polanyi, M. (1959) *The Study of Man*. Chicago: University of Chicago Press.

Posner, M. I. (1973) *Cognition: An Introduction*. Glenview, IL: Scott, Foresman.

Pruyser, P. (1979) An essay on creativity. *Bulletin of the Menninger Clinic*, 43:294–353.

Roland, A. (1972) Imagery and symbolic expression in dreams and art.

International Journal of Psycho-Analysis, 53:531–539.

Rosenberg, E. H., and Medini, G. (1978) Truth: A concept in emergence. *Contemporary Psychoanalysis*, 14:424–433.

Rosenblatt, A. D., and Thickstum, J. T. (1977) Modern psychoanalytic concepts in a general psychology. *Psychological Issues Monograph* 42/43.

Schachtel, E. (1947) On memory and childhood amnesia. In: *Metamorphosis*. New York: Basic Books, 1959, pp. 279–322.

Schachtel, E. (1959) *Metamorphosis*. New York: Basic Books.

Schachtel, E. (1966) *Experiential Foundations of Rorschach's Test*. New York: Basic Books.

Schachtel, E. (1973) On attention, selective inattention, and experience: An inquiry into attention as an attitude. In: *Interpersonal Explorations in Psychoanalysis*, Ed. E. G. Witenberg. New York: Basic Books, pp. 40–66.

Schafer, R. (1976) *A New Language for Psychoanalysis*. New Haven: Yale University Press.

Schimek, J. G. (1975) A critical re-examination of Freud's concept of unconscious mental representation. *International Review of Psycho-Analysis*, 2, 171–187.

Spence, D. P. (1982) *Narrative Truth and Historical Truth: Meaning and Interpretation in Psychoanalysis*. New York: Norton.

Sullivan, H. S. (1940) *Conceptions of Modern Psychiatry*. New York: Norton.

Sullivan, H. S. (1953) *The Interpersonal Theory of Psychiatry*. New York: Norton.

Viderman, S. (1979) The analytic space: Meaning and problems. *Psychoanalytic Quarterly*, 48:257–291.

Winnicott, D. W. (1971) *Playing and Reality*. Middlesex, England: Penguin, 1980.

Wolstein, B. (1981) The psychic realism of psychoanalytic inquiry. *Contemporary Psychoanalysis*, 17:399–412, 595–606.

Wolstein, B. (1982) The psychoanalytic theory of unconscious psychic experience. *Contemporary Psychoanalysis*, 18:412–437.

Afterword

At the time this article was written, I had yet to encounter hermeneutics. Donald Spence's (1982) book on narrative truth was published just as the article was going to press, Roy Schafer's (1983) first collection of papers on clinical hermeneutics had yet to appear, and I had not yet started to read the work of hermeneutic philosopher Hans-Georg Gadamer. And so the conception of unconscious experience as unformulated did not originally derive from a hermeneutic reading of psychoanalysis, as much of my later work has. While unformulated experience did eventually turn out to slip easily into a hermeneutic perspective, it originated in the much more intuitive sense that experience was emergent, that it was not hidden and whole but continuously in the process of being constructed. A few years after the article appeared, I began to understand the idea of unformulated experience as an expression of psychoanalytic constructivism (Protter, 1985, 1988; Stern, 1985, 1992; Mitchell, 1988, 1993; Hoffman, 1991, 1994; Aron, 1996), a clinical variety of the postmodern critique of language that had already swept through philosophy, literary criticism, and European psychoanalysis and was beginning to revise the questions asked in the social sciences.

I think differently now about what defines experience as formulated or unformulated. From this 1983 article, one gets the impression that unformulated experience is defined by its lack of structure and that the process of formulation is a matter of structuring it. But that cannot be. Prereflective experience *must* have a certain kind and degree of structure; its structure is what makes it meaningful to refer to in the first place. This structure is nonverbal, however, and, because it is nonverbal, we are incapable of taking critical distance from it: we cannot reflect on it. Why? Because in order to reflect, we must adopt an explicitly verbal perspective on the unformulated. Such a perspective does not merely label, but actively participates in the shaping of the eventual reflective experience. And so, today I would say that what defines whether experience is unformulated is simply whether or not one has taken a verbal-linguistic perspective on it.

A revised and greatly expanded description of the concept of unformulated experience appears elsewhere in book form (Stern, 1997). The points made in this brief postscript are developed there in detail.

References

Aron, L. (1996), *A Meeting of Minds: Mutuality in Psychoanalysis.* Hillsdale, NJ: The Analytic Press.

Hoffman, I. Z. (1991), Discussion: Toward a social-constructivist view of the psychoanalytic situation. *Psychoanal. Dial.*, 1:74–105.

———— (1994), Dialectical thinking and therapeutic action in the psychoanalytic process. *Psychoanal. Quart.*, 63:187–218.

Mitchell, S. A. (1988), *Relational Concepts in Psychoanalysis.* Cambridge, MA: Harvard University Press.

———— (1993), *Hope and Dread in Psychoanalysis.* Cambridge, MA: Harvard University Press.

Protter, B. (1985), Toward an emergent psychoanalytic epistemology. *Contemp. Psychoanal.*, 21:208–227.

———— (1988), Ways of knowing. Some epistemic considerations for an autonomous theory of psychoanalytic praxis. *Contemp. Psychoanal.*, 24:428–526.

Schafer, R. (1983), *The Analytic Attitude*. New York: Basic Books.

Spence, D. P. (1982), *Narrative Truth and Historical Truth: Meaning and Interpretation in Psychoanalysis*. New York: Norton.

Stern, D. B. (1985), Some controversies regarding constructivism and psychoanalysis. *Contemp. Psychoanal.*, 21:201–208.

——— (1992), Commentary on constructivism in clinical psychoanalysis. *Psychoanal. Dial.*, 2:331–363.

——— (1997), *Unformulated Experience: From Dissociation to Imagination in Psychoanalysis*. Hillsdale, NJ: The Analytic Press.

Toward a Relational Individualism: The Mediation of Self Through Psychoanalysis

(1986)

Nancy J. Chodorow

▼   ▼   ▼   ▼   ▼

Editors' Introduction

Nancy Chodorow has been a major presence within contemporary psychoanalytic theorizing for over two decades. Her book *The Reproduction of Mothering*, published in 1978, has had a great impact on understandings of gender development, gender identity, family dynamics, and social roles, both within and beyond the psychoanalytic community. Prior to Chodorow's work, there was an enormous rift between the feminist tradition and psychoanalysis. Like Juliet Mitchell in England, Chodorow opened up bridges between these two traditions, thereby creating what has become an extremely rich, generative, and influential conceptual domain.

Traditional psychoanalytic wisdom had approached gender differentiation and the beginnings of gender development with reference to the penis/phallus (for Freud, in terms of the castration complex and penis envy; for Lacan, in terms of the phallocentric symbolic order). Chodorow drew together currents from various object relations theories to develop an approach to gender differentiation and gender development with reference to the differing fates of the

child's primary identification with the mother, located within the particularities of parenting practices of contemporary Western culture.

In this influential paper Chodorow extends her concerns even further
to the very nature of self-organization and development. She contrasts a more classical analytic model, based on ideals of autonomy
and control, in which the self is shaped through oedipal struggle with
the father, with an object relations account of a self that "in its very
structure [is] fundamentally implicated in relations with others." This
perspective is grounded on a very different understanding of the
nature of autonomy, an autonomy always in the context of connectedness, always embedded in a relational field of both internal and
external object relations.

Chodorow's relational sensibility derived from different sources than
those of many of the other authors in this volume. She has not drawn
explicitly on the literature of interpersonal psychoanalysis. Her vision
of a relational matrix composed of interactions between self and others in both the interpersonal and the intrapsychic domains emerged
from the convergence of her studies in object relations theories and
feminism. But, in the originality of her vision, she anticipated many of
the later basic principles of subsequent relational thought: the permeability of boundaries between self and others, a constructivist/rela-
tional epistemology, and an intrinsically social view of the self and
interactive model of the analytic process. She writes:

> [W]hat is central to an analysis and must be constantly kept at the
> forefront of the analyst's awareness is an affective and cognitive
> exchange between two people . . . analysis focuses primarily on
> experiences of the self in both internal and external relationship
> rather than on the analysis of resistances and defenses.

Chodorow's groundbreaking book *The Reproduction of Mothering*
(1978, University of California) anticipated many of the themes that
were later to become major features of the relational movement in
psychoanalysis. Her early contributions on the relational foundations
of self experience and related issues are also to be found in *Feminism
and Psychoanalytic Theory* (1989, Yale). The papers in Part II of that
volume, including the essay published here, explore various features
of "Gender, Self, and Social Theory." Her more recent thinking on
these areas appears in *The Power of Feelings: Personal Meaning in
Psychoanalysis, Gender, and Culture* (1999, Yale).

Toward a Relational Individualism:*
The Mediation of Self Through Psychoanalysis

▼ ▼ ▼ ▼ ▼

Psychoanalysis begins with a radical challenge to traditional notions of the individual self. As Freud, with characteristic modesty, puts it:

> In the course of centuries the *naive* self-love of men has had to submit to two major blows at the hands of science. The first was when they learnt that our earth was not the centre of the universe but only a tiny fragment of a cosmic system of scarcely imaginable vastness. This is associated in our minds with the name of Copernicus, though something similar had already been asserted by Alexandrian science. The second blow fell when biological research destroyed man's supposedly privileged place in creation and proved his descent from the animal kingdom and his ineradicable animal nature. This revaluation has been accomplished in our own days by Darwin, Wallace and their predecessors, though not without the most violent contemporary opposition. But human megalomania will have suffered its third and most wounding blow from the psychological research of the present time which seeks to prove to the ego that it is not even master in its own house, but must content itself with scanty information of what is going on unconsciously in its mind.[1]

According to Freud, then, we are not who or what we think we are: we do not know our own centers; in fact, we probably do not have a center at all. Psychoanalysis radically undermines notions about autonomy, individual choice, will, responsibility, and rationality, showing that we do not control our own lives in the most fundamental sense. It makes it impossible to think about the self in any simple way, to talk blithely about the individual.

At the same time, however, psychoanalysis gives us an extraordinarily rich, deep, and complex understanding of whatever it is that is not the simple self we once thought we were, and it explains how whatever this is develops. "What is going on unconsciously in its mind" are forces and structures beyond conscious control or even knowledge: sexual and aggressive drives within the id; primary-process thinking with no respect for time, logic, reality, or consistency; powerful ideas and wishes that anxiety and repression have removed from consciousness and that defenses

---

* Reprinted from *Reconstructing Individualism: Autonomy, Individuality, and the Self in Western Thought,* (ed. Thomas C. Heller, Morton Sosna, and David E. Wellbery with permission of the publishers, Stanford University Press. © 1986 by the Board of Trustees of the Leland Stanford Junior University.

like resistance, isolation, and denial work to ensure will not reappear there; conflict, as these wishes and ideas seek recognition and meet with resistances and defenses; superego pressures that once were felt to come from recognized external forces but now operate relatively independently, fed by aggressive drives turned inward. This fragmentation of structure, function, and process that the psychoanalytic metapsychology describes affects the everyday subjective experience of self, lending what Freud recognized as a certain unease to expressed certainties about autonomous individuality and sparking a fierce opposition to his theories.

Even though Freud radically undermined notions of the unitary and autonomous individual, we can also see psychoanalysis, in its endless, reflexive involvement with self-investigation, as a particularly intense scrutiny of the individual, the apogee of the development of individualism in Western culture.[2] From the earliest days of psychoanalysis until the present, cultural thinkers, artists, and writers have celebrated the fragmented self that psychoanalysis portrays, denigrating character in literature, romanticizing the lack of agency, meaning, morality, and authorship.

Freud, however, wanted to resolve the paradox he created, to use the scrutiny of individual and self not to celebrate fragmentation but to restore wholeness. He could not accept that the self is the outcome of messy unconscious processes and a warring structure, that it disallows individual morality, autonomy, and responsibility; he wanted to reconstitute the individual and the self he had dissected. That metapsychological dissection shows who we are, but the clinical project of psychoanalysis is to develop individual autonomy and control in the self. As Freud put it, "Where id was, there shall ego be. It is a work of culture—not unlike the draining of the Zuider Zee."[3] And where an overwhelming, punitive superego was, there shall a conscious ego be. These goals, I think, have to be made very clear. Freud, and later psychoanalysts, did not just give up in despair; that is, although he did despair that the dikes could keep back the Zuider Zee entirely, he certainly wanted to give it a good try. All analysts probably want to restore a certain wholeness and agency to the self.

In this paper, I discuss two psychoanalytic solutions to the dilemma posed by Freud's challenge to individualism and the self, two different conceptions of wholeness and agency. These solutions are not mutually exclusive: they overlap each other in psychoanalytic thought and in theory and therapy. One solution is, in essence, to reconstitute, or resuscitate, the traditional autonomous self of the pristine individual; the other is to reconstruct a self that is in its very structure fundamentally implicated in relations with others. Because the mediation of self through psychoanalysis happens within the psychoanalytic process, we must examine this mediation in clinical practice as well as in theory.[4]

In the traditional model, based on Freud's drive theory along with his late structural theory, "where id was, there shall ego be," maturation and psychic health consist in rational ego control over the insistent drives, reducing the tyranny of the superego in order to harmonize conscience and wish, ego-ideal and ego-actuality. Internal conflict, then, is between different aspects of the psychical personality; reduction of this conflict will presumably lead to fulfillment in the external world, although traditional psychoanalysis does not specify how that will happen. The developmental model here is the oedipal struggle between self and father, where the Oedipus complex—the relational complex itself— is "smashed to pieces" and leaves in its wake a superego "so inexorable, so impersonal, so independent of its emotional origins."[5] Autonomy is key: although the superego is originally formed in response to parental prohibitions and the relationship to parents, this relational history ceases to be actively part of one's psychic makeup. The focus on individual autonomy is extended in Heinz Hartmann's work on ego psychology, which contributes to psychoanalytic metapsychology the notion of autonomous, conflict-free ego spheres; it is also reflected in the work of Heinz Kohut, who assesses the psychic functioning of the bipolar self in terms of ambitions and ideals.*

An alternative psychoanalytic view of the individual and the self emerges, not from Freud's structural discussions or from the exhortation that "where id was, there shall ego be," but from his essay "On Narcissism." Here, Freud notes how libido can be directed alternately toward objects (other people) or toward the self. He calls these forms "object libido" and "ego libido," and he locates psychic wholeness in a delicate balance between them. In Freud's view here, exclusive investment in the self with no connection to the other creates the narcissistic

---

*Kohut is somewhat paradoxical in terms of the antinomy I am trying to develop here. On the one hand, he is seen as an object-relations theorist par excellence, who locates disorders of the self squarely in early failures of the mirroring and idealizing relationship to mother and father. He is contrasted (and contrasts himself) with the classical theorists in his focus on the self and the self's disorders, as opposed to the classical concern with conflict. Yet on the other hand, his goals for the self—ambitions and ideals mediated by skills and talents—could not be more individualist. In his version, the object-relations route is to lead to individual fulfillment of individual goals. Where Freud, Hartmann, and others assume that harmonizing internal conflict will somehow harmonize relations with the external world, Kohut seeks to harmonize external relations to enable internal resolution. See his *Analysis of the Self* (New York, 1971) and *Restoration of the Self* (New York, 1977).

neuroses and psychoses; relatedness is the sine qua non of mental health. At the same time, he warns against the opposite danger, complete investment in the object—as in slavish unrequited love, which debases the self and deprives it of energy. As he puts it, "A strong egoism is a protection against falling ill, but in the last resort we must begin to love in order not to fall ill, and we are bound to fall ill if, in consequence of frustration, we are unable to love."*

The developmental theory Freud begins to describe in the same essay points toward a maturation of belongingness or connectedness (such as Carol Gilligan outlines)[6] instead of ego autonomy and control. He proposes that in its original libidinal state the infant has two love objects, "itself and the woman who tends it," and conceptualizes development in terms of what happens to these two libidinal attachments: in the best case, unproblematic self-regard and lack of self-punitiveness on the one hand, and "true object love," loving a person as a complement to and not an extension of the self, on the other.

Just as Hartmann and others picked up from Freud's metapsychology and developmental theory an emphasis on the autonomous ego and rational superego, so other post-Freudian psychoanalysts have expanded upon the theory of narcissism. Object-relations theorists conceptualize the infant in terms of its cognitive narcissism and primary libidinal relatedness—that is, its inability to distinguish itself conceptually from its primary caretaker and other objects in the world, even while it feels itself in, and gets gratification from, a relationship to an other.[7] As cognitive narcissism gives way to a sense of bounded self, internality and externality come to have both a simple cognitive and a complex affective reality.** On the physi-

---

* "On Narcissism: An Introduction" (1914), *The Standard Edition of the Complete Psychological Works of Sigmund Freud*, ed. James Strachey (London, 1953–66), XIV, p. 85. Freud in this essay still makes object-relatedness residual. Thus he assumes that libido proceeds onto the object as a spillover from narcissism: "What makes it necessary at all for our mental life to pass on beyond the limits of narcissism and to attach the libido to objects? The answer which would follow from our line of thought would once more be that this necessity arises when the cathexis of the ego with libido exceeds a certain amount." And although he notes the *two* original love objects of the infant (mother and self), he and his followers go on as if primary narcissism precedes any object-directedness and is the exclusive original state of the infant.

** Recent infancy research claims that the infant's cognitive sense of separateness is innate, rather than developed in the manner described by Mahler and

cal level, the infant comes to be unproblematically aware of its own boundaries and separateness. On the affective level, as the infant defines a self out of the mother-child matrix, the early flux of projections and introjections ensures that some aspects of that self are likely to have originally been perceived or experienced as aspects of the primary other or others, and aspects of the other may have originally been felt as aspects of the self.[8] On a psychological level, then, even the apparent boundaries of the individual do not separate in any simple way the pristine individual from the rest of the world.

The core of the self, or self-feeling, is also constructed relationally. Michael Balint locates the primary feeling of self in terms of the sense of fit or lack of fit with the primary caretaker; Winnicott characterizes as "the capacity to be alone" a sense of individuality and autonomy that includes the internalization of the benign but uninvolved presence of the mother. The development of psychic structure begins with this basic self-feeling and self-structure, which includes relatedness to and aspects of the other, and it continues through internalizations and splittings-off of internalized self-other representations to create an inner world consisting of different aspects of an "I" in relation to different aspects of the other. Psychological disorders, the problem of the fragmented individual, are seen here not so much in terms of conflict and defenses but rather in terms of problematic self-other relationships, which themselves internally constitute low self-esteem, self-punitiveness, lack of control, and so forth.*

Thus, the object-relations perspective gives us a very different notion of the construction of individuality than does the classical analytic account. In the classical account, the inner world is conceived in terms of different aspects of the psychical personality, and the goal is reduction of conflict among these. The classical account accords some recognition to the implicit relatedness of the individual: Freud claims that "the superego continues to play the part of an

---

others. Such a revision of our understanding of the infant's mental capacities does not undermine the understanding of the affective and object-relational components of sense of separateness and relatedness that I discuss here. See Daniel N. Stern, "The Early Development of Schemas of Self, Other, and 'Self with Other,'" in Joseph D. Lichtenberg and Samuel Kaplan, eds., *Reflections on Self Psychology* (Hillsdale, NJ, 1983).

* In the course of this development, what were originally unstructured and unorganized drive potentials come to be differentiated into aggressive and libidinal components, given affective meaning and organized by attachment to aspects of the inner world. See Edith Jacobson, *The Self and the Object World* (New York, 1964).

external world for the ego, although it has become a portion of the internal world," and he also mentions the role of identifications in the formation of the ego-ideal.[9] But these origins are not stressed in accounts of psychic functioning or models of the psychic constitution; instead, autonomy and the resolution of conflict are seen in terms of modes of ego functioning.

By contrast, the object-relations model, although it recognizes the role of defenses in ego functioning (understanding these defenses as operating in terms of an internal sense of self in relationship and of internal objects) and acknowledges the desirability of conflict-free ego spheres, conceptualizes the self as inexorably social and intrinsically connected. Thus, both views challenge the traditional notion of the pristine individual, but one does so without fundamental recourse to the "outside world." In neither view is the self unitary, but in object-relations theory it is also not apart from the other. Joan Riviere—an associate of Melanie Klein, who first made projection, introjection, and the role of internal objects central in psychoanalytic theory—puts the position as follows:

> We tend to think of any one individual in isolation; it is a convenient fiction. We may isolate him physically, as in the analytic room; in two minutes we find he has brought his world in with him, and that, even before he set eyes on the analyst, he had developed inside himself an elaborate relation with him. There is no such thing as a single human being, pure and simple, unmixed with other human beings. Each personality is a world in himself, a company of many. That self, that life of one's own, which is in fact so precious though so casually taken for granted, is a composite structure which has been and is being formed and built up since the day of our birth out of countless never-ending influences and exchanges between ourselves and others. . . . These other persons are in fact therefore parts of ourselves, not indeed the whole of them but such parts or aspects of them as we had our relation with, and as have thus become parts of us. And we ourselves similarly have and have had effects and influences, intended or not, on all others who have an emotional relation to us, have loved or hated us. We are members one of another.[10]

Riviere, like Freud, points to the threat that this conception of the individual poses:

> The "inner world," like other psychoanalytical concepts, meets with a twofold resistance; on the one hand, the incapacity to understand it, and on the other a direct emotional rejection of it . . . an acute reaction which arises, as experience teaches, from an acute anxiety. . . . When this proposition meets with an intense emotional rejection there is clearly a direct association in the hearer's mind of this idea with danger, as though

anything inside one which is not "oneself" pure and simple is and must be dangerous—or pathological.[11]

Object-relations theory does not need to idealize a hyperindividualism; it assumes a fundamental internal as well as external relatedness to the other. The question is then what kind of relation this can or should be. The relational individual is not reconstructed in terms of his or her drives and defenses but in terms of the greater or lesser fragmentation of his or her inner world and the extent to which the core self feels spontaneous and whole within, rather than driven by, this world. Even the senses of agency and autonomy remain relational in the object-relations model, because agency develops in the context of the early relationship with the mother and bears the meaning of her collaboration in and response to it. Separation and autonomy are not so crucial to development, because the model assumes the permeability of boundaries and focuses instead on the nature of the inner world and the inner core of self, whose implicit relatedness is acknowledged in its very structure. Paraphrasing Freud, we might say that the goal in the object-relational reconstruction of the individual is: where fragmented internal objects were, there shall harmoniously related objects be; and where false, reactive self was, there shall true, agentic self be, with its relationally based capacity both to be alone and to participate in the transitional space between self and other self that creates play, intimacy, and culture.

Object-relations psychoanalysis, in reformulating the psychoanalytic conception of self, also reformulates a self for social theory and analysis.[12] This self is intrinsically social, and, because it is constructed in a relational matrix and includes aspects of the other, it can better recognize the other as a self and, ultimately, attain the intersubjectivity that creates society. This self's full historical grounding contrasts with that of the drive-determined individual. The grounding of the object-relational self derives from an appropriation and interpretation of experienced relationships and accordingly varies by individual, culture, period, gender, and so forth. By contrast, the self of the drive-determined individual is originally constructed not through historically grounded experience but from universal and unchanging drives; this leads to a more abstract and universalist view of the self. (Insofar as this latter self has historical grounding, that grounding also derives from its object-relational history, the "precipitate of abandoned object-cathexes"[13] that it contains.) We might speculate that a fully social and historical conception of self provides an alternative to the autonomous ego and responsible, nonpunitive superego as a solution to the problems of morality, responsibility, and so forth posed by the psychoanalytic dissolution of the individual.

Psychoanalytic knowledge of the individual and the self is developed in theoretical and in metapsychological writings, but this knowledge is originally derived from the clinical setting, the analytic situation. Thus, an investigation of this setting can give further insight into the differentiated or relational self and help us decide between classical and object-relations models.

It would seem that the epistemological setting provided by the analytic situation requires that the knowledge of self emerging within it be relational, because this situation is a reflexively constructed collaboration in which analyst and analysand, through their interaction, create a history, or story, of the analysand's life.[14] Engagement with others as subjects (an engagement moderated by objectivity) is central to clinical practice, as opposed to metapsychology. In fact, this practical activity, empathetically involved with and taking account of another's interests, while objectively assessing the other and the self, in some ways illustrates a desirable sociality in general. A clinically derived view of the self also seems to require a historical as well as a social view of the self because of this concretely based engagement. Thus, a clinical perspective on the self seems to require engagement with the other, no matter what your theory.

Nevertheless, psychoanalysts have developed two clinical approaches, which reflect—though less starkly than the theory, for reasons I have suggested—the two approaches to the individual I have discussed. The first approach is popularly caricatured in the silent, uninvolved, blank-wall analyst, the object of a transference brought entirely from past experiences and relationships, who says little except, "What comes to mind?" or "umhmm," and occasionally offers brief nuggets of interpretation.* Analytic technique here consists in analyzing resistances and defenses that prevent the analysand from acknowledging transference feelings. The relentless analysis of all the analysand says in terms of these resistances will eventually lead to an acknowledged transference relationship, which can then be analyzed to bring out and resolve early developmental material. This assumes that what is going on in the analysis has nothing to do with any actual relationship to the analyst or with the reality

---

*As we know from Freud and others this is hardly the stance that Freud himself took. He took walks with patients, talked to their relatives, gave and got cigars, and in the case of Dora was quite happy to attempt to browbeat her into submitting to his definition of the intrapsychic and interpersonal situation. Yet officially his interpretive stance was closer to the classic model of interpretation of resistances. In addition, as I mention below, he felt that countertransference signified inadequacy on the part of the analyst. See on this Samuel Lipton, "The Advantages of Freud's Technique as Shown in His Analysis of the Rat Man," *International Journal of Psycho-Analysis*, 58 (1977), 255–73.

of the person of the analyst, that this relationship is entirely transference and as such is entirely one-way. There is also a "therapeutic" or "working" alliance between analyst and analysand,[15] but this is merely an agreement made with the unneurotic parts of the analysand's ego to work on change, in tandem as it were, and does not involve any reciprocity or acknowledged connection.[16]

In this view, what the analyst does is to help the analysand reorganize a psychic organization and mental processes conceived as drives, superego, ego defenses, and resistances. In Freud's original view, countertransference—strong feelings about the analysand or about particular moments in the analysis, feelings perhaps evoked by the analysand—was always an unwelcome intrusion and a sign of the analyst's own inadequate analysis. The later classical model recognizes countertransference but prescribes that it should count for little in the analysis.

This view of the analytic process corresponds with and nicely reinforces a metapsychology that posits a pristine individual who is all ego and id, and whose autonomous ego must take more and more spheres of control from id, unconscious ego defenses, and superego. Nonetheless, in spite of formal intention the clinical situation almost requires some recognition of the interpersonal construction (and reconstruction) of a self. Various residual concepts in the classical account of technique (none formally acknowledged in theory and all requiring justification and scrutiny in the individual case), much like the Ptolemaic epicycles, point to an alternative formulation of the analytic process and the selves involved in it. The relentless interpretation of resistances is sometimes avoided for considerations of "tact" and "timing"—if pointing them out might lead to the creation of even more ego defenses by the analysand. Deviations from technique (in revealing information about yourself, in allowing the analysand to sit up, in responding to questions) are occasionally allowed if these will help the analytic work by making the analysand more secure. Similarly, building a therapeutic alliance may depend partly on the analysand's trust in the analyst's good intent and may therefore require the analyst to indicate such intent.

All of these, of course, are ways to acknowledge that the actual relationship between analyst and analysand matters, that change in the analysand depends at least partly on the nature and meaning of that relationship. An alternative clinical position makes this engagement and its consequences more explicit. Formulated variously by Michael Balint, Heinz Kohut, Frieda Fromm-Reichman, Margaret Little, Leo Stone, Harold Searles, D. W. Winnicott, and others, this position proposes, not that the analyst should participate equally in a real relationship (always answering questions about her or himself, always being supportive and responsive), but that what is central to an analysis and must be constantly kept at the forefront of the analyst's awareness is an affective and cognitive exchange between two people.[17] Choices in technique accordingly have the aim of enhancing this relationship so that the analytic work can progress; analysis focuses primarily on experiences of the self in both internal and external relationship rather than on the analysis of resistances and defenses.

In this model the analyst's attentiveness to and investigation of countertransference are a crucial part of every analysis, not a holdover to be avoided. Moreover, countertransference involves all feelings evoked in the analyst, and these feelings are not seen as purely neurotic. As Elizabeth Zetzel puts it: "Many analysts today believe that the classical conception of analytic objectivity and anonymity cannot be maintained. Instead, thorough analysis of reality aspects of the analyst's personality and point of view is advocated as an essential feature of transference analysis and an indispensable prerequisite for the dynamic changes."[18] These "many analysts" would claim that a focus on the analyst's own reactions will provide the best clue to what is going on with the patient (and with the analyst's self as well). Thus, they would explicitly recognize that the analysand's self is reconstructed in and through both conscious and unconscious interaction with the analyst.

The focus on countertransference points to a final, important part of the first psychoanalytic formulations of the self: psychoanalytic knowledge of the self originally concerned the self of the analyst as well as the self of the patient. Thus, Freud first learned about the unconscious, resistance, and repression from his hysterical patients, but he learned about dreams and the Oedipus complex from self-analysis.[19] And in the countertransference, perhaps not only the self of the analysand is reconstructed or reconstituted; the analyst's self may be changed, or at least better understood, as well.[20] Thus, knowledge of the other and knowledge of the self, construction of the self and construction of the other, are intimately related.

Psychoanalytic theory radically challenges our understanding of ourselves as whole, autonomous individuals, then seeks to reconstruct that wholeness and autonomy. It poses two solutions to this goal in its metapsychology and attempts them in its therapeutic technique and understanding. But the therapeutic setting can, finally, produce knowledge and self-knowledge only of a relational self. And psychoanalysis can only know the self in the analytic situation; anything else is ungrounded speculation. Thus, when we investigate psychoanalytic theory and practice, we see a historical progression from a view favoring a pure, differentiated individuality, based on rigid notions of autonomous separateness, toward a relational individualism.

Notes

I am indebted to Ann Swidler and Abby Wolfson for very helpful responses to an earlier version of this paper and to Peter Lyman for general conversations about these issues. The argument in this paper is part of a larger project formulated in various ways over the past several years by Jessica Benjamin, Jane Flax, Evelyn Fox Keller, and myself. I have benefited from discussion and correspondence with all of them as well as from their work. See Benjamin, "The End of Internalization: Adorno's Social Psychology," *Telos*, 32 (1977); "Authority and the Family Revisited, or, A World Without Fathers?" *New German Critique*, 13 (1978); "Rational Violence and Erotic Domination," in Hester Eisenstein and Alice Jardine, eds., *The Future of Difference* (Boston, 1980); and "The Oedipal Riddle: Authority, Autonomy, and the New Narcissism," in John Diggins and Mark Kamm, eds., *The Problem of Authority in America* (Philadelphia, 1981); Flax, "Critical Theory as a Vocation," *Politics and Society*, 8 (1978); "Political Philosophy and the Patriarchal Unconscious," in Sandra Harding and Merrill B. Hintikka, eds., *Discovering Reality: Feminist Perspectives on Epistemology, Metaphysics, Methodology, and the Philosophy of Science* (Boston, 1983); and "On Freud: Narcissism, Gender and the Impediments to Intersubjectivity," unpublished paper; Keller, *A Feeling for the Organism* (San Francisco, 1983); and *Reflections on Gender and Science* (New Haven, 1985). Sherry Ortner first suggested to me the formulation "relational individualism."

1. Sigmund Freud, "Introductory Lectures on Psycho-Analysis" (1915–16), in James Strachey, ed., *The Standard Edition of the Complete Psychological Works of Sigmund Freud* (London, 1953–66), XVI, 285.

2. See Michel Foucault, *The History of Sexuality*, I (New York, 1978), and Fred Weinstein and Gerald M. Platt, *The Wish to Be Free* (Berkeley and Los Angeles, 1969).

3. Sigmund Freud, "Dissection of the Psychical Personality" (1933), in Strachey, ed., *Works*, XXII, 80.

4. The polarity I discuss is found in personality psychology as well as within psychoanalytic theory. See Avril Thorne, "Disposition as Interpersonal Constraint," (Ph.D. diss., University of California, Berkeley, 1983). But for a very different argument, for individualism in personality psychology, see Gordon Allport, *Personality: A Psychological Interpretation* (New York, 1937), who argues in his opening paragraphs not against a more relational conception of personality but against the scientific psychological attempt to cut up the self into nomothetically derived aspects that can be studied across persons without regard to their situatedness in the makeup of the whole person.

5. Sigmund Freud, "Some Psychical Consequences of the Anatomical Distinction Between the Sexes" (1925), in Strachey, ed., *Works*, XIX, 257.

6. See Carol Gilligan, *In a Different Voice: Women's Conceptions of the Self and Morality* (Cambridge, Mass., 1982), and "Remapping the Moral Domain: New Images of the Self in Relationship," in Heller et al. (Stanford, 1986).

7. See Michel Balint, *Primary Love and Psycho-Analytic Technique* (New York, 1965), and *The Basic Fault* (London, 1968); W. R. D. Fairbairn, *An Object-Relations Theory of the Personality* (New York, 1951); Harry Guntrip, *Personality Structure and Human Interaction* (New York, 1961), and *Schizoid Phenomena, Object-Relations and the Self* (New York, 1969); Edith Jacobson, *The Self and the Object World* (New York, 1964); Margaret S. Mahler, Fred Pine, and Anni Bergman, *The Psychological Birth of the Human Infant* (New York, 1975); and D. W. Winnicott, *Collected Papers: From Paediatrics to Psychoanalysis* (London, 1958), *The Maturational Processes and the Facilitating Environment* (New York, 1965), and *Playing and Reality* (New York, 1971).

8. See on the primary creation of internality and externality, Hans Loewald, "Internalization, Separation, Mourning and the Superego" (1962), in his *Papers on Psychoanalysis* (New Haven, 1980), and Jacobson, *The Self*.

9. Sigmund Freud, "Outline of Psychoanalysis" (1940), in Strachey, ed., *Works*, XXIII, 106.

10. Joan Riviere, "The Unconscious Phantasy of an Inner World Reflected in Examples from Literature," in Melanie Klein, ed., *New Directions in Psychoanalysis* (London, 1977), pp. 358–59. This essay and quote came to my attention in Norman O. Brown, *Love's Body* (New York, 1966), p. 147.

11. Riviere, p. 347.

12. I discuss this further in "Beyond Drive Theory: Object Relations and the Limits of Radical Individualism," *Theory and Society*, 14, no. 3 (1985), 271–319.

13. Sigmund Freud, *The Ego and the Id* (1913), in Strachey, ed., *Works*, XIX, 29.

14. See Roy Schafer, "Narrative in the Psychoanalytic Situation," *Critical Inquiry*, 7 (1980), 29–53.

15. See Elizabeth R. Zetzel, "Therapeutic Alliance in the Analysis of a Case of Hysteria," in *The Capacity for Emotional Growth* (New York, 1970), and other papers in that volume; and Ralph Greenson, *Technique and Practice of Psychoanalysis* (New York, 1967).

16. For the most fully formulated account of this position, see Charles Brenner, *Psychoanalytic Technique and Psychic Conflict* (New York, 1976). For a lively account of the debate, see Janet Malcolm, *The Impossible Profession* (New York, 1980).

17. See Balint, *Primary Love* and *The Basic Fault*; Heinz Kohut, *Analysis of the Self* (New York, 1971) and *Restoration of the Self* (New York, 1977); Frieda Fromm-Reichman, *Principles of Intensive Psycho-therapy* (Chicago, 1950); Margaret Little, *Transference Neurosis and Transference Psychosis* (New York, 1981); Leo Stone, *The Psychoanalytic Situation* (New York, 1961); Harold Searles, *Countertransference and Related Subjects* (New York, 1979); and D. W. Winnicott, *Maturational Processes* and *The Piggle* (New York, 1977).

18. Elizabeth R. Zetzel, "Current Concepts of Transference," *International Journal of Psycho-Analysis*, 37 (1956), 374. A discussion of gender in the creation of psychoanalytic theory is beyond the scope of this essay. I note, however, that women analysts were particularly central to focusing psychoanalytic interest on the importance of countertransference. See Fromm-Reichman, *Principles*;

Annie Reich, "On Counter-Transference," *International Journal of Psycho-Analysis*, 32 (1951), 25–31; Lucia Tower, "Countertransference," *Journal of the American Psychoanalytic Association*, 4 (1956), 224–55; Margaret Little, "Counter-Transference and the Patient's Response to It," *International Journal of Psycho-Analysis*, 32 (1951), 32–40; Paula Heimann, "On Counter-Transference," *International Journal of Psycho-Analysis*, 31 (1950), 81–84; and Mabel Blake Cohen, "Counter-Transference and Anxiety," *Psychiatry*, 15 (1952), 501–39. I noticed this while reading Peter Loewenberg, "Subjectivity and Empathy as Guides to Counseling," unpublished paper.

19. See Josef Breuer and Sigmund Freud, *Studies on Hysteria* (1893–95), in Strachey, ed., *Works*, II; and Sigmund Freud, *The Interpretation of Dreams* (1900–1901), in Strachey, ed., *Works*, IV and V. See also Nellie Louise Buckley, "Women Psychoanalysts and the Theory of Femininity: A Study of Karen Horney, Helene Deutsch, and Marie Bonaparte" (Ph.D. diss., University of California, Los Angeles, 1982), who suggests that the dominant psychologies of women emerged from their own life histories, if not their own self-analyses.

20. See the introduction to Harold Searles, *Collected Papers on Schizophrenia and Related Subjects* (New York, 1965); and Little, *Transference Neurosis*.

Afterword

This paper was a contribution to a 1984 symposium at Stanford University, "Reconstructing Individualism: Autonomy, Individuality, and the Self in Western Thought" (Heller, Sosna, and Wellbery, 1986). This symposium provided a forum in which philosophers, historians, literary critics, and social scientists addressed individualism, individuality, authenticity, and other related concepts in the wake of the postmodern unease and critique of such concepts that had begun to permeate many fields. My contribution was written just as I was embarking on psychoanalytic training, and it was my first attempt to locate without reference to gender the implications of the account of gender development and critique of psychoanalysis that I had developed previously. I, along with those few other psychoanalytic feminist writers of the 1970s, had argued in that earlier work (1974, 1978, 1979), that our relational and object relational accounts had implications for psychoanalysis and psychology as a whole, not just for our understandings of female psychology or the psychology of gender (see also Miller, 1976; Dinnerstein, 1976; Benjamin, 1977, 1978; Keller, 1978; Gilligan, 1982). Although I have chosen a nonfeminist piece for inclusion in this collection, I think it important not to obscure its genealogy in my psychoanalytic feminist writings, nor to obscure, I believe, the genealogical role of psychoanalytic feminism more generally in the current prominence of relational psychoanalysis and in the content of many of its claims.

The context and early formulations of the argument for a relational psychoanalysis found in "Toward a Relational Individualism" can be found in my psychoanalytic feminist writings of the 1970s. In these writings, I more or less intuitively synthesized a version of relational psychoanalysis. I was influenced especially by a Fairbairn/Guntrip-derived object relations theory (Fairbairn, 1952; Guntrip, 1961), with its insistence on libido as object seeking, its Kleinian-derived conception of psychic structure as an internal ego-object world, and its focus on introjection and projection as primary processes, and by minimal reading of Klein. (As I have noted elsewhere, the lack of American recognition of Kleinian theory in the 1970s cannot be overestimated.) I relied on assumptions of primary sociality derived from Balint's (1965) argument for primary love and Winnicott's (1960) claim that "there is no such thing as an infant [but only a unit of infant and maternal care]." I found a model in Loewald's (1980) account of the creation of ego and reality, or self and other, through primary and secondary internalizations and externalizations and of psychic structure as fluid rather than fixed. These theories met my own discoveries about the relational self-constructions of women and men and my predilections as a psychoanalytic anthropologist-sociologist to accord meaning and influence to "external" as well as "internal" reality. (This background also gave me some grounding in interpersonal and cultural school psychoanalysis—Sullivan, Horney, Fromm—and their 1930s culture and personality anthropologist colleagues, but, as a social scientist moving toward psychoanalysis, I was leery of any theories that seemed too culturally determinist of the psyche.)

In particular, in *The Reproduction of Mothering* (1978) and the articles that preceded that book, I developed concepts of gender psychology that centered not so much on what I now call subjective gender—the sense of self as gendered—but more on observed differences in relational constructions of the psyche (see my discussion of these distinctions in Chodorow, 1996). I argued that women developed what I called a self-in-relation, in contrast to the typical masculine self that denied relation, and that men and women created differently constructed internal worlds. I highlighted psychoanalytic concepts that did not privilege separateness over connection. In "Family Structure and Feminine Personality" (1974) I claimed that "ego strength' is not completely dependent on the firmness of the ego's boundaries" and pointed approvingly to Guntrip's (1961) description of Fairbairn's notion of mature dependence, "characterized by full differentiation of ego and object, . . . a capacity for valuing the object for its own sake and for giving as well as receiving; a condition which should be described not as independence but as mature dependence" (cited in Chodorow, 1974, pp. 61–62). *The Reproduction of Mothering* (Chodorow, 1978) itself portrays the psyche in terms of an inner object world composed of ego in relation to internalized others and development centrally as a process and product of unconscious communication between mother and child.

My feminist concerns, finally, alerted me early to the dangers of objectification of the mother, pushing me toward views of psychological growth that did not require rejection of or distancing from the mother but that acknowledged her subjectivity in particular and thus the subjectivity of the other more generally. Especially, my feminist relational theory essay, "Gender, Relation, and Difference in Psychoanalytic Perspective" (1979), made strong claims for a relational self, as it addressed some of the general meanings of separation-individuation, differentiation, and selfhood in the context of a discussion of gender differentiation and attitudes to the mother. In these formulations, I was led to pay particular attention to the intrinsic intersubjectivity (although I did not use the word) of selfhood and psychic life. It is worth quoting that essay extensively here. In my rethinking of separation-individuation, I follow the now-discredited Mahlerian and Freudian notion that the child is originally symbiotically or narcissistically fused with the mother, but my account of differentiation and the development of self is otherwise consonant, I believe, with Stern's (1985) revised account. I suggest, following Mahler-Freud, that "separateness . . . is not simply given from birth, nor does it emerge from the individual alone" (p. 102). But I add:

> separateness is defined relationally; differentiation occurs in relationship: '*I*' am "*not-you.*" Moreover, "*you,*" or the other, is also distinguished. The child learns to see the particularity of the mother or primary caretaker in contrast to the rest of the world. Thus [in a Loewaldian vein], as the self is differentiated from the object world, the object world is itself differentiated into its component parts [pp. 102–103].

I continue:

> Adequate separation, or differentiation, involves not merely perceiving the separateness, or otherness, of the other. It involves perceiving the person's subjectivity and selfhood as well. . . . This interpretation implies that true differentiation, true separateness, cannot be simply a perception and experience of self-other, of presence-absence. It must precisely involve two selves, two presences, two subjects. Recognizing the other as a subject is possible

only to the extent that one is not dominated by felt need and one's own exclusive subjectivity. Such recognition permits appreciation and perception of many aspects of the other person, of her or his existence apart from the child's/the self's. Thus, how we understand differentiation—only from the viewpoint of the infant as a self, or from the viewpoint of two interacting selves—has consequences for what we think of as a mature self [pp. 103–104].

One can be separate from and similar to someone at the same time. For example, one can recognize another's subjectivity and humanity as one recognizes one's own, seeing the commonality of both as active subjects. . . . At the same time, the other side of being able to experience separateness and commonality, of recognizing the other's subjectivity, is the ability to recognize differences with a small "d," differences that are produced and situated historically [p. 105].

I conclude that "differentiation is not distinctness and separateness, but a particular way of being connected to others" (p. 107).

These conclusions led to the more general advocacy of relational and intersubjective accounts of individuality and psychoanalysis found in "Toward a Relational Individualism." But, before moving on to that work, I want to reiterate both the feminist roots (among other roots) of our contemporary focus on intersubjectivity and the significance (developmentally, in psychic life, in the clinician's view of the mother, and in clinical practice) of an intersubjective relational psychoanalysis for maternal subjectivity and our attitudes toward women. Again, to quote from "Gender, Relation, and Difference":

The view that adequate separation-individuation, or differentiation, involves not simply preceiving the otherness of the other, but her or his selfhood/subjectivity as well, has important consequences, not only for an understanding of the development of selfhood, but also for perceptions of women. Hence, it seems to me absolutely essential to a feminist appropriation of psychoanalytic conceptions of differentiation. Since women, as mothers, are the primary caretakers of infants, if the child (or the psychoanalytic account) only takes the viewpoint of the infant as a (developing) self, then the mother will be perceived (or depicted) only as an object. But, from a feminist perpective, perceiving the particularity of the mother must involve according the mother her own selfhood. This is a necessary part of the developmental process, though it is also often resisted and experienced only conflictually and partially [I could have added, here, both by infants and by psychoanalysts]. Throughout life, perceptions of the mother fluctuate between perceiving her particularity and selfhood and perceiving her as a narcissistic extension [an incontrovertible fact, I believe, that must be a developmental achievement, if Stern's claim that she is not originally perceived narcissistically is correct], a not-separate other whose sole reason for existence is to gratify one's own wants and needs [Chodorow, 1979, p. 104].

"Toward a Relational Individualism" in a few pages sets out the contrasts between my own then-version, based on available readings at that time as well as the very beginnings of my own clinical experience, of relational psychoanalytic theory and classical structural-ego psychological psychoanalysis. I begin with the problem of individuality, a problem to which I still return (see Chodorow, 1998, 1999). This framing was dictated by the constraints of the conference topic, but I believe it is still to the point. Relational, intersubjective, or two-person psychoanalytic approaches, I sometimes fear, take us away from our equally important investigations and conceptualizations of the unbelievable complexities of the individual psyche and unconscious fantasy and of the goals of psychoanalysis. These are, finally, to help an individual to expand her own self-awareness, to integrate her own unconscious and conscious (or transference, fantasy, and reality), to repair and forgive herself, to recognize and accept her own life as the life she has led, thus owning projection, to link her own past and present, to enhance aliveness, being, psychic movement, and range, over deadness, nonbeing, constriction, and rigidity.

Briefly, my essay begins from and challenges Freud's structural-psychoanalytic project—"where id was, there shall ego be"—and parodies this dictum with an object-relational revision: "where fragmented internal objects were, there shall harmoniously related objects be. . . ." As I have put it more recently:

> Psychological life involves continuous projection and introjection, continuous attempts to manage threatening affects and objects, so that parts of the self come to be located in the other, and parts of the other come to be located within the self. Our internal world is a complex and continually changing creation, and the constructions of inside and outside shift accordingly. . . . Not only, as Freud suggested, is the ego not master in its own house. Where the house begins and ends, what's inside it and what's outside, is never self-evident [Chodorow, 1998].

In a related vein, my argument in "Toward a Relational Individualism," that the epistemological setting of the analytic situation requires a more relational or two-person conception of the psyche and psychic change, describes an internal contradiction in classical psychoanalytic technique that presaged and almost required the emergence of our current situation. Noting first that what were classically called parameters were really ways of recognizing the actual relationship between analyst and analysand, I focus on clinical writers who describe the analytic experience as a cognitive and affective interchange between two people, who argue that analytic change takes place in and through interaction with the analyst, who question rigid analytic employment of conceptions of objectivity and anonymity, who see countertransference experience and understandings as resources rather than impediments, and who advocate continuous attention to the analyst's subjectivity and participation. And in the current period, it seems to me, almost everyone has become some version of a relational psychoanalyst. They may indicate this by focusing on the analyst's subjectivity, the use of the self, the containing of projective identifications, the use of projective identification to know the patient's psychic reality, the transference use of the analyst, the patient as interpreter of the analyst's experience, transference as a total situation, investigating countertransference enactments, judicious self-disclosure, of the analytic third.

It is sobering and perhaps too self-revealing to acknowledge that I still agree with this argument developed 15 to 25 years ago concerning the relational nature of the psyche and of analytic change. My ideas have of course been elaborated since, both as a result of the uncontrovertible experience of clinical practice and through participation in professional reading and interchange, so that my recently completed book, *The Power of Feelings: Personal Meaning in Psychoanalysis, Gender, and Culture* (1999) now takes hundreds of pages to elaborate my understanding of the complexities of the psyche, of the analytic relationship, and of the ways that analytic change is both firmly within the individual (within both individuals) and also firmly an intersubjective process between ourselves and our patients.

At the same time, as I indicated earlier, I believe our criticisms of one-person psychologies may have been overdone. I still have little sympathy for what I have sometimes thought of as the vulture model of ego-psychological technique—sitting and waiting to pounce on resistances that emerge entirely from within the patient—or for the overvaluation of ego rationality and ego and superego autonomy against a focus on unconscious fantasy and psychic reality. But I found myself, in writing a concluding chapter to *The Power of Feelings*, on "Psychoanalytic Visions of Subjectivity," wanting a both/and model and being drawn to some very old-fashioned psychoanalysts. As I reflected on the big questions that must be in the back of our minds as we do analytic work—what kind of a life do we envision for our patients or ourselves? what constitutes a desirable subjectivity or selfhood?—I found myself thinking about (emphatically nonmainstream) ego psychologists deeply interested in individuality, specifically about Loewald (1980) and Erikson (e.g., 1950 and 1959). And I found myself not drawn to the contemporary, seemingly odd pairing of relational psychoanalysis and postmodernism, in which those very psychoanalysts who consider themselves relational or intersubjective, who challenge one-person psychologies from the perspective of the inevitable two-ness of the analytic encounter, also challenge individual wholeness and depth of experience from the perspective that the subject (and intersubject?) is always split, destablized, and shifting. Loewaldian and Eriksonian goals, it seems to me, are conceptualized, in spite of their origins in the mother–child matrix or the analytic encounter, as distinctly within the individual. For Loewald, unconscious, infantile fantasies give intensity and depth to current experiences, or as he also puts it, transference and fantasy enliven reality and make it meaningful. In his view, the individual oscillates between the psychotic core of fusion and oedipal individuation and autonomy. For Erikson, ego integrity requires our recognition that our life, however contingent, is the only life we have and could have led (as Winnicott puts it, 1960, analysis requires gathering impingement into omnipotence). These are, finally, not relational goals: they are goals for individuation in which, at most, projection, or relationship have been taken within and transformed. Similarly, Kleinian and object relational measures of psychic health and functioning, symbolization for example (e.g., Klein, 1930, or Segal, 1957), or finding one's unknown thought (Bollas, 1987), however they depend on the infant–mother or analytic field for their development, are, finally, one-person experiences. These internal, intrapsychic goals, I believe, must complement our increasing focus on the Winnicottian or Lewinian analytic field and the centrality of intersubjective recognition, both developmentally and in the analytic encounter. But in spite of all of these caveats, I nonetheless believe that "Toward a Relational Individualism" sets out with succinct clarity much of what is at stake, and what has been much contested, especially within the different American psychoanalyses, for the last many years.

References

Balint, M. (1965), *Primary Love and Psycho-Analytic Technique*. New York: Liveright.
Benjamin, J. (1977), The end of internalization: Adorno's social psychology. *Telos*, 32:42–64.
———— (1978), Authority and the family revisited: Or, a world without fathers? *New German Critique*, 13:35–57.

Bollas, C. (1987), *The Shadow of the Object: Psychoanalysis of the Unthought Known*. New York: Columbia University Press.

Chodorow, N. J. (1974), Family structure and feminine personality. In: *Feminism and Psychoanalytic Theory*. New Haven, CT: Yale University Press, 1979, pp. 45–65.

———— (1978), *The Reproduction of Mothering*. Berkeley: University of California Press.

———— (1979), Gender, relation, and difference in psychoanalytic perspective. In: *Feminism and Psychoanalytic Theory*. New Haven, CT: Yale University Press, pp. 99–113.

———— (1996), Theoretical gender and clinical gender: Epistemological reflections on the psychology of women. *J. Amer. Psychoanal. Ass.*, 44/Suppl.:215–238.

———— (1998), Psychoanalytic visions of subjectivity. Contribution to Symposium, "The Concept of the Individual in Psychoanalysis Today." San Francisco Psychoanalytic Institute Extension Division and California Pacific Medical Center Department of Psychiatry. San Francisco, September 19.

———— (1999), *The Power of Feelings: Personal Meaning in Psychoanalysis, Gender and Culture*. New Haven, CT: Yale University Press.

Dinnerstein, D. (1976), *The Mermaid and the Minotaur*. New York: Harper & Row.

Erikson, E. (1950), *Childhood and Society*. New York: Norton.

———— (1959), *Identity and the Life Cycle: Selected Papers*. New York: International Universities Press.

Fairbairn, W. R. D. (1952), *An Object-Relations Theory of the Personality*. New York: Basic Books.

Gilligan, C. (1982), *In a Different Voice*. Cambridge, MA: Harvard University Press.

Guntrip, H. (1961), *Personality Structure and Human Interaction*. New York: International Universities Press.

Heller, T. C., Sosna, M. & Wellbery, D. E., eds. (1986), *Reconstructing Individualism: Autonomy, Individuality, and the Self in Western Thought*. Stanford, CA: Stanford University Press.

Keller, E. F. (1978), Gender and science. In: *Reflections on Gender and Science*. New Haven, CT: Yale University Press, 1985, pp. 75–94.

Klein, M. (1930), The importance of symbol-formation in the development of the ego. In: *Love, Guilt and Reparation & Other Works 1921–1945*. New York: Delta, pp. 219–232.

Loewald, H. (1980), *Papers on Psychoanalysis*. New Haven, CT: Yale University Press.

Miller, J. B. (1976), *Toward a New Psychology of Women*. Boston: Beacon.

Segal, H. (1957), Notes on symbol formation. In: *Melanie Klein Today, Vol. 1: Mainly Theory*, E. B. Spillius. London: Routledge, pp. 160–177.

Stern, D. N. (1985), *The Interpersonal World of the Infant*. New York: Basic Books.

Winnicott, D. W. (1960), The theory of the parent-infant relationship. In: *The Maturational Processes and the Facilitating Environment*. New York: International Universities Press, 1965, pp. 37–55.

Theoretical Models and the Analyst's Neutrality

(1986)

Jay R. Greenberg

▼   ▼   ▼   ▼   ▼

Editors' Introduction

In this often-cited article, Jay Greenberg develops several of the most fruitful values and conceptual strategies to be used by subsequent relational authors. Drawing on the broad distinction he and Mitchell had introduced three years earlier, in their book *Object Relations in Psychoanalytic Theory*, between the drive and relational models, here Greenberg considers the implications of those contrasting models for the nature of the analyst's stance and participation. These were problems that were to occupy him over the next several years and culminated in his 1991 book, *Oedipus and Beyond*.

Greenberg demonstrates an attitude toward theory that is respectful yet not reverent. Whereas earlier critics of classical psychoanalysis (for example, within the interpersonal psychoanalytic tradition) often portrayed the classical clinical approach as theory driven, suggesting the possibility of a freer, less technique-laden practice, Greenberg suggests that all clinical practice is, necessarily, theory driven. What is called for is not an impossible freedom from theory, but a close study of the way one's theory is implicated in one's practice. In Greenberg's conceptual methodology, and a general tendency within subsequent relational theorizing in general, the issue is not so much whether a theoretical principle is true or not, but what the implications are for the analyst's stance of believing in it. (In 1988 Lawrence Friedman was to develop a similar approach to comparative theory in *The Anatomy of Psychotherapy*.)

Also characteristic of Greenberg's methodology is an interest in the reclamation and mining of important classical concepts. He first explores the meaning of the concept in Freud's original usage—here, the significance of the principle of neutrality vis-à-vis the analyst's detached objectivity within the drive model and the philosophy of science of Freud's time. He finds the original meanings rife with anachronistic assumptions and obstructive of thoughtful clinical judgement. "Neutrality is a burdoned term."

Greenberg then considers what meaning a concept of neutrality might have, recontextualized within current relational principles. In the relational model, the analyst cannot choose whether or not to participate in the process. This does not imply for Greenberg (in contrast to some relational authors) that technique is irrelevant or impossible. Technique, in Greenberg's lights, becomes even more important, because principles of technique, whether explicit or implicit, shape the ways in which the clinician participates.

Greenberg then offers a relational definition of neutrality as a goal, rather than a set of behaviors, a striving for a kind of balance, rather than an indifference or inactivity. The kind of balance the analyst ought to aim for, Greenberg offers, is a balance between safety and danger, the familiar and the unknown, the old and the new, always within the highly idiosyncratic features of each analytic dyad.

Greenberg has been one of the key figures within the relational community in developing a disciplined way of thinking through clinical process and clinical judgement despite the abandonment of the traditional guidelines supplied by classical precepts and prohibitions. His redefinition of neutrality from something to do to something to think about in each interactive context has helped make it possible to broaden the range of options for participation that a thoughtful relational clinician can consider as part of his repertoire. Thus, Greenberg concludes that a greater emotional openness, self-revelation, and the expression of judgments all can serve the goal of neutrality, when "applied judiciously" in some clinical circumstances. Likewise, reserve and anonymity, the safeguards of classical technique, can have a detrimental, highly nonneutral impact in some clinical circumstances.

Greenberg is very careful here, and throughout his subsequent writings, to stress that none of these behaviors is ever always correct or useful. For Greenberg, as for other relational authors in recent years, analytic restraint is equally important as analytic expressiveness as an option within the clinician's repertoire in negotiating the terrain within the analytic relationship between safety and risk, old and new.

This essay was reworked and integrated into other aspects of Greenberg's influential contributions in *Oedipus and Beyond: A Clinical Theory* (1991). Chapters 9 and 10 provide clinical applications of Greenberg's reconsideration and revision of classical concepts like neutrality. Many important further developments in Greenberg's explorations of the interactive features of the analytic relationship have appeared in papers since, including: "Psychoanalytic Technique and the Interactive Matrix" in *The Psychoanalytic Quarterly* (1995, 64:1–22). "Psycho-analytic Words and Psychoanalytic Action: A Brief History" in *Contemporary Psychoanalysis* (1996, 32:195–214).

Theoretical Models and the Analyst's Neutrality*

▼　　▼　　▼　　▼　　▼

Few issues in psychoanalysis are quite so muddled, or tend to generate quite so much confusion in the mind of the clinician, as the relationship between theory and technique. There are many reasons for this, all related in one way or another to the poor match between the kind of work that theory-making is, and the kind of work that clinical practice is. One aspect of this is the inescapable but jarring mismatch between an activity which is inherently public and one which is fundamentally private. Theorizing, necessarily, is done publicly. Theoretical contributions by their nature must be written down or spoken aloud. When they are debated, all participants have access to what is said, if not necessarily to what is meant. Technique, on the other hand, is obviously private. There exists no record of all the transactions constituting an analysis, nor could such a record exist, even in principle.

Because of this, the translation of theoretical principles into technical precepts eludes outside observation. Theory applied is, inevitably,

* Originally published in *Contemporary Psychoanalysis*, 22(1):89–106, 1986. Reprinted by permission. This is a slightly revised version of paper read as Invited Address, Division of Psychoanalysis, American Psychological Association, Los Angeles, California, August 25, 1985.

theory interpreted. Personal predilection gives the application an idio-syncratic, and decisive, cast. By the time it is run through the analyst's particular vision of human life, not to mention his personality, the impact of theory is difficult to trace.

It is a commonplace that no beneficial analysis can be accomplished "by the book," that is, by simple application of theoretical premises to the life history of an individual analysand. However, to deprive technique of the influence of theory altogether is equally harmful. It is certainly true, as Joseph Sandler (1983) has noted, that every analyst—at least preconsciously—holds a theory in mind. Theory-making as a formal discipline requires the analyst to articulate his own assumptions and to assess them with respect to alternatives which inform the work of others. This discipline prevents retreats to the kinds of naive and sterile claims that have given psychoanalysis a bad press within the broader intellectual community—claims that we have subordinated theory to intuition, empathy, or pragmatism.

Despite the poor fit between theory and technique, it is nevertheless possible to draw important technical conclusions from broad theoretical premises. Mitchell and I have addressed this extensively with respect to one technical issue—the analyst's interpretive armamentarium. We have documented the ways in which the theoretical model which an analyst implicitly or explicitly holds will determine the content of his interpretations (Greenberg and Mitchell, 1983). In this paper, I will address the implications that models have for the analyst's stance within the psychoanalytic situation. I will be particularly concerned with the much maligned but, as I hope to demonstrate, still useful concept of analytic neutrality. I will discuss the origin of the neutrality concept in Freud's early theory, the problems which remain attached to it because of its roots in that theory, and the improvements which can emerge from re-defining it on the basis of modified theoretical premises.

In our book, Mitchell and I distinguished two major competing models which have dominated the history of psychoanalytic theory: we labeled them the drive/structure model and the relational/structure model. The drive/structure model originated in the early work of Freud, and was developed and maintained in his later work and in that of his major followers within the "orthodox" psychoanalytic tradition. The relational/structure model was prefigured in the early dissents of Adler and Jung and emerged fully, albeit independently, in the theories of Fairbairn and Sullivan. It has been developed in various ways by many of those typically designated as object relations or interpersonal theorists. The models themselves are broad groupings of theories—they are envelopes which contain compatible although by no means identical points of view.

Approached from the perspective of their implications for the analyst's clinical stance, two characteristics distinguishing the models require special mention. First, the drive/structure model is an individual psychology while the relational/structure model is a field theory. This decisively affects the way that each model understands the position of the analyst as an observer. Secondly, the models attribute psychic structure, the source of regularity and pattern in emotional life generally and in psychopathology particularly, to different processes. The drive model understands structure as the transformation of original drive energies, while the relational model sees structure as the developmental sequelae of early interpersonal exchanges. I will address each of these fundamental premises in turn, beginning with the premises of the drive model.

Freud's model of the analyst's role is based on the position of the observing scientist as that was understood in the 19th century. The Spanish philosopher Ortega y Gasset critically characterized this scientific attitude well:

> At last man is to know he truth about everything. It suffices that he should not lose heart at the complexity of the problems, and that he should allow no passion to cloud his mind. if with serene self-mastery he uses the apparatus of his intellect, if in particular he uses it in orderly fashion, he will find that his faculty of thought is ratio, reason, and that in reason he possesses the almost magic power of reducing everything to clarity, of turning what is most opaque to crystal, penetrating it by analysis until it is become self-evident (1940, pp. 170–171).

Compare Freud's statement in a letter to Theodore Reik that "scientific research must be without presumptions. In every other kind of thinking the choice of a point of view cannot be avoided" (1928, p. 196, my italics).

Freud's comment embodies a formulation which contemporary philosophers would consider to represent an outmoded, not to say particularly presumptuous, motion about the nature of scientific investigation. Derived from the Cartesian philosophy of science, which Ortega mocks, this formulation holds essentially that the observer stands outside of his observational field. His externality brings with it a kind of uninvolvement, using that word in its structural and emotional senses. It is this very uninvolvement that allows the impartial application of reason, and which facilitates the emergence of truth.

Freud did not develop a comprehensive, systematic set of principles regarding the analyst's clinical stance. His comparison of technique to the rules of chess, emphasizing the near infinite variability of procedures during the prolonged middle phase of analysis, suggests that full systematization is undesirable or even impossible (Freud, 1913). I suspect that Freud—in contrast to many of his followers—had an inclination to give the individual clinician wide berth and to let technique evolve out of the peculiar mix of personalities that creates and defines each analytic encounter. At the same time, his individual technical guidelines do hang together; they have much in common because they share a root in his attitude toward science. The posture of "evenly-hovering attention," the "blank screen" or "reflecting mirror" analogies, and the suggestion of an attitude of "surgical detachment" (Freud, 1912; 1913) and derive from the idea of the externality, objectivity, and impartiality of the analyst-observer.

If a philosophy of science dictates the desirability and even the possibility of externality and full impartiality, we still need a psychology to define the force among which the analyst must be impartial. This is where the psychodynamic and structural hypotheses of the drive/structure model are decisive. To state these briefly, the model holds that psychic structure, with the partial exception of autonomous ego aspects of the undifferentiated matrix, evolves out of the transformation of the energy of constitutionally determined sexual and aggressive drives. On the basis of different levels of exposure to environmental influence, and consequently with different degrees of distance from the original drive aims, the three structures, id, ego and superego, emerge. Each structure embodies a more or less consistent pattern of needs—it is this relative consistency of the structures themselves and of the balance among them that allows us to conceptualize a regularity which we call personality and/or psychopathology. It is also these structures, and their mutual influences, which constitute the observational field for the drive model analyst.

The philosophical and psychological premises of the drive model converge in the technical principle of neutrality. Freud himself used the term neutrality rarely. It first appears in the context of advice to analysts about how to handle patients' declarations of love. Responding in kind, whether encouragingly or discouragingly, will defeat the analysis, Freud warns, and he goes on to say that ". . . we ought not to give up the neutrality toward the patient, which we have acquired through keeping the counter-transference in check" (1915, p. 164). Freud went no further in spelling out what he intended neutrality to mean. In fact, despite its being a keystone of the traditional conceptualization of the analytic posture, a formal definition of neutrality did not appear until Anna Freud suggested one in 1936. In *The Ego and the Mechanisms of Defense* Anna Freud wrote:

It is the task of the analyst to bring into consciousness that which is unconscious, no matter to which psychic institution it belongs. He directs his attention equally and objectively to the unconscious elements in all three institutions. To put it in another way, when he sets about the work of enlightenment, he takes his stand at a point equidistant from the id, the ego, and the superego (1936, p. 28).

Notice in this the assumptions I have been discussing. There is the objectivity borne to externality, the rationality leading to enlightenment, the impartiality of the reasonable observer. Also, of course, there are the dynamic forces contained within the tripartite organization of the structural model. Joseph Lichtenberg has summarized this: ". . . the dictatorship of truth and reason irrevocably commits itself to being open-minded—each element in the individual—impulses, ego, and superego will therefore receive the position it deserves" (1983, p. 207).

The neutrality concept is not particularly popular in many analytic circles recently. To understand why, let us turn to the *Oxford English Dictionary*. There neutrality is defined in various ways. For the analyst, the first definition is useful as well as dangerous: "Not assisting or actively taking the side of either party in the case of a war or disagreement between . . . states, remaining inactive in relation to the belligerent powers." This is close to what Anna Freud had in mind, but notice the stress on inactivity. Some analysts mistakenly believe that impartiality is best achieved through inactivity. But even if inactivity is possible politically, as the dictionary suggests, it is never possible interpersonally. Hoffman (1983) and Wachtel (1982) have both argued persuasively that no behavior of the analyst can be considered simply inactive. Rather, all the analyst's behaviors must be understood as activity of one sort or another.

Because of this difficulty, even among those currently relying on neutrality as the keystone of a correct clinical posture, there remains considerable confusion about how it is best expressed within the psychoanalytic situation. Considered broadly, there is general agreement that neutrality has to do with not imposing values on the patient and with keeping countertransference in check. Chused has nicely characterized a neutral attitude as "a nonjudgmental willingness to listen and learn" (1982, p. 3). Poland has put it this way: "Neutrality is the technical manifestation of respect for the essential otherness of the patient" (1984, p. 289). The plot thickens, however, when it comes to realizing these attitudes in terms of technical procedures—for example, in determining their relationship to issues such as level of responsiveness, expressions of encouragement, or enforcement of conditions of abstinence (see Panel, 1984). Most authors who use the term translate it into behaviors such as non-responsiveness or anonymity. There is a tendency when discussing neutrality to equate non-alignment and colorlessness.

These clinical applications of the neutrality concept are reflected in subsidiary definitions in the dictionary. Indifference and colorlessness appear there among the meanings of the term (see Poland, 1984). On this account, as a summary statement of an analytic stance, "neutrality" seems pallid, failing to capture the intensity of the emotional experience that clinical encounters are or should be. Many clinicians feel that as a term neutrality is too cold and aloof, that it doesn't convey the kind of affirmation that patients not only need but typically get in a well conducted treatment.

Why should psychoanalysis be stuck with a concept which inextricably ties impartial acceptance of all parts of the patient's personality to the analyst's inactivity and non-expressiveness? The reason, I believe, is traceable to neutrality's roots in the epistemological premises of the drive/structure model. There is a direct line from the Cartesian stress on the observer's potential externality and objectivity to the drive model's equation of non-alignment with non-participation. Inactivity in the interest of discovery is at least an apparently logical next step.

Clearly, neutrality is a burdened term. Some analysts believe that it should be abandoned altogether. However, despite its limitations, I see some important advantages in retaining neutrality as both a concept and a term. Especially in the context of its formal definition as a kind of "equidistance," neutrality conveys the idea that the analyst should occupy a certain position and that the position should be a balanced one, that it should be between something and something else. This is a particularly important prescription for the analyst, who is continuously buffeted by a variety of forces, pushed and pulled into responding in one way or another. The temptation to ally oneself with one or another force in the patient's personality, to favor one of his tendencies at the expense of others, is always present. In the face of this, neutrality is a necessary, if incomplete, way of expressing an optimal analytic stance. The connotations of indifference are unfortunate, but this is not sufficient reason to discard it. Further, the term is in use and I have not been able to come up with an apt replacement.

If we are going to retain the term, however, we must be careful what we mean by it. Neutrality itself is far from a neutral word: any definition of it inevitably changes with alterations in the underlying theory. When Freud first introduced the term, he was talking about the need for the analyst to resist countertransferential pressures. He was not talking about equidistance from psychological structures, as Anna Freud was later in her definition, nor could he have constructed the concept in those terms. At the time of the technical papers, Freud was working with the topographic model; the mind was divided into the systems Ucs., Pcs., and Cs.: the very goal of analysis was to make the unconscious conscious. Any notion of equidistance awaited a crucial theoretical change: the tripartite structural model with its inherent idea that there are unconscious elements in alll psychic structures.

In fact, Anna Freud's formulation is not simply a derivative of fair-mindedness. The classic definition appears in the context of her argument for the legitimacy of studying and analyzing the ego: it is not only technical prescription, but also theoretical polemic. As Lichtenberg (1983) notes, this argument was directed against the large number of analysts who refused to abandon the older system, in which ego functioning was considered the sort of superficial study that could be of interest only to academic psychologists.

Just how tied neutrality is to an underlying theoretical system becomes clear in light of another consideration. When Anna Freud defined neutrality, she was operating out of a model that viewed the Oedipus complex as the core issue both in development and in treatment. Working with the Oedipus complex as classical analysts did, and do, makes a number of assumptions about the patient, of which two are especially relevant here. First, it is assumed that the patient has achieved a set of structured goals (that is, instinctual aims) which has consistency and coherence over time and across a variety of different situations. Secondly, it is assumed that the patient is an independent agent capable of active pursuit of these goals, although this may be interfered with on the basis of internal conflict. The "neutrality" of the analyst is an equidistance from all the forces operating within this sort of person.

However, as many analysts have come to appreciate the importance of developmental residues from the preoedipal years, the very vision of the patient as an autonomous, active agent has become a departure from neutrality. More accurately, I should say that the assumption of autonomy and activity is a departure from neutrality for those who accept the theoretical emendations of recent developmental theory. It is a departure because it involves an implicit rejection of the earliest developmental needs, seeing these as secondary to defensive retreats from the oedipal situation. On the other hand, for those who maintain an unmodified classical perspective, the serious consideration which is often given to preoedipal development may constitute non-neutrality, for example by being too accepting of the patient's passivity or of his regressive defenses.

These considerations make it clear that a theoretical model based on radically different psychological and epistemological assumptions requires a redefinition of neutrality from that currently in use. The relational/ structure model rests on such alternative assumptions. However, there has been no attempt to formulate the required redefinition. I now propose to do so after reviewing the fundamental theoretical premises on which such a definition would be based.

As I mentioned earlier, the theories comprising the relational model are field theories. Based not on Cartesian rationalism but on a philosophy of science informed by Heisenberg's uncertainty principle and Einstein's relativity theory, the relational model postulates an analyst who is, in Sullivan's (1954) phrase, a "participant observer" or, in Fairbairn's, an "interventionist" (1958). These concepts are not themselves technical prescriptions (i.e., suggestions that one ought to participate or to intervene), they are statements of fact from a particular philosophical perspective (Greenberg, 1981).

From the psychodynamic point of view, every relational model theory postulates some idea of an internal object world, or a representational world. This is a stable, structured set of images consisting of transformations of relationships with other people (Sandler and Rosenblatt, 1962). Sullivan's "personifications" and "illusory others" and Fairbairn's "internal objects" are the constituents of the representational world in their particular versions of the relational model. The representational world of the relations/structure model theorists is not simply a collection of images, however—it has both motivational and structural properties. Put very briefly, the represented experiences constitute both a guide to what is desirable, expectable, or anxiety-ridden in human relationships, and also a template for judging contemporary experience with others.

Combining these two relational model premises, we arrive at the following formation: the analyst inevitably participates somewhere within a historical continuum of the patient's relationships with others. That is, he "fits" somewhere into the patient's representational world, either assimilated into an old relational pattern or experienced as new, and different from that the patient has experienced before. To reiterate: that he participates is not a choice; technique is a matter of specifying how he should participate. With respect to the neutrality concept, a relational model revision of Anna Freud's concept of equidistance would "place" the analyst somewhere within the historical continuum of the patients' relationships. I will take this up shortly, but first must take a brief detour through another aspect of the psychoanalytic situation.

A theme which is being increasingly stressed in recent discussions of the psychoanalytic process is the need to create what Schafer (1983) has aptly termed an "atmosphere of safety." (See also the "atmosphere of tolerance" of Sandler and Sandler [1983] and the "conditions of safety" of Weiss [1982].) Only under conditions of perceived security can the patient risk elaborating the thoughts, fantasies, and feelings which need to be brought to light and examined if analysis is to proceed beneficially (see Myerson, 1981a, 1981b). In the absence of this sense of safety, as Schafer puts it, "the analysand could not take on what he or she ventures to confront during the analysis, and instead would continue simply to feel injured, betrayed, threatened, seduced, or otherwise interfered with or traumatized" (1983, p. 32). In agreement with Schafer, I see an intimate connection between the analyst's neutrality and the patient's experience of safety.

The stress on the need for safety depends on an important theoretical assumption that, although prefigured in Freud's late writings and in some of Hartmann's work, was developed most fully in the work of relational model theorists. This is the assumption that repression always has an interpersonal component; it takes place in a context that determines when a feeling or impulse is dangerous (see Myerson, 1977). Both Schafer's and Myerson's work stress the importance of creating an atmosphere in which the conditions under which repression once became necessary are not recreated. In terms of the relational model premises which I have spelled out, the atmosphere of safety would depend on the analyst's ability to create conditions in which the patient perceives him as a new object. Strachey (1934) conceptualized this as the need to breach the vicious circle of projection/introjection through which archaic bad object relationships keep being re-created. I think Schafer implicitly recognizes this in his statement that without the atmosphere of safety the patient would continue to feel injured, betrayed and so on.

Ironically, however, the analytic situation cannot be too safe. I mean, of course, that there has to be room for transference, with all the dangers that the eruption of threatening feelings within the context of an archaic relationship entails. Many patients—and, I hasten to add, some analysts too—eagerly and defensively embrace the emergence of the analyst as a "new" object. They embrace him eagerly because there is genuine relief from a life of relationships gone awry; they embrace him defensively because the "good" therapeutic relationship temporarily de-fuses conflict. But the analyst who is too much a new object has fallen into a trap: it is in working through the disruptions of safety (and, thus, in its re-establishment) that the most important progress occurs.

I am suggesting here that there is a need to strike a kind of balance between danger and safety, which can be roughly translated as striking a balance between being seen by the patient as an old or a new object.

This recalls the relational model concept of a historical continuum within the representational world. It is also reminiscent of Anna Freud's idea of neutrality as equidistance, although when addressing operations within the representational world I prefer a term like "optimal tension" to equidistance because of its dynamic connotations.

This brings me to the new definition of analytic neutrality. In my contribution to a panel discussion on this issue, I have suggested that neutrality is best understood not as a behavior or series of behaviors, but as the goal on all the analyst's behaviors (Greenberg, 1986). I said that neutrality is a work like "democracy," which refers to a kind of government rather than to the particular laws that implement it. With this in mind, we are in a position to define neutrality from the perspective of the relational model: Neutrality embodies the goal of establishing an optimal tension between the patient's tendency to see the analyst as an old object and his capacity to experience him as a new one.

This revised definition is not simply terminological; it has important technical implications that will occupy the reminder of this paper. For one thing, as defined within the terms of the drive model, neutrality has a static ring to it; it implies that the "neutral" analyst occupies a fixed position. That is, from one analysis to another, the neutral posture would always look more or less the same. This accords well with the model of the analyst as 19th century scientist which informed Anna Freud's thinking.

Under my proposed reformulation, the activity of the neutral analyst is always dependent upon the quality of the patient's relationships with others. The analytic behaviors which implement the goal of optimal tension between old and new necessarily vary with the openness to new experience of a particular patient's internal object world. Generally speaking, the silence and anonymity which constitute unmodified classical technique enable the patient to include the analyst in his internal object world, while a more active or self-revealing posture established the analyst as a new object. Thus, with a patient who is firmly encased in a closed world of internal objects, the analyst will have to assert his newness more affirmatively to achieve an optimal level of tension, while with the more open patient just such assertiveness would constitute an impediment to the development of transference and to insight about it. Neutrality is thus not to be measured by the analyst's behaviors at any moment, but by the particular patient's ability to become aware of and to tolerate his transference.

The value of establishing a neutral atmosphere is closely related to Schafer's recent, stated, formulation of ego-syntonicity. Schafer wrote:

. . . the concept of ego-syntonicity has always referred to those principles of constructing experience which seem to be beyond effective question by the person who develops and applies them. . . . Metaphorically,
they are the eye that sees everything according to its own structure and
cannot see itself seeing. . . .

One might say that these principles are beyond question in so far as the
person treats the relevant questions about them *not as questions but as
evidence.* . . .

In undertaking the analysis of a character problem, one counts on there
being some diversity of experiential principles. . . . The point of access
may be some well-guarded for of thinking hopefully, some shrugged-off
way of esteeming oneself realistically, or some shyly hidden but stable
kind of loving (1983, pp. 144–146).

Schafer's point applies equally to the representational world of many
patients. The patient can become aware that he is assimilating the analyst into his world of archaic internal objects only when he has already
become aware that there is an alternative possibility. Unless he has some
sense of the analyst as a new object, he will not be able to experience
him as an old one. The inability to achieve this balance is responsible
for many analytic failures. If the analyst cannot be experienced as a new
object, analysis never gets under way; if he cannot be experienced as an
old one, it never ends.

In distinguishing between neutrality as a goal and the specific actions
that support and implement it in my earlier paper it was my intention
to cast analytic behaviors such as emotional openness, self-revelation,
and even expressing judgments in a new light. The theoretical framework developed here further clarifies these relationships. That is, I think
that these behaviors, which are typically thought of as *prima facie* nonneutral, may actually contribute to neutrality when judiciously applied
with the right patient. Conversely, the traditional, purely interpretive posture which Glover (1955), for example, feels defines neutrality may actually detract from it. Let me develop this possibility.

In his important writings on relational aspects of the psychoanalytic
situation, Myerson has pointed out that in bringing material into analysis, patients express ". . . a need or determination to know something
about as well as *from* the analyst. The analysand wants to ascertain how
the analyst would react if he were to express his desire or anger more
directly as well as what the analyst thinks is the nature of his experience" (1981a, p. 98). This fits well with my idea about the need to see
the analyst as a new object.

Let me take as an example a set of circumstances which arises frequently. Many analysands need to know something about the analyst because they are frightened of the impact that their transference fantasies (including the perceptions of which these fantasies are generally eleborations) have on their analysts. Transference represents an assault on the analyst's sense of self, a point on which analysts as theoretically different as Levenson (1972), Racker (1968), Sandler (1976), and Searles (1965, 1979) have been especially eloquent. For a patient to experience his own transference fully, including its assaultive aspects (and here I include so-called positive as well as negative transferences) he must be able to assume that the analyst will experience the impact of that transference differently than the original objects did. The patient must be able to probe the analyst's weak spots, to get beneath his professional calm and reserve, either with some confidence that the probing will not be murderously destructive or with a firm belief that the analyst—having promulgated the free-association rule—is significantly responsible for his own reactions to what comes up. Compare Myerson's emphasis on the child's need for parents who can allow him "to discover for himself that if he acts upon or expresses his desire or his anger sometimes at least, nobody will hurt him or be hurt by him or reject him and that even when someone is upset by his actions, that person bears some responsibility for this reaction" (1981b, p. 178).

Let me suggest a few commonplace examples that arise in analyses. Levenson has mentioned that patients often have thoughts about being younger than their analysts, and more attractive, leading more active and varied sex lives. Many patients are richer than their analysts, or plan to be. Many are more creative or ambitious; they look forward to being more successful. Many are simply younger, and have reactions organized around their having more years to live. All of these realistic perceptions intermingle with fantastic, archaic loving and hateful intentions to give the individual transference its unique character. But the patient must worry if the analyst can stand it, both in terms of the intensity of archaic feeling involved and also in terms of the awesome reality.

These concerns are often at the core of what Gill (1982) has called "resistance to the awareness of tranference." The patient feels responsible for destroying the analyst's (presumably) fragile sense of self. Both impulse and perception must be denied in favor of maintaining the analyst and the analytic relationship. In these circumstances, some analysands will hear any interpretive intervention as a condemnation, specifically, a condemnation borne of the analyst's fragility and sense of having been damaged. Interpretation, whether defense, impulse, or affect is stressed, is experienced as blame, as holding the patient culpable for his transferencee wishes and perceptions. Needless to say, it will be as hard for the patient to become conscious of his anxiety or guilt about the destructive impact he is having on the analyst as it was for him to gauge his effect on his parents. The insidious effect of the analyst's anonymity will thus be to confirm the patients worst fears about intense, erotic, hateful, or even simply loving feelings. The technical problem is how to avoid creating and sustaining a vicious circle. In this context, the goal embodied in the concept of neutrality becomes especially important. The central question of technique is determining the behaviors that support the neutral posture.

Chused has suggested recently that for child patients who had intrusive or over-controlling parents, the non-responsive posture of the classical analyst facilitates the development of a new, growth-promoting object relationship. Her formulation can be read as an updating of Hartmann's "principle of multiple appeal of interpretations." Hartmann suggested that ". . . the incidental effects of interpretation . . . frequently transcend our immediate concern with the specific drive-defense setup under consideration, and . . . are not always predictable" (1951, p. 152). Chused updates Hartmann by indicating that there is multiple appeal not only to interpretations themselves, but to all the analyst's behaviors.

The allegiance of both these authors to the premises of the drive/structure model make it difficult for them to follow through the logic of their important insights. Hartmann, although he speaks approvingly of ". . . variations of our technical principles according to each patient's psychological structure, clinical symptomatology, age level, and so on" (1951, p. 144), is unable to develop a systematic basis for such variations, or to systematically trace their effects. Similarly, although Chused acknowledges that the analyst's behavior can be the source of genuine structural change, she cannot allow that for some patients the non-responsiveness which characterizes her classical vision of neutrality may thwart the possibility of any treatment.

Reformulating neutrality within the terms of the relational model allows a consistent approach to these problems. For example, there are many patients for whom analytic reserve is simply too close to the aloof, self-protective posture with which their parents guarded themselves against their children's erotic, competitive, challenging or hostile impulses. With these patients, reserve and anonymity can actually detract from neutrality, by confirming the patient's sense of having harmed the analyst. For all intents and purposes the patient's rage turns the analyst into the damaged, archaic object. Self-revelation can be the road back to neutrality under these circumstances. This is an especially likely situation in the case of the patient who is most locked into the constraints of his internal object world.

Along the same lines, there are some patients who were exposed to parental indifference bordering on neglect. For these people, the traditionally neutral non-judgmental attitude can be genuinely dangerous. Under these circumstances, passing judgment on the patient's behavior (e.g., that it is provocative or self-destructive) or on important people in the patient's life (e.g., a disturbed or cruel lover or relative) can be essential to the establishment of neutrality. Schafer is referring to something similar when he says that "It is not a departure from neutrality to call a spade a spade" (1983, p. 4).

Let me conclude with an example of the sort of behavior that can support neutrality as I have redefined it within the terms of the relational model. I would stress in this connection that I don't think what I will be describing is terribly unusual from the point of view of current clinical practice. I do think, however, that these are interventions which are not typically included in case reports, because there is no theoretical framework for encompassing their effects, and that my new definition will enable them to be more comfortably included in our technical bag of tricks.

The patient is a middle-aged, married man who came to analysis because of an obsession about a woman with whom he had recently had a brief flirtation that had come to nothing. Although he presented himself as simply wanting to be rid of thoughts about the woman, with very little encouragement he quickly came to care less about the obsession itself, and to become more interested in his sense of chronic dissatisfaction with his life at home and at work.

Within a relatively short time, some fairly dramatic improvements occurred in this man's life. The obsession disappeared, but more importantly, he began to feel generally more open to people in a way that he described as making life far richer than it had been. The scope of his involvement with people and activities grew dramatically. He reported liking himself better and being less anxiously self-absorbed. He acquired new interests.

Depite all these changes, the patient felt that there was a distance between him and me that placed limits on his potential for full self-exploration and growth within the analysis. He felt that he had "no relationship" with me, that I was distant, aloof, and inscrutable. For instance, I didn't answer his questions, preferring instead to demand (as he saw it) his fantasies. Also, he objected to my ways of running my practice. He could not see why I charged for missed sessions. He could understand being charged if he missed for frivolous reasons, but when he did miss it was always unavoidable. And why didn't I even tell him why I did what I did, beyond brief references to my need for some finan-cial stability? Was I just a small-minded cheapskate who hid behind the convenient mask of analytic anonymity?

As the work proceeded, more details of the transference emerged. My failure to answer questions and the demand for fantasies was, as he experienced it, fundamentally a sadistic and voyeuristic exercise for me: I loved to see him squirm and to come up with fantasies that were "wrong." Also, I used both my sadism and my analytic status to pro-tect myself from his own assaults—fundamentally, I was afraid of him and, more pointedly, afraid of my own weakness.

The elaboration of these fantasies was essentially affectless. The patient could not allow himself to feel very much about what was emerg-ing because he was convinced that what he saw was true. We were able to connect the fantasies historically to his perception of his father, a weak, frightened man who had been jilted by his mother and who had carried a torch for her all his life. The father had taken a great deal of his helpless anger out on his own—from criticizing his penis size and taking him for hormone shots as a small child, to denigrating his very real school and work accomplishments later on. Still, he claimed, there was no real involvement. We both learned a good deal as we constructed his transferential feelings in terms of defense against and reaction to his relationship with his father, but nothing much changed. The "bottom line" for the patient was that I was like his father or, as he put it other times, "analysis" is too much like his father.

Over a period of time, I came to believe that perhaps these com-plaints were justified; perhaps unmodified anonymity was too much like the begrudging, self-protective attitude which the patient had experienced as coming from his father. This led to a change in tone in the sessions. For example, during an exchange organized around some sessions can-celled because of bad weather, the patient again asked me why I per-sisted in the small-minded practice of charging him when I knew perfectly well that he had a good reason for not coming. This time, I told him that, although I had no doubt that it would have been impos-sible or extremely difficult for him to make the appointments, I charged him because I didn't want to be in the position of judging whether he had good reasons or not. Further, I said that I thought it would be dis-respectful for me to pass on the validity of his reasons for missing a ses-sion on any particular occasion, and that I felt most comfortable simply relying on guidelines established in advance.

The patient, surprised and pleased, responded "Oh, why didn't you tell me that before?" I said that it was because I hadn't thought it would be helpful, but that perhaps I had been wrong. This opened up a period of sustained anger—the first expressions of anger beyond the potshots or hit and run attacks that had characterized the earlier work.

During this time, which lasted for several weeks, the patient thought seriously of ending the analysis. Why had I been so like his father for so long, why should he have to put up with and suffer for my mistakes. He also was clearly afraid of what he as feeling. He speculated that maybe it was all for the good, that it was better to feel something for me than nothing. He sought reassurance that this was a sign of analytic progress, but I did not give it to him. In fact, I said, it was possible that the anger was the first step in the end of the analysis, that it was something to be taken very seriously.

As the anger subsided, the patient was able to react more directly to my having told him why I charged for the session and, more important, that I respected him. His reaction was, of course, not unambivalent. He had a dream in which he, an avid tennis player, was playing with John McEnroe. He had the sense that he could beat McEnroe, or at least give him a good game, but he noticed that although several of his own shots were out, McEnroe was calling them good, giving the patient a break. He was able to hear and elaborate my interpretation—that he felt I was toying with him, letting him think he was in my league, building him up for a harsh disappointment. This was the first time that he was able to connect in a full emotional way with a transference implication of one of his dreams.

In the context of these exchanges, the patient rather quickly became able to experience and accept both angry and admiring or even loving feelings toward me. The analysis took a decisive turn, and the material clearly had a more powerful emotional impact on him. Moreover, he subsequently reported that during the period of greatest anger he had, for the first time in the analysis, felt "really myself."

I see my departure from anonymity—a departure which with my new definition I can say promoted neutrality—as relatively minor. It also came well into the analysis. With other patients, the more active technique must come earlier (sometimes from the first session) or be more dramatic. Notice that my intervention did not truncate the most intense or regressive transferential feelings. In fact, the patient could not have tolerated sustained rage until after I had ventured to become less anonymous. Nor did the change in my position make things more comfortable in any conventional sense. The change enable the patient to feel that what I did was not self-protective, hostile and small-minded in the way he had experienced his father. This enhanced his sense of analytic safety, but that in turn allowed the emergence of a range of feelings that were at least temporarily more dangerous to both of us and to the continuation of the analysis itself than the earlier indifference had been.

Defining neutrality as optimal tension between the patient's experience of us as old or new objects gives a clear reference point in the patient's experience for evaluating our interventions, and for monitoring our technique throughout the course of an analysis. By relying on this standard, we have a good chance of maintaining the neutral posture, which I continue to believe best serves the goals of psychoanalytic treatment.

References

Chused, J. (1982) The role of analytic neutrality in the use of the child analyst as a new object. *Journal of The American Psychoanalytic Association* 30:3–28.

Fairbairn, W. R. D. (1958) On the nature and aims of psycho-analytical treatment. *International Journal of Psycho-Analysis* 39:374–385.

Freud, A. (1936) *The Ego and the Mechanisms of Defense*, New York: International Universities Press.

Freud, S. (1912) Recommendations to physicians practicing psychoanalysis. *Standard Edition* 12.

Freud, S. (1913) On beginning the treatment: Further recommendations on the technique of psychoanalysis. *Standard Edition* 12.

Freud, S. (1915) Observations on transference love (Further recommendations on the technique of psycho-analysis III). *Standard Edition* 12.

Freud, S. (1928) Appendix to Dostoevsky and parricide. *Standard Edition* 21.

Gill, M. (1982) *Analysis of Tranference*, Volume 1. New York: International Universities Press.

Glover. E. (1955) *The Technique of Psycho-Analysis*. New York: International Universities Press.

Greenberg. J. (1981) Prescription or description: The therapeutic action of psychoanalysis. *Contemporary Psychaoanalysis* 17:239–257.

Greenberg. J. (1986) The problem of analytic neutrality. *Contemporary Psychaoanalysis* 22:76–86.

Greenberg, J. and Mitchell, S. (1983) *Object Relations in Psychoanalytic Theory*. Cambridge, MA: Harvard University Press.

Hartmann, H. (1951) Technical implications of ego psychology. In: *Essays on Ego Psychology*. New York: International Universities Press.

Hoffman, I. (1983) The patient as interpreter of the analyst's experience. *Contemporary Psychoanalysis* 19:389–422.

Levenson, E. (1972) *The Fallacy of Understanding*. New York: Basic Books.

Lichtenberg. J. (1983) Is there a Weltanschaunng to be developed from psychoanalysis? In: *The Future of Psychoanalysis*. Goldberg. A. ed. New York: International Universities Press, pp. 203–238.

Myerson. P. (1977) Therapeutic dilemmas relevant to the lifting of repression. *International Journal of Psycho-Analysis* 58:453–462.

Myerson, P. (1981a) The nature of the transactions that enhance the progressive phases of psychoanalysis. *International Journal of Psycho-analysis* 62:91–103.

Myerson. P. (1981b) The nature of the transactions that occur in other than classical analysis. *International Review of Psycho-Analysis* 8:173–189.

Ortega y Gasset, J. (1940) History as a system. In: *History as a System and Other Essays Toward a Philosophy of History.* New York: Norton, pp. 165–233.

Panel (1984) The neutrality of the analyst in the analytic situation. R. Lieder, reporter. *Journal of The American Psychoanalytic Association* 32:573–585.

Poland, W. (1984) On the analyst's neutrality. *Journal of The American Psychoanalytic Association* 32:283–299.

Racker, H. (1968) Transference and Countertransference. New York: International Universities Press.

Sandler, J. (1976) Counterfransference and role-responsiveness. *International Review of Psycho-Analysis* 3:43–47.

Sandler, J. (1983) Reflections on some relations between psychoanalytic concepts and psychoanalytic practice. Interntional Journal of Psycho-Analysis 64:35–45.

Sandler, J. and Rosenblatt, B. (1962) The concept of the representational world. *Psychoanalytic Study of the Child* 17:128–145.

Sandler, J. and Sandler, A. (1983) The second censorship the three box model and some technical implications. *International Journal of Psycho-Analysis* 64:413–425.

Schafer, R. (1983) *The Analytic Attitude.* New York: Basic Books.

Searles, H. (1965) *Collected Papers on Schizophrenia and Related Subjects.* New York: International Universities Press.

Searles. H. (1979) *Countertransference and Related Subjects.* New York: International Universities Pess.

Strachey. J. (1934) The nature of the therapeutic action of psycho-analysis. *International Journal of Psycho-Analysis* 15:127–159.

Sullivan, H. S. (1954) *The Psychiatric Interview.* New York: W.W. Norton and Co.

Wachtel, P. (1982) Vicious circles: The self and the rhetoric of emerging and unfolding. *Contemporary Psychoanalysis* 18:259–273.

Weiss. J. (1982) Psychotherapy research: Theory and findings. theoretical introduction. Psychotherapy Research Group. Department of Psychiatry. Mount Zion Hospital & Medical Center, Bulletin 5.

Afterword

Reading this paper a decade and a half after I wrote it, I am struck both by aspects of it that feel familiar—representative of me as I work and think today—and by aspects that feel somewhat quaint. First, I remain quite comfortable with the idea that the analyst's stance changes and should change in the work with each individual analysand, I also continue to believe, more strongly than ever, that one cannot know whether a particular way of engaging an analysand will be useful or destructive in advance. We can only do the best we can in any moment and evaluate the effects later on.

On a second point, I realize that I was generalizing something quite personal about my experience of doing analysis. When I am working at my best, I feel a powerful tension between wanting to provide a new and more benign experience for my patients and wanting to tolerate the painful sense of being the archaic bad object. Today, I think a great deal about the need to exercise restraint on my own tendencies to enact the role of the new, good object. I like the way that the paper conveys some of that tension, and I like the way I translated the personal experience into the idea of maintaining a technical stance that embodies a feeling of "optimal tension," for the analysand and also for the analyst.

What seems most foreign in my rereading is that the paper conveys a sense of certainty that the analyst can conceive and actualize a way of participating that is ultimately clear and purposive. I am not entirely sure just how I was thinking when I first wrote it, but in the years since I have learned from my own experience and from the work of others (notably Irwin Hoffman) that a great deal of what goes on in treatment is inaccessible to anybody's awareness, in the moment or perhaps forever. So I think that the paper conveys the possibility of a planfulness that should be a part of the way we think about our work, but that we also must realize is most often honored in the breach. I would like anybody reading the paper today to keep in mind that there is much more inadvertence in the analytic encounter than I described. Taking adequate account of the effects of inadvertence is critical, especially because the argument in my paper has important consequences for our understanding of the therapeutic action of psychoanalysis.

So much for my own reflections. Most of the criticism of the paper by others has been directed toward my decision to retain the term neutrality. To many, the term is inseparable from the technical canon that I intend to reject and is therefore compromised and misleading. I have spent a good amount of time going back and forth between wishing that I had been able to find a better term and feeling satisfied about the ambiguity that comes with packaging new wine in an old bottle. In the final analysis, I have come to believe that it suits my own sensibility to think of technique as poised between the old and the new, between what can be negotiated in a relationship and what remains irretrievably private and beyond relational engagement. I believe that all of us, analyst and analysands alike, are always in and always outside our relationships. Neutrality is an abrasive term, and the abrasiveness itself conveys some of the strain I was trying to describe. That, of course, is hindsight, but even in the face of others' criticism and my own doubts, I still can't think of a better way to express what I had in mind.

The Wings of Icarus:
Illusion and the Problem of Narcissism

(1986)

Stephen A. Mitchell

▼   ▼   ▼   ▼   ▼

Editors' Introduction

Choosing a representative selection from among the numerous influential publications by Stephen Mitchell was not an easy task, but in "The Wings of Icarus" Mitchell established certain key conceptual strategies that would come to characterize much of the rest of his work. As the leading spokesperson for the emerging relational approach within contemporary psychoanalysis, Mitchell establishes the fundamental idea that, at least as it influenced the psychoanalytic mainstream in the United States, the legacy of Freud's drive theory was to underemphasize the role of actual interpersonal relationships in the development of mental life. Offering an alternative to drive theory as the cornerstone of psychoanalytic metapsychology, Mitchell places relations with others, internal and external, real and imaginary, at the center of the theoretical edifice, and the framework of the relational tapestry replaces what was a one-person psychology.

As has become characteristic of his conceptual methodology, Mitchell first lays out before his readers two contrasting approaches to a problem, and then he shows how, by examining the problem from a different level of abstraction, one can find a third alternative that reconciles the tensions between the first two. Here, he compares two dramatically contrasting and incompatible approaches to the problem of narcissism: narcissism as illusion versus narcissism as the growing edge of the self; narcissism as defensive versus narcissism as the basis of creativity and growth. Mitchell demonstrates how these opposing theoretical understandings led to contradictory technical recommendations in the work of Kernberg and Kohut.

Penetrating beneath the surface of these seemingly irreconcilable theories, Mitchell reveals a surprising structural similarity, namely, that both of these approaches assume a model of mind in which narcissism operates intrapsychically rather than as a mode of connection to important others. As Mitchell writes, they "isolate the figure within the relational tapestry." Mitchell then offers a synthetic approach that avoids the pitfalls of each, by treating narcissism as a learned pattern of integrating relationships and serving as an important vehicle for maintaining intimate connections with others.

Mitchell then lays out what has become a defining feature of his therapeutic method. Viewing the patient's longings for admiration and idealization as "invitations" to the analyst to participate with the patient in a particular way, Mitchell proposes that the analyst has no choice but to respond in some way—neutrality, or nonparticipation, is not an option. Mitchell proposes that the analyst respond by joining the patient in the narcissistic integration by playfully allowing for some admiration and idealization while also heightening the patient's curiosity by questioning how it is that the patient feels so locked into participating with others in just these limited ways. Mitchell's approach to psychopathology is to understand it as an unnecessary limitation on the patient's options in life, and his view of treatment is to discover experientially with patients that other choices remain available, so as to expand their interactional repertoire as well as their abilities to reflect on these life choices.

Mitchell is unique as a psychoanalytic writer in that he first zooms in on the minute details of the trees in the analytic forest and then swoops up to a higher level of abstraction to provide a bird's eye view, revealing a clearing through the timber. With clear, elegant, and persuasive writing, Mitchell's metaphors are unforgettable and his balanced approach allows him to sail through analytic space without suffering the fate of Icarus.

"The Wings of Icarus" was expanded into chapters 7 and 8 of Mitchell's broad historical overview and critical synthesis of relational theorizing in *Relational Concepts in Psychoanalysis: An Integration* (1988, Harvard). In *Hope and Dread in Psychoanalysis* (1993, Basic Books).

Mitchell further explored the theoretical and clinical implications of the emerging relational paradigm in psychoanalysis, including the concept of multiplicity in relation to self-organization and self-states, narcissistic and otherwise. Chapters 7 and 8 of *Hope and Dread* further explored the analyst's response to the patient's needs and wishes introduced in this early paper. In *Influence and Autonomy in Psychoanalysis* (1997, The Analytic Press) Mitchell explored the implications of relational theory for clinical practice, demonstrating that we achieve autonomy and authenticity through interpersonal influence rather than despite it.

The Wings of Icarus:
Illusion and the Problem of Narcissism*

▼　　▼　　▼　　▼　　▼

Although he had been using the term for some years prior Freud formally introduced the concept of narcissism into psychoanalytic theory in 1914 on the heels of Jung's painful defection from the psychoanalytic community. The theory of narcissism was largely a response to the conceptual challenge posed by Jung's critique of Freudian theory. Freud's libido theory had provided a powerful and compelling account of the various forms of neurosis, tracing them through complex associative pathways of transformation and disguise, to conflicts over libidinal wishes. Jung objected to what he felt was the narrowness of this account of human motivations, arguing that other kinds of issues, totally independent of sexuality, played a central role in mental health and psychopathology, particularly in psychotic disturbances such as schizophrenia. To meet Jung's challenge and to save his larger ambitions for libido theory, Freud had to account for schizophrenia in libidinal terms, to derive it interpretively from psychosexual wishes and conflicts.

In order to bring schizophrenia within the explanatory sway of libido theory, Freud expanded his view of the nature and developmental course of psychosexuality. Libido does not originate in the array of various infantile component instincts which Freud had unveiled beneath neurotic symptomatology. These various wishes constituting infantile psychosexuality are already a secondary phase in the course of libidinal development, in which libido has taken on objects in the external world. Prior to this turn outward, Freud argued, the

* Originally published in *Contemporary Psychoanalysis*, 22(1), 107–132, © 1986 W. A White Institute.

totality of the infant's desire is directed towards the child's own self, discharged inwards. By introducing narcissism as a pre-stage of object relations, Freud was able to generate a plausible (although misleading and inaccurate) account of schizophrenic phenomenology and symptomatology as the product of a libidinal regression beyond infantile parental imagoes (the fixation points for the neuroses), back to an obliviousness regarding the external world and others characteristic of an original state of primary narcissism.

The introduction of the concept of narcissism, however, had larger implications than providing a theory of schizophrenia. By granting self-love a position prior to object love and in a continual reciprocal relation to it, Freud opened up for psychodynamic consideration the whole realm of issues and phenomena pertaining to self-regard and self-esteem regulation. The concept of narcissism allowed the drive model to address itself to the kinds of questions which were to become central to subsequent relational model theorists such as Sullivan, Kohut and others—questions like: How does a person come to experience and visualize himself the way he does? How does self-regard develop, and how is it maintained? Over the subsequent history of psychoanalytic ideas, the problem of narcissism—the development and maintenance of self-image and self-esteem—has become a common realm into which all psychoanalytic theories, classical, ego-psychological, interpersonal and object-relational have forayed. Although narcissism is often discussed in connection with more severe characterological disturbances, conceptualizations of, and technical recommendation for, narcissistic phenomena have had an enormous influence on clinical practice across all diagnostic groupings.

Illusion as Defense

In unveiling narcissism as a powerful undercurrent within human experience, Freud pointed to the similarities among: the megalomania of the schizophrenic, the magical thinking of "primitive" (non-western peoples), the blinding infatuation of the lover, and the "childish," doting adulation of parents towards their offspring. The common element in these states, Freud argued, is "overvaluation"—whatever is being considered, whether in oneself or in another, is inflated in importance, its powers exaggerated, its unique perfections extolled. Thus, narcissism entails the attribution of illusory value. Freud's (1914) metaphor of the amoeba and its oscillatory protoplasm, now extending outwards into the world, now retreating back into the central body, highlights the reciprocal relationship Freud saw between engagement with reality (and other people) and narcissistic illusions. For Freud, narcissistic illusions (even when they are transferred through idealization onto love objects), ultimately draw one away from involvements with others and the gratifications they provide.

Although an explorer of the darkest, most irrational dimensions of human experience, Freud was a supreme rationalist in his sense of social, moral and scientific values. Rationality, fueled by sublimation, represents the highest and most felicitous development of the human mind. The discontents we suffer in civilization are the necessary price of its uplifting advantages. Unless impeded by neurosis, developmental progress is characterized by a movement from primary process to secondary process, from the pleasure principle to the reality principle. Psychoanalysis as a treatment facilitates this process whereby the irrational and fantastic are brought under the sway of the rational and the real—"where id was, ego shall be." In this larger context, Freud regarded narcissistic illusions as the inevitable residue of the most primitive and infantile state of mind, and therefore, as both unavoidable and dangerous. Precisely because narcissism, by definition, entails illusory overvaluation, it runs counter to reality, and beckons as an ever-tempting defensive retreat. In Freud's view, withdrawal from reality is always perilous, the ultimate threat being the total loss of connection with the real world (the schizophrenic state) and the less devastating threat posed by the vulnerable loss of self suffered by the unrequited lover, whose narcissism is transferred to the beloved and never returned.

Freud's stress on the defensive function of illusions has been largely maintained in what one might consider the mainstream of contemporary Freudian thought, although exactly what is being defended against varies in different accounts, depending on the larger set of theoretical premises which shape that account.

Kernberg (1975) combines the traditional approach to narcissism as a defense with concepts borrowed from Melanie Klein's vision of the mental life of the child. For Kernberg, pathological narcissism is the outcome of a particular primitive defensive operation, a fusion of ideal self, ideal object, and actual self images, serving as a defense against pathologically augmented oral aggression. In Kernberg's account, the infant is overloaded with primitive aggressive impulses. He experiences himself and, projectively, other people as well, as essentially sadistic, and this aggressive outlook dominates his early experience. Sticking close to Klein's account of "envy" (1957), Kernberg portrays the narcissistically-prone infant as so frustrated and hateful as to be unable to tolerate hope, the possibility of anyone offering him anything pleasurable or sustaining. So little is forthcoming, the child concludes, and with such ill-will toward him, it is better to expect nothing, to want nothing, to spoil and devalue everything that might be offered. So, a "grandiose self" is established—complete, perfect, and self-sustaining. This position serves as both an expression of and a defense against the explosive oral aggression, and the only secure resolution in a world experienced as treacherous and sinister. The maintenance of the grandiose self becomes the central psychodynamic motive, resulting in a contemptuous character style and a disdainful manner of relating to others.

Primitive idealization of others is also characteristic of personalities organized around a grandiose self, according to Kernberg, but the idealization has little to do with any real valuing of others. Rather, Kernberg's narcissistic patient projects his own grandiose self image onto others when it becomes impossible to sustain within himself, and also uses idealization as a secondary defense, along with splitting, to ward off and conceal the hateful and contemptuous devaluation of others.

In this account, narcissistic illusions have a perniciously sabotaging effect on psychoanalytic treatment. Based on the illusions of self-sufficiency and perfection of the gradiose self, they undercut the very basis on which the psychoanalytic process rests, the presumption that the analysand might gain something meaningful from someone else (in this case the analyst). Despite what might be considerable psychological suffering and a genuine interest in treatment, the analysand whose character is organized around a grandiose self cannot allow the analyst to become important enough to him to really help him. The analyst and his interpretations must be continually devalued, spoiled, to avoid catapulting the patient into a condition of overpowering longing, abject dependency and intolerable hatred and envy.

In terms of technique, Kernberg argues that transferential illusions concerning either the self or the analyst must be interpreted quickly and vigorously, their unreality pointed out, their defensive purpose defined. Anything less represents a failure to deal with the subversive impact of narcissistic illusions on the analytic process itself, and seriously obstructs the possibility for any beneficial effects of the analytic treatment. This traditional emphasis on aggressive interpretation of narcissistic phenomena derives in part from the original view of "narcissistic neurosis" as unanalyzable, and narcissistic defenses as generating the most recalcitrant resistances to the analytic process (see, for example, Abraham, 1919).

Rothstein (1984) has presented a rich amalgam of dynamic formulations which he portrays as an "evolutionary" extension of Freud's structural model (from which he has deleted virtually all energic considerations). The result is a psychodynamic account which stresses conflict among various relational motives, and puts a particular stress on the importance of the actual relationship to significant others. The most pervasive influence on Rothstein's perspective, particularly with regard to more severe disorders, is Mahler's depiction of the process of separation-individuation from an original symbiotic matrix. Hence, Rothstein's approach to narcissism is a blend of Freud's original formulations and Mahler's more contemporary view of the child's struggle for relational autonomy.

Rothstein distinguishes Freud's phenomenological portrayal of narcissism as a "felt quality of perfection" from his metapsychological treatment of narcissism (as the libidinal cathexis of the ego). Rothstein adds symbiosis to Freud's account of primary narcissism and sees narcissistic illusions as based developmentally on pre-individuated experiences of a perfect self fused with a perfect object. The loss of this original state of perfection is a severe narcissistic blow, an inevitable developmental insult which is traversed only by reinstating the lost narcissistic perfection in the ego ideal. By identifying with the narcissistically tinged images of the ego ideal, the child softens the otherwise unbearable pain of separation. "Narcissistic invested identification is the sole condition under which the id can give up its objects and is a fundamental concommittent of primary separation individuation. The pursuit of narcissistic perfection in one form or another is a defensive distortion that is a ubiquitous characteristic of the ego" (1984, p. 99). Thus, like Freud, Rothstein sees some residues of primary narcissism as inevitable, reestablished in the ego ideal. For Rothstein, with his Mahlerian perspective, the loss of infantile narcissism has an additional bite, since it represents not just the loss of grandeur and perfection, but the loss of the original symbiotic state. Accordingly, narcissistic illusions operate as defensive retreats not only from disappointments in reality in general, but also from anxiety and dreads connected with separation. For Rothstein, "narcissistic perfection is a defensive distortion of reality" (1984, p. 98). Like all defenses within the ego psychological model, narcissism itself is neither healthy nor pathological; some defenses are necessary, and serve adaptive functions within the psychic economy. Therefore, although a total relinquishment of narcissistic illusions is impossible, it is the goal of analysis, in Rothstein's view, to identify and work through the salient narcissistic investments.

Although proceeding from a very different set of basic assumptions concerning the motivational and structural underpinings of emotional life, the major theorists within the interpersonal tradition have taken an approach to the phenomenon of illusions, the clinical implications of which, surprisingly, are often quite similar to the mainstream orthodox approach from Freud to Kernberg to Rothstein. Sullivan sees idealization as a dangerous, self-depleting security operation, and stresses the "cost" to the patient of "thinking the doctor is wonderful" (White,

1952, pp. 134–135). He recommends challenging the patient's assumptions that the analyst is so different from other people, often a product of inexperience in taking risks with others, and sees extended periods of idealizations as reflecting a kind of countertransference acting out. "The effective restriction of idealization is dependent on the physician's own freedom from personality warp" (1972, p. 343). Similarly, Sullivan regards grandiosity as a dynamic for covering over feelings of insecurity through "invidious comparison" between oneself and others.

> The hostile performance is in essence an accelerating spiral of desperate attempts to prop up a steadily undermined security with the result that the patient is more and more detested and avoided . . . If the patient will be alert to how small he feels with anybody who seems to be at all contented or successful in any respect, then he may not have need for this hateful superiority—which is hateful in part because he hates himself so much, being unable to be what he claims to be (quoted in White, 1952, pp. 138–139).

Although he does not develop an explicit technical procedure for the handling of illusions, one gets the clear message throughout Sullivan's writings that the analyst is in no way being helpful by failing to address the patient's overvaluation of either himself or the analyst. Both kinds of illusions are seen as propping up a shakey sense of self-esteem and operating as an obstacle to the development of the analysand's own resources and self-respect.

Fromm takes an even dimmer view of the place of illusion within emotional life. Fromm sees psychodynamics within the general context of certain inescapable realities of the human condition, among which are finitude and separateness. Two general kinds of responses are possible to this condition, progressive, productive responses which accept the existential realities and create meaningful ties to others, and regressive, destructive responses, based on a self-deluding denial of the realities of the human condition. Overvaluing illusions concerning self or others from whom one derives some compensatory reassurance are regressive self-deceptions within Fromm's perspective and must be dealt with as such. "For the narcissistic person, the partner is never a person in his own right or in his full reality; he exists only as a shadow of the partner's narcissistically inflated ego" (1964, p. 107). In fact, at several points Fromm accuses Sullivan, in his emphasis on protecting the analysand's need for security, of being, in effect, soft on illusions (1955, p. 30; 1970, p. 31). Since in Fromm's view, ". . . intense narcissism implies an inability to experience reality in its fullness" (1964, p. 82ftn), anything short of a continual interpretive challenge of the analysand's overvaluing illusions concerning both himself and the analyst would be an expression of counter-transferential contempt on the analyst's part, a disrespectful collusion in the analysand's flight from reality and meaning.

Thus, although deriving from very different psychodynamic traditions and assumptions, the major lines of theorizing within orthodox theory, Freudian ego psychology, and interpersonal theory all converge in an essentially similar technical approach to the clinical phenomenon of narcissistic illusions. The latter are viewed as regressive defenses against: frustration, separation, aggression, dependence, and/or despair. Transferential illusions concerning either the self or the analyst must be interpreted, their unreality pointed out, their defensive purpose defined. The technical confluence of approaching illusion as defense in Sullivan and Fromm with drive model derived approaches is interesting because, as we shall see below, the larger framework of interpersonal psychoanalysis can also generate an approach with a different sort of clinical emphasis, which is capable of being integrated with other relational model theorists.

Illusion as Growth

In recent years, there has emerged an alternative view of infantile mental states and the narcissistic illusions which are thought to derive from them. The most important contributors to this very different perspective have been Winnicott and Kohut who, each in his own distinct fashion, regard infantile narcissism and subsequent narcissistic illusions in later life as the core of the self and the deepest source of creativity. Here the prototypical "narcissist" is not the child, madman or savage, but the creative artist, drawing on overvaluing illusions for inspiration.

Although he did not often write about "narcissism" per se, Winnicott's entire opus revolves around the issue which we have seen is central to that domain: the relationship between illusion and reality, between the self and the outside world. For Winnicott, the key process in early development is the establishment of a sense of the self experienced as real. Winnicott portrays the infant as becoming aware of spontaneously arising needs. The key feature of the necessary "facilitating" environment provided by the mother is her efforts to shape the environment around the child's wishes, to intuit what the child wants and provide it. The infant's experience is one of scarcely missing a beat between desire and satisfaction, between the wish for the breast and its appearance, for example. The infant naturally assumes that his wishes produced the object of desire, that the breast, his blanket, in effect his entire world, is the product of his creation. The mother's provision and perfect accommodation to the infant's wish creates what Winnicott terms the "moment of illusion." Thus, in the earliest months of life, Winnicott's "good enough mother" is invisible, and it is precisely her invisibility which allows the infant the crucial megalomaniacal, solipsistic experience which Winnicott characterizes as the state of "subjective omnipotence." In his view, a relatively prolonged experience of subjective omnipotence is the foundation upon which a healthy self develops.

Winnicott's vision of health (which is equated with the capacity for play), entails a freedom to move back and forth between the harsh light of objective reality to the soothing ambiguities of lofty self-absorption and grandeur in subjective ommipotence. In fact, Winnicott regards the reimmersion into subjective omnipotence as the ground of creativity, in which one totally disregards external reality and develops one's illusions to the fullest. This view of the development of the self led Winnicott to redefine both the analytic situation and the analytic process. Whereas Freud saw the analytic situation in terms of absti-nence (instinctual wishes emerge and find no gratification), Winnicott sees the analytic situation in terms of satisfaction, not of instinctual impulses per se, but of crucial developmental experiences, missed parental functions. The couch, the constancy of the sessions, the demeanor of the analyst—these become the "holding environment" which was not provided in infancy. Freud saw the analytic process in terms of renunciation; by bringing to light and renouncing infantile wishes, healthier and more mature forms of libidinal organization become possible. Winnicott sees the analytic process in terms of a kind of revitalization; the frozen, aborted self is able to reawaken and begin to develop as crucial ego needs are met.

Although Winnicott doesn't apply this model of treatment to the problem of narcissistic illusions per se, its implications are clear. The patient's self has been fractured and crushed by maternal impingement, creating the necessity for a premature adaptation to external reality and a disconnection from one's own subjective reality, the core of the self and the source of all potential creativity. The analyst's task is to fan the embers, to rekindle the spark. He must create an atmosphere as recep-tive as possible to the patient's subjectivity; he must avoid challenging the patient in any way which could be experienced as an impingement, an insistence once again on compliance with respect to external reality. Therefore, narcissistic illusions, in Winnicott's model, are neither defenses nor obstructions. The patient's illusions concerning both himself and the analyst represent the growing edge of the patient's aborted self; as good-enough-mothering entails an accommodation of the world to sustain the infant's illusion, good-enough-analysis entails an accommodation of the analytic situation to the patient's subjective reality, a "going to meet and match the moment of hope" (1945, p. 309).

The more explicit technical implications of this new understanding of the meaning of narcissistic illusions were developed by Kohut. In Kohut's account, the appearance of narcissistic illusions within the analytic situation—primitive grandiosity or idealization—represent the patient's attempt to establish crucial developmental opportunities, a selfobject relationship which was not available in childhood. These phenomena represent not a defensive retreat from reality, but the growing edge of an aborted developmental process which was stalled because of parental failure to allow the child sustained experiences of illusions of grandeur and idealization. Thus, the appearance of narcissistic illusions within the analytic relationship constitutes a fragile opportunity for the revitalization of the self. They must be cultivated, warmly received, and certainly not challenged, allowing a reanimation of the normal developmental process through which the illusions will eventually be transformed, by virtue of simple exposure to reality, in an emotionally sustaining environment, into more realistic images of self and other. Kohut sees the dangers of interference, analogous to Winnicott's notion of "impingement" as very great indeed, and warns against even "slight over-objectivity of the analyst's attitude or a coolness in the analyst's voice; or . . . a tendency to be jocular with the admiring patient or to disparage the narcissistic idealization in a humorous, kindly way" (1971, p. 263). Anything short of a warm acceptance of narcissistic illusions concerning both the self and the analyst runs the risk of closing off the delicate, pristine narcissistic longings and thereby eliminating the possibility of the reemergence of healthy self-development.

There is a striking symmetry between these two approaches to narcissistic illusions; from the point of view of each, the approach of the other borders on the lunatic. From Kohut's point of view, the kind of methodical interpretive approach to narcissistic transferences recommended by Kernberg is extremely counterproductive, suggesting a countertransferential acting out, involving a difficulty in tolerating the position in which the narcissistic transferences place the analyst, arousing anxiety concerning his own grandiosity (in the idealizing transference) or envy of the patient's grandiosity (in the mirroring transference). Thus, Atwood and Stolorow (1984) feel that the oral rage Kernberg sees in "borderline" patients is actually an iatrogenic consequence of his technical approach. Methodical interpretation of the transference is experienced by the narcissistically vulnerable patient as an assault, and generates intense narcissistic rage, which Kernberg then regards as basic and long-standing, requiring the very procedures which have created it in the first place. From the vantage point of selfpsychology, Kernberg is continually creating the monster he is perpetually slaying.

Similarly, from the more traditional point of view (both in terms of drive theory and interpersonal theory), the Winnicott/Kohut approach is an exercise in futility. An unquestioning acceptance of the patient's illusions with the assumption that they will eventually diminish of their own accord represents a collusion with the patient's defenses; the analytic process is thereby subverted, and the analyst never emerges as a figure who can meaningfully help the patient in any real way. From the traditional vantage point, the Winnicott/Kohut approach suggests what Loewald (1973) has termed a countertransferential "over-identification with the patient's narcissistic needs" (p. 346). Loewald further suggests that Kohut's avoidance of any focus on "an affirmation of the positive and enriching aspects of limitations" of self and others constitutes a "subtle kind of seduction of the patient" (p. 349). As Kernberg notes, unresolved narcissistic conflicts in the analyst "may foster excessive acceptance as well as rejection of the patient's idealization . . . to accept the admiration seems to be an abandonment of a neutral position" (1975, p. 298).

Illusion as defense; illusion as the growing edge of the self—these two approaches are closely linked to the larger divergent perspectives Greenberg and I (1983) have termed the drive paradigm and the relational paradigm respectively. They have generated an exciting controversy within the analytic literature, partially because they are dramatically contrasting and mutually exclusive, which is often the case with competing psychoanalytic theories, in their polarized swings of the pendulum back and forth. Thus, theories generated out of the relational model (like Winnicott's and Kohut's) often underemphasize precisely those aspects of human experience that seem to have been overemphasized in the drive model. This controversy also demonstrates dramatically the extent to which concepts like neutrality, countertransference and empathy are theory-bound. It is a mistake to regard one of these approaches as more "empathic" than the other. They simply proceed (empathically) from different assumptions about what is going on. Empathy and countertransference are clearly in the eye of the beholder!

I strongly suspect that the majority of analysts work in neither of these two sharply contrasting ways, that most of us struggle to find some mid-point, undoubtedly reflective of our own personality and style, between challenging and accepting narcissistic illusions. Because subtlety and tone are crucial here, it is difficult to formulate such an approach in simple, schematic terms. The following model is offered as a framework for locating such an approach conceptually and in terms of technique. I consider the perspective I am about to describe as based on what I would call a synthetic, relational model, combining Sullivan's emphasis on what actually goes on between people, past and present, with Fairbairn's elucidation of the residues of interpersonal relations in ties to "bad" objects. Models are containers of clinical ideas. While the containers themselves generally cannot be meaningfully mixed, since their basic assumptions are mutually exclusive, it is often possible to place some of the content, the clinical and technical insights, from one container into another. The traditional approach to narcissism highlights the important ways in which narcissistic illusions are used defensively, but misses their role in health and creativity and in consolidating certain kinds of developmentally crucial relationships with others. The Winnicott/Kohut approach has generated a perspective on narcissism which stresses the growth-enhancing function of narcissistic illusion, but overlooks the extent to which they often constrict and interfere in real engagements between the analysand and other people, including the analyst. It is possible to draw upon the clinical wisdom in both these contributions by viewing narcissistic illusions in the context of their role in perpetuating stereotyped patterns of integrating relationships with others (Sullivan) and in maintaining ties to early objects (Fairbairn).

A Synthetic Approach

All varieties of narcissistic illusions are generated throughout the life cycle: grand estimations of one's own capacities and perfection, an infatuation with the larger-than-life qualities of others whom one loves and/or envies, and fusion fantasies of an exquisite, perfect merger with desirable or dreaded others. The determination of emotional health vs. psychopathology, when it comes to narcissistic illusions, seems to have less to do with the actual content of the illusions, and more to do with the attitude of the person about that content. Thus, all of us probably experience at various times feelings and thoughts just as self-enobling as the most grandiose narcissist, just as devoted as the most star-struck idealizer, just as fused as the most boundaryless symbiosis-seeker. The problem of narcissism concerns issues of character structure, not mental content. It is not so much what you do and think that is the problem but your attitude toward what you do and think, how seriously you take yourself. How can this subtle issue of attitude be conceptualized?

Consider Nietzsche's theory of tragedy. Life is lived on two fundamental dimensions, Nietzsche suggests. On the one hand, we live in a world of illusions, continually generating transient forms and meanings with which we play and quickly discard. This facet of living Nietzsche terms the Apollonian, Apollo being the god of the dream, of art and illusion. On the other hand, we are embedded in a larger unity, a universal pool of energy from which we emerge temporarily, articulate ourselves, and into which we once again disappear. This facet of living Nietzsche terms the Dionysian, Dionyses representing re-immersion into this larger unity and, in Nietzsche's system, standing for the inevitable undoing of all illusions, all individual existence. Nietzsche establishes "the tragic" as the fullest, richest model of living, and the truly tragic represents a balance between the Apollonian and Dionysian dimensions. The tragic man (this must be disentangled from all pejorative connotations of this word) is one who is able to fully pursue his Apollonian illusions and also is able to relinquish them in the face of the inevitable realities of the human condition. The tragic man regards his life as a work of art, to be conceived, shaped, polished and inevitably dissolved. The prototypical tragic activity is play, in which new forms are continually created and demolished, in which the individuality of the player is continually articulated, developed and relinquished.

Picture the beach at low tide, endless sand offering itself as material for creation. Three different approaches are possible. The fully Apollonian man builds elaborate sandcastles, throwing himself into his activity as if his creations would last forever, totally oblivious of the coming tide which will demolish his productions. Here is someone who ignores reality and is therefore continually surprised, battered and bruised by it. The fully Dionysian man sees the inevitability of the leveling tide, and therefore builds no castles. His constant preoccupation with the ephemeral nature of his life and his creations allows him no psychic space to live and play. He will only build if his productions are assured of immortality, but unlike the Apollonian man, he suffers no delusions in this regard. Here is someone tyrannized and depleted by reality. The third option is Nietzsche's tragic man, aware of the tide and the transitory nature of his productions, yet building his sandcastles nevertheless. The inevitable limitations of reality do not dim the passion in which he builds his castles; in fact, the inexorable realities add a poignancy and sweetness to his passion. The tragicomic play in which our third man builds, Nietzsche suggests, is the richest form of life, generating the deepest meaning from the dialectical interplay between illusion and reality.

Nietzsche's model provides a useful framework for conceptualizing some of the clinical issues concerning narcissism. Healthy narcissism reflects the same subtle dialectical balance between illusion and reality; illusions concerning oneself and others are generated, playfully enjoyed and relinquished in the face of disappointments. New illusions are continually created and dissolved. Pathological narcissism represents what we might regard as an Apollonian fixation—illusions are taken too seriously, insisted upon. In some narcissistic disturbances, narcissistic illusions are actively and consciously maintained; reality is sacrificed in order to perpetuate an addictive devotion to self-enobling, idealizing, or symbiotic fictions. This is the approach of the first man on the beach, blindly building away. In some narcissistic disturbances, narcissistic illusions are harbored secretly or repressed; the preoccupation with the limitations and risks of reality lead to an absence of joyfulness or liveliness —even a paralysis. Any activity is threatening, because it inevitably encounters limitations, and these are felt to be unacceptable. This is the approach of the second man on the beach, holding out for immortality and waiting for the tide in despair.

What is the etiology of such disturbances? What determines whether one will be able to negotiate the delicate balance between illusions and reality in healthy narcissism or whether one will suffer an addictive devotion to illusions resulting in either a removal from reality or a despair in the face of it? The key factor resides in the interplay between illusions and reality in the character-forming relationships with significant others. The development of the balance necessary for healthy narcissism requires a particular sort of relationship with a parent, in which the parent is able to comfortably experience both the child and himself in both modes, in playful illusions of grandiosity, idealization and fusion, and in deflating disappointments and realistic limitations. The child naturally generates lofty self-overvaluations, glowing overvaluations of the parent, and boundaryless experiences of sameness and fusion. The ideal parental response to these experiences consists of a participation coupled with the capacity to disengage, a capacity to enjoy and play with the child's illusions, to add illusions of his or her own, and to let the illusions go, experiencing the child and himself in more realistic terms. Thus, the parent participates with the child in requisite experiences characterized by shifting idealization and aggrandizements, now the child is elevated, now the parent, now both together.

Consider the position of the child in relation to a parent who, in one way or another, takes these kinds of illusions extremely seriously, whose own sense of security in fact is contingent upon them. Such a parent insists on specific overvaluations of the child or himself or both. These illusions have become addictive for the parent, and they become a dominant feature in the possibilities for relatedness which such a parent offers the child. The more addictive are the illusions for the parent, the more unavoidable they become for the child, who feels that the only way to connect with the parent, to be engaged with him, is to participate in his illusions. Such a child must regard himself as perfect and extraordinary and be seen by the parent that way, to be seen at all; or, he must worship the parent as perfect and extraordinary to become real and important to the parent. Further, children tend to pick up how crucial such illusions are for the parent's shaky sense of self-esteem. Helene Deutsch (1937) noted long ago the role of parental "induction" in cases of "folie a deux," where the adoption by the child of the parent's delusion represents "an important part of an attempt to rescue the object through identification with it, with its delusional system" (p. 247).

In such circumstances, sustaining parental illusions becomes the basis for stability and maintaining connections with others, the vehicle for what Fairbairn terms the "tie to bad objects," or what Robbins (1982) has more recently termed "pathological efforts at symbiotic bonding." Here illusion is no longer the spontaneously generated, transitory, playful creation of an active mind. Illusions are insisted upon with utmost seriousness by significant others, and they become the necessary price for contact and relation. Ogden (1982) writes of

> . . . the pressure on an infant to behave in a manner congruent with the mother's pathology, and the ever-present threat that if the infant fails to comply, he would cease to exist for the mother. This threat is the muscle behind the demand for compliance: "If you are not what I need you to be, you don't exist for me." Or in other language, "I can see in you only what I put there. If I don't see that, I see nothing" (p. 16).

This is true not just for the infant, but throughout childhood and later into adulthood. Every analyst is familiar with the dread adult patients frequently feel in connection with major characterological change; they anticipate a profound sense of isolation from parents (alive or dead), who related to them, seemed to need so much to relate to them, only through their now loosened and about to be transcended character pathology (see Searles, 1958).

Thus, addictive parental illusions generate learned modes of contact in the child who will come to develop narcissistic difficulties, modes of contact which are felt to be the only alternative to the impossible option of no contact at all. The more addictive the illusion for the parent, the more unable the parent to experience the child in any other way, the more brittle is the child's personality, precariously anchored around those same illusions. If the parent is not able to play at illusion-building and relinquishment, to offer a full and variegated emotional presence to the child, the latter participates in what is provided, and these forms of participation become the learned basis for all future interpersonal relations.

The mythological figure of Icarus vividly captures this powerful relationship between the child and the parent's illusions. Daedalus, the builder of the Labyrinth, constructs wings of feathers and wax, so he and his son Icarus can escape their island prison. The use of such wings requires a true sense of Nietzsche's dialectical balance; flying too high risks a melting of the wings by the sun; flying too low risks a weighing down of the wings from the dampness of the ocean. Icarus does not heed the warning he receives. He flies too close to the sun; his wings melt, and he plunges into the ocean, disappearing beneath a clump of floating feathers.

All of us have been born of imperfect parents, with favorite illusions concerning themselves and their progeny buoying their self-esteem, cherished along a continuum ending with compulsive addictiveness. We have all come to know ourselves through participation with parental illusions, which have become our own. Like Icarus, therefore, we have all donned Daedalus's wings. It is the subtleties of parental involvement with these illusions which greatly influences the nature of the flight provided by those wings, whether one can fly high enough to enjoy them and truly soar, or whether the sense of ponderous necessity concerning the illusions leads one to fly too high or to never leave the ground.

In both prior approaches to narcissism, pathological grandiosity and pathological idealization are understood as operating within the internal psychic economy of the individual. They are viewed largely as internally generated phenomena, either as defensive solutions to anxiety, frustration and envy, or as spontaneously arising, pristine, early developmental needs. Kohut's approach suffers from this constraint just as much as the more traditional approach. Illusion is treated not as a normal product of mental activity throughout the life cycle, but located within the earliest developmental phases. And illusions within the psychoanalytic situation are treated as reflective of the early developmental needs, in pure form, rather than as learned modes of connection with others, as the stereotyped and compulsive patterns of integration they have become. Ever since Freud's abandonment of the theory of infantile seduction, the legacy of drive theory on the subsequent history of psychoanalytic ideas has included an underemphasis of the role of actual relationships on the evolution of mental structures and content. With respect to narcissism, both these traditions isolate the figure within the relational tapestry and, in so doing, overlook the extent to which grandiosity and idealization function as relational modes, arising as learned patterns of integrating relationships, and maintained as the vehicle for intimate connections with others. To regard these phenomena solely in terms of individual psychic economy is like working with only half of the pieces of a jig-saw puzzle.

The major theorists I have been considering do not fail to notice this facet of narcissistic phenomena. They are all too astute as clinicians to do so. The problem is that the specifics of parental character and fantasy do not fit into the theoretical model, so they are noticed clinically and then passed over when major etiological dynamics are assigned or technical approaches developed. The subtleties of the parents' personalities, the ways in which they required the child to maintain narcissistic illusions, are lost, as the parents are viewed in a binary fashion, simply either as gratifying or not gratifying infantile needs (drives or relational). Within both traditions, however, there has been movement toward rectifying this problem. From the drive theory side, for example, Rothstein has placed increasing emphasis on the role of the actual relationships in the generation and maintenance of narcissistic illusion, and Michael Robbins (1982) has written of the ways in which narcissistic phenomena operate as shared illusions, "drawing on grandiose fantasies of idealized objects." From the (self psychology) relational model side, there has been recent discussion of the parents, not simply in terms of their failure to provide self-object functions for the child, but also in terms of their use of the child as a self-object.

Clinical Implications

Models attempting to illuminate the meaning and function of narcissistic phenomena necessarily imply a clinical posture by the analyst which best facilitates their resolution; therefore, theories of narcissism tend to appear together with a recommended technical approach. I have suggested that narcissistic illusions are usefully understood neither solely as a defensive solution for an internal psychic economy, nor solely as a pure efflorescence of infantile mental life, but most fundamentally as a form of participation with others. From this perspective, the main function of grandiosity and idealization in the analytic situation is as a gambit, an invitation to a particular form of interaction.

Viewing narcissistic illusions as invitations casts the analyst's response in a different sort of perspective. The patient requires some participation from the analyst to complete the old object tie, to connect with the analyst in a consciously or unconsciously desired fashion. If grandiosity is involved, some expression of admiration or appreciation may be requested, or at least an attentive noninterference; if idealization is involved, some expression of pleasure at being adored may be requested, or at least an acknowledgement of the patient's devotion. Often, a participation in a mutually admiring relationship is requested—both the analyst and analysand are to be considered truly distinguished and special, and alike in some unusual fashion. Responding to such an invitation in a way that is analytically constructive is a tricky business, not able to be captured in a simple formula. Often what is most crucial is not so much the words, but the tone in which they are spoken. The most useful response entails a subtle dialectic between joining the patient in the narcissistic integration and also simultaneously questioning the nature and purpose of that integration, both a playful participation in the patient's illusions and a puzzled curiosity about how and why they came to be the sine qua non of the analysand's sense of security and involvements with others.

It is easiest to define the sort of analytic posture I have in mind by locating it between the kinds of recommended positions which have accompanied the major theoretical traditions. On the one hand, an aggressively interpretive approach misses the need of the analysand to establish the narcissistic integration and runs the risk of discouraging the gambit and driving the transference underground. Grandiosity and idealization interpreted as defenses against anxiety, aggression, and separation are not appreciated as efforts to reach the object through familiar patterns, preferred modes of connection and intimacy. Thus, in Kernberg's discussion of these issues, narcissistic configurations are understood as defenses against anxieties generated by oral aggression within early object relations, rather than as expressions of these object relations as entrenched familial patterns throughout childhood. The danger here is of encouraging resistances to the expression and establishment of these key transferential configurations and compliance with what can only be experienced as the analyst's insistence on less narcissistic, more "real" perceptions and relations.

On the other hand, a receptive, unquestioning approach misses the function of the narcissistic integrations in perpetuating old object ties, and runs the risk of consolidating them. Stolorow and Atwood, drawing on the self-psychology tradition, regard these narcissistic illusions as the product of the patient's effort "to establish in the analytic transference the requisite facilitating intersubjective context that had been absent or insufficient during the formative years and that now permitted the arrested developmental process to resume" (1984, p. 83). Here narcissistic illusions are simply reflected and encouraged, as a device for remobilizing a stalled developmental process, and presumed to dissolve of their own accord in the face of reality and the analyst's empathic understanding of the patient's naturally arising disappointments. The danger of not appreciating illusions as vehicles for preserving entrenched familial patterns is of encouraging resistances to the resolution of these transferential configurations, and what can only be experienced as the analyst's own investment in and encouragement of compulsive narcissistic illusions.

Why can't the analyst simply remain "neutral," neither demanding change nor encouraging perpetuation, but simply silent or descriptively interpretive? If one is invited to a dance, one either attends in some fashion, or does not attend in some fashion. Remaining silent, refusing to respond, constitute responses, and are experienced by the analysand as responses. It is striking in this regard that Kohut and Kernberg consider their own approaches to be neutral, and that of the other to be a departure from neutrality. In my view, each is right about the other, but misses the extent to which his own posture is a form of participation and is inevitably experienced by the analysand in that way.

The most constructive form of participation steers through the narrow passage between the contrasting dangers of complicity and challenge, reflecting a willingness to play, an acceptance of the importance of the narcissistic integration as a special and favored mode of relation, yet also a questioning as to why it must be this and only this way. This posture is similar to the kind of ideal parental response to the child's illusions described above. The parent is receptive to the child's illusions about himself and the parent, but with a light touch, conveying a sense of pleasure without the pressure of necessity. The analyst's response to the analysand's transferential gambits should reflect that same openness to playful participation. Although it is useful to view such an analytic posture in connection with parent–child interactions, it does not entail an infantilization of the analysand. An ability to play together, including a participation in each other's illusions, is a crucial dimension not only of adult–child relationships, but of adult–adult relations as well.

In the specifically analytic relationship, the analyst's response to the analysand's narcissistic integrations is necessarily accompanied by curiosity, and a pursuit of the analytic inquiry into the meaning of the integrations. Where did the analysand learn this particular pattern of relatedness? What was riding on these illusory notions within the analysand's early significant relations with others? What were its pleasures? Its costs? The latter question is particularly important.

Analysands who integrate relations with others around grandiose claims tend to believe passionately that this is the best sort of relationship to have. They seek out admirers and discard those who don't admire them as uninteresting. (Patients who harbor secret grandiose claims believe just as passionately that being the object of devoted admiration is the acme of interpersonal satisfaction, but fear they will never be successful in attaining this goal.) The analytic inquiry into these phenomena necessarily opens up important questions. How did this asymmetrical form of relatedness become so highly treasured? One frequently discovers that it was the vehicle for the closest bonds within the family, or shared familial fantasies about how closer bonds might be achieved. Does the analysand assume that the passion of parental investments in overvaluing him is the most intense sort of connection he can hope for with others? The analysand is generally unaware of what is lost in such asymmetry, that relationships structured around another's admiration of and devotion to him precludes his excitement about and enjoyment of them, his opportunity to take pleasure in them not simply as reflectors of his own glory, but as different, interesting and admirable in their own right.

It is important that the analytic inquiry into grandiose illusions and relationships and what the patient believes, notices and doesn't notice about them, avoid a moralistic tone. Relationships structured around grandiosity are problematic because they truncate the analysand's experience, not because they are unfair or unseemly. The focus should be on what is gained and what is missing in these relationships, and the analysand's limited awareness of both. The analyst's capacity to constructively explore these issues with the analysand is contingent upon an appreciation of this central point. The danger is of the analyst secretly or unconsciously believing that entitlement and grandiose claims are in fact a precious and preferred way of life. This leads either to a more or less subtly conveyed insistence that the patient renounce his claims, motivated by the analyst's envy ("If I can't have this, you certainly can't.") or a vicarious enjoyment in allowing the analysand an envied and tabooed pleasure denied to himself ("I'm too 'mature' to indulge myself in this precious entitlement, but I can grant it to you.").

The analyst's over-identification with the analysand's grandiose claims represents a failure to appreciate how much these claims undermine and sour the analysand's involvements with other people and isolate him in a confusing and often paranoid fashion. The analysand may come to feel more and more that only his analyst is really "sensitive" to him. An additional danger in working with this sort of transference is the analyst's own conflictual longings to idealize coming to play a role in his admiration of the analysand, which can lead to either the analyst's own investment in the analysand's grandiosity and a difficulty in allowing him to move past this integration, or anxiety in the face of the analysand's grandiosity and an interference with the unfolding of this narcissistic integration.

Analysands who integrate relations around idealizing others also tend to believe passionately that this is the best sort of relationship to have. Life is seen as extremely complicated and perilous. The easiest and safest strategy for living is to find someone who seems to be very secure and successful, to have all the "answers," and to apprentice oneself to him or her. For the price of considerable devotion, the idealized object will take the disciple under wing, protecting him, leading him, guiding him along the path they have already cut through the obstacles of life. Analysands integrating relationships on this basis are convinced that such an idealized bond is a very precious, very special tie. Sullivan would ask of patients idealizing the analyst, "Can they afford it?" It is precisely the cost of idealization which the analysand doesn't notice.

Feuerbach, the 19th century German philosopher, argued that religion is, necessarily, a form of human self-alienation, that characteristics and powers attributed to "god" within any religion are inevitably a reflection of human resources which the inhabitants of that culture are frightened to own. "God" becomes a screen on which are projected dissociated aspects of the self. Although this is an oversimplified account of religion, idealization in human relations often does reflect this masochistic, projective process. Because of disturbed earlier relationships, there is a terror of individuation and self-development. The analysand fears that finding his own path means isolation, a fear often originating in the context of relationships with parents who demand adoration and deference as the price of involvement. For such an analysand, the only way to insure human contact is to find someone to go first, to remain always in someone's shadow. The presumption is that all others are as brittle and demanding of deference as the parents, as frightened of the analysand's self-development. They fear that to emerge from the parent's/analyst's shadow is to lose the parent/ analyst. Such an analysand generally doesn't appreciate how much mental effort he expends in propping others up, convincing himself that the other is always more advanced along whatever line he himself is pursuing. Despite recurring inevitable disappointments, the analysand doesn't grasp that life is too idiosyncratic for anyone else's solutions to be a helpful shortcut to reaching one's own.

As with the analysis of grandiose illusions, the inquiry into idealizing illusions also must avoid a moralistic tone. The problem with idealization is not that it is childish (as Freud noted), but that it limits possibilities. Analysands who compulsively integrate relationships on an idealizing basis remain perpetual disciples and can never fully allow themselves to experience their own strengths and resources fully. Further, they often secretly harbor the suspicion that the object of their idealization is flawed and brittle, that a close look at the analyst's full humanity would ruin them both. A danger in the analytic exploration of these issues is of the analyst's over-identifying with the analysand's idealizing longings, secretly or unconsciously believing that being under the wing of (or sexually surrendering to) a bigger, more powerful figure is a preferred way of life. This may lead either to a more or less subtly conveyed insistence that the analysand renounce his claims, motivated by the analyst's envy, or a vicarious enjoyment in allowing the analysand an envied and tabooed pleasure denied to oneself. An additional danger is of the analyst enjoying too much being the object of idealization, so that he has trouble releasing the analysand from the narcissistic integration, or of fearing that he will enjoy being the object of idealization so much that he can't allow the analysand this experience.

Analysand's manifesting narcissistic transferences need to either be admired by or to idealize the analyst (sometimes both) at least for a time, in order to feel involved, to feel that something important is happening. The issue of timing is very complex and only determinable within the complexities of each individual case. Bromberg (1983) has described a shifting "empathy-anxiety balance" as the context within which treatment takes place, and argues that for narcissistic patients, the beginning of treatment must be weighted heavily on the side of empathy. "For certain of these individuals more than others, analytic success depends upon being able to participate in an initial period of undefinable length, in which the analysis partially protects them from stark reality which they cannot integrate, while performing its broader function of mediating their transition to a more mature and differentiated level of self and object representation" (p. 378). These analysands are generally extremely sensitive to the manner in which the analyst reacts to their illusions and gambits. The analytic posture I am describing conveys both a willingness to participate as well as a curiosity as to the constrictive limits which this form of participation allows. To return to the metaphor of the dance invitation, I am not proposing going to the dance and constantly grousing about the music, but enjoying the dance offered, together with a questioning of the singularity of the style. How did it come about the analysand learned no other steps? Why does the analysand believe that this is the only desirable dance there is? Most analysands need to feel their own dance style is appreciated in order to be open to expanding their repertoire.

Relational model theorists tend to regard the analytic relationship as really two simultaneous relationships—a neurotic form of integration (Loewald's "old" object; Fairbairn's "bad" object) that dissolves over time, and a healthier form of integration (Loewald's "new" object; Fairbairn's "good" object) that is slowly consolidated. The analyst's participation is essential to the establishment of the narcissistic integration; the analyst's questioning is essential to its dissolution and the establishment of a richer form of relation.

The analyst's descriptions, interpretations and questions all provide the analysand with a form of participation which operates outside of the narcissistic integration. What is provided in this sort of interaction is an opportunity for the analysand not so much to renounce illusions as to experience them in a broader context, not as constrictive limits to his relations with others, but as possible forms of enriching interactions. The analyst's own ease in engaging and disengaging in illusions about himself and others is crucial to this process. One might think of it in terms of the analysand learning and/or internalizing a kind of "love of life," sustaining without illusions yet continually enriched by them.

References

Abraham, K. (1919) A particular form of neurotic resistance against the psychoanalytic method. In: *The Evolution of Psychoanalytic Technique*, ed. Bergmann, M. and Hartmann, F. New York: Basic Books, Inc., 1976.

Atwood, G. and Stolorow, R. (1984) *Structures of Subjectivity: Explorations in Psychoanalytic Phenomenolgy*. Hillsdale, NJ: The Analytic Press.

Bromberg, P. (1983) The mirror and the mask: On narcissism and psychoanalytic growth. *Contemporary Psychoanalysis*, 19:359–387.

Deutsch, H. (1937) Folie à deux. In: *Neuroses and Character Types*. New York: International Universities Press, 1965.

Fairbairn, W. R. D. (1943) Repression and the return of bad objects (with special reference to the "war neuroses". In: *An Object Relations Theory of the Personality*. New York: Basic Books, Inc., 1952.

Freud, S. (1914) On narcissism: An introduction. *Standard Edition*, 14:117–140.

Fromm, E. (1955) *The Sane Society*. Greenwich, CT: Fawcett.

Fromm, E. (1964) *The Heart of Man*. New York: Perennial.

Fromm, E. (1970) *The Crisis in Psychoanalysis*. Greenwich, CT: Fawcett.

Greenberg, J. and Mitchell, S. (1983) *Object Relations in Pscyoanalytic Theory*. Cambridge, MA: Harvard University Press.

Kernberg, O. (1975) *Borderline Conditions and Pathological Narcissism*. New York: Jason Aronson.

Kernberg, O. (1984) *Severe Personality Disorders: Psychotherapeutic Strategies*. New Haven: Yale University Press.

Klein, M. (1957) *Envy and Gratitude*. In: *Envy and Gratitude and Other Works*, 1946–1963. New York: Delacorte Press, 1975.

Kohut, H. (1971) *The Analysis of the Self*. New York: International Universities Press.

Kohut, H. (1977) *The Restoration of the Self*. New York: International Universities Press.

Loewald, H. (1973) Heinz Kohut: *The Analysis of the Self*. In: Papers on Psychoanalysis. New Haven: Yale University Press, 1980.

Nietzsche, F. (1972) The birth of tragedy. In: *The Birth of Tragedy and the Geneology of Morals*. New York: Doubleday Anchor.

Ogden, T. (1982) *Projective Identification and Psychotherapeutic Technique*. New York: Jason Aronson.

Robbins, M. (1982) Narcissistic personality as a symbiotic character disorder. *International Journal of Psycho-Analysis*, 63:457–474.

Rothstein, A. (1984) *The Narcissistic Pursuit of Perfection*. New York: International Universities Press.

Searles, H. (1958) Positive feelings in the relationship between the schizophrenic and his mother. In: *Collected Papers on Schizophrenia and Related Subjects*. New York: International Universities Press.

White, M. (1952) *The Contributions of Harry Stack Sullivan: A Symposium*. New York: Hermitage House.

Winnicott, D. (1945) Primitive emotional development. In: *Through Paediatrics to Psycho-Analysis*. London: Hogarth Press, 1958.

Afterword

As Lewis Aron points out in his introduction to this early paper of mine, it has many features that were to become basic to a kind of conceptual strategy that I employed in a great deal of my subsequent writing. I was interested in exploring the possibility of a synthetic, integrative relational model for thinking psychodynamically. I was exploring what it would be like to think about narcissistic "illusions" as forms of participation with others, both real interpersonal others and in terms of internal object relations. I wanted to find a way of drawing on the clinical wisdom of prior traditions of psychoanalytic theorizing, yet to set those clinical insights into a theoretical context that made sense to me and opened up my own clinical options. A good deal of the writing I have done since then has applied this same methodology to other fundamental areas of human experience (e.g., sexuality [1988] and aggression [1993].) This paper was expanded into chapters 5 and 6 of *Relational Concepts in Psychoanalysis* (1988).

One major aspect of my subsequent thinking that is reflected here (although in some sense it might be considered implicit) is the notion of discontinuity and multiplicity in states of mind and self-organizations. I began writing about multiplicity in 1991, and this theme became elaborated in my next book, *Hope and Dread in Psychoanalysis* (1993). Since that time, there have been many important contributions to this approach to self-experience that have had a considerable influence on my own thinking and clinical practice. Most notable have been the major contributions on varieties of dissociation, both traumatic and therapeutic, by Jody Messler Davies, Philip Bromberg, and Stuart Pizer. If I were writing "The Wings of Icarus" today, I would probably argue that a key factor in whether various narcissistic states such as grandiosity and idealization function constructively or destructively is the relationship between these states and other, discontinuous states and self-organizations. At the time I was writing this paper I had not yet begun to appreciate the extent to which relational thinking was moving us into ways of thinking about self-experience that were quite different from the more linear, singular self inherent in both the defense and developmental models.

Another major development in my thinking and clinical work since this paper was written concerns the impact of current developments in epistemology, feminism, and the philosophy of science, many of them linked closely with the current intellectual climate associated with postmodernism. I've been greatly and gratefully influenced in these areas by my association with colleagues who have made important contributions: Jessica Benjamin, Charles Spezzano, Adrienne Harris, Muriel Dimen, and Virginia Goldner. These themes were explored in chapters 1 & 2 of *Hope and Dread in Psychoanalysis* and especially in chapters 7 & 8 of the more recent *Influence and Autonomy in Psychoanalysis* (1997). If I were writing "The Wings of Icarus" today, I would take up in greater depth the epistemological complexities of concepts like actuality, fantasy, illusion, and so on.

Another major line of theorizing that I have been very caught up with since that time in which I also have been stimulated by the work of others concerns the exploration of the dense complexities of the interactions between analyst and analysand and the interpenetration of their subjective worlds. Here I have been particularly enriched by the work of Irwin Z. Hoffman, Jay Greenberg, Thomas Ogden, and Lewis Aron. If I were writing "The Wings of Icarus" today, I would explore in considerably more detail the joint participation of analysand and analyst in mutually generated experiences of grandiosity and idealization.

It is absolutely astounding for me to reflect on how much has changed in psychoanalytic thought and practice since the mid-80s, when I was working on this essay. In those days, we were struggling to break free of a "classical" metapsychology and technique that many of us experienced as extremely deadening, both for the generation of new ideas and in trying to grasp what is at stake in the clinical process. These days, the conceptual landscape strikes me as much more open and vital, with rich work developing in many different directions. One of my own recent interests involves something of a return to my earlier concerns—the function of idealization, not in narcissism but in romance (Mitchell, 1997).

References

Mitchell, S. (1988), *Relational Concepts in Psychoanalysis*. Cambridge, MA: Harvard University Press.

———— (1991), Contemporary perspectives on self: Toward an integration. *Psychoanal. Dial.*, 1:121–147.

———— (1993), *Hope and Dread in Psychoanalysis*. New York: Basic Books.

———— (1997), *Influence and Autonomy in Psychoanalysis*. Hillsdale, NJ: The Analytic Press.

Recognition and Destruction: An Outline of Intersubjectivity

(1990)

Jessica Benjamin

▼   ▼   ▼   ▼   ▼

Editor's Introduction

No one who takes pleasure in ideas can fail to find the writings of Jessica Benjamin a source of delight, surprise, and reflection. One of the most profound psychoanalytic theoreticians of this generation, she turns concepts upside down and inside out, arranging and rearranging them in relation to each other to expand their possibilities and enrich our experience.

We have chosen this essay from among her many influential writings because in it Benjamin outlines her position on one of the themes that has dominated her work, the problem of how we relate to the fact of the other's independent consciousness. It is in and through the exhaustive and systematic examination of this question that Benjamin has brought together feminist studies and intersubjectivity theory. Thus, her profound contributions both to a feminist psychoanalysis and to psychoanalytic feminism do not result simply from bringing these two movements into dialogue with each other. Rather, Benjamin's unique approach evolved from her creative recognition that these two domains were intricately and necessarily connected in solving the problem of understanding how separate subjects can recognize each other as equivalent centers of experience.

Benjamin's thinking is characterized by her ability to maintain an approach of both/and rather than of either/or. Where we all tend to collapse the tension in an argument toward one side or the other, Benjamin has managed better than most to keep the tension, holding out for a theoretical space that makes room for complexity and paradox. Thus, as seen in this essay, her approach demands that psychoanalysis include the study of both the intrapsychic and the intersubjective. For Benjamin, subjectivity is established through processes of both recognition (affirmation) and destruction (negation), that the child is viewed as moving along a developmental path toward both separation-individuation and connection and mutuality. Never settling for easy resolution of difficult problems, Benjamin draws on her philosophical background in critical theory and insists that simple reversals do not advance our thinking. Instead, only by moving beyond complementarity toward the recognition for both sides of a dialectic can we further the development of our understanding.

In this essay, Benjamin lays out her critique of the traditional developmental assumptions of psychoanalytic ego psychology as they were popularized in Mahler's (and her colleagues) separation-individuation theory. She shows how classical theory took the perspective of the child's movement away from the mother toward separation and individuation rather than highlighting the equally important movement toward mutual recognition and attachment. Benjamin links this bias in the theory to its view of the (m)other as an object instead of as a separate subject. Here is where she links the most penetrating findings of feminism with the most important implications of developmental psychoanalysis, namely, that by defensively objectifying the mother of early infancy—by eliminating feminine subjectivity—we confine ourselves to an intrapsychic world in which we can relate only to objects and hence can establish neither our own subjectivity or the subjectivity of others. Benjamin thus shows the essential need to maintain both intrapsychic theory, with its exploration of our relations to objects, and intersubjectivity theory, in which there may be a meeting of minds.

Benjamin credits Stolorow and his colleagues with introducing the term intersubjectivity into psychoanalytic discourse. Stolorow and collaborators define intersubjectivity as the field of intersection of two subjectivities, but theirs is not a developmental theory and they do not distinguish subject-object relations from intersubjective ones, more narrowly defined. Stolorow is referring essentially to the *mutual regulation* that characterizes all human relationships. In this essay, however, Benjamin distinguishes her version of intersubjectivity theory by emphasizing that she views intersubjectivity as a developmental progression with a series of key moments of transformation. In her model, intersubjectivity is a developmental achievement that entails the only gradually and imperfectly acquired capacity for *mutual recognition*.

Drawing on Hegel's master–slave analogy, Benjamin shows that the need for recognition entails the fundamental paradox that, in the very moment of realizing our own independent will, we are dependent on another to recognize it. She then draws heavily on Winnicott's notions of object relating and object usage to demonstrate the need for both recognition and negation in the establishment of human subjectivity. Benjamin thus succeeds in combining the depth of psychoanalytic developmental observation with contemporary gender studies and feminism to reconstruct the theory and practice of psychoanalysis so that "where objects were, subjects might be."

Benjamin's *The Bonds of Love: Psychoanalysis, Feminism, and the Problem of Domination* (1988, Pantheon) introduced a powerful and influencial approach to the relationship between psychoanalysis and feminism by drawing on Hegel's concept of "recognition" to explore the development of human subjectivity and the themes of domination and submission in the polarities of gender formation. In *Like Subjects, Love Objects: Essays on Recognition and Sexual Difference* (1995, Yale), which includes this early essay, Benjamin further developed an integration of various currents of psychoanalytic developmental theory with her own version of intersubjectivity theory. In her recent *Shadow of the Other: Intersubjectivity and Gender in Psychoanalysis,* (1998, Routledge) Benjamin continues the provocative conversation between critical social theory and intersubjective psychoanalysis by further exploring the paradoxes of gender complementarity and the dialectics of authority in the analytic situation.

Recognition and Destruction:
An Outline of Intersubjectivity

▼　　▼　　▼　　▼　　▼

We are all of us born in moral stupidity, taking the world as an udder to feed our supreme selves: Dorothea had early begun to emerge from that stupidity, but yet it had been easier to her to imagine how she would

Originally published in *Psychoanalytic Psychology*, 7(suppl.):33–47. © 1990 Lawrence Erlbaum Associates, Inc.

> . . . become wise and strong in his strength and wisdom, than to con-
> ceive with that distinctness which is no longer reflection but feeling . . .
> that he had an equivalent center of self, whence the lights and shadows
> must always fall with a certain difference.
>
> George Eliot, *Middlemarch*, p. 243.

In recent years analysts from diverse psychoanalytic schools have converged in the effort to formulate relational theories of the self (Eagle, 1984; Mitchell, 1988). What these approaches share is the belief that the human mind is interactive rather than monadic, that the psychoanalytic process should be understood as occurring between subjects rather than within the individual (Atwood and Stolorow, 1984; Mitchell, 1988). Mental life is seen from an intersubjective perspective. Although this perspective has transformed our theory and our practice in important ways, such transformations create new problems. A theory in which the individual subject no longer reigns absolute must confront the difficulty that each subject has in recognizing the other as an equivalent center of experience (Benjamin, 1988).

The problem of recognizing the other emerges the moment we consider that troublesome legacy of intrapsychic theory, the term "object." In the original usage, still common in self psychology and object relations theories, the concept of object relations refers to the psychic internalization and representation of interactions between self and objects. While such theories ascribe a considerable role to the early environment and parental objects—"real" others—they have taken us only to the point of recognizing that "where ego is, objects must be." For example, neither Fairbairn's insistence on the need for the whole object nor Kohut's declaration that selfobjects remain important throughout life addresses directly the difference between object and other. Perhaps the elision between "real" others and their internal representation is so widely tolerated because the epistemological question of what is reality and what is representation appears to us, in our justifiable humility, too ecumenical and lofty for our parochial craft. Or perhaps, because we are psychoanalysts, the question of reality does not really trouble us.

But the unfortunate tendency to collapse other subjects into objects cannot simply be ascribed to this irresoluteness with regard to reality. Nor can it be dismissed as a terminological embarrassment that could be dissolved by greater linguistic precision (see Kohut, 1984). It is instead a symptom of the very problems in psychoanalysis that a relational theory should aim to cure. An inquiry into the intersubjective dimension of the analytic encounter would aim to change our theory and practice so that "where objects were, subjects must be."

What does such a change mean? A beginning has been made with the introduction of the term intersubjectivity for the analytic situation (Atwood and Stolorow, 1984; Stolorow, Brandchaft, and Atwood, 1987), defining intersubjectivity as the field of intersection between two subjectivities, the interplay between two different subjective worlds. But how is the meeting of two subjects different from one in which a subject meets object? Once we have acknowledged that the object makes an important contribution to the life of the subject, what is added by deciding to call this object another subject? And what are the impediments to the meeting of two minds?

To begin our inquiry, we must address this question: what difference does the other make, the other who is perceived as truly outside, not within our mental field of operations? Isn't there a dramatic difference between the experience with the other perceived as outside the self and the subjectively conceived object? Winnicott (1971) formulated the basic outlines of this distinction in what may well be considered his most daring and radical statement, "The Use of an Object and Relating Through Identifications." Since then, with a few exceptions (Eigen, 1981; Modell, 1984; Ghent, 1989), there has been little effort to elaborate Winnicott's juxtaposition of the two possible relationships of the subject to the object. Yet, as I show here, the difference between the other as subject and the other as object is crucial for a relational psychoanalysis.

The distinction between the two types of relationships to the other can emerge clearly only if we acknowledge that both are endemic to psychic experience and hence both valid areas of psychoanalytic inquiry. If there is a contradiction between the two modes of experience, then we ought to probe it as a condition of knowledge rather than assume it to be a fork in the road. Other theoretical grids that have bifurcated psychoanalytic thought—drive theory vs. object relations theory, ego vs. id psychology, intrapsychic vs. interpersonal theory—insisted on a choice between the two opposing perspectives. I am proposing, instead, that the two dimensions of experience with the object/other are complementary, even though they sometimes stand in an oppositional relationship. By encompassing both dimensions, we can fulfill the intention of relational theories: to account both for the pervasive effects of human relationships on psychic development and for the equally ubiquitous effects of internal psychic mechanisms and fantasies in shaping psychological life and interaction.

I refer to the two categories of experience as the intrapsychic and the intersubjective dimensions (Benjamin, 1988). The idea of intersubjectivity, which has been brought into psychoanalysis from philosophy (Habermas, 1970, 1971), is useful because it specifically addresses the problem of defining the other as object. Intersubjectivity was deliberately formulated in contrast to the logic of subject and object that predominates in Western philosophy and science. It refers to that zone of experience or theory in which the other is not merely the object of the ego's need/drive or cognition/perception, but has a separate and equivalent center of self.

Intersubjective theory postulates that the other must be recognized as another subject in order for the self to fully experience his or her subjectivity in the other's presence. This means, first, that we have a need for recognition and second, a capacity to recognize others in return—mutual recognition. But recognition is a capacity of individual development that is only unevenly realized, in a sense, the point of a relational psychoanalysis is to explain this fact. In Freudian metapsychology the process of recognizing the other "with that distinctness which is no longer reflection but feeling" would appear, at best, as a background effect of the relationship between ego and external reality. Feminist critics of psychoanalysis have suggested that the conceptualization of the first other, the mother, as an object underlies this theoretical lacuna: cultural antithesis between male subject and female object contributed much to the failure to take into account the subjectivity of the other. The denial of the mother's subjectivity, in theory and in practice, profoundly impedes our ability to see the world as inhabited by equal subjects. My purposes are to show that, in fact, the capacity to recognize the mother as a subject is an important part of early development; and to bring the process of recognition into the foreground of our thinking.

I suggest some preliminary outlines of the development of the capacity for recognition. In particular I focus on separation-individuation theory, showing how much more it can reveal when it is viewed through the intersubjective lens, especially in the light of the contributions of both Stern and Winnicott. Because separation-individuation theory is formulated in terms of ego and object, it does not fully realize its own contribution. In the ego-object perspective the child is the individual, seen as moving in a progression toward autonomy and separateness. The telos of this process is the creation of psychic structure through internalization of the object in the service of greater independence.

As a result, separation-individuation theory focuses on the structural residue of the child's interaction with the mother as object; it leaves the aspects of engagement, connection, and active assertion that occur with the mother as other in the unexamined background. This perspective is infantocentric: Typical studies of mother-child interaction will formulate the mother's acts of independence as a contribution to the child's self-regulation but not to the child's recognition of her subjectivity. (see, e.g.,

Settlage et al., 1991). This perspective also misses the *pleasure* of the evolving relationship with a partner from whom one knows how to elicit a response, but whose responses are not entirely predictable and assimilable to internal fantasy. The idea of pleasure was lost when ego psychology put the id on the backburner, but it might be restored by recognizing the subjectivity of the other.

An intersubjective perspective helps to transcend the infantocentric viewpoint of intrapsychic theory by asking how a person becomes capable of enjoying recognition with an other. Logically, recognizing the parent as subject cannot simply be the result of internalizing the parent as mental object. This is a developmental process that has barely begun to be explicated. How does a child develop into a person who, as a parent, is able to recognize her or his own child? What are the internal processes, the psychic landmarks, of such development? Where is the theory that tracks the development of the child's responsiveness, empathy, and concern, and not just the parent's sufficiency or failure?

It is in regard to these questions that most theories of the self have fallen short. Even self psychology, which has placed such emphasis on attunement and empathy and has focused on the intersubjectivity of the analytic encounter, has been tacitly one-sided in its understanding of the parent-child relationship and the development of intersubjective relatedness. Perhaps in reaction against the oedipal reality principle, Kohut (1977, 1984) defined the necessary confrontation with the other's needs or with limits in a self-referential way—optimal failures in empathy (parallel to analysts' errors)—as if there were nothing for children to learn about the other's rights or feelings. Although the goal of self psychology was to enable individuals to open "new channels of empathy" and "intuneness between self and selfobject" (Kohut, 1984, p. 66), the self was always the recipient, not the giver of empathy. The responsiveness of the selfobject, by definition, serves the function of "shoring up our self" throughout life; but at what point does it become the responsiveness of the outside other whom we love? The occasionally mentioned (perhaps more frequently assumed) "love object," who would presumably hold the place of outside other, has no articulated place in the theory. Thus, once again the pleasure in mutuality between two subjects is reduced to its function of stabilizing the self, not of enlarging our awareness of the outside, nor of recognizing others as animated by independent though similar feelings.[1]

---

1. My remarks may be more apt for Kohut than for self psychology as a whole, which has recently shown an impetus to correct this one-sidedness and to include the evolution of difference in relation to the other (e.g., Lachmann, 1986) as well as the relationship to the "true" object (Stolorow, 1986).

In this essay I outline some crucial points in the development of recognition. It is certainly true that recognition begins with the other's confirming response that tells us we have created meaning, had an impact, revealed an intention. But very early on we find that recognition between persons—understanding and being understood, being in attunement—begins to be an end in itself. Recognition between persons is essentially mutual. By our very enjoyment of the other's confirming response, we recognize her in return. I think that what the research on mother-infant interaction has uncovered about early reciprocity and mutual influence is best conceptualized as the development of the capacity for mutual recognition. The frame-by-frame studies of face-to-face play at three to four months have given us a kind of early history of recognition.

The pathbreaking work of Stern (1974, 1977, 1985) and the more recent contributions of Beebe (1977, 1985, 1988) have illuminated how crucial the relationship of mutual influence is for early self-development. They have also shown that self-regulation at this point is achieved through regulating the other: I can change my own mental state by causing the other to be more or less stimulating. Mother's recognition is the basis for the baby's sense of agency. Equally important, although less emphasized, is the other side of this play interaction: the mother is dependent to some degree on the baby's recognition. A baby who is less responsive is a less "recognizing" baby, and the mother who reacts to her apathetic or fussy baby by overstimulation or withdrawal is a mother feeling despair that the baby does not recognize her.

In Stern's (1985) view, however, early play does not yet constitute intersubjective relatedness. He instead designates the next phase, when affective attunement develops at eight or nine months, as intersubjectivity proper. This is the moment when we discover "there are other minds out there!" and that separate minds can share a similar state. I would agree that this phase constitutes an advance in recognition of the other, but I think the earlier interaction can be considered an antecedent, in the form of concrete affective sharing. Certainly, from the standpoint of the mother whose infant returns her smile, affective sharing is already the beginning of reciprocal recognition. Therefore, rather than designate the later phase as intersubjective relatedness, I would rather conceptualize a development of intersubjectivity in which there are key moments of transformation.

In this phase, as Stern (1985) emphasizes, the new thing is the sharing of the inner world. The infant begins to check out how the parent feels when he is discovering a new toy and the parent demonstrates attunement by responding in another medium. By translating the same affective level into another modality, for instance, from kinetic to vocal—

the adult conveys the crucial fact that it is the inner experience that is congruent. The difference in form makes the element of similarity or sharing clear. I would add that the parent is not literally sharing the same state, since the parent is (usually) excited by the infant's reaction, not the toy itself. The parent is in fact taking pleasure in *contacting the child's mind.*

Here is a good point to consider the contrast between intersubjective theory and ego psychology, a contrast Stern makes much of. The phase of discovering other minds coincides roughly with Mahler's differentiation and practicing subphases, but there is an important difference in emphasis. In the intersubjective view, the infant's greater separation, which Mahler emphasizes in this period, actually proceeds in tandem with, and enhances the felt connection with, the other. The joy of intersubjective attunement is: This other can share my feeling. According to Mahler (Mahler, Pine, and Bergman, 1975), though, the infant of ten months is primarily involved in exploring, in the "love affair with the world." The checking back to look at mother is not about sharing the experience, but about safety/anxiety issues, "refueling." It is a phase in which Mahler sees the mother not as contacting the child's mind, but giving him a push from the nest.

While Stern emphasizes his differences with Mahler, I think the two models are complementary, not mutually exclusive. It seems to me that here intersubjective theory amplifies separation-individuation theory by focusing on the affective exchange between parent and child and by stressing the simultaneity of connection and separation. Instead of opposite endpoints of a longitudinal trajectory, connection and separation form a tension, which requires the equal magnetism of both sides.

Now it is this tension between connection and separation that I suggest we track beyond the period of affective attunement. If we follow it into the second year of life, we can see a tension developing between assertion of self and recognition of the other. Translating Mahler's rapprochement crisis into the terms of intersubjectivity, we can say that in this crisis the tension between asserting self and recognizing the other breaks down and is manifested as a conflict between self and other.

My analysis of this crisis derives, in part, from philosophy, from Hegel's (1807) formulation of the problem of recognition in *The Phenomenology of Spirit*. In his discussion of the conflict between "the independence and dependence of self-consciousness" Hegel showed how the self's wish for absolute independence conflicts with the self's need for recognition. In trying to establish itself as an independent entity, the self must yet recognize the other as a subject like itself in order to be recognized by the self, immediately compromising the self's absoluteness and posing the problem that the other could be equally absolute and independent. Each self wants to be recognized and yet maintain his absolute identity: the self says, I want to affect you, but I want nothing you do or say to affect me, I am who I am. In its encounter with the other, the self wishes to affirm its absolute independence, even though its need for the other and the other's similar wish give the lie to it.

This description of the self's absoluteness covers approximately the same territory as narcissism in Freudian theory, particularly its manifestation as omnipotence: the insistence on being one (everyone is identical to me) and all alone (there is nothing outside of me that I do not control). Freud's (1911, 1915) conception of the earliest ego with its hostility to the outside, or its incorporation of everything good into itself, is not unlike Hegel's absolute self. Hegel's notion of the conflict between independence and dependence meshes with the classic psychoanalytic view in which the self does not wish to give up omnipotence.

But even if we reject the Freudian view of the ego, the confrontation with the other's subjectivity and the limits of self-assertion is a difficult one to negotiate. The need for recognition entails this fundamental paradox: in the very moment of realizing our own independent will, we are dependent upon another to recognize it. At the very moment we come to understanding the meaning of I, myself, we are forced to see the limitations of that self. At the moment when we understand that separate minds can share similar feelings, we begin to find out that these minds can also disagree.

Let us return to Mahler and her associates' (1975) description of rapprochement, and see how it illustrates the paradox of recognition and how the infant is supposed to get out of it. Prior to rapprochement, in the self-assertion of the practicing phase, the infant still takes herself for granted, and her mother as well. She does not make a sharp discrimination between doing things with mother's help and without it. She is too excited by *what* she is doing to reflect on who is doing it. Beginning about 14 months a conflict emerges between the infant's grandiose aspirations and the perceived reality of her or his limitations and dependency. Although now able to do more, the toddler is aware of what she or he can't do and what she or he can't make mother do—for example, stay with her or him instead of going out. Many of the power struggles that begin here (wanting the whole pear, not a slice) can be summed up as a demand: "recognize my intent!" The child will insist that mother share everything, participate in all her or his deeds, acquiesce to all her or his demands. The toddler is also up against the increased awareness of separateness, and, consequently, of vulnerability: she or he can move away from mother—but mother can also move away from her or him.

If we reframe this description from the intersubjective perspective, the infant now knows that different minds can feel differently, that he or she is dependent as well as independent. In this sense, rapprochement is the crisis of recognizing the other, specifically of confronting mother's independence. It is no accident that mother's leaving becomes a focal point here, for it confronts the child not only with separation but with mother's independent aims. For similar reasons, the mother may experience conflict at this point; the child's demands are now threatening, no longer simply needs, but expressions of his or her independent (tyrannical) will. The child is different from her mental fantasy, no longer *her* object. He may switch places with her: from passive to active. He, not she, is now the repository of omnipotence once attributed to the "good" all-giving mother. How she responds to her child's and her own aggression depends on her ability to mitigate such fantasies with a sense of real agency and separate selfhood, on her confidence in her child's ability to survive conflict, loss, imperfection. The mother has to be able to both set clear boundaries for her child and to recognize the child's will, to both insist on her own independence and respect that of the child—in short, to balance assertion and recognition. If she cannot do this, omnipotence continues, attributed either to the mother or the self; in neither case can we say that the development of mutual recognition has been furthered.

From the standpoint of intersubjective theory, the ideal "resolution" of the paradox of recognition is for it to continue as a *constant tension* between recognizing the other and asserting the self. However, in Mahler et al.'s (1975) theory the rapprochement conflict appears to be resolved through internalization, the achievement of object constancy—when the child can separate from mother or be angry at her and still be able to contact her presence or goodness. In a sense, this sets the goal of development too low: it is difficult and therefore sufficient for the child to accomplish the realistic integration of good and bad object representations (Kernberg, 1980). The sparse formulation of the end of the rapprochement conflict is, shall we say, anticlimactic, leaving us to wonder, is this all? In this picture, the child has only to accept mother's disappointing her; she or he does not begin to shift her or his center of gravity to recognize that mother does this because she has her own center.

The breakdown and recreation of the tension between asserting one's own reality and accepting the other's is a neglected aspect of the crisis, but it is equally important. This aspect emerges when we superimpose Winnicott's (1971) idea of destroying the object over Mahler's rapprochement crisis. It is destruction—negation in Hegel's sense—that enables the subject to go beyond relating to the object through identification, projection, and other intrapsychic processes having to do with the subjectively conceived object. It enables the transition from relating (intrapsychic) to using the object, carrying on a relationship with an other who is objectively perceived as existing outside the self, an entity in her own right. That is, in the mental act of negating or obliterating the object, which may be expressed in the real effort to attack the other, we find out whether the real other survives. If she survives without retaliating or withdrawing under the attack, then we know her to exist outside ourselves, not just as our mental product.

Winnicott's scheme can be expanded to postulate not a sequential relationship but rather a basic tension between denial and affirmation of the other (between omnipotence and recognition of reality). Another way to understand the conflicts that occur in rapprochement is through the concepts of destruction and survival: the wish to absolutely assert the self and deny everything outside one's own mental omnipotence must sometimes crash against the implacable reality of the other. The collision Winnicott (1971) has in mind, however, is not one in which aggression occurs "reactive to the encounter with the reality principle," but one in which aggression "creates the quality of externality" (p. 110). When the destructiveness damages neither the parent nor the self, external reality comes into view as a sharp, distinct contrast to the inner fantasy world. The outcome of this process is not simply reparation or restoration of the good object, but love, the sense of discovering the other (Eigen, 1981; Ghent, 1990).

The flipside of Winnicott's analysis would be that when destruction is not countered with survival, when the other's reality does not come into view, a defensive process of internalization takes place. Aggression becomes a problem—how to dispose of the bad feeling. What cannot be worked through and dissolved with the outside other is transposed into a drama of internal objects, shifting from the domain of the intersubjective into the domain of the intrapsychic. In real life, even when the other's response dissipates aggression, there is no perfect process of destruction and survival; there is always also internalization. All experience is elaborated intrapsychically, we might venture to say, but when the other does not survive and aggression is not dissipated it becomes almost exclusively intrapsychic. It therefore seems to me fallacious to see internalization processes only as breakdown products or defenses; I would see them rather as a kind of underlying substratum of our mental activity—a constant symbolic digestion process that constitutes an important part of the cycle of exchange between the individual and the outside. It is the loss of balance between the intrapsychic and the intersubjective, between fantasy and reality, that is the problem.

Indeed, the problem in psychoanalytic theory has been that internalization—either the defensive or the structure-building aspects (depending on which object relations theory one favors)—has obscured the component of destruction that Winnicott (1964, p. 62) emphasizes: discovering "that fantasy and fact, both important, are nevertheless different from each other." The complementarily of the intrapsychic and intersubjective modalities is important here: as Winnicott makes clear, it is in contrast to the *fantasy* of destruction that the *reality* of survival is so satisfying and authentic.

Winnicott thus offers a notion of a reality that can be loved, something beyond the integration of good and bad. While the intrapsychic ego has reality imposed from the outside, the intersubjective ego discovers reality. This reality principle does not represent a detour to wish fulfillment, a modification of the pleasure principle. Nor is it the acceptance of a false life of adaptation. Rather it is a continuation under more complex conditions of the infant's original fascination with and love of what is outside, his appreciation of difference and novelty. This appreciation is the element in differentiation that gives separation its positive, rather than simply hostile, coloring: love of the world, not merely leaving or distance from mother. To the extent that mother herself is placed outside, she can be loved; separation is then truly the other side of connection to the other.

It is this appreciation of the other's reality that completes the picture of separation and explains what there is beyond internalization—the establishment of shared reality. First (1988) provided some very germane observations of how the toddler does begin to apprehend mutuality as a concomitant of separateness, specifically in relation to the mother's leaving. The vehicle of this resolution is, to expand Winnicott's notion, cross-identification: the capacity to put oneself in the place of the other based on empathic understanding of similarities of inner experience. The two-year-old's initial role-playing imitation of the departing mother is characterized by the spirit of pure retaliation and reversal—"I'll do to you what you do to me." But gradually the child begins to identify with the mother's subjective experience and realizes that "I could miss you as you miss me," and, therefore, that "I know that you could wish to have your own life as I wish to have mine." First shows how, by recognizing such shared experience, the child actually moves from a retaliatory world of control to a world of mutual understanding and shared feeling. This analysis adds to the idea of object constancy, in which the good object survives the bad experience, the idea of recognizing that the leaving mother is not bad but independent, a person like me. By accepting this, the child gains not only her own independence (as traditionally emphasized) but also the pleasure of shared understanding.

Looking backward, we can trace the outlines of a developmental trajectory of intersubjective relatedness up to this point. Its core feature is recognizing similarity of *inner* experience in tandem with difference. We could say that it begins with "We are feeling this feeling," and then moves to "I know that you, who are an other mind, share this same feeling." In rapprochement, however, a crisis occurs as the child begins to confront difference—"you and I don't want or feel the same thing." The initial response to this discovery is a breakdown of recognition between self and other: I insist on my way, I refuse to recognize you, I begin to try to coerce you, and therefore I experience your refusal as a reversal: you are coercing me. As in earlier phases, the capacity for mutual recognition must stretch to accommodate the tension of difference, in this case to accept the knowledge of conflicting feelings.

In the third year of life this tension can be expressed in symbolic play. The early play at retaliatory reversal may now be a kind of empowerment in which the child feels "I can do to you what you do to me." But then the play expands to include the emotional identification with the other's position, and becomes reflexive so that, as First puts it, "I know you know what I feel." In this sense, the medium of shared feeling remains as important to intersubjectivity in later phases as in early ones. But it is now extended to symbolic understanding of feeling so that "you know what I feel, even when I want or feel the opposite of what you want or feel." This advance in differentiation means that "we can share feelings without my fearing that my feelings are simply your feelings."

The child who can imaginatively entertain both roles—leaving and being left—begins to transcend the complementary form of the mother-child relationship. The complementary structure organizes the relationship of giver and taker, doer and done to, powerful and powerless. It allows one to reverse roles, but not to alter them. In the reversible relationship, each person can play only one role at a time: one person is recognized, the other negated; one subject, the other object. This complementarily does not dissolve omnipotence, but shifts it from one partner to the other. The movement out of the world of complementary power relations into the world of mutual understanding thus shows us an important step in the dismantling of omnipotence: power is dissolved, rather than transferred back and forth in an endless cycle between child and mother. Again, this movement refers not to a one-time sequence or final accomplishment, but an ongoing tension between complementarily and mutuality.

When mutual recognition is not restored, when shared reality does not survive destruction, complementary structures and "relating" to the inner object predominate. Because this occurs commonly enough, the intrapsychic, subjectobject concept of the mind actually fits with the dominant mode of internal experience. This is why—notwithstanding our intersubjective potential—the reversible complementarity of subject and object conceptualized by intrapsychic theory illuminates so much of the internal world. The principles of mind Freud first analyzed—reversal of opposites like active and passive, the exchangeability or displacement of objects—thus remain indispensable guides to the inner world of objects.

But even when the capacity for recognition is well-developed, when the subject can use shared reality and receive the nourishment of "other-than-me substance," the intrapsychic capacities remain. The mind's ability to manipulate, to displace, to reverse, to turn one thing into another is not a mere negation of reality, but the source of mental creativity. Furthermore, when things go well, complementarily is a step on the road to mutuality. The toddler's insistent reciprocity, his or her efforts to reverse the relationship with the mother, to play at feeding, grooming, and leaving her, is one step in the process of identification that ultimately leads to understanding. It is only when this process is disrupted, when the complementary form of the relationship is not balanced by mutual activity, that reversal becomes entrenched and the relationship becomes a struggle for power.

The attempt to reverse the mother's omnipotence within the context of complementary structures may shed light on the problem of male dominance. One important mental structure that has perpetuated male power is the complementarily in which male = subject and female = object. As feminist theory has repeatedly pointed out, the failure of psychoanalysis to formulate a perspective in which the mother appears as subject limits our understanding of the infant as well. Insofar as the mother-infant relationship postulated by much psychoanalytic thinking was framed in terms of subject-object complementarity, the theory reproduced the prevalent cultural stance toward woman as mother. In other words, there is both a formal fit and a dynamic relationship between subject-object relations and male-female relations. Formally, the reversible, complementary structure of the mother-infant dyad dovetails with later representations of self-other relations as power relationships. Dynamically, the omnipotent mother of this dyad becomes the basis for the dread and retaliation that inform men's exercise of power over women. Thus the adult relation between men and women becomes the locus of the great reversal, turning the tables on the omnipotent mother of infancy.

The intersubjective view of development offers a contrast that throws this reversal into bold relief. It shows that within the maternal dyad mutuality exists alongside complementarily, and the child engages in the first struggles for recognition. This is in direct contrast to the implicit assumption, from Freud up to the current work of Chasseguet-Smirgel (1986), that the acceptance of reality and the separation from the mother are brought about through the intervention and internalization of the oedipal father. In this view, the mother remains archaic and omnipotent in the child's mind and omnipotence must be counteracted by power of the oedipal father. The underlying premise is that the problem of recognition (that is, narcissism) cannot be worked on or resolved within the relationship to the primary other; it requires the intercession of an outside other, a third term, the "Name of the Father" as Lacan (1977) explicitly proposed. In other words, two subjects alone can never confront each other without merging, one being subordinated and assimilated by the other. This position justifies a split in which the mother's power is displaced onto the father, and he serves as the independent other whom the (boy) child recognizes and with whom he struggles.

But, according to the intersubjective theory of destruction and recognition, differentiation does take place within the maternal dyad. Omnipotence can be counterbalanced and in this sense overcome. For it is not necessary that the fantasy of maternal omnipotence be dispelled, only that it be modified by the existence of another dimension—mutual recognition. From this perspective, the problem lies not in the unconscious fantasy of maternal omnipotence per se. Rather, the dread of the mother that has been linked to domination in the masculine stance toward women (Horney 1932; Stoller, 1975) becomes problematic when not counterbalanced by the development of intersubjectivity.

Horney's (1932) remarks on male dread of woman illustrate how the loss of intersubjectivity affects the subject as well as the object: "'It is not,' he says, 'that I dread her; it is that she herself is malignant, capable of any crime, a beast of prey, a vampire, a witch, insatiable in her desires. She is the very personification of what is sinister'" (p. 135). The projective power of this fantasy reflects the predominance of the intrapsychic over the intersubjective: "she is that thing I feel." The lack of intersubjectivity in this psychic situation can be conceptualized as the assimilation of the subject to the object, as the lack of the space in between subjects. As Ogden (1986) puts it, the existence of potential space between mother and child allows the establishment of the distinction between the symbol and the symbolized. The subject who can begin to make this distinction now has access to a triangular field—symbol, symbolized, and interpreting subject. The space between self and other can exist and facilitate the distinction, let us say, between the real mother and the symbolic mother; this triangle is created without a literal third person.[2] Lacking that space, the mother becomes the dreaded but tempting object; the subject is overwhelmed by that object since it really is "the thing in itself" (Ogden, 1986). In the denial of the other's subjectivity the exercise of power begins.

The creation of this space within the relationship between infant and mother is an important dimension of intersubjectivity, a concomitant of mutual understanding. This space is not only a function, as Winnicott emphasized, of the child's play alone in the presence of the mother, but also of play between mother and child, beginning with the earliest play of mutual gaze. As we see in First's (1988) analysis of play with identification with the leaving mother, the transitional space also evolves within the communicative interaction between mother and child. Within this play, the mother is simultaneously "related to" in fantasy, but "used" to establish mutual understanding, a pattern that parallels transference play in the analytic situation. In the elaboration of this play the mother can appear as the child's fantasy object as well as other subject without threatening the child's subjectivity.

The existence of this space is ultimately what makes the intrapsychic capacities creative rather than destructive; perhaps it is another way of referring to the tension between using and relating. Using, that is recognizing, implies the capacity to transcend complementary structures, but not the absence of them. It does not mean the disappearance of fantasy or of negation but that "destruction becomes the unconscious backcloth for love of a real object" (Winnicott, 1971, p. 111). It means a balance of destruction with recognition. In the broadest sense, internal fantasy is always eating up or negating external reality—"While I am loving you I am all the time destroying you in (unconscious) fantasy" (p. 106). The loved one is being continually destroyed but its survival means that we can eat our reality and have it too. From the intersubjective standpoint, all fantasy is the negation of the real other, whether the fantasy's content is negative or idealized; just as, from the intrapsychic view, external

---

2. Of course, the satisfactory development of this space may generate or become associated with the intrapsychic representation of the third person, even in children with one parent. The point here is not to disqualify oedipal representations, but to say that the oedipal father is not the way out of an otherwise engulfing maternal dyad. More likely, the traditional formulation of the oedipal relationship, which has emphasized identification with an idealized male power as the payoff for renouncing the mother, represents a fantasy "solution." But when the symbolic father does substitute for the space between mother and child, the mother's existence as an object of desire remains terrifying; the oedipal repudiation of femininity, with its disparagement of women, then becomes a further obstacle to the creation of intersubjective space.

reality is simply that which is internalized as fantasy. The ongoing inter-play of destruction and recognition is a dialectic between fantasy and external reality.

In the analytic process, the effort to share the productions of fantasy changes the status of fantasy itself, moving it from inner reality to inter-subjective communication. The fantasy object who is being related to or destroyed and the usable other who is there to receive the communica-tion and be loved complement each other. What we find in the good hour is a momentary balance between intrapsychic and intersubjective dimensions, a sustained tension or rapid movement between the patient's experience of us as inner material and as the recognizing other. This sus-pension of the conflict between the two experiences reflects the success-ful establishment of a transitional space in which the otherness of the analyst can be ignored as well as recognized. The experience of a space that allows both creative exploration within omnipotence and acknowl-edgment of an understanding other is, in part, what is therapeutic about the relationship.

The restoration of balance between intrapsychic and intersubjective in the psychoanalytic process should not be construed as an adaptation that reduces fantasy to reality, but rather as practice in the sustaining of con-tradiction. When the tension of sustaining contradiction breaks down, as it frequently does, the intersubjective structures—mutuality, simultaneity and paradox—are subordinated in favor of complementary structures. The breakdown of tension between self and other in favor of relating as sub-ject and object is a common fact of mental life. For that matter, break-down is a common feature within intersubjective relatedness—what counts is the ability to restore or repair the relationship. As Beebe and Lachmann (1988) have proposed, one of the main principles of the early dyad is that relatedness is characterized not by continuous harmony but by continuous disruption and repair (Beebe and Lachmann, 1991; Tronick, 1989).

Thus, an intersubjective theory can explore the development of mutual recognition without equating breakdown with pathology. It does not require a normative ideal of balance which decrees that breakdown reflects failure, and that the accompanying phenomena—internalization/ fantasy/aggression—are pathological. If the clash of two wills is an inher-ent part of intersubjective relations, then no perfect environment can take the sting from the encounter with otherness. The question becomes how the inevitable elements of negation are processed. It is "good enough" that the inward movement of negating reality and cre-ating fantasy should eventually be counterbalanced by an outward movement of recognizing the outside. To claim anything more for intersubjectivity would invite a triumph of the external, a terrifying psychic vacuity, an end to creativity altogether. A relational psychoanalysis should leave room for the messy, intrapsychic side of creativity and aggression; it is the contribution of the intersubjective view that may give these elements a more hopeful cast, showing destruction to be the "other" of recognition.

References

Atwood, G. & Stolorow, R. (1984), *Structures of Subjectivity*. Hillsdale, NJ: The Analytic Press.

Beebe, B. (1985), Mother-infant mutual influence and precursors of self and object representations. In: *Empirical Studies of Psychoanalytic Theories, Vol. 2*, ed. J. Masling. Hillsdale, NJ: The Analytic Press, pp. 27–48.

———— & Lachmann, F. (1988), Mother-infant mutual influence and precursors of psychic structure. In: *Frontiers in Self Psychology: Progress in Self Psychology, Vol. 3*, ed. A. Goldberg. Hillsdale NJ: The Analytic Press, pp. 325.

———— & Lachmann, F. (1991), The organization of representation in infancy: Three principles. Unpublished manuscript.

———— & Stern, D. (1977), Engagement-disengagement and early object experiences. In: *Communicative Structures and Psychic Structures*, ed. N. Freedman & S. Grand. New York: Plenum Press.

Benjamin, J. (1988), *The Bonds of Love*. New York: Pantheon.

Chasseguet-Smirgel, J. (1986), *Sexuality and Mind*. New York: New York University Press.

Eagle, M. (1984), *Recent Developments in Psychoanalysis*. Cambridge, MA: Harvard University Press.

Eigen, M. (1981), The area of faith in Winnicott, Lacan and Bion. *Internat. J. Psychoanal., 62*, 413–433.

Eliot, George. (1871), *Middlemarch*. Harmondsworth, Eng.: Penguin, 1965.

Fairbairn, W. R. D. (1952), *Psychoanalytic Studies of the Personality*. London: Routledge & Kegan Paul.

First, E. (1988), The leaving game: I'll play you and you'll play me: The emergence of the capacity for dramatic role play in two-year-olds. In: *Modes of Meaning*, ed. A. Slade & D. Wolfe. New York: Oxford University Press, pp. 132–166.

Freud, S. (1911), Formulation on the two principles in mental functioning. *Standard Edition*, 12:213–226. London: Hogarth Press, 1958.

———— (1915), Instincts and their vicissitudes. *Standard Edition*, 14:11–140. London: Hogarth Press, 1957.

Ghent, E. (1989), Credo: The dialectics of one-person and two-person psychologies. *Contemp. Psychoanal.*, 25:169–211.

———— (1990), Masochism, submission, surrender. *Contemp. Psychoanal.*, 26:108–136.

Habermas, J. (1970), A theory of communicative competence. In: *Recent Sociology, No. 2*, ed. H. P. Dreitzel. New York: Macmillan.

———— (1971), *Knowledge and Human Interests*. Boston: Beacon.

Hegel, G. W. F. (1807), *Phenomenologie des Geistes*. Hamburg: Felix Meiner, 1952.

Horney, K. (1932), The dread of women. In: *Feminine Psychology*. New York: Norton, 1967.

Kernberg, O. (1980), *Object Relations Theory and Clinical Psychoanalysis*. New York: Aronson.

Kohut, H. (1977), *The Restoration of the Self*. New York: International Universities Press.

———— (1984), *How Does Analysis Cure?* ed. A. Goldberg & P. Stepansky. Chicago: University of Chicago Press.

Lacan, J. (1977), *Ecrits, A Selection*. New York: Norton.

Lachmann, F. (1986), Interpretation of psychic conflict and adversarial relationships: A self psychological perspective. *Psychoanal. Psychol.*, 3:341–355.

Mahler, M., Pine, F. & Bergman, A. (1975), *The Psychological Birth of the Human Infant*. New York: Basic Books.

Mitchell, S. (1988), *Relational Concepts in Psychoanalysis*. Cambridge, MA: Harvard University Press.

Modell, A. (1984), *Psychoanalysis in a New Context*. New York: International Universities Press.

Ogden, T. (1986), *The Matrix of the Mind*. New York: Aronson.

Settlage, C. F., Bemesderfer, S. J., Rosenthal, J., Afferman, J. & Spielman, P. M. (1991), The appeal cycle in early mother-child interaction: Nature and implications of a finding from developmental research. *J. Amer. Psychoanal. Assn.*, 39:987–1014.

Stern, D. (1974), The goal and structure of mother-infant play. *J. Amer. Acad. Child Psychiat.*, 13:402–421.

———— (1977), *The First Relationship*. Cambridge, MA: Harvard University Press.

———— (1985), *The Interpersonal World of the Infant*. New York: Basic Books.

Stoller, R. (1975), *Perversion*. New York: Pantheon.

Stolorow, R. (1986), On experiencing an object: A multidimensional perspective. In: *Progress in Self Psychology, Vol. 2*, ed. A. Goldberg. New York: Guilford, pp. 273–279.

———— Brandchaft, B. & Atwood, G. (1987), *Psychoanalytic Treatment*. Hillsdale, NJ: The Analytic Press.

Tronick, E. (1989), Emotions and emotional communication. *Amer. Psychol.*, 44:112–119.

Winnicott, D. W. (1964), *The Child, the Family and the Outside World*. Harmondsworth, Eng.: Penguin.

———— (1971), The use of an object and relating through identifications. In: *Playing and Reality*. London: Tavistock.

Afterword

By way of an afterword, I will sum up some of the implications of what I have written about intersubjectivity, especially in relation to discussion that has unfolded in the last decade. I use the term intersubjectivity to refer not merely to the generalization that we operate in the presence of two persons, in an interpersonal field, but to the specific matter of recognizing the other as an equivalent center of being. My usage derives from the philosophical move made by Habermas from the primacy of a subject who knows or transforms the object to a subject who communicates with other subjects. This line of thinking, which goes back to Hegel, is rather different from that of Stolorow and Atwood (1992; Atwood and Stolorow, 1984), whose definition of intersubjectivity refers to all interplay between different subjective worlds. That definition does not tell us how the intersubjective differs from the interpersonal, a term formerly used to denote the matrix of relationships that compose psychic life. Nor does it sufficiently distinguish subjects from objects, as in the all-important issue of how a child comes to recognize the mother as a separate subject rather than internalize her as an object. In my view, it is only by postulating that recognition that we can confer on intersubjectivity a distinct and specific meaning.

I use the term intersubjectivity, like Stern (1985), to describe the developmental achievement of recognition (see Aron, 1996). I think of the intersubjective as a complement to the aspects of psychic life elaborated by the intrapsychic theory of object relations. Intersubjectivity adds to the object relations perspective a notion that our representations and relationships can be charted on the axis of the tension between recognizing and negating the other. In line with Ogden's (1994) suggestion, both perspectives can include an awareness of interpersonal relations, but the intersubjective dimension refers to a specific axis of these relations. Lacan (1988), whose notion of intersubjectivity also stems from the Hegelian notion of a struggle for recognition, was the first to insist on the distinction between object relations and intersubjectivity. His conception of the imaginary and the symbolic was in some ways roughly parallel to Winnicott's (1971) distinction between relating to and using the object. As I see it, our mental life is always located somewhere on that tension between relating to the object and recognizing the outside other, between contact with outer reality and omnipotence. Each relationship is always definable in terms of the movement of negation and recognition, each moment the other appears to us more or less as object or subject, or rather in some combination thereof.

The problem with the approach that equates the intersubjective with the interpersonal field of object relations is that it may attribute psychic failure or conflict to the impact on developing capacities (deep structure) by an interpersonal environment (as in Gentile, 1998)— as if to say that, in a good-enough enironment, psychic conflict would be minimal. My view is that the converse is equally true: failure at the level of interpersonal relations must be explained by the inherently problematic and conflictual makeup of the psyche.(NB: only equally true, results and causes fluctuate in continual figure-ground reversal depending on our perspective.) In this ongoing switch of perspectives, we can start either from the relational configuration or the inherently problematic negotiation of recognition on the axis of intersubjectivity.

My model of intersubjective development proposes an endemic psychic tension within the individual, one that is not reducible to, although manifested in, the conflict between individual wills and interests (as in Slavin and Kriegman, 1992). Our psychic makeup is such that we are torn between omnipotence, the illusion of control, on the one hand, and the wish for contact with the different, the external, the not-me, on the other. The "solution"—insofar as we may speak of one—to this conflict is that, as Ogden (1986, 1994) has promised, we become dialecticians who can hold such opposites in tension. But at best such tensions are necessarily first dealt with by splitting (Ogden, 1986). The problem, then, is not merely that we need others to develop our intersubjective capacities, but that, even in an optimal interpersonal environment, reconciling inner and outer reality (Winnicott, 1969) is a strain. Just as Freud posited an inherent conflict in intrapsychic life between eros and death, so can we posit an inherent conflict in intersubjective life between eros and narcissism, recognition and omnipotence. The tension that we ideally imagine between these continually breaks down and has to be accomplished over and over.

We theorize about destruction because in analysis we experience breakdowns in recognition, tests of the dialogic process. Of course, surviving in real life is a good deal harder than theorizing about it. What we experience as analysts is that the patient is engaged in negating our analytic "goodness" and so destroying an aspect of our subjectivity. Quite frequently, we know we react by being unable to think, by losing the internal intersubjective space in which reflection is possible. Surviving this breakdown of recognition and restoring a creative tension requires a stepping out of the oppositional dynamic without either submitting to or resisting the projection. It is the effort to define this possibility—stepping out of the ever-repeating stream

of enactment and breakdown into the space of intersubjectivity—
that so much of our current work thematizes.

The issue that arises is how we use our subjectivity when breakdowns
of recognition come into play. Our effort is to formulate the common
subjective experience of being an analyst, in particular, the experience within breakdowns. In this effort we have come to highlight the
moment when both interpretation and empathy fail, or do not even
have a chance, when our subjectivity really is on the line. In other
words, we have reached an understanding that the crisis or "crunch"
(Russell, cited in Pizer, 1998), the point at which the patient presents
the real difficulty that needs mending, really is often experienced as
the moment of maximum attack on our subjectivity (as analysts and
as persons). This destruction is inevitable when we work in "basic
fault" areas, where traumatic repetition is so emotionally powerful
that understanding appears to the patient as useless, or self-protective, or as a coercive response aimed to dislodge the patient's realistic, self-protective opposition. When we work on this fault line, simple
recognition is no longer possible, and the effort to remain good, caring, and empathic will only exacerbate the dillema. Destruction continues until survival becomes possible at a more authentic level.

What we observe in the most subtle and the most extreme moments
of negation is that the relationship is thrown onto the axis of reversible
complementarity, the seesaw in which our stances mirror each other
(Lacan, 1988). For instance, the patient is wondering why the analyst
doesn't get it when the patient has tried to show her a hundred times.
The analyst feels defeated by the patient's refusal of her understanding, and the patient is convinced the analyst doesn't understand or
can't help. It is as if neither person can transcend this clash of wills
and perspectives but can only submit or resist. The analyst feels
ashamed of being unable to think her way through the clinch or has
a guilty fear of acting in a retaliatory fashion.

Characteristically, the dynamic pattern of interaction includes a collapse of the space in which it is possible to think, to work with the
difference between my view and yours (see Ringstrom, 1998; Slavin
and Kriegman, 1998). In this all too familiar and yet compelling
dynamic we are often aware of the felt negation of our or the other's
separate subjectivity. We are thrown into the mode of reversible complementarity in which the partners face off as the absolute selves
Hegel described: only one viewpoint or feeling can prevail. This is
what Ogden (1994) calls the subjugating third: submitting to or resisting the other's projection seems to be the only choice.

Now, while classical method suggested that if one had known and offered in time the right interpretation of the content of the patient's transference this would not have happened, self psychology countered that such insistence on interpretation re-presented an empathic failure to grasp the patient's subjective experience of misattunement. From the intersubjective standpoint, we could say that both perspectives aimed to dissolve the resistance, on the analyst's or the patient's part, to what is felt as submission to the other's view—but this aim was already embedded in the complementary demand, "submit or resist." Each perspective critiques the other's point of view: the classical standpoint is seen as in danger of becoming lodged in a demand that the patient submit to the analyst's view, whereas self psychology is seen as correcting for this by leaning toward submission to the patient's view. The question becomes, is it possible to formulate this embeddedness in complementarity in a somewhat different way? For instance, as the question of how we speak of breakdown during a breakdown?

Intersubjective theory formulates the problem of resistance in this way: it asks how it is possible to restore the process of identification with the other's position without losing our own, rather than submit to or negate the other (Benjamin, 1998). This accomplishment has been variously understood, especially by Lacan (1988), as creating a point of thirdness. The third allows us to mediate between two different points of view; a third line opens up a space where two points offer only a line back and forth between two poles. The intersubjective level aims to transform differences from the register of power, in which one partner asserts his or her meaning, will, need over the other (I know best because I am the analyst) to an understanding of the meaning of the struggle (What feeling or aim is at stake in this difference between us.) Here I agree with Lacan (1988) that the chief commitment of psychoanalysis is to release the psychic hold of the power struggle and to establish the commitment to recognition, the dialogic process itself. There must be, as Ringstrom (1998) has proposed, a move to the level of metacommunication—which is one good way to think of the third. Ogden (1994) has referred to this as "the recognizing third," a subcatgegory of a more general "analytic third," a separate dyadic entity. In my view, however, the third appears only in the relationship of recognition, the space that mediates the two partners' viewpoints, preventing the collapse of tension.

As we know, supervision frequently serves to break up clinches in the dyadic complementarity, because the third person tries to mediate and hold in mind both points of view. This, in effect, amounts to a restoration of the dialogic process. But when we are in it, how do we restore a dialogue about the breakdown with the patient? How do we speak about breakdown of recognition during breakdown? How does the analyst unhook from her investment and move to a view that can encompass two separate subjectivities? The primary intersubjective experience of affect attunement cannot simply be reinstated. Rather, difference must be negotiated at the level of speech so that your meaning does not annihilate mine, or action must be taken to recreate externality and reestablish the intersubjective space. Analyzing how this reopening of intersubjective space works in the dyad seems to be the project at the center of relational theory today.

This project involves not only discussing how our individual countertransference contributes to breakdown but also analyzing what kind of creative, even desperate, acts the analyst may take in the interaction to restore intersubjective space. There is a wide range of discussion already of the contribution of the analyst's subjectivity (Mitchell, 1993; Aron, 1996): the analyst's use of subjectivity in becoming aware of unconscious affective exchange (Natterson, 1991; Bollas 1992; Ogden, 1994), the analyst's change within the interaction (Ringstrom, 1998; Slavin and Kriegman, 1998) or spontaneous action within situations of enactment (Davies, 1994; Hoffman, 1994), to name only a few. While the pivotal point in many an account of release from the complementary power struggle is the one at which the analyst reflects on her own reaction and so creates internal space, in many other accounts it is a spontaneous movement in the interaction that transforms the tension in the dyad. We cannot afford to privilege only the internal work of reflection and leave hidden and undiscussed the actions that change the other and ourselves. For it is often the case that we break through by speaking—"acting"—in such a way that we manage to bring our subjectivity back into play forcefully yet carefully enough to create externality (Cooper, in press). This might occur through controlled acknowledgment of anger, through ruefully humorous commentary, through admission of being stumped and helplessness (Maroda, 1991). Likewise, we have begun to delineate the ways that the patient is active in breakdown and repair, helping us unconsciously to contain affect (Cooper, in press), to tolerate the "countertransference strain" (First, 1993), repeating in order to give us another chance at survival. Such description brings us to a different view of mutuality in the affective interplay of analysis.

We are aware of the underlying dialogic property of our internal mental life, the imagined presence of the other through which we find space for thinking and feeling (Spezzano, 1996). The notion of a third implies that there is quality to this otherness that is external to the reversible complementarity, something outside just me and you to which we orient ourselves in order that the dialogue sustain a tension between the selves rather than collapse into oneness. Only from this standpoint can we be separate-yet-connected beings capable of a desire that does not endlessly reflect the other's desire—a condition in which we are doomed to either be what the other wants, or make the other be what we want (see Lacan, 1988). Such a hall of mirrors could be the end result of any version of ego psychology or object relations that sees all relations to others in terms of their internalization as psychic structure. As I have pointed out elsewhere, if the patient is merely to take the analyst as his ideal, then there is no external other, no space of intersubjectivity (Benjamin, 1995). Therefore I have stressed that dialogue is not merely the means to an end but a goal in itself, a source of pleasure, providing an erotic potential for play alongside of (though easily mixed up with) the idealizing aspects of the transference.

Here I am speaking of play, of the primary dialogic forms of mutual recognition that first create thirdness—"first" developmentally speaking, but also often first in the therapeutic dyad. From my perspective it is as important to describe the process of creating the space of thirdness through play as it is to focus on the breakdown that we experience in the reversible complementarity. Thirdness is another way of defining an essential aspect of the relationship of recognition, of conceiving the intersubjective space. We might ask, what creates the third, where does it come from? I am not proposing to answer this question. While it is clear that symbolic capacities are associated with thirdness, I do not know that we can speak of cause. Rather, it seems to me that symbolic capacity and thirdness are effects of the mental work of containing and communicating affect.

I can only say here that affective, symbolic play, which allows two partners to construct a dialogue, has led me to think of the third in terms of the music or dance that two partners follow. "Following the music" is like the process described in infancy research by which the partners don't necessarily match each other's moves but, rather, both align to a third pattern or direction of affects (Beebe and Lachmann, 1988). This following embodies the paradoxes of transitional experience: it is as if we were sight-reading an unknown score. We make it up as we go, yet it feels as though we are oriented to something outside. It feels discovered as well as invented. As in musical improvisation, there may not be one right way to go, but there are definitely wrong notes that can be anticipated or, more often, heard as soon as they are sounded. What we hear in the other's speech depends on how much, how deeply we have built up a history, a complex pattern of reciprocal understanding: it is as important for the patient to understand the analyst's thought process, although perhaps in a different way, as for the analyst to understand the patient. This coconstructed history of dialogue is ultimately the container, what holds the analytic couple.

It is the acknowledgment of mutual influence, that both partners contribute to its content, which allows the "law" to be a matter of cocreated interpretation and play rather than strict construction. But this coconstructed, mutual relationship still has important elements of asymmetry, as emphasized by Aron (1996) and Hoffman (1994). As in playing music together, we are oriented by certain limits and opportunities set by the reality of our partner's capacities and state. What orients us in an ongoing way as we try to expand the exploration within analytic space is a commitment not only to the rules (what Hoffman has called "the book," which may vary for each of us) but to following what appears to be the dyadic pattern. If we no longer have the security of one theory, one master narrative of this pattern, we require it less because we do not claim to offer certainty; our commitment is to offer a process, an exploration, a willingness to risk not knowing and failing to understand, an engagement of two subjectivities. The intersubjective perspective offers not a specific content but, rather, suggests that we be guided by the palpable distinction between submitting to an other's viewpoint (whether it be the patient or the others who train and appraise us) and subordinating ourselves to certain kinds of necessity, for example, the necessity of maintaining the asymmetrical frame, of not challenging transitional experience, of accepting without judgment. As in a mother's awareness of her child's limits, we are able to see the analysand's traumatic breakdown, anxiety, defenses, inability to sustain tension not as willful or resistant. It is often precisely when we feel ourselves reacting as though something *were* being done to us that we know we have lost the third space, and we are back in the reversible dyad of resistance and submission. We then scour the possibilities of self-analysis, theory, interaction for an opening out toward analytic interaction.

What I am hoping to suggest here is the way that our sensitivity to the quality of thirdness, to what we might call the realization of intersubjectivity, now holds the place that was to be occupied in Freud's schema by a specific content of interpretation. Such a notion of thirdness in dialogue is essential to the relational project; otherwise, the rejection of objectivism in favor of coconstruction would lead to an infinitely regressing hall of mirrors experience. The dialogue is a transitional process that gives us the sense that what we have attained is both inevitable and contingent, transcending the arbitrary and yet springing from the spontaneous creation of each partner.

Both the uncertainty of our knowledge and the necessity of struggling toward mutual accommodation of difference are contained in this conception of dialogue. It is the constantly renewed commitment to restoring the thirdness of intersubjectivity that allows us to get beyond a struggle of your meaning versus my meaning, to a sense of working together to transcend complementarity in favor of mutual recognition.

While the psychoanalytic idea of a third term as a solution to the dyadic struggle of absolute selves was originally elaborated by Lacan (1988), I have offered a rather different perspective on it here. My differences with Lacan, to which I can only allude, concern his associating of the third with language and the paternal function, with the oedipal father's prohibition, indeed with castration. As in Freud's thinking, a specific content is privileged: the symbolic father is what makes it possible to move out of the imaginary, mirroring relation with the mother into the world of speech, of recognition. This location of recognition in the structure of oedipal renunciation, as if that were the primary limit on omnipotence, strikes me as highly problematic. By contrast, I have suggested (Benjamin, 1995) that the mothe–infant relationship already contains this thirdness in the very form of communicative dialogue (see Ogden, 1986, 1994, for related formulations; also Green, 1975) prior to the child's symbolic process to language.

This perspective suggests a diffent way to cast the relationship between intersubjectivity and gender. Gender is deeply entwined with the paradigmatic form of complementarity that forecloses space and leads to a breakdown of mutuality. This form of splitting, in which the opposing terms of negation and recognition are attributed to separate partners, has a powerful iteration in the sadomasochistic relationship (Benjamin, 1988) with its gendered association to masculinity and femininity (see Benjamin, 1995, 1998 for further elucidation). I suggested that gender difference as we know it—a set of oppositional, mutually exclusive and determining categories—can be understood as a complementary structure based on splitting. Such splitting is necessarily intertwined with the reversible complementarity that founds the relation of domination and submission, for it demands that each partner play only one side, sacrificing part of self, one doer and one done to. The basic paradigm for this split is articulated in the masculine assertion, "I am subject, you are my reflecting object; you incarnate what I refuse to own," which fits neatly with the split between activity and passivity that Freud so often associated with masculinity and femininity. The ultimate implication of maintaining the tension between destruction and recognition is an overcoming of this split such that both partners can be subjects. Likewise, reconstituting the tension between activity and passivity brings about a different possible sexual relation.

I find this long-ignored connection compelling: that the development of intersubjectivity in our mental life depends on the overcoming of gender splitting, on reconfiguring the tension between passivity and activity so that each partner can be both author and agent, owner and expresser of tension (Benjamin, 1998). These considerations bring us to an expanded form of the proposition that the mother must be seen not merely as the child's object but also as another subject. We must add to this proposition that the very idea of two subjects requires a rethinking of the idea of sexual subjectivity and the relations of gender. From this perspective I believe it is clear how the rethinking of gender dovetails with the intersubjective understanding of how recognition between subjects breaks down into the reversible complementarity of doer and done to. The parallels between our clinical experience and the broader cultural experience of gender have only begun to be explored.

References

Aron, L. (1991), The patient's experience of the analyst's subjectivity. *Psychoanal. Dial.*, 1: 29–51.

Aron, L. (1996), *A Meeting Of Minds: Mutuality in Psychoanalysis.* Hillsdale, NJ: The Analytic Press.

Atwood, G. & Stolorow, R. (1984) *Structures of Subjectivity: Explorations in Psychoanalytic Phenomenology.* Hillsdale NJ: The Analytic Press.

Beebe, B. & Lachmann, F. (1988), The contribution of motherinfant mutual influence to the origins of self and object relations, *Psychoanal. Psychol,*, 5:305–337.

Benjamin, J. (1991), Commentary on Irwin Hoffman's discussion, "Toward a social constructivist view of the psychoanalytic situation." *Psychoanal. Dial.*, 1: 525–534.

———— (1995), *Like Subjects, Love Objects: Essays on Recognition and Sexual Difference.* New Haven, CT: Yale University Press.

———— (1998), *Shadow of the Other: Intersubjectivity and Gender in Psychoanalysis.* New York: Routledge.

Bollas, C. (1992), *Being a Character: Psychoanalysis and Self Experience.* New York: Hill & Wang.

Cooper, S. (in press), *The Objects of Hope: Sources of Influence in Psychoanalysis.* Hillsdale, NJ: The Analytic Press.

Davies, J. M. (1994), Love in the afternoon: A relational reconsideration of desire and dread in the countertransference. *Psychoanal. Dial.*, 4:153–170.

First, E. (1993), Countertransference strain and the use of the analyst. *Psychoanal. Inq.*, 13:264–273.

Gentile, J. (1998), Listening for deep structure: Between the a priori and the inter-subjective. *Contemp. Psychoanal.*, 34:67–90.

Green, A. (1975), The analyst, symbolization and absence in the analytic setting. In: *On Private Madness*. Madison CT: International Universities Press, 1986.

———— (1994), Dialectical thinking and therapeutic action in the psychoanalytic process. *Psychoanal. Quart.*, 63:187–217.

Lacan, J. (1988), *The Seminars of Jacques Lacan, Book I*, ed. J. A. Miller (trans. J. Forrester). New York: Norton.

Maroda, K. (1991). *The Power of Countertransference*. Chichester, NY: Wiley.

Mitchell, S. (1993), *Hope and Dread in Psychoanalysis*. New York: Basic Books.

Natterson, J. (1991), *Beyond Countertransference*. Northvale, NJ: Aronson.

Ogden, T. (1986), *The Matrix of the Mind*. Northvale, Aronson.

———— (1994), *Subjects of Analysis*. Northvale, NJ: Aronson.

Pizer, S. (1998), *Building Bridges: Negotiating of Paradox in Psychoanalysis*. Hillsdale NJ: The Analytic Press.

Ringstrom, P. (1998), Therapeutic impasses in contemporary psychoanalytic treatment: Revisiting the double bind hypothesis. *Psychoanal. Dial.*, 8:297–316.

Slavin, M. & Kriegman, D. (1992). *The Adaptive Design of the Human Psyche: Psychoanalysis, Evolutionary Biology, and the Therapeutic Process*. New York: Guilford Press.

———— & ———— (1998), Why the analyst needs to change. *Psychoanal. Dial.*, 8:247–285.

Spezzano, C. (1996), The three faces of two-person psychology: Development, ontology, and epistemology. *Psychoanal. Dial.*, 6:599–622.

Stern, D. (1985), *The Interpersonal World of the Infant*. New York: Basic Books.

Stolorow, R. & Atwood, G. (1992), *Contexts of Being: The Intersubjective Foundations of Psychological Life*. Hillsdale, NJ: The Analytic Press.

Winnicott, D. W. (1969), The use of an object and relating through identification. In: *Playing and Reality*. New York: Basic Books, 1971, pp. 86–94.

Masochism, Submission, Surrender: Masochism as a Perversion of Surrender

(1990)

Emmanuel Ghent

▼　　▼　　▼　　▼　　▼

Editors' Introduction

Emmanuel Ghent has suggested that the analyst's beliefs play an immensely important role in psychoanalysis but that we tend to obscure the significant influence of our personal convictions and philosophies by referring to our belief systems as theories. In this deeply penetrating article, Ghent puts forward his own "credo," his belief in the fundamental need of people for the expansion and liberation of the self, the letting down of defensive barriers, and the dismantling of false self. It is in the careful attention that he pays to the universal human need for transcendence that Ghent's own belief system may be classified as a spiritual one. His psychoanalytic goal is not insight, information, or understanding alone, but, rather, transformation, a radical change in people's nature as they come into contact with the frozen parts of themselves that are yearning to be reached, known, and recognized. Ghent draws our attention to the intimate etymological relations between *healing*, making *whole*, and *holy*, thus spelling out his own personal vision of psychoanalysis as a sacred task.

211

Ghent's paper is not only philosophical, however, for he makes the significant clinical distinction between submission and surrender, and in so doing he illuminates the clinical realm of sadomasochistic phenomena and a host of related symptomatology. Whereas submission carries the connotation of defeat and is accompanied by resignation, surrender means, not subjugation, but transcendence and acceptance. The critical insight of the paper is that masochism is a perversion or distortion of this longing to surrender, to let go of defensiveness, of the wish to be penetrated, for one's essence to be known and recognized. "Submission, losing oneself in the power of the other, becoming enslaved in one or other way to the master, is the ever available lookalike to surrender," Ghent writes.

Among the most weighty implications of Ghent's clinical approach is the affirmative and hopeful sensibility conveyed by the emphasis that his theory gives to positive and healthy motivations that are disguised by what looks from the outside to be masochism, perversion, and the full range of human self-destructiveness and aggression. Ghent emphasizes our fundamental strivings for growth and development, "the impulse to psychic healing," our longings to know and be known by the other, to come clean, "yielding the defensive superstructure, being known, found, penetrated, recognized" in an accepting and safe environment. Ghent is careful, however, not to neglect or minimize the dark side of psychic life; he recognizes the evil and potential for destructiveness inherent in sadomasochistic relations. Rather than emphasize fundamentally destructive motives and the resistance's to their recognition, however, he highlights the many ways in which what looks like perversion is "a living testimonial of the urgency with which some buried part of the personality is screaming to be exhumed."

Perhaps the central project of relational psychoanalysis has been the synthetic integration of the interpersonal and object relations traditions. Ghent's work has been among the most important contributions making that convergence vital and generative. Schooled in interpersonal psychoanalysis, with its extensive exploration of the interactive nature of the analytic relationship, Ghent has become one of the most insightful interpreters of Winnicott's creative journeys to the roots of creativity and a personal sense of meaning.

Emmanuel Ghent's "Credo: The Dialectics of One-Person and Two-Person Psychologies" (1989, *Contemporary Psychoanalysis*, 25:169–211) was among the first major statements elucidating the modern relational approach with its attention to both the intrapsychic and the interpersonal, internal and external object relations, and one- and two-person psychologies. In "Paradox and Process" (1992, *Psychoanalytic Dialogues*, 2:135–159), Ghent elaborated on paradox as a key term in efforts to transcend simple dichotomized thinking in psychoanalysis. "Interaction in the Psychoanalytic Situation" (1995, *Psychoanalytic Dialogues*, 5:479–491) examines the shift from an informational to a transformational perspective on change processes in contemporary psychoanalysis and explores the play of interaction and recognition in the emergence of wishes and needs.

Masochism, Submission, Surrender: Masochism as a Perversion of Surrender*

▼   ▼   ▼   ▼   ▼

Surrender, in striking contrast to masochism, is a word that is seldom encountered in the psychoanalytic literature, and even then it often bears an ambiguous meaning. My goal in this paper is to give the term a certain clarity of definition and to study its relation to submission and masochism, which I regard as antitheses to surrender. In order to span the full compass of the meaning I give to surrender, my plan is to broaden the scope implied by the title and touch on some other issues that are related to surrender: object usage (Winnicott, 1969) and its perversion in the form of sadism, creativity, and the apperception of threatening meaning.

Let me say at the outset that by masochism I mean all that is customarily intended by the term including both its sexual and characterological meanings. By perversion I mean something akin to distortion, corruption, diversion, misconstruction. The meaning I will give to the term "surrender" has nothing to do with hoisting a white flag; in fact, rather than carrying a connotation of defeat, the term will convey a quality of liberation and expansion of the self as a corollary to the letting down of defensive barriers. I hope the meaning of surrender, in its most inclusive sense, will gradually reveal itself as we encounter it in a variety of contexts. Nor am I convinced that "surrender" is the right word for what I would like to convey. Alternative words will crop up from time to time and perhaps help give form to the conception.

The thrust of this paper is not to challenge or discredit the vast lit-

* First presented at New York University Postdoctoral Program in Psychoanalysis, December 2, 1983. Originally published in *Contemporary Psychoanalysis*, 26(1):108–135. © 1990 W. A. White Institute.

erature on masochism and the ever sharpening insight into its psychic functions and meanings, but to attempt to illumine the shroud of mystery that still hangs over this curious human phenomenon—the seeking out of submission, pain or adversity—by drawing attention to another dimension that in my view plays a major and often deeply buried role in its varied expressions.

By way of circling around the meaning of surrender I would like first to draw upon a paper by Michael Eigen (1981), a remarkable analysis of the work of Winnicott, Lacan and Bion in which he locates a dimension of faith that underlies some of their most basic conceptions. "By the *area of faith*," Eigen says, "I mean to point to a way of experiencing which is undertaken with one's whole being, all out, 'with one's heart, with one's soul, and with all one's might.' " Faith, surrender, the beginnings of creativity and symbol formation all intersect in the world of transitional experiencing "when the infant lives through a faith that is prior to a clear realization of self and other differences."

Later, with object usage, there comes a new awakening in which "the core sense of creativeness that permeates transitional experiencing is reborn on a new level, insofar as genuine not-me nutriment becomes available for personal use." One might imagine the subject saying to the object, "I went all out, completely vulnerable, in the faith [or surrender] that someone was out there—and it turned out to be true, as I could only have known by destroying you with all my might, and yet here you are. I love you."

Throughout this paper I imply that there is, however deeply buried or frozen, a longing for something in the environment to make possible the surrender, in the sense of yielding, of false self. "For this to occur," Winnicott (1954) says, there must be "a belief in the possibility of a correction of the original failure represented by a latent capacity for regression." Here, regression and surrender are close relatives.

In describing the course of an analysis, Winnicott (1954) wrote, "The false self gradually became a 'caretaker self,' and only after years could a caretaker self become handed over to the analyst, the self surrender to the ego. . . . The theory is being put forward of regression as part of the healing[1] process" (p. 281). The yearning for surrender of this false self

---

1. It is worth noting here the relation between *healing*, making *whole*, and *holy*, all of which are etymological cognates. In this connection note Winnicott's (1971, pp. 28–29) description of false self as "missing the boat," or at times simply as "missing," "being absent." In the old testament the Hebrew word designating *sin* has as its literal meaning *to miss* as in "missing the boat," "missing an opportunity to be present, alive" (Fromm, 1966, p. 132). The cure for *miss-*

is emphasized by Winnicott: "The organization that makes regression useful has this quality distinct from the other defense organizations in that it carries with it *the hope of a new opportunity* (italics added) for an unfreezing . . ." (Winnicott, 1954). My point here has been to highlight the centrality, despite its buried secrecy, of a *longing* for the birth, or perhaps rebirth, of true self.

As tags of meaning begin to attach to our notion of surrender, it seems to take on the sense of being in some way the obverse of resistance. Resistance is the name given to motivational forces operating against growth or change and in the direction of maintenance of the status quo. Surrender might be thought of as reflective of some "force" towards growth, for which, interestingly, no satisfactory English word exists. Submission, on the other hand, either operates in the service of resistance, or is at best adaptive as an expedient. The superstructure of defensiveness, the protections against anxiety, shame, guilt, anger are, in a way, all deceptions, whether they take the form of denial, splitting, repression, rationalizations, evasions. Is it possible that deep down we long to give this up, to "come clean," as part of an even more general longing to be known, recognized? Might this longing also be joined by a corresponding wish to know and recognize the other? As to the developmental origins of such longings I would locate them as being rooted in the primacy of object-seeking as a central motivational thrust in humans.

To develop further the meaning of surrender, some features that characterize it may be enumerated:

1. It does not necessarily require another person's presence, except possibly as a guide. One may surrender "in the presence of another," not "to another" as in the case of submission.
2. Surrender is not a voluntary activity. One cannot choose to surrender, though one can choose to submit. One can provide facilitative conditions for surrender but cannot make it happen.

---

ing is to become whole through surrender; the cure for sinning, in this sense, is to come alive, to be present in full awareness, authentic, centered in true self, holy. Rycroft (1966) has observed that "there would seem to be no necessary incompatibility between psychoanalysis and those religious formulations which locate God within the self. One could, indeed, argue that Freud's Id (and even more Groddeck's It), the impersonal force within which is both the core of oneself and yet not oneself, and from which in illness one becomes alienated, is a secular formulation of the insight which makes religious people believe in an immanent God . . ."

3. It may be accompanied by a feeling of dread and death, and/or clarity, relief, even ecstasy.
4. It is an experience of being "in the moment," totally in the present, where past and future, the two tenses that require "mind" in the sense of secondary processes, have receded from consciousness.
5. Its ultimate direction is the discovery of one's identity, one's sense of self, one's sense of wholeness, even one's sense of unity with other living beings. This is quite unlike submission in which the reverse happens: one feels one's self as a puppet in the power of another; one's sense of identity atrophies.
6. In surrender there is an absence of domination and control; the reverse is true in the case of submission.
7. It is easily confused with submission and often confounded with it for exploitative purposes. Certainly in life they are often found together. Considering the central thesis of this paper, that submission be viewed as a defensive mutant of surrender, this juxtaposition should not be surprising. (Nonetheless they are intrinsically very different.)
8. The distinction I am making between surrender and submission helps clarify another pair that are often confused. Resignation accompanies submission; it is heavy and lugubrious. Acceptance can only happen with surrender. It transcends the conditions that evoked it. It is joyous in spirit and, like surrender, it happens; it cannot be made to happen.

In the West surrender has meant "defeat." In the East it has meant transcendence, liberation. In the West "ego", as used in the vernacular, has meant one's strength, rationality, a very close relative, until recently, of one's self. In the East "ego" has meant maya, (dream, the illusion of one's self), a concept close to Lacan's "the Imaginary" or Winnicott's "unit self" world of identifications and projections, or Fairbairn's closed inner world. The goal in all of these systems is the awakening from the "dream world." In the East, to quote Heinrich Zimmer (1954), "the primary concern—in striking contrast to the interest of modern philosophers of the West—has always been, not information but transformation, a radical changing of man's nature and . . . a renovation of his understanding both of the outer world and of his own existence." Perhaps we see vestiges of this distinction in the schism between analysts whose emphasis is informational (insight is what cures) as against those for whom the focus is transformational (with cure comes insight). Seen in this light the controversial "short hour" of Lacan acquires new meaning, its intent and sometimes effect being to at least momentarily awaken the analysand from the world of the Imaginary, the dream . . . and perhaps provide a glimpse of something closer to the Real.

It has been said that there are no gurus, only disciples. The guru creates an illusion—an illusion which permits the disciple to yield, surrender false self, and therein have a chance at finding himself. The process may be thought of as allowing the disciple to re-enter the exhilarating world of transitional experiencing—wherein the guru is the transitional object. The "ego," false self, "mind" wants to argue; the guru won't argue. He knows that all engagement at this level reinforces the strength of the "ego" (false self). Surrender in this sense does not need a guru. The indirect object of the surrender could as well be a tree, the sun, God . . . anything or anyone that will not impinge with its own "ego." The process is what is important; the object to whom one surrenders is irrelevant. However, because we are so impressed by our "ego," we need to find something or someone who so totally transcends our experience, whose presence is so total and affirming that we will take a chance on surrendering. Hence the guru, and in a different world, the analyst. He is an excuse, an ally for true self to come forth.

For most of us in the West this notion of surrender is something so foreign as to be barely comprehensible. Perhaps a detour into the world of art or creativity in general will serve as a bridge to grope into the meaning of surrender as distinguished from submission. Marion Milner (1957), in paraphrasing Jacques Maritain (1953), says that "any 'explanation of art which is only in terms of the context of repressed wishes . . . leaves out what is essential . . . to art. It leaves out this deliberately fostered getting in touch with, not just hidden wishes but *a different way of functioning* (italics added); and a way of functioning which is essential if something new is to be created."

In her book, *On Not Being Able to Paint*, Milner (1950) drew attention to another phenomenon that I would include under the umbrella of meaning provided by the word surrender. She speaks of "the blanking out of ordinary consciousness when one is able to break free from the familiar and allow a new unexpected entity to appear." One's ordinary sense of self seems temporarily to have disappeared. Composers often have the feeling that the musical idea comes from some source external to themselves; Mozart said he was not a composer, merely an amanuensis to God. This subjective "blanking out" as in the so-called oceanic feeling, or as "emptiness," the beneficent state of being that is at the center of the *Tao*, have been likened by analysts to the state of blissful satisfaction at mother's breast. Milner goes on to ask if these may not also reflect an essential part of the creative process, not just of painting, but of living: 'May they not be moments in which there is a plunge into no-differentiation which results (if all goes well) in a re-emerging into a new division of the me-not-me . . . ?"

I have already hinted at the notion that these phenomena that I am encompassing as surrender are not mere descriptions of a particular way of functioning, but are as well characterized by a quality of need, mostly operating out of awareness, yet seemingly with a relentlessness that is not easy to account for in traditional psychoanalytic terms. By "need" I am not implying that there is something like an inborn instinct for the integration of self. My view rather is that in normal development the most primitive functions and needs of the infant, when adequately responded to and interacted with by the environing others, give rise to ever more sophisticated and complex conative structures, which later we recognize as having the valence or motivational quality of need. Milner (1969), too, seems to imply something akin to a need, when towards the end of her deeply compelling book, *The Hands of the Living God*, she concludes, "Certainly, some patients seemed to be aware, dimly or increasingly, of a *force* in them to do with growth, growth towards their own shape, also as something that seemed to be sensed as *driving them* to break down false inner organizations which do not really belong to them; something which can also be deeply feared, as a kind of creative fury that will not let them rest content with a merely compliant adaptation; and also feared because of the temporary chaos it must cause when the integrations on a false basis are in process of being broken down in order that a better one may emerge" (pp. 384–385; italics added).

We are left with many questions: Is this phenomenon a different kind of integrative force? If so, what is its nature, and what are its antecedents in the developing human? My hunch is that there is something like a universal need, wish or longing for what I am calling surrender and that it assumes many forms. In some societies there are culturally sanctioned occasions for its realization in the form of ecstatic rituals and healing trances. In other societies, perhaps most notably in Japan where the psychology of *amae*² is so central to one's way of being, something akin to

---

2. I am grateful to Dr. Jean-Yves Roy of Montreal for having brought to my attention the work of Takeo Doi (1973, 1986) on the psychology of *amae* and its relation to the phenomenon of surrender. The word *amae* has variously been translated as dependence, a form of love, the play of indulgence. In some contexts, the verb *amaeru* conveys a meaning of surrender that resembles its usage in this paper. The *amae* psychology underpins a sense of oneness between mother and child, and plays an indispensable role in the development of a healthy spiritual life (Doi, 1973, p. 75). Zen *satori* (enlightenment) might be looked upon as an affirmation of *amae* (p. 77). The person who seeks *amae* often experiences frustration, with the result that some people turn to Zen and other religions,

surrender is experienced as almost universally desired and desirable. In many people in our own culture the wish for surrender remains buried; in some it is expressed in creative and productive ways, and in others its derivatives appear in pathological form, deflected away from normal channels by that most unwelcome price-tag: dread. I suspect further that this dread is something that we have encountered in other contexts and have conceptualized as annihilation anxiety, dread of dissolution, ego fragmentation and so on. Perhaps what I am saying is that just as in so many other aspects of living, where there is a dread, so, too, there is a wish, a longing, however disguised its expression may be. Poets have captured in a line or two what takes the rest of us pages of gropings to contact. (Rilke, 1912, p. 21) confides in us about his experience of surrender when he writes

> . . . For Beauty's nothing but beginning of Terror we're still just able to bear, and why we adore it so is because it serenely disdains to destroy us.

The intimate relation between dread and wish is as old as psychoanalysis. Guntrip (1969) spoke of ego dissolution in two seemingly opposite ways; it reflected the deepest dread and at the same time was inseparable from the ultimate longing of the frozen-in true self to be discovered. Eigen (1973) noticed with surprise how a number of patients had spontaneously undertaken periods of profound abstinence for the sake of their personal development.

> It was as though a reaction to the over-stimulating pleasure orientation had begun to set in. . . . The practical-social milieu was viewed increasingly as lacking in crucial respects and discounted as a place one could want to take root in. Neither people nor things seemed any longer to offer the promise, pleasure or satisfaction 'similar' patients just some years before had compulsively sought. . . . The process took place 'blindly' and was often frightening. Most generally, patients felt they were being drawn down out of the world as though by a magnet towards a sense of self they knew they had at bottom. . . . Often a state of seemingly endless, painful emptiness preceded the clear experiencing of this I-kernel.

Many therapists would be frightened by this, viewing it as either depression or withdrawal or even a heralding of psychosis. As I under-

---

while others out of a similar motivation are driven to the pursuit of beauty (p. 79). In the West, freedom has usually meant freedom from dependence, and we see it in the celebration of autonomy at the expense of human connection. At the root of the *amae* psychology of the East is the reverse emphasis: the freedom to bond, rather than the Western focus on freedom from bondage (pp. 84ff).

stand it, however, what Eigen is describing is a phase in successful analysis when the patient begins to get in touch with what Winnicott (1965) referred to as that "true, silent, inviolable self, beyond all usual communication with the outside world." The self structure described by Eigen (1973), unlike the regressed ego of Guntrip, is "intensely alive and active. . . . It is experienced in an aura of power. . . . The respite here is not passivity in the womb, not a sleep, but an active seeing stillness, compact and electrifying."

The main hypothesis of this paper is that it is this passionate longing to surrender that comes into play in at least some instances of masochism. Submission, losing oneself in the power of the other, becoming enslaved in one or other way to the master, is the ever available lookalike to surrender. It holds out the promise, seduces, excites, enslaves, and in the end, cheats the seeker-turned-victim out of his[3] cherished goal, offering in its place only the security of bondage and an ever amplified sense of futility. By substituting the appearance and trappings of surrender for the authentic experience, an agonizing, though at times temporarily exciting, masquerade of surrender occurs: a self-negating submissive experience in which the person is enthralled by the other. The intensity of the masochism is a living testimonial of the urgency with which some buried part of the personality is screaming to be exhumed. This is not to be minimized as an expression of the longing to be healed, although so often we bear witness to its recurring miscarriage.

Having put forth a substantial portion of my thesis, it now feels essential to place it in perspective. The literature on masochism is vast and this is clearly not the place for a critical review. In the early years of psychoanalysis masochism was seen essentially as an expression of drive derivatives, or as a superego phenomenon (Freud, 1924). Later, based on the work of Reich (1933), Horney (1935), Berliner (1947), Menaker (1953) among others, it was seen as a defensive reaction of the ego. Brenman (1952) showed how masochism served a multiplicity of functions at the same time. Stolorow and Lachmann (1980) add yet another function: that "masochistic activities may . . . represent abortive (and sometimes primitively sexualized) efforts to restore and maintain the structural cohesion, temporal stability, and positive affective coloring of a precarious or crumbling self representation" (p. 30). The formulation I am suggesting is not intended to replace others but to add a depth of focus to them. It has a paradoxical relation to the self-psychology formulation in that it implies in the long run a strength-

---

3. For purposes of expressive clarity I will at times use the masculine pronoun generically; it is not intended to convey any gender significance.

ening, a wholling of the self; on the other hand, it implies that a surrender, a controlled dissolution of self-boundaries is at times *sought*, not only feared; that the masochistic phenomena are symptoms of the derailment or distortion of a wish, not just the defense against a fear. As in Eigen's (1981) formulation about "The Area of Faith in Winnicott, Lacan and Bion," there is a tone of sought-after vitality and joy, rather than escape from doom.

Masochistic phenomena have often been traced to deprivation, traumata and developmental interferences suffered in the early preoedipal years. Stolorow and Lachmann (1980, pp. 30–31) suggest that these early traumata would also leave their mark by interfering with the development of a cohesive and stable self-representation. The masochistic tendency then would serve to shore up the lack of cohesion of the self. An alternative view might be that in response to these early traumata a false self based on compliance is built up. This eventuates in a continuing longing to surrender this false self in the hope of a "new beginning" (Balint, 1968). Any movement in this direction would likely lead to the re-experience of the mortification and annihilation anxiety that first led to the development of the false self. One might expect a certain "invitation" of masochism and a submissive attitude, "mistaking" submission for surrender, since submission, as in the perversion of surrender, is the closest the person has likely come to knowing about surrender. Winnicott (1974), in "The Fear of Breakdown," threw further light on what I am generically calling the longing to surrender. In effect, he identified the fear of breakdown as really being the fear of re-experiencing, and the wish to re-experience, the breakdown that has already occurred so early in life that it cannot be remembered. I will deal with this more fully in connection with the role of surrender in the apperception of meaning.

An appropriate question arises from this melange of masochism and surrender. What are the roots in experience that eventuate in this clinical picture? Perhaps a partial answer is to be found in an earlier paper by Winnicott (1950–55, pp. 211ff.) a study on what he called motility and what we might now call activity, or assertiveness. He described three patterns. In one, the healthy pattern, through motility the world outside the baby is constantly being discovered and re-discovered so that contact with the environment is an experience of the individual. Only under these conditions may the individual start to exist. In the second pattern the environment impinges on the baby and instead of a series of individual experiences there is a series of reactions to impingement. Under these circumstances, only withdrawal allows an individual existence.

In a third pattern, which is extreme, this is exaggerated to such a degree that there is not even a resting place for individual experience, and the result is a failure in the primary narcissistic state to evolve an individual. The 'individual' then develops as an extension of the shell rather than of the core, and as an extension of the impinging environment. . . . The individual then *exists by not being found.*

In the second and third patterns it is only through environmental impingement that the motility potential becomes a matter or experience. Here is ill health. To a lesser or greater degree the individual *must* be opposed and only if opposed [I would add: or imposed upon] does the individual tap the important motility source. This is satisfactory while environment consistently impinges, but environmental impingement must continue . . . and must have a pattern of its own, else chaos reigns, since the individual cannot develop a personal pattern" (italics all in the original).

For our purposes, what bears emphasis is that in the second and third pattern the individual or "non-individual" that has developed in an atmosphere of impingement has a continuing need for environmental impingement. I believe Winnicott is identifying here at least one source of the masochistic syndrome, pointing to the need for patterned impingement. Is this a euphemism suggestive of a need to be the object of sadistic experience? "Impingement" is not far from "penetration." The deeper yearning, which remains invisible behind compulsive masochistic activity (in itself needed to forestall chaos or disintegration), is the longing to be reached and known, in an accepting and safe environment. The individual then becomes free to use his or her own motility to discover and be discovered in such a way that contact with the environment can become an "experience of the individual."

Fantasies of being raped can have all manner of meanings, often superimposed. Among them, in my clinical experience, one will almost always find, sometimes deeply buried, a yearning for what I am calling surrender. Erotic fantasies in relation to the analyst (usually, but by no means only, in the case of a female patient with male analyst) or the wish to make love with the analyst so very often turns out to have as its root the intense longing to surrender in the sense of giving over, yielding the defensive superstructure, being known, found, penetrated, recognized. The closest most of us come to the experience of surrender is in the moment of orgasm with a loved one. Little surprise it should be then for the sexual scene to be the desired focus for such letting-go. It is not primarily the sex that is longed for except as the vehicle for the glimpse of surrendered bliss that we are speaking of. Sometimes the roles are reversed and the fantasy is of the analyst's total surrender with the patient. This turns out ultimately to be a half-way house on the way to the ultimate longed-for goal of self-surrender and being known in one's nakedness. Often the erotic fantasies have a distinctly masochistic flavor, as, for example, in being forced, tricked, seduced into lovemaking, or being overpowered by the sheer masterfulness of the other. The masochistic expression here is the disguise, or what I am calling the perversion of the wish for surrender. If by mischance the analyst should enter into the patient's real world in sexual response, the masochism of the patient soon flourishes, and all hope of what the patient had really longed for, genuine surrender, is lost. The fantasy of rape is a foil for the disguised expression of the longing for surrender. Real rape, be it by the penis, or the "ego" (psychological rape, no matter how subtle), violently forecloses and, by not recognizing or not caring about the genuine longing, has deeply betrayed it. It is important to emphasize that I am not trying to reduce the entirety of an erotic transference to this dynamic; many other layers are often involved and have to be dealt with.

The sexual arena is not the only area where passionate, even ecstatic intensity lends itself to being a masochistic substitute for surrender. The excitement of recklessness or dangerous, near-death activities is another, as is the pull to manifest infantilism and helpless demandingness. Both of these quasi-masochistic configurations—and there are others—can be very intense and can function as disguised expression of the longing for surrender.

In the analytic situation this longing for, dread of, and pain in, surrender is most frequently first encountered in the defensive reactions that are designed to contain the impulse, a kind of compromise where the impulse is deflected and only appears in some disguised, distorted form. Sometimes the patient, experiencing the beginnings of the dread we are speaking of, attributes it to the dangerousness of the analyst, his or her intrusiveness, malevolence, empathic unresponsiveness, seductiveness. Often enough, some expressions of these features may well appear and even be fanned by an intensifying transference–countertransference interaction. An erotic transference may develop, or a paranoid transference, or masochistic or sadistic acting out, even a variety of negative therapeutic reaction. But what is common to all of these manifestations of the impulse towards, and dread of, surrender is some aspect of masochism.

Perhaps a few vignettes will illustrate what I mean by masochism as a perversion of surrender. A borderline young woman, exceedingly demanding, whiny and manipulative, left the session with an involuntary smile saying, "That was a good session," implying that this time, in contrast to all others, I had not failed her. During the session I had remained firm but gentle against a barrage of demands and complaints. At one point I had said "You know, I somehow think that if you had your way you would feel deeply disappointed." She smiled involuntarily and after a long, very unwonted silence, said, "You mean if I win, I lose?" I said, "The part of you that's hiding, and we're trying to find, she's the loser." Another long silence. Next day her first words were, "You really got through to me," and then she reported with much embarrassment, that after the session she had gone home, beat herself, forced a stick into her anus and masturbated with fantasies of being tortured. My understanding of the sequence was that she had felt her defensive barrier come down, there had been a glimpse into the possible existence of an undefended lovable self and with it the nascent excitement of a beginning surrender. Quickly the impulse to surrender had to be redefined in terms of false self, as its masochistic counterpart. Feeling reached, known, "gotten through to," was translated into "penetrated" (in its ambiguous meaning) and beaten. A momentary new reality was translated back into the old familiar inner reality; the impulse to surrender (she had often said, "Please do not let me fool you") had to be experienced as its perversion, masochism.

A professional woman of 30 dreamed, "I am hiding under the table from what seems to be the forces of repression, Franco men. There is a man with a gun there. He had a black beard. I had to get a secret message, a very important message that concerned the secret location of our forces, to an older man. I was extremely nervous and did not think I would be able to do it; yet actually I did. Still I felt I had not done well enough." Among the various meanings reflected in the dream is the one that concerns us here: that the very impulse to be known, to get the vital message through to the analyst about her secret inner strength—this impulse had to be experienced in the context of pain and the dread of being killed or raped. It is as if this woman (as the masochist) needs the powerful force of violence, the fascist with the gun (that is, the image of the analyst as sadist), because only under his presence and force is she able to get the secret to the old man. In other words, "I have to invite danger and perhaps sex with the analyst, that is, be the masochist, in order to provide the cover for getting the secret message to the analyst, the wish to surrender and be known.

Masud Khan (1973) makes the convincing point that "all perversions accrue from a symbiotic complicity between two persons, which is both unconscious and empathic." He then goes on to describe in his characteristically vivid style a young woman who had for years been in a state of inertia and depression. Slowly but surely she was won over by a man who tantalized, excited her to intense passion, and degraded her; in his power she felt totally helpless. Khan notes, however, how the relationship with the lover helped her exteriorize her psychic pain and her rage, and furthermore, initiated experience for her. He reflects on how the pervert has a great advantage over a therapist in being able to mobilize the "passive will" in a person inasmuch as he can initiate and execute experiences through his "active will." Nonetheless, the therapist is not without the exercise of his will and power, as manifested for example by the various demands made by the analytic setup, which, if not adhered to, the analyst treats as resistance.

During the course of therapy, this same patient began asking him frequent questions as to how she should behave in various social situations. When these went unanswered, the patient would withdraw into a torpor not unlike the original depressed, apathetic state that preceded the love affair. "Once I had decided to answer her questions," Khan observes, "what followed was very revealing. She would instantly accept and agree to what I said. But then she would *play around* with what I had said: question and correct it until she would find the right solution for herself. I was very struck by her capacity to play with different possibilities of conduct, once I had suggested a course. If I abstained she would invariably go inert and become resourceless. This use of the analyst's will and power with which she could identify and internalize, proved extremely helpful to her." My reading of the situation is that the patient had identified with the analyst's power in the sense that she became the "active will," and he yielded (surrendered) to her initiative in such a way that there developed, to use Winnicott's words, "an area of play in the analytic situation" (Winnicott, 1968).

Khan asks, "How was playing in the 'analytic contract' different for this patient from participating in 'games' that her lover had made her an accomplice to during her 'perverted contract.'" He then answers: "The crucial difference seemed to [lie] in the different *use* of the patient by her lover and by her analyst. . . . Her lover compelled her into the role of his 'subjective object.'" That is, he forced her to play a passive part in his inner drama.

> He had to devalue and disrupt all functions in her that gave her a separate identity and existence. . . . What she had experienced was merely an intensely excited and passive surrender to his will. . . . In the analytic contract, per contrast, she sought help to be enabled to find her own will and power in her life situation. The empathy she required was in the service of the actualization of her own capacities and functions towards personal autonomy (p. 208).

To return to the theme of this presentation, I would describe her relation to her lover not at all as surrender but as that of submission, a pseudo-surrender, a masochistic object of the sadist. Anna Freud (1952) has diagnosed the emotional predicament in perversion formation as the dread of emotional surrender. It is surrender, in the sense I have defined, that the patient was longing for, the wish to be found, recognized, penetrated to the core, so as to become real, or as Winnicott put it in another context "to come into being."

In this case with the lover we witness the perversion of the process, where instead of the patient's autonomy being freed and her identity found, she becomes a captive puppet. With the analyst, on the other hand, a mild kind of surrender, again in the sense that I mean it, has occurred, incidentally on the part of the analyst as well as the patient, with the result that the patient feels found, enriched and more whole.

Sadism as a Perversion of Object Usage.

It is difficult to do justice in a few paragraphs to Winnicott's concept of object usage (Winnicott, 1969) as against object relating. Yet, as a preamble to the question whether there is a formulation for sadism analogous to the one I am proposing for masochism, it merits review. In transitional experiencing the mother allows, encourages, the infant to bathe in the illusion that she or some part of her is part of baby. With the evolution of creative play and the very gradual disillusion by the mother, the baby discovers and in effect, creates, bit by bit, both self and external reality. In object *relating* both self and other are perceived largely through projections and identifications. The self at this stage may be thought of as a "unit self" in that relating can be described in terms of an "isolate," the individual subject; the object then is the subjectively perceived object. The *use* of an object, object-usage, however takes object-relating for granted. New features enter that involve the nature and behavior of the object in external reality. "The object, if it is to be used, must necessarily be real in the sense of being part of shared reality, not a bundle of projections" (p. 88). Winnicott gives an almost diagrammatic example:

> Two babies are feeding at the breast; one is feeding on the self in the form of projections, and the other is feeding on (using) milk from a woman's breast. . . . The change does not come about automatically, by maturational process alone. . . . Mothers, like analysts, can be good or not good enough; some can and some cannot carry the baby over from relating to usage. [This transition] is the most difficult thing, perhaps, in human development . . . [and] the most irksome of all the early failures that come for mending. . . . The change [from relating to use] means that the subject destroys the object [as subjective object] and the object, if it survives destruction, is now real. . . . 'Hullo object!' 'I destroyed you.'

'I love you.' 'You have value for me because of your survival of my destruction of you' [p. 89].

In effect, destruction has created the reality, placed the object outside the self. The word 'destruction' may seem out of place here in what might naively appear to be a piece of straightforward development. Yet it is needed "not because of the baby's impulse to destroy, but because of the object's liability not to survive" (Winnicott, 1969). The varieties of nonsurvival include retaliation, withdrawal, defensiveness in any of its forms, an overall change in attitude in the direction of suspiciousness or diminished receptivity, and finally, a kind of crumbling, in the sense of losing one's capacity to function adequately as mother, or in the analytic setting, as analyst.

This conception of development involving the difficult passage from object relating to object use implies a radical departure from the usual analytic notion that aggression is reactive to the encounter with external reality (the reality principle). Here it is destructiveness that creates the very quality of externality.

But the main reason for this discussion of the development of the capacity for object usage is to explore its relation to surrender, masochism, and now, sadism. The essence of both transitional experiencing and the transition into object usage is the heady and wonderful world of creative experiencing wherein self and other have the opportunity to become real. Failures in either or both of these developmental currents lead to the development of one or other variety of false self; from the baby's point of view they might well be called failures of faith.

A principal cause of failure in transitional experiencing is what has already been referred to as impingement by the caretaker. We have seen how this intrusiveness interferes with true experiencing or "coming into being," with the distressing result that for the infant to "exist," continuing impingement is required. Here we saw the beginnings of masochism. I have suggested also that in many people there is an impulse to surrender, perhaps in order to reengage that area of transitional experiencing, the miscarriage of which impulse or longing appears as masochism or submission.

I now suggest the possibility that failure of the transition from object relating to object usage would result from a different (but probably related) failure of the caretaker: retaliation, defensiveness, negativity on the part of the caretaker or crumbling of her or his effectiveness. In either case the triple misfortune is that the subjective object never becomes real but remains a bundle of projections, and externality is not discovered; as a corollary the subject is now made to feel that he or she *is* destructive; and finally, fear and hatred of the other develops, and with them, characterological destructiveness comes into being. In short we have the setting for the development of sadism (in what remains a unit self, a self as isolate), the need to aggressively control the other as a perversion of object usage, much as we have seen in masochism as a perversion of surrender. An excerpt from a session will perhaps add a little flesh and blood:

> I desperately want you to stay in control no matter how hard "the mouth with teeth" tries to destroy you—not destroy you as a person, but as a competent analyst. I need you to be strong, to never "explain" anything. If you explain, I feel it as defensive and, therefore I am back in control and I have forced you to defend yourself. The mouth that babbles on vindictively and vengefully needs to be allowed out and to be here. Don't tell him to give up control. He also wants to give up control but will do so only if he feels your strength not to be afraid of him in his full presence.

There is a reciprocity here—a wish for surrender (which in this excerpt reveals only hints at masochism), a plea for what we have been calling object usage, and an awareness that what now exists as biting sadism is a derivative of the wish to discover the reality of the other, and thereby truly experience the self.

Here we see an outreaching, penetrative version of surrender. Earlier we saw how a defensive mutation of the longing to be recognized, deeply known, penetrated, a desire for what might be called "receptive" surrender, becomes transformed into a seeming quest for submission, submergence of self. Now we come upon another version of surrender, the complement of the earlier variety. We see it here in the desire to deeply know, penetrate, discover the other. One might say that the longing is to dive deeply into the other, or, in Winnicott's terms, "use" the other, and discover what might be called "true other" in contrast to the false other. False other corresponds either to the false image of the other or the false self of the other. If the other has not been destroyed in the process, false other turns out to be (or to have been) the false image or representation of the other. On the other hand, if the other was destroyed, rendered useless, then the false other corresponds in all probability to the false self of the other.

Use of an object is not a very felicitous expression, because it too closely resembles the vernacular "using the other as a sexual object," as well as "objectification." Perhaps better words to express Winnicott's meaning would be un-cover, dis-cover, penetrate. Unfortunately, except for "penetrate," these do not easily permit the ambiguity that "use" affords wherein attack may be the effect, although not at all the intended goal, which by contrast is to dis-cover, or to un-cover the real other in lieu of the subjective other. We seem to need a word as a container of the meaning that resides in both aspects of the phenomenon under discussion, what might be called the autoplastic and the alloplastic versions of surrender. The lack of such a word points up the foreignness of these conceptions to our ordinary way of thinking. Perhaps this is an expression of the awkwardness in our own language of expressing the opposite of intentionality, a state of being that is not marked by active conscious goal-seeking. Even in expressing this thought I seem to require locutions that frame it in terms of what it is not. Yet the frequency with which reference is made in the psychoanalytic literature to Keats' famous lines "on negative capability" (Rosen, 1960; Green, 1973; Hutter, 1982), attests to its being a focus of some importance.

The sexual experience can be, for example, an instance where the meaning of surrender and object usage almost lose their distinctive meaning, and blend. On the surface it appears as though the woman is surrendered, and the man "using the object," that is, active. But in the kind of interaction we are speaking of, each is surrendered and one might say, involved in object usage, in the sense of un-covering, dis-covering the reality of the other.

In my view love and hate are not opposites. The real polarity is between love and fear. Only when there is no fear, love flourishes. When fear or anxiety is present, it often becomes manifest in a reactive and compensatory form as hatred (or indifference), with the result that love and hate (or love and indifference) appear to be the polarities. The successful use of the object, or being used by the object in the form of surrender, is one's bid at overcoming the fear of the other. Hence, the successful use and surrender, in which both survive the use and have therefore transcended fear of the other, are necessary precursors in the development of love. In fact, a deep sense of love is what is actually felt in either of these experiences.

The Apperception of Disorganizing Meaning.

I would like now to shift focus and explore the relevance of our notion of surrender to another group of phenomena. The area I am looking at has to do with what might be called the apperception of disorganizing meaning, and has bearing on the so-called repetition compulsion and the question of identification. We encounter, daily, in our practice the phenomenon of a patient who can say, "my mother was sadistic," and describe events to nail down the assertion, and yet one has the impression that the patient ends up with the feeling of "but somehow I can't believe it's true." The patient seems not to have been able to "take in" the perception of what he or she has witnessed. It is as if the perception would shatter the prevailing belief system and induce chaos were a complete perceptual letting-go to occur, a surrender to the experience. A total revision of one's perception of, in this case, mother, would have to happen in which the image of mother being sadistic would reside alongside and integrated with other images of mother.

A brief illustration: Many years ago, while vacationing in the country, my three-year-old niece noticed that my knee was scratched and bleeding slightly. She immediately said, "Oh! Blood! You have a cut. (slight pause). I'll go get you a band-aid. (slight pause). How did it happen?" I, jokingly: "We were playing in the sand and your mom pushed me!" She: "There's no cut. I don't see any blood." I: "That was just a joke; your mom didn't push me; I fell." She (greatly relieved): "That blood needs a band-aid." She immediately went off to fetch a band-aid. The story well illustrates that if a perception is threatening to a belief, either the belief or the perception has to go. In this case the idea that good mommy could cause harm to someone was so unacceptable that the perception, as long as it carried significance that would be disorganizing, had to be denied. In other words it could not be "taken in." In older children and adults a perception may be registered but its significance denied; we refer to this as the mechanism of isolation.

Another way of looking at this process is that the child's developing perceptual and cognitive skills probably outgrow the meanings he or she can safely take in. Surrender to "what is" would, in some instances, lead to a disorganizing, threatening state of being. A compromise develops, driven by the wish to surrender to the perception, and opposed by the threat it implies. The result is the masochistic solution; recurring situations are created in which each fresh opportunity for clarity is subverted by the dread, which by now is so shrouded in history as to feel nameless and "existential." Again, as we have seen earlier in our discussion of surrender, the dread and the wish are two sides of the same coin. The wish is to return to the scene of the dread and expresses not so much the wish "to master the experience" as to integrate the experience.

In effect, I am suggesting that some instances of masochism may be rooted in a deep quest for understanding, for undoing the isolation. It is as if with one mind the person is setting up situations in which he is "done in" or caused pain by the other, an authority, friend, lover, and with the other, is struggling with the inner question that remains tantalizingly unanswered: What happened? How did it happen? A loved one could not have done that to me! That is inconceivable. Then how did it happen? He did it! . . . but somehow I cannot "take it in." It just cannot be. Maybe next time I can create a situation that's more clear. . . . Then I will be able to "take it in, perceive, conceive it."

Masochism, rather than being an expression of some "aggressive drive turned inward" may, at least in some circumstances, be a distorted representation of what I have called the wish to surrender, or as in this context, to confront and "take in" the inner truth, to perceive self and other as they really are, that is, without regard to the false selves erected out of compliance to early authorities. This compulsion to repeat, masochistically, self-destructive behavior may turn out to be another form of trying to "take in" some reality, in this case the unthinkable destructiveness of a significant other. The act of "taking in" may involve a considerable degree of disorganization in order for this to be possible and, by analogy to the creative moment in art, it may mean that one has to give up, surrender the conventionalized "surface mind" view of an object, a tree or whatever, and allow the gestalt free "depth mind" (Ehrenzweig, 1953) to take over. This may mean a transition to a period of chaos in the "depth mind" before the new reality can be taken in and comprehended or expressed.

In discussing the negative therapeutic reaction, Esther Menaker (1969, p. 90) touches on this very question even using the same expression, "take in." She writes, "the patient is faced with the single ultimate choice: will he choose growth or refuse it—can he *take in what is* [italics added], *permit the resultant disorganization of the status quo of the self. . . ?"*

There is more yet to be said about this issue, the wish and dread of "taking in" experience. I am thinking of Winnicott's "axiom" (Davis and Wallbridge, 1981, p. 50) that *"the clinical fear of breakdown is the fear of breakdown that has already been experienced"* (Winnicott, 1974). He asks,

> Why does the patient go on being worried by this that belongs to the past? The answer must be that the original experience of primitive agony cannot get into the past tense unless the ego can first gather it in [cf. "take it in"] to its own present time experience and into omnipotent control now (assuming the auxiliary ego-supporting function of the mother (analyst)). . . . In other words, the patient must go on looking for the past detail which is *not yet experienced*. This search takes the form of looking for this detail in the future.

Winnicott (1974) goes on to extend this fear of breakdown to related issues such as the fear of death (annihilation) and the feelings of emptiness and non-existence. He adds, "When Keats was 'half in love with easeful death' he was, according to the idea I am putting forward here, longing for the ease that would have come if he could 'remember' [or I would add, 'take in'] having died; but to remember he must experience death now."

"Beinglessness" was the word discovered recently by a patient as he was groping for the sensation that crept over him like death when no one was there to assuage the urgent needy feelings for someone to "fill him up," to continuously affirm his existence. "It looks like I need admiration," he said, "but that's not it; it's as if I need someone to keep telling me I'm alive—or else I sink into horror—just that horror that I could feel the beginnings of when the word 'beinglessness' came to me." As deep as the dread of that state, so too is the pull to revisit it, to dig around the edges of it. I am suggesting that by reaching into the is-ness of the circumstances that led to that horror, or the events that did not happen that might have otherwise brought him into being, he is unconsciously seeking a chance to come solidly into being. As the session in question came to a close the patient said, "I have to hold onto this place and never forget it. If I lose it would be like the most important page of a book torn out. The book would be meaningless." Although in this instance it did not happen, the search, the wishing for surrender to experience, may miscarry, and in its miscarried forms may well bear the marks of masochism.

I would like now to address a related issue, another outcome that may result from the incomplete "taking-in" of experiences whose full and meaningful apperception would be disorganizing. This outcome is usually thought of as "identification with the aggressor." But what does this phrase mean? How does it happen? I have found myself wondering if the wish to perceive, "take in," comprehend something may require a certain quality of activity. It has long been known that in order to perceive a triangle, the child first has to move his eyes from point to point, and, eventually, after many repetitions of this motoric act, he becomes able to perceive and, still later, to conceive, a triangle (Hebb, 1949). Schilder (1964) similarly ties motility with perception. "Primitive perception is a state of motion. . . . Development is in the direction of the elimination of the inner motion of the perception." If what is being perceived would require inner disorganization to a degree greater than the child can handle, is it possible that a child does something analogous to what a painter does in trying to express an aspect of reality that is beyond formulation? The painter uses his available medium, paint, to represent "the unthinkable." Could it be that the child or infant uses *his* available medium, his quite plastic self as his medium, separates part of it and makes a creative representation of what he has partially perceived in the external reality? Is this perhaps another example of how, under adverse environmental conditions, the impulse to surrender, in this case the let-go, the taking-in, of this is-ness of the "unthinkable" situation, goes awry, now resulting not simply in masochism, but in an identification with the aggressor in whatever style characterizes the aggressor.[4]

Many of us have had the experience of a spouse or good friend chiding us in irritation, "You are behaving just like your father!" If and when we recover from our injured innocence and reflect on the event in question, we, at times, with a little self-analysis, dis-cover exactly what unique version of subtle hostility we were engaging in. At that moment, if we are lucky, another insight may break into consciousness with the thought, "Oh, I see! So that's what father was up to when he did such and such!" The identificatory process has finally paid off; it has at last revealed what one had not been able to see, "take in," recognize, or understand in the father.

In discussing Francis Bacon, "the skillful and challenging artist of our time who goes on and on painting the human face distorted significantly," Winnicott (1967) conjectures, "In looking at faces he seems to need to be painfully striving towards being seen, which is at the basis of creative looking" (p. 114). I would like to add to the conjecture that he is painfully striving to perceive something that he has not dared to see. If this be the case, it would be a kind of intermediate example between the painter who represents with paint what he cannot "take in" and the child who does the same with his self.

Surrender, Masochism and the Creative Process.

I would like now to return to the notion, shared by Ehrenzweig (1953) and Milner, that "this self-destruction is perhaps a distorted, because frustrated, form of self-surrender which is inherent in the creative process" (Milner, 1958). Much of Milner's analytic work has been an exploration into the pathology of the creative process. In particular her paper, *The Role of Illusion in Symbol Formation* (Milner, 1952) offers

---

4. I recently came across a paper by Minna Emch (1944) in which she describes a phenomenon in children that adds weight to this hypothesis. "When the . . . experience is one which *cannot yet* be assimilated by the child, the 'next best' tool at its command is the *attempt* to know through an attenuated repetition of the disturbing stimulus-experience, especially as it relates to the mediator of that experience." She adds that both observations of children and clinical material from adults indicate that this attempt at knowing, by acting out the likeness of a situation, takes place very early, and may result in patterns of astonishing mimicry and even the "most caustic of caricatures" (p. 14).

deeper insight into the meaning I have given to the word surrender. She describes a young girl of eleven who

> fervently and defiantly scribbled on every surface she could find. Although it looked as if it were done in anger, interpretation in terms of aggression only led to increase in the defiance. In fact, the apparent defiance did not change until I began to guess that the trouble was less to do with faeces given in anger and meant to express anger, than with faeces given in love and meant to express love [p. 106].

Milner gradually came to look upon the scribbling in a fresh way:

> By refusing to discriminate, and claiming the right to scribble over everything, the young patient was trying to deny the discrepancy between the feeling [she experienced] and the expression if it; by denying completely my right to protect any of my property from defacement she was even trying to win me over to her original belief that when she gave her messes lovingly they were literally as lovely as the feelings she had in giving of them. . . . She was struggling [with the problem of the identity of the symbol with the thing symbolized . . .] with the very early problem of coming to discriminate . . . between the lovely feeling in giving [making, creating] the mess and the mess itself [p. 107].

Although this was written long before Winnicott's paper on object usage, it provides a wonderful example of a "good-enough analyst" who was able to carry this girl over the tortuous path from object relating to object usage. Had this not occurred, the child's efforts to discover the real object and thereby real self—(cleared of the debris of the identifications and projections that kept alive the confusion of symbol with thing symbolized)—would have been defined as sadistic; the patient would likely have developed into what we think of as a sadistic, narcissistic woman.

Fortunately, Milner's perspicacity enabled her to recognize the child's struggle with the agony of disillusion in giving up the belief that everyone must see in her dirt what she sees in it. Another patient, a young boy said, "'My people' are to see these empty trucks and 'think it's gods.' In fact, Milner muses, "he is saying what the poet Yeats said: 'Tread softly, because you tread on my dreams'" (p. 107).

We ought also to "tread softly" on patients' masochism and submissiveness. These too are often expressing in a disguised and a distorted way a deep yearning to be found and recognized. Unlike Milner's children they are not so much defacing her walls as their own walls. They too are "struggling with the problem of the identity of the symbol and the thing symbolized," in this case between the longing to yield control, to give up one's protective superstructure (as the thing symbolized) and inviting rape and other overpowering action (as the symbol).

We must note, of course, that acting out is no solution. It would not help Milner's patients if all she did was let the children scribble on the wall and celebrate the scribbles as their expressions of love. The same is true of submissive masochistic behavior. What is needed in both cases is that the patient get in touch with, and be validated in, the real longing to be recognized, known, perhaps penetrated with enough gentleness that the patient can feel safe enough to discover his or her own motility, while still having a symbolic foot in the need for continuing impingement, the absence of which would be so unfamiliar as to evoke panic or chaos.

Growth and Healing.

In reviewing the territory covered by the term surrender, a subtext is revealed. The longing for surrender seems to emerge as a special detail in a more inclusive picture: growth and the restitution of impeded growth, healing. The literature abounds with papers and discussions of resistance; yet how little we study the vagaries of the force that is on the side of psychic healing, the impulse to grow, to surrender, to let-go. If this paper has said anything, it is that the pain and suffering of the masochist (and less obviously the sadist, at least in some instances) may well be the excuse the caretaker self has devised to get the true self to where it has a chance of being found, a signal that something deep inside is rent, a tear in the self, that unbeknown to its bearer, seeks healing, and that the masochistic patterns, especially if a certain satisfaction and pleasure accrues, are really expressions of the patient's efforts at self-cure. Masud Khan (1970, p. 97) has said, "Very few illnesses in a person are difficult to handle and cure. What however, is most difficult to resolve and cure is the patient's practice of self-cure." Chasseguet-Smirgel (1983) goes even further. In her explorations of the meaning of perversions she writes, "I consider that perversion is one of the essential ways and means [a person] applies in order to push forward the frontiers of what is possible and to unsettle reality. I see perversion not just as disorders of the sexual nature affecting a relatively small number of people [but] as a dimension of the human psyche in general, a temptation in the mind common to us all." The underlying theme, as Menaker (1969) suggests, is about growth, the healing and expansion of the self. She asks: "Will the patient choose it or refuse it?" Will he or she let us into the living kernel from which true growth is possible—and are we up to the challenge?

Let us not overlook the role of masochism and surrender in being a member of our profession. What other occupation requires of its practitioners that they be the objects of people's excoriations, threats and rejections, or be subjected to tantalizing offerings that plead "touch me," yet may not be touched? What other occupation has built into it the frustration of feeling helpless, stupid and lost as a necessary part of the work? And what other occupation puts its practitioners in the position of being an onlooker or midwife to the fulfillment of others' destinies. It is difficult to find a type of existence, other than that of the psychoanalyst, who fits this job description. In a sense it is the portrait of a masochist. Yet I suspect that a deep underlying motive in some analysts at least, is again that of surrender, and their own personal growth. It may be acceptably couched in masochistic garb or denied by narcissistic and/or sadistic exploitation. When the yearning for surrender is, or begins to be, realized by the analyst, the work is immensely fulfilling and the analyst grows with his patients.

Michael Polanyi (1958), the physical-chemist who turned his brilliance to sweeping inquiries into how the scientist works and to the psychology of thought, wrote: "We owe our mental existence predominantly to works of art, morality, religious worship, scientific theory and other articulate systems which we accept as our dwelling place and as the soil of our mental development. Objectivism has totally falsified our conception of truth, by exalting what we *can* know and prove, while covering up with ambiguous utterances all that we know and *cannot* prove, even though the latter knowledge underlies, and must ultimately set its seal to, all that we *can* prove" (quoted in Brenman-Gibson, (1976)). Some of the ideas addressed in this paper are at the level of hunches, and demand the follow-up of intellectual rigor as well as careful observation in our clinical work to see whether they stand the test of careful scrutiny. Also, in stressing the complexity of the matters at hand, it is important to remind ourselves that in the flush of putting forth one set of ideas, many other complicating considerations have been put aside and remain to be integrated.

Overview

As used in this paper, surrender, implies not defeat but a quality of liberation and "letting-go." I have explored the thesis that at least in some instances masochism is the result of a distortion or perversion of a deep longing for surrender, a yearning to be known, recognized, "penetrated," and often represents the miscarriage of a wish to dismantle false self. Similarly, some instances of sadism are traceable to the obverse of this phenomenon: a failure in the consummation of a more active "penetrative" type of surrender as in object usage. Successful transition from object relating to object usage involves an act of surrender and risk-taking on the part of the infant (or later, patient), as well as a degree of surrender on the part of the facilitating caretaker, or later, analyst. To round out the conception of surrender I have touched on related issues such as creativity and the apperception of disorganizing meaning.

References

Balint, M. (1968). *The Basic Fault: Therapeutic Aspects of Regression*. London: Tavistock.

Berliner, B. (1947). On some psychodynamics of masochism. *Psychoanalytic Quarterly*, 16:459–471.

Brenman, M. (1952). On teasing and being teased: and the problem of "moral masochism." *The Psychoanalytic Study of the Child*, 7:264–285. New York: International Universities Press.

Brenman-Gibson, M. (1973). Notes on the study of the creative process. In: *Psychological Issues, Monograph 36, Psychology versus Metapsychology*. New York: International Universities Press, 1976, pp. 326–357.

Chasseguet-Smirgel, J. (1983). Perversion and the universal law. *International Review of Psycho-Analysis*, 10:293–301.

Davis, M., & Wallbridge, D. (1980). *Boundary and Space, an Introduction to the Work of D. W. Winnicott*. New York: Brunner/Mazel.

Doi, T. (1973). *The Anatomy of Dependence*. Tokyo: Kodansha International.

Doi, T. (1986). *The Anatomy of Self*. Tokyo: Kodansha International.

Eigen, M. (1973). Abstinence and the schizoid ego. *International Journal of Psycho-Analysis*, 54:493–498.

Eigen, M. (1981). The area of faith in Winnicott, Lacan and Bion. *International Journal of Psycho-Analysis*, 62:413–433.

Ehrenzweig, A. (1953). *The Psycho-Analysis of Artistic Vision and Hearing*. London: Routledge & Kegan Paul.

Emch, M. (1944). On the 'need to know' as related to identification and acting out. *International Journal of Psycho-Analysis*, 25:13–19.

Freud, A. (1952). A connection between the states of negativism and emotional surrender. In: *Indications for Child Analysis and Other Papers*. New York: International Universities Press, 1968. Referred to by Khan (1972, p. 222).

Freud, S. (1924). The economic problem of masochism. *Standard Edition*, 19:159–170. London: Hogarth Press, 1961.

Fromm, E. (1966). *You Shall Be As Gods: A Radical Interpretation of the Old Testament and Its Tradition*. New York: Holt, Rinehart and Winston.

Green, A (1973). On negative capability. *International Journal of Psycho-Analysis*, 54:115–119.

Guntrip, H. (1969). *Schizoid Phenomena, Object Relations and the Self*. New York: International Universities Press.

Hebb, D. O. (1949). *The Organization of Behavior*. New York: Wiley.

Horney, K. (1935). The problem of feminine masochism. *Psychoanalytic Review,* 22:241–257.

Hutter, A. D. (1982). Poetry in psychoanalysis: Hopkins, Rosetti, Winnicott. *International Review of Psycho-Analysis*, 9:303–316.

Khan, M. M. R. (1970). Towards an epistemology of cure. In: *The Privacy of the Self*. New York: International Universities Press, 1974, pp. 93–98.

Khan, M. M. R. (1973). The role of will and power in perversions. In: *Alienation and Perversions*. New York: International Universities Press, 1979, pp. 197–209.

Khan, M. M. R. (1972). Pornography and the politics of rage and subversion. In: *Alienation and Perversions*. New York: International Universities Press, 1979, pp. 219–226.

Maritain, J. (1953). *Creative Intuition in Art and Poetry*. New York: McClelland.

Menaker, E. (1953). Masochism—a defense reaction of the ego. *Psychoanalytic Quarterly*, 22:205–220. Also in: *Masochism and the Emergent Ego, Selected Papers of Esther Menaher*, ed. L. Lerner. New York: Human Sciences Press, 1979.

Menaker, E. (1969). Will and the problem of masochism. In: *Masochism and the Emergent Ego, Selected Papers of Esther Menaher*, ed. L. Lerner. New York: Human Sciences Press, 1979.

Milner, M. (1950). *On Not Being Able to Paint*. London: Heinemann, and New York: International Universities Press, 1957.

Milner, M. (1952). The role of illusion in symbol formation. In: *New Directions In Psycho-Analysis*, eds. M. Klein, P. Heinemann, R. E. Money-Kyrle. London: Tavistock, 1955, pp. 82–108.

Milner, M. (1958). Psychoanalysis and art. In: *Psychoanalysis and Contemporary Thought*, ed. J. D. Sutherland. London: Hogarth, and New York: Grove (1959).

Milner, M. (1969). *The Hands of the Living God*. New York: International Universities Press.

Nass, M. (1984). The development of creative imagination in composers. *International Review of Psycho-Analysis*, 11:481 –492.

Polanyi, M. (1958). *Personal Knowledge: Towards a Post-Critical Philosophy*. Chicago: University of Chicago Press, 1964. Quoted in Brenman-Gibson (1973).

Reich, W. (1933). *Character Analysis*. New York: Orgone Institute Press, 1949.

Rilke, R. M. (1912–1922). *Duino Elegies*. Trans. J. B. Leishman and S. Spender. New York: Norton, 1939.

Rosen, V. H. (1960). Imagination in the analytic process. *Journal of the American Psychoanalytic Association*, 8:229–251.

Rycroft, C. (1966). Causes and meaning. In: *Psychoanalysis Observed*, ed. C. Rycroft. New York: Coward-McCann, p. 22.

Schilder, P. (1964). *Contributions to Developmental Neuropsychiatry*. New York: International Universities Press. Quoted by Nass (1984).

Stolorow, R. D., & Lachmann, F. M. (1980). *Psychoanalysis of Developmental Arrests*. New York: International Universities Press.

Winnicott, D. W. (1950–1955). Aggression in relation to emotional development. In: *Through Paediatrics to Psycho-Analysis*. New York: Basic Books, 1975.

Winnicott, D. W. (1954). Metapsychological and clinical aspects of regression within the psycho-analytical set-up. In: *Through Paediatrics to Psycho-Analysis*. New York: Basic Books, 1975, pp. 278–294.

Winnicott, D. W. (1965). *The Maturational Processes and the Facilitating Environment*. New York: International Universities Press.

Winnicott, D. W. (1967). Mirror role of mother and family in child development. In: *Playing and Reality*. London: Tavistock, 1971, pp. 111–118.

Winnicott, D. W. (1968). Playing: a theoretical statement. In: *Playing and Reality*. London: Tavistock, 1971, pp. 38–52.

Winnicott, D. W. (1969). The use of an object and relating through identifications. In: *Playing and Reality*. London: Tavistock, 1971, pp. 86–94.

Winnicott, D. W. (1971). *Playing and Reality*. London: Tavistock.

Winnicott, D. W. (1974). The fear of breakdown. *International Review of Psycho-Analysis*, 1:103–107.

Zimmer, H. (1951). *Philosophies of India*, ed. J. Campbell. Princeton, NJ: Bollingen Series, Princeton University Press.

Afterword

While much remains to be said about surrender, I will confine myself to one issue in this brief afterword. Back in 1983, when I wrote "Masochism, Submission, Surrender," I was at pains to distinguish sharply between surrender and submission, pointing out how, despite surface similarities, they were fundamentally different processes, so much so that submission at times served as a substitute for, or a defense against, the experience of surrender. By referring to submission as the alienated lookalike to surrender, I was focusing keenly on the potential for being seduced into a position of submission while yearning for surrender.

While I still hold to the critical distinction between surrender and submission, I think it is important to draw attention to certain ways in which these two phenomena not only are in opposition to each other, but also are, in a certain sense, joined in a symbiotic relation to one other.

Sometimes by design, either conscious or unconscious, or by an accident of fate, one finds oneself in a submissive position or in a position of suffering brought on by the actions of another. Consciously one may rue the day that this anguish was brought into being.

Oftentimes it is only later, sometimes much later, that one comes to recognize that some very real growth took place in the context of the suffering and that one ultimately emerged the richer for the experience. How to account for this paradoxical situation? I believe that a most important ingredient is the wisdom and equanimity, and even creativity, that accrue from the confrontation with one's narcissistic sense of omnipotence in which the feeling of helplessness is dealt with by a deep sense of transformative acceptance.[1] It is not difficult to see that an act of meaningful surrender has occurred; but the element of surrender, in contrast to the feeling of submission, becomes apparent only at a later stage of the process. The story of Job may serve as an exemplar of this type of experience (see Milner, 1959, for an extended discussion of Blake's representation of Job's ordeal and transcendence).

I think there are times when one may put oneself into a masochistic or submissive position in order to taste surrender, as if by "faking it" one is afforded a glimpse of the real thing. It happens often enough that, after starting out with the subjective feeling of "faking," by enacting some emotional expression, a point comes when, to one's utter astonishment, it has come to feel real. Thus, what may begin as a contrived act of obeisance may before long yield a foreshadowing of genuine surrender. The ritual formalisms of zen practice require one to participate in gestures of deference and obeisance to the master. In many traditions where enlightenment is the goal and surrender through intensive meditation is the means, the seeker puts himself or herself entirely in the hands of the master. As Fauteux (1997) puts it, "Obedience to a religious superior or to a Zen roshi can help overcome the unconscious resistance of the false self to experiencing the true self. It puts a person outside the limited and egocentric self in order to learn from the other just how limited and egocentric is his false self" (p. 19). Acts of worship, in many religious traditions, may involve a profound submission that may even include practices of mortification; the goal, however, is surrender. An exotic illustration of worshipful practices may be found in Tantric worship of the woman as a path toward attaining a state of enlightenment.

> In the *Caṇḍamahāroṣaṇa-tantra*, Vajrayogini describes how this Tantric worship is to proceed. A yogi and yogini should seclude themselves in a hermitage to practice together. After gazing at each other and attaining single-minded concentration, the woman

---

1. The vitalizing transcendence of acceptance needs to be sharply distinguished from resignation with its penumbra of festering resentment.

should address the man, affirming that he is her son and husband, brother and father, and claiming that for seven generations he has been her servant and slave, purchased and owned by her. He in turn should fall at her feet, press his palms together in a gesture of reverence, and declare his devotion and humble servitude to her, asking her to grace him with a loving glance. She will then draw him to her and kiss him, direct his mouth to between her thighs, and embrace and pinch him playfully. She guides him in how to make the offering of pleasure to her [Shaw, 1994, p. 155].

In a different and rather more familiar venue, we encounter the observation of Otto Rank (1972), "but the patient shows at the same time another will [beyond that of challenging the therapist's will (resistance)] , that is the will to yield, to submit himself which is what brings him as a seeker for help to the therapist. . . . At the time of his coming [for therapy] the will to submit has the upper hand" (p. 464).

But in bringing the mind to bear upon the not infrequent conjunction of submission or masochism with surrender, I can find no more telling words than those of Michael Parsons's (1990) celebration of Marion Milner,

An interest in the wilder parts of nature introduces [in Marion Milner] a preoccupation with volcanic eruption which seemed to symbolize her inner turmoil. . . . To her surprise she discovered a profound wish to submit herself, not just to an ideal good, but to something overwhelmingly powerful regardless of whether it were good or evil: a desire to have her will broken and her sense of self destroyed, even if only momentarily, by something alien. This seemed a masochistic self-abasing impulse. She remembered, however, the gesture of internal poverty she had discovered in *A Life of One's Own*,[2] the deliberate abandonment of her hopes, her strivings and even her sense of herself as a person. That involved the same submission and willingness to be nothing, but by conscious acceptance. When she could make this internal act of sacrifice her anxieties and feelings of inadequacy gave way to serenity and her mind produced creative ideas about what had been hopeless problems. Although she did sometimes treat herself masochistically she came to see this not simply as a bit of pathology but the distortion of an impulse which, when properly understood and used, might be a key to well-being [pp. 415–416].

Despite the necessary brevity of this afterword, I feel it essential, in order to avoid major misunderstandings, to touch on two riders to the thesis I have presented.

---

2. Milner's first book, written under the pen name of Joanna Field.

The first point is by far the more important. I hope it will be understood that I do not mean that surrender is necessarily fused with submission. I wish only to convey the sense that the lookalike status of submission and surrender is not entirely accidental. The great danger of my drawing attention to submission as a ticket of admission to the experience of surrender is the ever-present peril of this impulse being exploited. The result of such a betrayal is the agony of defeat rather than the serenity of surrender.

The second point has to do with what the reader may experience as an omission. In this chapter I hope it is clear that there are two main species of surrender. For want of better names, they might be referred to as the receptive and the active, or penetrative, modes. It follows, then, that an important analogue of the conjunction between surrender and submission as described in this afterword might derive from the more active sense of surrender that in the text of the chapter was dealt with under the rubric of the use of an object, or discovering externality, or "letting go." This active form of surrender may seem, on the surface, to be the opposite of surrender; but deeply it, too, involves a sense of surrendering, of going "all out, with one's heart, with one's soul, and with all one's might" (Eigen, 1981) in total vulnerability. Much as with surrender and submission, it may make its first appearance in conjunction with the impulse to dominate and impose oneself. Creativity will often be found lurking in these precincts.

References

Eigen, M. (1981), The area of faith in Winnicott, Lacan and Bion. *Internat. J. Psycho-Anal.*, 62:413–433.

Fauteux, K. (1997), Self-reparation in religious experience and creativity. In: *Soul on the Couch: Spirituality, Religion, and Morality in Contemporary Psychoanalysis*, ed. C. Spezzano & G. G. Gargiulo. Hillsdale, NJ: The Analytic Press.

Milner, M. (1959), Psycho-analysis and art. In: *Psychoanalysis and Contemporary Thought*, ed. J. D. Sutherland. New York: Grove Press.

Parsons, M. (1990), Marion Milner's "answering activity" and the question of psychoanalytic creativity. *Internat. Rev. Psycho-Anal.*, 17:413–424.

Rank, O. (1936), The basis of a will therapy. In: C. Thompson, M. Mazer & E. Witenberg, *An Outline of Psychoanalysis*, New York: Modern Library, 1955.

Shaw, M. (1994) *Passionate Enlightenment: Women in Tantric Buddhism*. Princeton, NJ: Princeton University Press.

The Patient's Experience of the Analyst's Subjectivity

(1991)

Lewis Aron

▼　▼　▼　▼　▼

Editor's Introduction

This is one of the most frequently cited papers within the relational literature, to which Lewis Aron made a major contribution in shaping the relational approach to the psychoanalytic process, both conceptually and in terms of clinical technique. He also helped build what were to become key bridges between important developments in psychoanalytic feminism, infant research and intersubjectivity theory and evolving relational thought and clinical practice.

Aron draws here on Hoffman's earlier paper, "The Patient as Interpreter of the Analyst's Experience." The thrust of Hoffman's paper was a critique of the fallacies underlying the blank-screen metaphor in its various contemporary manifestations. The patient's (transferential) interpretations of the analyst's (countertransferential) experience cannot usefully be understood as distortions, Hoffman persuasively demonstrated. Aron extends this approach, bringing in contributions from infant research and intersubjectivity theory and arguing that the patient's efforts to reach the analyst as a person represent a key dimension of the analytic situation. Not only is it impossible for the analyst to remain opaque, Aron is suggesting, the patient's curiosity about, and discovery of, the analyst in deeply personal terms is essential to what is curative about the analytic process.

243

Aron richly develops the analogues between the analytic situation and the child–mother relationship. He draws heavily on contemporary feminist critiques (especially Jessica Benjamin's) of traditional psychoanalytic developmental portrayals of the mother. Just as earlier authors (e.g., Winnicott) minimized the importance of the subjectivity of the mother for the healthy development of the baby, so have analytic authors minimized the crucial importance of the subjectivity of the analyst for the vitality and authenticity of the analytic process. By introducing this vision of the analytic relationship, Aron emphasizes the reciprocal influence of analysand and analyst on each other, their mutuality and intersubjectivity, that were to become hallmarks of his important later contributions (see especially 1996).

Another feature of Aron's conceptual methodology, to which readers were introduced in this article, is his thoughtfulness and multifaceted consideration of all sides of complex clinical situations. Despite his contribution to the explosion of the myth of the analyst's opaqueness, Aron carefully considers the complexity of the factors bearing on what the analyst says explicitly about his own countertransferential experience, including the analyst's own conflicts about being known. Providing the patient the richest, most deeply analytic experience is always the highest concern.

Accompanying the conceptual innovations, Aron offered in this article an approach to clinical technique that was to have considerable impact on the shaping of a specifically relational clinical sensibility. Merton Gill had proposed a systematic scrutiny of the patient's associations for thoughts and feelings about the analyst, "allusions to the transference." But Gill's approach was largely interpretive. Aron is suggesting and illustrating a more open-ended inquiry into not just the patient's interpretations of the analyst but his broader experience of the analyst as a person. Aron provides an open invitation to the patient to use the analyst as a vehicle for self-exploration and self-discovery. There is something in Aron's deep curiosity about and authentic openness to the patient's experience, despite the cost to the analyst's own anxieties and self-esteem, that has become a kind of signature feature of the relational clinical sensibility.

Aron's seminal contributions on the analyst's subjectivity and the interactive nature of the analytic relationship were integrated and expanded in A Meeting of Minds: Mutuality in Psychoanalysis (1996, The Analytic Press). Of particular relevance are: chapters 3 and 4, which explore various features of the analyst's subjectivity; chapter 5, which deals with the mutuality of the interaction between the two participants in the analytic situation; and chapter 8, in which Aron considers the thorny problem of the analyst's self-disclosure. "Clinical Choices and the Relational Matrix" (*Psychoanalytic Dialogues*, 1999, 9:1–29) is a recent contribution considering the implication of an appreciation of mutuality and the analyst's subjectivity for psychoanalytic technique and supervision. Other major contributions have included original scholarship and editorial overseeing of both *The Legacy of Sándor Ferenczi* (coedited with Adrienne Harris, 1993, The Analytic Press) and *Relational Perspectives on the Body*, (coedited with Frances Sommer Anderson, 1998, The Analytic Press).

The Patient's Experience of the Analyst's Subjectivity

▼   ▼   ▼   ▼   ▼

The purpose of this paper is to highlight the clinical centrality of examining the patient's experience of the analyst's subjectivity in the psychoanalytic situation. Although many cultural, social, and scientific developments have contributed to a relational view of the psychoanalytic process, I believe that the shift to an intersubjective perspective has emerged predominantly out of our accumulated clinical experience in psychoanalytic work with patients. I would like to begin by noting some developments in two areas not directly related to clinical psychoanalysis: feminist thought and infancy research. My purpose is not to base clinical theory on the grounds of laboratory research nor to rest it on the movement to rectify social inequities; rather, because the implications of an intersubjective view are being clearly spelled out in these areas, they provide an illustration of what I mean by intersubjectivity.

Only with the recent development of feminist psychoanalytic criticism has it become apparent that psychology and psychoanalysis have contributed to and perpetuated a distorted view of motherhood (Dinnerstein, 1973; Chodorow, 1978; Balbus, 1982; Benjamin, 1988). In all of our theories of development, the mother has been portrayed as the object of the infant's drives and as the fulfiller of the baby's needs. We have been slow to recognize or acknowledge the mother as a subject

Reprinted from *Psychoanalytic Dialogues*, 1(1), 29–51, The Analytic Press, Inc. © 1991.

An earlier version of this article was first presented at the spring meeting of the Division of Psychoanalysis, American Psychological Association, April 5, 1990.

in her own right. In discussing the prevalent psychological descriptions of motherhood, Benjamin (1988) recently wrote:

> The mother is the baby's first object of attachment, and later, the object of desire. She is provider, interlocutor, caregiver, contingent reinforcer, significant other, empathic understander, mirror. She is also a secure presence to walk away from, a setter of limits, an optimal frustrator, a shockingly real outside otherness. She is external reality but she is rarely regarded as another subject with a purpose apart from her existence for her child [p. 24].

Benjamin has argued that the child must come to recognize the mother as a separate other who has her own inner world and her own experiences and who is her own center of initiative and an agent of her own desire. This expanding capacity on the part of the child represents an important, and previously unrecognized, developmental achievement. Benjamin has proposed that the capacity for recognition and intersubjective relatedness is an achievement that is best conceptualized in terms of a separate developmental line, and she has begun to articulate the complex vicissitudes involved in this advance. This developmental achievement is radically different from that which has previously been described in the literature. The traditional notion of "object constancy" is limited to the recognition of the mother as a separate "object." What is being emphasized from an intersubjective perspective is the child's need to recognize mother as a separate subject, a need that is a developmental advance beyond viewing mother only as a separate object. Dinnerstein (1976) anticipated this when she wrote, "Every 'I' first emerges in relation to an 'It' which is not at all clearly an 'I.' The separate 'I'ness of the other person is a discovery, an insight achieved over time" (p. 106).

Intersubjectivity refers to the developmentally achieved capacity to recognize another person as a separate center of subjective experience. Stern's (1985) description of the developmental progression of the sense of self has begun to draw attention to the domain of intersubjective relatedness in which the nature of relatedness expands to include the recognition of subjective mental states in the other as well as in oneself. Recent theorizing about the construction of internal representations of self and others (Lichtenberg, 1983; Beebe and Lachmann, 1988a; Stern, 1989) has just begun to consider the child's emerging ability to attribute subjectivity or internal states to others and to explore the ways in which these internal states can be interpersonally communicated.

Winnicott (1954–1955) anticipated the importance of an intersubjective perspective and provided a preliminary hypothesis regarding the establishment of intersubjectivity. He expanded Klein's depressive position to include the development of the capacity for "rush" (p. 265), which he contrasts to the state of "ruthlessness" that exists prior to the development of the capacity to recognize the other as a separate person. Winnicott (1969) elaborates a theory of "object usage" that describes the process by which the infant destroys the object, finds that the object survives destruction, and therefore is able to surrender omnipotence and recognize the other as a separate person. Other theorists who have been examining the nature and development of intersubjectivity include Stern (1985), Ogden (1986), Kernberg (1987), Stolorow, Brandchaft, Brandchaft, and Atwood (1987), and Bollas (1989). It was perhaps Lacan (Miller, 1988) who, in his seminars of the mid-1950s, first discussed the implications of intersubjectivity within the psychoanalytic situation. I will not elaborate here on the developmental aspects of intersubjectivity since my present aim is to discuss intersubjective psychology as it is related to clinical psychoanalysis.

The theory of intersubjectivity has profound implications for psychoanalytic practice and technique as well as for theory. (It should be noted that in my understanding of intersubjectivity I have been influenced by Benjamin [1988] and that my approach to psychoanalytic technique is quite distinct from that being developed by Stolorow, Brandchaft, and Atwood [1987].) Just as psychoanalytic theory has focused on the mother exclusively as the object of the infant's needs while ignoring the subjectivity of the mother, so, too, psychoanalysis has considered analysts only as objects while neglecting the subjectivity of analysts as they are experienced by the patient.

The traditional model of the analytic situation maintained the notion of neurotic patients who brought their irrational childhood wishes, defenses, and conflicts into the analysis to be analyzed by relatively mature, healthy, and well-analyzed analysts who would study the patients with scientific objectivity and technical neutrality. The health, rationality, maturity, neutrality, and objectivity of the analyst were idealized, and thus countertransference was viewed as an unfortunate, but hopefully rare, lapse. Within the psychoanalytic situation, this bias, which regarded the patient as sick and the analyst as possessing the cure (Racker, 1968), led to the assumption that it was only the patient who had transferences. Furthermore, it was as if only the patient possessed a "psychic reality" (see McLaughlin, 1981) and the analyst was left as the representative of objective reality. In sum, if the analyst was to be a rational, relatively distant, neutral, anonymous scientist-observer, an "analytic instrument" (Isakower, 1963), then there was little room in the model for the analyst's psychic reality or subjectivity, except as pathological, intrusive countertransference.

As is well known, it is only in the most recent decades that countertransference has been viewed as a topic worthy of study and as potentially valuable in the clinical situation. For Freud (1910), countertransference reflected a specific disturbance in the analyst elicited in response to the patient's transference and necessitating further analysis of the analyst. Contemporary theorists are more inclined to take a "totalistic" (Kernberg, 1965) approach to countertransference and view it as reflecting all of the analyst's emotional responses to the patient and therefore useful as a clinical tool. Rather than viewing countertransference as a hindrance to the analytic work that should be kept in check or overcome and that should, in any event, be kept to a minimum, most analysts today recognize the ubiquity of analysts' feelings and fantasies regarding patients and hope to utilize their own reactions as a means to understand their patients better. Psychoanalysis has thus broadened its data base to include the subjectivity of the analyst. It has not yet, however, sufficiently considered the patient's experience of the analyst's subjectivity.

In my view, referring to the analyst's total responsiveness with the term countertransference is a serious mistake because it perpetuates defining the analyst's experience in terms of the subjectivity of the patient. Thinking of the analyst's experience as "counter" or responsive to the patient's transference encourages the belief that the analyst's experience is reactive rather than subjective, emanating from the center of the analyst's psychic self (McLaughlin, 1981; Wolstein, 1983). It is not that analysts are never responsive to the pressures that the patients put on them; of course, the analyst does counterrespond to the impact of the patient's behavior. The term countertransference, though, obscures the recognition that the analyst is often the initiator of the interactional sequences, and therefore the term minimizes the impact of the analyst's behavior on the transference.

The relational approach that I am advocating views the patient–analyst relationship as continually established and reestablished through ongoing mutual influence in which both patient and analyst systematically affect, and are affected by, each other. A communication process is established between patient and analyst in which influence flows in both directions. This approach implies a "two-person psychology" or a regulatory-systems conceptualization of the analytic process (Aron, 1990). The terms transference and countertransference too easily lend themselves to a model that implies a one-way influence in which the analyst responds in reaction to the patient. The fact that the influence between patient and analyst is not equal does not mean that it is not mutual. Mutual influence does not imply equal influence, and the analytic relationship may be mutual without being symmetrical. This model of the therapeutic relationship has been strongly influenced by the recent conceptualizations of mother-infant mutual influence proposed by Beebe and Lachmann (1988b).

Others have also suggested that we abandon the term countertransference. Olinick (1969) suggested the alternative eccentric responses in the "psychology of the analyst," but I see no advantage to the pejorative term eccentric. Bird (1972) broadened the meaning of the term transference and sees it as the basis for all human relationships. He then suggests referring simply to "the analyst's transferences." This strategy, however, leads to terminological confusion, such as in Loewald's (1986, p. 280) discussion of the importance of analyzing the patient's countertransference to the analyst's transference. McLaughlin (1981) convincingly argues for abandoning the term countertransference. He writes, "The term countertransference particularly cannot accommodate the intrapsychic range and fullness of the analyst's experiences vis-a-vis his patient" (p. 656).

In a seminal paper, Hoffman (1983) draws together the work of theorists from a wide variety of psychoanalytic schools. These theorists share a radical social and perspectival concept of psychoanalysis that recognizes that patients make plausible inferences regarding aspects of their analysts' experience. Hoffman advances a view of psychoanalytic technique that makes central the analysis of the patient's interpretations of the analyst's experience. In many respects the present paper may be seen as my efforts to grapple with and elaborate on the implications of Hoffman's contribution. While Hoffman entitles his paper "The Patient as Interpreter of the Analyst's Experience," he continues to refer to the patient's interpretation of the analyst's countertransference. Because of my objections to the implications of the term countertransference, I prefer to describe the focus of this paper in terms of the patient's experience of the analyst's subjectivity.

Racker (1968) was one of the first to make the technical recommendation that "analysis of the patient's fantasies about countertransference, which in the widest sense constitute the causes and consequences of the transference, is an essential part of the analysis of the transferences" (p. 131). Gill (1983) puts it simply and directly, although in my view this point has not received nearly the attention it deserves: "A consequence of the analyst's perspective on himself as a participant in a relationship is that he will devote attention not only to the patient's attitude toward the analyst but also to the patient's view of the analyst's attitude toward the patient" (p. 112).

Since, from a classical perspective, the analyst was viewed as participating with the patient in only a minimal way (Gill, 1983), very little attention was given to the impact of the individual analyst and the impact of the analyst's character. Analysts did not consider that patients would inevitably and persistently seek to connect with their analysts by exploring their own observations and inferences about their analyst's behavior and inner experience.

Wolstein (1983) has pointed out that resistances are defensive efforts by patients to cope with a particular analyst and that these resistances must therefore be patterned by the patient to accommodate to some aspect of the analyst's unconscious psychology. The point is that the patient could find a specific defense or resistance to be effective only if in some way it was designed to match the personality of the patient's particular analyst. Therefore, the ultimate outcome of successfully analyzing resistances is that patients would learn more not only about their own psychologies but also about the psychology of others in their lives, particularly about the psychology of their analysts. Wolstein (1988) writes:

> Nothing was more natural than for patients to turn the strength of this new awareness and reconstruction toward the psychology of their immediately environing others—especially their psychoanalysts—and describe the perceived aspects of countertransference against which they thought they had gone into resistance [p. 9].

The implications of this point are enormous, for it means that as resistances are analyzed, patients not only expose more of their own unconscious but also gain awareness of hitherto unnoticed, dissociated, or repressed aspects of the psychology of their analysts. In spite of extended training analyses, analysts might not be aware of some of what their patients notice. Some of the observations that patients make about their analysts are likely to be unpleasant and anxiety-provoking. Therefore, analysts might back off from exploring the patient's resistances because of their own anxieties and resistances (Racker, 1968; Gill, 1982; Hoffman, 1983).

Of course, it is often argued that patients can and do fantasize about the analyst's psychology and that therefore the successful result of analysis of these fantasies is that patients learn more about their own psychology than about that of their analyst. My point here is that these fantasies are not endogenously determined, drive-determined, autistic creations of patients, nor are they purely the result of expectations derived from past interpersonal experiences. Rather, these fantasies may additionally be seen as patients' attempts to grapple with and grasp, in their own unique and idiosyncratic way, the complex and ambiguous reality of their individual analyst (see Levenson, 1989). Ultimately, an analysis of these fantasies must contribute to a clearer understanding of both the patient's and the analyst's psychologies.

I believe that patients, even very disturbed, withdrawn, or narcissistic patients, are always accommodating to the interpersonal reality of the analyst's character and of the analytic relationship. Patients tune in, consciously and unconsciously, to the analyst's attitudes and feelings toward them, but inasmuch as they believe that these observations touch on sensitive aspects of the analyst's character, patients are likely to communicate these observations only indirectly through allusions to others, as displacements, or through descriptions of these characteristics as aspects of themselves, as identifications (Lipton, 1977; Gill, 1982; Hoffman, 1983). An important aspect of making the unconscious conscious is to bring into awareness and articulate the patient's denied observations, repressed fantasies, and unformulated experiences of the analyst (Racker, 1968; Levenson, 1972, 1983; Hoffman, 1983).

All children observe and study their parents' personalities. They attempt to make contact with their parents by reaching into their parents' inner worlds. The Kleinians have emphasized this point vividly through concrete metaphors of the infant's seeking literally to climb inside and explore the mother's body and to discover all of the objects contained inside. Children imagine with what and with whom their mothers are preoccupied. They have some sense, although they may have never thought about it, as to how their mothers related to their own mothers. There is now empirical research that documents that a mother's internal working model of her relationship with her own mother affects her child's attachment to her (Main, Kaplan, and Cassidy, 1985). The child acquires some sense of the characters who inhabit the mother's and father's inner worlds and of the nature of the relations among these inner objects. Most important, children formulate plausible interpretations of their parents' attitudes and feelings toward the children themselves. Children are powerfully motivated to penetrate to the center of their parents' selves. Pick (1985) states this idea in Kleinian language: "If there is a mouth that seeks a breast as an inborn potential, there is, I believe, a psychological equivalent, i.e. a state of mind which seeks another state of mind" (p. 157).

If, as McDougall (1980) asserts, "a baby's earliest reality is his mother's unconscious" (p. 251), then patients' psychic reality may be said to implicate their analyst's unconscious. Patients have conscious and unconscious beliefs about the analyst's inner world. Patients make use of their observations of their analyst, which are plentiful no matter how anonymous the analyst may attempt to be, to construct a picture of their analyst's character structure. Patients probe, more or less subtly, in an attempt to penetrate the analyst's professional calm and reserve. They do this probing not only because they want to turn the tables on their analyst defensively or angrily but also, like all people, because they want to and need to connect with others, and they want to connect with others where they live emotionally, where they are authentic and fully present, and so they search for information about the other's inner world. An analytic focus on the patient's experience of the analyst's subjectivity opens the door to further explorations of the patient's childhood experiences of the parents' inner world and character structure. Similarly, patients begin to attend to their observations about the characters of others in their lives. This development is an inevitable and essential part of how patients begin to think more psychologically in their analyses. The analytic stance being described considers fantasies and memories not just as carriers of infantile wishes and defenses against these wishes, but as plausible interpretations and representations of the patient's experiences with significant others (Hoffman, 1983). This point was anticipated by Loewald (1970), who wrote, "The analysand in this respect can be compared to the child—who if he can allow himself that freedom—scrutinizes with his unconscious antennae the parent's motivations and moods and in this way may contribute—if the parent or analyst allows himself that freedom—to the latter's self awareness" (p. 280).

In the clinical situation I often ask patients to describe anything that they have observed or noticed about me that may shed light on aspects of our relationship. When, for example, patients say that they think that I am angry at them or jealous of them or acting seductively toward them, I ask them to describe whatever it is that they have noticed that led them to this belief. I find that it is critical for me to ask the question with the genuine belief that I may find out something about myself that I did not previously recognize. Otherwise, it is too easy to dismiss the patients' observations as distortions. Patients are often all too willing and eager to believe that they have projected or displaced these feelings onto their analyst, and they can then go back to viewing their analyst as objective, neutral, or benignly empathic. I encourage patients to tell me anything that they have observed and insist that there must have been some basis in my behavior for their conclusions. I often ask patients to speculate or fantasize about what is going on inside of me, and in particular I focus on what patients have noticed about my internal conflicts.

For instance, a patient said that when he heard my chair move slightly, he thought for a moment that I was going to strike him. I asked the patient to elaborate on what he thought I was feeling, what he thought was the quality and nature of my anger, what he had noticed about me that led him to believe that I was angry in this particular way, and how he imagined that I typically dealt with my anger and frustration. I asked the patient what he thought it was like for me to be so enraged at him and not to be able to express that anger directly, according to his understanding of the "rules" of psychoanalysis and professional decorum. I asked him how he thought I felt about his noticing and confronting me with my disguised anger.

I choose first to explore the patient's most subtle observations of me, which reflect my attitudes toward the patient as well as my character and personal conflicts, in preference to examining either the patient's own projected anger or the displaced anger of others in the patient's current or past life. All of this anger ultimately needs to be explored, but following Gill's (1983) recommendations, I begin with an analysis of the transference in the here and now, focusing on the plausible basis for the patient's reactions. It is important to note that I proceed in this way whether or not I am aware of feeling angry at that point. I assume that the patient may very well have noticed my anger, jealousy, excitement, or whatever before I recognize it in myself.

Inquiry into the patient's experience of the analyst's subjectivity represents one underemphasized aspect of a complex psychoanalytic approach to the analysis of transference. A balance needs to be maintained between focusing on the interpersonal and the intrapsychic, between internal object relations and external object relations. While at times exploring patients' perceptions of the analyst serves to deepen the work, at other times this focus is used defensively, by patient and analyst, to avoid the patient's painful inner experience (see Jacobs, 1986, p. 304 for a clinical illustration of this problem). For each time that I ask patients regarding their experience of me, there are other times that I interpret their focus on the interaction with me as an avoidance of their inner feelings and of looking into themselves.

While asking direct questions about the patient's observations of the analyst is often necessary and productive, the most useful way to elicit the patient's thoughts and feelings about the analyst's attitudes is to analyze the defenses and resistances that make these thoughts and feelings so difficult to verbalize. Asking patients direct questions about their experience of the therapeutic relationship entails the disadvantage that it may appeal to more surface and conscious levels of discourse. The analyst needs to listen to all of the patient's associations for clues as to the patient's experience. Often the patient fears offending the analyst and provoking the analyst's anger by confronting the analyst with aspects of the analyst's character that have been avoided. Patients fear that they are being too personal, crossing over the boundary of what the analyst is willing to let them explore. Patients are especially likely to fear that if they expose the analyst's weaknesses and character flaws, the analyst will retaliate, become depressed, withdrawn, or crumble (Gill, 1982).

Implicit in this fear are not only the patient's hostility, projected fears, or simply the need to idealize the analyst but also the patient's perception of the analyst's grandiosity, which would be shattered by the revelation of a flaw. The patient's expectations of the analyst are related to the ways in which the patient's parents actually responded to their children's observations and perceptions of them. How did their parents feel about their children's really getting to know who they were, where they truly lived emotionally? How far were the parents able to let their children penetrate into their inner worlds? Was the grandiosity of the parents such that they could not let their children uncover their weaknesses and vulnerabilities? To return to the rich Kleinian imagery of the infant's attempts in unconscious phantasy to enter into the mother's body, we may wonder whether the violent, destructive phantasies encountered are due only to innate greed and envy or whether they are not also the result of the frustration of being denied access to the core of the parents. Could these phantasies be an accurate reflection of the child's perceptions of the parents' fears of being intimately penetrated and known?

What enables patients to describe their fantasies and perceptions of the analyst is the analyst's openness and intense curiosity about patients' experience of the analyst's subjectivity. The patient will benefit from this process only if the analyst is truly open to the possibility that patients will communicate something new about the analyst, something that the patient has picked up about the analyst that the analyst was not aware of before. If, on the other hand, the analyst listens to the patient with the expectation of hearing a transference distortion and is not open to the likelihood and necessity of learning something new about himself or herself, then the analysis is more likely to become derailed or to continue on the basis of compliance and submission to authority.

The recognition of the analyst's subjectivity within the analytic situation raises the problem of the analyst's self-disclosure. The issues involved by the analyst's self-revelations are enormously complex and can only be touched on here. There are, however, a few comments that should be made because they are directly raised by the line of inquiry advocated in this paper.

When patients are encouraged to verbalize their experiences of the analyst's subjectivity, it is most likely that they will put increased pressure on the analyst to verify or refute their perceptions. It is extremely difficult and frustrating for patients to be encouraged to examine their perceptions of the analyst's subjectivity and then to have their analyst remain relatively "anonymous." Once analysts express interest in the patient's perceptions of their subjectivity, they have tantalized the patient

(Little, 1951) and will surely be pressured to disclose more of what is going on inside themselves. Furthermore, the ways in which analysts pursue the inquiry into the patient's perceptions of themselves are inevitably self-revealing. I assume that one reason that analysts have traditionally avoided direct inquiry into the patient's experience of the analyst's subjectivity is that they recognized that pursuing this line of inquiry would unavoidably result in self-disclosure.

Self-revelation is not an option; it is an inevitability. Patients accurately and intuitively read into their analyst's interpretations the analyst's hidden communications (Jacobs, 1986). In unmasking the myth of analytic anonymity, Singer (1977) pointed out that the analyst's interpretations were first and foremost self-revealing remarks. It cannot be otherwise since the only way we can truly gain insight into another is through our own self-knowledge, and our patients know that fact.

Hoffman (1983) emphasized that patients know that the psychology of the analyst is no less complex than that of themselves. He challenged what he termed "the naive patient fallacy," the notion that the patient accepts at face value the analyst's words and behavior. For analysts simply and directly to say what they are experiencing and feeling may encourage the assumption that they are fully aware of their own motivations and meanings. The analyst's revelations and confessions may tend to close off further exploration of the patient's observations and perceptions. Furthermore, we can never be aware in advance of just what it is that we are revealing about ourselves, and when we think we are deliberately revealing something about ourselves, we may very well be communicating something else altogether. Is it not possible that our patients' perceptions of us are as plausible an interpretation of our behavior as the interpretations we give ourselves? If so, then it is presumptuous for the analyst to expect the patient to take at face value the analyst's self-revelations. Pontalis (cited in Limentani, 1989) asks, "What is more paradoxical than the presupposition that: I see my blind spots, I hear what I am deaf to . . . and (furthermore) I am fully conscious of my unconscious" (p. 258).

We hope that we, as analysts, have had the benefit of an intensive analysis of our own, but this in no way ensures that we have easy access to our unconscious or that we are immune from subtly enacting all sorts of pathological interactions with our patients. This recognition has led to our contemporary acceptance of the inevitability of countertransference. Whereas in the past idealized, well-analyzed analysts were thought to have no countertransference problem, today's idealized analysts are thought to be so well analyzed that they have immediate and direct access to their unconscious. It is well to keep in mind that the trouble with self-analysis is in the countertransference! When analysis is viewed as a coparticipation (Wolstein, 1983) between two people who are both subjects and objects to each other, then the analyst can read the patient's associations for references to the patient's perceptions of the analyst's attitudes toward the patient. This method provides additional data with which analysts can supplement their own self-analysis. In this way the analyst and patient coparticipate in elucidating the nature of the relationship that the two of them have mutually integrated.

Bollas (1989) advocates that analysts need to establish themselves as subjects in the bipersonal analytic field. Bollas encourages analysts to reveal more of their internal analytic process to their patients, for example, describing to a patient how the analyst arrived at a particular interpretation or sharing with the patient the analyst's associations to a patient's dream. He argues that if the analyst's self-disclosure is congruent with who the analyst really is as a person, then the disclosure is unlikely to be taken as a seduction. In establishing themselves as subjects in the analytic situation, analysts make available to the patient some of their own associations and inner processes for the patient to use and analyze. It is important to note that Bollas's revelations have a highly playful and tentative quality in that he does not take his associations or "musings" as containing absolute truth but rather puts them into the analytic field and is prepared to have them used or destroyed by the patient. Furthermore, Bollas is reserved and cautious in his approach because of his awareness that an incessant flow of the analyst's associations could be intrusive, resulting in "a subtle takeover of the analysand's psychic life with the analyst's" (p. 69). Bollas's clinical contributions are enormous, but while I agree that analysts should be available to the patient as a separate subject, the danger with any approach that focuses on analysts' subjectivity is that analysts may insist on asserting their own subjectivity. In the need to establish themselves as separate subjects, analysts may impose this on the patient, thus forcing the patient to assume the role of object. Analyst's imposition of their own subjectivity onto their patients is not "intersubjectivity"; it is simply an instrumental relationship in which the subject-object polarities have been reversed.

In my view self-revelations are often useful, particularly those closely tied to the analytic process rather than those relating to details of the analyst's private life outside of the analysis. Personal revelations are, in any event, inevitable, and they are simply enormously complicated and require analysis of how they are experienced by the patient. We as analysts benefit enormously from the analytic efforts of our patients, but we can help them as analysts only if we can discipline ourselves enough to put their analytic interests ahead of our own, at least temporarily.

The major problem for analysts in establishing themselves as subjects in the analytic situation is that because of their own conflicts they may abandon traditional anonymity only to substitute imposing their subjectivity on patients and thus deprive patients of the opportunity to search out, uncover, and find the analyst as a separate subject, in their own way and at their own rate. While a focus on the patient's experience of the analyst needs to be central at certain phases of an analysis, there are other times, and perhaps long intervals, when focusing on perceptions of the analyst is intrusive and disruptive. Focusing exclusively on the presence of the analyst does not permit the patient temporarily to put the analyst into the background and indulge in the experience of being left alone in the presence of the analyst. Analysts' continuous interpretations of all material in terms of the patient-analyst relationship, as well as analysts' deliberate efforts to establish themselves as separate subjects, may be rightfully experienced as an impingement stemming from the analysts' own narcissistic needs. To some degree this outcome is inevitable, and it can be beneficial for a patient to articulate it when it happens.

Winnicott (1971) has suggested that psychoanalysis occurs in an intermediate state, a transitional space, transitional between the patient's narcissistic withdrawal and full interaction with reality, between self-absorption and object usage, between introspection and attunement to the other, and between relations to a subjective-object and relations to an object, objectively perceived, transitional between fantasy and reality. In my own clinical work I attempt to maintain an optimal balance between the necessary recognition and confirmation of the patient's experience and the necessary distance to preserve an analytic space that allows the patient to play with interpersonal ambiguity and to struggle with the ongoing lack of closure and resolution. A dynamic tension needs to be preserved between responsiveness and participation on the one hand and nonintrusiveness and space on the other, intermediate between the analyst's presence and absence. My manner of achieving this tension is different with each patient and varies even in the analysis of a single analysand. I believe that each analyst-patient pair needs to work out a unique way of managing this precarious balance. The analysis itself must come to include the self-reflexive examination of the ways in which this procedure becomes established and modified. Analysis, from this perspective, is mutual but asymmetrical, with both patient and analyst functioning as subject and object, as coparticipants, and with the analyst and patient working on the very edge of intimacy. The question of the degree and nature of the analyst's deliberate self-revelation is left open to be resolved within the context of each unique psychoanalytic situation.

In my initial attempts to present these thoughts to varying groups of colleagues and students, I was struck by the overwhelming tendency on the part of my listeners to focus the discussion on the issue of the analyst's self-revelation. I wondered why analysts were so eager to discuss self-revelation when it was not the main point of the paper. In my view, what is important is not the analyst's deliberate self-disclosure but rather the analysis of the patient's experience of the analyst's subjectivity. The very expression by patients of their perceptions of the analyst leads to the establishment of the analyst as a separate subject in the mind of the patient. So why do analytic audiences focus on self-revelation?

I believe that people who are drawn to analysis as a profession have particularly strong conflicts regarding their desire to be known by another, that is, conflicts concerning intimacy. In more traditional terms these are narcissistic conflicts over voyeurism and exhibitionism. Why else would people choose a profession in which they spend their lives listening and looking into the lives of others while they themselves remain relatively silent and hidden? The recognition that analysts, even those who attempt to be anonymous, are never invisible and, furthermore, the insight that patients seek to "know" their analysts raise profound anxieties for analysts who are struggling with their own longings to be known and defensive temptations to hide.

How is it that psychoanalysis, which is so concerned with individual subjective experience and with the development of the child's experience of the other, for so long neglected the exploration of intersubjectivity? Why has it taken so long for us to recognize that we must develop a conception of the other not only as an object but as a separate subject, as a separate psychic self, as a separate center of experience?

For most of its history psychoanalysis has been dominated by the metapsychology of drive theory. Freud conceived of mind as a closed energy system fueled by biological drives pressing for discharge. This model of mind is based on the notion that there are drives striving for gratification and that the ego regulates, channels, and defends against these drives while attempting to find objects suitable to meet their fulfillment. Within this theoretical framework the other person is "objectified"—seen as the "object" of the drive. Because the focus of the theory is on the vicissitudes of the drives, the role of the other is reduced to that of the object of the drives, and the only relevant variable is whether the person is gratifying or frustrating the drive. The dimension of gratification-frustration becomes the central if not the exclusive characteristic of the object since the object's individual subjectivity is of no relevance in as much as they are an object. Only with the shift in psychoanalysis away from drive theory and toward a relational theory of the development of the self and of "object relations" (that is, of inter-personal relations—conscious and unconscious, real and fantasied, exter-nal and internal [Greenberg and Mitchell, 1983]) could psychoanalysis begin to study the other not as an object but as a separate subject (Chodorow, 1989). Adopting a "two-person psychology" or a relational perspective opens up the possibility for the investigation not only of sub-ject-object relations but of subject-subject relations. As Mitchell (1988a) has recently stated, "If the analytic situation is not regarded as one sub-jectivity and one objectivity, or one subjectivity and one facilitating envi-ronment, but two subjectivities—the participation in and inquiry into this interpersonal dialectic becomes a central focus of the work" (p. 38).

It should be clear that it is not only the classical drive/structure metapsychology that narrows our view of people, deprives them of sub-jectivity, and reduces them to objects. This limitation is true of any aso-cial, "one-person" psychology. (For a discussion of asocial paradigms, see Hoffman, 1983; for a discussion of one-person psychologies, see Aron, in press). For example, Kohutian self psychology provides an important contribution to clinical psychoanalysis in its emphasis on the need for the analyst to be responsive and empathic and in its recogni-tion of the vital experience of emotional attunement in the analytic process. Self psychology, however, maintains the classical view that who the analyst is as a unique character is irrelevant to the process of the analysis. Kohut (1977) wrote that the patient's transferences were defined by "pre-analytically established internal factors in the analysand's per-sonality structure" (p. 217). The analyst's contribution to the process was limited to making "correct" interpretations on the basis of empa-thy with the patient. Similarly, Goldberg (1980) has stated:

> Self psychology struggles hard not to be an interpersonal psychology . . . because it wishes to minimize the input of the analyst into the mix . . . It is based on the idea of a developmental program (one that may be innate or pre-wired if you wish) that will reconstitute itself under certain conditions [p. 387].

In the self-psychological model, the analyst is restricted to being a self-object, focusing only upon what the patient (as subject) needs from the analyst (as object). It is important to recognize that in this respect self psychology does not differ from the classical model (see Hoffman, 1983). For classical analysts, the function of the psychoanalytic situation, and in particular of free association, "is to ensure that what emerges into the patient's consciousness is as far as possible endogeneously determined" (Arlow, 1980, p. 193). If the analyst is analyzing correctly, the patient's associations are not seen as largely or predominantly determined by the current interpersonal relationship with the analyst. The psychoanalytic situation is thought to represent "a standard, experimental set of conditions" (Arlow, 1986, p. 76) whose purpose is to minimize external stimuli so as to allow the spontaneous unfolding, from within, of derivatives of drive and defense. Both the classical model, with its focus on drive and defense, and the self-psychological model, with its reliance on the notion of a "developmental program," require that the psychoanalytic situation remain free of the contaminants of the analyst's subjectivity so that the patient's transferences can "unfold" in pure form from within. The presuppositions of a one-person psychology demand that the only psychology in the consulting room that should matter is that of the patient. The patient's subjectivity, the patient's transferences, the patient's psychic reality are there to be examined. The person of the analyst is ignored in favor of a conception of an "analyzing instrument," and the subjectivity of the analyst is to be kept out of the equation so as to produce an objective experimental situation. (I recognize that this critique of Kohutian self psychology may not apply to certain post-Kohutian developments within the self psychology school. For a similar but more thorough critique of Kohut's self psychology as a one-person psychology, see Bromberg, 1989 and Ghent, 1989.)

Similar objections could be raised regarding the clinical stance taken by psychoanalysts of the British object-relational school and of the American interpersonal school. The metaphors of the analyst as "good enough mother" and "holder" (Winnicott, 1986) or as "container" (Bion, 1970) and "metabolizer" of the patient's pathological contents have been extremely useful inasmuch as they have drawn attention to nonverbal and subtle exchanges and to the ways in which the analyst needs to respond to these "primitive communications." The danger with these metaphors, however, is not only that the patient may be infantilized and deprived of a richer and more complex adult kind of intimacy, as Mitchell (1988b) rightly points out, but that the analyst is similarly instrumentalized and denied subjective existence. Instead of being seen as subjects, the mother and the analyst are transformed into the baby's and the patient's "thinking apparatus" (Bion, 1970). The blank screen has simply been replaced with an empty container, free of the analyst's psychological insides (Hoffman, 1983; Levenson, 1983; Hirsch, 1987). In parallel to this view, Chodorow (1989, p. 253) has recently pointed out that most object-relations theorists still take the point of view of the child, with mother as the object, and do not take seriously the problem of the subjectivity of the mother.

While contemporary interpersonal analysts (Levenson, 1972, 1983; Wolstein, 1983) emphasize the analyst's personal contributions to the patient's transferences, this emphasis was not true of Sullivan's clinical position. Sullivan saw the therapist as an "expert" on interpersonal relations who would function as a "participant-observer" in conducting the analytic inquiry, and as an expert he assumed that the therapist could avoid being pulled into the patient's interpersonal entanglements (see Hirsch, 1987). Sullivan's interpersonal theory, while interpersonal in its examination of the patient's life, was asocial inasmuch as it neglected the subjectivity of the therapist as inevitably participating in the analytic interaction. Sullivan's description of the principle of participant-observation soon brought attention to the analyst's subjective experience and the patient's perceptions of the analyst's experience, which became the focus of attention for later interpersonal analysts. Historically, Hirsch attributes the contemporary interpersonal focus on the participation of the analyst to the influence of Fromm. I see this clinical movement, which emphasizes the contribution of the analyst's subjectivity, as deriving more from the influence of Thompson in the United States and Balint in England, both of whom were deeply influenced by and attempted to extend the later contributions of Ferenczi. Ferenczi was the first analyst seriously to consider the impact of the analyst's subjectivity within the analytic situation (see Dupont, 1988), and the origins of relational theory and practice can be traced back to the conflict between Freud and Ferenczi.

I will conclude by highlighting eight clinical points:

1. The analytic situation is constituted by the mutual regulation of communication between patient and analyst in which both patient and analyst affect and are affected by each other. The relationship is mutual but asymmetrical.
2. The analyst's subjectivity is an important element in the analytic situation, and the patient's experience of the analyst's subjectivity needs to be made conscious.
3. Patients seek to connect to their analysts, to know them, to probe beneath their professional facade, and to reach their psychic centers much in the way that children seek to connect to and penetrate their parents' inner worlds. This aggressive probing may be mistaken for hostile attempts at destruction.
4. Self-revelation is not a choice for the analyst; it is an inevitable and continuous aspect of the analytic process. As patients resolve their resistances to acknowledging what they perceive interpersonally they inevitably turn their gaze toward their analysts, who need to help them acknowledge their interpersonal experience.

5. Establishing one's own subjectivity in the analytic situation is essential and yet problematic. Deliberate or surplus self-revelations are always highly ambiguous and are enormously complicated. Our own psychologies are as complicated as those of our patients, and our unconsciouses are no less deep. We need to recognize that our own self-awareness is limited and that we are not in a position to judge the accuracy of our patients' perceptions of us. Thus, the idea that we might "validate" or "confirm" our patients' perceptions of us is presumptuous. Furthermore, direct self-revelation cannot provide a shortcut to, and may even interfere with, the development of the patient's capacity to recognize the analyst's subjectivity.

6. It is often useful to ask patients directly what they have noticed about the analyst, what they think the analyst is feeling or doing, what they think is going on in the analyst, or with what conflict they feel the analyst is struggling. The major way to reach this material, however, is through analysis of the defenses and resistances that inhibit the expression of each patient's experience of the analyst.

7. Focusing exclusively on the presence of the analyst and on establishing the analyst's subjectivity does not permit the patient temporarily to put the analyst into the background and indulge in the experience of being left alone in the presence of the analyst. This focus may be experienced by patients as an impingement that disrupts their encounter with their own subjective experiences. Instead of leading to an intersubjective exchange, analysts' insistence on asserting their own subjectivity creates an instrumental relationship in which the subject-object polarities have simply been reversed.

8. The exploration of the patient's experience of the analyst's subjectivity represents only one aspect of the analysis of transference. It needs to be seen as one underemphasized component of a detailed and thorough explication and articulation of the therapeutic relationship in all of its aspects.

References

Arlow, J. A. (1980), The genesis of interpretation. In: *Psychoanalytic Explorations of Technique: Discourse on the Theory of Therapy*, ed. H. P. Blum. New York: International Universities Press, pp. 193–206.

——— (1986), Discussion of transference and countertransference with the difficult patient. In: *Between Analyst and Patient: New Dimensions in Counter-*

transference and Transference, ed. H.C. Myers. Hillsdale, NJ: The Analytic Press, pp. 75–86.

Aron, L. (1990), One-person and two-person psychologies and the method of psychoanalysis. *Psychoanal. Psychol.*, 7:475–435.

Balbus, I.D. (1982), *Marxism and Domination: A Neo-Hegelian, Feminist, Psychoanalytic Theory of Sexual, Political, and Technological Liberation*. Princeton, NJ: Princeton University Press.

Beebe, B. & Lachmann, F.M. (1988a), The contribution of mother-infant mutual influence to the origins of self- and object representations. *Psychoanal. Psychol.*, 5:305–337.

——— & ——— (1988b), Mother-infant mutual influence and precursors of psychic structure. In: *Frontiers in Self Psychology: Progress in Self Psychology, Vol. 3*, ed. A. Goldberg. Hillsdale, NJ: The Analytic Press, pp. 325.

Benjamin, J. (1988), *The Bonds of Love: Psychoanalysis, Feminism, and the Problem of Domination*. New York: Pantheon Books.

Bion, W. R. (1970), *Attention and Interpretation*. London: Heinemann.

Bird, B. (1972), Notes on transference: Universal phenomena and the hardest part of analysis. *Jounal of the American Psychoanalytic Association*, 20 267–301.

Bollas, C. (1989), *Forces of Destiny: Psychoanalysis and Human Idiom*. London: Free Association Books.

Bromberg, P. M. (1989), Interpersonal psychoanalysis and self psychology: A clinical comparison. In: *Self Psychology: Comparisons and Contrasts*, ed. D. W. Detrick & S. P. Detrick. Hillsdale, NJ: The Analytic Press, pp. 275–291.

Chodorow, N. (1978), *The Reproduction of Mothering: Psychoanalysis and the Sociology of Gender*. Berkeley: University of California Press.

——— (1989), *Feminism and Psychoanalytic Theory*. New Haven, CT: Yale University Press.

Dinnerstein, D. (1976), *The Mermaid and the Minotaur: Sexual Arrangements and Human Malaise*. New York: Harper & Row.

Dupont, J., ed. (1988), *The Clinical Diary of Sandor Ferenczi*. Cambridge, MA: Harvard University Press.

Freud, S. (1910), The future prospects of psycho-analytic therapy. *Standard Edition*, 11:141–151. London: Hogarth Press.

Ghent, E. (1989), Credo: The dialectics of one-person and two-person psychologies. *Contemp. Psychoanal.*, 25:169–211.

Gill, M. M. (1982), *Analysis of Transference I: Theory and Technique*. New York: International Universities Press.

——— (1983), The interpersonal paradigm and the degree of the therapist's involvement. *Contemp. Psychoanal.*, 19:200–237.

Greenberg, J. R. & Mitchell, S. A. (1983), *Object Relations in Psychoanalytic Theory*. Cambridge, MA: Harvard University Press.

Hirsch, I. (1987), Varying modes of analytic participation. *J. Amer. Acad. Psychoanal.*, 15:205–222.

Hoffman, I.Z. (1983), The patient as interpreter of the analyst's experience. *Contemp. Psychoanal.*, 19:389–422.

Isakower, O. (1963), In: Minutes of the faculty meeting of the New York Psychoanalytic Institute, November 20.

Jacobs, T. J. (1986), On countertransference enactments. *J. Amer. Psychoanal. Assn.*, 34:289–307.

Kernberg, O. F. (1965), Notes on countertransference. *J. Amer. Psychoanal. Assn.*, 13:38–56.

——— (1987), Projection and projective identification: Developmental and clinical aspects. In: *Projection, Identification, Projective Identification*, ed. J. Sandler. Madison, CT: International Universities Press, pp. 93–115.

Kohut, H. (1971), *The Analysis of the Self*. New York: International Universities Press.

Langs, R. (1982), *Psychotherapy: A Basic Text*. New York: Aronson.

Levenson, E. (1972), *The Fallacy of Understanding*. New York: Basic Books.

——— (1983), *The Ambiguity of Change*. New York: Basic Books.

——— (1989), Whatever happened to the cat? Interpersonal perspectives on the self. *Contemp. Psychoanal.*, 25:537–553.

Lichtenberg, J. D. (1983), *Psychoanalysis and Infant Research*. Hillsdale, NJ: The Analytic Press.

Limentani, A. (1989), *Between Freud and Klein: The Psychoanalytic Quest for Knowledge and Truth*. London: Free Association Books.

Lipton, S. D. (1977), Clinical observations on resistance to the transference. *Internat. J. Psycho-Anal.*, 58:463–472.

Little, M. (1951), Counter-transference and the patient's response to it. *Internat. J. Psycho-Anal.*, 33:3240.

Loewald, H. W. (1986), Transference-countertransference. *Journal of the American Psychoanalytic Association*, 34:275–287.

McDougall, J. (1980), *Plea for a Measure of Abnormality*. New York: International Universities Press.

McLaughlin, J. T. (1981), Transference, psychic reality, and countertransference. *Psychoanal. Ouart.*, 50:639–664.

Main, M. Kaplan, N. & Cassidy, J. (1985), Security in infancy, childhood and adulthood: A move to the level of representation. In: *Growing Points in Attachment: Theory and Research*, ed. I. Bretherton & E. Waters. Monographs of the Society for Research in Child Development, Serial 209. Chicago: University of Chicago Press, pp. 66–104.

Miller, J-A., ed. (1988), *The Seminar of Jacques Lacan. Book I: Freud's Papers on Technique 1953–1954*, trans. with notes J. Forrester. New York & London: W. W. Norton.

Mitchell, S. (1988a), Changing concepts of the analytic process: A method in search of new meanings. Presented at the Relational Colloquium of the New York University Postdoctoral Program in Psychoanalysis.

——— (1988b), *Relational Concepts in Psychoanalysis: An Integration*. Cambridge, MA: Harvard University Press.

Ogden, T. H. (1986), *The Matrix of the Mind: Object Relations and the Psychoanalytic Dialogue*. Northvale, NJ & London: Aronson.

Olinick, S.L. (1969), On empathy and regression in service of the other. *British Journal of Medical Psychology*, 42:41–49.

Pick, I. B. (1985), Working through in the counter-transference. *Internat. J. Psycho-Anal.*, 66:157–166.

Racker, H. (1968), *Transference and Countertransference*. New York: International Universities Press.

Rosenfeld, H. (1986), Transference–countertransference distortions and other problems in the analysis of traumatized patients. Presented to the Kleinian analysts of the British Psycho-Analytical Society, April 30, 1986.

Singer, E. (1977), The fiction of analytic anonymity. In: *The Human Dimension in Psychoanalytic Practice*, ed. K. Frank. New York: Grune & Stratton, pp. 181–192.

Stern, D. N. (1985), *The Interpersonal World of the Infant*. New York: Basic Books.

—— (1989), The representation of relational patterns: Developmental considerations. In: *Relationship Disturbances in Early Childhood: A Developmental Approach*, ed. A. J. Sameroff & R. N. Emde. New York: Basic Books, pp. 52–69.

Stolorow, R. D. Brandchaft, B. & Atwood, G. E. (1987), *Psychoanalytic Treatment: An Intersubjective Approach*. Hillsdale, NJ: The Analytic Press.

Winnicott, D. W. (1954–1955), The depressive position in normal development. In: *Through Pediatrics to Psycho-Analysis*. New York: Basic Books, 1975.

—— (1969), The use of an object. *Internat. J. Psycho-Anal.*, 50:711–716.

—— (1971), *Playing and Reality*. Middlesex, England: Penguin.

—— (1986), *Holding and Interpretation: Fragments of an Analysis*. London: Hogarth Press.

Wolstein, B. (1983), The pluralism of perspectives on countertransference. *Contemp. Psychoanal.*, 19:506–521.

—— (1988), Introduction. In: *Essential Papers on Countertransference*, ed. B. Wolstein. New York: New York University Press, pp. 115.

Afterword

My clinical study of the patient's experience of the analyst's subjectivity led me to think more and more about the various ways in which mutuality played a role in the psychoanalytic situation. At first, I was troubled by the artificial distinction that some theorists were making between analysts who believed in mutuality and those who believed in asymmetry. It seemed to me that these were two distinct dimensions of psychoanalytic conceptualization and that one could recognize the various ways in which psychoanalysis was inevitably asymmetrical but nevertheless acknowledge that there were many areas where some degree of mutuality was central to the work. This led me to differentiate between symmetry and mutuality.

Symmetry refers to a correspondence in form or arrangement on either side of a dividing line or plane. In mathematics, for example, we designate as symmetrical an equation whose terms can be interchanged without affecting its validity. Symmetry implies a similarity, and even a quantitative equality, between the two sides. Mutuality means reciprocity and commonality. It refers to what we have between us; for instance, a mutual agreement is one we both understand and consented to, and a mutual friend is a friend we have in common. Mutuality implies reciprocation, community, and unity through interchange. Lack of mutuality, by contrast, connotes difference and separateness, a lack of sharing.

The definition of mutuality does *not* include symmetry or equality. Two people may be said to have formed a mutual admiration society when they hold each other in high esteem or share reciprocal mirroring or idealization. There need be no assumption, however, of quantitative equality or functional symmetry for the term mutual to be applied. That a mother and an infant exert mutual influence in certain interactions does not imply that they influence each other equally or in identical ways. Similarly, one may speak of mutuality between patient and analyst without advocating that they maintain identical functions or implying that they are equal in status or power.

Although in many important respects psychoanalysis is a mutual endeavor, it is, nevertheless, inevitably asymmetrical. While influence and regulation move in both directions, that influence is not necessarily equal or identical. Patient and analyst do not have the same or equivalent roles, functions or responsibilities. Psychoanalysis, then, is mutual but inevitably asymmetrical—inevitably because it is the patient seeking help from the analyst, who is the professional and is invested with a certain kind of authority and responsibility.

Mutuality should not be mistaken for an evasion of difference and conflict between patient and analyst, nor should it imply an emphasis only on kindness and gratification. Mutuality does not preclude a focus on the dark side of human experience. There may be mutual conflict, mutual resistances, mutual aggression, or hatred; and there may be mutual enemies. Mutuality must always be balanced by separateness, difference, and autonomy, or else it degenerates into merger or fusion. Furthermore, I have emphasized that the exploration of the patient's experience of the analyst's subjectivity is only one aspect of the analysis of the transference–countertransference matrix and that this focus needs to be balanced with the recognition that for long periods of time the patient needs to feel "left alone in the presence of the analyst" without the analyst's bringing his or her own subjectivity onto the center of the analytic stage.

As I continued to explore the meaning of mutuality, and to contrast it with symmetry, I became aware that mutuality was too broad a concept to be meaningfully utilized and that much finer distinctions needed to be made. I began by distinguishing mutual recognition, which Benjamin had included in her elaboration of intersubjectivity theory, from mutual regulation, which Stolorow and his colleagues maintained was central in their version of intersubjectivity theory. When I revised "The Patient's Experience of the Analyst's Subjectivity" for my (1996) book, *A Meeting of Minds*, I elaborated on the various theoretical approaches to intersubjectivity theory in the light of these differentiations.

In *A Meeting of Minds* I went on to examine a wide variety of dimensions of the psychoanalytic situation in which mutuality played a role. These included discussions of mutual recognition, mutual regulation, mutual transferences, mutual resistances, mutual empathy, mutual regressions, mutual affective involvement, mutual enactments, mutual generation of data, and mutual analysis. I used this scheme to explore many issues that I had only touched on in the 1991 article: interpretation as an expression of the analyst's subjectivity; enactment, interaction, and projective identification; technical considerations regarding self-disclosure; as well as ethical and boundary considerations in a relational approach.

In my most recent work, I continue to build on and elaborate ideas that were touched on in this earlier article. I have become increasingly persuaded that psychoanalytic technique can be articulated only with due consideration given to the individuality of the analyst and the analyst's need to work in a way that is compatible with and responsive to his or her own subjectivity. Clinical choices are always made within the relational matrix, one pole of which is constituted by the analyst's subjectivity.

I have begun to research analytic stalemates and have found that impasses are often created through mutual collusion and mutual resistances. When an analysis gets stuck it is often because, in some way, the analyst has deeply identified with the patient in some way that the analyst does not want to recognize, and the patient cannot go further with the analytic process until the analyst finds some way to own this identification. Along similar lines, I have begun to articulate a theory of therapeutic action that emphasizes mutual projections, mutual identifications, and mutual affective exchanges as important aspects of the development of reflexive self-functioning.

Having focused on a meeting of minds, I became aware that I may have inadvertently shortchanged the significance of the body. A two-person psychology is really a two-body psychology, it is not just a meeting of minds but of persons including bodies. This realization led to my collaboration with Frances Sommer Anderson on the collection, *Relational Perspectives on the Body* (Aron and Anderson, 1998). It is not necessary for relational psychoanalysis to deemphasize bodily matters in its focus on persons in relation. Following a suggestion of Stephen Mitchell, we set out to investigate what happens to the centrality of the body in relational theory.

Building on our growing recognition that our impact on our patients is not limited to the neutral interpretation of meanings but, rather, that we continually exert a personal influence on our patients, I have called on analysts to acknowledge *the irrepressible influence of the analyst's subjectivity*. This recognition is in striking contrast to the mainstream Freudian tradition that considered the elimination of "suggestion" as the hallmark of psychoanalysis, with the rationale that this was in the best interest of protecting the patient's autonomy. Acknowledging the irrepressible influence of the analyst's subjectivity does more to enhance mutual recognition and mutual regulation and paradoxically by better defining the analyst's contributions to the analysis, preserves the patient's autonomy and freedom.

References

Aron, L. (1996), *A Meeting of Minds: Mutuality in Psychoanalysis*. Hillsdale, NJ: The Analytic Press.
——— & Anderson, F. S. (1998), *Relational Perspectives on the Body*. Hillsdale, NJ: The Analytic Press.

Dissociative Processes and Transference–Countertransference Paradigms in the Psychoanalytically Oriented Treatment of Adult Survivors of Childhood Sexual Abuse

(1991)

Jody Messler Davies, Ph.D.
Mary Gail Frawley, Ph.D.

▼   ▼   ▼   ▼   ▼

Editors' Introduction

Why would we include, in a collection of seminal papers documenting the relational psychoanalytic tradition, an article on so specific a topic as the treatment of adult survivors of childhood sexual abuse? The answer is that in this groundbreaking article Davies and Frawley introduced controversial topics that have become central to a contemporary relational sensibility. While the article focuses on the specifics of treating a very particular population, in so doing the authors presented a quintessentially relational view of the psychoanalytic approach sui generis.

Davies and Frawley begin by acknowledging that historically psychoanalysis has been guilty of contributing to society's unconscionable denial of the reality of childhood sexual abuse. They attempt to correct for the tension and mistrust that have existed between psychoanalysts, on one hand and those who specialize in the treatment of sexual abuse and who research trauma, on the other. The project of reconciling these traditions leads them to a new exploration of the early history of psychoanalysis and Freud's initial point of departure from his "seduction theory" as well as from his contemporaries who were engaged in the study of trauma along quite different lines.

Davies and Frawley's investigation leads them to propose that psychoanalysis reintroduce the notion of dissociation. They highlight that, unlike repression, conceptualized as defending against drives, dissociation consists of the splitting off of certain experiences so as to preserve and protect the internal object world. Along with the shift from repression to dissociation comes a recognition that analysis cannot take place in the verbal realm of interpretation alone but, rather, requires the active participation of the analyst, as the patient reenacts the crucial self- and object-relational scenarios of her traumatic childhood.

"Working with adult survivors of childhood sexual abuse within a relational model implies the cocreation of a transitional space in which therapist and patient together are free to reenact, create context and meaning, and ultimately recreate in newly configured forms the central organizing relational matrices of the patient's early life," the authors write. Davies and Frawley beautifully illustrate the "kaleidoscope" that is constituted by the continual shifts between various relational configurations as patient and analyst alternate roles: the good, perfect child; the naughty, omnipotent child; the terrified, abused child; the adolescent protector self; the omnipotent, nurturing rescuer and savior; the helpless, masochistic victim; the sadistic abuser; and the denying, mystifying neglector.

Within the relational approach spelled out here, dissociation, the reenactment of traumatic interpersonal relations, and the experience and integration of the affects that accompany them compose the core of psychoanalytic treatment. Clinicians must be willing and able to work within the powerful and rapidly shifting relational paradigms of transference and countertransference unleashed by the psychoanalytic process.

Subsequent papers by Davies on some of the knottiest, most difficult transference–countertransference experiences have demonstrated the power of the clinical methodology Davies and Frawley developed here. Clinical technique has been notoriously difficult to teach in a way that avoids reductiveness and excessive formalism. One of the surprises of this paper and the book that developed from it was its remarkable utility in conveying an approach to clinical practice that provides a conceptual map while, at the same time, conveys a sense of the complexity and intensity of analytic engagement.

The article by Davies and Frawley was extensively expanded and elaborated in their extremely influential book *Treating the Adult Survivor of Childhood Sexual Abuse: A Psychoanalytic Perspective* (1994, Basic Books). They integrate much of the extensive literature in the fields of trauma research and clinical psychoanalysis. Their application of relational concepts to the understanding of dissociation and transference–countertransference configurations with respect to the treatment of traumatic sexual abuse has had wide application to clinical work with all patients. Davies has extended the conceptual methodology developed in this early work into controversial and wide-ranging theoretical and clinical concerns. In "Love in the Afternoon: A Relational Reconsideration of Desire and Dread in the Countertransference" (*Psychoanalytic Dialogues*, 1994, 4:153–170) Davies explored the mutual participation of both members of the analytic dyad in a tense analytic stalemate, in which the analyst was able to constructively employ a selective disclosure of erotic countertransference. Davies has further explored the issues surrounding this complex technical problem in the recent paper "Between the Disclosure and Foreclosure of Erotic Transference–Countertransference Processes: Can Psychoanalysis Find a Place for Adult Sexuality" (*Psychoanalytic Dialogues*, 1998, 8:747–766). In "Multiple Perspectives on Multiplicity" (*Psychoanalytic Dialogues*, 1998, 8:195–206) Davies builds on her notion of the relational unconscious and the imagae of a kaleidoscope as a metaphor for the mind as a multiply organized, associationally linked network of meaning organization and understanding.

Dissociative Processes and Transference–Countertransference Paradigms in the Psychoanalytically Oriented Treatment of Adult Survivors of Childhood Sexual Abuse*

▼   ▼   ▼   ▼   ▼

Only recently, and still amid great controversy, have mental health professionals returned to the issue of treating, from a psychoanalytic perspective, the adult survivor of childhood sexual trauma. The growing awareness of the actualities of childhood abuse, in concert with the burgeoning numbers of men and women seeking professional help in

* Originally published in *Psychoanalytic Dialogues*, 2(1):5–36. © 1991 The Analytic Press, Inc.

dealing with long-term residual effects of their abusive experiences, has created a desperate need for psychoanalytically trained clinicians educated in this area and alerted to the specific needs of this patient population.

It is our contention that we can afford to sacrifice, in this context, neither clinical experience and sophistication, nor a thorough, working understanding of the maladaptive intrapsychic organizations typical of the psychological adjustments of adult survivors of childhood sexual abuse. Analysts must be alerted both to the specific constellations of reality preserving/distorting defenses used by adult survivors and to the particular transference-countertransference paradigms that represent the introduction of these defenses into the intersubjective field of the analytic work. The analyst's attention to his or her own pattern of reaction, be it primary or counter to the patient's reaction, is of paramount importance and must assume an organizing function in any attempt to interpret a central therapeutic configuration. We firmly believe that it is within the context of an informed analytic treatment that adult survivors can best move beyond the pervasive guilt and shame that are their unique legacy, to deal with the underlying defensive compromises that make continued experiences of victimization and abuse a lifelong pattern.

The tension and mistrust that exist between psychoanalysis and the field of childhood sexual abuse are, of course, historic. To date, many classical analysts persist in their denial of the realities of childhood sexual abuse, a denial we believe to be unconscionable, given the incontrovertible results of current, quality research on the subject. Though it is not our intention in the present paper to review fully the incidence and demographics of childhood sexual abuse in this country, we do believe that inclusion of certain key statistical findings serves to substantiate our conviction that a reconciliation between psychoanalysts and researchers in the field has become an emergent clinical and social necessity.

All available, current research points to the same conclusions. Actual sexual molestation of children is, and for a long while has been, a reality of life in our society. It will not be dismissed, and it will not be isolated by race, religion, or socioeconomic classification. Our best current estimate is that between 20 and 35% of all women have had unwanted sexual encounters with adult males sometime before their 18th birthday, and 8.5 to 15% report that such contact was with a close family member (Russell, 1986). Between 1 and 4.5% of all women report having been sexually abused by a biological father, adoptive father, or stepfather (Finkelhor, 1979; Herman, 1981; Herman and Hirschman, 1981; Russell, 1983, 1984, 1986). These studies were intentionally conducted on nonclinical, primarily middle-class populations; in many cases the populations consisted entirely of randomly selected college students.

Findings across studies were remarkably consistent, and all researchers agreed that if there was error, it was to underestimate the actual incidence of abuse. Unfortunately, the findings on the incidence of sexual abuse of male children are much less consistent and therefore less conclusive. Finkelhor (1979) places the figures at 8.6% for general abuse and 1.5% for abuse by a close family member. More research on the abuse of male children is a necessity.

Clearly, the time has come to reopen a serious psychoanalytic dialogue about the specific psychological sequelae of early childhood sexual trauma. Our intention in the present paper is to focus on the clinical manifestations and therapeutic implications of dissociation as it is used defensively by adult survivors. Our belief is that dissociation, more than any other clinical phenomenon, is intrinsic to the intrapsychic structure and organization of this patient group and, to a large extent, is pathognomic of it. Though contemporary psychoanalytic discussion of dissociation in victims of abuse is minimal and will be reviewed below, our belief in the primacy of this clinical phenomenon emerges out of a confluence of three other bodies of empirical data. These are the areas of childhood sexual abuse (Briere, 1989; Courtois, 1989); trauma and posttraumatic stress disorders (van der Kolk, 1987; Krystal, 1988; Ulman and Brothers, 1988); and specific dissociative disorders, including multiple personality disorders (Putnam, 1989; Ross, 1989). From these disparate areas of investigation comes confirmation of the recurring connection between childhood trauma, particularly physical and sexual trauma, and the process of dissociation. Indeed, a recent empirical study of 278 university women found that a measure of dissociation could successfully discriminate between abused and nonabused subjects when no other measures were employed (Briere and Runtz, 1988).

In the present paper we use the concept of dissociation to refer to an organization of mind, not unlike splitting, wherein traumatic memories are split off from associative accessibility to the remainder of conscious thought, but rather than being repressed and forgotten, as would be the case in a topographical/structural model, they alternate in a mutually exclusive pattern with other conscious ego states. As with splitting, the clinical question is not what is conscious and what is unconscious but, rather, what is available and conscious to the patient at a particular point in time, and what clinical interventions best serve the purposes of integration. Unlike splitting, in which the goal is to protect the good object from the murderous impulses of an angry, frustrated self, dissociation aims to protect the person from the overwhelming memory of traumatic events and the regressive fantasies that these memories trigger.

It will become clear, however, that our position differs significantly from the classical position, which regards dissociation as a regressive defense against the overwhelming aggressive and libidinal drive derivatives stimulated by early sexual and aggressive assault. Though our view preserves the importance of powerful sadomasochistic struggles, we view dissociation not merely as a defense against drive but, rather, as a process that preserves and protects, in split-off form, the entire internal object world of the abused child. We believe that in making contact with the split-off, dissociated, child persona within the abused adult, we free these archaic objects to work their way into the transference-countertransference paradigms through projective-introjective mechanisms and, in so doing, enable patients to work through each possible configuration within the therapeutic relationship.

The following discussion is divided into three sections: (1) a brief, historical review of the concept of dissociation, (2) a review of the more contemporary psychoanalytic writing on the concept of dissociation, (3) a clinical description of dissociation as it appears in the treatment of adult survivors of childhood sexual abuse, including a specific discussion of the transference-countertransference dilemmas that emerge when treating patients whose intrapsychic structure depends heavily on dissociative mechanisms.

Dissociation in Historical Context

The legacy of mistrust and misunderstanding between psychoanalysts and those in the field of childhood sexual abuse had its inception in the very earliest period of psychoanalytic thought and writing. The much debated process of Freud's (1896) wholehearted commitment to, and subsequent rejection of, the "seduction hypothesis" is, by now, well known to those familiar with the history of psychoanalytic thought. Although it is not within the scope of this paper to analyze the reasons behind Freud's rejection of a hypothesis he had believed in so intensely, we do wish to examine the impact that this change of heart ultimately came to exert on the direction of psychoanalytic thought and practice.

Though Freud came to doubt that early sexual trauma could account for all neurotic manifestations and turned the attention of the psychoanalytic community, therefore, from the realities of childhood trauma to the complexities of infantile fantasy and intrapsychic structuralization, he did dramatically underestimate the incidence of actual sexual abuse and inadvertently cast aside an enormously rich body of literature on the nature of intrapsychic processes specific to adult survivors of childhood sexual abuse. Only today is this literature beginning to resurface, as Freud's conclusions about the psychical integration of infantile traumatogenic events are subject to empirical study. Indeed, Freud's (Breuer and Freud, 1893–1895) earliest psychoanalytic writings on the predisposition to altered states of consciousness and ego dissociation and splitting in the victims of childhood sexual trauma are almost entirely supported by the results of contemporary research (van der Kolk, 1987; Krystal, 1988; Ross, 1989; Putnam, 1989; Ulman and Brothers, 1988).

Clearly, Freud believed that his early hysterical patients had been sexually abused. In "The Aetiology of Hysteria" Freud (1896) concluded:

> If you submit my assertion that the aetiology of hysteria lies in sexual life to the strictest examination, you will find that it is supported by the fact that in some eighteen cases of hysteria I have been able to discover this connection in every single symptom, and, where the circumstances allowed, to confirm it by therapeutic success [p. 199].

Later in the same paper he wrote:

> I therefore put forth the thesis that at the bottom of every case of hysteria there are one or more occurrences of premature sexual experience, occurrences which belong to the earliest years of childhood but which can be reproduced through the work of psychoanalysis in spite of the intervening decades [p. 203].

In this context we turn back to Breuer and Freud's earlier clinical papers in and attempt to review their prescient description of the clinical manifestations of early sexual overstimulation in their adult hysterical patients. The theme of dissociation and the dual nature of consciousness, with which we are particularly concerned in this paper, assume a central role throughout their early writing. In their "Preliminary Communication, The Mechanism of Hysterical Phenomena" (Breuer and Freud, 1893–1895), the authors state unequivocally:

> The longer we have been occupied with these phenomena the more we have become convinced that the splitting of consciousness which is so striking in the well-known classical cases under the form of "double conscience" is present to a rudimentary degree in every hysteria, and that a tendency to such a dissociation, and with it the emergence of abnormal states of consciousness (which we shall bring together under the term "hypnoid") is the basic phenomenon of this neurosis. . . . Ideas which emerge in them are very intense but are cut off from associative communication with the rest of the content of consciousness [p. 12].

Though Freud later moves in a direction that stresses the repression of traumatic events within a topographical model of the mind, wherein there is a layering of levels of consciousness depending on the acceptability of the memories (later impulses) contained therein, he and Breuer are, at this time, still describing in their hysterical patients not a layering but an alternation of differing experiences of consciousness. It is not that one group of associations is conscious and one group unconscious; rather, they are independent, mutually exclusive ego states, associatively unavailable to each other, which alternate depending on the patient's emotional state, the stimulation of traumatic memories, and the particular configuration of transference-countertransference material operative at a particular time.

In the first of his published case studies, that of Frau Emmy Von N., Freud describes the phenomenon unmistakably:

> What she told me was perfectly coherent and revealed an unusual degree of education and intelligence. This made it seem all the more strange when every two or three minutes she suddenly broke off, contorted her face into an expression of horror and disgust, stretched out her hand towards me, spreading and crooking her fingers, and exclaimed, in a changed voice, charged with anxiety: "Keep still! Don't say anything! Don't touch me!" She was probably under the influence of some recurrent hallucination of a horrifying kind and was keeping the intruding material at bay with this formula. These interpolations came to an end with equal suddenness and the patient took up what she had been saying, without pursuing her momentary excitement any further, and without explaining or apologizing for her behavior—probably therefore without herself having noticed the interpolation [Breuer and Freud, 1893–1895, p. 49].

The case studies in this volume contain many such evocative examples of recurrent dissociative episodes. Unfortunately, Freud's abandonment of the seduction theory in September 1897 relegated these early clinical and theoretical conceptualizations to the ancillary position of scientific history. For the most part, clinicians today read "Studies on Hysteria" to learn about the early stages in the development of psychoanalysis and Freud's struggles to develop a working model of the mind and to elucidate a technique that would overcome the powerful forces of repression, unconscious conflict, and symptom formation. The brilliant clinical descriptions so richly depicted in the text and so pertinent to work with adult survivors of childhood sexual abuse were to be lost for many years to come.

Not until the work of Sándor Ferenczi did the actualities of early childhood trauma and their psychologically devastating sequelae again become the focus of serious psychoanalytic inquiry. Ferenczi (Freud's pupil, analysand, and, after Fliess, his closest personal friend) would eventually jeopardize his relationship with Freud and his respect and esteem within the psychoanalytic community to promulgate his belief in the primacy of these events. In a letter to Freud dated December 25, 1929, Ferenczi writes:

> In all cases where I penetrated deeply enough I found uncovered the traumatic-hysterical bases of the illness. . . . The critical view that I gradually formed during this period was that psychoanalysis deals far too one-sidedly with obsessive neurosis and character analysis—that is, ego psychology—while neglecting the organic-hysterical basis of the analysis. This results from overestimating the role of fantasy, and under-estimating that of traumatic reality, in pathogenesis . . . [Dupont, 1988, p. xii].

Unfortunately, the presentation of these views (Ferenczi, 1932) and their ultimate publication (Ferenczi, 1949) led to an irreconcilable break with Freud, and ultimately, during the last years of his life, Ferenczi was branded by Jones (1961) and other members of the international psychoanalytic community, as the victim of an emotional and mental breakdown.

Psychoanalytic politics notwithstanding, the publication of Ferenczi's clinical diaries (Dupont, 1988) clearly put to an end speculation about his mental deterioration and provided the most profoundly insightful observations, to date, on the psychological adaptation and resultant psychopathology of childhood sexual traumata. In treatment observations on four different patients, Ferenczi touched upon the major theoretical and technical issues facing those analysts working with this population. Of course, dissociation and ego splitting assume a position of some primacy, but also included in the diaries are comments about identification with the aggressor, somatization of early abusive memories, inclinations toward certain countertransferential pitfalls, and some of the masochistic elements inherent in the psychoanalytic situation that exacerbate the resistance of those with a history of abuse.

In a diary entry dated January 12, 1932, Ferenczi revealed his own particular view of the dissociated ego states he observed in his patients. Ferenczi's metaphors were a far cry from the "hysterical," "delirious," "hallucinating" images referred to by Freud and Breuer. To Ferenczi the dissociated state included more than a set of associatively isolated traumatic memories; he described the dissociated state as a whole person, a child, and the delirious quality of that child as the reactivation in the treatment setting of the traumatically overstimulating, abusive situation.

The patient Ferenczi (Dupont, 1988) refers to here had been sadistically abused over a long period of time by several family members. Ferenczi writes:

> A being suffering purely psychically in his unconscious, the actual child, of whom the awakened ego knows absolutely nothing. This fragment is accessible only in deep sleep, or in a deep trance, following extreme exertion or exhaustion, that is, in a neurotic (hysterical) crisis situation. Only with great difficulty and by close observance of specific rules of conduct can the analyst make contact with this part: the pure repressed affect. This part behaves like a child who has fainted, completely unaware of itself, who can perhaps only groan, who must be shaken awake mentally and sometimes also physically. If this is not done with total belief in the reality of the process, the "shaking up" will lack persuasiveness as well as effectiveness. But if the analyst does have that conviction, and the related sympathy for the suffering being, he may by judicious questioning (which compels the sufferer to think) succeed in directing this being's reflective powers and orientation to the point where it can say and remember something about the circumstances of the shock [p. 9].

So complete and ill-spirited was Ferenczi's ostracism from his dearest friends and oldest colleagues, that it would be many years before any other analyst would again raise the specter of real trauma and sexual abuse, and then only in ways that revealed obvious conciliatory overtures toward the classical psychoanalytic theory.

Contemporary Psychoanalytic Literature

This injunction against serious consideration of childhood sexual abuse was powerfully effective within the psychoanalytic community for many years. Written discussions of this very important clinical phenomenon are dramatically sparse in the subsequent psychoanalytic literature, and papers pertaining to the long-term sequelae of such abuse are even more unusual. Those articles that do exist, for the most part, follow a traditional psychoanalytic line, one that downplays the effects of actual trauma and stresses, instead, regression to more dangerously primitive fantasies and to earlier forms of psychosexual excitation and discharge (Greenacre, 1950, 1967; Shengold, 1967, 1989; Dewald, 1989). In the clinical work with adult survivors of abuse, specific discussion of dissociation can be found in the literature, but here again the concept is embedded in a drive theory model of psychopathology, and its interrelationship to early childhood trauma, though mentioned, is oddly understated.

Fliess (1953) was the first writer to call attention to what he regarded as the intrinsically hypnotic factors within the analytic situation. He attempted to demonstrate how certain patients could exploit these factors and, in so doing, bring about what he termed "the hypnotic evasion." This term referred to a self-induced alteration in consciousness, marked by a mild sleepiness or emotional withdrawal, which could be used as a defense against unacceptable transference fantasies, usually of a sexual nature. To Fliess, the alteration in consciousness was a resistance, employed to defend against unacceptable impulses. Clearly, the analyst's task was to interpret the defensive use of this hypnotic evasion and, in so doing, render the unconscious fantasy accessible to interpretation.

In a series of moving clinical vignettes, Dickes (1965) attempts to communicate the pervasiveness of this type of alteration in consciousness as seen in clinical practice. For the first time, he ties this type of defense directly to childhood experiences of sexual or physical abuse. Dickes says: "Childhood events as described in my patients offer some clues to the development of a pathological hypnoid state in the adult. This adult state is often a repetition of a childhood hypnoid state which occurred as a means of warding off intolerable feelings due to overstimulation and abuse" (p. 397). Dickes, however, maintains the classical position that hypnotic evasion is a resistance to treatment and a defense against unconscious aggressive and libidinal fantasy. He, too, stresses the primacy of interpretation of unconscious drive derivatives as the single most important factor in the treatment.

Of all contemporary psychoanalytic writers, no one has studied the effects of early childhood abuse as thoroughly as Shengold (1963, 1967, 1971, 1975, 1979, 1989). Proceeding from the work of Fliess and Dickes, Shengold stresses the centrality of what he calls "autohypnotic states" in the mental lives of adult survivors. He believes that the autohypnotic state essentially relieves the patient from the burden of being responsible for what is said and felt during the analytic hour. Though he also maintains a classical drive model and views autohypnosis as "the ego's need to defend against drive tensions" (1989, p. 141), Shengold adds two very significant perspectives to what has heretofore been described. He stresses the possibility that autohypnosis can also be used to facilitate drive discharge, a phenomenon that transcends the defensive functions described above. Here the alteration in consciousness is used to facilitate a traumatic reenactment, either within or outside of the transference, and to deny the experience of significant gratification of libidinal and aggressive impulses. In addition, Shengold describes how the hypnotic state can bring about a "concentrated hypercathexis of perceptory signals" that enhances one's awareness of peripheral stimuli and evokes a state of what he terms "hypnotic vigilance" (p. 143). Though it stems from the simultaneous need to defend against the derivatives of instinctual drive or their discharge, the process, as described in clinical vignettes, appears inadvertently to heighten the patient's sensitivity to a range of other experiences within the therapeutic relationship.

In moving from a position that regards autohypnosis as merely an ego defense against instinctual impulses to one that recognizes that the dissociative state involves the possibility of an expansion of awareness, Shengold moves somewhat closer to our own position, though by no means close enough. Our belief is that the expansion of awareness goes far deeper than Shengold describes. Rather than viewing the dissociative experience as a resistance to the analytic work, we view it much as Freud viewed the dreams of his early analytic patients—as "the royal road" to otherwise unavailable, split-off experience and memory. We believe that only within the dissociative state can the analyst come to understand the internal object world of the abused child and that only within this state can the split-off self and object representations play themselves out in the transference-countertransference configurations. Contrary to Shengold's position that the analyst must be hypervigilant himself to such instances of autohypnosis because they represent the patient's evasion of responsibility for what is thought, felt, and said in the analytic space, we believe such a traditional "resistance interpretation" to be counterproductive.

Our hope in this paper is to show that only by allowing ourselves to enter, rather than interpret, the dissociative experience; to encourage temporarily the evasion of responsibility; and to expect that unwitting reenactments, gratifications, and frustrations will be the hallmark, and not the downfall, of the analytic work will the patient and therapist come to occupy the same relational matrix. By our clinical description we hope to demonstrate that only from within this shared field can the analyst hope to experience, contain, comprehend, and ultimately interpret the fragmented, ever-shifting projective, introjective, counterprojective processes that come, ultimately, to define our most profound levels of participation in the analytic endeavor.

We turn now to a clinical description of this phenomenon and to an analysis of the transference-countertransference paradigms that emerge in a system where dissociative mechanisms play such a central role.

The Child Imago and Dissociative Processes

Most survivors of childhood abuse are faced with the dilemma of having to negotiate the external, interpersonal worlds of friendship, school, authority, career, and so on, in spite of the fact that, relatively early on, they have been betrayed by a person with whom they share one of the most intimate relationships of their lives. It is remarkable to observe the degree to which most survivors can painstakingly erect the semblance of a functioning, adaptive, interpersonally related self around the screaming core of a wounded and abandoned child. This adult self has a dual function; it allows the individual to move through the world of others with relative success and at the same time protect and preserve the abused child who lives on, searching still for acknowledgment, validation, and compensation. The impact of this essential splitting and dissociation at the core of the personality and its effects on all later personality development form the body of this paper.

In the preceding review of early classical literature, we have attempted to demonstrate a critically important point. The patient who was sexually abused as a child is not an adult patient with particularly vivid memories of painful childhood experiences existing in the context of other, happier, more loving times. We stress here that this child is a fully developed, dissociated, rather primitively organized alternative self. In this regard, we speak concretely, not metaphorically. It is imperative that the therapist who begins working with an adult who has survived significant childhood sexual abuse understand that he or she is, in fact, undertaking the treatment of two people: an adult who struggles to succeed, relate, gain acceptance, and ultimately to forget and a child who, as treatment progresses, strives to remember and to find a voice with which to scream out his or her outrage at the world.

The dissociated child-self has a different ego structure, a more primitive and brittle system of defenses, a fuller and more affect-laden set of memories and has clearly become the repository for the patient's intense, often overwhelming rage, shame, and guilt. We often find the child with a different wardrobe, facial expressions, body postures, voice quality, and set of linguistic expressions. "She" takes on the persona of a timid little girl; "he," of an awkward preadolescent whose emergent sexuality has lagged behind that of his chums.

It should be noted that dissociation exists along a broad continuum, with coexistent, alternative ego states moving in ever-shifting patterns of mutual self-recognition and alienation. It is not uncommon for the child-self to contain several different personas, often with different access to historical information and memory. Common among these personas are the good, perfect child, the naughty, omnipotent child, and, ultimately, the terrified, abused child. Given the frequent coexistence of these alternative states, we do not believe that they represent true multiple personality organizations. In most instances the adult and the child are at least partially aware of each other's existence; it is the child's incestuous secret and overwhelming rage about which the adult is often completely ignorant. We would be remiss, however, in not reporting that although not all adult survivors of childhood sexual abuse show multiple personality structures, the best current estimate is that between 88 and 97% of all multiple personalities have experienced significant sexual abuse, physical abuse, or both in childhood (Putnam, 1989; Ross, 1989).

Although the adult and the child are, in most situations, aware of each other, they are not friends. They have entirely different emotional agendas and live in a constant state of warfare over whose needs will take priority at any given time. Each feels entirely abandoned by the other. The child believes that the adult has "sold out" by progressing with her life as a grown-up. After all, grown-ups are bad and do bad things. To become one of them is the ultimate betrayal. The child takes every opportunity, therefore, to subvert the adult's attempts to separate from her past and her identity as a victim, to become a part of the outside world. She uses the techniques she was taught by her abusive parent (other) to undermine the confidence of her other self: seduction, cajoling, manipulation, and threat of abuse (in this case self-inflicted). As she herself felt invaded, she often invades the unexpecting, conscious sensorium of the adult in inappropriate and disruptive ways, causing great confusion and disorientation, at times bringing to a halt whatever activity the adult was engaged in at that moment. She stands in relation to her adult-self—a provocateur, with a terrorist's commitment to a program of unrelenting insurgence.

On her end the adult persona "hates" the sadistic and disruptive child with bitter intensity. On the most conscious level, the adult views the child as a demanding, entitled, rebellious, and petulant pain in the neck. If she remembers being sexually abused in childhood, she blames her child-self for the abuse and thereby refortifies her insistence on the child's thorough and complete badness. She was "the seductress," and, as one patient announced with burning rancor in her first session, "She got what she deserved. . . . It was coming to her."

It is almost incomprehensible to us that here the patient is talking about herself, the part of herself that was rather sadistically abused as a child and abused by her own father. We see, though, the effectiveness of the dissociation that spares both the adult persona and the father from the full impact of the child's rage. The hate is turned back upon the child, who has, after all, been well trained in the art of self-victimization.

In situations where the patient has not yet recovered actual memories of childhood sexual abuse, she stands in relation to her demanding and disruptive child-self as a passive and mystified player who gives voice to the child's tantrums, mood swings, and demands without exactly understanding why. "It's as if a voice rises up in me," reported one patient. "I know it's my voice. . . . I recognize the sound of it . . . but it's so odd, I have no idea what the voice is going to say. All I know is that usually it says something to get me into trouble." If the disparity between the intensity of the child's rage and shame and the content of her thoughts becomes severe enough, the patient may experience full dissociative episodes where the child is given full reign to express, remember, and reenact, without any conscious recollection of the experience. As is the case with true multiple personalities, patients, for example, report losing time and suddenly finding themselves in the middle of a situation but not remembering how they got there. One patient would report, with some regularity, sitting down to write business reports only to find that they had already been done and done to perfection! "It's like the shoemaker and the elves," she would say. "I go to sleep and when I wake up, there it is!" This particular patient entered treatment because of persistent problems on her job. Though it was immediately clear that her personal life was also extremely restricted, she kept these issues out of the early phase of her treatment by insisting that a social life was completely unimportant to her. On her job, the patient was considered a truly brilliant and incisive thinker whose written analyses supported and gave direction to much of her firm's ongoing work. She however, was, completely incapable of presenting her written work either within her office or to clients. She was terrified of being looked at, exposed, and penetrated by the stares of others. A severe inhibition, based in large measure upon dissociated exhibitionistic urges, would give rise to the most paralyzing experiences of humiliation and shame in these situations. The inhibition was so complete that others would often be called upon to present the patient's work to clients. To make matters worse, the patient was considered moody and demanding, with a reputation among colleagues for being "entitled and difficult to get along with."

With no conscious recollection, then, of the ongoing sexual abuse by her father between the ages of 1 and 12, the patient had perfectly re-created the emotional climate of these confusing early years in her present work life. She was gifted, special, and favored in some way that remained quite a mystery to her. Since she had no memory of writing her "brilliant" reports, she could hardly value herself for writing them, as others valued her. Despite her vague sense of specialness, she also felt despised and abused by her colleagues. She felt deserving of this abuse since she agreed that her behavior was often demanding and unpredictable. The patient herself experienced these abrupt mood swings and outbursts of demanding, entitled behavior as ego-alien intrusions, and on occasion when the affect was most intense, she had no recollection of them at all. Without the memories that would spur compassion for this "other self," the patient was filled with fear and self-loathing.

> *Patient:* It's like there's this baby part of me. . . . She's scared and pitiful sometimes, and I hate her for that . . . but then she turns hateful and demanding. . . . She won't be satisfied. . . . I try, but I can't. She wants more and more, but I don't know of what. She won't leave me alone, and she won't grow up. Sometimes I think she takes over completely, and part of me gets scared of what she'll do. I go away, I think. . . . I just can't bear to listen.

> *Therapist:* It seems to me she's likely to stay around until someone hears what she's trying to say.

> *Patient:* The less attention she gets, the better. The only thing I can do is ignore her . . . starve her out . . . otherwise, she'll never leave. If I give her nothing at all, maybe she'll go away and leave me alone. [quietly] Maybe she'll die. . . . I really want her to die.

Here again are the hatred and death wish for the child-self, not, this time, the omnipotent seductress who is blamed by the adult for her own abuse, but the raging and entitled child who makes her pain clear but keeps its source a mystery to all, including herself. Not yet on the analytic scene, but struggling to emerge, is the terrified child, living in a dissociated world of perpetual abuse and terrorized not only by the actions of another but by the prospect of speaking her own words and knowing her own mind.

It is almost always the adult-self who presents herself for treatment. Either she is struggling with overt, nightmarish memories of childhood, or, in her amnesia, she is plagued with one or many of a list of vague, debilitating complaints: sexual dysfunction, depression, intense guilt, poor self-esteem, self-destructive impulses, drug and alcohol abuse, and so on (Gelinas, 1983). Only slowly and after much careful testing does the child persona begin to make her presence known. She may step forth boldly and dramatically, as in the development of sudden panic attacks or in the eruption of painful and frightening somatic complaints. The child may also enter quietly, almost imperceptibly. The therapist may first become aware of her presence by an oddly childish mannerism—a way of wiping away tears or twisting a lock of hair. At other times, the child may signal her arrival with a subtle change in vocabulary, grammar, body postures and movements, different styles of clothing, a particular voice or facial expression. Many times the therapist's first awareness of change has to do with a perceived shift in the nature of the transference or in his or her own experience of the countertransference. Regardless, however, of the specific manner of entrance, it is most often the case that the child enters the analytic scene sometime before the recovery or disclosure of specific memories of past abuse begins.

The reasons here are clear. From the child's perspective the analyst is, as yet, an unknown quantity, a stranger. True, she has been listening, but what she has heard has been limited by the nature of the adult-analyst interaction. From the child's point of view, the analyst and the adult interviewed and chose each other. It is they who have evolved a relationship and have begun to define the limits of their trust and to deal with painful and intimate issues. As a dissociated self system with a separate object world and ego structure, the child has been kept very far away from the analytic field. The child has had little or no impact on the analytic relationship, and this relationship has affected her only insofar as she has perceived enough trust between the analyst and the adult to encourage her participation. To be sure, the emergence of the child in the treatment signifies that the early work has proceeded well and that the heart of the treatment is about to begin.

There are now two different patients on the analytic scene: an adult-self whom the analyst has already begun to know and an elusive child-self who appears and disappears at will; introducing endless confusion into the analytic process. It behooves us to pause here and take a closer look at this child-self system and at the ways in which he or she attempts to engage the analyst in playing out unconscious wishes, dreams, and fears.

Without question, the most singularly important thing to understand about the child is that he or she exists only in the context of a perpetually abusive, internalized object relationship. This aspect of the self and this aspect of the object have been literally ejected from the patient's more integrated personality functioning and allowed to set up an independent existence for the sake of pursuing its separate needs. Let us propose, as others have done (see, for example, Kernberg, 1976; Volkan, 1976; Ogden, 1986), that mature personality organization is an amalgam and integration of a multitude of widely varying self experiences and object experiences, each with its own unique affective-ideational-instinctual charge. This integration leads ideally to internal representations of the self and object that are wide ranging, at times contradictory, but not mutually exclusive. Love and hate coexist, are modulated by each other and give rise to the potential for ambivalence and mourning, as well as intense passion and ambition.

In the patient who has been sexually abused, the child aspect of the self representation, along with that of the abusing other and their complex system of emotional connection and exchange, is cordoned off and isolated from the rest of the personality. It remains virtually frozen in time, the images unmodulated by any others of a different, perhaps gentler nature. These images become the embodiment of the murderous rage and pernicious self-loathing that drive the child in his or her relationships with others. In their intensity they fuel the psychotic-level terrors of annihilation and world destruction that so infuse the patient's internal experience. The child cannot grow. Her anger and self-hatred go untempered, therefore unintegrated. Her world is a world of betrayal, terror, and continued emotional flooding. Her reality has been penetrated by a hostile, invasive force and her perceptions tragically distorted by her abusive experiences. What is bad she is told is good; what hurts is something she has been told she secretly wants and asks for. Her body aches. Her mind is in a constant state of upheaval and confusion. When, as a child, she turned to those around her for a way out, she was confronted either with threats and further abuse or with neglect and formidable denial. The child is incapable of expecting anything different from the analyst. She experiences herself as terrified, completely alone, and helpless. Only the adult persona can ask for and receive help. The child cannot ask, and it is, indeed, a long while before the analyst's "help" begins to penetrate the formidable dissociative barriers.

The extreme dissociation of the abused child into a separate self and object system is, essentially, an attempt by the patient at damage control. As physicians attempt to isolate and remove a potentially invasive malignancy before it can affect healthy tissue, the adult survivor of childhood sexual abuse attempts to isolate and eject the toxic introject and accompanying self representation before the capacity to trust oneself and others is entirely destroyed. The child-self may be condemned to a world of unrelenting paranoia, but the adult persona, having ejected these toxic experiences, attempts a rudimentary integration where self and object representations coalesce at a higher level of development. Indeed, the adult persona of many of our patients is marked by a rather hypomanic defensive style, where aggression is routinely projected and then denied. The adult in these instances takes on an air of uncanny innocence. He or she is often eager, if not compulsively driven, to help others. The consummate self-denier, the patient is unaware of the ways in which others take advantage of her well-intentioned need to help and equally unaware of her own resentment at often being taken advantage of. She struggles but fails to make sense of her complete inability to say no. Others seem to be capable of possessing her completely.

Clearly, the balance attained here between adult and child is tenuous at its best, with a codetermined impairment of ego functioning that makes successful adaptation virtually impossible. Secondary process thinking is subject to the constant intrusion of more primitive ideational strains. Reality testing is impaired by the pathological defensive patterns and the dissociative trends that give rise to a confusing duality in functioning. Somatic complaints are rampant, and the struggle against self-abusive urges is constant and unrelenting. Unlike diseased tissue that can be rendered harmless, once removed, the child-self is fully aware of her extradition and can wage an insidious campaign against the adult and thus make any successful adaptation even more unlikely.

Often at this precise moment of crisis, as adult and child are beginning to come together and memory of childhood abuse threatens to emerge and overwhelm the adult sensorium, a third persona can appear. This is an adolescent protector-self aspect of the personality who conveys a tough, streetwise, intensely cynical view of the world. She comes equipped with a truly dazzling array of impulsive, acting-out, self-abusive symptomatology designed to preoccupy the adult, befuddle and distract the therapist, and, above and beyond all else, obfuscate the threatening emergence of the child-self and her traumatogenic memories. The compendium of delinquent and self-abusive behavior includes stealing, truancy, pathological lying, burning, cutting, and the entire spectrum of anorexic-bulimic symptomatology.

The adolescent persona has no memories of specific childhood abuse and, rather than understanding her delinquent, self-abusive behavior as symptomatic of an earlier trauma, she often uses her own abusiveness to excuse a general attitude of parental neglect, indifference, or hurtfulness. The adolescent must at all cost contain the child, but the only methods of containment and control available to her are the cruel and sadistic methods she experienced as a child. The adolescent persona is, in essence, the clinical manifestation of the sadistic introject in its dissociated adult form. Certainly this extreme resolution cannot work indefinitely, and the adult, at great unconscious risk, enters psychoanalytic treatment.

Once the participation of all the psychic players has been assured, the goal and direction of the analytic treatment are relatively straightforward. Of tantamount importance is the integration of the adult and child personas' experiences. This involves, above all else, the recovery and disclosure of as many memories of early sexual abuse as possible, including, of course, the actual memories as they emerge for the patient; the fantasies and secondary elaborations that arise in the patient's associations, dreams, or memories; and a full, affectively integrated reliving and working through of the traumatic overstimulation, terror, and dissociation. Only when the patient witnesses the dissociation during the course of treatment does she become truly convinced of its existence.

Only then can she begin to anticipate and circumvent the experience and thus obviate it at times of heightened emotionality and excitement. As the adult listens to the child's words and slowly begins to understand their significance, new meaning is given to previously inexplicable symptoms. The acceptance and integration proceed slowly, but ideally the interpenetration of these two personas provides each with some compensation for this intensely painful process.

The adult, no longer terrified of the child's experiences, comes to appreciate the reasons for her rage and to acknowledge its justification. There is a new compassion for this former enemy and a wish to heal her wounds. Because the adult slowly comes to allow the child back into a shared consciousness, she can also provide the child with some sorely needed parenting. In providing understanding and acceptance for her child-self, the adult can go a long way toward gratifying a painfully frustrated developmental need. The child, on the other hand, is no longer driven to undermine the adult's successes. Her program of insurgence can, at last, come to an end. The adult's thought processes are no longer subject to constant invasion and disruption. In addition, the adult is revivified by once again integrating the child into her inner world. In excising the dangerous child persona, many other important childlike capacities have been lost to her. The child, now freed from her painful and all-consuming burden, is released to discover, perhaps for the first time, these other capacities and to bring them back to the adult, who also experiences them anew. Vitality and the shameless passion known only to children can reinfuse the adult's interpersonal world. Play and fantasy, for so long dangerous, regressive forces, will enrich her internal life and breathe creativity into her practical, survival-oriented mind. Ambition, always too close to aggression and exhibitionism, either dissociated or inappropriately acted out, can assume a more readily modulated position and spur the adult to a greater enjoyment of her successes. One patient, for example, presented her dysphoric, anhedonic, rigid adult-self for treatment. Some time later, when she had made considerable progress in integrating the dissociated child-self, she reported to her analyst a day spent at an amusement park. She had ridden the fastest rides, eaten cotton candy, flown a balloon, and reveled with delight in all these pleasures. In her next session she began to muse about returning to school for a master's degree in her field.

This is the force and these are the consequences of integration. But during this intensely painful phase of treatment, the forces of integration exist in a constant battle with the ever-ready tendencies toward dissociation and disorganization. For during this phase adult and child together must come to terms with the two most deadening realities: the first, the realities of the abuse that occurred and the second and perhaps more diffIcult fact, a childhood that was destroyed and will never be reclaimed. It would appear, in this regard, to be a universal fantasy among all adult survivors of childhood sexual abuse that once the horrible facts of the abuse become known, the world will be moved to provide a new and idealized, compensatory childhood. This fantasy had always been the antidote, the daily painkilling drug that became an addiction for the tortured child. She fed herself, in one patient's words, "daily doses, prn for pain," in order to go on living. Often the renunciation of this wish proves to be even more unimaginable for the child than accepting the realities of her abuse. Acknowledging the impossibility of bringing this fantasy to realization represents a betrayal of her most sacred inner self. Often this issue gives rise to the most serious suicidal ideation, a threat that must, particularly in this context, be taken seriously. Even when suicide is not an issue, however, renunciation of this idealized, compensatory childhood almost always results in a refortification of dissociative defenses and hatred for the child-self. Through a purely childlike piece of logic, the dissociated self believes some form of these words uttered by one patient:

> If what happened to me was unfair . . . if I did not deserve it, then I would get what I did deserve . . . what all the other children had. If people only knew, they would make sure that I got it. If I am not going to get it, even now when they know the truth . . . then I must have deserved what happened to me after all. I must be bad.

Another patient:

> This is too much. I can deal with the abuse . . . I think . . . maybe I can. But the idea that this is all there will ever be, that when I think of being little, all I will feel is pain and terror . . . that's too much. . . . I can't live with that. I want to feel what I see in the eyes of little children. You [therapist] say I deserve this . . . so why can't I? The sense of safety, I want a place that's safe. I want to get into trouble and be mischievous . . . safe trouble . . . usual trouble. I want someone else to do the worrying and the punishing. I'm tired. You say I can feel some of these things as a grown-up. . . . You tell me about them. But how can I feel them when I'm not sure what they are . . . words. It's like trying to describe a color to someone who was born blind.

This underlying theme, which runs throughout the treatment, does call forth periods of the most profound and intractable mourning. It tests a patient's determination to survive the threat of overwhelming disorganization, and it challenges the analyst's capacities to withstand his patient's despair and the limitations of his own abilities to alleviate suffering. Above all else, the analyst must allow the patient to experience and express his grief in full measure. This expression must be unencumbered by a need to appear better for the analyst's sake. The patient must recognize and come to terms with the finality and irreversibility of the traumatic loss. This is a long and arduous process of working through intense rage and profound pain. Every resistance possible will be called up by the patient to avoid this mourning process, and the analyst will inevitably be swept up into a maddening conundrum of elusively shifting transference-countertransference enactments. The child will hold on, first, to her denial, then, to her expectation of compensation, with a ferocity that the analyst may not have experienced previously. In addition, the analyst may experience some trepidation about allowing such primitive transference paradigms to play themselves out and about tolerating such extreme regressive disorganization in a previously functional patient. Our contention, however, is that this regressive process is unavoidable and that only by allowing the child-self to emerge, speak, and mourn will the emotional trauma be healed and the structural insufficiencies mended.

In attempting to analyze this kaleidoscopic pattern of rapidly changing transference-countertransference resistances to the mourning process, the therapist must keep in mind what has been learned about the internal object world of the dissociated child-self. Specifically, the internal object world of this child-patient is organized around the representations of only three major players: a victim, an abuser, and an idealized, omnipotent rescuer. Any resistances that emerge during the analytic process will represent some fantasied relationship among these three. Unless all combinations and permutations are reexperienced and worked through in the transference-countertransference analysis, the treatment will not be complete.

Indeed, many attempts at analyzing adult survivors of childhood sexual abuse fail because both the therapist and the patient become locked into acting out one particular paradigm to the exclusion of, and as a resistance to, any others. The most common deadlock would appear to occur when the therapist assumes the role of omnipotent rescuer and the patient that of the helpless victim. The patient fails to experience her own potential for growth and change and instead credits the analyst with supreme power over her. In many ways this occurrence is a natural, perhaps a necessary precursor to analyzing more complex object relationships, and it can inadvertently contribute to the establishment of a powerful working alliance. The therapist, quietly listening to the patient's memories of overwhelming childhood terror and helplessness, is deeply moved. He relates to his own experiences of terror and helplessness; he perhaps places his own children or fantasied children in such a hideous predicament. Empathic concern for the abused, helpless child is surely the countertransference response most readily and nonconflictually available to the analyst. His grandiose fantasies of rescuing a frightened child represent perhaps the best part of himself or herself. The child, for her part, has found an ally at long last, someone who will listen, care, and respect her particular needs for support, while she recovers and works through memories of her abuse. The analyst will tolerate the patient's regression during this time and provide the necessary ego support to make the working through, mourning process possible. Indeed, some therapeutic modifications may become necessary, for example, double sessions, additional sessions, phone contact between sessions. A safe holding environment must be created to contain the intense affective discharge and ego disorganization that will accompany the traumatic levels of stress reawakened during periods of the treatment.

The therapist's very willingness to accede to the patient's often necessary demands for extra-analytic contacts, however, gives rise to a major therapeutic dilemma. As the analyst struggles to rescue the tortured child from her endless nightmare, he or she may inadvertently interfere with the mourning process—which must go on—by refortifying the child's expectation that complete compensation will be made to her. It is eventually from the analyst, who seems so eager to help, that this compensation will come to be expected. The child, who at first needs certain modifications in analytic technique to begin the recovery and mourning process and to tolerate the regressive disorganization that ensues, eventually comes to expect and demand these interventions as evidence of the analyst's real concern for her and devotion to her. The treatment parameters thus lose their original ego-supportive function and become symbolic expressions of the analyst's love. They become "the stuff that compensation is made of." An entirely different transference paradigm now exists. The demands that were at first reasonable and uttered with quiet urgency become more strident and entitled. They slowly call for greater sacrifices on the part of the analyst and become increasingly difficult to keep up with. The relationship has, in essence, become an addiction for the patient, who must receive larger and larger infusions of compensation to be satisfied. As with any addiction, each dose stimulates an inevitable demand for more, and ultimately the demands can simply not be met. One must remember that though the child demands ever-increasing expressions of love as compensation, she has in her dissociated state never experienced anything but abuse, neglect, and betrayal. The analyst must, therefore, fail her. This experience is all she has known.

What has happened? It appears that in attempting to prove himself trustworthy to his ever-doubting patient, by acceding to necessary and sometimes unnecessary demands, the analyst has acted out a masochistic surrender and in so doing has reawakened and called forth the sadistic introject within the patient, that is, that part of the patient who is closely identified with her own abuser. This sadomasochistic reenactment is even further intensified by the fact that in presenting himself as an omnipotent rescuer, the therapist becomes, in Fairbairn's (1944) terms, an "exciting bad object," one who stimulates and awakens deep-seated desires that cannot at the same time be gratified.

The patient who was sexually abused as a child is vigilantly defended against those who make promises and attempt to resuscitate hope. Promises are broken, and hope leads inevitably to disappointment. Only self-sufficiency and a renunciation of all dependency needs create a margin of safety. To refortify her counterdependent defenses against the "exciting" analyst, the patient calls upon the sadistic introject to launch a full-scale attack upon the therapist's integrity and competence. It becomes the mission of the abuser, within the abused-child persona, to trap the therapist into revealing the emptiness of his promises, thereby rescuing the frightened child from giving hope, in the form of a trusting relationship to the analyst, another chance. Paradoxically, the mechanism of failure begins with the analyst's most ardent wish to help and rescue. It is by dint of his need to be seen as the good and nurturing rescuer, that the analyst assures his position as the exciting, therefore dangerous deceiver who must be destroyed. Hear the desperation in one patient's protest, occurring at a moment when the analyst had done something that truly moved her:

> Oh, no, you don't, get away from me. . . . Please . . . don't you understand? I hate you! I must hate you. You're too dangerous. You're the biggest threat of all. It would kill me to have it happen again . . . to be deceived. There isn't any hope left . . . none. . . . Well, maybe some. But I'm begging you, please . . . there's very little. If you're not sure . . . if you can't go all the way, then please go away and leave me alone.

On one level we hear the cries of the terrified, abused child recoiling from the presence of her seducer. They are in the latent meaning, of the language and not the manifest content, of the passage "Please, I beg you, please don't; go away, don't touch me again, or I will die." Here the patient clearly perceives the analyst, who has dared come too close, as a dangerous seducer.

The analyst, however, is at a most delicate choice point. To the extent that he backs off, he re-creates the neglect and denial of all the adults who originally failed to rescue the abused child. To the extent that he reassures the patient of his ability to "go all the way," he sets in motion the sadistic introject who will set about the task of proving that the analyst just does not have what it takes and that he in no way means what he says. The analyst's best intentions, experienced as dangerously seductive, must be spoiled. Whether by dint of ineptitude or deceit, the patient views the analyst as unhelpful.

The patient, on the other hand, has gone from the role of helpless victim to that of a demanding, insatiable, and constantly critical abuser. She seduces the analyst into rescue attempts, doomed to fail. The analyst has moved from his cherished role as savior to the increasingly masochistic role of victim who will do, say, give anything to appease the encroaching other. Via projective identification and counteridentification, the patient experiences herself as a victim but is experienced by the analyst as a seductive abuser; the therapist experiences himself as concerned and available, determined to rescue, while to the patient he is cruelly withholding or dangerously seductive.

Our contention is that all of these paradigms will be played out in the transference-countertransference; that they are intrinsic to the work with adult survivors of childhood sexual abuse. The patient must experience herself as all: victim, abuser, and savior; and the analyst must do the same. Therapist will seduce patient, and patient will seduce therapist as a part of the natural process of intimate bonding. Both will think long and hard, during the course of this work together, about the nature of abuse and the differences between benign and malignant seduction.

Here we take strong exception to the classical psychoanalytic position of the analyst as dispassionate commentator on the vicissitudes of the patient's instinctual life. Even when this position is expanded to include issues of ego, defense, and adaptation, our belief is that an approach based exclusively on verbal interpretation of impulse, prohibition, and gratification will inhibit the emergence of dissociated states and, with them, the recovery and disclosure of specific traumatogenic memories. We contend that adherence to such standard analytic fare fosters compliance by the adult persona and, inadvertently, collusion with the essential pathological duality at issue. Only by entering, rather than interpreting, the dissociated world of the abused child, can the analyst "know," through his own countertransferences, the overwhelming episodes of betrayal and distortion that first led to the fragmentation of experience.

As with all analytic work, it is ultimately the analyst's ability to both participate in and interpret the unfolding historical drama and to relate this history to current interpersonal difficulties, that encourages the progression of insight, integration, and change. Parts assigned in the dramatic productions of patients for whom powerful dissociative trends predominate, are, however, fluid and ever-changing. They are assigned, reassigned, and assigned again. Both therapist and patient must be willing to read all parts and reinterpret the action from each different perspective. Only in this way can the full range of interpersonal possibilities, as motivated by dissociated matrices of internalized self and object relationships, become realizable.

Our belief is that the interpretive process within the analytic experience is the only way to end the constant cycle of dissociation, projection, projective identification, and reintrojection that makes the history of abuse not only a painful memory, but an ongoing reality. We stress, here, the word "process." Included in our conceptualization of the transformational aspects of the treatment are the patient's experience of the analyst's availability and constancy, the analyst's willingness to participate in the shifting transference-countertransference reenactments, and, finally, his or her capacity to maintain appropriate boundaries and set necessary limits. Though verbal interpretation provides the patient with a highly significant, cognitive conceptualization of the analytic experience, we believe the experience itself to be equally mutative.

It is particularly the analyst's ability to work within the transference to familiarize the patient with the sadistic introject that will lead to the greatest analytic change. The analyst's true talent will be tested in trying to accomplish this work without making the patient enormously guilty or refueling the cycle of child-hate for another go-around. The abuser within the child persona is, after all, the part of the patient who was determined to survive and who borrowed from her abusive parent ways of protecting the more vulnerable parts of herself. She turned a passive trauma into an active one, gave the world good reason to be angry with her, and thus reconfirmed with her current interpersonal problems the belief that she must always have been hateful and therefore responsible for her own abuse.

Though we believe that this interpretive analytic work with adult survivors of childhood sexual abuse must occur within a safe and relatively nurturing environment where the therapeutic alliance is strong enough to survive the relentless battering of projective mechanisms we have described, we wish to stress in the most unequivocal terms our belief that it is ultimately the interpretation of primitive pathological structures, in the context of this nurturing containment, that makes reintegration, growth, and healing possible. The positive working alliance between analyst and patient is necessary but not sufficient to accomplish such profound change. The notion that treatment is curative because it provides the patient with the attention and devotion that were missing originally is, to our way of thinking, a significant failure in empathy, for it fails to take into account the patient's lifelong struggle with the sadistic forces, now internalized and self-abusive, that so pervaded her early years. It also sets in motion the process described above whereby the analyst becomes the target of constant assault and can find himself in a position of masochistic surrender vis-á-vis the patient.

Certainly, the patient needs to know that the analyst cares and is moved by her difficult struggle. She needs to feel the analyst's presence and support as terrifying memories flood her consciousness. She needs to know that the analyst is flexible enough to make certain therapeutic modifications and accommodations when regression and disorganization threaten to become too overwhelming. But in doing battle with sadistic forces, in working through experiences of murderous rage and dreams of retaliation, and in contending with the deadening hopelessness and fear of attachment, the patient, in addition to all else, needs to sense the analyst's strength. The patient needs to know that the analyst can protect herself at the same time that she cares for others and that she can say no to unreasonable demands and set appropriate boundaries. At the height of the most intense struggles to control and dominate the therapist and extract additional concessions as proof of concern, the patient is often, in disguised form, testing the therapist's capacity to set limits and establish boundaries. Only in this way, by sensing that the analytic structure is sound, can the patient give way to the most intense inner struggles. The patient can rest assured that the analyst will be neither gobbled up by insatiable demands nor moved to a form of retaliation against the patient that could destroy the treatment entirely.

Finally, a word about the tendency toward dissociation in adult survivors of childhood sexual abuse and classical psychoanalytic conceptualizations. Unfortunately, it is not difficult to see how early psychoanalysts became convinced of the accuracy of Freud's rejection of the seduction theory and why so many patients were for so long willing to be convinced of an interpretation that so defied their most terrifying experience. Surely, the classical theory, which regarded sexual abuse memories as fantasized oedipal victories, a theory in which the child was the perpetrator and not the victim of abuse, served only to revivify the patient's pathological, defensive splitting and dissociation, rather than helping to mend the internal breach. Both patient and therapist colluded in accepting a system of beliefs that set back the recovery and disclosure of memories by denying their reality and labeling them oedipal fantasies, wish-fulfillment fantasies of the child's own creation.

Adults who have been sexually abused as children are only too willing to believe that the nightmarish memories that begin to flood their waking thoughts are not real. It is a most heartfelt wish to be convinced that what they begin to perceive as a traumatically overwhelming past is merely a fantasy of their own creation. Certainly, when the dissociative and projective tendencies described above engender such intense hatred for the child-self and when the fantasies are viewed as the child's creation, the patient is relieved to turn the entire issue around and make, first, the fantasies and then, ultimately, the abuse itself the child's own fault. These haunting, as yet dimly illuminated perceptions, which cause such panic and terror for the patient during recovery and disclosure, can once again be denied. They are bad thoughts, belonging to an evil child-self, and as such are intellectualized, discredited, and dismissed via classical interpretation.

The clinical danger of such an approach is twofold. Certainly, it represents a secondary betrayal of the child whose original abuse was ignored, denied, and unattended to by the significant adults in his life. In addition, the therapist's denial of facts that are struggling so mightily to emerge deals a serious blow to a system of reality testing already damaged by an intricately interwoven set of pathological defenses needed to keep the truth from awareness.

The analyst, too, must initially favor a system of interpretation that allows him to avoid confronting the reality of widespread sexual abuse among children. In particular, there is a need to deny the traumatic childhood terror of patients with whom the analyst has developed a close and intimate bond.

For all of these reasons it is easy for the adult and analyst to agree on a theory that appears to silence the child and at the same time make sense out of her nightmares. This approach has the added advantage of not causing regressive ego disorganization, but rather, of strengthening preexisting defenses and allowing the adult to resume control of her life. As long as the patient remains in treatment, the child knows she will be safe. She may choose not to speak directly in this treatment, for fear that her words will be ignored or misunderstood; however, she does experience a holding effect wherein she knows she is safe, both from the dangers outside and from the sadistic introjects within.

In the most traditional sense we have here a transference cure, whose limited effectiveness does not become clear until after the treatment has been terminated. Every analyst who works with adult survivors of sexual abuse is confronted regularly with patients who have "completed" other treatments but have yet to open up for analytic scrutiny the raw, primitive, internal world of the abused child-self.

Vastly different is the treatment that ensues when the analyst accepts the reality of early childhood sexual abuse, when he is familiar with current research and understands how to distinguish such a reality from wishful oedipal fantasy. We, by no means, wish to imply here that the latter does not exist as an important clinical entity, accounting for a wide-ranging spectrum of neurotic symptomatology, but the presentation of these two clinical phenomena is so vastly different that they can be recognized as such and treated each in the appropriate way. Here we will touch upon just a few of the key distinctions.

The most telling distinction is that the patient struggling with problems related to unresolved oedipal conflict is unlikely to present with the severe symptomatology and ego fragmentation described earlier. The phenomenological presentation of oedipal material is also markedly different from that of sex abuse memories. Oedipal fantasies, while frequently disturbing to the patient, do not carry the imagistic or affective intensity of sexual trauma memories. Further, the anxiety surrounding oedipal material is usually a response to the murderous rage felt toward the same-sex parent. It does not evoke the explicitly and precociously sexual material graphically reported by sex abuse survivors. Oedipally derived anxiety, in fact, is usually warded off from direct subjective experience. It is, instead, manifested in classical, neurotic, compromise formations. When the patient discusses her oedipal conflict in treatment, her ego functioning will most often remain intact.

Anxiety connected to sex abuse memories, on the other hand, is linked directly to the sexual aspects of the survivor's relationship with the perpetrator. Most often this anxiety is not successfully warded off through symptom formation but, rather, is subjectively experienced by the patient, who frequently feels flooded by the memories and their associated affects. Severe impairment of ego functioning, flashbacks, and intrusive thoughts about the abuse often result. Finally, oedipal fantasies are most likely to be reported in symbolic form; the analyst hears derivatives of the conflict rather than fully formed memories. In contrast, the sex abuse survivor quite often relates vivid, highly affectively charged, direct memories of her abuse. Even the survivor who remains amnesic about her abuse will proffer derivatives that are more violent, less romantic, and more threatening to ego functioning than will the oedipal patient.

If, with all this in mind, the analyst communicates to her patient that she accepts the reality of childhood sexual abuse, and that she is willing, with her patient, to think and speak the forbidden, the child, who has never spoken, will listen. She hears the possibilities, and though it may be some time before she makes her appearance, the construction of the groundwork necessary for such an emergence has begun. The analyst has earned the child's attention. Now she must remember that though she addresses the adult patient some of the time, the listening child, with her very separate agenda, takes in every word and filters it through the matrix of her own internal system of object-related needs, wishes, and fears.

References

Briere, J. (1989), *Therapy for Adults Molested as Children*. New York: Springer.
―――― Runtz, O. (1988), Symptomatology associated with childhood sexual victimization in a non-clinical adult sample. *Child Abuse & Neglect*, 12:51–59.
Breuer, J. & Freud, S. (1893–1895), Studies on hysteria. *Standard Edition*, 2. London: Hogarth Press, 1955.
Courtois, C. A. (1988), *Healing the Incest Wound*. New York: Norton.
Dewald, P. A. (1989), Effects on an adult of incest in childhood: A case report. *J. Amer. Psychoanal. Assn.*, 37:997–1014.
Dickes, R. (1965), The defensive functions of an altered state of consciousness. *J. Amer. Psychoanal. Assn.*, 13:356–403.
Dupont, J. (1988), *The Clinical Diary of Sandor Ferenczi*, trans. M. H. Balint & N. Z. Jackson. Cambridge, MA: Harvard University Press.
Fairbairn, W. R. D. (1943), The repression and the return of bad objects. In: *Psychoanalytic Studies of the Personality*. London: Routledge & Kegan Paul, 1984, pp. 59–81.
―――― (1944) Endopsychic structure considered in terms of object relationships. In: *Psychoanalytic Studies of the Personality*. London: Routledge & Kegan Paul, 1984, pp. 82–136.
―――― (1949), Steps in the development of an object relations theory of the personality. In: *Psychoanalytic Studies of the Personality*. London: Routledge & Kegan Paul, 1984, pp. 152–161.
Ferenczi, S. (1932), The passions of adults and their influence on the character development and sexual development of children. Presented at International Psycho-Analytic Congress, Wiesbaden.
―――― (1949) Confusion of tongues between the adult and child. *Intemat. J. Psychoanal.*, 30:225–230.
Finkelhor, D. (1979), *Sexually Victimized Children*. New York: Free Press.
―――― (1984), *Child Sexual Abuse*. New York: Free Press.
Fliess, R. (1953), The hypnotic evasion. *Psychoanal. Ouart.*, 22:497–511.
Freud, S. (1896), The aetiology of hysteria. *Standard Edition*, 3:189–221. London: Hogarth Press, 1962.
Gelinas, D. (1983), The persisting negative effects of incest. *Psychiat.*, 46:312–332.
Greenacre P. (1950), The prepuberty trauma in girls. In: *Trauma, Growth and Personality*. New York: International Universities Press, pp. 204–223.
―――― (1967), The influence of infantile trauma on genetic patterns. In: *Psychic Trauma*, ed. S. S. Furst. New York: International Universities Press, pp. 108–153.

Herman, J. (1981), *Father-Daughter Incest*. Cambridge, MA: Harvard University Press.

──── Hirschman, L. (1981), Families at risk for father–daughter incest. *Amer. J. Psychiat.* 138:967–970.

Jacobson, E. (1949), Observations on the psychological effect of imprisonment on female political prisoners. In: *Searchlights on Delinquency*, ed. K. R. Eissler. New York: International Universities Press, pp. 341–368.

──── (1959), Depersonalization. *J. Amer. Psychoanal. Assn.*, 7:581–610.

Jones, E. (1961), *The Life and Work of Sigmund Freud*. New York: Basic Books.

Kernberg, O. (1976), *Object Relations Theory and Clinical Psychoanalysis*. New York: Aronson.

Krystal, H. (1988), *Integration and Self-Healing*. Hillsdale, NJ: The Analytic Press.

Ogden, T. (1986), *The Matrix of the Mind*. Northvale, NJ: Aronson.

Putnam, F. (1989), *The Diagnosis and Treatment of Multiple Personality Disorders*. New York: Guilford Press.

Ross, C. A. (1989), *Multiple Personality Disorder*. New York: Wiley.

Russell, D. E. H. (1983), The incidence and prevalence of intrafamilial and extrafamilial sexual abuse of female children. *Child Abuse and Neglect.* 7:133–146.

──── (1984), The prevalence and seriousness of incestuous abuse: Stepfathers vs. biological fathers. *Child Abuse and Neglect*, 8:15–22.

──── (1986), *The Secret Trauma*. New York: Basic Books.

Shengold, L. (1963), The parent as sphinx. *J. Amer. Psychoanal. Assn.*, 11:725–751.

──── (1967), The effects of overstimulation: Rat people. *Internat. J. Psychoanal.*, 48:403–415.

──── (1971), More about rats and rat people. *Internat. J. Psychoanal.*, 52:277–288.

──── (1975), Soul murder. *Internat. J. Psychoanal. Psychother.*, 3:366–373.

──── (1979), Child abuse and deprivation: Soul murder. *J. Amer. Psychoanal. Assn.*, 27:533–559.

──── (1989), *Soul Murder*. New Haven, CT: Yale University Press.

Ulman, R. & Brothers, D. (1988), *The Shattered Self*. Hillsdale, NJ: The Analytic Press.

van der Kolk, B. (1987), *Psychological Trauma*. Washington, DC: American Psychiatric Press.

Volkan, V. D. (1976), *Primitive Internalized Object Relations*. New York: International Universities Press.

Afterword

The agenda for this paper, like that of the book which followed, *Treating the Adult Survivor of Childhood Sexual Abuse: A Psychoanalytic Perspective* (Davies and Frawley, 1994) was an integration of contemporary trauma theory with an emerging relational model of mind and psychoanalytic technique. We began writing this paper with a fundamental question at its heart. To the extent that traumatic experience involves overwhelmingly intense and uncontainable affective experience that floods and overrides essential cognitive processes; to the extent that traumatic experience has therefore eluded meaningful internalization, codification, and symbolic, verbal articulation, how can psychoanalysis, a primarily verbal modality, seek to be therapeutic?

The multiple answers we posed were all organized around the fundamental belief that it was, indeed, only within a psychoanalytic treatment that had the potential to recreate consciously unavailable experience in the transitional arena of transference–countertransference enactment that such a therapeutic agenda could be met. Thus it was not simply the working through of specific trauma related memory but the reactivation in the transference–countertransference experience of archaic, dissociated object relationships specific to the intrapsychic negotiation of and accommodation to traumatic childhood sexual abuse that would be most therapeutically efficacious. Such reactivation of early self–other schemas of organization and "meaning-making" activity seemed indispensible to both the reclaiming of historical continuity necessary for self-cohesion and integration and the contextualization of present-day interpersonal difficulties that imprison adult survivors of childhood trauma in endless cycles of abusive and victimizing relationship, oftentimes including failed therapeutic ones.

In this article we stressed the reactivation, in transference–countertransference processes, of three prototypical personae: the abused child, the abuser, and a fantasized, omnipotent savior, all of whom volleyed in ever-shifting kaleidoscopic patterns between patient and analyst in therapeutic reenactments of archaic relational bonds. The book (Davies and Frawley 1994) incorporated one additional persona, that of the "unseeing, denying other" into these schemas, and a later paper by Davies (in press) introduces the personae of the "evacuated child" and the "omnipotent manager" as well. Though never attempting to be exhaustive in our articulation of predominant transference–countertransference paradigms, we hoped that setting out these transference–countertransference "landmarks," if you will, had the potential to serve as a set of orientation points during the oftentimes passionate and mind-boggling reenactments so endemic to this work.

We view this article as one of the first clinical applications of a uniquely different, still emerging relational model of mind and therapeutic action. As first posited by Mitchell (1991), this model views the multiplicity of self as normal and universal. The effect of trauma (Rivera, 1988) is not to create multiplicity—this is to be expected; the effect of trauma is to drive a dissociative wedge between these different states, making them mutually inaccessible to simultaneous consciousness. As further elaborated in our article, the dissociative processes leading to the fragmentation of these self–other configurations occurred not only because of the overstimulating, overwhelming effect of traumatic affects, but, in addition, because of the irreconcilable nature of conflicting identifications specific to experiences of profound parental betrayal. This model of mind involved the loose organization of multiple self–other representational schemas, schemas that included uniquely different internalizations of memory, affect, and cognitive meanings. The therapeutic agenda set forth in this article and in the book that followed involved an expanded awareness and integration of these multiple self–other configurations; a growing capacity to be simultaneously aware of multiple perspectives in any given situation; and the facillitation of a mourning process in which the longed-for, idealized compensatory objects could be relinquished in favor of real relationships. Such a mourning process involved an analytic attitude that could simultaneously hold an awareness of the reparative limitations of any therapeutic endeavor and an appreciation of the implicit gratifications that could, paradoxically, create, at least in small measure, the very experience that must be ultimately mourned and relinquished. Analytic neutrality, in this context, could then be redefined as maintaining the capacity to move fluidly among the different concordant and complementary identifications involved in each self–other configuration and avoiding the pitfalls of becoming locked into the repetitive reenactment of any one transference–countertransference paradigm.

At the time that our 1992 article and our 1994 book were published, the reconsideration of dissociation as an important process of psychic organization was just beginning to elicit interest within psychoanalysis. Since then our articulation of the development, vicissitudes, and treatment of dissociation, in both its normative and its pathological manifestations, has grown and become elaborated, informing thinking, for both of us, in a number of diverse areas. In a later series of articles, Davies (1996a, b, c; 1997, 1998a, in press) expanded on the notion of multiple self–other organizations as configuring a model of mind and internal representational structure, borrowed in part from late 19th-century "preanalytic" writings on trauma, yet more consistent with emerging "postclassical" relational-developmental-cognitive thought. Within this model, conflict emerges out of a need to internalize irreconcilable identifications, and that which cannot be integrated into the more overarching organizational schemas can become split-off, unintegrated representational units, each with its own potential sense of purpose and agency. Introducing the idea of "therapeutic dissociation," Davies (1997, 1998) described how the analyst could encourage a partial "dehomogenization" of these incompletely integrated self–other experiences by "inviting" them into the clinically significant reenacts within the transference–countertransference arena and, by so doing, provide a safe space within which previously foreclosed aspects of experience could begin to contextualize, renegotiate, and reconstruct earlier dysfunctional accomodations and alliances. In such a way psychoanalytic experience proceeded from working within these dissociated self–other states, inhabiting rather than interpreting the transference–countertransference processes.

Frawley-O'Dea (1997a) continued her expansion and elaboration of the centrality of dissociative phenomena by demonstrating how these processes elucidated transference–countertransference paradigms emerging in group psychotherapy with adult survivors of childhood sexual abuse. Moving out of the consultation room and into the supervisory setting, she began to delineate the manner in which dissociative processes at play in the supervised treatment often come to infuse the supervisory relationship through parallel processes which can be disorienting and disturbing for both supervisor and supervisee (Frawley-O'Dea, 1996, 1997b).

Since both the 1992 article and the 1994 book predated much of the intense controversey over the reliability of memories of childhood sexual abuse, both authors offered later articles on this complex subject. Davies (1996a, b, 1997) reviewed the arguments on both sides of the controversey and focused on the transference–countertransference enactment of issues having to do with repression, dissociation, and reality testing within the therapeutic relationship. Frawley O'Dea (1997c) attempted to elaborate manifestations of dissociation occurring at the level of culture and society which have contributed to the marginalization of discourse regarding trauma, especially the victimization of children within their own families.

Since working with adult survivors of childhood sexual abuse often involves the intense erotization of transference–countertransference processes, both of us have made significant contributions to this difficult, itself dissociated, aspect of clinical discourse (Davies, 1994a, 1998a; Frawley-O'Dea, 1998). In this most recent work we struggle to disentangle the universal incestuous themes that infuse myth, culture, and interpersonal process for all psychoanalytic patients from the concrete actualization of incestuous behavior that so compromises developmental and interpersonal processes in patients who have been sexually abused. It is clear that the psychoanalytic discourse regarding dissociation to which we contributed almost a decade ago has provided an enormously helpful additional lens through which to view aspects of the psychic organization of individuals, groups, organizations, and cultural phenomena.

References

Davies, J. M. (1994a) Desire and dread in the analyst: A response to Gabbard. *Psychoanal. Dial.*, 4:503–509.

——— (1994b) Love in the afternoon: A relational reconsideration of desire and dread in the countertransference. *Psychoanal. Dial.*, 4:153–171.

——— (1996a) Linking the pre-analytic with the postclassical: Integration, dissociation, and the multiplicity of unconscious process. *Contemp. Psychoanal.*, 32:553–575.

——— (1996b) Dissociation, repression, and reality testing in the countertransference: The controversey over memory and false memory in the psychoanalytic treatment of adult survivors of childhood sexual abuse. *Psychoanal. Dial.*, 6:189–218.

——— (1996c) Maintaining the complexities, *Psychoanal. Dial.*, 6:281–294.

——— (1997) Dissociation and therapeutic enactment. *Gender and Psychoanalysis*, 2:241–257.

——— (1998a) Some thoughts on the nature of desires, erotic and otherwise: A response to discussions by Cooper, Gabbard, and Hoffman. *Psychoanal. Dial.* 8:805–823

——— (1998b) Between the disclosure and foreclosure of erotic transference-countertransference processes: Can psychoanalysis find a place for adult sexuality? *Psychoanal. Dial.*, 8:747–766.

——— (1998c) The multiple aspects of multiplicity: Symposium on clinical choices in psychoanalysis. *Psychoanal. Dial.*, 8:195–206.

——— (1998d) Fairbairn and Janet: Repression and dissociation. In *Fairbairn, Then and Now*, ed. N. J. Skolnick & D. Scharff. Hillsdale, NJ: The Analytic Press, pp. 53–69.

——— (in press) Getting cold feet, defining safe-enough borders: Dissociation, integration and multiplicity in the analyst's experience of the transference-countertransference process. *Psychoanal. Quart.*

——— & Frawley, M. G. (1994) *Treating the Adult Survivor of Childhood Sexual Abuse: A Psychoanalytic Perspective*. New York: Basic Books.

Frawley-O'Dea, M. G. (1998). What's an analyst to do?: Shibboleths and "actual acts" in the treatment setting. *Contemp. Psychoanal.*, 34:615–633.

———— 1996. Supervision amidst abuse: the supervisee's perspective. In *Psychodynamic Supervision*, ed. M. Rock. Northvale, NJ: Aronson.

———— (1997a). Transference paradigms at play in psychoanalytically oriented group therapy with female adult survivors of childhood sexaul abuse. *Internat. J. Group Psychother.*, 47:427–441.

———— (1997b). Who's doing what to whom?: supervision and sexual abuse. *Contemp. Psychoanal.*, 33:5–17.

———— (1997c). Patients, politics, and psychotherapy in the true/false memory debate. In *Memories of Sexual Betrayal*, ed. R. Gartner. Northvale, NJ: Aronson.

Mitchell, S. M. (1991), Contemporary perspectives on self: Toward an integration. *Psychoanal. Dial.*, 1:121–148.

Rivera, M. (1989), Linking the psychological and the social: Feminism, poststructuralism and multiple personality. *Dissociation*, 2:24–31.

Gender as Contradiction

(1991)

Adrienne Harris

▼   ▼   ▼   ▼   ▼

Editors' Introduction

Among Freud's most famous contributions are his great case histories. Students of psychoanalysis have come to think of these memorable characters as old friends: Dora, Little Hans, the Rat Man, and the Wolf Man. Even the key players in the lives of his patients have left lasting impressions—think of Herr K or the cruel captain. So it is all the more significant, as Adrienne Harris points out in this timely and frequently cited essay, that in his description of the "Psychogenesis of a Case of Homosexuality in a Woman," Freud left his patient nameless, and the case has subsequently been greatly neglected in the literature. Hence Freud contributed to the forgotten fate of this young woman, a lesbian and a feminist.

Harris is well known, not only as one of the principle contributors to clinical psychoanalysis and postmodern feminism, but also as grounded in developmental psychology and particularly developmental psycholinguistics. It is not surprising, therefore, that her essay is wide ranging and deeply penetrating into both gender and sexuality, emphasizing social, cultural, and historical factors along with a careful attention to Freud's language and literary style. Harris also touches on critical historical factors that shaped the writing of Freud's case history. To round out her essay, she provides insightful comparisons of Freud's case with two contemporary women drawn from her own clinical experience.

Harris uses the insights of feminism and postmodernism to reexam-
ine what psychoanalysis means by gender, and she clearly articulates
a view of "gender as contradiction," emphasizing that at times gender may be thick and reified and at other times it may seem porous
and insubstantial, "simultaneously tenacious and evanescent." In
Harris's vision, a grasp of gender as shifting constructions in no way
sacrifices gender as passionately affective. Harris's article encourages
psychoanalysts to champion the more radical aspects of Freud's contributions about gender and sexuality and question the meaningful-
ness of thinking in terms of such "natural," binary, stable categories
as homosexual and heterosexual, masculine and feminine. Her work
is in line with other relational analysts (especially Ghent and Benjamin)
who have laid stress on contradiction, paradox, and maintaining tension among various polarities. In this, all these thinkers follow
Winnicott and, like him, recognize the need for fluidity and playfulness in respect to gender and identity. Among the most important
ways in which this article has influenced contemporary psychoanalysis is in its encouraging them to think of subjectivity as including multiple genders and multiple embodied selves, a way of thinking that
nicely dovetails with other currents in recent relational theorizing such
as Bromberg's work on dissociation and Mitchell's and Davies's explorations of multiple selves.

The unique combination of a sophisticated background in developmental psychology, philosophy and political theory that Harris brings
to her exploration of the contradictions of gender in this early essay
were further evidenced in later essays. They include "Aggression, Envy
and Ambition: Circulating Tensions in Women's Psychic Life" (*Gender
and Psychoanalysis*, 2:291–325), in which Harris explores the negotiation of separation and rapproachement, anxieties about the meanings of aggression, and the power of envy in identifications and object
ties, and "Psychic Envelopes and Sonorous Baths: Sitting in the Body
in Relational Theory and Clinical Practice" in *Relational Perspectives
on the Body* (ed. L. Aron & F. S. Anderson, The Analytic Press, 1998,
pp. 39–64), in which she argues that psychoanalysis is a theory of
body–mind integration and that relational theory must grapple more
thoroughly with this project by focusing on what she terms *bodies in
relationship*. In the forthcoming *The Softly Assembled Self:
Developmental Theory for Relational Psychoanalysis* (The Analytic
Press), Harris draws on 25 years of teaching developmental theory to
closely examine its problematic status for relational psychoanalysis.
She explores such controversial topics as: constructivism, linguistics
and speech practices, identity and multiplicity, gender, sexuality, and
the body.

Gender as Contradiction*

▼　　▼　　▼　　▼　　▼

Gender is one of the most contested concepts in contemporary social thought and social life. Gender has provided an organizing principle for social movements and critical analyses. In some contexts, it has been seen as an inalienable fact of life and biology. Gender has also been viewed as a troublesome set of shackles, best broken off and discarded. In the last two decades, our understanding of gender experience has undergone profound critique and reframing within psychoanalytic thought and practice (Mitchell, 1975; Chodorow, 1976; Dinnerstein, 1976; Benjamin, 1988).

This article makes a contribution to these ongoing debates by considering gender as a point of paradox. Gender can be as core and coherent an experience as any structure of self and subjectivity. But gender can also mutate, dissolve, and prove irrelevant or insubstantial. In short, gender can be as fragile, as unreliable, or as tenacious as any structure of defense or layer of the self.

I begin this consideration of gender and contradiction through an extended discussion of Freud's (1924) essay on the case of homosexuality in a woman. A critique of the case, using contemporary clinical examples, is the launching point for an analysis of gender dilemmas. The aim is to challenge monolithic models of gender and to argue that a paradoxical model of gender as simultaneously tenacious and evanescent is faithful to Freud's radical vision of sexuality.

"She Was in Fact a Feminist."

This is Freud's summary judgment of a young girl sent to him by her father. The father is determined to disrupt the passionate attachment formed by his daughter for an older, disreputable woman. But this young girl is not ill, has no symptoms, and has no noticeable motivation to give up her lover. She has, however, in the throes of conflict with her father and the older woman, made a serious suicide attempt.

Rounding up the usual suspects, Freud summarizes his patient's "masculinity complex":

---

* Originally published in *Psychoanalytic Dialogues*, 1(2):197–224. © 1991 The Analytic Press, Inc.

A spirited girl, always ready for romping and fighting, she was not at all prepared to be second to her slightly older brother; after inspecting his genital organs she had developed a pronounced envy of the penis and the thoughts derived from this envy still continued to fill her mind. She was in fact a feminist [p. 169].

If "she was in fact a feminist," she was a feminist quite without the protection and support of feminism. Through recent work in psychoanalytic feminism, the widening theory of transference and countertransference (inherent in relational perspectives) and through a semeiotics-based mode of reading psychoanalytic narratives, I want to recuperate and position the woman in this case. For she is not positioned. Strikingly, the woman Freud treated and mistreated in this case, has been almost completely effaced. Eclipsed under the generic terms given in the title, a "case of homosexuality in a woman," she is denied her real name on the grounds of medical discretion, but also, inexplicably, denied a metaphoric displacement into pseudonym. Without even the luxury of disguise, this woman is relegated to object status. Introduced descriptively as "a beautiful and clever girl of eighteen," she remains throughout the essay nameless and virtually speechless. In the course of an extended discussion of sexual object choice, the patient loses not only her name, but even her gender in the slippage, midparagraph, to the masculine pronoun:

Further unfavorable features in the present case were the facts that the girl herself was not in any way ill (she did not suffer from anything in herself . . . thus restoring *his* bisexuality. After that it lay with *him* to choose whether *he* wished to abandon the path that is banned by society and in some cases *he* has done so [pp. 150–151; italics added].

If we cannot encounter her subjectivity, can we come closer to her desire? Again, Freud's language relegates this desire to the margins. The particular love object of our nameless, subjectless heroine is also barred from subjectivity by Freud's language. The lover is variously described by Freud as *cocotte* or *demimondaine* or, contemptuously "society lady," in quotes. Freud uses these quotation marks as a kind of linguistic semaphore signaling instructions on how to read this term, so that we get its ironic twist. This lady, who is no lady, is Other who slips perversely in a degraded circuit of sexuality—with men, with women, in a social space outside the realm of bourgeois security and family. Like Dora's governess, or the beautiful white body of Frau K, this is a love outside legitimacy. The sexual woman, the object of homosexual desire and the subject of bisexual sexuality, is marginal and degraded. Even the young girl's longings for this woman are rendered in another language: *"Che poco spera e nulla chiede"* (p. 160). The *cocotte* enbodies an illicit, free-ranging desire. A woman's desire is presented paradoxically as exotic, dangerous, and degraded.

In this reading of Freud, I want to set contradiction center stage. Published in 1920, the essay depends on the core ideas of the "Three Essays" (Freud, 1905a), glances laterally though enigmatically at "The Interpretation of Dreams" (Freud, 1900), and prefigures the later essays on femininity and female sexuality. It has a crucial and underestimated place in the development of Freud's thought and holds some of the subtlest writing on sexuality and identity that exists in Freud's canon. There are, of course, a number of different strategies for reading Freud's theory of sexuality. Grossman and Kaplan (1988) sort out what they term "commentaries" on gender within Freud's writing. They note many instances in which Freud produces a simplified trait theory of gender, but they also extract from Freud's work a commentary in which gender is preserved as a psychodynamic category. Mitchell (1988), on the other hand, draws out the biological tropisms in Freud and in drive theory. Freud's essay on the case of female homosexuality contains ample evidence for each of these readings, reminding us that the arduous task Freud set himself—to build an account of sexual object choice and identity that broke with previous biological models—was one he both succeeded at and failed.

In this essay, Freud both perpetuates and breaks with the conventional patriarchal thinking on homosexuality and femininity. Freud's contradictions are embodied in the very circumstances of agreeing to undertake the analysis. As with Dora, he has responded to a father's insistence that a daughter be brought to heel. This father, "an earnest, worthy man, at bottom very tenderhearted," actually reacts to his daughter's homosexual tendencies with "rage," "threats," and "bitterness." Should psychoanalysis fail, the father's fallback position is "a speedy marriage. . . . to awaken the natural instincts of the girl and stifle her unnatural tendencies" (p. 149). Tracking the voice of patriarchy through this essay, we hear the outraged voice of the father of a disobedient, rebellious girl. Freud's alliance and, I would suggest, his identification with this father thus undermine his theoretical claims for the constructed and complex dynamics in all forms of sexuality and identity.

This essay exemplifies a historically new censorious attention to female friendship. The girl's relationship to her love object, so disagreeable to her father, is characterized as an instance of the devotion of friendship taken to excess. Carol Smith Rosenberg (1985) identifies a shift late in the 19th century when female friendship, which had formerly enjoyed much social and moral approval, became problematic and pathological. Freud's essay shows the unmistakable signs of a cautionary tale on the forms and fate of female friendship, on the potentially dangerous connections between women. This narrative of danger is one theoretical move through which deviance can be constructed. Empowered scientific discourse simultaneously lights up female desire and problematizes it.

Yet Freud places so many cool and rigorously argued ideas before the reader. Following the radical insight of the "Three Essays," Freud traces out the view that sexuality and identity can never be simply some hard-wired, constitutionally driven forms but, rather, that the formation of sex and identity operates like the rules of grammar. As Chomsky (1965) demonstrated formally in the case of language, any given sentence has no inherent linkages or simple linear connections. His theory of generative grammar demonstrates that all human language creatively combines elements according to a set of special combinatorial rules, which permit many optional selections and arrangements. If we extend this analogy to the sphere of sexuality, any human experience of sexuality and identity is built on a unique and particular sexual sentence in which the elements of subjectivity, action, and object are never inherent or inevitable. Unlinking aim from object and allowing the play of sexual forms and symbolic meanings for bodies, selves, and acts are the radical core of Freud's theory of desire and gender.

The theoretical revolution Freud (1924) proposes is set within an essay whose opening paragraph enigmatically invokes the law and whose closing paragraph evokes gender surgeons and a rather horrible prefiguring of fascist medicine: "the remarkable transformations that Steinach has effected in some cases by his operations" (p. 171).

We can track the contradictions in the tonal variations in Freud's voice and stance in regard to this patient. A Foucaultian twinning of science and power sets a doomy beginning to the essay. A hitherto hidden practice, homosexuality in women, ignored by the law and neglected by psychoanalysis, is to be excavated to make "a claim" on our attention. At the very beginning, the patient is brought into Freud's sight-lines. All the exits seem closed off. "It is possible to trace [the origin of this case] in complete certainty and almost without a gap" (1924, p. 147). But later, Freud likens treatment to a train ride (though which of Freud's trains is not so clear). "An analysis falls into two clearly distinguishable phases" (p. 152). In the first the analyst does the explaining; and in the second "the patient himself gets hold of the material put before him" (p. 152). The analyst is then a powerless passenger, sitting passively with ticket in hand until the patient-engineer agrees to start the journey. Ticket and seat offer up only the "right" and the "possibility" of voyage, never the necessity. But perhaps what was in sight here was "a journey to another country," the preoedipal home of femininity. Freud (1931) wrote his own Baedeker to this country in his essay on femininity by sketching out the trip into that terrain of womanhood as a place of gaps and silences, a place without certainty, a "pre-Minoan-Mycenaen civilization" whose tourism Freud left finally to the women analysts.

Late in the essay and late in the short-lived treatment, Freud must acknowledge that gaps yawn open in the "hypocritical dreams" in which revenge and the wish to please are reverberating transforms of each other, played out in respect to Freud and to the father.

> Warned through some slight impression or other, I told her one day that I did not believe these dreams, that I regarded them as false or hypocritical, and that she intended to deceive me just as she habitually deceived her father. I was right: after I had made this clear, this kind of dream ceased [p. 165].

Freud's harshness and the sermonizing admonitions in his commentary to the patient about her wish to distort and deceive her analyst are stunning. Then the tone shifts, and in a more wondering, open register, so different from the imperious voice of his conclusions about this patient, Freud speculates on how little we know of whom and why we love. "It would seem that the information received by our consciousness about our erotic life is especially liable to be incomplete, full of gaps, or falsified" (pp. 166–167). These unsettled and unsettling moments in the essay are its golden possibilities.

The contradictions move not merely through the structure and style of the essay but in the alternation between the theory and the particularities of the treatment. We should take up what Freud says, not what he does. Views on the manifold causes of homosexual object choice and homosexual identity and the subtlety of parallel dynamics in respect to a child's connection to mother and to father are lost to the rigid choice Freud makes as analyst in his insistence on the conventional oedipal structure, the primacy of disappointment in losing the father's love.

"Her Facial Features Were Sharp"

Within the body of this essay, Freud (1924) establishes his commitment to the independence of physical constitution, mental traits, and love object choice. The idea that sexual object choice is necessarily fixed and immutable is undermined in various ways. In the discussion of situational homosexuality, the power of setting to shape drive and counter inhibition is considered. In the discussions of motives for accepting treatment, the person's youth, vulnerability, and commitment to family and object ties are all proposed as elements in the shaping of sexuality. Indeed, in the very term "choice," the role of consciousness and the multiplicity of options, decisions, and reflections are all raised in regard to experiences that are often considered to be immutable. Paradoxically, Freud also describes the entrenched resistance of sexual object choice.

Freud seems to speak here against two different literary and scientific traditions. In regard to one, medical psychiatry, with its commitment to taxonomies and the rigid alignment of constitution and sexuality, Freud marks his great revolutionary stance, the disjunction of body and culture. But in repudiating the idea of a "third sex," he also speaks against a politicizing polemic of the 19th century that sought to carve out a psychic and social space for homosexual persons (see Weeks, 1979, for an analysis of these historical developments). It is interesting that psychoanalysis is still poised against both these traditions, though they themselves are so implacably oppositional.

Political works in gay liberation have often refused any account of sexuality as a developmental achievement and have considered that a constitution-based sexual identity offered safer and securer ground for a politics and a life-style organized around sexual object choice and homosexual identity. This politicized stance served another important function, namely to protect gay people from institutional practices that privilege one gender (male) and one object choice (heterosexual) as unremarkable and thus unquestioned, while homosexuality becomes a developmental dilemma that needs to be understood. Gender identity and sexuality can perhaps be "freely" investigated only in a social, institutional, and therefore political situation in which everything may be put in question and nothing is fixed or "natural." This utopian possibility was sketched in Freud's theory of sexuality and was at the heart of his method in the technique of "free" association. This hope for a freedom to question, this radical skepticism, is also psychoanalytic feminism's deepest utopian vision.

Conventional thinking in psychoanalysis, in academic psychology, and in psychiatry frequently opted for the apparent security of a biologically based treatment of sexuality. Freud defers from considering "the problem of homosexuality," yet this essay requires that we consider homosexuality not as a problem but as a solution, the solution any child might make to the dynamics of a family, the conflicted process of object choice.

There is a magisterial flow to the final section of the essay. Sexual object choice is achieved, not given. Any individual contains and, in some forms, retains multiple sexual needs and objectives. Only a reflective, psychoanalytically based study of an individual's history yields some understanding of the relative potency of homosexual and heterosexual libido. Femininity is connected to maternal attachment. The oedipal moment is a developmental hinge for boy and girl in which each must give up the mother, though with differing symbolic meanings attached to each repudiation. But as Freud always insisted, nothing is ever fully given up, merely displaced.

Yet how curious the final paragraph. Freud makes a pitch for a hermeneutic method for psychoanalysis as opposed to prescriptive and predictive scientism. Then enigmatically he speaks of a masculinity that fades into activity and a femininity that fades into passivity. And, finally, he counterposes powerful surgery against a puny, feminized, castrated psychology. As against the more phallic, surgical interventions of Steinach, Freud presents psychoanalysis in rather the same way as he presents the female genital: "When one compares the extent to which we can influence it with the remarkable transformations that Steinach has effected in some cases by his operations, it does not make a very imposing impression" (p. 170).

Even more curious is the final sentence: "A woman who has felt herself a man and has loved in masculine fashion, will hardly let herself be forced into playing the part of a woman, when she must pay for this transformation, which is not in every way advantageous, by renouncing all hope of motherhood" (p. 172). If a woman homosexual were to give up her hermaphroditic organs, she would be one sex but would be deprived of motherhood. She would be doubly punished through a loss of masculinity and a loss of that phallic possibility offered to femininity, the birth of a child. From the high ground of theory, the writing drifts into enigma and defeated retreat. This movement has continued to operate within psychoanalysis. Lacan (1977) initially sought to recuperate Freud's notion of a complex and fragmentary sexuality but ends in a position that displaces women, conflates them with the place of the Other, and mystifies social power by a reified treatment of language's relation to subjectivity. Chasseguet-Smirgel (1966, 1986) critiques phallic monism but puts in its place biologically based feminine and masculine drives.

It is tempting to ask whether, within psychoanalysis, there are two genders or one. As in comparable debates about a one-person or two-person psychology, we can inquire whether psychoanalysis makes a commitment to a one-gender (male) or two-gender system. Could gender fluctuate like any system of meaning? But if we insist on the symbolic meaning of the body, can we, in our practice and our theories, tolerate the ambiguity and instability of these profoundly personal and ideologically charged categories of experience?

In Freud's treatment of this patient his own insights fail him. He tells us that this sharp-featured, tall girl has a body that evokes that of her father and a mind that echoes this body: sharp, imperious, tough. Constitution as an explanation for homosexual identity and object choice is rejected in theory but sneaks in the back door of practice and countertransference.

"She Changed into a Man"

As Freud sets out the case, he puts into a play a fascinating set of possibilities, a complexity of attachments and identifications. The girl faces a set of relational problematics to which sexual object choice could offer a resolution. First, there is the girl's relation to her mother, an attractive young woman who Freud thinks may be content with a daughter who refuses to compete with her.

One strand of explanation woven throughout the case material is that the primary object choice for the girl, the mother, is never fully given up but transferred to other mothers and finally to the lady love. In this way, the patient continues a "masculine protest" (which for Freud never quite attains the legitimacy of male identification).

We can take a moment to look at the Freudian position on the differences between male identification and masculine protest. The former is thought to rise wholesomely from libido and desire; the latter is thought to be a more unsavory outcome of aggression. This position only restates the valuative judgment and double standard in different terms. The problem still remains. Why would a girl's identification with her father arise solely from envy and aggression? Jessica Benjamin (1988) addresses this question by proposing a legitimate role for a girl's identificatory love for her father and examining the conflicts and inhibitions that arise for women when this process of loving identification is thwarted.

Alternatively, a feminine object choice is the resentful consolation prize after an oedipal defeat. In this case, mother gets father's boy baby (when the girl is five or six and again in adolescence), and the daughter spurned gives up men altogether and "changes into a man." The spoiling of her chances for a love object lead, in extreme form, to an abandonment of gender identity. The changeling now enacts the conventions of male love.

This interpretation allows us to see the contradictions in the theory of normative male heterosexual choice that Freud brings to bear on the case of this young girl. He lays out the unconscious dynamic of masculine love, both in its oedipal and its narcissistic components. Certain men choose an idealized yet degraded woman lover. Freud understands this choice as an aspect of masculine idealized love operating as a defensive distortion within the Oedipus complex. This scene goes as follows. An idealized pure love develops for a degraded creature who is really a stand-in for mother. In the boy's fantasy, mother stays with father only for protection and convenience; her sexual love for father is degraded and bad, and she saves her purity for the devoted son. The boy loves a pure mother and will save her from the degradation of heterosexuality.

There is also the narcissistic element in mature male object choice. The man defers to the pleasure and the narcissistic preoccupations of the lover: "the humility and the sublime overvaluation of the sexual object . . . the renunciation of all narcissistic satisfaction and the preference for being the lover rather than the beloved" (p. 154). This position is somewhat of a theoretical double standard. A man's love of women is cast in the language of submission and deferral, of living through the narcissism and pleasure of the Other. A comparable construction in a woman would have been tagged with the epithet of masochism. This aspect of male love of women, perhaps the theoretical twin of penis envy in a woman, has none of that construct's negative play. The central point to extricate from this piece of theory that Freud produces is the feature of distortion and defense in normal heterosexual development that is nonetheless not introduced as a "problem."

Freud's interpretive solution to this patient's problem is a relational solution: sexuality and desire are at the mercy of object relations. Choosing a woman or rechoosing a woman comes after a defeat and a disappointment in respect to her longing for her father. She seems then, to Freud, to have jumped tracks from a positive to a negative oedipal complex, changed into a man, taken on a rebellious struggle with her father (surely a version of the oedipal identificatory struggles of father and son), and fallen in love with a mother substitute, whom symbolically she will win back from the degraded sexualilty of heterosexual life.

For a contemporary reader of this case who operates with the insights of object relations theories, the intersubjective treatment of transference and countertransference, and the current appreciations of the potency of maternal attachment, the question is how to decide between the alterative models of identity and object choice that Freud sets up.

I want to take up first the fate and form of Freud's patient's primary love object, her mother, who consistently deserts her for men, for father, and for flirtations and male attention. The most crucial abandonments were for a male baby sibling when she is five or six and at yet another crucial developmental juncture, adolescence. The trauma of these narcissistic injuries might well be measured in the girl's obliteration of any thought that these births were psychically disruptive. But perhaps the trauma resurfaces, disguised, in an attempted solution when she begins to play with a three-year-old boy. Freud connects this play to maternal and feminine identification. But it is also possible that the identification is with the rapprochement boy, an alter ego who represents her child self before the narcissistic (and obviously also oedipal) disaster. If she is a little boy, she retains the exclusivity of her mother. There is not yet a new baby boy. Also if she retains "boyness," the discovery and despairing loss associated with femininity are warded off. Did she change into a man or simply always stay one, imagining within her family that to be loved by mother you have to be a boy? As a mother's boy, she looks for an adored love object and seeks to love an ego ideal that Chasseguet-Smirgel (1985) has always connected to the longing for narcissistic healing and reunion with the preoedipal mother.

At the same time, many factors (father and culture) prevent her from occupying the privileged position of adult masculinity. Perhaps one compromise solution is to be a rebellious "boy" in a failed relation to a heterosexual women. Loving the "cocotte" serves multiple functions. It symbolically plays out the oedipal defeat and the preoedipal possibilities and hope, also finally defeated. The suicide attempt signals the futility, not merely the oedipal enactment of the wish for father's baby. Rather, we are back at the railroad as the girl fallen on the tracks, symbolically expresses having nowhere to go, and is caught in a preoedipal and oedipal no person's land. Her chastity then arises from confusion and a double inhibition. This enactment of futility could also preserve the elements Freud sees in the suicide attempt, its mixture of hate and excitement. Stasis and refusal remain the fundamental stance, hidden behind a mask of compliance and interest.

The suicide attempt, however, demands a closer look. It is introduced as an example of her mixture of openness and deceitful disobedience. "She paid for this undoubtedly serious attempt at suicide with a considerable time on her back in bed, though fortunately little permanent damage was done. After her recovery she found it easier to get her own way than before" (p. 148). We might note Freud's rather chilling refusal to privilege the girl's despair, to see the integrity and seriousness of her hopelessness and her confusion. Lauffer and Lauffer (1989), working on adolescent breakdown and suicide attempts, consider some adolescent suicidal crises as expressions of intolerable conflict over the integration of gender, body ego, and sexuality.

One poignant dilemma for this girl is the contradiction between the preoedipal and oedipal mother, the mother of longed-for exclusivity and the mother who rivalrously reserves the ground of femininity for herself. We cannot know, in this woman's case, whether she chooses masculine identity as a solution to defeat at mother's hands, at father's, or at both. We know more, I suspect, of the creative resolution of her object choice as it preserves the complexity of her sexuality.

Freud suggests that the patient's love object is a complex solution, a fusion of male and female object choice, the expression of homosexual and heterosexual libido. An object choice ideally represents a world of multiple sexualities and the preserving of all prior forms of loving. The love object technically must be one gender or another, that is, formally either female or male, but unconsciously and symbolically, this object choice is a multilayered, multisexed creation. It is not, of course, that the gender identity of the lover is unimportant, but that it both expresses a powerful resolution of conflicting aims and preserves all elements of the conflict.

In formal identity terms, the patient makes a homosexual object choice. But in the more subtle terms of identity and unconscious meaning, I read this patient's love relation as a heterosexual object choice in which a fictive "boy" chooses a mother to idealize and save from an oedipal father. Despite Freud's reading of the girl's disappointment in respect to her father, the transference-countertransference deadlock suggests this oedipal battle has not been conceded. The mother's body and feelings are still contested zones.

"Russian Tactics" by the Patient, So the Analyst "Breaks It Off"

Like an Escher engraving, the question of who drives and who buys a train ticket and sits waiting on this treatment journey is constantly fluctuating. "In the case of our patient, it was not doubt but the affective factor of revenge against her father that made her cool reserve possible . . . As soon as I recognized the girl's attitude to her father, I broke off treatment" (p. 164). Freud claims to see through the false self-analysis and the subterfuge, a repetition of tactics with the father. He sees that envy and defeat are the real project, refuses the charade, and stops the work.

There is now a tradition of thought in object relations theory, notably the work of Little (1981) and Bollas (1987) and others in which countertransference is viewed as an induced experience of the object history of the patient. Using that model in this case, we might ask how this clever girl of 18 maneuvers Freud to play out the father, to act out the rejecting and rejected patriarch, and to admit defeat by referral to a woman analyst.

In another enactment, Freud's response to the dream reports is to make a transference interpretation, not a dream interpretation. The reporting of dreams of marriage and heterosexual happiness is given transference meaning as an enactment of the wish to deceive the father by presenting him with "hypocritical" dreams. Although he uses the judgmental term hypocritical in the footnoted section in "The Interpretation of Dreams" (1900), he simply presents the dual level, manifest and latent, in any dream and notes that dreams disguise just as they express. Worth remarking on is the dream example he uses—a dream in which his relation with Fliess is played out and hidden (Freud, 1900, p. 52). This hidden association can be connected to the poetic paragraphs earlier in the essay, in which Freud invokes the mystery of not knowing why or whom one loves. I am suggesting a buried countertext of rivalries involving Freud, Fliess, and Tausk in a complex scenario of love and contest.

The enactment of silenced, disowned countertransference in this treatment is the story of father-son rivalry. Freud plays out the struggle of father versus girl-who-is-really-a-boy and consistently relates to the patient both as a ridiculous rival for male terrain and as a girl refusing to give up the position of masculine protest and accept and internalize the analyst's interpretations. I would say it is less clear that she wants these interpretations (for Freud the symbolic equivalent of the father's babies) than that she wishes to be the boy to mother and thus comes into a situation of difficult rivalry with her father and then with Freud.

Freud interprets the patient's single quoted comment in the essay, "How very interesting," as an intellectualized defense. Yes, but also a masculinized one. We are two colleagues sitting here discussing a patient we have in common, who happens to be me. How very interesting. This patient practices, as Freud suggests, a Russian tactic: an entrenched, defensive resistance against which penetration must fail. Freud notes with some exasperation the mildly interested attention the girl gives to the analytic work. He sees resistance, certainly. But perhaps she is calm because he was so obviously off target. Freud presses on as if he were treating a young girl who is vengeful because she was betrayed by her father. One thinks of Winnicott (1971) glimpsing one gender masked behind another. In the daring move Winnicott makes in making the acquaintance of the "girl" in his male patient, the treatment lights up and moves.

In this case there are evocations of Freud's (1905b) work with Dora. Both are cases of resistant, oppositional young women, and both are treatment struggles in which shame and defeat are the stakes. Dora votes with her feet and gives Freud notice as though he were a servant. This other patient, "the clever and beautiful girl of 18," from "a family of good standing, beautiful and well made, . . . a spirited girl, always ready for romping and fighting, . . ." (1924, p. 169) is sent away. In Freud's language we can note that the oedipal blow of castration has been struck: "I broke it off." This girl must not dare to inhabit male space, to represent phallic desire. He recommends that she be dispatched to a woman analyst. And here is the complexity of the defeat/victory, for perhaps he has sent the fox into the henhouse.

There are two moments in the clinical management of this treatment that are striking. The first arises when the girl's dreams are rejected as "hypocritical." The second is the censorious tone in which the analysis is ended. Both these moments may be seen as instances in which Freud, the stern, gate-keeping patriach, refuses the rivalry of this fictive boy, this woman who appears to make a claim for masculinity. This refusal raises a question in respect to masculine identification in women. When, for whom, and with whom is it permitted? In Helene Deutsch's analysis, which Freud conducted, her masculine identification, her father complex, was left deliberately unanalyzed. In the essay on femininity, female analysts as a group are given a kind of dispensation from the humiliating requirement to confess penis envy and repudiate phallic aims (Freud, 1931).

The date of his first publication of Freud's essay is 1920. Drawing on Jones's (1957) biographical treatment of this period and Roazen's (1969) book on Freud's young colleague, Victor Tausk, I propose a linkage between these biographical events and the themes of this case. Tausk's suicide occurred in July 1919. Freud's complex preoccupations with Tausk and his death are evidenced in a rather cold, dispassionate interpretation of the suicide as a loss to the "father ghost," an interpretation that he includes in a frank letter to their mutual friend, Frau Lou Salomé. Later that year, Freud produced a respectful obituary, as Roazen (1969) has noted, the longest obituary Freud wrote. Jones (1957) records that Freud wrote the essay on this case of homosexuality in the fall of 1919, thus in the immediate aftermath of Tausk's suicide and in the same period as the composition of the obituary. In the obituary, Tausk is described as "passionate," "sharp," and "brilliant," several terms also used to describe Freud's young suicidal patient.

These links between the events surrounding Tausk's death and the writing of the case are evocative not causal. Nonetheless, I interpret the end of this young woman's treatment as both castration and reparation. It enacts the father's punishment of a contesting son, a guilty repetition of Freud's treatment of Tausk. Freud had earlier refused to take Tausk into analysis and had sent him instead, in a humiliating move, to work with Helene Deutsch, an analyst quite junior in experience and reputation to Tausk. Then, when Deutsch was overwhelmed by this analytic task and found herself using her sessions with Freud to talk over the work with Tausk, Freud forces a choice: Deutsch could give up her work

with Tausk or her analysis with Freud. She abandoned Tausk, and several months later he killed himself. There is one other parallel between
Tausk and the young patient discussed in Freud's case. Tausk died grue-
somely, shooting himself in the head and simultaneously hanging himself. Roazen interprets this suicide as a double death, reflecting both the
loss of Freud and the failure of a love relationship. Tausk had been
poised against a double loss, as the young woman patient is at the
moment on the railroad tracks when she is threatened with rageful abandonment by her father and the loss of her love for the cocotte. The resolution of the case acknowledges a potential healing power in the
mother-analyst, for Freud recommends turning the errant "boy" over to
a woman analyst. I read this referral as a symbolic reparation to Tausk
and perhaps also to Deutsch.

Yet the danger in this way of thinking and in Freud's own language
as he announces the resolution to this case is that mother and father analysts become a newly reified category. What if we could imagine the term
"woman analyst" as a provisional title for a range of analytic responses
or strategies? This construct would make a theoretical space for the
"woman" analyst (which could, of course, be an aspect of any analyst)
to hear rivalry, masculinity, competitiveness, and ambition without tri-
angulating. Maternal identity in the analyst is usually invoked in issues
of separation or preoedipal functioning. Here is a position not for an
oedipal mother who will be object, but for an oedipal mother who could
be subject as well, untempted to do same-sex battle with a child who is
trying to assert self in adult psychic territory.

To summarize this reading of the case, I hope to suggest some advantages to reading gender identity as a complex, multiply figured, and fluid
experience. This view is in contradiction to work on core gender identity, such as that of Fast (1984), but it does not preclude experiences of
the sort Coates (in press) has written about in which young boys feel
profoundly in opposition to their gender. In fact, Coates's interpretation
of gender identity disorder in boys, in which a disruption in gender coincides with a disruption in separation experience and self-structure, rather
supports this view that gender can become heavily freighted with meaning and can be put to the service of crucial psychic work.

The position I am suggesting is one in which gender is neither reified
nor simply liminal and evanescent. Rather, in any one person's experience, gender may occupy both positions. Gender may in some contexts
be as thick and reified, as plausibly real as anything in our character. At
other moments, gender may seem porous and insubstantial. Furthermore,
there may be multiple genders or embodied selves. For some individuals

these gendered experiences may feel integrated, ego-syntonic. For others, the gender contradictions and alternatives seem dangerous and frightening and so are maintained as splits in the self, dissociated part-objects. Any view of sex, object choice, or gender that grounds these phenomena as categories of biology or "the real" misses the heart of Freud's radical intervention in our understanding of personality. Biologically determined theories keep such experiences as gender and sexuality outside the system of meaning itself. To be meaningful, these experiences must be understood as symbolizable. Gender, then, and the relation of gender to love object can be understood only by acts of interpretation. In that way the density of their unconscious and conscious elaborations are brought into the realm of language. Only with the reflective narratives on which psychoanalysis depends, can we know the complex meaning of "masculine," "feminine," "boy," "girl," "same," "different."

In the remainder of this paper I want to begin to translate this perspective into clinical work and refuse any monolithic, single-determinant, and single-dynamic theory of homosexuality or gender. This view is not a prescription for total relativism or for the idea that everyone is everything and all choices are equally plausible or equally privileged. Any experienced gender- or sexuality-based identity or sexual choice arises in a historical and culturally laden context that becomes part of the internal experience of gender.

In considering two contemporary clinical examples in the light of Freud's work, I will keep formal gender identity as a point of comparison. I consider the consciously experienced totality of being a male or female person, as Lacan (1977) noted, a necessary fiction. I will therefore write about my work with two women who use love objects as points of identification as well as desire. The symbolic meaning of these loves undermines the surface meanings of their choices. I have also chosen to highlight women's problem of masculine or father identification as well as the complexity of conscious and unconscious gender meanings. These two women are preoccupied with and conflicted over the meaning and symbols of masculinity as internal aspects of ego functioning and of self-structure. As gender identity and sexual choice become more complex, so the constructs of maternal and paternal imagoes become more complexly figured as they appear, develop, and alter in the patients' internal worlds as aspects of gender identity and self. Each woman, in unique ways, struggles with the complexity of her gender identifications and the ways in which her body reflects and at the same time spoils identity.

"I Don't Like To Be Encumbered"

This statement is my patient Hannah's explanation of a routine of daily workouts at the gym and her refusal to risk weight gain by giving up smoking. For Hannah, flesh itself symbolizes encumbrance, the entangling encumbrance of need and desire. A beautiful and delicate young woman, an aspiring performer, always freshly turned out, she seems the platonic form of the lovely, contemporary urban girl. As her mother wryly observed, in a town where girls cannot find a date, Hannah always has a line of suitors. At first glance, then, not an obvious case of masculine identity.

Indeed, considering her relationships to her father and stepfather, there is no simple stage of idealization, no obvious clear point of connection to an admired and enabling male parent. Her own father was positioned in the family as the degraded outsider. Her stepfather was quite an exciting, powerful figure but never offered Hannah entry into the charmed circle of his life in the artistic world.

Each life arena in which aggression, activity, and mobility may hold sway has been excruciatingly difficult for Hannah to occupy. She is torn and enraged with frustration over her career and her possibilities, she is furious in the knowledge that she must thwart herself from having the success and contentment she longs for, she is furious that she cannot seem to stop her mind from turning on itself and destroying any sense of ampleness or possibility. The prohibition on action touches many spheres of life, both fundamental and trivial. The capacity for sexual pleasure, learning to drive and securing a license, serving at tennis, succeeding at intellectual projects at a university, being hired by an employer-each of these experiences, which entail accepting one's own power and wish, has been powerfully forbidden, and only grudgingly have the rights and access been won.

The daughter of a seductive and intrusive father, she spent many early confusing years (her parents divorced when she was an infant) listening to her father bind her to him in complex identifications against the maternal family and against society. This father kept his daughter in a folie a deux of outsiders and oddballs. Later in her adolescence he treated her as his perfect feminine object. In a kind of seductive initiation into exhibitionism, she would be told in any public setting that all eyes were on her, that everyone wanted her. The unspoken implication was that she, the one wanted, was Daddy's. Yet this understanding has given way to a deeper and more unsettling possibility, for Hannah had always sensed her father's investment in attracting the interest of young men. One of her favorite dramatic monologues is the scene from

Suddenly Last Summer in which a beautiful young girl discovers she has been bait for her male homosexual companion's interest in young men. This scene reappears in fantasy in many guises, a sort of disabling myth. Hannah's father's feminine identification and homosexual desires disrupt her own possibilities for display and power, that is, not only must she deal with her own fantasies of grandiose display and exhibitionism, the delight in being seen and admired, but she must also struggle with the complex projections of her father's exhibitionist and homosexual desires, which contaminate her fantasy life.

One of the *Suddenly Last Summer* subtexts is that the man is devoured, cannibalized by the objects of his desire. Desire can be fatally dangerous. Her guilty excitement in her complicity in this scene is also powerful and problematic. Desire and the desire for empowered visibility are contaminated from many points of view. One of Hannah's psychic solutions follows the line of masochistic fantasy in which she becomes wildly excited and out of control, is desired, and then is attacked. The behavioral outcome of these conflicts is the avoidance of any moment of success or visible empowerment.

Identification and attachment to her mother have become problematic in another way. In the marital dynamic, the mother ruled, and the father was defeated and castrated. So her mother, in the world of work and in her interactions with Hannah's father, embodies phallic power and hegemony. Her mother's understanding of her own life connects efficacy, ambition, and power to her liberation from men altogether. One of the tasks of Hannah's adolescence was to begin to integrate and manage the meaning for herself of her mother's lesbian identification and its correlation with greater happiness and power for her mother. There is one other feature of this confusing family dynamic—the preoedipal mother. For Hannah, this relation is split between her mother and grandmother. Her memories of the mother of her early childhood are terrifying. An angry, unhappy woman, furious at any evidence of need in a child, corrosively contemptuous of weakness or dependency, her mother discovered a capacity to parent and love a child only upon the birth of Hannah's younger brother, when Hannah was six. This injury to narcissism has been excruciating for Hannah to acknowledge. It remains layered in feelings of shame and self-doubt. The grandmother is sweet, somewhat ineffectual, a comforting but distanced presence. As an internal object, this grandmother is no match for the murderous mother, so derisive of need or weakness, so contemptuous of Hannah's striving for competition.

Where is masculinity? Primarily, in Hannah's relation to her body, which is experienced and maintained as a place of phallic triumph. She lifts weights, works out, monitors appetite, eats sensibly if somewhat obsessively, and contains in her own body the fusion of masculine and feminine ideals. To draw on Bertram Lewin's (1933) idea of the body concretizing as a phallic object, we can say that Hannah at the gym is pure phallus, pure object; she embodies the male desire, but as its object, and is thus usually rendered powerless to act in any personal way on her own authority.

Second, there is her relationship to men. She is never without a boyfriend for very long and always chooses handsome, aggressive men. What is powerfully clear in these relationships is that they are founded as much on processes of identification as on processes of desire. She wants to be with these men and to be like them. What she enjoys is a life on male turf, hanging out at clubs, late night poker games. She prides herself on being able to outdo, outtalk, outdrink, and outplay any boyfriend and his coterie of male buddies. Her relations with men are a mixture of object choice and identification. In these heterosexual object relations, which she finds compelling and exciting, she is also working out masculine identification. A recent, intriguing analysis of this process is found in Mikkel Borch-Jacobsen's *The Freudian Subject* (1988). Drawing on Freud's work on dream interpretation, he notes the placement or displacement of some wish or desire into being the one who possesses the desired object: if I cannot have something for myself, I will be like one who can or does. Hannah then encounters, in her wish to be subject like these hypermasculine men, the paradox that they themselves insist on highly conventional feminine attitudes in women.

Finally, she plays out in her analysis her idea and ideal of masculine identification. I am experienced as a version of her well-meaning, ineffectual grandmother-distanced, unskilled, impotent in regard to the treatment. Any insight she will have to develop for herself. She attends her analysis politely, dutifully, but without hope of her change or of my efficacy. She monitors and maintains all systems of control. She cannot know or experience any need for me. She can need analysis in some abstract sense, but her sessions with me are lined up with duty visits to grandmother and other burdensome obligations. To feel need in her analysis would to be give in to terrifying possibilities, to be, in her derisive words, "a betty," apparently a code word she uses to signify any dependent, weak girl. It is also a term her mother reserves for her girlfriends. She is depressed but bewildered whenever a separation from the analysis presents itself. Sessions are canceled for headaches and stomach aches, but, if I question the absences, there are angry outbursts at the banality of my suggestions, at the ordeal of having to come for analysis that cannot help because she is hopeless. There is, above all, the terrible, degrading idea that if she needs her analyst, she is hopelessly female and I will become the triumphant, contemptuous, masculinized figure to whom she must submit.

"Look Ma, No Cavities"

A greeting at the beginning of a session. BK continues: "The good news is that I went to the dentist. No cavities. The bad news is that I went to the gynecologist." BK tells more than a medical history. The good news is that she could be a boy, my boy, teeth without holes, body without messy insides. The bad news is that it is not the whole truth; she is a girl with a long-standing relationship to gynecology and its ministrations. Perhaps the analyst can cast the deciding vote.

I have chosen this "homosexual" patient to challenge to idea of "homosexuality" as a monolithic, simple, transhistorical category. An important guide in this work has been Eisenbud's (1982) paper on lesbian identity. BK has her own form of ironic linguistic markers, humorous commentaries that embrace and transform conventional descriptions of lesbian identity. She uses the term "little butch" as a self-description but lives this identity in a social and personal space that is marked by feminism and by urban culture. Freud's patient was struggling with conflicts in male identification while simultaneously living within the conventions of respectability and bourgeois culture. BK experiences and expresses symbolically through her body, a more frankly male identification but complexly set within a woman-based scene.

Male identification for BK works and does not work. In the urban world she inhabits, part subculture, part community, she has constructed a personal, social, and occupational world in which boyish style, feminist stance, and working-class identity all coexist. Her self structures mix and disrupt. Crew-cut, always in pants, shorts, or work suits, tattooed, she has fashioned a body ego and self-presentation that express her identification through the blurring of gender boundaries. Moreover, she has found a way to live in a social world in which this stance is unremarkable. She tailors her name to suit her particular notion of her gender and gives up a rather feminine name, first for androgynous nicknames and later for initials.

In work, she is socially permitted and has permitted herself to choose a working-class, skilled trade and to live out an occupational life akin to her father's. But she cannot permit herself fully to thrive and succeed in this world. She thwarts herself, doubts that she can bear the "responsibility" of the full title of tradesman. She stays defensively at the level of "helper," occasionally having to defeat the practitioners of equal-opportunity programs by deliberately failing various exams. Her dream life is full of images of work-mates driving cars while she is stuck in parking lots or is never quite in the driver's seat. Nothing can occur to disrupt the reign of the idealized father. Does fear of male retaliation play a role in her inhibition? Perhaps. But loyalty and love also play a role. And recently she has come upon the shadowy idea that she cannot have what she wants at work and also live a gay lifestyle. That idea, though certainly plausible at a social level, given cultural homophobia, runs against some reality on her job. A gay woman, BK's age, obtained a senior administrative position. The practical possibilities of advancement seem to make the psychic taboos against such successes even fiercer. BK tells me she cannot come to know this woman, and she avoids any contact. Indeed she assures me that this whole problem of work and success is impossible to think about, unknowable. To underscore this point, she brings in a dream in which she was decapitated.

BK is the daughter of an adored and idealized father, who ran a store. As he appears in her material, the father is warm, funny, big, and hairy (there are many gorilla dreams both scary and fun). He is seen as responsible, hardworking. Curiously, he is the only parent about whom any memories of feeding and sensory care remain. His deli was the source of treats and food. There is an evocative memory of this father sitting in the kitchen and dozing by a stove on which eggs are boiling. This vision of the responsible, docile father giant is a source of warmth and identity. There is also melancholy in this memory. The father's exhaustion signals his ordeal in caring for his wife, BK's mother, who progressively declined to invalidism from multiple sclerosis, an ordeal that seems to have contributed to the father's early death.

Her mother, by contrast, was experienced as first absent, then horribly controlling, and later sick and frighteningly debilitated. When BK was two, a sister was born, and her mother simultaneously began the slow, inexorable slide to debility. A double loss experienced by BK because of the mother's preoccupation both with the new baby and with her mysterious and terrifying illness. What seems relevant here is that B K enters all relationships with the conviction that she cannot be interesting, that the other will be bored and drift away, and that a rival may at any moment exclude her. In a dream early in treatment she is at a cafe, and a waitress wants her to spoon cocaine over her Rice Krispies. She spies her former girlfriend buying coffee and rolls to go. BK reports a panicky feeling as she tries to see if the bag the lover is holding is "big enough to hold food for two." She is riven with jealously.

In a striking and powerful way, BK has used sexual excitement and later drugs to regulate tension and to cover separation anxiety and depressive loss. Constant masturbation, a lifelong habit of thumb sucking, and, in her childhood, the frantic excitement of sports and sex play with boys were placed against the constriction and anxiety of school and home. BK was a child who could play hard and wildly but who often felt speechless at school. Outside, she felt alive and sure. Inside, she felt ashamed, silent, bored, and boring. In the wildness of outdoor play, she remembers pulling down boys' pants "to have a look." As an adolescent this frantic quest for identity and soothing emerged in an intense sexual and love relation with a boy. Locked in combat with her mother over this relationship, she experienced in it a quality of absolute desperation, an obsessional and addictive tie later overlaid with drugs. The potency and power of this experience are a mix of desire and identity. At this time BK seems most determined to inhabit and have pleasure in a homosexual space as one of the boys, freed from the maternal eye and control and looking for pleasure and freedom. I am terming "homosexual" her love of a young adolescent boy in that it is a choice of an object experienced as same-sexed, at least in unconscious fantasy.

This period coincided with the escalation of the mother's illness. In a dream that takes place in the street and back alley of her childhood, she is trying to escape on a bicycle as her mother comes toward her. But it is BK who is wearing the hospital gown, which is covered with shit. She is humiliated, carrying her mother's shame, the horror at physical collapse and loss of control. Associating to the dream, BK tearfully remembers the ordeal of caring for her mother during this preadolescent and adolescent period. The mother lost bladder control; an operation was performed that permitted catheterization, a duty both father and daughter had to perform. This memory allowed us to make sense of a series of dream images in which flaps of skin, sores on feet, and catheterized genitals could now be understood in terms of her desperation to repudiate a femininity that seemed ill and damaged and a female genital that was sordid and shameful.

Behind the memories of a shamed and damaged mother is a depressed and withholding mother, a silent mother who is longed for. An evocation of this mother partially inspires the lovers chosen in adulthood. Romantic enactment is always orchestrated around bringing a woman to life. For BK, as she says, pleasure for herself is "at best second." Her relationships are primarily heterosexual in the sense that BK enacts symbolically the role of "boy/butch" courting mother. She is, in symbolic terms, not exactly the same sex as her love object. In making this claim, I am preserving Freud's insight into the distinction between biology and culture and Lacan's insistence on the fictive nature of sexuality and gender.

What is developing for this patient within the realm of object choice is quite interesting. There is a new willingness to have pleasure, not merely to give it. This willingness seems to require greater comfort with an experience she is calling "being baby," a passivity that is frightening but fascinating. There is some wonderment at the possibility that pleasure might occur for her and for another person from acts of incorporation, being inside.

In these more ample relationships, she combines excitement with personal connection, although at key moments threaten to recapture or imitate or outdo some fantasied primal scene, BK draws back to a mode of phallic play, of deferral. Taking her lover away for a weekend was to be a time when, in her words, she could "be daddy." Things went well until the moment for sex. It was a Sunday afternoon, a time, BK later remembered, when her parents would shoo the children away so they could make love. At that moment, BK, to her surprise, turned away from the bedroom and went out to play softball.

BK has a quality about her that has always puzzled me. For a person with such a florid and elaborate sexual history, the term "latency" does not exactly hold. Yet, stylistically, BK lives like a latency boy. Her apartment is full of toys, games, and projects. She builds rockets, takes craft classes, does handiwork for friends. In this way she is caught as boy, not able to inhabit adult masculinity, and this inhibition is sharply problematic to her in her work. "It's natural for them. They always knew how to do it." She is talking about her workmates, and if we hear penis envy here, we can think of Marie Torok's (1966) account of that structure as a defensive move against owning and inhabiting one's own life, body, and prospects. "In penis envy, there is a projection into the Other of some desire, deemed natural to that other and treated as fundamentally unavailable to the self" (p. 140).

Conclusion

Despite the shortcomings and contradictions in Freud's work with his patient, there is still an astonishing richness in his ideas of sexuality and gender. This complexity in the structure of anyone's gender and object choice now meets up with the analyses in feminism and in current deconstructionist and semiotic theory. These perspectives argue for a multiply figured and multiply determined model of gender, for the fluid and fragmentary nature of desire, and for the potency of culture to shape and construct both identity and desire.

What might be helpful is to maintain a contradictory model of gender in which it is a serious, fully lived, conscious experience of self, often "core" to one's being, and at the same time it can dissolve or transmute under our very gaze. Ann Snitow (1989) has recently argued for this approach as one that keeps in play the currently unresolvable conflicts within and around this category.

We might try to hold to a paradox. What is persistent is that gender and sexuality are fluid and unsettled and labile. What can be consistently addressed is the disruptive and complex and multiply determined developments that end up in adult identity and adult love. Giving up commitments to a bifurcation of normality and abnormality where object choice and identity are concerned means that other criteria can be watchfully considered.

The French psychoanalytic school proposes a definition of perversion as one in which difference is refused. Yet Chasseguet-Smirgel and others using this framework often secure "difference" as a solely biological term. But "nature" is no guarantee of difference. A more promising line of thought is in Winnicott's (1971) criteria for normal versus pathological play, which are echoed in McDougall's (1980) consideration of perversion as the enactment of a rigidly programmatic and fetishistic object relation, a refusal of fluidity and playfulness in respect to sex and identity.

Yet even with a revitalized vision of the complexity of gender structure and sexual choice, there is still the problem of politics, culture, and power. Freud's theory of the construction of the relation of sexual aim and object, of the free play of associations and symbolic meaning that arise for any child in regard to the body can sound remarkably idealistic. Our society marks some practices as wholesome and some as pathological, and these markings hold powerful meanings for all of us. Feminist and gay liberation texts have revalenced the degraded positions of homosexual practices and refused patriarchal culture hegemony. What is needed is a theory that recognizes the social power of categories like gender and sexuality in both conscious and unconscious experience but can also account for the way in which these categories, at certain moments, lose salience and become more porous. Benjamin's (1988) ground-breaking work holds that promise.

Hannah and BK, each in her own way, express the rage and conflict they feel at the absence of social power. But whatever binds them as women struggling with the phallic position, the differences are equally profound. BK lives her life in a community of women and gay people. Her lovers are women, even as she wryly worries that not all lesbian women like to hear her talk about "disks and being inside people." Hannah competes and lives in a rather relentlessly heterosexual world as a woman who hates the feminine in herself while operating fully within the conventions of femininity in dress, look, and style. She groans, "The only good thing about being a girl is the clothes."

In one of those coincidences about which psychoanalysis teaches us to be curious, during a week in which I was revising this paper, both Hannah and BK brought in stories about dancing. BK talked about the pleasure of dancing with her shirt off at a Gay Pride Day dance, and she contrasted this pleasure with the shame she felt looking at her body with her T-shirt on. Covered, she felt female and saw rolls of flesh. Uncovered, she felt full and pleased and safe. Hannah had gone to a benefit at which there were mostly gay men. She also talked of the pleasure in dancing freely. Why this freedom for Hannah in a crowd of gay men? She would say, graphically, "No one stares at your tits." I would theorize that at this moment she is freed from pure object status and can inhabit her own subjectivity. Yet the contradiction comes in her meticulous development of her body along ideals and stereotypes of feminine beauty. Hannah's ideally slim, feminine body concretizes phallic power, but as object. It is phallic power more in enactment than in conscious function. This conflict, lived at the level of the body, is a thwarting of a masculine identification that could infuse her subjectivity. In both these women's experiences, masculine life and possibility are highly idealized. Maleness seems to equate with freedom itself. Torok's (1966) analysis of penis envy notes this defensive stance in women as the idealizing into masculinity, desires and possibilities too dangerous to own as aspects of self.

At this point historically, we need to understand the psychic costs of contesting for entry as a subject in the Symbolic order, a privileged psychic space from which women are barred, both in unconscious fantasy as well as in social reality. We need a theory to encompass the complexity of rebellion in masculine and feminine character, its liberating potential and its painful costs. We need a theory of gender with room for both reified categories and fluid new forms of social and personal life. Psychoanalysis and Freud's radical model of sexuality, as he theorized it in the essay on homosexuality in a woman, can be one crucial resource in such a project.

References

Benjamin, J. (1988), *The Bonds of Love*. New York: Pantheon Press.

Bollas, C. (1987), *The Shadow of the Object*. New York: Columbia University Press.

Borch-Jacobsen, M. (1988), *The Freudian Subject*. Stanford: Stanford University Press.

Chasseguet-Smirgel, J. (1966), *Feminine Sexuality*. Ann Arbor: University of Michigan Press.

────── (1986), *Sexuality and Mind*. New York: Basic Books. (1985), *The Ego Ideal*. New York: Norton.

Chodorow, N. (1976), *Tne Reproduction of Mothering*. Berkeley: University of California Press.

Chomsky, N. (1965), *Aspects of a Tneory of Syntax*. Cambridge, MA: MIT Press.

Coates, S. (in press), The ontogenesis of gender identity disorder in boys. *J. Amer. Acad. Psychoanal.*

Dinnerstein, D. (1976), *The Mermaid and the Minotaur*. New York: Harper & Row.

Eisenbud, R. (1982), Early and later determinants of lesbian identity. *Psychoanal. Rev.*, 69:85–109.

Fast, I. (1984), *Gender Identity: A Differentiation Model*. Hillsdale, NJ: The Analytic Press.

Freud, S. (1900), The interpretation of dreams. *Standard Edition*, 4 & 5. London: Hogarth Press, 1953.

────── (1905a), Three essays on the theory of sexuality. *Standard Edition*, 7:135–246. London: Hogarth Press, 1953.

────── (1905b), Fragment of an analysis of a case of hysteria. *Standard Edition*, 7:7–122. London: Hogarth Press, 1953.

────── (1924), Psychogenesis of a case of homosexuality in a woman. *Standard Edition*, 18:145–174. London: Hogarth Press, 1955.

────── (1931), Female sexuality. *Standard Edition*, 21:223–242. London: Hogarth Press, 1961.

Grossman, W. & Kaplan, D. (1988), Three commentaries on gender in Freud's thought: A prologue to the psychoanalytic theory of sexuality. In: *Fantasy, Myth and Reality*. New York: International Universities Press.

Jones, E. (1957), *The Life and Work of Sigmund Freud*, Vol. 3. New York: Basic Books.

Lacan, J. (1977), *Ecrits*. New York: Norton.

Lauffer, M. & Lauffer, M. (1989), *Developmental Breakdown and Adolescent Psychopathology*. New Haven, CT: Yale University Press.

Lewin, B. (1933), The body as phallus. In: *The Selected Writings of Bertram D. Lewin*. New York: Psychoanalytic Quarterly Press, 1973.

Little, M. (1981), *Transference Neurosis and Transference Psychosis*. New York: Aronson.

McDougall, J. (1980), *Plea for a Measure of Abnormality*. New York: International Universities Press.

Mitchell, J. (1975), *Psychoanalysis and Feminism*. New York: Basic Books.

Mitchell, S. (1988), *Relational Concepts in Psychoanalysis: An Integration*. Cambridge, MA: Harvard University Press.

Roazen, P. (1969), *Brother Animal: The Story of Freud and Tausk*. New York: Knopf.

Rosenberg, C. (1985), *Disorderly Conduct*. New York: Knopf.

Snitow, A. (1989), A gender diary. In: *Rocking the Ship of State: Towards a Feminist Peace Politicis*, ed. A. Harris & Y. King. Boulder, CO: Westview Press.

Torok, M. (1966), The significance of penis envy for a woman. In: *Feminine Sexuality*, ed. J. Chasseguet-Smirgel. Ann Arbor: University of Michigan Press, pp. 135–169.

Weeks, J. (1979), *Coming Out: A History of Homosexuality from the Nineteenth Century to the Present*. New York: Quartet Books.

Winnicott, D. W. (1971), *Playing and Reality*. London: Tavistock.

Afterword

In the years since this essay was first published, the emergent theoretical sophistication in regard to gender and sexuality has been striking. I revisit this work with a significantly deepened understanding of Judith Butler's (1992) theoretical innovations and with the benefit of many developments in theory and clinical psychoanalysis. In the clinical material in my essay I was reaching to talk about two problems that are now center stage for a number of writers, most signally Benjamin (1995, 1996) and Chodorow (1992).

First, gender as a monolithic, essential, pregiven category is now so thoroughly deconstructed, fractured, and complexly re-represented as to be but a shell of its former self. I could just begin to consider the distinction between overt gender or sexual identity and the lived internal experience of gender in fantasy. Drawing on feminist psychoanalytic work and on the emerging forms of queer theory, one can now see that the fluidity of gendered experience in forms of identity and in sexuality seems so much more complex and multifaceted. Phillip Bromberg (1994, 1996) has also provided a deep and subtle reading of the internal/interpersonal landscape as a site of multiple and shifting self-states.

The inadequacies of language and many forms of representation to signify the experience of being or loving are striking. The dichotomizing principles of a binary gender system and a binary linguistic system distort as well as elaborate. It is much clearer to me now that questions of gender development must address variation and multiple functions changing over time and within any one individual. Freud's essay and much of our critical history of studying gender have been riveted to the question, "What do women want?" but now the contemporary questions are much more: What does gender do? What does gender mean? What is its dialectical practice in relation to living and loving? To some extent, the term gender must now, ironically, be set off in quotation marks. This practice, signaling gender terms' problematic status, appears as early as Riviere's 1929 paper on femininity as a masquerade. It is most highly developed within queer theory, a theoretical development often in productive tension with psychoanalysis (Butler, 1993; Dean, 1993). Within this perspective, reified forms of identity are political or rhetorical strategies rather than essences.

Second, my essay was headed toward an examination of the instable relation of identification and desire. Chodorow (1992), in her ground-breaking paper on heterosexuality as an achievement or compromise formation remarks on the unquestioned assumption in psychoanalysis that identification and idealization of the same-sex parent fuels desire for the opposite sex.

> There are two major problems with such accounts. First, one is left without a sense of the motivation for such shifts in identificatory choices. More important, the account does not tell us how *identi-fication*—an ego choice which might well tell the developing child whom he or she ought to love in order to be like the identificatory object—relates to erotization [p. 287].

Benjamin has also been describing the complex interactions of identificatory love and oedipal and postoedipal structures. Concerned with maintaining the contradictions between renunciation and retention of identities and loves, she argues for a more pluralistic and multiply configured model of love and being.

The elision of homosexual identity, so palpable in Freud's case history, has provoked the great theory battles in psychoanalysis in respect to both gender and sexuality. In a number of contemporary books, Lesser and Domenici (1995) O'Connor and Ryan (1994), Schwartz (1998), and Magee and Miller (1998), homosexual, and in particular lesbian, experiences are being written into discourse. In this rich and diverse range of publications, identities are being moved from the margins, or else margins are claimed to have their own place of privilege. The homosexual women, in Freud's case history is about to have her own book, an edited collection of essays in which this essay will also be reprinted (Lesser and Schoenbrun, in press).

This exercise in rereading and in writing an afterword is an opportunity for self-reflection. One of the pervasive and fascinating instabilities in much modern and postmodern thought is that of the position of the writer. Who is the author of this article that I wrote? I wrote it, in part as an act of piratical launching of my own ship, my own adventure in various skirmishes and power struggles in the field. Of course, such a private enterprise would be unimaginable without the great armada of feminism. But in the years since, an author's subjectivity and countertransference to the text, along with the fluidity and interchangability of reader and writer, are now commonplace cultural ideas. I arrive at some new questions. "Every text, however metaphysical, always produces gaps which announce breaches in the metaphysical circle: the points at which the textual process subverts what its 'author' intended to say. . . . The process of enunciation always subverts the utterance" (Zizek, pp. 154–155). Where would this author find some of Harris's slips, the point of "metonymical dissipation of the text"?

Given my critique of Freud's presentation of a seamless argument, I am struck by the tightness of my own writing. The rigidity of a "phallic" literary practice, an attempt to be one of the boys. "Russian tactics" in the writer. Both in the case itself and in my own clinical material, I see how taken I was with details of the masquerades of masculinity and femininity, and I appreciate the powerful autobiographical elements and identifications. From the patient I called Hannah, I trace my interest in Riviere and feminine performances. I recognize also how much my immersion in psychoanalysis as a profession has entailed a very particular enactment and engagement with femininity and its decorative elements.

I can see now that this essay is one beginning of my interest in theorizing tomboys, an interest in the fate and meaning of masculinity in women. Yet how thoroughly both the original essay and my commentary subsume a psychoanalytic theory of sexuality into the analysis of gender, a trope Benjamin (1996) has noted in much feminist and postfeminist theory. While the tomboy figure is both gender stereotyped and a gender outlaw, sexuality is more ambiguously situated. Consider the "boy" of the essay, or the self-styled "little butch," or the girl with masculine identifications in my clinical examples: do they love as homosexual or heterosexual, and are those terms secured by object or by subject? Silverman (1988) in an essay on Henry James describes him as a writer who "can be said to enclose homosexuality in heterosexuality and heterosexuality within homosexuality" (p. 173). It seems to me now that an exploration into homosexuality and masculine identifications in girls would open up the jouissance located in the doubleness of the tomboy girl and would raise questions of bisexual fantasy laced through sexual life and through multiple identifications.·

In my essay I seem preoccupied with control and repression. But I wonder now about Freud's fascination with a masculine woman. Hughes (1991), in a biographical essay on Riviere, describes Freud's relationship to his analysand/translator as quite distinctly mentoring.

Hughes quotes a letter from Freud in which Riviere is encouraged to write her own material. Sarah Kofman's (1985) reading of Freud in the essays on femininity insists on the excitement and its dangers in relation to women as much as the more usual feminist focus on Freud's fear of engulfment and identification with the feminine. The riddle of femininity provokes curiosity, and in this Kofman would have us notice Freud's desires, his excitement, and his identifications.

References

Benjamin, J. (1995), *Like Subjects Love Objects*. New Haven, CT: Yale University Press.
——— (1996), In defense of gender ambiguity. *Gender & Psychoanal.*, 1:27–44.
Bromberg, P. (1994), Speak that I may see you! Some reflections on dissociation, reality and psychoanalytic listening. *Psychoanal. Dial.*, 4:517–547.
——— (1996), The multiplicity of self and psychoanalytic relationship. *Contemp. Psychoanal.*, 35:509–535.
Butler, J. (1993), *Bodies That Matter*. New York: Routledge.
Chodorow, N. (1992), Heterosexuality as a compromise formation. *Psychoanal. Contemp. Thought*, 15:267–304.
Dean, T. (1993). Transsexual identification, gender performance theory and the politics of the real. *Literature & Psychol.*, 39:1–27.
Hughes, A. (1991), Joan Riviere: Her life and work. In: *The Inner World and Joan Riviere*, ed. A. Hughes. London: Karnac Books.
Kofman, S. (1985), *The Enigma of Woman*. Ithaca, NY: Cornell University Press.
Lesser, R. & Domenici, T. eds. (1995), *Disorienting Sexuality*. London: Routledge.
——— & Schoenbrun, eds. (1999), *That Obscure Subject of Desire: Freud's Female Homosexual Revisited*. New York: Routledge.
Magee, M. & Miller, D. (1998), *Lesbian Lives*. Hillsdale, NJ: The Analytic Press.
O'Connor, N. & Ryan, J. (1994), *Wild Desires and Mistaken Identities*. London: Virago.
Riviere, J. (1929), Womanliness as a masquerade. *Internat. J. Psycho-Anal.*, 10:303–313.
Schwartz, A. (1998), *Sexual Subjects*. New York: Routledge.
Silverman, K. (1992), *Male Subjectivity at the Margins*. New York: Routledge.
Zizek, S. (1989), *The Sublime Object of Ideology*. London: Verso.

The Negotiation of Paradox in the Analytic Process

(1992)

Stuart A. Pizer

▼   ▼   ▼   ▼   ▼

Editors' Introduction

This paper by Stuart Pizer brings together and captures many currents and features that have been important in the development of relational theorizing and clinical practice.

A signature feature of Pizer's approach is the extension of key features of Winnicott's contributions from specific developmental phases and needs to a more general relational context.

In his development of the concept of paradox, Pizer joins writers like Donnel Stern and Charles Spezzano in developing an epistemology compatible with a relational perspective. Pizer emphasizes not just complexity (as in Freud's concepts of conflict and overdetermination, Waelder's concept of multiple-function, and Brenner's concept of compromise-formation), but contradiction. In contrast to the linear, cause-and-effect determinism of traditional analytic interpretation, Pizer recommends the growth-enhancing value of cultivating and sustaining tension and ambiguity. There is an extension here of Winnicott's discussion of paradox in terms of specific developmental passages to a more general epistemic take on life and reality, which, Pizer suggests, is one of the most precious things the analytic experience offers patients.

Pizer also broadens Winnicott's notions of transitional experience and object usage in rich, descriptive frameworks for viewing creative intersubjective exchange. And negotiation of paradox becomes a way of understanding not just sticky moments of impasse between analysand and analyst but the basic nature of the analytic relationship, in its playful, mutually shaping give-and-take. Pizer takes the powerful developmental metaphors Winnicott provides and interpersonalizes them, making them more reciprocal, and, following Aron, making room for the analyst's subjectivity.

One of the most important features of this paper is its extended clinical example, in which Pizer demonstrates the application of complex theoretical concepts in a rich depiction of clinical process. The tone is, at the same time, very thoughtful, open, and also playful. It provides a vivid illustration of one style through which a wide range of relational theoretical concepts have been brought to life in analytic practice.

Stuart Pizer's contributions on paradox and negotiation have been expanded into the recently published *Building Bridges: The Negotiation of Paradox in Psychoanalysis* (1998, The Analytic Press). In that work, the case of Donald, which Pizer introduced in this early paper, is explored further, along with other vivid clinical examples, to develop the rich applicability of the concepts of paradox and negotiation in terms of the psychoanalytic process and also other major domains of contemporary life, like gender and politics.

The Negotiation of Paradox in the Analytic Process*

▼   ▼   ▼   ▼   ▼

A patient reports the following incident in the course of a "good-enough" analysis with a good analyst. He was lying on the couch, in the midst of whatever associations, when he was distracted by a smell as if someone were spraying trees in the neighborhood. He registered this impingement by saying, "I smell insecticide spray." From behind the couch, the analyst's voice replied, "It is neither insecticide nor spray. It is something burning." The patient shrugged internally and went on with whatever his associations had been. At the end of the session, when the patient walked out to the street, he saw a tank truck from a nursery service, such as might spray insecticide, parked in front of his analyst's house. He muttered, "Sonofabitch," not being certain at that moment whether he was referring to his analyst or himself. The patient began the following day's session with reference to this experience. A psychother-

---

* Originally published in Psychoanalytic Dialogue, 2(2):215–240. © 1992 The Analytic Press, Inc.

apist himself, the patient raised the issue of the analytic frame defined in terms of psychic reality and external reality as interpreted by analytic authority. He questioned his analyst's attitude of certainty and his own attitude, as patient, of uncertainty. The patient further noted that whatever he had been implicitly communicating by saying, "I smell insecticide spray," whatever he had been seeking to bring into play—particularly with an analyst whom he knew to be an avid gardener—had been derailed by the analyst's peremptory response. At this point, the analyst affirmed, "This is the danger of too much certainty in the countertransference. I recognize that my remark served to close exploration rather than open it."

For me, this analytic moment illustrates the feeling of being up against a nonnegotiable stance on the part of one's analyst. Notably, the patient's protest had served to initiate a return to negotiation between them, as the analyst was able to recognize and acknowledge how he had ruptured analytic potential space. This chapter is about the process of negotiation as an intrinsic vehicle of the therapeutic action of psychoanalysis. I examine the nature of analytic negotiation and its relationship to paradox, with particular focus on the implicit place of this concept in the writings of Winnicott. I conclude with clinical material that illustrates the negotiation of paradox in the course of a treatment.

Negotiation is intrapsychic, interpersonal, and intersubjective, and it is vital to our biological existence.[1] Negotiation is intrapsychic in the sense that we must each mediate within ourselves the containment and expression of drive and affect, or inner contradiction and multiplicity, as well as the tension in living between engagement in the fresh potentials of the present moment and enmeshment in the conservative grip of repetition of our past experience; thus, negotiation is an ego function necessary for the internal management of paradoxical experience. Negotiation is interpersonal in the sense that we are always arranging with one another matters of desire, safety, anxiety, power, convenience, fairness, and so on. Negotiation is intersubjective in the sense that we constantly influence one another, consciously and unconsciously, from infancy onward in a myriad of ways, from minute adjustments to gross adaptations. So it is that we experience the fine choreography of infant and mother attaining, rupturing, and repairing states of attunement and

---

1. Other writers (e.g., Racker, 1968; Sandler, 1976; Goldberg, 1987; Adler, 1989; Bollas, 1989; Mitchell, 1993; Modell, 1990; Russell, unpublished; Slavin and Kriegman, 1990, 1992; Bromberg, 1995) have converged on the issue of negotiation in the analytic process, either as an implicit factor in their thinking or an explicit term in their discourse.

affective communion (Stern, 1985; Beebe and Lachmann, 1992) or, in adulthood, the intersubjective exchange of the forces of projective identification by which we shape, and, in turn, are shaped by our partners. In these ways, collusive relationships are forged around the negotiation of mutually invested defenses and repetitions, and therapeutic or mutually enhancing relationships are created and evolved through an ongoing negotiation that allows for self-expression, spontaneity, and self-realization in a context of safety, respect, and reciprocity.

I believe that, in the psychoanalytic process, the transference–countertransference tapestry is woven between analysand and analyst through a process of intersubjective negotiation. Much of what is essentially mutative in the analytic relationship is rendered through mutual adjustments that occur largely out of awareness in both parties. Only some of this process need ever become conscious to patient or analyst or be explicated through interpretation. The moments of explicit or implicit negotiation between analyst and patient may mark a discernible unit within the analytic process, as distinct from the analytic modes of historical narrative, reconstruction, interpretation, and reflection (although, as we shall see, even interpretation is a matter always subject to negotiation between both parties to the process).

The analyst, as he or she receives a patient's transference communications, is continually monitoring within himself or herself such questions as, What are you making of me? Can I accept this or that construction of me based on my own subjective sense of myself, my integrity, my commitment to the analytic framework as I see it, and my sense of our analytic mission? As a result, the analyst, whether making genetic or here-and-now interpretations (which, in themselves, have importance), is recurrently saying to the patient, "No, you can't make this of me. But you can make that of me." In turn, the patient receives the analyst's response with relief, gratitude, frustration, hurt, and the like and proceeds to generate further associations that seek to negotiate among past impressions, current experience, and future potential in this field of interplay between two subjectivities. Indeed, it may be the patient who, in response to an analyst's genetic or transference interpretation, declares, "No, you can't make this of me. But you can make that of me." In short, the very substance and nature of truth and reality—as embodied both in transference–countertransference constructions and in narrative reconstructions —are being negotiated toward consensus in the analytic dyad. The important therapeutic yield of these ongoing and recurrent negotiations goes beyond such products of negotiation as an accepted insight, a retrieved recollection, or a self-analytic reflection on the mind's defensive patterns. Essential as these analytic products surely are, I believe they are secondary to the therapeutic *action* of psychoanalysis, which is the engagement of two persons in a process of negotiation that, to borrow a phrase from Loewald (1960), is "an intervention designed to set ego development in motion."

I further believe that people looking back on their successful analyses commonly recall as particularly significant those moments in which their analyst seemed to step outside his or her accustomed position in a way that registered arrival at a deep recognition of the patient's essential being, an epiphanic state of rapport (perhaps marked by humor or sadness), or an affirmation of the personal caring that had spanned the vicissitudes of their relationship. While such moments may come as a surprise to the patient, they do not have the quality of coming from out of the blue or from out of some "left field" in the analyst's psyche, nor are they some whimsical bestowal or slip in analytic attitude. Rather, they have the quality of the analyst's yielding to some subtlety of being in the patient, some subtlety of their relatedness over time, which allows for a freshly discovered play in the analytic framework. These enactments by the analyst have been prepared for over time in the analytic partnership that has made them feasible, viable, and usable. Mitchell (1993) has made note of such analytic moments and attributed them to a negotiation between patient and analyst over the requisite countertransference response to the patient's relational needs, as differentiated from an enacted countertransference gratification of the patient's desires. As Mitchell observes,

> What may be most crucial is *neither* gratification nor frustration, but the process of negotiation itself, in which the analyst finds his own particular way to confirm and participate in the patient's subjective experience yet slowly, over time, establishes his own presence and perspective in a way that the patient can find enriching rather than demolishing [p. 196].

I would add that, while the process of negotiation does unfold "slowly, over time" and while moments of sublime, spontaneous rapport may be rare (and perhaps need not be frequent), the give-and-take of subjectivity, desire, stricture, and demand between patient and analyst is continual, recurrent, and always somehow new and incomplete. Out of this two-person process of negotiation, one may find emerging a patient's growing capacity to encompass wider experiential possibilities within his or her range of negotiable options in living, a growing trust and hope for participation in an increasingly negotiable interpersonal world, and a growing synthetic facility for bridging the inescapable paradoxes of human separateness and connection—in short, ego development set in motion by the analytic process.

Winnicott, that artful dodger of a psychoanalytic author, comfortably nestled in a British literary tradition that conveyed sense through nonsense, was profoundly sensitive to the elemental paradoxes that shape our being and our development (Phillips, 1988). Paradox requires negotiation, and Winnicott's theory is built on paradox.

Perhaps the most widely recognized statement of paradox in Winnicott's writings is in his paper on "Transitional Objects and Transitional Phenomena." As Winnicott (1951) wrote:

> We cannot ignore . . . an intermediate area of *experiencing*, to which inner reality and external life both contribute. It is an area that is not challenged, because no claim is made on its behalf except that it shall exist as a resting-place for the individual engaged in the perpetual human task of keeping inner and outer reality separate yet interrelated [p. 2].

Thus, out of need, the infant creates the mother's breast, which is there to be found. Later, the child makes of the first not-me possession, such as his Teddy or Blankie, a personal object imbued with life from the subjective world along with sentient qualities from the objective world. According to Winnicott, "The transitional object and the transitional phenomena start each human being off with what will always be important for them, i.e. a neutral area of experience which will not be challenged" (p. 12). Within the paradox of transitional space lies the potential for creative play. Within the preservation of paradox lies the necessity for an ongoing process of negotiation.

Probably the most profound spiritual paradox elucidated by Winnicott is the essential human need to communicate juxtaposed with the essential human need to remain incommunicado. On one hand, we need to experience our connection with objects in the external world in order to feel real. Winnicott recognized the terror to which we are subject if we feel threatened by submergence in the boundless ocean of our own subjectivity. Our psychic life requires both the limits encountered through our abutment with externality and the nourishment provided by other-than-me substance. Even to enjoy our solitude, we need to achieve the state of "ego-relatedness" that Winnicott (1958a) described as the product of the paradoxical experience in infancy of being alone in the presence of another. On the other hand, Winnicott grasped that, as the infant becomes increasingly competent, the mother who anticipates her baby's needs before her baby signals is no longer "good enough." What was once exquisitely empathic can become traumatically invasive, and the loss of inviolable privacy is an annihilation.

Winnicott (1958a) suggests that, when growth takes place under the best of circumstances, the child comes to possess "three lines of communication" (p. 188). The first is *"for ever silent"* and constitutes a non-negotiable retreat to relaxation within the subjective world of the inviolable self. The second is "explicit, indirect and pleasurable" and consists of the capacity for language; and, as Stern (1985) has argued (following Vygotsky, 1962), the meaning of language is negotiated in each child–parent dyad. Thus, language equips the child, for life, with the competence to reveal while concealing, to portray an approximation of experience, to achieve consensual validation without utter exposure. Finally, Winnicott's third line of communication is that *"intermediate* form of communication that slides out of playing into cultural experience of every kind" (p. 188). This third area of communication, then, is the area of shared symbols, where the most intimate negotiations occur in the overlap between the subjective worlds of self and other, where two people may engage in the creative exchange of gestures, or squiggles,[2] and construct mutually useful metaphors. When Winnicott shifts the scene to the analytic process, he writes, "Here there is danger if the analyst interprets instead of waiting for the patient to creatively discover" (p. 189). Winnicott is referring to the crucial importance of the negotiation of meaning between analyst and patient, through linguistic approximations and with an attitude of joint creation and a sensitivity to mutual regulation.

As I see it, the process of psychoanalysis may be conceived as an exchange of "squiggles" between adults without pencil and paper. By such an exchange, mostly verbal, of marks and "re-marks" offered in evocative and resonant sequence, analyst and patient become cocreators of a relational construction that represents and communicates a place of intersection of their separate experiences together over time. Neither the analyst's "squiggle"—be it interpretation, clarification, confrontation, empathic reflection, or self-disclosure—nor the patient's "squiggle"—be it historical narrative, transference impression, manifest dream, or other association—constitutes an X-ray rendering of "the self's core." Rather, analyst and patient, in their use of what Winnicott terms "explicit, indirect" communication—that is, language—become an intersubjective partnership for the

---

2. "Squiggling" refers to the Squiggle Game used by Winnicott (1971b) in his therapeutic consultations with children. In the service of providing the child a sense of comfort and freedom, and the opportunity for a spontaneous or creative gesture that might crystallize the child's self-awareness, Winnicott employed this paper and pencil game. He would make a mark, a line or doodle, on the paper and ask the child to complete it. In turn, he would complete initial marks supplied by the child. Through this reciprocal exchange, representations of impulse, need, affect, or fantasy would take shape and come into focus.

collaborative creation of a shared culture of usable, and reusable, reverberative images. As analyst and patient come into play in the area of illusion, they create metaphorical renderings of the approximate meaning of their shared transference–countertransference experience (see Chapter 2 for further elaboration of the use of metaphor).

Human self-interest constitutes another basic paradox. We are not only consumers, but also providers. We realize our selves both through the care we receive and the care we give. This fundamental paradox of our nature is entailed in Winnicott's (1962a, 1963b) notion of the principal human drive: toward development. On one hand, it is easy for us to read Winnicott's theory of human development as a kind of infant advocacy theory. From this perspective, development seems to mean the development of a spontaneous self, the achievement of ego integration and psychosomatic unity, and the capacity to use environmental provision for internal robustness and a sense of subjective mastery over the external world. On the other hand, if we trace Winnicott's developmental schema from the phase of absolute dependence through relative dependence and toward independence, we may ask, What are the qualities of "independence"? In this manifestly baby-centered theory, which reminded the psychoanalytic field of the significance of the real facilitating environment in psychological development, we each grow to an adulthood in which we provide the facilitating environment for the next generation. Having once been babies, we now become mothers, fathers, or analysts. Our destiny, as we grow toward independence, is to develop the capacities whereby we may contribute back to the world, by our own adaptations, the holding environment for the nourishment of others. In a sense, reflecting the Kleinian roots in Winnicott's thinking, this generativity constitutes our reparation for our own earliest voracious feeding upon the world that held us in the bliss of our subjectivity. Although Winnicott describes the "primary maternal preoccupation" of the "good-enough" mother as a kind of temporary illness, this state is not based on maternal masochism or sentimentality. It is closer to primary creativity, the mother's illusion that she continues to create her baby while she is merged with it by "almost 100% adaptation" to its needs. The analyst, in moments of "primary analytic preoccupation," is fortunate to experience a similar joy at being found and used. But what of the human abhorrence of being found? If, as Winnicott has argued, to be found is to be violated, how do we willingly allow ourselves to be found by the infant or the analysand who needs to conjure us for personal usage?

How has the mother actually managed to survive as a separately existing center of need, affect, intensity, and will while adapting to her infant's moment-by-moment imperatives? The answer is implied in

Winnicott's (1968) observation that, whereas the baby has not been a mother before—or even a baby—the mother has both been a baby and played at being a mother. Hence, the mother survives in her position as mother by having recourse to her survival as a baby, past, present, and future. Within herself, the mother must find ways of retaining access to her own ruthlessness through her dependence on the actual sustaining support of others; through memory, fantasy, and projection—including her fantasies of utterly creating her baby and utterly destroying her baby; and through her anticipation of her baby's development toward independence, as she has developed in her own course of time. The mother also knows, from her own experience as infant and child, that she is contributing both to her own survival and to her child's growth by imposing a disillusioning process as she introduces frustration where her needs and her baby's emerging tolerance intersect. Similarly, in analysis, the analyst has already been both a baby and a patient and has previously played at being an analyst. The analyst's survival of a patient's ruthlessness reflects the analyst's continued connection with his own inner ruthlessness.[3] The analyst, then, survives as an analyst by surviving as a patient, with his memories of patienthood; his projections of patienthood; his own fantasies of primary creativity and utter destructiveness toward his patient; and his anticipation of his patient's potential for development, including a firmer tolerance for the essential disillusioning process delivered through optimal frustrations (including interpretations). This very process within the analyst, surviving as a patient, constitutes the analyst's ongoing, self-analytic use of the countertransference and the opportunity to change and grow as a person while responsibly fulfilling his role to survive as analyst.

In the developmental process, as it approximately follows this course, the infant comes to recognize that its mother has endured its ruthless usage and has survived. The infant has been able to make of mother what it needed, and yet mother has been capable of remaining herself. This recognition allows for the emergence of love for the mother, a love that is not only libidinally based but also grounded in an identification with the mother of quiet moments of care and rapport. From this juncture in the child's development, the capacity for ruthlessness is joined by a capacity for concern for the object of ruthlessness that has survived destruction. Now the child is ready to become a full partner in the give-and-take of negotiation.

---

3. Of course, this juncture is also where the analyst's or the mother's repetitions and actual destructiveness may predominate, introducing nonnegotiable elements that deform the relationship and its yield.

Ruthlessness, however, is never given up. Winnicott's theory is not one of conflict, renunciation, and compromise formation in the classical sense. His theory is of paradox, the acceptance of paradox, and the negotiation of paradox. Herein lies another step toward answering our question of how the "good-enough" mother and the analyst have been equipped by their own development to remain unfound and unannihilated even as they are there to be found and used. Winnicott (1969) described what happens after the infant has destroyed the subjectively conceived object and faced its sturdiness—if, indeed, it has survived—and passed from relating to using:

> A new feature thus arrives in the theory of object-relating. The subject says to the object: "I destroyed you," and the object is there to receive the communication. From now on the subject says: "Hullo object!" "I destroyed you." "I love you." "You have value for me because of my destruction of you." "While I am loving you I am all the time destroying you in (unconscious) *fantasy*" [p. 90].

How profound are the implications of the last sentence! For, as Winnicott went on to say, "Here fantasy begins for the individual." I suggest that Winnicott here was deftly indicating the place of a dynamic unconscious in his theory. From this perspective, we may understand the unconscious to be the private repository of our most all-out, ruthless tendencies. It constitutes the taproot of our capacity to deconstruct the external world, to destroy the object as we find it, and to re-create it to suit our subjectivity. Clearly, we cannot afford to reveal to those near and dear to us that this full-tilt, ruthless potential underlies our every interaction. Hence, the core of the self remains hidden away, while we engage in interactions that accommodate the separate nature of the Other. As we have seen, these interactions are mediated by language, including metaphor, which is both explicit and indirect, and by play in the area of overlap between two subjectivities, wherein the ruthless potential in both parties may achieve a tolerable intersection. Thus, we negotiate with others, and the yield of this negotiation will not be based on compliance, reaction formation, or subjugation to the extent that we retain access to the ruthless base of our own subjective world while exercising our capacity for concern for the other. In this model, repression may be adaptive. It allows us to engage in negotiation while keeping alive within us what Winnicott called "a backcloth of unconscious destruction." A recognition of the adaptive function of repression, from the perspective of evolutionary biology, has been introduced into psychoanalytic thinking by the work of Slavin and Kriegman (1990; Slavin, 1990). In Winnicott's theory, repression is adaptive; it is dissociation that compromises psychological health by alienating our negotiations from their ruthless and creative taproots within the true self.

The passage from object relating to object "usage" is a crucial developmental attainment. From this juncture we may carry through life the capacity to poise at the threshold between ruthlessness and ruth, to straddle the paradox of our isolation and our connectedness, to retain our spontaneity while doing maternal or psychoanalytic work. In the psychoanalytic process, the analyst serves a dual holding function. On one hand, when indicated, the analyst adapts to the needs of the patient and thereby brings to the patient the experience and the hope of a negotiable world. On the other hand, the analyst tries his best to hold on, hold fast, and hold up, seeking to survive "the patient's destructive attacks," which Winnicott (1969) understood to be "the patient's attempt to place the analyst outside the area of omnipotent control, that is, out in the world" (p. 91). The analytic frame that the analyst maintains (for example, by interpreting rather than remaining enmeshed in projective identifications) represents the staunch durability of external reality; whereas the analyst's adaptations (for example, offering some personal information requested) present to the patient a world that is negotiable. And, in the intermediate area of intersection between the subjective worlds of analyst and patient, negotiation may be playful, creative, and mutually enlivening, and it may lead to ego development.

A word about analytic neutrality is relevant here. I have always liked Loewald's (1960) description of neutrality as "a love and respect for the individual and for individual development" (p. 229). I suggest, however, that neutrality may be defined as the analyst's responsibility to maintain the area of illusion for ongoing negotiation. The frame for the therapeutic action of analysis is provided by the continuing existence of paradox that requires negotiation between both parties. The negotiation of paradox is the transaction that articulates the potential in potential space at the intersection of transference and countertransference. From this perspective, analytic abstinence, interpretation, enactment, or disclosure may, at any given moment, preserve or violate potential space between analyst and patient. Silence, empathic observation, interpretation, metaphorical construction, evocative association, squiggling, laughter, and confrontation may all serve to maintain the area of illusion and are thus to be regarded as potential analytic responses within a stance of neutrality. Even some personal information about the analyst may, in some instances, open the field of association for the patient rather than truncate it.

The gauge of the analyst's neutrality is not whether he restricts his responses to interpretation, refrains from self-disclosure, or introduces his own personal imagery into the analytic discourse. The gauge of neutrality is whether a self-disclosure is the product of a jointly developed negotiation that exists between analyst and patient, that is evoked by the patient's need for something to go on, and that is used as a "personal object" for the patient's self-articulation; neutrality is violated to the extent that self-disclosure entails some personal information "bestowed" by the analyst out of his own urgency. Or the gauge of neutrality is whether the analyst's silence is a nonnegotiable stance imposing barrenness or lack of affect between analyst and patient; whether an enactment has violated or destroyed potential space by collapsing paradox with the intrusion of the analyst's all-too-concrete substance, which is neither created nor found, but inflicted; whether an interpretation, like a squiggle, manages to evoke, clarify, or connect while preserving paradox, and does not foreclose the patient's freedom of response and personal construction, within a range of what Modell (1990) calls the "multiple levels of reality" in the transference. The criterion for an analyst's neutrality thus becomes the maximizing of the creative potential in the negotiation of paradoxes preserved in the shared area of illusion, in the overlap of the play of two subjectivities. Greenberg (1986) was pointing in a similar direction when he stated the paradox that, unless the analyst is enough of a new object, the analysis does not begin; and, unless the analyst is enough of an old object, the analysis does not end.

A Case Report

The following case report illustrates how both patient and therapist change as they find and use their points of intersection in the unfolding process of negotiation during the course of a treatment. Several years ago, a 26-year-old man—whom I will call Donald—came to me for therapy and said that he needed to learn how to conduct relationships and how to enrich his life. His manner was one of stolid and remote sobriety. He worked in a technical field and felt stunted in his career as well as in his personal life. He had virtually no friends outside of work acquaintances, except for a married couple whom he visited frequently. He stayed at their home to dog-sit, baby-sit, or tutor the wife in a technical subject. I sensed the vacancy of Donald's life when I called him at home and heard him say on his answering machine, "You have reached the home of 443-1413."

Donald presented me with a formative history of early loss, disruption, parental unreliability, and relative poverty in inner-city Chicago. His father died before he was two. His mother, living next door to her own capricious mother, related to Donald on the basis of her own whims and needs in an invasive and controlling way. She did not permit him vigorous physical activity; bike riding was banned because of her inordinate worry about his congenital orthopedic problem. Donald retreated into science fiction. There was no family member with whom Donald could share his precocious intellectual interests. Donald did enjoy one stable and reliable relationship with his maternal grandfather, a modest man who worked double shifts but, nevertheless, maintained a benign and consistent interest in Donald when he was at home. This grandfather's dying and death toward the end of Donald's college years delivered a serious blow. Donald had engaged in his first sexual relationship during the weeks his grandfather was dying. This relationship ended abruptly with Donald's sense that the young woman had betrayed him and that he had betrayed his grandfather and his Catholic upbringing by dalliance with her. Since that time, he had not been open to another relationship.

We had our work cut out for us. Perhaps the first negotiation I faced with Donald was the question of whether or not we could undertake it together. I felt daunted by the challenge of working with him toward significant structural change, given the degree of his schizoid withdrawal. I noted how thoroughly he avoided eye contact and how, while speaking in his affectless manner, he held one arm extended over the back of the couch and drummed in an amazing, complex digital pattern. He seemed dissociated from me, from affect, and from his own fingers as they discharged energy in rapid precision tapping. I noticed another aspect of Donald that bore heavily on my choice of working with him: his body odor. I could not tolerate his smell, although, during our first weeks of meeting, I tried. The odor lingered in my office for a few more patient hours after he left. I questioned whether I could work with Donald under the distancing influence of my struggle to defend against his smell. So, with my heart in my mouth, I raised the issue with him. This issue forced on us a difficult and significant negotiation that would haunt the treatment to follow, as well as provide us with a central metaphor to which we could return in our explorations. When I asked Donald whether he used deodorant, he said he had never used one nor had he noticed his smell. No one had ever taught him about the use of deodorant. When he came to our next session, he had bathed carefully and had used a deodorant. He quite openly began by asking, "Is this OK?" Yes, the deodorant had worked. Donald adopted the use of deodorant, although sometimes he forgot, and in his rush to get to my office on a hot summer day, his smell would return. I reminded him a few times, and Donald began to keep a deodorant stick in his car for insurance and for extra use before his sessions.

With this response of Donald's, I chose to work with him. I felt moved by his earnestness and gentlemanly decency, I respected his intelligence and determination as valuable strengths, and I cared about the poignancy of his desire to surmount his meager early provisions.

The first several months of Donald's therapy focused on his family relationships: how, at an early age, he had walled himself in from his mother's intrusiveness and capriciousness while becoming the "fixer" in his chaotic household and how he still avoided going home for Christmas to face outrageous presents he had asked his mother not to buy with money she did not have (but would recurrently solicit from him) and her seven dogs roaming, unruly and ungroomed, throughout the house. I attempted linking interpretations aimed at connecting boundary issues with his mother and his current "triangle" with the married couple he frequently visited. We also talked about Donald's missing father and how hard it is to be a self-made man who lacks a paternal legacy.

For extended periods, the affective tone between us was largely formal, emotionless, arid. Donald avoided or broke eye contact. He usually drummed on the couch in his mechanical finger patterns as he spoke. Sometimes, when my empathic response conveyed that I was moved by Donald's loneliness or low expectations, my affect-laden utterances had a visible effect on him. Donald withdrew. His eyes took on the glaze of dissociation. When I asked him what was happening, he would say, "I didn't hear your words" or "I went far away." I took this withdrawal to be a sign of Donald's intolerance for closeness or affective rapport. I thought about the hazards of a therapist's seeming to hover or crowd a schizoid patient. I adjusted myself accordingly, to give Donald room. I would not intrude more of my affect than he seemed to be able to assimilate. Rather than pursue him, I would wait nearby for signs that he was ready to approach me.

Concurrently, Donald asked me for more guidance. He requested that I recommend life activities, seminars, and so on that would augment his therapy. He asked for readings that would tell him what was wrong with him and how therapy would help. He wondered aloud if he should see another therapist, because we were not producing changes. He felt stuck.

I felt fluctuations of hope and pessimism and never settled into one or the other. Sometimes I would feel in conflict over my own optimism and accuse myself of projecting my own wishes for Donald—a false hope in the face of so much history of hurtful commission and omission. I refused to recommend readings. I feared that Donald would find in descriptions of the schizoid personality the pessimism of so many authors about treatment prospects. Since Donald often took things categorically, I worried that he would make extreme inferences from flat-out statements about prognosis. I also generally do not recommend readings in therapy. With Donald, I understood him to be asking for a kind of tutorial alternative to the treatment process. I was also resisting my own developing countertransference wish to take Donald in hand as a sponsor and guide, a fantasy reciprocal to his longing for a father. More personally implicated in my resistance was my memory of my own first analyst, who had offered me liberal advice on living, a kind of apprenticeship in the good life, in return for my admiration of his superiority. I knew, with benefit of hindsight, how superficially gratifying and relieving this analyst's guidance had been, and what a subversion and abandonment of true, structuralizing analytic work. Thus, I balked at the temptation to "educate" Donald in living and hoped for greater gain by preserving the intermediate area of therapeutic process.

Donald and I continued along in low gear until, unwittingly, we crossed a threshold in our relationship by a pivotal negotiation just prior to my second July vacation break. In the third week of June, Donald announced that he was uncertain whether he could make our final pre-vacation Friday appointment owing to a tentatively scheduled business trip. I asked him what flexibility he had in scheduling this trip. He explained that he was participating in a conference that involved several people and he did not see how he could initiate a request that might inconvenience several others. For my part, I was aware that our separations had their impact on Donald. He had told me after my first July vacation that he had felt abandoned and despairing. Knowing that the predictable structure of our relationship served an important framing function, I offered him the option of a back-up session on Saturday if he should, in fact, be out of town on Friday. I told Donald that, although Saturday was indeed July 1 and, in a formal sense, within the boundary of my vacation, I would still be in town and that I would rather see him on Saturday than leave us both uncertain whether or not we would have the opportunity to say good-bye.

In return, I asked if he might undertake to determine whether he had more say than he assumed over his part in the scheduling of the business conference. Donald came to his next session pleased and excited. He had spoken up at work and arranged to give his presentation on Wednesday and leave the conference on Thursday. We could keep our regular time on Friday. He was pleased to have taken this more active stance for himself and relieved not to impose on me and feel beholden to me for a July 1 meeting. Nevertheless, he reported having felt astonished that I had offered him the Saturday time during my vacation. He said he never before had experienced any arrangement in his world that accommodated to his needs or took his wants into account. I was saddened and moved by his feeling my gesture to be a kind of positive trauma, a jolting interruption of his assumptions about a nonnegotiable universe. My offer of the Saturday back-up appointment was not a self-conscious or calculated choice to bestow on Donald a "corrective emotional experience." Rather, it was a direct negotiation necessitated by our time constraints that happened to strike him with metaphorical significance.

While this moment between us felt potentially pivotal, it clearly did not pass a noticeable magic wand over our work. On my return from vacation, Donald continued to flounder in his efforts to find a way to feel that he was using our relationship. He expressed frustration over not knowing what to say, not knowing how therapy works. Once again, he asked me for readings. I asked him why he wanted to study the schematics before entering the process. Soon thereafter he became involved with a woman who seemed, from his descriptions, to have a very limited capacity for intimacy. Donald eventually broke up with her. He felt disappointed and, I think, somewhat embittered, as if to say, "So much for relationship."

Meanwhile, in my office, Donald and I oscillated between contactful and distanced moments. Donald continued to avert his gaze, and I reacted by reminding myself that I had to make an extra effort not to withdraw even while I so often felt deprived of engagement and affective rapport. At moments I resented his complex digital finger drumming. I felt like shouting, "Stop drumming and look at me when you speak!" I did not say this. I chose tact. At times I withdrew into my own reciprocal detachment. Donald initiated a new ritual. At the end of our meeting, as he walked to the door, he turned and looked back at me, and, as we held a moment's eye contact, he nodded. I found myself nodding reciprocally. Once begun, this ritual became our invariant pattern of leave-taking at the end of each session. I would wait for Donald to reach the doorway, he would turn, our eyes would meet and hold contact, and, usually with a smile and a nod, he would be out the door.

While this pattern of last-minute engagement took hold between us, Donald continued in our sessions to talk about his current life and his family history, with few moments of sustained contact between us. At one point, he informed me that he had discovered, on his own, Miller's (1981) *Prisoners of Childhood* and had found her book to be a revelation: here was a therapist who appeared to be a "sympathetic character." He asked me again to recommend further readings. I declined. Soon after, he reported that, since I would not recommend readings to instruct him in the use of psychotherapy, he had gone to the public library and begun to make his way alphabetically through the shelves on psychotherapy and psychoanalysis. He had read Arlow and Brenner, and his despair only increased. His reading confirmed his worst fears; he was expected somehow, on his own, to find the right things to say that would unlock my insightfulness so that I would finally grant him my interpretations. Meanwhile, I was expected to remain uninvolved, leaving him to work out for himself how to say the magic words that would yield my explanations and solutions to his life.

Hearing him, I relented on the issue of readings. I offered him some articles by Kohut and Tolpin on the development of the self through a psychoanalytic "dialogue." I lent him my copies to photocopy. I recommended that, at the library, he skip ahead and read some Winnicott. Donald[4] reported to me that his reading of Tolpin, Kohut, and Winnicott began to restore the hope he had first found in reading Miller. I am sure that my recommending and lending these readings contributed to that new hope. In his reading of these authors, Donald found people who seemed to understand him and his needs. Perhaps there were such people in this world. Perhaps he could find some similar experience with me. He began to see the potential for resuming the development of the self in a therapeutic interaction, even in the wake of massive, early childhood environmental failure. Months later, he explained to me that he had created out of Kohut, Miller, and Winnicott a transitional object that represented a benevolent and caring therapist. In his frustration over the limits of our closeness, he took steps toward me through this bridging metaphor of a therapeutic relationship. But would we truly follow this direction? From Donald's perspective, it was hard to see evidence that we had yet.

I returned from my next July vacation to face a new threshold in our therapy. Donald was angry and challenging (although he denied anger and said he was "upset"). He required to know whether I cared about him. Was my interest real? Was I merely practicing my technique with him? Is his participation real, or was he only mastering techniques of being with people? Was our relationship real?

---

4. As I write this narrative, a realization flashes on me. Why had I, over the past two days of sifting through my notes and synthesizing this clinical material, chosen for my patient the pseudonym of Donald? When I had thought of it, it had felt just right. But my only referents were Donald Trump, Donald Duck, and my next-door neighbor. Did I really want to use a name with those associations? Why does this name feel right? Now, in the text before my eyes, I see "Winnicott. Donald." The connection emerges out of repression. In writing this paper, I had created my own internal transitional object and metaphor. Neither Winnicott nor my patient nor myself alone, this narrative is my own negotiated amalgam.

In the first of these postvacation sessions in which Donald issued his ultimatum to our therapy, he embodied his challenge in what I felt was a particular way of conveying the paradoxes of our experience together. He delivered a metaphor between us. That is, while I sat and faced his anger and his disappointment and clearly heard his direct statement of his need to know from me that I cared, I felt myself unable to summon a caring feeling from within. Instead, I was recoiling. On this hot August day, he smelled again, and I felt put off. What could I offer at this moment? An insincere bromide? A refusal of his direct request for a sign of closeness? I chose to address explicitly the paradox before us and to ask if we could consider together its import. I told him that on a day in which he urgently asks for my caring response, he comes to me with his body odor unmodified. Yes, he says. He has just recently stopped using deodorant. I ask whether he connects the two. No, he does not. I venture for him to consider whether conflict and anger are expressed in his asking for closeness just when he discontinues his use of deodorant. Are you enacting your dread of the very closeness you so urgently request? Are you angrily saying, Show me a sign that you will struggle some on my behalf; care for me without my making it easy? None of these conjectures rang a bell for Donald, but he did immediately resume his use of deodorant.

In the months that ensued, our sessions were devoted repeatedly to shared reflections on our past years together. Donald often would begin a session with yet another question or protest about how our work had developed. At one point he told me he had never believed I understood what his life was like. He experienced too much disparity between us. He did not feel like a match for me. After all, he had no background of his own to bring to his part in a relationship. He had nothing to go on. He felt shame and did not expect that we could meet on common ground. He assumed it was up to him to do something different to make it better, but all he knew to do was to tell me more life history. He also had to worry about distancing me with his smell and probably in other ways as well. I reminded Donald that, in our early days, when I responded to his life story with affective warmth, he had signaled me that he went far away within himself where he could not hear me. He replied that, since he had felt that he could not match me, he had not known how to respond. He added, "I didn't mean stay away, but, help me." I replied, "Then my tact was not what you most needed." He returned, "And yet, there's a point there. I had nothing. And I couldn't take things in either. And there was nothing you could do."

Donald soon reported to me that he now began to hear me say some of the supportive and affirmative things about him and his work with me that he had missed all along. He also informed me that he could begin now to use my interpretations because he was becoming able to hear them as something other than a criticism. Soon thereafter, Donald said that he did not much need our ritual good-bye at the door anymore. He voiced his recognition of our unspoken ritual and said that he now saw it as a way to deal with his question of whether I held him in mind between sessions. He had been testing whether my connection with him lasted even up to the threshold of my office door or whether he would find a sign that I had already turned away from him. He also said that he would not like it if I ever tolerated his smell and hid from him that I did not feel good about being with him.

I came to recognize an unconscious, unacknowledged negotiation that had been transpiring between us over time, an essential paradox, perpetually unresolvable, which had contributed to the shaping of potential space between us. Donald was profoundly in need of a father. He needed to grieve the loss of his father and the loss of what Bollas (1989) would call a potential "future" that his father's living presence might have enabled him to elaborate for himself. I could not be his father, both because this role would be untrue and because Donald's grief had to be allowed without denial. Yet, in a way that was also utterly true, we both had to wait until Donald became, over time, like a son to whom, in my own countertransference, I could feel like a father. I could not recognize this paradox before I had overcome my own resistance to giving Donald the readings he requested. Several times Donald has said to me, "I will never receive the guidance I always wanted" or "I can't have the parenting I missed." Or, more within the idiom of transference, he would say, "I wish you could have told me what to say first. Couldn't you have spelled out what this process would be? I wish you had guided me and told me what to do." At one point, Donald said, "I know I need a father. And I look to you to replace him. And you can't." I responded with, "No. I can't. We both know I can't. And yet, we both know you have to find something here to go on."

With this paradox actively on my mind, I thought of my work with Donald as potentially a good treatment to use for clinical illustration in this chapter. I asked his permission, which he readily gave. He was pleased to think that his therapy might benefit others.

Soon afterward, Donald reported a dream (there had been just a few reported dreams thus far in his therapy). In his dream, he was with me in my office. We had a detailed conversation, which he does not remember. The central element of this dream is the feeling that we were connected and informal with each other—just the feeling he had wanted with me all along. He woke up feeling very good.

One therapeutic agenda that Donald now announced was his need to address his growing sense of anger toward his mother. He said he would have to bring either his anger or his mother into my office. He was mortified at the thought of being anything like her. He then recalled how he had been kept in his crib until he was five or six and how he would jump in the crib to break through the bottom. He recalled throwing his orthopedic device down the stairs, to be rid of it (his stepfather had whipped him and put him back in his crib). He remembered hitting his mother once and upsetting her more than once during his adolescence by telling her sadistically that she had never been a good mother. When I noted to him that he could reach her only in this sadomasochistic way, he said, "That's why I knew I had to move out as soon as I could. I was afraid of that. I was bigger than she." I suggested that he understandably needed to be able to protest in some form.

Interspersed with this material was Donald's redoubled protest toward me. Why had I so rigidly refused at first to recommend readings? Why had I not spoken more words of affirmation and encouragement? If I had doubted the prospects of a successful treatment, why did I not have the integrity to refer him on to someone else? Further, Donald protested, "Why didn't you understand the time I stopped using deodorant again? You called it anger. It was despair. I had tried everything here I knew how to try. I was about to give up. So I gave up on myself." I acknowledged here the convincing sense of Donald's own interpretation. I also felt rebuked and put to the test. In the face of Donald's disappointment and anger, I was on tenterhooks and expected him to quit this therapy abruptly. I responded to what questions I could and wondered if we would survive. I am reminded here of what Winnicott (1956) wrote. While the therapist's adaptations to the patient allow the patient to relax the "caretaker self" and permit a regression to dependence, the therapist's failures of adaptation offer occasion for the patient's protest. As I see it, protest, like the "antisocial gesture," is a sign both of anger and of hope—the hope for a negotiable environment that will heed the protest as a signal of distress. Protest in the transference is the patient's act in the present to renegotiate relational failures of the past that occurred prior to the ability to protest. The current protest is, to paraphrase Russell, both now and then. Paradoxically, the safety of therapy permits the risk of protesting the failures of the therapist. Donald asked me why he had to suffer so long in this therapy the feelings of disconnection, disappointment, abandonment, and helplessness. Why could I not help him avoid all this suffering by a more structured and instructional agenda? My understanding of this quandary, as I conveyed to him, was that our crucial work was to find our way out of this feeling together, which required that first we find ourselves in the feeling.

Donald expressed an interest in the subject of this chapter. I told him that, of course, he would have the opportunity to read it. I added that it was about negotiation in analysis and the Winnicottian paradoxes of ruthlessness and concern, isolation and connectedness. Donald responded that he had trouble with Winnicott's concept of ruthlessness. He said that if this perspective were applied to himself, he was afraid of developing an attitude of "What's in it for me?" He feared an internal pendulum swing by which he would become lazy and self-interested and abandon the one set of values he had ever internalized and embraced: the religious catechism teaching him to be good, sacrifice for others, put himself last, and "serve." He panicked that he might forget who he was and lose hold of the meaning of life. I explored this anxiety, which he was able to associate not only with his Catholic education but also with his fear of dying young as his father had ("You might die any day and face Judgment") and his fear of destructive impulses toward his mother. I asked Donald if he worried that my perspective might be a corrupting influence on him. He said that he did not regard my ideas or me as unsound, just unsuited to him. For him, "selfishness" and "self-assertiveness" were indigestible notions. He just did not understand how a child could or should be encouraged to be ruthless.

In that session, perhaps moved, in part, by a concern that I had imposed on Donald some half-developed theoretical ideas that seemed to him all-too Mephistophelian, I told him an anecdote about my own childhood. At age five or six, in the late 1940s, I had one major toy, a red tricycle. These tricycles were still hard to come by in the gradual postwar conversion to consumer goods. One summer evening, while my parents, my red tricycle, and I were waiting for the elevator, an elderly lady joined us. As we entered the elevator, she admired my tricycle and said she had been unable to find one to buy for her grandchild. So I handed over mine, on the spot. The elevator stopped at the fourth floor, she got out with my red tricycle, the door shut, and my tricycle was gone. My parents had stood by, stunned, and permitted the incident to happen. I told Donald that now, as a parent, I would say to the elderly woman, "That's a child. Why are you taking the tricycle?" I would have a long talk with my child about what is too little and what is too much to give. And, if I were that elderly lady's therapist, I certainly would not counsel her to develop her ruthless side.

Donald thanked me for telling him this story; he said it helped. At the next session, he said he had been angry at the old woman for taking advantage of my childish generosity. He then told me a story of his own. He had a friend when he was seven or eight and liked to visit that boy's home and play with his friend's GI Joes. He gave his friend his extra Erector set box to store the toy soldiers. Donald's mother discovered what he had done, became angry, and made him take back his box. He then secretly defied his mother and again gave his friend the box. Apparently, my story had evoked in Donald the lost memory of a childhood time when he had actively participated in a friendship. While it was understood that Donald and I could not be friends and he had protested our lack of common ground, he now met my story with one of his own. After telling me his story, Donald expressed some anxiety about violating my privacy by knowing something about me. After all, I had said earlier in his treatment that I would not talk about myself, although he had repeatedly indicated his need for a more personal sense of me. I inquired further about Donald's anxiety. Did he feel I had violated the boundaries of therapy with my story? Was I, like his mother, losing control and abandoning a position of responsibility? No. What Donald realized was that he had just gotten what he wanted, and getting what he wanted made him anxious. He wondered about his own manipulativeness. I asked him, "Are you afraid you've somehow manipulated me into handing over to you a red tricycle in the form of a story?" Yes, this possibility did make him anxious. He feared his own capacity for "aggressive manipulation" to get what he wanted. He was afraid to take responsibility for wanting, for self-interest. He was supposed to be the one who could give away and do without.

I was then able to link this pattern to his posture early in therapy of waiting in retreat for me, with my presumed omniscience, to intuit and provide what he needed to get going. I told him, "As we've said before, partly you didn't believe or trust what I gave was really meant if you had to ask. But, partly, we can understand now that you kept yourself passive out of fear of actively asserting yourself to get what you want." Following this interpretation came several sessions in which Donald expressed sadness—more an affect of discouragement, which he said was not despair now—that all his choices in life had been arbitrary and reactive; that he had never been guided by desire; that he had never developed a sense of his own needs; that he felt close to grieving now the absence of family conditions in which he could have found his "internal desires." He said he felt left with a handicap, that the best he could do was to fit in with others when he chose; but that he had no negotiating position of his own based on his internal standards.

In the months that followed, Donald took the first steps in years to overcome his sense of being stalled in his career. He began a job search and ultimately negotiated an improved position within his own company. He reported feeling that "categorical change" had occurred within him. He was feeling consistently "plugged in." He called it "structural change." I also saw structural change in Donald. For example, his defense against his anger and aggression was now not so much dissociation, passivity, and schizoid withdrawal. Recently he has shown evidence of higher order defenses, such as displacement. Reading Bollas's new book, which I had recommended (and which he admired), he said, "I read Bollas saying it's difficult to treat schizoid patients, and I think, 'You asshole. Try harder.'" Instantly, Donald recognized his displacement and with pride affirmed that he had noted it as quickly as I had.

Donald has taken a more active part in shaping our relationship. If I am late, he firmly asks, "Why were you late?" If my attention drifts, sometimes he says, "Where did you go?" And Donald has begun again to date. He reports that, rather than being overwhelmed by shyness and anxiety, he can now remain present and explore with a woman what they have in common and what they feel for each other. He affirms with pride that he can now "negotiate a relationship." He notes his ability even to break up, kindly yet firmly and straightforwardly, with a woman who was falling for him, because he felt too little potential for intimacy to develop between them. In treatment, when he tells me that what he needs now as the unfinished work of his therapy is a greater feeling of intimacy between us, he is not drumming his digital finger patterns; he is looking me in the eye and pointing his finger straight at me. We share humor; I can tell him, "I'm glad I finally recommended readings; when would you have ever gotten to the Ws?"

Donald still continues to question why his therapy with me took the path it has and the time and the pain. He wishes he had been able to push at me—"nail you to the wall"—during the long stretch when I frustrated his needs and he remained unable to convey himself to me. He quotes me to myself from our early sessions, and I feel appalled. Could I really have said that? We continue to wonder. We have considered how, in my reluctance to evoke the transference risks of being too much like his invasive mother and perhaps drive him away, I had exposed us to the transference risks of my being too much like his dead father, too absent for Donald, and thus had driven him into despair. Even so, my presence, perhaps evocative of his grandfather, was allowing for the experience of continuity, safety, essential protest, and metaphorical realization. Now Donald begins to wonder where his own love has lain hidden. He wants to feel that he can vitalize a relationship and not just weigh it down.

Donald says he is beginning to see what we were doing together. "The trouble is," he says, "I never had anyone in my past whom I could trust and depend on and who would be reliable and responsive and still be themselves. I had plenty of people in my family being themselves, but that's why I couldn't rely on them. I had you being responsive, but I didn't think you were being yourself. I needed something in the middle."

Something in the middle. Donald brings our attention back to that middle area of experience between analyst and patient, between the subjective and the external, between the repetition and the renegotiation—the Winnicottian area of illusion where two people may intersect and negotiate the paradoxical reality of the analytic process.

In summary, the product of a negotiation in the analytic process may be an agreement about fees, an arrangement about scheduling, or an adjustment about such delicate matters as the use of deodorant. These issues are important in themselves; they permit the relationship to continue. At another level, the product of an analytic negotiation may be the resolution of a conflict, a shift in the patient's representational world, or a mutually sensible narrative construction. At the level of transference–countertransference, the product of a negotiation may be a jointly accepted understanding of a patient's repetition or an analyst's failure. But the crucial function of negotiation in psychoanalysis is that it constitutes the intersubjective process that delivers the therapeutic action. While engaged in the process of analytic negotiation, the patient experiences his participation in a kind of duet. He uses his voice to render the imperatives and the potentials in his own subjective world and hears the analyst's voice offering other-than-me substance that, in moments of grace, he may find and use to effect transformations in the core of the self. The structure-building potential of this process lies in the extension, articulation, and elaboration of the patient's internal capacity to remain competently, genuinely, and creatively engaged in ongoing negotiations. Negotiation is never complete; it is a living process. In a "good-enough" analysis, we prepare ourselves for playing in life's duets by discovering our own musicality.

Afterword

I feel considerable affection for this paper and am grateful for the epigenesis of ideas it launched. Since I wrote it eight years ago, I have completed a book, *Building Bridges: The Negotiation of Paradox in Psychoanalysis* (1998), in which this article now stands as chapter 1. When I revisit this paper, I face the paradox that it is now both inside me and outside me; it is both me *then* and me *now*, and I feel the simultaneous identification and discontinuity that attends any revisiting. Like any text, written or dreamed, it is both a fixed entity and a prompter of emergent, and divergent, associations. I see that it contains implicitly the book that needed to be unpacked from within it.

During the eight years of developing the ideas in "The Negotiation of Paradox," I have been influenced by exposure to the parallel and convergent arrival of contributions from several psychoanalytic thinkers whom I consider colleagues, friends, and kindred spirits. Lewis Aron, Jessica Benjamin, Philip Bromberg, Jody Messler Davies, Adrienne Harris, Barbara Pizer, and the late Paul Russell are prominent among them, and I particularly note the ongoing enlivenment and guidance of Stephen Mitchell's thinking. Reactions to my article in print have been valuable challenges to me to clarify what I mean by what I say in this paper and have given me the opportunity to reflect on the limitations or implications in what, or how, I communicate here. If I were to change this essay now, Winnicott (whose voice and sensibility I still love) would be a less singular conceptual font from which my thinking flows. (Actually, this paper grew out of my teaching of Winnicott's work and a panel presentation honoring his contributions.) Now, with my ground water fed by a greater multiplicity of sources, one effect would be a somewhat lessened tone of idealization of the possibilities (or necessity) for perfect maternal, or analytic, adaptation to the needs of the dependent other as a pre-stage of negotiation. I would, thus, further emphasize how the intersubjective/relational process of negotiation is always conducted at the raw edge of the nonnegotiable, reflecting the imperatives, the passions, and the limitations of each member of the duet. And, as I develop in my book, I would elaborate how the loving, integrative, and constructive tendencies that sponsor negotiation continually encounter ruthless and destructive promptings, along with a multiplicity of contradictory self-states (in both parent and child, analyst and patient) that complicate the nature of any process in which there is a bridging of "selves." I would articulate how the tolerance of paradox represents a developmental achievement that allows analyst and patient to straddle paradoxical states of despair and hope, absence and presence, repetition and change, in relationship. And I would further clarify how the negotiation of paradox differs from the negotiation of conflict.

Finally, some follow-up about Donald: In the spring of 1991, I shared this paper with Donald for his consideration and approval before publication. He loved it; and we enjoyed together the irony that, having initially refused to recommend readings for Donald, I was now *writing* for Donald and about *us*. Very soon thereafter (within three months), however, Donald announced that he wanted to end his therapy. I thought, *What* have I *done!?* Had I foreclosed Donald's therapy by handing him this paper? Donald told me he knew I would worry about the timing and abruptness of his leaving; he even declared that, while the "books" might not, in theory, endorse his choice, it simply *felt* right to him. Having seen the film *Cinema Paradiso* (about a dozen times) and identified with the relationship between the youth and the projectionist, Donald felt ripe to pursue some wider experience that might then serve as a basis for his further therapeutic explorations. He told me he felt as if he were "leaving home" for the first time.

A year later, Donald contacted me. Now involved in a relationship with a woman, he asked to consult me about it. The therapy that followed led to Donald's decision to undertake a five-time-a-week analysis that lasted four more years. During his analysis, Donald revisited his grief for his father and his frustration that I could not *be* his father. In a deeper way, Donald and I negotiated the paradox that, as his analyst, I *was* what I *was not* for him. That is, my presence represented an absence that he could, finally, address in an analytic potential space. Through enactment, recollection, dream, and metaphor, Donald constructed a way of feeling both alone and companioned (Pizer, 1996).

As Donald's analysis neared its end, he had advanced in his career, pursued intimate relationships, bought a home, and taken up the hobbies of building furniture and reading Eastern philosophy. As we approached termination (see Pizer, 1998), Donald made a statement that, for me, remarkably rendered the therapeutic action of his analysis. Donald said, "I thought I'd come here to fix my life. The only way I could think was in a kind of linear, logical, problem-solving way. Now, it's like my mind works differently, at least sometimes. Now my mind is more like the scent of a spring day."

References

Adler, G, (1989), Transitional phenomena, projective identification, and the essential ambiguity of the psychoanalytic situation. *Psychoanal. Quart.*, 58:81–104.

Beebe , B. & Lachmann, F. (1992), The contribution of mother-infant mutual influence to the origin of self- and object representations. In N. J. Skolnick & S. C. Warshaw (eds.), *Relational Perspectives in Psychoanalysis*. Hillsdale, NJ: The Analytic Press, pp. 83–117.

Bollas, C. (1989). *Forces of Destiny*. London: Free Association Books.

Bromberg, P. M. (1995), Resistance, object-usage, and human relatedness. *Contemp. Psychoanal.*, 31:173–191.

Goldberg, A. (1987), Psychoanalysis and negotiation. *Psychoanal. Quart.*, 56:109–129

Greenberg, J. (1986), Theoretical models and the analyst's neutrality. *Contemp. Psychoanal.*, 22:87–106

Loewald, H. (1960), On the therapeutic action of psychoanalysis. In: *Papers on Psychoanalysis*. New Haven, CT: Yale University Press, 1980, pp. 221–256.

Miller, A. (1981), *Prisoners of Childhood*. New York: Basic Books.

Mitchell, S. (1993), *Hope and Dread in Psychoanalysis*. New York: Basic Books

Modell, A. (1990), *Other Times, Other Realities*. Cambridge, MA: Harvard University Press

Phillips, A. (1988), *Winnicott*. Cambridge, MA: Harvard University Press.

Pizer, S. (1996), Negotiating potential space: Illusion, play, metaphor, and the Subjunctive. *Psychoanal. Dial.*, 6:689–712.

––––––– (1998), *Building Bridges: The Negotiation of Paradox in Psychoanalysis*. Hillsdale, NJ: The Analytic Press.

Racker, H. (1968), *Transference and Counter-transference*. New York: International Universities Press.

Russell, P. (unpublished), Crises of emotional growth (a.k.a. the theory of the crunch).

Sandler, J. (1976), Countertransference and role-responsiveness. *Internat. Rev. Psycho-Anal.* , 3:43-47.

Slavin, M. (1990), The dual meaning of repression and the adaptive design of the human psyche. *J. Amer.Acad. Psychoanal.*, 18:307–341.

––––––– & Kriegman, D. (1990), Toward a new paradigm for psychoanalysis: An evolutionary biological perspective on the classical-relational dichotomy. *Psychoanal. Psychol.*, 7 (suppl.):5–31.

––––––– & ––––––– (1992), *The Adaptive Design of the Human Psyche*. New York: Guilford.

Stern, D. (1985), *The Interpersonal World of the Infant*. New York: Basic Books.

Vygotsky, L. (1962), *Thought and Language*, ed. & trans. E. Hanfmann & G. Vakar. Cambridge, MA:MIT Press.

Winnicott, D. W. (1951), Transitional objects and transitional phenomena. In: *Playing and Reality*. New York: Basic Books, 1971, pp. 1–25.

––––––– (1956), On transference. *Internat. J. Psycho-Anal.*, 37:386–388.

––––––– (1958), The capacity to be alone. In: *The Maturational Processes and the Facilitating Environment*. New York: International Universities Press, 1965, pp. 29-36.

——— (1962a), Providing for the child in health and crisis. In: *The Maturational Processes and the Facilitating Environment*. New York: International Universities Press, 1965, pp. 64–72.

——— (1963), From dependence towards independence in the development of the individual. In: *Maturational Processes and the Facilitating Environment*. New York: International Universities Press, 1965, pp. 83–92.

——— (1968), Communication between infant and mother, and mother and infant, compared and contrasted. In: *Babies and Their Mothers*. Reading, MA: Addison-Wesley, 1987, pp.89–103.

——— (1969), The use of an object and relating through identifications. In: *Playing and Reality*. New York: Basic Books, 1971, pp. 86–94.

——— (1971a), Playing: A theoretical statement. In: *Playing and Reality*. New York: Basic Books, pp.38–52.

——— (1971b), *Therapeutic Consultationas in Child Psychiatry*. New York: Basic Books.

Three Realms of the Unconscious

(1992)

Robert D. Stolorow
George E. Atwood

▼　　▼　　▼　　▼　　▼

Editors' Introduction

Robert Stolorow and George Atwood are among the leading pioneers of the intersubjective approach. It was they and their collaborators in the 1970s who introduced the term intersubjectivity into the vocabulary of the psychoanalytic community in this country. These authors have long argued for a paradigm shift in the field toward a dyadic systems perspective and have been most articulate and persuasive in their radical critique of "the myth of the isolated mind." By highlighting the mutuality of regulation in intersubjective systems, "An intersubjective field is a system of *reciprocal mutual influence,*" Stolorow and Atwood differentiated themselves from classical and even from the contemporary self psychology with which they had been loosely associated.

Stolorow and Atwood have been prolific contributors to the field. Our choice of this paper, "Three Realms of the Unconscious," for this anthology is based on our recognition that critics have suggested that relational approaches to psychoanalysis neglect the unconscious. In this chapter, not only do Stolorow and Atwood persuasively argue that the unconscious is at the heart of the psychoanalytic enterprise, but they clearly articulate and elegantly illustrate three distinct realms of the unconscious: the prereflective unconscious, the dynamic unconscious, and the unvalidated unconscious. With this systematization of unconscious structure and experience, Stolorow and Atwood expand psychoanalytic theory by including traditional conceptualizations of repression as well as the more recently emerging examination of dissociation. They demonstrate not only that the boundaries of the mind are determined by its "internal structure" but also that mind itself is inherently relational and therefore the parameters of defense and repression are highly contextual. Furthermore, in making these differentiations in the realms of the unconscious, the authors clarify the important differences between conceptualizations of psychic structure and psychic content.

In this chapter, the reader will encounter certain notions that have become highly influential within relational circles. In addition to the conceptual shift from the isolated mind to the intersubjective, a second transformation is from the study of instinctual drive derivatives to exploring affect states. Perhaps most important is the idea of "organizing principles," those unconscious structures that shape and thematize a person's experience. From an intersubjective perspective, psychoanalysis is fundamentally the investigation and articulation of these organizing principles through the examination of the ways in which they pattern the analytic relationship according to developmentally preformed meanings and themes. Stolorow and Atwood remind the reader, however, that the analyst's own subjectivity, that is, the analyst's own organizing principles, codetermine the unfolding of the analytic relationship.

Stolorow and Atwood have been particularly convincing in making the link between objectivist epistemology and the myth of the isolated mind. While some theorists have suggested that these are two separate and independent dimensions of psychoanalytic theory, Stolorow and Atwood see them as tied together. The intersubjective viewpoint, with its emphasis on "the constitutive interplay between worlds of experience leads inevitably to an epistemological stance that is best characterized as perspectivalist." It is precisely in bringing together the systemic focus on the intersubjective context and the epistemological critique of objectivism that intersubjectivity theory has been so influential for the emerging relational tradition.

The project of recontextualizing the concept of the unconscious in intersubjective/relational terms was evident in *Faces in a Cloud: Subjectivity in Personality Theory* (Stolorow and Atwood, 1979, Aronson). They present psychobiographical depictions of the lives and theories of Freud, Jung, Reich, and Rank to illustrate the ways in which the conscious and unconscious dimensions of the subjective world of the theorist are inevitably translated into metapsychological conceptualizations. In *Contexts of Being: The Intersubjective Foundations of Psychological Life* (1992, The Analytic Press), which includes the current essay, Stolorow and Atwood expose what they call the "myth of the isolated mind" in traditional psychoanalytic theory, presenting new understandings of the unconscious, fantasy, mind-body relations, trauma, therapeutic alliances and treatment impasses. In the recent *Working Intersubjectively: Contextualism in Psychoanalytic Practice*, (1997, The Analytic Press), Orange, Atwood and Stolorow present the latest phase of their evolving intersubjective approach in terms of the methodology of contextualism.

Three Realms of the Unconscious*

▼   ▼   ▼   ▼   ▼

In this chapter we extend our intersubjective framework to a reconsideration of a cornerstone of all psychoanalytic thought—the concept of unconscious mental processes.

In an earlier attempt to reconceptualize the unconscious, we (Atwood and Stolorow, 1984) distinguished two forms of unconsciousness that are important for psychoanalysis—the prereflective unconscious and the more familiar dynamic unconscious. Both differ from Freud's (1900, 1915) "preconscious" in that they can be made conscious only with great effort. The term prereflective unconscious refers to the shaping of experience by organizing principles that operate outside a person's conscious awareness:

> The organizing principles of a person's subjective world, whether operating positively (giving rise to certain configurations in awareness) or negatively (preventing certain configurations from arising), are themselves unconscious. A person's experiences are shaped by his psychological structures without this shaping becoming the focus of awareness and reflection. We have therefore characterized the structure of a subjective world as *prereflectively unconscious*. This form of unconsciousness is not the product of defensive activity, even though great effort is required to overcome it. In fact, the defenses themselves, when operating outside a person's awareness, can be seen as merely a special instance of structuring activity that is prereflectively unconscious [Atwood and Stolorow, 1984, p. 36].

---

* Originally published in *Contexts of Being: The Intersubjective Foundations of Psychological Life* © 1992 The Analytic Press, Inc.

In our view of psychological development, we pictured these prereflective structures of experience as crystalizing within the evolving interplay between the subjective worlds of child and caregivers. Prime examples are those organizing principles, traditionally covered by the term *superego*, that derive from the child's perceptions of what is required of him to maintain ties that are vital to his well-being.

In reconsidering the dynamic unconscious, we first attempted to formulate its essence in experience-near terms, stripped of metapsychological encumbrances:

> [R]epression is understood as a process whereby particular configurations of self and object are prevented from crystalizing in awareness. . . .
> The "dynamic unconscious," from this point of view, consists in that set of configurations that consciousness is not permitted to assume, because of their association with emotional conflict and subjective danger. Particular memories, fantasies, feelings, and other experiential contents are repressed because they threaten to actualize these configurations [Atwood and Stolorow, 1984, p. 35].

Later we (Stolorow et al., 1987) proposed that the psychological phenomena traditionally encompassed by the concept of the dynamic unconscious derive specifically from the realm of intersubjective transaction that Stern (1985) refers to as "interaffectivity"—the mutual regulation of affective experience within the developmental system. We wrote:

> The specific intersubjective contexts in which conflict takes form are those in which central affect states of the child cannot be integrated because they fail to evoke the requisite attuned responsiveness from the caregiving surround. Such unintegrated affect states become the source of lifelong inner conflict, because they are experienced as threats both to the person's established psychological organization and to the maintenance of vitally needed ties. Thus affect-dissociating defensive operations are called into play, which reappear in the analytic situation in the form of resistance. . . . It is in the defensive walling off of central affect states, rooted in early derailments of affect integration, that the origins of what has traditionally been called the "dynamic unconscious" can be found [pp. 91–92].

From this perspective, the dynamic unconscious is seen to consist not of repressed instinctual drive derivatives, but of affect states that have been defensively walled off because they failed to evoke attuned responsiveness from the early surround. This defensive sequestering of central affective states, which attempts to protect against retraumatization, is the principal source of resistance in psychoanalytic treatment, and also of the necessity for disguise when such states are represented in dreams (Stolorow, 1989).

The shift from drives to affectivity as forming the basis for the dynamic unconscious is not merely a change in terminology. As we discussed in chapter 1, the regulation of affective experience is a property of the child-caregiver system of reciprocal mutual influence. If we understand the dynamic unconscious as taking form within such a system, then it becomes apparent that the boundary between conscious and unconscious is always the product of a specific intersubjective context.

With its focus on the vicissitudes of unconscious mental processes, psychoanalysis has, until quite recently, had little to say about the ontogeny of consciousness. It is our view, as we stated in chapter 1, that the child's conscious experience becomes progressively *articulated* through the validating responsiveness of the early surround. The child's affective experience, for example, becomes increasingly differentiated and cognitively elaborated through the attuned responsiveness of caregivers to his emotional states and needs (Socarides and Stolorow, 1984/85). Such attunement must, of course, be communicated in a form that coincides with the child's unfolding psychological capacities.

It follows from this conception of consciousness becoming articulated within an intersubjective system that two closely interrelated forms of unconsciousness may develop from situations in which the requisite validating responsiveness is absent.[1] When a child's experiences are consistently not responded to or are actively rejected, the child perceives that aspects of his own experience are unwelcome or damaging to the caregiver. Whole sectors of the child's experiential world must then be sacrificed (repressed) in order to safeguard the needed tie. This, we have suggested, is the origin of the dynamic unconscious. In addition, other features of the child's experience may remain unconscious, not because they have been repressed, but because, in the absence of a validating intersubjective context, they simply never were able to become articulated. In both instances, the boundary between conscious and unconscious is revealed to be a fluid and ever-shifting one, a product of the changing responsiveness of the surround to different regions of the child's experience. We believe that this conceptualization continues to apply beyond the period of childhood and is readily demonstrated in the psychoanalytic situation as well, wherein the patient's resistance can be seen

---

1. In an earlier work (Stolorow et al., 1987), we suggested that massive developmental failure in the function of validation of perception is an important factor in the predisposition to psychotic states.

to fluctuate in concert with perceptions of the analyst's varying receptivity and attunement to the patient's experience. The idea of a fluid
boundary forming within an intersubjective system contrasts sharply with
the traditional notion of the repression barrier as a fixed intrapsychic
structure, "a sharp and final division" (Freud, 1915, p. 195) separating
conscious and unconscious contents.

During the preverbal period of infancy, the articulation of the child's
experience is achieved through attunements communicated in the sensorimotor dialogue with caregivers (Stern, 1985). During this earliest
phase, unconsciousness results from situations of unattunement or misattunement. By the middle of the second year, the child is able to use
symbols, making language possible. This is a momentous step in the
development of consciousness because henceforth the child's experience
increasingly becomes articulated by being encoded in verbal symbols. As
Stern (1985) emphasizes, symbols make possible "a sharing of mutually
created meanings about personal experience" (p. 172). With the maturation of the child's symbolic capacities, symbols gradually assume a
place of importance alongside sensorimotor attunements as vehicles
through which the child's experience is validated within the developmental system. In that realm of experience in which consciousness
increasingly becomes articulated in symbols, unconscious becomes coex-
tensive with unsymbolized. When the act of articulating an experience
is perceived to threaten an indispensable tie, repression can now be
achieved by preventing the continuation of the process of encoding that
experience in symbols. At this point in the development of consciousness, aspects of Freud's (1915) formulation of the process of repression
can be seen to apply: "A presentation which is not put into words . . .
remains thereafter in the *Ucs.* in a state of repression" (p. 202).

To summarize, we can distinguish three interrelated forms of unconsciousness: (1) the *prereflective unconscious*—the organizing principles
that unconsciously shape and thematize a person's experiences; (2) the
dynamic unconscious—experiences that were denied articulation because
they were perceived to threaten needed ties; and (3) the *unvalidated
unconscious*—experiences that could not be articulated because they
never evoked the requisite validating responsiveness from the surround.
All three forms of unconsciousness, we have emphasized, derive from
specific, formative intersubjective contexts.

We believe that this experience-near conceptualization of the unconscious, its different realms and their origins, provides a definitive answer
to those critics (e.g., Kernberg, 1982) who claim that an empathic-intro-
spective psychology of the subjective world can only remain a psychology of the conscious, and also to those theorists (e.g., Rubinstein, 1976)

who argue that the existence of unconscious mental processes can be explained only by resorting to experience-distant concepts borrowed from neurobiology. We define the stance of sustained empathic inquiry as a method for investigating the principles *unconsciously* organizing experience. By emphasizing the analyst's *investigative* activity, this definition supplies an antidote to those countertransference-based misconstruals of analytic empathy that amalgamate it with a requirement literally and concretely to fulfill a patient's selfobject longings and archaic hopes.

It is our view that the mode of therapeutic action of psychoanalytic treatment differs in each of the three realms of unconsciousness that we have described. Psychoanalysis is, above all else, a method for illuminating the prereflective unconscious, and it achieves this aim by investigating the ways in which the patient's experience of the analytic relationship is unconsciously and recurrently patterned by the patient according to developmentally preformed meanings and invariant themes. Such analysis, from a position within the patient's subjective frame of reference, with the codetermining impact of the analyst on the organization of the patient's experience always kept in view, both facilitates the engagement and expansion of the patient's capacity for self-reflection and gradually establishes the analyst as an understanding presence to whom the patient's formerly invariant ordering principles must accommodate, inviting syntheses of alternative modes of experiencing self and other.

The dynamic unconscious becomes transformed primarily through analysis of resistance, that is, the investigation of the patient's expectations and fears in the transference that if his central affective states and developmental longings are exposed to the analyst, they will meet with the same traumatogenic, faulty responsiveness that they received from the original caregivers. Such analysis, always taking into account what the patient has perceived of the analyst that has lent itself to the patient's anticipations of retraumatization, establishes the analytic bond as a gradually expanding zone of safety within which previously sequestered regions of the patient's experience can be brought out of hiding and integrated.

Analytic attention to the realm of the unvalidated unconscious probably makes a contribution to all analyses, but is especially important in the treatment of patients who have suffered severe developmental derailments in the articulation of perceptual and affective experience. These are patients, often prone to fragmented, disorganized, or psychosomatic states, for whom broad areas of early experience failed to evoke validating attunement from caregivers and, consequently, whose perceptions remain ill-defined and precariously held, easily usurped by the judgments of others, and whose affects tend to be felt as diffuse bodily states rather than as symbolically elaborated feelings. In such cases, the analyst's investigation of and attunement to the patient's inner experiences, always from within the patient's perspective, serves to articulate and consolidate the patient's subjective reality, crystalizing the patient's experience, lifting it to higher levels of organization, and strengthening the patient's confidence in its validity. This, we contend, is a foundation stone of the sense of self, a selfobject function so vital and basic that we designate its appearance in analysis by a specific term—the *self-delineating selfobject transference* (Stolorow e al., 1992).

Let us turn now to a visual analogy that we have found useful in discussions of these ideas with students and colleagues. Our purpose here is not to introduce a new topographic model of the mind, complete with reified spatial metaphors, but rather to highlight certain interrelationships between the three forms of unconsciousness once they have become established in the course of development. Imagine a building with several floors and a basement that lies below the surface of the ground. Consciousness corresponds here to the parts of the building above ground level; the higher floors represent those areas of awareness in which a person has achieved comparatively greater development and integration. The dynamic unconscious appears in the basement of the structure below ground and out of sight. Here lie the contents that are driven out of conscious awareness, because of their association with intolerable conflict and subjective danger. The prereflective unconscious has no concrete counterpart in this image, but, rather, corresponds to an architect's blueprint, which sets out the plan according to which a building is constructed. A blueprint may be thought of as a set of organizing principles that specify a pattern of relationships between the various parts of the building. Prereflective structures of experience likewise are not specific subjective contents, but are the principles that organize those contents into characteristic patterns. The unvalidated unconscious appears in our analogy in the form of bricks, lumber, and other unused materials left lying around the building and in the basement, materials that were never made part of the construction but that could have been. These various objects represent experiences that have never been articulated and integrated into the structure of consciousness and that in consequence remain largely unconscious as long as the requisite validation continues to be absent.

Clinical Illustration

In what follows, we illustrate, through a discussion of a dream, the different forms of unconsciousness. The dream we have selected is a very brief one that occurred at the onset of a psychotic episode experienced by a 19-year-old woman.

> The dreamer stood in a country setting before a small structure that she said resembled an outhouse. Looking inside, she found a toilet. As she peered into the bowl, the water began gurgling, foaming, and then rising and overflowing. The flow became more and more agitated until an explosive geyser of unidentified glowing material erupted from the toilet, increasing in violence without apparent limit. At this point the dreamer awoke in terror.

The nuclear formative situation of this patient's childhood history involved severe sexual exploitation by her father. Commencing at the age of two, her father had used his daughter for primarily oral sexual gratification several times each week. These practices, carried out late at night, were kept entirely secret from other family members and continued well into the patient's teenage years. This was a family that maintained an image of great normalcy before the community. It kept a well-tended lawn, participated in neighborhood life, and regularly attended church. A profound division thus existed between the normal life carried on during the day and the nighttime sexual practices between father and daughter. Once she was old enough to realize that their relationship was not the one all fathers and daughters had, her father instructed her never to speak of their physical intimacy; he explained that other people had not evolved to the point where they could understand what was taking place. He also pressured her to enjoy the sexual episodes, which he said were akin to the practices of royal families during other historical eras. The father told her that what was taking place between them heralded the future of parent-child relations. Her need to comply with his vision of their special relationship was reflected during the period of her psychosis in a delusion that she had been sent to earth by God to have sexual intercourse with all the men on the earth in order to lighten their spirits and lift their gloomy moods. The tie to the mother was also deeply problematic. On one occasion when the patient was six and told her mother something of what had been occurring with her father, she was screamed at and beaten for making up lies. The truth about the incest did not begin to emerge until her midteens, when another child in the family complained about the father's sexual behavior.

During her childhood years, the patient appeared to be a well-adjusted girl. She had many friends, received excellent grades in school, and tried to make her parents proud. The only sign of difficulty she showed was a tendency toward daydreaming, which her teachers and parents encouraged her to curb. Cordoning off the nighttime experiences of sexual molestation and blocking from awareness the destructive impact of these experiences, she consciously identified with the talented, normal child she was known as. Allowing herself to experience or express the confusing tangle of emotions occasioned by the incest threatened her ties to the people closest to her, notably her mother and father. As will be seen, a clear consciousness of what was transpiring also had a disintegrating effect on her sense of her own selfhood.

Hints of the nature of the effects of her situation, however, made an appearance in her recurring dreams. Two repeating nightmares haunted her early and middle childhood years, dreams that were elucidated only many years later as part of her psychotherapy. In one dream she stood in the kitchen of her family's home and noticed the presence of strange dark spots on the floor. Above each spot, any object or part of an object vanished and was annihilated. Observing this, she was terrified to see that the dark spots were beginning to expand, leaving less and less area in the light. In the dream she began to step and jump awkwardly between the growing spots in a desperate effort to avert her own annihilation. This dream emerged during the therapeutic sessions as a child's expression in metaphorical symbols of the increasing threat to her psychological survival that she was experiencing in her family. In the second recurrent dream, she lay prostrate as her body was pulled alternately in opposite directions by two arrays of strings with little hooks on them caught under her skin. Small elf-like creatures pulled on these strings, stretching her skin first in one direction and then in the other direction. This dream came to be understood as concretizing the contradictory pulls on her sense of her own self by her two fathers: one, the loving, responsible father of the daylight world; and the other, the leering sexual abuser who inhabited her nights. Here we find an additional and perhaps even more central motive for her separating off and repressing so much of the incest experience. To the extent that she remained conscious of all that was taking place in the home, during the night as well as the day, she faced the threat of being pulled apart and ultimately ripped into pieces by the contradictions that had been imposed upon her.

Let us return now to the dream that is the focus of our discussion and examine it from the standpoint of the distinctions between the various forms of unconsciousness. The dynamic unconscious in this case, consisting in sectors of experience that have been sacrificed in order to safeguard needed ties and protect a sense of self-integrity, is represented in the dream by the underground material that lay beneath the outhouse. The dream actually portrays not the dynamic unconscious, but rather a breakdown of repression and the invasion of consciousness by what earlier was dynamically unconscious. In terms of the patient's life, we could say that the contents of the dynamic unconscious here consisted principally of the overwhelming affects generated by her situation in her family, affects that were never fully articulated or communicated to anyone.

The prereflective unconscious in the dream appears in the geometry of the imagery, wherein there is a spatial division between the world above—the daylight, public, conscious realm of a loving family—and the world below—the nighttime, mostly unconscious life of betrayal and incest. A profound and central invariant principle organizing the patient's subjective universe pertained to this dichotomy, according to which vitally needed acceptance by others is gained and protected through the systematic driving underground of one's own emotional truths. The outhouse in the dream, a symbolic receptacle for such unacceptable contents, provided a channel for expunging those areas of her subjective life that threatened the integrity of the daytime world of her family.

The unvalidated unconscious appears in the dream in the undifferentiated, unidentifiable nature of the glowing material that erupted from the toilet. What came up, it will be recalled, was not specific objects that could be identified and labeled, and that would have corresponded to a set of specifically articulated feelings and memories. It was, rather, an overwhelming mass of something she did not recognize. The experiences it had been necessary for this patient to eliminate from her conscious life had never been acknowledged or validated by anyone; indeed, they had been specifically invalidated by both parents: by the father when he redefined the incest as a special rite and insisted that she enjoy it, and by the mother when she angrily punished her daughter for making up lies. This patient, at the outset of her treatment, did not have what one could call emotional knowledge of what had happened to her. She was cognitively aware of the incest, though not of its vast extent, but she had no feeling that she had been victimized, abused, or exploited. Likewise she knew that her mother had ignored her situation, but she had never experienced a sense of betrayal or abandonment by her mother. The exploration of the patient's history within the validating context of the analytic dialogue resulted in the emergence, element by element, in a process extending over nearly two decades, of a more complete emotional sense of the devastating position she had occupied in her family. Of great assistance in the exploration was a detailed investigation of the various delusions and hallucinations she developed during the period of her psychosis, which seemed to encode or otherwise be associated with previously unconscious features of her traumatic history, features that had been submerged in her accommodation to her parents' needs. The result of this illumination was a gradual redefinition of her identity to incorporate the felt reality of having been victimized, exploited, and betrayed as the central experiences of her childhood.

The dynamic unconscious and the unvalidated unconscious coincide with one another in this case; the patient's repressed emotional reactions to her family situation were parts of experiences that had never been validated by anyone during her childhood years. What emerged from repression at the onset of her psychotic episode was not clear memories and feelings, which could then perhaps have been integrated into her conscious life; her experience at that time was, instead, one of being flooded by disorganizing emotional impressions that she could not understand or articulate. Although sharp distinctions between the different forms of unconsciousness can be drawn theoretically, in the realm of clinical reality, as this case illustrates, the different forms are likely to become manifest in intricately amalgamated ways.

References

Atwood, G. & Stolorow, R. (1984), *Structures of Subjectivity: Explorations in Psychoanalytic Phenomenology*, Hillsdale, NJ: The Analytic Press.

Freud, S. (1900), The interpretation of dreams. *Standard Edition*, 4 & 5. London: Hogarth Press, 1953.

———— (1915), The unconscious. *Standard Edition*, 14:159–204. London: Hogarth Press, 1957.

Kernberg, O. (1982), Review of *Advances in Self Psychology. Amer. J. Psychiat.*, 139:374–375.

Rubinstein, B. (1976), On the possibility of a strictly clinical psychoanalytic theory. In: *Psychology Versus Metapsychology*, ed. M. Gill & P. Holzman. Madison, CT: International Universities Press, pp. 229–264.

Socarides, D. D. & Stolorow, R. (1984/85), Affects and selfobjects. *The Annual of Psychoanalysis*, 12/13:105–119. Madison, CT: International Universities Press.

Stern, D. (1985), *The Interpersonal World of the Infant*. New York: Basic Books.

Stolorow, R. (1989), The dream in context. In: *Dimensions of Self Experience: Progress in Self Psychology, Vol. 5*, ed. A. Goldberg. Hillsdale, NJ: The Analytic Press, pp. 33–39.

———— Atwood, G. & Brandchaft, B. (1992), Three realms of the unconscious and their therapeutic transformation. *Psychoanal. Rev.*, 79:25-30.

———— Brandchaft, B. & Atwood, G. (1987), *Psychoanalytic Treatment: An Intersubjective Approach*. Hillsdale, NJ: The Analytic Press.

Afterword

In this chapter we have shown that three forms of unconsciousness central to psychoanalysis—indeed, the very boundary between conscious and unconscious—can be grasped as emergent properties of ongoing intersubjective systems. In other works (Stolorow and Atwood, 1992; Stolorow, Brandchaft, and Atwood, 1987), we demonstrated the same for such fundamental theoretical problems as emotional conflict, mind–body relations, trauma, and fantasy and such important clinical phenomena as transference and resistance, therapeutic action and impasses, and borderline and psychotic states. We pictured all these as taking form at the interface of reciprocally interacting worlds of experience.

We hope it is clear that we seek not to eliminate psychoanalysis's traditional focus on the intrapsychic, but to *contextualize* the intrapsychic. The problem with classical theory was not its focus on the intrapsychic, but its inability to recognize that the intrapsychic world, as it forms and evolves within a nexus of living systems, is profoundly context dependent and context sensitive. We (Stolorow and Atwood, 1992) previously addressed this issue as follows:

> The concept of an intersubjective system brings to focus *both* the individual's world of inner experience *and* its embeddedness with other such worlds in a continual flow of reciprocal mutual influence. In this vision, the gap between the intrapsychic and interpersonal realms is closed, and, indeed, the old dichotomy between them is rendered obsolete. . . . [p. 18].

Pushing this line of argument further, we contend that the very distinction between one-person and two-person psychologies—at the heart of much current debate in psychoanalysis—is obsolete, because the individual and his or her intrapsychic world are included as a subsystem within the more encompassing relational or intersubjective suprasystem (Stolorow, 1997). We ought to speak instead of a *contextual psychology*, the subject matter of our most recent book (Orange, Atwood, and Stolorow, 1997) offering contextualism as a broad-based philosophy of psychoanalytic practice.

References

Orange, D., Atwood, G. & Stolorow, R. (1997), *Working Intersubjectively: Contextualism in Psychoanalytic Practice.* Hillsdale, NJ: The Analytic Press.

Stolorow, R. (1997), Dynamic, dyadic, intersubjective systems: An evolving paradigm for psychoanalysis. *Psychoanal. Psychol.,* 14:337–346.

——— & Atwood, G. (1992), *Contexts of Being: The Intersubjective Foundations of Psychological Life*. Hillsdale, NJ: The Analytic Press.
——— Brandchaft, B. & Atwood, G. (1987), *Psychoanalytic Treatment: An Intersubjective Approach*. Hillsdale, NJ: The Analytic Press.

Shadow and Substance:
A Relational Perspective on
Clinical Process

(1993)

Philip M. Bromberg

▼ ▼ ▼ ▼ ▼

Editors' Introduction

Freud's break with his mentor Joseph Breuer was precipitated to some extent over their disagreement about the primacy of hypnoid states in the etiology of hysteria. Since then, psychoanalysts have by and large turned their attention away from the study of states of consciousness and dissociative phenomena to concentrate on conflict and repression. In a long series of theoretically groundbreaking and clinically sophisticated articles, Philip Bromberg has developed a penetrating and highly influential approach to the study of dissociative mental states in development, psychopathology, the normal human mind, and, most important, in the psychoanalytic situation.

Bromberg's work derives from the convergence of two strikingly different sensibilities. On one hand, Bromberg is an interpersonal analyst par excellence, with a plain-speaking forthrightness, a finely honed sense of the mutual impact of people on each other, and a distaste for the abstractions of theorizing. On the other hand, Bromberg has a keen appreciation of the most deeply private domains of experience, the hidden recesses, the nuances of "innerness" within which personal existence is preserved. This combination has generated a unique vision of finely textured conceptualizations of the psychoanalytic process that captures some of its deepest contrasts: sameness and difference, safety and growth, the emotional connections that make a deeply personal life possible and the immutably private.

Bromberg's papers, all written with a poet's sensitivity to language and imagery, generate an immediate experience in the reader of the importance of careful listening. But what comes through repeatedly in Bromberg's clinical illustrations is that he listens not only to his patients' various selves, but for his own reactions and split-off states of awareness. Bromberg teaches his readers to listen not just to patients' words or to their own inner dialogue, but also to the way in which the analytic narrative is enacted nonverbally as a living entity between patient and analyst. "Patients, in fact, do not reveal their unconscious fantasies *to* the analyst: They *are* their unconscious fantasies and live them with the analyst through the act of psychoanalysis, which includes the analyst's subjectivity as well as the patient's," he writes.

Bromberg is an influential contributor who has elaborated a view of mind as comprising multiple selves and a wide range of self-states. He emphasizes how both conflict and trauma organize, structure, and disrupt mental life, and he clarifies how dissociative states result when trauma disrupts one's capacity for self-reflection. By attending to the subtle shifts in one's own self-states and by viewing these shifts within the relational context of ongoing enactments with the patient, psychoanalysis helps patients to tolerate conflict and ambiguity. For Bromberg, "Health is the ability to stand in the spaces between realities without losing any of them. This is what I believe *self-acceptance* means and what *creativity* is really all about—the capacity to feel like one self while being many."

Bromberg's major contributions to relational theory and clinical practice have been collected, revised and updated, along with new clinical contributions, in the recently published *Standing in the Spaces: Essays on Clinical Process, Trauma, and Dissociation* (1998, The Analytic Press). Included are "On Knowing One's Patient Inside Out: The Aesthetics of Unconscious Communication" (*Psychoanalytic Dialogues*, 1991, 1:399–422), and "Standing in the Spaces: The Multiplicity of Self and the Psychoanalytic Relationship" (*Contemporary Psychoanalysis*, 1996, 32:509–535). In the former essay, Bromberg examines the paradoxical quality of the psychoanalytic relationship as an intersubjective field that is both "inside" and "outside," while in the latter he focuses on such clinical topics as trauma, dissociation, and regression, within a perspective of the mind as a configuration of shifting, nonlinear, discontinuous states of consciousness in an ongoing dialectic with the healthy illusion of unitary selfhood.

Shadow and Substance:
A Relational Perspective on Clinical Process*

▼   ▼   ▼   ▼   ▼

Brigid, a young female servant to an archbishop—a girl loving and lovable, unworldly and selfless—is tormented by a secret: She receives visitations advice, and instructions from her name-saint, Saint Brigid, with whom she converses regularly. The archbishop, her employer, is a cynical and domineering man, certain of his wisdom. Except for the uncharacteristic tenderness he feels for his servant, he is privately tormented by his own secret: his inner isolation and absence of authentic spiritual or human feeling despite his uncompromising adherence to accurate interpretation of church doctrine. His genuine wish to help the young girl is framed by his conviction that her experience is simply a symptom of the illness from which she must be rescued, because true religious experience cannot take such a personal form. In the course of his efforts to help her, he finds that Brigid's resistance slowly leads him to encounter painful aspects of his own nature; Brigid cannot claim her perceptions of him as her own, however, and can confront the canon only as a conduit for the words of Saint Brigid, who commands her to speak them. He tries to dismiss her perceptions as further evidence of her illness, but (to parody Samuel Johnson) a diagnosis of psychotic transference is the last refuge of a beleaguered analyst. His insistence on the priority of his own truth only makes her more and more desperate to reach him personally. Ultimately, but too late to save her from death, he is able to allow her humanness to directly reach his, where the absolute rightness of his own truth gives way to a shared reality and to his ability to experience the world through her eyes as well as his own.

What I have just summarized is, of course, one of the masterpieces of Irish playwriting, *Shadow and Substance*, a work written by Paul Vincent Carroll (1937/1941) and first performed at the Abbey Theatre in Dublin. The play has meanings at many levels, including historical,

---

* Originally published in *Psychoanalytic Psychology,* 10(2):147–168 © 1993 Lawrence Erlbaum Associates, Inc.

sociopolitical, religious, and spiritual. But what is most relevant to my topic is the level of meaning that overrides differences in sex, social class, and role definition. It is a nakedly honest portrayal of the painful struggle in simply being human, a nonjudgmental recognition of the inevitable and lifelong collision of selfhood and empathy; it is an encounter, both glorious and ignoble, between the self-preservative power of one's subjective truth and the self-transformational power of human relatedness, between personal reality and interpersonally negotiated reality, and often between self-aggrandizement and love.

My choice of title for this article was influenced not only by the play, however. I also wished to convey in a single phrase my view of the unconscious as a reality that is "inside," "outside," and simultaneously both—a phenomenon (a) that an analyst, at certain moments, subjectively senses as a shadowy presence peeking out from the unsymbolized and unshared reaches behind his[1] patient's eyes; (b) that he at other moments objectively observes in his patient's associations, dreams, parapraxes, and transferential behavior; and (c) that he, most powerfully of all, experiences as a manifest presence living in the shared world of intersubjective reality jointly constructed by himself and his patient as they coexist in the analytic process.

As psychoanalysts, we hope to succeed where the archbishop could not; we hope that the process of psychoanalysis and our use of interpretation will not become an act of indoctrination (either failed or successful) and that a consensually constructed reality will begin to develop before the patient "terminates." But on what do we base this hope? What do we believe is the relation between the human personality in its capability for change and the unique role of the psychoanalyst that allows us to entertain such a hope even though other efforts have failed? In the face of the strong adaptational value that resides in the stability of an individual's sense of personal identity, why should anyone agree to go through an internally disorganizing process that systematically tampers with stability? In other words, it might reasonably be asked why self-equilibrium is not always preserved at the expense of growth. Why should anyone ever change? The answer is self-evident but thought-provoking: The human personality possesses the extraordinary capacity to negotiate stability and change simultaneously, and it will do so under the right conditions. This attribute is, in fact, the basis of what we rely on to make clinical psychoanalysis possible. How we understand this

---

1. I have used the male gender designation in this article for convenience of exposition. Unless I am referring to a specific individual, it is intended to represent the male or female pronoun interchangeably.

remarkable capability of the mind, how we conceptualize it structurally and psychodynamically, and what we see as its clinical implications (i.e., the optimal conditions for it to occur) are the questions that shape psychoanalytic theory and practice.

Much has happened to the psychoanalytic conception of the human mind and to its notions of consciousness and unconsciousness since Freud, in his case history of Katharina (Breuer & Freud, 1893–1895), stated that he "should like at this point to express a doubt as to whether a splitting of consciousness due to ignorance is really different from one due to conscious rejection" (p. 134). Since then, there have been quite a few "changes of mind," including, several times, Freud's own. I was trained in interpersonal psychoanalysis and paid particular attention to the thinking of Harry Stack Sullivan (1953, 1954), whose pragmatic conception of the mind emphasized dissociation, observable reality, and the field of interpersonally communicable data. Although there have been scattered appearances throughout history, the term *relational* as applied to psychoanalysis entered our vernacular approximately 10 years ago through the contemporary classic, written by Greenberg and Mitchell (1983), that distinguished between a *drive/structure* and a *relational/structure* model of psychoanalysis, further elaborated by Mitchell (1988) into a *drive/conflict* and *relational/conflict* distinction. Partly as a result of the unprecedented and continuing dialogue among the major post-classical schools of analytic thought—Freudian, interpersonal, self-psychological, and British object-relational—the boundary between what psychoanalysts consider psychic reality and what they conceptualize as observable reality has become increasingly permeable. "Within the mind" and "between people" no longer delimits two discrete and unambiguous domains of experience (intrapsychic and interpersonal). What is meant by fantasy and reality, and by unconscious and conscious, has thus become more interesting and complex.

Freud's view of consciousness and unconsciousness is embedded in the idea of a self or psyche that is inherently unitary and structured archeologically in terms of a particular layer's degree of access to awareness; thus, we find his topographical conceptions of unconscious, preconscious, and conscious. I do not suggest that these distinctions have been lost or that they are not worthwhile. My argument, rather, is that we are moving increasingly in the direction of a model in which our view of what is conscious and what is unconscious is informed by a conception of the mind as a nonlinear, dialectical process of meaning construction, organized by the equilibrium between stability and growth of one's self-representation—the balance between the need to preserve meaning (the ongoing experience of "being oneself") and the need to construct new meaning in the service of relational adaptation that Sullivan (1940) called *interpersonal adjustive success* (p. 97).

Further, I suggest that the way analysts conceptualize reality in terms of past and present is also changing. The clinical focus is not as much on discovering past roots of current problems—as though past experience and present experience are discretely stratified in the memory bank of a unitary "self"—as on exploring the way in which the self-states comprising a patient's personal identity are linked to each other, to the external world, and to the past, present, and future. In a seminal article on the experience of temporality, Loewald (1972) wrote:

> When we consider time as psychoanalysts, the concept of time as duration, objectively observed or subjectively experienced, loses much of its relevance. We encounter time in psychic life primarily as a linking activity in which what we call past, present, and future are woven into a nexus. . . . The individual not only *has* a history which an observer may unravel and describe, but he is history and makes his history by virtue of his memorial activity in which past-present-future are created as mutually interacting modes of time. (pp. 407–409)

From this perspective, the "contents" of a patient's mind and what constitutes memory and time at any given moment are psychoanalytically contained not in an image of memory retrieval from an archive of historically organized information, but by what Bach (1985) called the ability to maintain "state constancy" (p. 187)—that is, in the interplay between an individual's capacity to access and cognitively process dissociated perceptual experience (past and present) and his felt vulnerability to potential traumatic disruption of his ongoing feeling of selfhood. One consequence of this shift in thinking is that postclassical analytic theory is now giving broadly based reconsideration to the phenomena of trauma and dissociation and their effect on both normal personality development and the process of clinical psychoanalysis.

In what is probably the most famous literary soliloquy ever written (Shakespeare, 1942), Hamlet ruminates on the pain that accompanies being alive and wonders whether death will end what he calls "the thousand natural shocks that flesh is heir to" (pp. 1066–1067). Shakespeare's choice of the word *shock* has always intrigued me. Why shock? Why is that word so particularly evocative? Why is it able to unmask the essential quality of human vulnerability that allows us to know what Hamlet feels at that moment—to know in our own souls the enemy that we are all helpless to oppose and possibly unable to escape even through death? Reik (1936), in *Surprise and the Psycho-Analyst*, a work considerably ahead of its time, stated:

The root problem of neurosis is not fear, but shock. In my opinion, *that problem remains insoluble until fear is brought into connection with the emotion of shock.* . . . Shock is the prime emotion, the first thing that the little living creature feels. . . . I hold that shock is in general characteristic of a traumatic situation, fear one of danger. *Shock is the emotional reaction to something that bursts in upon us, fear the reaction to something that comes with a menace.* Fear is itself a signal preceding shock, it anticipates the emotion of shock in miniature, and so protects us from it and from its profound and harmful effects. (pp. 267–268)

Recall that Freud (1926) made the distinction between a danger situation and a situation that actually becomes traumatic, stating that the essence and meaning of the traumatic situation *"consists in the subject's estimation of his own strength compared to the magnitude of the danger and in his admission of helplessness in the face of it"* (p. 166, italics added). He emphasized that it is not the source of the danger that is primary, but whether the affect is subjectively experienced as overwhelming. The person is psychologically overstimulated such that he loses the capability of perceiving and instead experiences a generalized flooding of affect—what Reik (1936) called *shock*. This idea may be our greatest unacknowledged debt to Freud—that what a person perceives in front of his eyes (so-called objective reality) is a construction that is partially shaped by his state of mind, not simply vice versa. "Psychic" reality, the world "behind" one's eyes, is thus in a continuing dialectic with perception, and our success as clinicians with any patient depends on our ability to work at the boundary between enactment and perception (most particularly, perception of the analytic relationship itself). That is, what we call psychic reality and observable reality—past experience and "here-and-now" experience, unconsciousness and consciousness—are partly subjective constructions that comprise the complex relational matrix that organizes human experience. Each, in its own way, is both "shadow" and "substance."

Dissociation, Enactment, and Clinical Process

It has long been recognized that every patient enters psychoanalysis with the same "illogical" wish—*the wish to stay the same while changing.* Traditionally, this recognition has been handled simply by the classical definition of *resistance*—the clinical phenomenon that "encompasses all of a patient's defensive efforts to avoid self-knowledge" (Moore & Fine, 1990, p. 168). Most postclassical theory, however, tends to subsume the "defense" component more and more into the broader context of a complex reality, a necessary illusion that configures and sustains the analytic situation as a playground for self-development that Winnicott (1967/1971) called the use of "potential space." Within this context, a primary task of the analyst's therapeutic role is to contribute to the viability of the patient's illusion that he can stay the same while changing. The analyst accomplishes this task by not attempting, through interpretation, to force a conceptual distinction among levels of reality in the patient's ambiguous self-experience, and by not insisting that the boundary between conscious and unconscious and between reality and fantasy be defined other than through a relational process of consensual negotiation (see also Ghent, 1992; Pizer, 1992). The goal is to enable the *experience* of self-growth—not simply its result or outcome—to be rewarding, to be one of transition rather than of traumatic "force feeding."

The transference-countertransference field, if looked at through this lens, is a dramatization of the patient's illusion, an externalization of the patient's internal communication with his own subjective phenomena in the form of an enactment with his analyst's reality. One dimension of the analyst's role is to create a therapeutic environment that allows this enactment to occur, and for him (the analyst) to participate in it and thus experience the illusion implicitly, not explicitly as through language. His job is not to correct the illusion but to know it with the patient so that the patient can make the most use of it creatively and imaginatively. The desired analytic outcome is not a surrender of the illusion as a distortion of reality but the patient's pleasurable construction of a more inclusive reality that emerges from his illusory experience and becomes linguistically symbolized by the consensual construction of new narrative meaning. *The heart of the process depends on the ability of the analyst to avoid imposing meaning so that the patient can feel free to enact new ways of being without fear of traumatically losing the continuity of "who he is."* As Friedman (1983) so evocatively put it, "Insight is the score that the patient learns while practicing on a well-tuned therapist" (p. 348).

From a relational standpoint, enactment defies categorization as either pathological or normal. Levi (1971) described it from an interpersonal perspective as

> the product of not just one, but two forces, contradictory and opposed; the one attempting to maintain the delimited self-system intact with its established boundaries and dissociations, and the other attempting to break down this organization . . . a powerful though perverted attempt at self cure. (p. 184)

The process of enactment, in analysis, often occurs in a dissociated self-state that is designed to communicate the existence of a "truth" that the patient is experiencing about the analyst, and that cannot be thought or said within the context of the self-other representation that the relationship is based on at the moment.

Consider, for example, the puzzling, unsettling, and multidetermined phenomenon referred to in the clinical literature as *delicate self-cutting*. Some patients threaten to hurt themselves physically but do not, whereas others may or may not threaten and really do it. Apart from a patient's past history, and even apart from the details of the patient's immediate life, an analyst often intuitively "knows," with a remarkably high degree of accuracy, which patient is likely to hurt himself and which is not. It has been my experience that, notwithstanding the multiplicity of factors that may be operating at a given moment in patients who do hurt themselves, such acts occur with impressively lower frequency in patients whose personality development could be considered organized more conflictually than dissociatively, and that an analyst will tend intuitively to worry less about the former than about the latter (i.e., patients who enact rather than think about their feelings toward themselves and toward significant objects, including the analyst). Patients who really *do it* are typically those who fluctuate among dissociated domains of reality, each with its own imperative truth.

In this connection, I am also reminded of certain patients who seem unable to tolerate analysts' holidays or vacation breaks. Analysts have sometimes discovered that giving a patient a phone number where, "if necessary," the analyst can be reached during the break provides a transitional object linkage that reduces abandonment anxiety. But . . . the more interesting issue arises not when this linkage "works" but when it does not. With the vast majority of patients, the result is that the patient does not call and does not feel any great sense of urgency to do so, despite a certain amount of anxiety. The linkage is enough, and the capacity exists for the person to experience and evaluate the relative balance among permission, necessity, and concern for the other person's needs. But with some patients, calls are indeed made, sometimes many calls, often to the analyst's surprise and even consternation (because this was not supposed to happen). In such instances the concept of "acting-out" is often applied, in my view usually inaccurately (even when it is not used retaliatively by a grouchy analyst). It tends to presume avoidance (through action) of a state of internal conflict, and it misses what is more frequently the revelation of a personality organization not yet sufficiently cohesive to hold simultaneously the need to make contact, the experience of having been given permission to do so, and the ability to empathize with the analyst's own legitimate limits, particularly when they have not been made explicit (usually because the analyst was less than candid about them). The reason that the analyst may not have chosen to spell out the fact that his offer was not equivalent to a continuously open telephone line varies from situation to situation, but certain patients are expert at spotting the inconsistencies between what someone says and the unverbalized aspect of what they "mean." These individuals have a nose for the slightest scent of hypocrisy, no matter how "well-meaning" the motive. The patient who does phone without "good" reason (from the analyst's perspective) is often in a dissociated self-state that permits access only to the need for contact and to the memory of having been given permission to call if necessary; in such a state, the felt need and the concept of "necessity" are experientially equivalent. The phone call is thus an enactment, much like certain forms of self-cutting, that is designed to make an impact on the object. To what end? It is not an easy question to answer with any degree of confidence. My strongest hunch is that it is an example of what Levi (1971) called "a powerful though perverted attempt at self cure" (p. 184). It involves a need to be known—in the only way possible, intersubjectively—through playing out with the analyst, in some mutually creative way that is different from the old and fixed patterning of self-other interactions, a version of the situation that led to the original need for dissociation; and through this relational act of sameness and difference to construct jointly an act of meaning (Bruner, 1990) that allows the dissociated threat of potential trauma to be cognitively processed.

Putnam (1992) called dissociation "the escape when there is no escape" (p. 104). It is a defense against trauma, which, unlike defenses against internal conflict, does not simply deny the self access to potentially threatening feelings, thoughts, and memories; it effectively obliterates, at least temporarily, the *existence* of that self to whom the trauma could occur, and it is in that sense like a "quasi-death." The rebuilding of linkages, the reentry into life, involves pain not unlike that of mourning. The return to life means the recognition and facing of death; not simply the death of one's early objects as real people, but the death of those aspects of self with which those objects have been united. At the point the patient begins to abandon the instant and absolute "truth" of dissociative reality in favor of internal conflict and human relatedness, the patient discovers that there is no path without pain. Russell (in press), in a recent article, speaks to the experience of the patient's recognition and processing of trauma as requiring the capacity for a particular kind of grief. "We have to presume," he writes, "that the pain accompanying this grief is extreme, among the most painful of life's experiences. We make this assumption because of the enormous psychological price that is paid to continue to avoid it."

A brief clinical vignette may help to illustrate this more vividly. A man in his late 30s had been seeing me three times a week for about 2 years and had lived since early adolescence in a state of timeless, purposeless, and concrete reality, marked by the ritual performance of daily activities that anchored him to what little sense of meaning life imparted. For many years he had been structuring his life by time spent in an apartment in New York and time spent in a weekend house in Vermont, each experience disconnected from the other, as if being lived by separate people. The regularity of this schedule and the regularity of his three visits each week to my office were each protected by him as a matter of life or death. If a session had to be canceled by either of us (including for holidays), it had to be replaced at almost any cost. One Monday morning, after returning from Vermont as usual, he arrived for his session even more unfocused and disconnected than he ordinarily was upon leaving one place and entering another. But there was a strange sadness to his voice that felt unfamiliar to me, and something additional that I could not quite put my finger on—there was almost what seemed like a hint of fright. He reported that he could not even remember why he was at my office other than that he was supposed to be, and then he quietly said, "Vermont is dead." There was something about his state of mind at that moment that was both so poignant and so unusual that I felt as if I were meeting him for the first time. "I am never going to have it again," he said. "It's not that I don't remember it. I do, but that just makes it worse. And right now, I am dead too; I have to look for something to do, to know why I'm here." "Where does that feel like it leaves you?" I asked. "It's just me and the world," he replied, continuing:

> I can't find a way to put all my other images of myself in the middle. This is all there is. I suppose it's liberating, but what I'm liberated into is a life that has death as a part of it. Maybe you can give me two weeks' worth of sessions as a single event, so they are linked, so they don't die, like Vermont died. When I leave Vermont, it dies, because it can never be there again in the same way. The memory only makes me sad.

Perception, Language, and Selfhood

Almost any human being, even in the most primitive of mental states, is able to use language as communicative speech—that is, to communicate his personal identity as an objective and enduring social reality that transcends the here and now. He is able to use his linguistic capacity not only to illuminate vocally what he feels and wants but to express through linguistic interaction who he believes he is, who he believes others are, and how accessible these self–other mental representations are to negotiated modification in the face of contradictory perceptions arising from social interchange—a process that Sullivan (1950) termed *consensual validation* (p. 214). No matter how idiosyncratic or impaired an individual's manner of interpersonal self-expression happens to be, it almost invariably conveys that it was shaped, for better or for worse, in an environment recognizably human regardless of its degree of dehumanization (Bromberg, 1984). The capacity to express linguistically one's experience of personal identity—who one is—is so fundamental to the essence of being human that in those rare instances when it is lost or altered in a central way, the experience is almost incomprehensible to others.

In the March 26, 1992 *New York Review*, Oliver Sacks wrote a piece called "The Last Hippie" about a patient he had treated. Sacks's patient, Greg, because of an unusually placed brain tumor that damaged both temporal and frontal lobe functioning, developed both episodic amnesia (an inability to transfer perceptual memory into permanent memory) and an incapacity to retain a sense of personal, unique identity,

> tending to "shallow" him, to remove genuine feeling and meaning, to replace these with a sort of indifference or frivolity. . . . Greg knew only presence, not absence. He seemed incapable of registering any loss—loss of function in himself, or of an object, or a person. (pp. 59–60)

This man, by most standards of prognostic evaluation, was hopeless, except for Sacks's perception that, although his frontal lobe damage had taken away his experience of personal identity,

> it had also given him a sort of identity or personality, albeit of an odd and perhaps primitive sort . . . by his relationship to and participation in an act of meaning, an organic unity, which overrode or bypassed the disconnections of his amnesia. . . . Music, songs, seemed to bring to Greg what, apparently, he lacked, to evoke in him a depth to which he otherwise had no access. Music was a door to a world of feeling, of meaning, a world in which Greg could, if only for a while, recover himself. (pp. 58–59)

It could be argued that the nature of the "organic unity" to which Sacks referred as "at once dynamic and semantic," is the heart of the interpretive process in psychoanalysis, what is often called "the words and music" of the analytic relationship. Sacks stated:

> It is typical of such flowing dynamic-semantic structures that each part leads on to the next, that every part has reference to the rest. Such structures cannot be perceived or remembered in part—they are perceived and remembered, if at all, as wholes. (p. 59)

Sacks concluded his essay with a question that I think has interesting implications for what I have called the shadow and substance of clinical process in psychoanalysis and its relation to dissociation, memory, and the interface between perception and self-narrative. He wrote the following:

> It is easy to show that simple information can be embedded in songs . . . but what does it mean to say, "This is December the 19th, 1991," when one is sunk in the profoundest amnesia, when one has lost one's sense of time and history, when one is existing from moment to moment in a sequenceless limbo? "Knowing the date" means nothing in these circumstances. Could one, however, through the evocativeness and power of music, perhaps using *songs with specially written lyrics* [italics added]—songs which relate something valuable about himself or the current world—accomplish something more lasting, deeper? (p. 62)

"Songs with specially written lyrics!" Perhaps not a bad way to conceive of analytic process: songs that bridge the space between a patient's inner reality (his preestablished view of who he is) and his perception of external reality as constructed through the analytic relationship: a harmonic joining of seeing and saying as an affectively organized flow of experience.

In brief, I am arguing that personal narrative cannot be edited simply by more accurate verbal input. Psychoanalysis must provide an experience that is perceivably (not just conceptually) different from the patient's narrative memory. Sullivan (1954), recognizing that self-discordant perceptual data must have an opportunity to structurally reorganize internal narrative for psychoanalysis to be a genuine "talking cure," emphasized the powerful relation between personality change and what he called "the detailed inquiry" (pp. 94–112) by the analyst. This phrase refers to the clinical reconstruction of perceptual detail, the recall of affects, areas of perception, and interpersonal data that are excluded from the narrative memory of the event as reported to the analyst. A central aspect of this process is that the patient-analyst relationship itself is inevitably drawn into the telling of the narrative and experienced by both parties as a living entity that must be continually renegotiated as the analysis proceeds. The core of the negotiation is that the *meaning* of the relationship is intersubjectively, though asymmetrically (see Aron, 1991; Hoffman, 1991) constructed out of the patient's self-narrative and the differences from it. It is in this sense that psychoanalysis breaks down the old narrative frame (the patient's "story") by evoking, through a process of negotiation, perceptual experience that doesn't fit it; *enactment is the primary perceptual medium that allows narrative change to take place.* Alternative, consensually validated narratives that contain events and experience of self–other configurations formerly excluded begin to be constructed. These events become symbolized not by words themselves but by the new narrative context that the words come to represent.

This view has implications that affect our concepts of neutrality, interpretation, anonymity, self-revelation, and many other dimensions of what we believe to be an acceptable analytic posture. For a patient in analysis to look into his own nature with perceptiveness and to creatively utilize what is being enacted, there must exist a simultaneous opportunity for the patient to look into the *analyst's* nature with an equivalent sense of freedom and security. For one thing, an analyst can no longer technically attempt to maintain an image of opaque neutrality without recognizing that it will be perceived by many patients as an injunction to see the analyst not as he really is and only to see him as different from the "other" (e. g., father, mother) except for transferential "distortions." Some patients, particularly those with personality disorders, will inevitably respond to this stance simply as an attempted extraction of their perceptual reality and either enter a prolonged analytic stalemate or learn to be "better" patients as part of their preexisting self-narratives (see Franklin, 1990; Greenberg, 1986, 1991a).

In a previous article (Bromberg, 1984, p. 440), I quoted from the work of Carlos Castaneda (1971, 1974) brief passages in which the shaman/sorcerer don Juan was trying (once again, unsuccessfully) to "explain" to Carlos why people remain stuck in their own limited versions of reality:

> Whenever we finish talking to ourselves the world is always as it should be. We renew it, we kindle it with life, we uphold it with our internal talk. Not only that, but we also choose our paths as we talk to ourselves. Thus we repeat the same choices over and over until the day we die, because we keep on repeating the same internal talk over and over until the day we die. (Castaneda, 1971, p. 263)

> [W]e are complacently caught in our particular view of the world, which compels us to feel and act as if we knew everything about the world. *A teacher from the very first act he performs, aims at stopping that view.* Sorcerers call it stopping the internal dialogue. . . . In order to stop the view of the world which one has held since the cradle, it is not enough to just wish or make a resolution. One needs a practical task. (Castaneda, 1974, p. 236)

This was Castaneda writing 20 years ago about the stubborn power of self-narrative to preserve itself and about what he wryly described as its ability to change only through negotiation with a "sorcerer" whose goal it is to facilitate commitment to a "practical task"—perhaps what Bruner (1990, p. xii) called an "act of meaning"—that will rewrite the internal dialogue. Judging from the number of times the words *hermeneutic* and *narrative* appear in the contemporary analytic literature, the therapeutic process of altering the internal dialogue is no longer simply the domain of sorcerers. It has been discovered by psychoanalysis, and the "practical task" in this context is the negotiation of the analytic situation. Schafer (1983) stated that, when you help the patient rewrite his story "in a way that makes change conceivable and attainable" (p. 227), you have done your job as an analyst. I tend to agree, but how does this model of analytic growth (if it is a model) speak to the act of what we do with our patients? Don Juan's *explanation* did not change Carlos's own story of reality despite the accuracy of what the shaman said. One's personal meanings do not change simply through the power of reason or convincing verbal explanation. Carlos became able to expand his vision of reality only when his relationship with his mentor led to actions within it that began to free him from the self-imposed reality that had defined its limits. In other words, he had to find a way to escape a relationship from which there was no escape other than through interpersonal action that changed its self-imposed story. The fact that Carlos later came to feel that he was "tricked" into these *acts of meaning* suggests an interesting comparison with certain aspects of the analytic relationship, but to develop this idea would take me too far from the present topic.

During my first year of graduate school, the instructor of our diagnostics class illustrated a point with a psychoanalyst-patient joke that I've never forgotten. This may serve equally well in the present context to vividly get at what self-narrative is not: neither a patient's spoken version of who he is, as when we conduct a formal "interview," nor something that can be changed or rewritten by the introduction (whether gently or abruptly) of a more accurate version. The joke is as follows:

"Doctor, I came to see you because I have a humiliating sexual problem that I have to talk about, but no one believes me."

"Don't worry, sir, this is my specialty; I promise I will take you seriously."

"Well, alright, but it really is very embarrassing. My problem is that my penis fell off." (Long pause while doctor thinks about how to respond.)

"I can tell, sir, that you are convinced that is what happened, and I am certain that your reasons for believing it are very important for us to talk about. I want to hear more about it, but I first want to assure you that it can't literally be true; penises don't just fall off."

"I knew you would say that; this is what makes it so hard to talk about. But this time I came prepared: Here! Look!" (Patient reaches into his jacket pocket and shows doctor what he is holding in his hand.)

"But that's not your penis; that's a cigar!"

"Oh, my God! I smoked my penis!"

It is my view that the essential quality of what Bruner (1990) calls an act of meaning lies in its being a relational act—an act mediated not by indoctrination (no matter how tactfully administered) but by consensually constructed interchange between the timelessness of one's internal "self-truth" and the immediacy of a discrepant, external perception of oneself as seen by an other. Only then can new meaning be cognitively conserved—that is, accommodated into one's internal dialogue, self-narrative, or unconscious fantasy, whichever phrase one chooses. To put it a bit more simply, the power of a relational act to alter self-truth is in the opportunity it presents to *perceive* an alternative version of reality rather than struggling to believe an alternative version that makes sense but has minimum interchange with self-narrative. Thus, if we conceive of perception as involving an interactive process of responsiveness to the world that operates on behalf of the motivation and behavior of the perceiver, then the information we perceive is given meaning by these very actions. It is a view of perception as a dynamic process, that in the world of human relatedness includes the dynamic interplay between two subjectivities that are always reading each other but are not always immediately aware of what they read. One might therefore suggest that *psychoanalysis is a process that is designed to enhance perception as its first act.*

But if this is so, then why do we laugh knowingly at "Oh, my God! I smoked my penis!"? There's the cigar, right in front of the patient's eyes. Why doesn't that perception lead the patient to consider the possibility that his reality might be worth questioning? Why does he instead create a logically possible but highly implausible crutch to support his self-truth? One answer, I think, is that new relational conditions were not yet present for his perception of the cigar to become part of a discrepant self-perception. By this I don't mean that the patient was looking at an inanimate object (the cigar) rather than at himself. The ability of an individual to allow his self-truth to be altered by the impact of an "other" (whether the other is an analyst or a sorcerer) depends on the existence of a relationship in which the other can be experienced as someone who, paradoxically, both accepts the validity of the patient's inner reality and participates in the here-and-now act of constructing a negotiated reality discrepant with it. Clinically, of course, the critical issue for any given person is the power held by the subjective truth of early self-other representations and the degree to which they are anchored in place by the dread of psychic trauma.

In the interchanges between Castaneda and don Juan, and between the patient and doctor in the joke,[2] the power of self-truth to remain unchanged was as yet unchallenged by perception. A relational context, an act of meaning, had not been constructed that could include the realities of both self and other. In both cases, the immediate perceptual context was an enactment of the patient's fixed, internal self-narrative, some "other" trying helpfully and logically to extract the person's own reality and replace it with theirs (albeit a "better" one). In both relationships, the "patients" acted in ways consistent with internal truth, so their self-narratives remained unchanged even in the face of convincing perceptual data (the cigar) and persuasive logic (don Juan's attempt at Socratic dialogue). In Piaget's (1936/1952) language, perceptual and cognitive experience was simply assimilated into the ongoing self-schema rather than the internal patterning of self-other representation having to accommodate discrepant data and to undergo structural reorganization. In other words, it is only when perception, in a relational mode, demands narrative accommodation that language, logic, and what we typically call "insight" become effective.

All this being said, isn't the entity we call *narrative* then somewhat elusive as a concept? Where is self-narrative located? It obviously is not to be found simply in the linguistic content of a patient's story, for example, in the words, "my penis fell off." Patients, in fact, do not reveal

---

2. Granted, there is the not insignificant issue of paranoia to be considered in this joke. Could it not be reasonably argued, however, that paranoia may be a special case of self-narrative that is highly—sometimes intractably—resistant to change even through relational negotiation, but that is no different in structure than any other? Perhaps it is the extremely dissociative isolation of the self-state that holds paranoid self-narrative, which makes what we call a "delusional" story virtually immune to perceptions inconsistent with it. It would therefore follow that as disjunctive perceptions become so powerful that the internal logic of the self-narrative cannot be reasonably maintained, the individual's efforts to hold his dissociated self-state intact by shoring up the narrative become more and more "irrational." As in the example of the cigar joke, the shoring up of narrative can include what Shapiro (1965) called the propensity of a paranoid person to "make brilliantly perceptive mistakes . . . [and to] be absolutely right in his perception and absolutely wrong in his judgement" (pp. 60–61). The dissociation must be preserved, sometimes at any cost, to prevent the return of unbearably traumatic self-experience.

their unconscious fantasies *to* the analyst: "They *are* their unconscious fantasies and live them with the analyst through the act of psychoanalysis" (Bromberg, 1989, p. 282), which includes the analyst's subjectivity as well as the patient's. In this sense, the patient's self-narrative is always in the interface between shadow and substance, and it is through the relational act of psychoanalysis that the patient, as his own narrative, comes to be known through enactment while telling his story. Shadow and substance are thus captured and reconstructed in a new domain of reality that is neither and both; a chaotic intersubjective field where the collision between narrative memory and immediate perception contains the simultaneous existence of multiple realities and disjunctive self-other representations. The chaotic nature of the intersubjective field at such times was evocatively portrayed, for example, by McDougall (1987), who, in her discussion of a case presentation, framed the description of her initial reaction to the case within her metaphor of the "psychoanalytic stage." She wrote:

> Much of the confused impression at first reading stems from the fact that these contradictory people in . . . [the patient's] psychic world are both talking at the same time. (When this occurs, whether within the analytic situation or in everyday life, it is difficult to hear what is being said!) (p. 224)

Dissociation and Conflict

I propose that structural personality growth in psychoanalysis is not simply a process of helping a patient change a unified, unadaptive self-representation to an equally plausible but more adaptive one, but rather a process of addressing individual subnarratives, each on its own terms, and enabling negotiation to take place between them (Bromberg, 1991). What do I mean by *subnarratives*? Simply that every person has a set of discrete, typically overlapping schemata of who he is, and that each is organized around a particular self-other configuration that is held together by a uniquely powerful affective state. There is increasingly strong evidence supporting the idea that the psyche does not start as an integrated whole that then becomes fragmented as a pathological process, but is nonunitary in origin; it is a structure that originates and continues as a multiplicity of self-other configurations or "behavioral states" (as Wolff, 1987, called them) that maturationally develop a coherence and continuity that comes to be experienced as a cohesive sense of personal identity—an overarching feeling of "being a self." Osborne and Baldwin (1982), for example, considered the fact that consciousness is discontinuous to be the most serious and overriding problem for all systems of psychotherapy. The data, they argued, are too powerful to be ignored any longer:

> We excerpt features of our experience rather than the whole and tend to conciliate parts into a compatible whole. Our consciousness is essentially a state of illusion embroidered by these processes upon a series of discontinuous moments of consciousness from our experience. (pp. 268–269)

In most people, the "illusion" (the general feeling of one's "sameness") is taken for granted. In other individuals, the experience of continuity and integrity of the sense of self is never taken for granted; it is absent either partially or totally, and it often involves a lifelong struggle to deal with the existence of relatively or totally dissociated self-states. Am I thereby implying that we are all, in one way or another, multiple personalities? No, I am not. I am suggesting that what we call the unconscious might usefully include the suspension or deterioration of linkages between self-states, preventing certain domains of self-experience (along with their respective constellations of affects, memories, values, and cognitive capacities) from achieving simultaneous access to the personality. The extent to which one's individual self-states are simultaneously accessible to awareness (what has been called the *observing ego*) is the criterion that analysts have traditionally used in determining whether a patient is "analyzable." The difference between patients who have classically been defined as analyzable and those who have been seen as unsuitable for analysis is from this perspective a matter of the degree to which the self-states are dissociated from one another.

Paradoxically, the goal of dissociation is to maintain personal continuity, coherence, and integrity of the sense of self and to avoid the traumatic dissolution of selfhood. How can this be? How can the division of self-experience into relatively unlinked parts be in the service of self-integrity? The most plausible answer has already been discussed: Self-experience originates in relatively unlinked self-states, each coherent in its own right, and the experience of being a unitary self (cf. Hermans, Kempen, & van Loon, 1992, pp. 29–30; Mitchell, 1991, pp. 127–139) is an acquired, developmentally adaptive illusion. It is when this illusion of unity is traumatically threatened with unavoidable, precipitous disruption that it becomes in itself a liability because it is in jeopardy of being overwhelmed by input it cannot process symbolically and deal with as a state of conflict.

When the illusion of unity is too dangerous to be maintained, what we call compulsivity and obsessional thinking may often serve primar-

ily to bolster the dissociative process by filling in the "spaces" and denying that they even exist. There is then a return to the simplicity of con-
creteness. Personality disorders of whatever type might, in this light, be
considered the characterological outcome of inordinate use of dissociation in the schematization of self-other mental representation; that is, an
identity organized, in part, as a proactive, defensive response to the
potential repetition of early trauma. A centrally defining hallmark of
such a patient would be the dominance of a concrete state of mind in
which the experience of internal conflict is only remotely and briefly possible (if at all), in the presence of data that requires looking at himself
through someone else's eyes. As a result of the subjective isolation of discretely organized realms of self-experience, data that are incompatible
with the ongoing self-state are denied simultaneous access to consciousness. Thus, unlike less dissociated personality organizations in which the
experience of conflict is structurally possible but psychodynamically
avoided, in a personality disorder the individual cannot hold conflicting
ways of seeing himself vis-à-vis his objects within a single experiential
state long enough to feel the subjective pull of opposing affects and dis-
cordant self-perceptions as a valid state of mind that is worth taking as
an object of self-reflection. The contents of the mind (affects, wishes,
beliefs, and so on) are not readily accessible to the reflective capacity of
the observing ego; the individual tends to experience his immediate subjective experience as truth and any response to it that contains the existence of data implying an alternative perspective as disconfirming and
thereby unthinkable.

Where there is little or no capacity for self-reflection, the analyst's
experience of the patient, if incompatible with the patient's present state
of mind, cannot be talked about as an object because the patient cannot conceive of the analyst's perspective as an object even potentially
belonging to the self, much less as something potentially observable. The
one vehicle for the expression of the patient's dissociated *data of
experience* (see also Boris, 1986) is through enactment in the analytic
relationship where the presence of these data is revealed in the intersubjectively linked transference-countertransference field and never in the
mind of the patient alone. The phenomenon is not *intra*psychic and can
be observed only through living it with the patient in the joint creation
of an intermediate reality that bridges the experiential void between the
patient's self-states and that helps sustain his essential experiential need
to stay the same while changing. In the proper analytic setting, there is
a chance, with the analyst, for the dissociated domains of self to play
out aspects of unsymbolized experience that will allow motoric, affective, imagistic, and verbal elements to coalesce with relevant narrative

memory in the context of something formerly unthinkable: a perceptual experience of the patient-analyst relationship as a dyadically constructed bridge, linking internal truth with a new, self-consistent, more flexible version of external reality. A basic dimension of analytic technique might then be conceptualized in terms of how the therapist negotiates the transition from relating to self-states that are dissociated to relating to the same patient when internal linkages begin to exist as part of an experientially consistent human alliance and analytic process.

What about the act of interpretation? Greenberg (1991b) stated that "an interpretation—complete or incomplete, exact or inexact, correct or incorrect—is as interactive as a handshake or a silence or a forgotten session." In the same vein, Bass (1992) felicitously noted:

> The analyst responds directly to what he perceives or believes to be that patient's needs, and in this sense his response is based on his interpretation of the patient's experience, even if he does not articulate an explicit interpretation with the patient. (p. 128)

I would certainly agree that interpretation as an event is given meaning that does not depend simply on the accuracy or exactness of the verbal content. Because any verbal interpretation is (inevitably) the analyst's own conceptual construction of reality, it is only containable within the patient's perceptual reality if it is consistent with the patient's experience of the analyst's attitude toward him while making it and consistent with the "felt" meaning of the behavior of both parties. Ogden (1991) referred to this idea as "an interpretation-in-action" and stated:

> I have on occasion allowed patients in states of near panic to make use of my waiting room as a place to spend time as they choose. I have later discussed with them the meaning of the experience of spending that time in my waiting room as well as the meaning of my allowing them to make use of me in that way. (p. 366)

Dissociation, as an ego function, is distinguished by the presence of a selectively amnesic mental state. As a global defense against ongoing trauma or the fear of potential trauma, it represents an adaptive hypnoidal capacity of the personality. It serves to protect against what Reik (1936) called *shock*: the real or perceived threat of being overwhelmingly incapacitated by aspects of reality that cannot be processed by existing cognitive schemata without doing violence to one's experience of selfhood and sometimes to sanity itself. The relation between dissociation and memory is central here. If we take seriously the growing body of research reviewed by Bonanno (1990), demonstrating the validity of Bartlett's (1932) proposal 61 years ago that memory cannot be conceived as an expanding library comprised of records of discrete events,

> but rather as a *process* involving bits and pieces of information that are continually interpreted and reconstructed during the course of remembering . . . and that the contents of what is recalled are dependent on the manner in which the memories are accessed," (Bonanno, 1990, pp. 175–176)

Then one of the primary features of dissociation becomes clearer— "the fallibility of memory for discrete and emotionally charged events" (p. 176). In the presence of new linguistic schemata that are experienced as fitting the perceptual event, symbolic consolidation is optimally possible; cognitive reorganization of narrative memory (what we call *insight*) will more and more integrally link the patient's potential for unitary self-experience to his ongoing perception of external reality. With highly charged emotional experiences, whether past or present, this is particularly difficult to accomplish because, in the interest of preserving ego stability, discrete, affectively intense events that are inconsistent with narrative memory are largely deprived of a self-context into which they can be accessed and cognitively processed.

As Laub and Auerhahn (1989) succinctly expressed it, "because the traumatic state cannot be represented, it is unmodifiable by interpretation . . . [and] what is required initially in the therapy is not elucidation of psychic conflict but . . . [that] the link between self and other must be rebuilt" (p. 392). The course of a successful analytic process thus involves periods of transition from the patient's primary use of dissociation and enactment in the transference-countertransference field to an increasing capacity to sustain the experience of internal conflict and to a growing commitment to taking the functioning of his mind as an analytic object in its own right. These periods, prior to a patient's full ability to experience the pull between opposing frames of self-reference without trauma, are often captured particularly vividly through patients' dreams[3] as they

---

3. Marcuse (1992) advanced a similar view that the meaning created from patients' reported dreams during analytic work is inherently relational in nature and demands that the distinction between what we have called latent (unconscious) content and manifest (conscious) content be reexamined: "I believe we need a model that frees us from the insistence on a radical distinction between manifest and latent content in dream analysis . . . [and] that the dichotomy tends to disappear in actual practice because the analyst's participation has a role in shaping what appears to be manifest or latent."

enter this transitional configuration of self-experience. The analytic process during such a transition typically involves a decrease in the patient's use of externalization, projective identification, and extractive introjection (Bollas, 1987) as primary modes of securing his dissociative boundaries, and a corresponding increase in recognition of the dissociative process and the fear of surrendering it. Because this recognition (except through dreams) may not be openly acknowledged by a patient for long periods of time, it is important that the analyst not lag too far behind in his own ability to process change, but it is equally critical that the analyst not impose his view of what he believes is going on with his patient.

The psychoanalytic transition from dissociation to the subjective experience of internal conflict is not one that has a linear beginning and end. In some patients, the initial shift is dramatic and involves a major personality reorganization, but the basic configuration is there in every analysis and is part of every treatment process during all phases. To put it as simply as possible, I argue that there is no such thing as an integrated self—a "real you." Self-expression and human relatedness will inevitably collide, just as they did in both Brigid and the archbishop, but health is not integration. Health is the ability to stand in the spaces between realities without losing any of them. This is what I believe *self-acceptance* means and what *creativity* is really all about—the capacity to feel like one self while being many.

I would like to conclude with a dream presented by a 45-year-old woman in her sixth year of treatment. For most of her life, she had virtually no perspective from which she could see herself except in the self-state that existed at the moment. This meant that she was unable to access either memory or imagination of herself in any context that was inconsistent with her ongoing state of mind. To say that she lacked an observing ego would be a more than fair statement. Her elaborately contrived modes of relating to disguise what was really a functional amnesia for many of her own actions had become her means of surviving in the real world. As she so often put it, "It's as if I can't *watch* myself. If only I was able to *watch* myself." The dream, which we both recognized was a powerful communication about the shift taking place in her current self-experience, came to be called by us, the dream of the "good watch."

> I was on the beach with my family and I could see a wave coming. I knew it was going to be a tidal wave and was scared, but not terrified. The tidal wave hit and my family disappeared. I was hit too, but I was picked up and put down a long way from where I was standing. I didn't know where I was. Then the scene shifted. I was in my apartment, and many people from my past were there. I had put a good watch on

the table. When the people left, the good watch was gone and there was cheap jewelry in its place. I was very upset—because I trusted them. Later, I discovered the good watch. But it was in a different place than I thought I had put it. Then I woke up.

As she was about to tell me the dream, she "forgot" it. She then "remembered" it, "forgot" it again, and finally "remembered" it enough to report it, but with obvious conflict. When she finished, she said, "I'm not sure now if I did find the good watch or if I'm just making it up." But for the first time there was a hint of playfulness in her eyes.

Acknowledgments

A draft of this article, sponsored by Division 39 of the American Psychological Association, was presented as an invited address at the Centennial Conference of the American Psychological Association in Washington, DC, August 15, 1992.

I acknowledge with gratitude the invaluable personal support and intellectual input of Dr. Leopold Caligor during all phases of the evolution of the manuscript.

References

Aron, L. (1991). The patient's experience of the analyst's subjectivity. *Psychoanalytic Dialogues, 1*, 29–51.

Bach, S. (1985). *Narcissistic states and the therapeutic process.* New York: Aronson.

Bartlett, F. C. (1932). *Remembering: A study in experimental and social psychology.* Cambridge, England: Cambridge University Press.

Bass, A. (1992). [Review of *Psychotic anxieties and containment: A personal account of an analysis with Winnicott*]. *Psychoanalytic Dialogues, 2*, 117–131.

Bollas, C. (1987). *The shadow of the object: Psychoanalysis of the unthought known.* London: Free Association Books.

Bonanno, G. A. (1990). Remembering and psychotherapy. *Psychotherapy: Theory, Research and Practice, 27*, 175–186.

Boris, H. N. (1986). Bion re-visited. *Contemporary Psychoanalysis, 22*, 159–184.

Breuer, J., & Freud, S. (1895). Studies on hysteria. *S.E., 2*.

Bromberg, P. M. (1984). Getting into oneself and out of one's self: On schizoid processes. *Contemporary Psychoanalysis, 20*, 439–447.

Bromberg, P. M. (1989). Interpersonal psychoanalysis and self psychology: A clinical comparison. In D. W. Detrick & S. P. Detrick (Eds.), *Self psychology: Comparisons and contrasts* (pp. 275–291). Hillsdale, NJ: The Analytic Press.

Bromberg, P. M. (1991). On knowing one's patient inside out: The aesthetics of unconscious communication. *Psychoanalytic Dialogues, 1*, 399–422.

Bruner, J. (1990). *Acts of meaning*. Cambridge, MA: Harvard University Press.

Carroll, P. V. (1941). Shadow and substance. In *Five great modern Irish plays* (pp. 217–232). New York: The Modern Library. (Original work published 1937)

Castaneda, C. (1971). *A separate reality: Further conversations with don Juan*. New York: Simon & Schuster.

Castaneda, C. (1974). *Tales of power*. New York: Pocket Books.

Franklin, G. (1990). The multiple meanings of neutrality. *Journal of the American Psychoanalytic Association, 38*, 195–220.

Freud, S. (1926). Inhibitions, symptoms and anxiety. *S.E.*, 20, 87–172.

Friedman, L. (1983). Discussion: Piaget and psychoanalysis, by A. Tenzer. *Contemporary Psychoanalysis, 19*, 339–348.

Ghent, E. (1992). Paradox and process. *Psychoanalytic Dialogues, 2*, 135–159.

Greenberg, J. R. (1986). Theoretical models and the analyst's neutrality. *Contemporary Psychoanalysis, 22*, 87–106.

Greenberg, J. R. (1991a). Countertransference and reality. *Psychoanalytic Dialogues, 1*, 52–73.

Greenberg, J. R. (1991b, December). *Psychoanalytic interaction. Paper presented at meeting of the American Psychoanalytic Association, New York*.

Greenberg, J. R., & Mitchell, S. A. (1983). *Object relations in psychoanalytic theory*. Cambridge, MA: Harvard University Press.

Hermans, H. J. M., Kempen, H. J. G., & van Loon, R. J. P. (1992). The dialogical self: Beyond individualism and rationalism. *American Psychologist, 47*, 23–33.

Hoffman, I. Z. (1991). Discussion: Toward a social-constructivist view of the psychoanalytic situation. *Psychoanalytic Dialogues, 1*, 74–105.

Laub, D., & Auerhahn, N. C. (1989). Failed empathy—A central theme in the survivor's Holocaust experience. *Psychoanalytic Psychology, 6*, 377–400.

Levi, A. (1971). *"We." Contemporary Psychoanalysis, 7*, 181–188.

Loewald, H. W. (1972). The experience of time. *The Psychoanalytic Study of the Child, 27*. 401–410.

Marcuse, J. J. (1992). *And what does this bring to mind?: Reflections on techniques of dream interpretation*. Manuscript submitted for publication.

McDougall, J. M. (1987). Who is saying what to whom? An eclectic perspective. *Psychoanalytic Inquiry, 7*, 223–232.

Mitchell, S. A. (1988). *Relational concepts in psychoanalysis*. Cambridge, MA: Harvard University Press.

Mitchell, S. A. (1991). Contemporary perspectives on self: Toward an integration. *Psychoanalytic Dialogues, 1*, 121–147.

Moore, B. E., & Fine, B. D. (Eds.). (1990). *Psychoanalytic terms and concepts*. New Haven, CT: American Psychoanalytic Association & Yale University Press.

Ogden, T. H. (1991). An interview with Thomas Ogden. *Psychoanalytic Dialogues, 1*, 361–376.

Osborne, J. W., & Baldwin, J. R. (1982). Psychotherapy: From one state of illusion to another. *Psychotherapy: Theory, Research and Practice, 19*, 266–275.

Piaget, J. (1952). *The origins of intelligence in children* (M. Cook, Trans.). New York: International Universities Press. (Original work published 1936)
Pizer, S. A. (1992). The negotiation of paradox in the analytic process. *Psychoanalytic Dialogues, 2*, 215–240.
Putnam, F. W. (1992). Discussion: Are alter personalities fragments or figments? *Psychoanalytic Inquiry, 12*, 95–111.
Reik, T. (1936). *Surprise and the psycho-analyst.* London: Kegan Paul.
Russell, P. L. (1993). Discussion of "Resentment, indignation, entitlement: The transformation of unconscious wish into need" by Peter Shabad. *Psychoanalytic Dialogues, 3:515–522.*
Sacks, O. (1992, March 26). The last hippie. *The New York Review,* pp. 53–62.
Schafer, R. (1983). *The analytic attitude.* New York: Basic.
Shakespeare, W. (1942). Hamlet, prince of Denmark. In W. A. Neilson & C. J. Hill (Eds.), *The complete plays and poems of William Shakespeare* (pp. 1043–1092). Cambridge, MA: Riverside.
Shapiro, D. (1965). *Neurotic styles.* New York: Basic.
Sullivan, H. S. (1940). *Conceptions of modern psychiatry.* New York: Norton.
Sullivan, H. S. (1950). The illusion of personal individuality. In *The fusion of psychiatry and social science* (pp. 198–228). New York: Norton.
Sullivan, H. S. (1953). *The interpersonal theory of psychiatry.* New York: Norton.
Sullivan, H. S. (1954). *The psychiatric interview.* New York: Norton.
Winnicott, D. W. (1971). The location of cultural experience. *In Playing and reality* (pp. 95–103). New York: Basic. (Original work published 1967).
Wolff, P. H. (1987). *The development of behavioral states and the expression of emotion in early infancy.* Chicago: University of Chicago Press.

Afterword

By way of afterword, I think it might be useful to place this chapter into somewhat broader context of my current thinking, that of the analytic situation seen not as the interplay between a "real relationship" and a "transferential relationship," but rather as a process of negotiation among "multiple real relationships"—that is, among the multiplicity of selves brought to it by both analyst and patient. The human mind is structured and dynamically organized by both trauma and conflict. Psychological trauma (independent of its severity) can be defined as the precipitous disruption of self-continuity through the invalidation of the patterns of interaction that give meaning to "who one is." It occurs in situations (explicitly or implicitly interpersonal) in which self-invalidation cannot be prevented or escaped and from which there is no hope of protection, relief or soothing. If the experience is either prolonged or assaultively violent, or if self-development is weak or immature, then the level of affective arousal is too great for the event to be experienced self-reflectively and given meaning through cognitive processing. Physiologically, what takes place is an autonomic hyperarousal of affect that cannot be cognitively schematized and managed by thought. Subjectively, the experience is that of a chaotic and terrifying flooding of affect that threatens to overwhelm sanity and psychological survival.

As a last resort, the mind falls back on its ultimate safety measure, what Frank Putnam (1992) has called "the escape when there is no escape"—its capacity for the *defensive* utilization of dissociation (the otherwise normal process of fluidly and creatively withdrawing consciousness from certain self-states while enhancing others), hypnoidally unlinking incompatible patterns of self-experience so that the domains of meaning that have been most adaptive to preserving sanity and survival are preserved by isolating in uncompromised purity, the self-other modes of interaction that define them.

What was formerly *normal* multiplicity—the loose configuration of multiple self-states that enables a person to "feel like one self while being many," becomes rigidified into a dissociative mental *structure* (the most extreme form of which we know as "multiple personality"), each self now uncompromisingly boundaried within its specific pattern of interpersonal engagement, which gives its self-meaning the cast of "truth." Because the individual states are *defensively* and rigidly isolated from one another, the dissociative structure has not only been restored but now is able to indefinitely *protect* the subjective sense of self-consistency and continuity by locating personal identity tightly within whichever self-state has access to consciousness and cognition at a given moment. The security of the personality is now linked to a trauma-based view of reality whereby the person is always ready for the disaster that he is sure is around the next corner, and some dissociated aspect of self is "on-call" to deal with it. The price that is paid is that the individual can no longer afford to feel safe even when he is.

Our work as analysts always involves enabling restoration of the links between these dissociated aspects of self to take place so that the conditions for intrapsychic conflict and its resolution can be present. Being attuned to shifts in his own self-states as well as those of his patient, and using this awareness relationally, an analyst furthers the capacity of a patient to hear in a single interpersonal context the voices of his other selves holding alternative realities that have been previously incompatible. The fear of traumatic flooding of affect slowly decreases along with the likelihood that opposing realities will automatically try to obliterate each other. Because there is less opposition between aspects of self, there is less danger that any individual self-state will use the gratification of being empathically supported in its own reality simply to further its individual sense of "entitlement" to priority within the personality. Translated into the traditional metapsychology of "pathological narcissism," a patient's investment in protecting the insularity of a so-called grandiose self diminishes as the need for dissociation is surrendered and replaced by the increased capacity to tolerate the existence of *conflictual* self-states. The capacity vitalizes a broadening experience of "me-ness" as simultaneously adaptational and self-expressive—an outcome that, I believe, most analysts would accept as the criterion of a successful treatment process.

An elaboration of this article can be found in my most recent book, *Standing in the Spaces: Essays on Clinical Process, Trauma, and Dissociation* (1998).

References

Bromberg, P. M. (1998), *Standing in the Spaces: Essays on Clinical Process, Trauma, and Dissociation*. Hillsdale, NJ: The Analytic Press.

Putnam, F. W. (1992), Discussion: Are alter personalities fragments or figments? *Psychoanalytic Inquiry, 12*:95–111.

Analytic Interaction: Conceptualizing Technique in Light of the Analyst's Irreducible Subjectivity

(1993)

Owen Renik

▼   ▼   ▼   ▼   ▼

Editors' Introduction

Reference to "the analyst's irreducible subjectivity," an expression introduced by Owen Renik in this provocative and persuasive paper, has become almost ubiquitous in the relational literature. The phrase irreducible subjectivity eloquently captures the central shift in epistemological stance accompanying the current relational approach: the critique of the analyst's epistemological authority; the inevitable limitations of the analyst's capacity for objectivity; the argument against conceptualizing the object of our investigation as an isolated mind, free of contamination by the analyzing instrument; a view of psychoanalysis as rooted in participant-observation, a two-person psychology, thoroughly intersubjective. Indeed, Renik endorses each of these reconstructions of psychoanalytic theory in the course of advancing his own radical thesis.

Renik's controversial writings have been particularly influential not only because of his compelling prose, but also because, unlike the vast majority of the contributors featured in this collection, Renik speaks with the prestige deriving from his position of power in the mainstream psychoanalytic establishment. Ironically, in the very act of critiquing the analyst's authority, Renik draws on his own institutional authority as Editor of the highly esteemed *Psychoanalytic Quarterly*, and as Program Chair of the American Psychoanalytic Association. These powerful institutional positions have magnified the radical edge of Renik's proposals.

In this article, Renik reviews Freud's early theoretical assumption, based on the 19th-century neurological model of the reflex arc, that impulses could take either the efferent or afferent paths and therefore that thought and motor activity were mutually exclusive. This presupposition led Freud to suggest that acting out needed to be blocked so that patients could achieve insight into their motivations. Similarly, Renik demonstrates that it led to the assumption that the analyst needed to refrain from activity so as to become aware of the countertransference. By way of contrast, Renik draws on his own clinical experience to suggest that awareness always follows from action, that is to say, "awareness of countertransference is always retrospective, preceded by countertransference enactment."

Renik's is a radically intersubjective and interactive approach. While analysts have heretofore needed to deny the influence of suggestion, he recommends that we acknowledge its inevitability and proceed to study its role. His position is that in doing good, constructive analytic work, the analyst is inevitably and necessarily personally, passionately, unpredictably, and even irrationally involved; and this is not to the detriment of the analytic process, but rather is what makes it dynamic, alive, and potent.

Analytic Interaction: Conceptualizing Technique in Light of the Analyst's Irreducible Subjectivity*

▼   ▼   ▼   ▼   ▼

Contemporary analysts acknowledge that every psychoanalysis inevitably consists of an interaction between the patient, with all his or her values, assumptions, and psychological idiosyncracies, and the analyst, with all his or hers. When we refer to a psychoanalytic interaction, we mean an

* Originally published in *Psychoanalytic Quarterly*, LXII:553–571, 1993. Reprinted by permission.

interaction between two complete psyches, and the realization that this is so has been exerting an increasing influence on the way we think about what actually takes place in treatment: various basic psychoanalytic concepts are currently coming up for reconsideration in light of the understanding that an analyst is a participant-observer. For example, Boesky (1990) recently proposed that each analytic couple negotiates its own unique forms of resistance—a valid and useful formulation, in my opinion, and one that shows just how far we have come from the image of the analyst as detached psychic surgeon, dissecting the patient's mental operations in an antiseptic field.

Yet, having said this, I would add that even our most up-to-date conceptions of the psychoanalytic process (the sequence of events that characterizes a successful clinical analysis) tend not to acknowledge fully the fact that clinical analysis is an interaction, in the sense just described. I think that despite our new understanding in principle, we retain an implicit obsolete theory of technique, evident in the model that most of us strive toward as we make moment-to-moment choices about whether and how to intervene with patients.

Let's consider the *action* that is involved in psychoanalytic *interaction*. A patient's expressions of his or her personal motivations in action during analytic sessions are expected and welcomed: speech is a form of action, and the things a patient says that proceed from his or her most intimate wishes, fears, and concerns, rational and irrational, make up the desired text that allows analysis of transference to take place.

What about actions on an analyst's part during sessions that proceed from his or her personal motivations? What role in the psychoanalytic process is played by the things an analyst says that proceed from his or her most intimate wishes, fears, and concerns, rational and irrational? Our conception of the analytic couple is clearly not symmetrical in this regard. According to the prevailing view, while an analyst's *awareness* of his or her personal motivations is certainly seen as useful, expression of them in action is not. Countertransference[1] fantasies are considered a rich source of information, but countertransference enactment is generally understood to be, in principle, a hindrance to analytic work.

An analyst is supposed to try to become aware of his or her emotionally determined urges *before* they get translated into speech or any other form of behavior. The goal is for the analyst to *imagine* how he or she might wish to act on an impulse before acting on it. Of course, recognizing human fallibility, an analyst expects to fail significantly in this endeavor; but concern about failure is ameliorated by the analyst's

---

1. To use the conveniently familiar term without, for the moment, discussing its disadvantages.

further expectation of being able to learn from his or her lapses and the patient's reaction to them. Our literature contains many accounts of how a countertransference enactment, once it occurs, can be put to use. It is important to note that such a turn of events, commonplace enough, is conceptualized as the productive exploitation *post facto* of a departure from model technique—the skillful recovery of an error. This is the conceptualization that is implicit, for example, even in Jacobs's (1986) beautifully evocative portrayals of the ubiquity and subtlety of countertransference enactment, the ways countertransference enactment can coincide with appropriate and generally accepted psychoanalytic procedure, and the yield of analytic work when the analyst becomes aware of countertransference enactments and their determinants.

According to the current consensual theory of psychoanalytic technique, as I understand it, countertransference awareness ideally takes the place of countertransference enactment, and it is toward the ideal of self-analysis forestalling personally motivated actions that an analyst continually strives. The principle of *awareness instead of action* guides analytic technique, though that principle is never, in practice, realized.

Thus, the fundamental conception we hold is of psychoanalysis as an interaction between two complete psyches, *but regrettably so*: our theory of technique directs the analyst to eliminate personally motivated action as much as he or she can. The current state of affairs is therefore a bit confusing: on one hand, tolerance for and interest in the intensely personal nature of an analyst's participation in clinical work has gained an increasing place in our thinking about psychoanalytic process and technique; but on the other hand, the theory we retain still conceptualizes the patient's psyche as a specimen to be held apart for examination in a field as free as possible from contamination by elements of the analyst's personal psychology.

Today's analysts readily acknowledge that dispassionate analytic technique is only an ideal, a goal approached but never perfectly achieved. However, this acknowledgment has the effect of helping us accommodate and perpetuate what is really a significant problem with our theory: we admit the fact that an analyst's individual psychology constantly determines his or her activity in analysis without taking systematic account of that fact in our conception of technique.

Everything I know about my own work and that of my colleagues leads me to the conclusion that an analyst's awareness of his or her emotional responses as they arise in the course of an analysis *necessarily* follows translation of those responses into action—i.e., awareness of countertransference is always retrospective, preceded by countertransference enactment. It is my impression that those instances in which we find ourselves able to profit from subsequent exploration of technical errors committed on the basis of the analyst's emotional involvement simply show us with unusual vividness what in fact is *invariably* the case; these "errors" differ from the rest of our preliminary countertransference enactments only in that circumstances conspire to bring them explicitly and dramatically to our attention.

Here is an everyday clinical sequence. A patient is describing her joyless marriage. As I listen, I am aware of a sense of immobility—I am sitting absolutely motionless in my chair, and my limbs feel heavy. Possible interventions come to mind, but I decide against them, one after the other; I have the feeling each time that what I might say just would not lead to anything useful. I note that the remarks I keep thinking of making all aim at a rather active investigation of my patient's situation—questions about her attitudes toward her husband and the future of their relationship, how she regards her options. I realize I have an urge to rescue her from her marriage and end her distress. The feeling is a familiar one to me, reminiscent of, among other things, my childhood wish to be my mother's savior.

We could summarize this vignette by saying that a piece of self-analysis led me to become aware of an omnipotent rescue fantasy generated by my own psychology, a fantasy that was not appropriate to my actual task as an analyst and my responsibilities toward my patient. The insight I gained was quite useful: keeping it in mind allowed me to avoid embarking on a mission of my own I might otherwise have pursued at my patient's expense. Thus, in this instance it was true that self-analysis forestalled analytically unproductive, personally motivated behavior on my part; awareness of a countertransference urge took the place of enactment of it, with beneficial results.

However, it was also true that before I became aware of it, the countertransference urge in question had already been determining my activity, my technique. The posture and the physical sensations I observed in myself were manifestations of an inhibition I was employing to guard against anxieties generated by my impulse to rescue my patient, and this driven passivity on my part was exerting a very significant influence on how I was listening to what my patient said, as well as on my interpretive efforts. The possible interventions that were coming to mind I rejected one after another, not because I had thought through the issue of their analytic utility, but because they carried a forbidden meaning for me. In fact, once I became more fully aware of my state of mind and some of its personal historical determinants, I allowed myself to facilitate more actively my patient's exploration of how she was dealing with her husband. The outcome of this line of investigation was analytically quite fruitful, too. Eventually, as you might expect, we even came to look into my patient's need to elicit rescue by me and her difficulty initiating her own efforts to extricate herself from her marital problems.

It seems to me that when we can look closely enough, we always see that an analyst's awareness of a personal motivation in the clinical situation has its origins in self-observation of a behavioral manifestation, in some form or other, of that motivation. Sometimes what the analyst notices about himself or herself can be an activity on the very finest scale of magnitude—a subtle kinesthetic tension, for example. It is tempting to believe that such microactivity remains essentially private and has no significant impact on the treatment relationship, so that, for all practical purposes, countertransference awareness can precede countertransference enactment. However, experience indicates otherwise. Even the slightest nuance of disposition influences how an analyst hears material, influences whether the analyst decides to remain silent or to intervene, influences how the analyst chooses his or her words and in what tone they are spoken if the analyst does make a comment, etc., all of which is of the greatest importance, as we know.

I would say that the data of introspection favor Darwin's (1872) conclusion that a motor behavior lies at the core of every affect. In the same vein, William James (1890) proposed that our awareness of emotion arises from observation of our actions—which was the case for me in the clinical experience I just recounted. I think James was right, and I believe the only reason that psychoanalysts look at things differently is that we have perpetuated, without realizing it, what is really an unsubstantiated and incorrect theory Freud put forward early in his thinking, as part of his beginning effort to account for dreams and hallucinations.

In *The Interpretation of Dreams* (1900), Freud developed a model of mental function based on the spinal reflex-arc (as the reflex-arc was understood by late nineteenth century neurology). According to that model, motivations are conceptualized as impulses that can take either one of two quite separate paths: the efferent, leading to motor activity, or the afferent, leading to fantasy formation via stimulation of the sensory apparatus from within. From this conceptualization, it follows that thought and motor behavior are mutually exclusive alternatives: to the extent that one acts, one will not think, and vice versa. Hence the notion that a patient's "acting out" should be blocked, so that his or her motivations will be made available for analysis in the form of fantasy; and hence the notion that an analyst should become aware of countertransference by *imagining* how he or she might behave in the clinical situation, not by *observing* how he or she actually has been behaving.

So far as I know, there has never been any empirical corroboration of this early protoneurological conceptualization of Freud's. Certainly, if one becomes aware of an unrealistic fantasy and of the irrational motivations that produce it, awareness often puts an end to enactment of the fantasy; and, if one remains determinedly unaware of an unrealistic fantasy and of the irrational motivations that produce it, enactment of the fantasy is more likely to continue. However, these observations, which every clinical analyst has had the opportunity to confirm, in no way support the premise that thought and motor action are mutually exclusive alternatives. Rather, there is every reason to believe that thought is a trial form of behavior involving highly attenuated motor activity. Freud in effect superseded his early reflex-arc model of mental function when he began to develop a sophisticated ego psychology (in *Inhibitions, Symptoms and Anxiety* [1926], Freud agreed with Darwin's view of emotion), though Freud never specifically reviewed and discarded his early model. In practice, we have increasingly gotten away from the assumption that a patient needs to frustrate his or her urges in order to think about them, but we have not gone as far in considering how an analyst's self-analysis takes place.

If we accept that an analyst's activity—including how an analyst listens and all the various moment-to-moment technical decisions an analyst makes—is constantly determined by his or her individual psychology in ways of which the analyst can become aware only after the fact, then we acknowledge the necessary subjectivity of even ideal analytic technique. Many authors have pointed to the participation of an analyst's individual psychology in analytic work. Atwood and Stolorow (1984), for example, define psychoanalysis as the "science of the intersubjective," stating: "Patient and analyst together form an indissoluble psychological system, and it is this system that constitutes the domain of psychoanalytic inquiry" (p. 64). Any number of analysts have written similarly.

Our difficulty has been in moving from broad epistemological assertions to a practical theory of analytic technique that takes account of the inherent subjectivity of every aspect of an analyst's activity. Just the fact that we still use the term interpretation would seem to indicate the extent to which we retain a conception of analytic technique as potentially objective, rather than inherently subjective—the extent to which we implicitly see the analyst trying to transcend his or her own psychology in order to deal with the patient's psyche "out there." The term interpretation dates from a conception of the psychoanalytic process that is now generally criticized, a conception in which the analyst decodes the patient's thoughts to reveal the unconscious, decides what hidden meanings lie beneath the manifest content of the patient's verbalizations—like the well-traveled railway conductor of Freud's famous analogy who tells the ignorant passenger where he is. In ordinary speech, interpretation refers to translation from one language to another, to exegesis of a religious text, to giving meaning to a work of art, etc. (see Dimon, 1992). The interpreter is always better informed than the recipient of the interpretation. In psychoanalysis, if we speak of an analyst making interpretations, our implication is that the analyst is better informed—despite the fact that the patient's psychic reality is the subject of investigation.

Schwaber (1992) has directly engaged the problem of the analyst's subjectivity in her extensive study of modes of analytic listening. Here is a clear statement by Schwaber of the way she sees the dilemma: "As analysts, we may agree with certain basic tenets: we should not impose our truths, whether or not theory laden; we should maintain our focus on the patient's inner reality. . . . But again and again, we fail to adhere to these precepts. *Despite our best intentions, we seem to have a fundamental disinclination to maintaining these positions*" (pp. 359–360).

I think that Schwaber articulates here, as she says, the generally agreed-upon basic conception of analytic technique. My own conclusion about subjectivity and analytic technique goes a bit farther, as will have been obvious from what I have already presented. Instead of saying that is it *difficult* for an analyst to *maintain* a position in which his or her analytic activity objectively focuses on a patient's inner reality, I would say that it is *impossible* for an analyst to be in that position *even for an instant*: since we are constantly acting in the analytic situation on the basis of personal motivations of which we cannot be aware until after the fact, our technique, listening included, is inescapably subjective.

Although I very much agree with the intent of Schwaber's recommendations, it seems to me pointless to ask an analyst to set aside personal values and views of reality when listening or interpreting. Everything an analyst does in the analytic situation is based upon his or her personal psychology. This limitation cannot be reduced, let alone done away with; we have only the choice of admitting it or denying it. I think we tend to give lip service to the important truth that an analyst cannot, ultimately, know a patient's point of view; an analyst can only know his or her own point of view. Thus, Schwaber has entitled her latest paper "Countertransference as a Retreat from the Patient's Vantage Point," and in it she urges the analyst, through attentiveness and humility, to reverse the retreat. If we are to take seriously the fact of an analyst's subjectivity, we need to question the concept of countertransference used as Schwaber has, the assumption that an analyst's personal responses can be isolated and subtracted from the rest of his or her analytic activity. It has been said, justifiably, that one person's countertransference is another person's empathy; I think we could equally add that one person's countertransference enactment is another person's good interpretation.

It is commonly asserted nowadays that an analyst is not and should not think of himself or herself as simply a reflecting mirror. Yet our usual underlying conception of technique asks the analyst to aspire to be a reflecting mirror, inasmuch as we encourage the analyst to be maximally objective by minimizing the influence of his or her individual psychology. This pursuit of a technical ideal that departs entirely from the true nature of clinical events, like the related effort to be aware of personal motivations before acting on them, can never be a successful strategy.

The unavoidable fact of the analyst's subjectivity is the psychoanalytic version of a universal and familiar scientific problem: the influence of the observing instrument on the thing observed. Consider an analogy from physics. Let us say that we want to ascertain the exact temperature of a glass of water. As soon as we introduce a thermometer into the water, we alter the temperature we want to measure. The change may be tiny, but it is certain. There is no way to eliminate this effect; but neither is there any need to. We only have to study it and take account of it. We establish the temperature, volume, and specific heat of the thermometer, use it to take the temperature of the water, the volume and specific heat of which are known, and calculate what the heat transfer must have been. We then use this information to obtain from our reading the true temperature of the water prior to introduction of the thermometer.

Analogously, in the analytic situation an analyst cannot eliminate, or even diminish, his or her subjectivity. However, an analyst can acknowledge his or her irreducible subjectivity and study its effects. Objectivity, in the Einsteinian rather than the Newtonian sense, requires that we do so. Our inclination is to think that the subjectivity of technique is a quantitative matter: that we become more or less emotionally involved at various moments, and that we can try to detect the extent to which we are acting on the basis of subjective considerations by noting our deviations from established baselines. It seems to me that, on the contrary, we are always completely personally involved in our judgments and decisions, and it is precisely at those moments when we believe that we are able to be objective-as-opposed-to-subjective that we are in the greatest danger of self-deception and departure from sound methodology.

What are the practical implications of a conception of analytic technique that accepts the analyst's constant subjectivity? For one thing, it means we discard a widely accepted principle of technique which holds that countertransference enactment, so called, is to be avoided. While emotional satisfaction for the analyst is clearly not an objective to be pursued, in and of itself, in making technical decisions, neither does recognition that a given course of action will serve the analyst's personal purposes constitute a contraindication to going forward. What distinguishes good technique from bad technique is not whether the analyst is gratified or reassured, consciously or unconsciously, by what he or she does; good technique can be gratifying or reassuring to the analyst, and bad technique frustrating or anxiety-provoking for the analyst, or vice versa.

Actually, analysts by and large tend to be quite conscientious, in my experience, so that interferences with optimal technique arise from constraining inhibitions and reaction formations designed to prevent satisfaction of some urge or another at least as often as from the direct pursuit of satisfaction per se. This was so for me with respect to my wish to rescue my patient in the vignette I presented. Elsewhere (Renik, 1993), I described how acting un-self-consciously on a wish to compete with and punish a patient was the basis for a very effective analytic intervention. I find, all in all, that the technique of beginning analysts tends to suffer more from stiffness than from an excess of spontaneity; and it seems to me that veteran analysts become more effective and comfortable not because they reduce the extent to which they act out of personal motivation, but because they become less defensive about it and more confident about being able to explore their patients' reactions to expressions of the analyst's personality.

An analyst can aim for maximum awareness of the personal motivations that determine his or her analytic activity without assuming that acting in a way that satisfies personal motivations will necessarily oppose the analytic process. Sometimes it is useful for an analyst to accept the need to act under the influence of personal motivations of which he or she has become aware before those motivations can be thoroughly investigated. I think this is the conclusion we reach if we follow, for example, Sandler's (1976) concept of "free-floating behavioral responsiveness" to its ultimate implications.

In this same vein, Jacobs (1991) makes the following assertion: "Reacting spontaneously with responses that inevitably include a mix of some personal as well as objective elements, the analyst uses his intuitive understanding of the patient's state of mind and character to make unconscious adjustment in his technique" (p. 12). Now, we may ask, why are these adjustments unconscious? Freud's (1915, p. 194) often-quoted comment, "It is a very remarkable thing that the Ucs. of one human being can react upon that of another, without passing through the Cs.," tends to mystify and glamorize the phenomenon a bit, I think, and distract us from considering that if the analyst's responses and technical "adjustments" are made unconsciously, it is likely because the analyst is motivated to remain unconscious of them—not a remarkable situation at all, but a very common and familiar one.

This brings us to a second implication of a theory of technique that accepts the analyst's constant subjectivity, namely, that unconscious personal motivations expressed in action by the analyst are not only unavoidable, but necessary to the analytic process. Here we enter into a crucial subject that deserves more extensive discussion than I can give it without departing from the immediate purposes of my presentation (for a fuller discussion, see Renik, 1993). For the moment, I will only suggest that it is precisely because of the analyst's capacity for self-deception, the analyst's *willingness to be self-deceived,* that he or she is able to enter spontaneously and sincerely into corrective emotional experiences with the patient without the presumption and hypocrisy of deliberate role-playing. These interactions provide a crucial series of gratifications and frustrations to the analysand that form the basis for a successful analytic process. Continuous examination of them as they occur, and the retrospective understanding continuously reached and refined, is what we usually refer to as the analysis of the transference. We can emphatically agree with Boesky (1990) when he observes, "If the analyst does not get emotionally involved sooner or later in a manner that he had not intended, the analysis will not proceed to a successful conclusion" (p. 573).

We come to a problematic third implication of a theory of technique that accepts the analyst's constant subjectivity. Since an analyst acting on his or her personal motivations is inherent in productive technique, how are we to say where analytic work leaves off and exploitation of the analytic situation by the analyst begins? There is no avoiding this very disconcerting question. In struggling to answer it, we cannot afford to deny the fact of an analyst's personal involvement.

What we have been used to calling countertransference, in the widest sense of the term, is the ever-present raw material of technique. We need to learn more about what combines with it in order to distinguish helpful analytic treatment from exploitation. We do not profit, ultimately, from the comforting but misconceived ideal of what is essentially an impersonal use of the self of the analyst in clinical analysis.

Instead of the analyst as surgeon or reflecting mirror, our guiding metaphor might be the analyst as skier or surfer—someone who allows himself or herself to be acted upon by powerful forces, knowing that they are to be managed and harnessed, rather than completely controlled. Of course, the forces with which an analyst contends in his or her work are internal ones. In this sense, perhaps we should think of effective clinical psychoanalytic practice as not unlike good sex, in that it is impossible to arrive at the desired outcome without, in some measure, relinquishing self-control as a goal. In making this analogy, of course, I am suggesting that interferences in both arenas may arise from the same causes.

By granting that the analyst's personally motivated behavior plays a constructive role in the analytic process, it might seem that we are opening the way for an "anything goes" attitude in analysis; but this is not really the case. Our traditional ideals of abstinence and transcendent objectivity provide no real protection at all against exploitation of the analytic situation by the analyst (as we have ample reason to know) because they advocate pursuit of an illusion. The notion that an analyst can minimize the personal involvement and subjectivity of his or her participation in clinical work offers only a false and dangerous complacency. An analyst's use of the clinical setting for personal gain is in fact more easily rationalized, and effective self-analysis impeded, by maintenance of the belief that countertransference is separate from technique.

We have no reason to believe that our prevailing theories about the analyst's personal motivations in relation to technique have helped us avoid exploiting our patients. Every effective clinician learns that appropriate gratifications for analyst and analysand are an essential feature of the successful analytic process; thus, the principle of abstinence is obviously flawed and does not provide an effective safeguard. In practice we struggle to determine which gratifications are effective and appropriate and which are counterproductive and exploitative, and in this context abuse can easily be excused as therapeutic. Actually, it is the ethical norms we establish and maintain in our analytic communities, rather than our theories, that prevent us from taking advantage of our patients. We do not have sex with our patients or borrow money from them for the same reasons that internists and surgeons refrain from doing these things with their patients (because responsible caregivers do not want to trade on the hopes and fears of people who rely upon them), not because we conceptualize that enactment of fantasies interferes with the analysis of transference.

Another implication of a conception of technique that accepts the analyst's subjectivity is that communication to the patient of even an implicit pretense of objectivity on the analyst's part is to be avoided. In this regard, perhaps we can look upon our continued use of the term *interpretation* as helpful in a way, since it constitutes an admission, really, that the analyst is always imposing his or her truth.

Hoffman (1983), in his paper "The Patient as Interpreter of the Analyst's Experience," cautions against the error of responding to a patient's speculations about the analyst's psychology as if their possible accuracy were not relevant. In issuing his warning, Hoffman joins those who emphasize that the analyst's interpretation of reality is not authoritative. I definitely agree, and I think it is also most important to add and to emphasize that neither is the patient's interpretation of reality authoritative. Surely there can be no privileged interpreter of reality within the analytic couple. Analyst and patient each develop their own interpretations of reality and operate on the basis of thetn. Progress in analysis occurs through the interaction between two individual interpretations; and though I think we generally find the interaction to be dialectical, it is by no means necessary for consensus to be achieved between patient and analyst on every point. In fact, I have the impression that when analytic work goes well, there are usually some matters about which analyst and patient agree to disagree, or to consider impossible to determine.

I would therefore take some issue with Schwaber's (1992) suggestion that the analyst focus on the patient's vantage point instead of the analyst's own. Certainly, the patient's exploration of his or her psychic reality is the objective of clinical analysis. However, sometimes the best way to facilitate a patient's self-exploration can be for an analyst to present his or her own, different interpretation of reality for the patient's consideration—even to present it as persuasively as possible, in order to be sure that the patient has taken full account of it. When an analyst feels constrained against doing this, an important tool is lost. Lipton (1977), for example, has discussed times when it is necessary for an analyst to introduce perspectives to which the patient will not come of his or her own accord, and I have suggested that the analyst communicating his or her own construction of reality is central to the analysis of certain fetishistic transference phenomena (Renik, 1992). I very much concur with Hoffman's (1992) view that if "analysts embrace the uncertainty that derives from knowing that their subjectivity can never be fully transcended . . . analysts can . . . 'speak their minds,' including expressing conviction about their points of view, even sometimes when they clash with those of their patients" (p. 287).

It seems to me a fundamental principle of analytic collaboration that an analyst's aim in offering an interpretation is not to have it accepted by the patient, but rather to have the patient consider it in making up his or her own mind. If the analyst is clear about this, then respect for the patient's autonomy—we might even say insistence on the patient's autonomy—comes through, and it can be useful for the analyst to communicate a definite point of view, even a sense of conviction about his or her own inferences. If, on the contrary, an analyst is not clear about the patient's autonomy, if an analyst holds persuading the patient to the analyst's own view as the goal of interpretation, then no amount of ostensible focus on the patient's vantage point will help—it can even act to keep the analyst's subjectivity covert, and therefore all the more insidious. An analyst is much more disposed to being inadvertently coercive toward agreement with his or her underlying assumptions when the analyst believes that he or she has been successful in putting aside subjectivity and allowing the patient's inner reality to determine the investigation.

To look at it from a slightly different angle, the problem with an analyst believing that he or she can transcend subjectivity and focus on the patient's inner reality is that it can promote idealization of the analyst. If an analyst communicates a feeling of being able to offer interpretations concerning the patient's psychic reality *not as that reality appears to the analyst through the lens of his or her own constructions, but from the patient's vantage point*, then the patient and analyst together become susceptible to colluding in a disavowal of the distinction between developing one's own meanings and accepting the meanings implicitly communicated by another. The analytic work relationship may be experienced like the relationship between mother and infant, in which giving meaning encourages development. So the analyst, like the good mother of early infancy, "understands" perfectly. While this is perhaps a necessary and useful illusion for a time in some treatments, if it persists the patient's autonomy is coopted in the name of empathy or analytic humility.

Psychoanalysis has frequently been criticized from without for being a clinical method that cultivates the patient's reliance on an idealized analyst, and analysts themselves have recognized this difficulty as a limiting factor, for example, in training analyses. I think we have much to learn on this score, in particular from French analysts, who are especially sensitive to the issue of subjectivity and its implications for technique. The French do not speak of analytic "training" (*éducation*, in French) because training means subordination of the trainee to the purposes of the trainer, e.g., what one does with a horse; they refer instead to the "formation" (*formation*) of the student analyst.

Although he may not have been successful himself in overcoming the problem, Lacan (1975) did repeatedly call attention to the ease with which an analyst is cast in the clinical situation as *le sujet supposé savoir*, the one who is supposed to know; and partly as a result of contending with Lacan's assertion, French analysts tend to operate with a particular mindfulness of the epistemological privacy of the patient's psychic reality. Interpretations are considered more as stimuli to the patient's self-investigation than as truths about the patient's mental life to be communicated to him or her. I have the impression that this helpful perspective on interpretation is one we too easily lose track of in the United States.

It seems to me that the most effective way to avoid danger of an analyst imposing his or her own subjective constructions upon a patient is not for the analyst to try to abandon those constructions, but rather for the analyst to acknowledge them and to make every effort to identify and question ways in which the analyst is idealized and his or her constructions given undeserved authority by the patient.

When we accept the subjectivity of analytic technique, we admit the role of suggestion in a successful analytic process, inasmuch as suggestion consists of the imposition by an analyst, wittingly or unwittingly, of his or her own views upon a patient. Many papers have been written about the fate of suggestion in clinical analysis. Since earliest days psychoanalysts have been at pains to distinguish psychoanalysis from other therapeutic modalities explicitly based on suggestion—at first from hypnotism and faith healing, then from the technical innovations recommended by Alexander and French, and more recently from systematic desensitization, cognitive therapy, and various other psychotherapies. It seems to me that this concern to preserve a psychoanalytic identity, so to speak, has occasioned a certain defensiveness. Analysts have often felt the need to deny the role of suggestion in analytic technique, whereas the truly scientific approach is to study the role of suggestion in effective analytic technique (see also Gill, 1991; Stolorow, 1990).

In our clinical lore, we have a group of maxims designed to counteract suggestion by reducing the analyst's subjective biases. We are cautioned to be modest, to remain open to surprise, to see ourselves as students who learn from our patients, to focus on the patient's inner psychic reality. I think all of these recommendations are well intended, and useful, as far as they go; but I also think it is very important that we realize that they are all double-edged swords—as I have already tried to point out with regard to some of Schwaber's suggestions—principles that can be inhibiting instead of liberating, if they are followed categorically. The reason that this is so, in my opinion, is that these recommendations substitute for a systematic, comprehensive theoretical conception of analytic technique that takes into account the unavoidable, pervasive subjectivity of the analyst. The more a theory of technique places the analyst in a position of authority as the privileged interpreter of reality, the greater the need to compensate by exhorting the analyst to humility. The more the theory of technique denies the inevitable subjectivity of technique, the stronger the call for objectivity on the part of the analyst. It has been my purpose to propose that we aim toward a revision in our basic theory of technique that will make it unnecessary for us to ask ourselves, in vain, not to be passionately and irrationally involved in our everyday clinical work.

References

Atwood, G. E. & Stolorow, R. D. (1984). *Structures of Subjectivity: Explorations in Psychoanalytic Phenonenology.* Hillsdale, NJ: Analytic Press.

Boesky, D. (1990). The psychoanalytic process and its components. *Psychoanal. Q.*, 59:550–584.

Darwin, C. (1872). *The Expression of the Emotions in Man and Animals.* Edited by F. Darwin. Chicago: Univ. of Chicago Press, 1965.

Dimon, J. (1992). A review of the literature. *Psychoanal. Inquiry*, 12:182–@195.

Freud, S. (1900). The interpretation of dreams. *S. E.*, 4/5.

——— (1915). The unconscious. *S. E.*, 14.

——— (1926). Inhibitions, symptoms and anxiety. *S. E.*, 20.

Gill, M. M. (1991). Indirect suggestion. In *Interpretation and Interaction. Psychoanalysis or Psychotherapy?* By J. D. Oremland. Hillsdale, NJ/London: Analytic Press.

Hoffman, I. Z. (1983). The patient as interpreter of the analyst's experience. *Contemp. Psychoanal.*, 19:389–422.

——— (1992). Some practical implications of a social-constructivist view of the psychoanalytic situation. *Psychoanal. Dialogues*, 2:287–304.

Jacobs, T. J. (1986). On countertransference enactments. *J. Amer. Psychoanal. Assn.*, 34:289–307.

——— (1991). *The Use of the Self. Countertrasference and Communication in the Analytic Situation.* Madison, CT: Int. Univ. Press.

James, W. (1890). *The Principles of Psychology.* New York: Dover, 1950.

Lacan, J. (1975). *Les écrits techniques de Freud.* Paris: Editions du Seuil.

Lipton, S. D. (1977). Clinical observations on resistance to the transference. *Int. J. Psychoanal.*, 58:463–472.

Renik, O. (1992). Use of the analyst as a fetish. *Psychoanal. Q.*, 61:542–563.

——— (1993). Countertrasference enactment and the psychoanalytic process. In *Psychic Structure and Psychic Change. Essays in Honor of Robert S. Wallerstein, M.D.*, ed. M. J. Horowitz, O. F. Kernberg & E. M. Weishel. Madison, CT: Int. Univ. Press, pp. 135–158.

Sandler, J. (1976). Countertransference and role-responsiveness. *Int. Rev. Psychoanal.*, 3:43–48.

Schwaber, E. A. (1992). Countertransference: the analyst's retreat from the patient's vantage point. *Int. J. Psychoanal.*, 73:349–362.

Stolorow, R. D. (1990). Converting psychotherapy to psychoanalysis: a critique of the underlying assumptions. *Psychoanal. Inq.*, 10:119–129.

Afterword

Looking back on this paper, I see it as marking a watershed for me in my thinking about clinical analysis. Once I accepted that an analyst's subjectivity is irreducible—that is, that an analyst as partici-

pant-observer cannot know the extent to which he or she is influenced by unconscious motivations—concepts like analytic neutrality, analytic anonymity, and enactment (meaning a discrete,
exceptional clinical events, rather than an ever-present aspect of
all clinical events) no longer made sense to me. It seemed to me
that they not only describe impossible-to-achieve goals, but they
are misconceived even as ideals to shoot for, since they're founded
on incorrect assumptions about how the mind works and how successful analytic results come about. I became concerned with the
destructive effects on clinical work of pursuing misguided technical guidelines based on these concepts. I wondered why they per-
sisted despite their disadvantages, and how we could best replace
them.

Subsequent critiques are forecasted in the paper, and I touch
upon two issues that I have come to regard as crucial to the development of a truly useful theory of analytic technique: the requirement that an analyst consistently play his or her cards face-up (an
ethic of self-disclosure) and the necessity for an experimental attitude toward technique that more fully authorizes the patient's
collaboration.

It is obvious from my references that, when I wrote the paper, I
was ignorant of relevant contributions that had already been made
by interpersonalist and relational analysts—an ignorance that tes-
tifies to the parochialism of my analytic upbringing. Nonetheless,
my impression is that the paper was not just a reinvention of the
wheel.

I insisted on a categorical view: that the analyst's subjectivity is
irreducible, that an analyst's awareness of a motivation is *invariably*
preceded by expression of it, in some form, in action. This uncompromising formulation of the state of affairs is even now controversial
among analysts of various theoretical orientations. There are many who
feel that, by stating the fundamental epistemological issues as I did in
this paper (as well as when addressing their clinical implications in later
papers). I exaggerate in order to make my point and go too far in a
new direction while trying to correct an old problem.

These colleagues see a danger of throwing out the baby with the bath
water. They believe that, yes, the analyst is always subjective, but
more subjective at some times than at other times and that the analyst can often tell when; yes, an analyst's motivations are often
expressed in action before coming into awareness, but not always. I,
on the other hand, continue to believe, as I did eight or more years
ago when I wrote this paper, that such moderation is really equivo-
cation and is a way of preserving a measure of unearned authority

for the analyst. Under the guise of bridge building between old and new, of not constructing straw men, clinical concepts like anonymity, neutrality, greater and lesser enactment, are seen in soft focus. Thus, they are preserved by being spared thorough scrutiny and full accountability—with destructive consequences to our patients and ourselves.

A Relational Model of Inquiry and Truth: The Place of Psychoanalysis in Human Conversation

(1993)

Charles Spezzano

▼　　▼　　▼　　▼　　▼

Editors' Introduction

Freud's introduction of psychoanalytic ideas to the world at large entailed considerable courage as well as ambition. Because psychoanalysis has always been such a prominent fixture of the world we live in, whether it is approved of or criticized and ridiculed, it is difficult for us to imagine the obstacles Freud faced in establishing credibility for his findings. The quasi-medical method of free association, when subjected to disciplined interpretation, generated dramatic hypotheses about the etiology of neurosis, childhood emotional life, and the nature of mind in general. To what sort of authority could Freud appeal in asking his contemporaries to take his claims seriously?

Although he was steeped in literature, philosophy, history, and, especially, archaeology, and although he was very interested in the interfaces of psychoanalysis with these other disciplines, Freud was careful to ground the truth claims of psychoanalysis in the general scientific *Weltanschauung* of his time. Psychoanalysis was a science, like any other science, Freud argued, with a specialized methodology (free association) and a delimited area of study (the unconscious.) This strategy has been largely preserved within the mainstream, traditional psychoanalytic community.

In many respects, over the past several decades, psychoanalysis has been hung with Freud's own petard. The weapon (scientific authority) Freud used to establish the credibility of psychoanalysis in his day has been broadly employed to discredit psychoanalysis in our day. There have been many lines of attack: psychoanalysis is not and cannot be a science; psychoanalysis has to date failed to prove its scientific credibility; psychoanalysis needs to be validated by some other science, like infant research or neurophysiology. And so on.

In this essay, which became the first chapter of his influential (1993) book *Affects in Psychoanalysis*, Charles Spezzano takes on the fundamental problem of truth claims in psychoanalysis. He calls for an abandonment of what he terms a "monadic" view of truth, in which there are right and wrong, true and false, theories and ultimate, final answers. He proposes, instead, what he terms a "relational" view of truth, grounded in "conversations" within communities of practitioners, in which the process itself is more important than the conclusions arrived at. There is no correct interpretation: there is always more to be said.

Spezzano's argument has important relevance for psychoanalysis in general; it amounts to an emancipation proclamation. Psychoanalysis is best regarded, Spezzano claims, not as an outpost of another discipline or world view. Psychoanalysis has every right to rest the value of the ideas it generates in the careful, disciplined ways we have been proceeding all along. Psychoanalysis has every right to be what it is; we no longer need be vulnerable to authority claims from various quarters that we should be something else, because their presumption of authority is no more foundationally grounded than our own.

Spezzano's argument also has particular relevance for relational psychoanalysis. He is dealing here with the truth claims of general psychoanalytic concepts and the relationship between psychoanalysis and other disciplines. But this macrocosmic view of inquiry and truth he is proposing (as he is well aware) is an analogue of the shifts reflected in the relational literature, in thinking about truth and authority within the microcosm of the analytic process. Here, too, the analyst's interpretation is no longer regarded as the ultimate authority with the final word; the conversation between analyst and patient, the disciplined and thoughtful process itself, has become more important than the truths arrived at. Spezzano has helped us—both as clinicians and as commentators on the human experience—to find ways of taking our ideas, very seriously without taking them too seriously, enjoining us, as he puts it, not to give up on truth, but to give up on "certainty about truth."

The "Relational Model of Inquiry and Truth" became the first chapter and methodological framework of Spezzano's groundbreaking exploration of that undertheorized domain, *Affect in Psychoanalysis: A Clinical Synthesis* (1993, The Analytic Press). Many influential articles have followed the themes introduced here, including "'Classical' vs. 'Contemporary' Theory: The Differences that Matter Clinically" (*Contemporary Psychoanalysis*, 1995, 31:20–46), which explores the subtle but important differences in theory of technique and clinical practice in various contemporary analytic schools, and "The Emergence of an American Middle School of Psychoanalysis" (*Psychoanalytic Dialogues*, 1997, 7:603–618), which explores various themes in contemporary relational theorizing and their connection to some recent currents in contemporary philosophy.

A Relational Model of Inquiry and Truth: The Place of Psychoanalysis in Human Conversation*

▼   ▼   ▼   ▼   ▼

There is but one truly serious problem facing psychoanalysts, we might say, paraphrasing Camus. Judging whether psychoanalysis is or is not worth doing amounts to answering the fundamental question. All the rest—whether people are driven by a need for pleasure or inexorably drawn out by a need for others, whether analysts interpret minds or immerse themselves in empathic dances—comes afterward.

Among the professions and scholarly disciplines, psychoanalysis stands out as a special target of concern. To my knowledge, no other professional activity or method of inquiry has been questioned so consistently on such fundamental grounds as ours. As professionals we are challenged to show that we do anyone any good. As scholars we are challenged to show that, during the first hundred years of our history, we have found out anything. Let me collapse both of these challenges into one question: does psychoanalysis generate any useful words about human life? Then, let me take this question back one step further. How would we know if we have generated any useful words about human life?

---

* Originally published in *Psychoanalytic Dialogues*, 3(2):177–208 © 1993 The Analytic Press, Inc.

Those critics, both within and outside psychoanalysis, who have most aggressively challenged us to prove ourselves have already suggested two approaches to answering this question: outcome studies and outside corroboration. In other words, if our theories are true, they should work in psychotherapy and they should be consistent with the truths established in other, perhaps more empirically solid, fields of research.

When the question *Does psychoanalysis generate useful words about human life?* is translated into *Is psychoanalysis true?*, it causes us, at times, to become frantic, partly because a negative answer suggests that we are charlatans and partly because the challenge usually comes from inside academia, an institution with which we have had a competitive relationship. Psychoanalysis is the only field of scholarly inquiry that houses itself outside the university. This aloofness was bound to produce competitive feelings. Then, too, we both promoted ourselves as, and accepted the promotional efforts of others to make us into, superscholars who, as I put it, speak the most privileged of languages—a language of the "true" unconscious reality through which all other scholar languages might have to pass to find out what they are "really" about.

To the extent that this was accepted as our position in the world of scholarship, it made some scholars from other disciplines frantic to ground themselves psychoanalytically, to show that what they had been doing not only still made sense when viewed psychoanalytically but could come to make even more and better sense when talked about in psychoanalytic language. Recently, the table has been turned, or at least made a two-way table, as both some psychoanalysts and some scholars from other fields have insisted that we ground ourselves in the languages of, and do not contradict the words spoken by, observers of children and measures of brain processes.

I take up this whole business of cross-disciplinary dialogue in this essay. I argue that such efforts have been seriously hampered by their having been undertaken with a monadic view of inquiry, discovery, and truth. I propose as a substitute a relational view of inquiry, discovery, and truth.

In the monadic model, one person alone encounters the world, finds something in it not previously observed or at least not observed in that way (often something that defies common sense, such as the earth's revolving around the sun), and then uses this observation to prove beyond a reasonable doubt that the truth has been established. Further, the conclusion of this process, if all goes well, is that what has been said is the final world. No further conversation about which heavenly body revolves around which is useful. Case closed.

In a relational, two-person model of inquiry, discovery, and truth there is always more to be said. The point, in fact, is to keep talking. Truth is not relative in the sense that it is anything anyone chooses to label as the truth. Nor is it proven at one time and then written in stone for all time. Truth emerges out of our conversations and confrontations, remains the truth for a time because no one can talk about the matter at hand in a more useful and compelling way, and then becomes not true or an irrelevant truth because someone does find another way to talk about the same matter that now seems more useful and more compelling.

To adherents of the monadic view, the relational view threatens us with chaos. Such a fear emerges because the monadic view generates a dichotomy, which, I will argue, is false. This dichotomy takes the form of arguing that psychoanalysis is either a quest for fixed, eternal truth or else a discourse that makes no truth claims—not out of modesty, but because it cannot make any. Once this dichotomy is set up, it generates the fear that only if psychoanalysis does something other than what it has been doing can it secure a place for itself, alongside other empirically solid disciplines, as a participant in the long-standing tradition of argument toward the truth. The other things we might do include the aforementioned outcome studies and grounding ourselves in the "findings" and languages of other disciplines, which are presumed to be inherently more empirically solid, as well as conducting experiments to prove or disprove the "hypotheses" that emerge from the clinical situation. To observe and talk about what we do are not enough. In fact, they inevitably remove us from the neighborhood of dispassionate pursuit of fixed, eternal truth and deposit us into what Erwin (1987) has called "the great language panic" in which truth is "a plastic, optional element, a variable incorporated to suit linguistic design" (p. 421).

This, I will argue, not only muddles the nature of what we have been doing but also distorts and idealizes what has been going on, and still goes on, elsewhere. There is, for example, a desire among some physicists to formulate a theory of everything, that is, to describe the fundamental stuff of nature, the foundation of all that exists. Superstring theory is a leading candidate for being accepted as this description. At some point, its central proposition—that these most ultimately fundamental things are tiny strings forming vibrating loops—may be considered as the truth.

At present, however, physicists have no way to test this proposition. In the past they found ways to test the proposition that the fundamental things in the world are ball-like particles, which are pushed and pulled by certain forces. This idea tested as true, but, it would now appear, that truth is something that can be revised. This temporality would suggest that scientific tests and experiments may not establish fixed, eternal truth.

The "experiment," as Shapin and Schaffer (1985) have argued, may be best viewed as a convention. Prior to the rise of the experiment as a convention, I would argue, active, critical argument was the foundation of truth, and, I would argue further, the experiment never actually displaced active, critical argument. There was a wish that it might, that it might turn out that we could simply conduct experiments and hold them up for others to see, with no words required.

The experiment, however, was just another thing to observe and about which to talk. Scientists conduct experiments *and* talk. After a sufficient number of certain kinds of experiments have been conducted, observed, and discussed, scientists say, "Enough," and begin to talk about some idea as true. Ball-like particles are the fundamental stuff, they have said. Now, some scientists are suggesting a new proposition, and some other scientists have ridiculed them.

To understand all of this as part of the scientific enterprise requires us to take the relational view of inquiry, discovery, and truth that I am suggesting. And, I will argue in this essay, it is necessary to take this same relational view in order to understand why so many cross-disciplinary efforts, involving psychoanalysts, have been unsuccessful.

Two Case Examples from the Psychoanalytic Literature

Consider two essays from the same issue of one of our journals, which I would like to examine because they highlight, with striking clarity, the way in which one body of literature from another discipline, in this case philosophy, can become evidence for two contradictory lines of argument in our discussions. In one essay (Hanly, 1988), the author argued that any attempt to ground psychoanalysis in hermeneutics rather than empirical science fundamentally undermines the psychoanalytic enterprise. He embraced Grünbaum's (1984) argument that psychoanalysis is either a natural and empirical science or nothing, even though that ultimately left him stuck with Grünbaum's subsequent argument that psychoanalysis is nothing. In the second paper (Sass and Woolfolk, 1988) the two authors argued that hermeneutics was an excellent place for psychoanalysis to ground itself. This might lead us to think that they would have considered Donald Spence, with his distinction between narrative and historical truth, to be an intellectual ally—but they did not. Spence, they said, did not try to ground psychoanalysis in hermeneutics, as it is usually assumed. He is, quite to the contrary, a closet empiricist who has suggested that psychoanalysis ground itself in extra-clinical, natural science observations—precisely the type of extraclinical, natural science observations in which Grünbaum insists psychoanalysis must ground itself to become a valid source of human knowledge.

The arguments in these articles raise several questions. Does psychoanalysis need to be grounded? If so, where should it ground itself? Does psychoanalysis have to choose between empirical science and hermeneutics for its core identity? If it does not need to be grounded, is it at least the case that its theories need to maintain consistency with the findings of some other disciplines? Why did so many analysts assume that Grünbaum had *demonstrated* the inadequacy of psychoanalytic inquiry rather than viewing his book as simply an argument? In other words, how could we believe that he had *proved* something by simple argument while at the same time believing that we had proved nothing by a hundred years of what he implied had been nothing but argument? What is wrong with searching for authority in another discipline?

First, I examine the two articles. Then I explore some possible answers to the questions they raise.

The Grünbaum Critique

Despite its complexity, I believe that Grünbaum's critique of psychoanalysis reduces to this: psychoanalysis is a bad experiment. No "findings" of any kind actually come from within psychoanalytic therapy sessions. Interpretations, reconstructions, or consensually validated understandings are contaminated beyond redemption by the possibility of suggestion. There is simply no way ever to distinguish reliably between patient and analyst's finding out and observing something and their inventing it. Thus psychoanalysis is not an instrument of scientific research. Clinical data are inherently epistemologically contaminated. Some interpretations or clinical findings are probably true, and some are probably false, but the ways of knowing available in analysis "cannot reliably sift or decontaminate the clinical data so as to identify those that qualify as authentic" (Grünbaum, 1984, p. 245).

Furthermore, Grünbaum has argued, even if clinical data were to be taken at face value as not being inherently contaminated by the possibility of suggestion, it would still be impossible to demonstrate that key psychoanalytic theories, such as repression or parapraxes, are true in any way. For example, even if Grünbaum accepted a psychoanalytic truth claim, like "All patients have unconscious oedipal desires" and even if he allowed that this had been conclusively demonstrated by the assertion on the part of every patient and analyst who ever undertook an analysis that it was only during the analysis that the patient became aware of such desires, he would still, he asserts, be able to argue that this does not prove that repression causes neurosis. It might simply be the case, for example, that as patients come to feel safe with the analyst and hopeful in his ability to help them feel better, they remember painful ideas they had forgotten and also relinquish symptoms they had become convinced they needed to survive emotionally. The two, however, have not been proven to be connected. Instead, it is equally possible that the analyst has been revealed as a human placebo rather than a discoverer of a universal psychic process called repression. Having already argued that analysis has no claim to have discovered any psychic content, Grünbaum now argues that it also has no claim to have established the existence of any psychic processes, such as repression. In fact, psychoanalysts cannot actually demonstrate that they know anything about human psychology, only that they talk about it in ways some people find interesting.

As a result, Grünbaum finds it understandable that as analysts we would welcome attempts to characterize psychoanalytic theories as good narratives rather than bad scientific statements. But while he finds it understandable, it is still, in his view, an abandonment of the quest to show that psychoanalysis generates any true words about human life in favor of settling for the position that psychoanalysts are interesting to listen to. And we are doomed to abandon such truth claims for psychoanalysis as long as we keep looking to the same flawed experiment, that is, therapy, to generate truth. We cannot rescue ourselves from this dilemma simply by escaping into the brand of philosophy known as hermeneutics, where we claim to be interpretive rather than empirical investigators.

In a review of Grünbaum's major work, *The Foundations of Psychoanalysis*, Hanly (1988) begins by approving of Grünbaum's argument that psychoanalysis must be viewed as a discipline aspiring to be an empirical science rather than a purely interpretive discipline wishing to make no claims about discovering objective truth. He uncritically accepts Grünbaum's characterization of hermeneutics as a unified school of thought whose scholars all agree that there is no possibility of objective truth in the human and social sciences and also agree that, as Hanly puts it, there is no "common psychic nature that evolves according to psychological laws of development independent of consciousness, self-knowledge, or will" (p. 522).

Actually, however, hermeneutics, like psychoanalysis, has its own internal debates about such topics as the viability of the search for universal objective truths. Despite this, Hanly, again granting Grünbaum unquestioned authority as the interpreter of all other philosophers of science, characterizes Habermas as the prototypical hermeneut. Not only am I arguing that there is no single philosopher who speaks for all hermeneuts, but, in addition, according to many accounts by philosophers, Habermas is viewed as having left the mainstream hermeneutic movement quite some time ago precisely because he does not believe we should embrace relativism or abandon the search for general theories about structures and systemic causes of pathology in the social sciences (Kelly, 1989–1990; Baynes, 1989–1990). Habermas's more recent position offers a framework for taking subjective and objective factors into account in attempts to understand social and psychological phenomena. Hanly has simply assumed that Grünbaum's decision to debate the Habermas of the early 1970s is the best way to examine the usefulness of all hermeneutics, while it may well be not even the best way to examine the usefulness of Habermas's writings.

Similarly, if, as Hanly does, we simply accept Grünbaum's premise that in the view of philosophy some forms of inquiry do provide access to ultimate truth, it is natural for us to want to be one of those disciplines. Because Hanly accepts this premise from Grünbaum as an undisputed or victorious opinion in philosophical debates on the subject, he is forced to agree with Grünbaum that we at least aspire to real scientific pursuit of knowledge and remain true to Freud, who saw psychoanalysis as having objective truth-seeking aims.

Once, however, he has sided with Grünbaum as the defender of the claim of psychoanalysis to *want* to be one of the "real," empirical sciences, Hanly is stuck with the other half of Grünbaum's argument: psychoanalysis is a fatally flawed attempt at empirical science. We can never prove that we discover real "facts" about the human mind or about anything else. It is always equally plausible that we create apparent confirmation for our theories by suggesting ideas to patients who then give them back to us, at which point we say, "See, this patient, too, has a mind the structure of which conforms to Freudian or self-psychological propositions." This criticism cannot be escaped simply by switching to another school of psychoanalysis, not even one that avoids theorizing about the mind. For Grünbaum the clinical situation is inherently incapable of yielding the truth, the whole truth, and nothing but the truth. Anything purportedly "discovered" there always might also be something other than the truth. It might be only our well-intentioned invention, accepted and elaborated by our patients in the shadow of our authority. We cannot even fall back on the argument that we are satisfied to observe and talk about what we observe, because we do not observe anything. We might like to fancy ourselves as participant-observers, but our method of participation—talking to, and suggesting ideas to, the object of our observation—so fundamentally contaminates the field in which we operate that there is nothing left to observe other than what we ourselves have put there. It is as if a group of alien interior decorators visiting some deserted planet talked all the inhabitants into filling their houses with exactly the same furnishings arranged in exactly the same way and then wrote home that they had "discovered" on this planet that the inhabitants had a universally unvarying way of decorating their homes.

Finding himself stuck with this Grünbaumian package deal, Hanly then follows many defenders of psychoanalysis against outside attack in leading off his defense by saying that Grünbaum is a flawed observer because he has never been analyzed. If Grünbaum was analyzed, he presumably would come to see what Hanly claims are the objective truths that "unconscious instinctual and ego processes are immune to suggestion" and that "an analytic observer is able to detect and interpret distortions of the process such as that brought about by defensive compliance" (p. 521). He adds to this a plea that analysis be granted a moratorium on having to prove that it knows anything for certain. "All that psychoanalysis need ask for or require is that the question of the probitive value of clinical observations be left open to be decided by experience" (p. 527). In other words, the question of the objectivity of psychoanalytic observation, Hanly is saying, should itself be allowed by Grünbaum to exist as an empirical question that simply has not been answered but that somehow, we must assume in reading Hanly, will, by some as yet unknown means, be answered in the affirmative and to Grünbaum's satisfaction.

At one point in his discussion Hanly argues that we cannot escape Grünbaum's demand that we clean up our empirical methodology by opting out of the natural science game because anyone who did that would be abandoning what he sees, along with Grünbaum, as Freud's agenda and, therefore, would suffer the fate of not being a real "Freudian." Analysts, seeking to escape Grünbaum's critique by abandoning the search for proof of a common psychic nature that evolves in a self-propelled and lawful fashion, are thereby designated as non-Freudians. Nonetheless, claiming that any opponent can no longer, by virtue of his arguments, call himself a Freudian is not a meaningful end to the kind of debate into which Hanly has entered. Nor can his opponent's arguments be dismissed on the basis that he has not had the same experiences and made the same observations as Hanly has, since the opponent's argument, in this case Grünbaum's argument, is precisely that the effects of suggestion cannot be distinguished from the effects of correct interpretation in any analysis, presumably including any analysis Grünbaum himself might undertake. Finally, ending a defense of psychoanalysis by asking Grünbaum to be fair and let us maintain the status of being a maybe-one-day empirical science seems to fall somewhat short of a satisfying outcome for our first century of scholarly effort.

The Controversy over Narrative Truth

The other article I want to examine as an example of the trouble we encounter when we appeal to the authority of scholars in other disciplines is of special interest, following the above account of Hanly's critique of those who do not want psychoanalysis to be seen as purely empiricist and positivistic, because the authors, Sass and Woolfolk (1988), criticize Donald Spence for *being* a closet empiricist and positivist. This, they argue, makes him overlook the obvious advantages of identifying psychoanalysis with contemporary hermeneutics—an identification they feel we should pursue because it offers us real legitimacy as a field of inquiry.

Sass and Woolfolk argue that Spence makes "the mistake" of dividing experience into a two-stage process in which perception of raw sense data is followed by projection of meaningful interpretation onto those data. Spence, as they characterize him, wants us to accept that our clinical interpretations are inherently relativistic and that if we want objective scientific knowledge, we must look to experiments that go beyond simply performing clinical analyses and then talking about them. Spence, they say, believes such splits are necessary only because he does not see that in contemporary philosophy there is a theory that allows us to make sense of the tension between—in fact, to bridge the gap between— subjective and objective in our clinical work. And ironically, writing in the same issue of the same journal as Hanly, they claim that this school of philosophy, which can save clinical psychoanalysis from being rejected as a failed effort really to know the truth, is none other than the same hermeneutics that, as we just saw, Hanly applauded Grünbaum for rejecting. So we have a fascinating debate in our own literature in which both sides interpret a particular brand of thinking from another field in a way that supports their arguments. Hanly and Grünbaum can reject, while Sass and Woolfolk embrace, hermeneutics because they have completely different readings of what hermeneutic philosophers have said.

The problem, Sass and Woolfolk argue, is that Spence does not understand hermeneutics. He, like Grünbaum and Hanly, believes contemporary hermeneuts exalt "subjective awareness over objectivity in the manner of 19th century romanticism or turn-of-the-century estheticism"

(Sass and Woolfolk, 1988, p. 431). What they are referring to is the notion of judging a work of art or a poem not in terms of its correspondence to some external reality but as an independent structure that possesses "a truth of internal coherence (Litz, 1979)." Their point is that, in Spence's view, psychoanalysts should be content to accept the story of the patient's life that they construct with a patient during an analysis as possessing only this truth of internal coherence and not factual, historical truth. Spence, as they read him, "argues that the hypotheticodeductive model of the natural sciences, with its notion of appeal to objective, independent facts for confirmation or disconfirmation of hypotheses, is inapplicable to the therapeutic encounter" (p. 431).

They find it ironic that Spence appeals to hermeneutics as a theory with which clinical psychoanalysis can ally itself in defending the value of narrative truth as distinct from historical truth. The rejection of such a distinction, they argue, is precisely what unites the three scholars whose ideas, as they see it, form the core of contemporary hermeneutic thinking: Heidegger, Gadamer, and Wittgenstein. In the view of hermeneutic philosophy, the very characteristics that Spence sees as later add-ons to immediate experience are, in fact, inherently bundled with it. Organization and meaning, including linguistic, social, and cultural patterning, are all intrinsic to immediate experience.

The Trouble with Debates About Who Really Knows

Consider the inherent trouble with debates about who really knows by starting with the foundation of Hanly's arguments. Hanly can be read as having crossed the bridge to philosophy at Grünbaum's invitation and, having arrived there, as having accepted Grünbaum's description of what is there. Grünbaum's version of what philosophers think about truth and knowledge became Hanly's guidebook.

If he had asked philosopher Richard Rorty, he would have heard a completely different answer about how philosophy might view truth, knowledge, and the psychoanalytic enterprise. Philosophy, Rorty (1979, p. 3) explains, for a long time viewed its purpose as the underwriting or debunking of claims to knowledge made by other scholars. Philosophers once unanimously viewed themselves as able to divide those other disciplines into three groups: those that represent reality very accurately, those that represent it fairly accurately, and those that largely misrepresent reality. By the early 20th century, however, this claim of philosophy to be the canopy of knowledge in the world was falling on deaf ears. Rorty writes, "The attempts of both analytic philosophers and phenomenologists to 'ground' this and 'criticize' that were shrugged off by those whose activities were purportedly being grounded or criticized" (p. 5). Facing this loss of power, says Rorty, the leading 20th-century philosophers began by trying to find some way convincingly to reestablish philosophy as the foundation of all thought. Unlike Grünbaum, each, in turn, gave up. In Rorty's estimation, knowledge is not what we can prove, in Grünbaum's sense of proof, but the best solution we currently have to a knowledge problem.

So, when Eagle (1985, p. 114), for example, refers to Grünbaum's *"demonstration* of the epistemically contaminated status of clinical data" (p. 174; italics added) in psychoanalysis, he is simply asserting that he has found Grünbaum's critique of the epistemic value of clinical data to be more persuasive than any defense of that he has read. It is a demonstration only if one first agrees (as Eagle does) with Grünbaum's key assumption—an assumption that Rorty urges us to set aside—that traditional scientific discourse is normal or quintessential discourse and that all other discourse should be modeled on it. And it is a demonstration only within Grünbaum's own theory of knowledge, which is no longer the only theory of knowledge in philosophy.

Hanly and Eagle both begin by assuming that, as a philosopher, Grünbaum knows something about knowing that nobody else knows so well. To drop that assumption would be to drop the notion that we should stop our psychoanalytic conversation as we have been conducting it simply because Grünbaum's voice has "an overriding claim" on our attention. Further, as Rorty (1979) has written:

> It would also be to drop the notion that there is something called "philo-sophical method" or "philosophical technique" or "the philosophical point of view" which enables the professional philosopher, *ex officio*, to have interesting views about . . . the respectability of psychoanalysis, the legitimacy of certain dubious laws, the resolution of moral dilemmas, the "soundness" of schools of historiography or literary criticism, and the like [pp. 392–393].

While philosophers may have interesting views on such topics, they do not have special knowledge about the quality of the knowledge of the other people involved in conversations on those topics. The potential usefulness of what Rorty calls "the kibutzing" philosophers may do on such topics usually results mostly from their ability to spot stale philosophical cliches with which others in the conversation who have not studied the history of philosophy may have only passing familiarity. Philosophers are welcome to participate in the psychoanalytic or historical or literary conversation, but the point in our field, as in any field, is that they are in the conversation and not transcendent to it.

A related observation can be made about Sass and Woolfolk's critique of Spence. Just as Hanly sees Grünbaum's philosophy of science as an authority, even though a hostile one, to which psychoanalytic reasoning and psychoanalytic claims to reliable knowledge must submit, Sass and Woolfolk see hermeneutics as a better, friendlier authority to which psychoanalysis should defer instead. It matters to them if Spence's thinking is in line with hermeneutic thinking because, despite a soft emphasis on this, they are clearly believers in the hermeneutic perspective and see this perspective as one in the mirror of which psychoanalytic interpretation and reconstruction appear as reasonable clinical and scholarly activities. In pursuit of this agenda, they note that Spence's argument for a dichotomy between perception and meaning is not in line with contemporary hermeneutics—and I agree with their assessment. But they then collapse the history-versus-narrative debate into the perception-meaning issue. The two, however, are not synonymous either within hermeneutics or within psychoanalysis. The proposition that perception takes place only with the infusion of meaning into the act of perceiving does not fully cover the issues raised in the debate over whether psychoanalytic life stories are accurate historical reconstructions or imaginative, even if useful, narrative constructions. That debate actually comes closer to the debate within hermeneutics over subjective and objective truth. That latter debate has not been resolved within hermeneutics any more than it has been within psychoanalysis.

As philosopher Michael Kelly (1989–1990) has pointed out, hermeneuticists have not resolved the basic question of "how to distinguish an objective, correct interpretation of a text from one that does violence to it" (p. iii). And hermeneuts still argue about whether hermeneutics is relevant only to texts or might also extend to events and other objects of human understanding. They have not even decided, says Kelly, whether philosophy should or should not abandon the quest for objective truths.

In fact, even philosophical argument itself is a topic of debate among philosophers. What characterizes the conversations of Hanly, Grünbaum, Spence, Sass, and Woolfolk and distinguishes them from everyday conversation is that they contain what the philosopher Michael Walzer (1989–1990) calls "authoritative moments," and they generate "authoritative claims." They are designed "to produce conversational endings, finished arguments, agreed-upon propositions—conclusions, in short, whose truth value or moral rightness the rest of us will be obliged to acknowledge" (p. 182). Agreement is the issue. At a certain level of agreement in certain domains of inquiry and discussion, what was previously one among many plausible truths becomes *the* truth, because everyone involved feels it explains things so well that no one has any interest in pursuing the conversation any further.

"There may be strong foundations for truth or rightness claims," Walzer hypothesizes, but agreement is still the most obvious one. In fact, he asks rhetorically, how would we know that one argument was stronger than another "unless we (or some of us, talking things through) agreed that it was? Even the agreement of one other person, who has begun by disagreeing, makes a strong impression; for we know how hard it is to get two intelligent people fixed on one conclusion" (p. 182). It is at least plausible to argue that this description applies equally well to psychoanalytic conversations—between patient and analyst as well as between analysts. The analyst talking to a patient or writing an article can always be heard to end with, "Wouldn't you agree?" Knowing that, says Walzer, Plato structured all his dialogues by inventing an affirming one-man chorus as a foil for himself—one who always answers, "Yes, of course, quite obviously," when Plato asks, "Wouldn't you agree?"

This, of course, happens only in books where the author can write the script for his imaginary debating opponent. Real philosophical conversations, Walzer reminds us—and the same can be said of our clinical work and our own scholarly debates—often do not end so neatly, "with one of the protagonists on his verbal knees, desperately searching for new ways to say yes" (p. 183). Agreements, when they are reached at all, "develop very slowly, over long periods of time; they are always rough and incomplete" (p. 183).

When we experience seemingly irresolvable disagreement in psychoanalysis, we may turn to another domain of inquiry in which questions similar to the ones with which we are struggling have been put to rest. In the cases I have been describing, the perception of homogeneity of opinion in philosophy of science or hermeneutics holds only if a subset of authorities from those domains is artificially selected as definitive authorities. Further, even if that entire other domain's inquiry had put to rest some question with which we were still actively struggling, that in itself would not automatically mean that nothing useful remained to be said on the issue from within psychoanalysis.

Talking Our Way Toward the Truth

In examining these two debates over the truth value and the knowledge in psychoanalysis, I have argued that the debates are impossible to resolve when they are engaged as they were by the participants. In each case I have shifted the focus from the content of the debate to consideration of what it means to engage in such arguments the way the participants have been engaged. Essentially, I see them as stuck in a two-century-old debate over whether truth is made or found. Once you enter that debate, there are only two positions you can take. If the answer is that truth is found, the next question becomes whether or not your method of inquiry is capable of finding any of it. Freud insisted that the psychoanalytic method of inquiry is capable of finding some of the truth. Grünbaum is correct about this. With this argument established, he has two tasks left. He must persuade his readers that the other basic position—that truth is made—is wrong, and then he must demonstrate that the psychoanalytic method cannot find truth.

What I am arguing here is that the statements *The truth is made* and *The truth is found* have themselves proven to be impossible to prove or disprove. How then do we choose among descriptions or languages for talking about the world? We do not actually do that. What we do is gradually develop the habit of talking in a certain way about the part of the world that interests us. To move from this way of thinking about what we do to thinking that we search for an essential human nature is not to become scientific but simply to "privilege some one among the many languages in which we habitually describe the world or ourselves" (Rorty, 1989, p. 6).

Freud privileged psychoanalytic language in that way, claiming that it was the language of the essence of human nature. Although this ultimately put psychoanalysis out on a limb from which it may or may not get down, for a while he appeared to be carrying the day. Other languages in which people had been in the habit of discussing human nature began to seem less useful, and so a significant portion of our culture stopped talking in them and began talking in psychoanalysis whenever possible. That, I believe, is one way to understand Auden's famous description of Freud as not simply a man with a theory but as "a whole climate of opinion."

Crossing Over to Psychoanalysis

Scholars from fields outside clinical psychoanalysis grew up in this climate of opinion. Some were persuaded to talk psychoanalysis about the objects of their attention, such as poems and plays and novels. A notable example is Frederick Crews, a literary critic. His adoption of, and subsequent disenchantment with, psychoanalytic language are worth examining because they highlight the fact that not only have we been intrigued by the possibility of talking in other languages, such as empiricism or hermeneutics, about our work, but scholars from other fields have traveled in the other direction across the interdisciplinary bridge and learned to talk psychoanalysis about their work. The results have been equally unsatisfying either way because the traveler to the other side thinks of himself as simply using another language but as finding some truth on the other side that had previously eluded him on his side of the bridge.

Crews (the course of whose critical career has been well documented by Litz, 1979) began as a detached chronicler of dogma in literary criticism. In fact, he first established his place in his discipline by parodying all attempts at dogma in criticism with what Litz (1979) characterized as "an ironic and detached attitude" (p. 67). Within a few years, however, he abandoned his detached skepticism about searchers for true understanding of texts. He found Freud and embraced Freudian dogma with the enthusiasm of a religious convert. In discussing works such as *Hamlet*, he now felt that only Freud could make sense of the play's contradictions, doubt, conflict, and gaps. The answers were below the surface of the play in its Freudian unconscious. Then, in the late 1960s, Crews, partly under the influence of the political debates of the day, retreated to a more moderate position on the value of Freudian understanding. It was useful, he felt, but carried with it dangers of reductionism and self-indulgent justification for destructive actions. By 1980, however, Crews had renounced his previous Freudian conversion with a vengeance. He wrote of having fallen under Freud's spell and his later coming to his senses and making his way back to "the enigmatic, uncathartic world we actually inhabit." The trouble, as I see it, is not that he defected but that he was converted in the first place. Crews clearly believed he had found the truth in Freud, and when he later realized the truth had eluded him, he felt betrayed. Had he begun by thinking Freud had a language to offer, he might have been able to try out this language as a way of talking about literature and then left it behind without the sense of bitterness he actually came to feel. He went looking for dogma, found it, embraced it, and then discovered that, like the dogmas he had previously satirized in his earlier writings, this one, too, did not offer permanent, objective truth. Having devoted himself to Freud as the beacon of all truth about life and literature, he sounds, in his rejections of Freud, as if he took it personally when he learned about Freud's questionable encounters with Emma Eckstein and Dora and about Freud's having taken seriously some of Fliess's "crackpot" doctrines.

Must Psychoanalysts Also Talk Child Development or Neuroscience?

This is just one example of the pitfalls of insisting that the world provide us with the truth about itself, the reality behind the appearances, the undistorted view of the whole picture. Whether we search for the truth about philosophy in Grünbaum or in hermeneutics or whether a scholar from outside our field comes looking to us for the truth, the end never comes, and no knowledge turns out to be the final truth. That is what is appealing about Rorty's way of talking about philosophy and all other disciplines as languages and about languages as tools. When you talk about truth, you ask who is right and who is wrong. When you talk about tools, the discussion gets reframed, and you ask how the tool works and what you can and cannot do with it.

Theories are intended to solve problems. It is possible, but not necessary, to specify that, in order to be useful or true, theories must specifically solve problems of prediction and control. But it is also possible to say that theories are useful or true when they solve conversational problems. New psychoanalytic theories appear when we want to discuss certain clinical problems with each other and with patients, but we perceive ourselves to be unable to discuss them adequately in the language of current theories.

This is, for example, how I read Greenberg and Mitchell's (1983) description of the evolution of psychoanalytic theorizing about object relationships. As Freudian theorists, one after the other, starting with Freud, found it difficult to talk about object relationships in the language of Freudian psychology, they gradually developed other languages in which they were more easily able to do that. That does not make object relations theory right and Freudian theory wrong; it simply means that some analysts found it easier to talk about certain topics they wanted to talk about in one language than in the other.

Similarly, the ways of talking about infant development that have evolved out of observational child research and the ways of talking about how human experience is organized that have evolved out of the neurosciences do not automatically have a claim on our attention. When we begin to think they do, it is usually because we are viewing their descriptions of things as the ways things really are. The distinction that is often made in this regard is to imagine that, because of some supposed greater inherent validity of the methods of inquiry of scholars who observe and measure children or brain-behavior relationships, they achieve certainty about the small segments of the world that they study while we sacrifice certainty about small matters in favor of exploring the big picture of an individual life-world. We become the game masters in this jigsaw puzzle-assembling view of psychology—the ones who take the bits and pieces of truth clarified by the observers and measurers and, if they appear relevant, fit them into one of our grand schemes. When, however, the bit players find an organizer and synthesizer of their own, as the infant development researchers found in Stern, we are thrown into a frenzy of accommodation and assimilation. In Stern's 1985 book the observers and measurers have come up with a big picture theory of their own. While we appear to have been filling in the gaps in our *knowledge* with interesting speculations and metaphors, they claim to have filled in the gaps in their copy of the same jigsaw puzzle with hard facts. And, having done this, they did not leave it to the clinician-theorists to decide if their observations and measurements had clinical relevance. Stern's book did not just offer a smorgasbord of observations from which we could pick and choose to bolster our theories. It pulled those observations together into a theory of development, the self, and therapy. In other words, Stern offered us a different language of the infant's world than analysts such as Mahler had done.

Consider the psychoanalytic discussion that Stern's book interrupted. Psychoanalysts had long been in the habit of speculating about the subjective states of infants based on their assessments of the subjective states of adults and older children. Since some patients seemed to alternate between extremes of love and hate toward the same person, analysts speculated that they had constructed good and bad mental representations of objects and that these representations were largely shaped around pleasurable and unpleasurable affective experiences—which implied that affect plays the key role in the construction of mental representations. This, of course, allowed analysts to dismiss experimenters studying cognitive development. Similarly, viewing some adults as seeking or experiencing psychic merger with their analyst, the story began to circulate that the roots of this analytic experience must lie somewhere in the preverbal stages of life. Mahler did not invent that conversation. She simply enhanced its legitimacy by observing young children and their mothers and arguing that her observations supported the notion that infants begin life merged with their caregivers and then hatch out of this state. Her elaboration of this process, in turn, was taken by some analysts as a model for the understanding of certain adult patients.

Stern goes all previous baby-watchers one better. He claims not simply that infant researchers observe babies but that they "talk" with them. He routinely describes experimenters as asking babies questions by giving them choices and the babies as answering by choosing. The baby is allegedly telling the experimenter about his mental processes. For example, in a 1988 paper, Stern discusses an experiment by Strauss in which the baby is shown a series of drawings of faces. Then, the baby, in Stern's language, is "asked" to "tell" the experimenter which of another series of drawings most reminds him of the first series. Babies tend not to choose from the second series a drawing of a face that is identical to any of those in the first series, but a drawing in which the positions of the facial features match the mathematical average of all of the positions of the features on the drawings in the first series. From this, Stern argues that babies construct prototypical memories or mental representations of multiple experiences. He then asserts that since babies do this with experimentally manipulated visual experiences, it is fair to assume they also do it with "lived-affective experiences" (p. 234). We all construct, he says, prototypical memories—what we generally call in psychoanalytic language mental representations—of such repeated events as Sunday evenings with the family or laughing with mother. So far, he is not saying anything different about mental representations than object relations theorists generally say about them—they are constructs, not copies of lived experiences. But, says Stern, since the psychological work done by the infant in forming a representation based on a mathematical averaging of distances between, and dimensions of, facial features is obviously just as much perceptual and cognitive as it is affective, "there is no reason to believe," as most psychoanalytic theorists have done, "that affect plays a special role in the organization of memories" (p. 236).

By carefully detailing the sequential, argumentative leaps Stern makes, I hope to have persuaded you that his theorizing is very similar to traditional psychoanalytic theorizing and all theorizing. He fashions interactive situations with babies and then talks about them, or he reads reports of others having done this and then talks about them. In his talking he speculates about the subjective experience of the infant, but his speculations are not privileged over those of psychoanalysts who decide to speculate about the subjective states of infants on the basis of conversations with patients who "tell" us that they alternately love and hate the same person and so are thereby "telling" us that they construct mental representations largely in affective terms.

Similarly, Stern's replacement of Mahler's developmental scheme is a replacement of one language with another—although it is presented as if it is a replacement of speculation with truth. Ultimately, Mahler and Stern end up trying to connect their observations of infants to the subjective states of adult patients—something that any of us may or may not find compelling if we are inclined to consider it critically. Instead of hatching, in a coming-and-going fashion, out of a natural state of autistic merger with their mothers. Stern's infants are aware from the start that they are physically separate and quickly develop a sense of being psychologically separate; that is, they subjectively experience a sense of agency and self-coherent existence in the context of intersubjective relatedness to an equally intentional caretaker. In Stern's way of talking, infants tell us this, but in my way of talking, Stern tells us this in the same way Mahler once told us the opposite.

It might appear that Stern replaced Mahler as the most popular interpreter of infancy because he had disproved her theories, but I would argue that he offered us a language in which we were ready to talk as a replacement for a language with which we had gradually become disillusioned. Stern's interpersonal and interactional language matched a language gradually taking hold in clinical psychoanalysis under the name of relational theory or two-person psychology. Both infant development researchers and psychoanalysts are part of a larger movement toward talking interpersonally and interactionally and away from talking isolated mind or autistic infant. The extent to which we would prefer to ground ourselves in Stern's book rather than view it as an addition to a language that is being developed is the extent to which we want there to be an authority from whom we can learn a truth that eluded our method of inquiry. Yet Sullivan, as Stern acknowledges, began talking this language a long time ago. But he was just another analyst claiming to have extracted a new truth from the same observations other analysts had been making. That, it turns out, is not as persuasive as saying that you have decided to talk that language because it is the language of the reality of the infant's world as you have observed it.

The other major extra-clinical domain in whose language some psychoanalysts are eager to ground psychoanalysis is neuroscience. A striking example of this uncritical eagerness can be found in the writings of Eagle (1985), especially in his assessment of the work of Rubenstein. The crux of Rubenstein's (1983) major argument can be taken directly from the following quotation: "The mental operations that interest psychoanalysis can also be viewed as physiological processes and sometimes, for proper understanding, have to be viewed that way" (p. 187). Rubenstein has elaborated this belief through a merger of two philosophical positions usually considered as diametrically opposed, one in which people are nothing but mechanisms and another in which human psychological life completely transcends nature and biology. He argues that both are true and that because both are true, explanations made from each perspective must remain consistent with those made from the other. If, therefore, psychoanalysts make statements about human psychology that have implications that contradict statements made by neuroscientists, psychoanalysts must revise their way of talking.

The way Eagle reads him, Rubenstein cleans up psychoanalytic discourse by replacing a casual and thoughtless use of concepts with a careful and detailed examination of them. The strength of Eagle's argument depends on whether or not we agree that we use concepts in the way he claims we do. For example, do we, as Eagle (1985, p. 85) claims, talk about unconscious mental events "without any apparent recognition" that this is a complex and ambiguous concept? And do we "typically" make interpretations and inferences in our clinical work "without any systematic attention to the nature of the evidence on which they rest"? How would we go about deciding whether analysts generally do that or not? I do not know. I do not think Eagle does either. That in itself appears to be a matter of discussion and agreement or disagreement rather than proof, but much of the significance Eagle attaches to Rubenstein's contribution to the psychoanalytic discussion rests on his acceptance of this as a factual statement about the current state of psychoanalytic discourse in therapy and in our literature.

Similarly, the power of Eagle's defense of Rubenstein's work depends heavily on his assumption that Rubenstein has "demonstrated" that clinical theory must be validated outside the clinical situation. Rubenstein has, I believe, argued for this but has not proven it. For example, he argues that when we infer the existence of unconscious motives in our patients, we must be making this inference because we have seen what we believe to be manifestations of these unconscious motives. The manifestations are proof of the motives, and the motives are the explanation of the manifestations. According to Rubenstein, the only way out of such circular talking is, as Eagle (1985) explains it, "to step out of the clinical context and look to nonclinical, including neurophysiological, evidence (p. 86)." Is it? Rubenstein and Eagle believe it is, but that is a position, not proof that it is. It is not even the same kind of discourse as Rubenstein engaged in to argue the circular character of inferring unconscious motives from their manifestations. It is, rather, simply an assertion that, if such apparent circularity is a problem, then the problem must be solved from outside the clinical situation.

It can also be argued, however, to the contrary, that circularity is not always a sign that something is inherently wrong with what is being said. As Mary Hesse (1980) has put it, there are times when the logic implied in an account, even a scientific account, is "virtuously rather than viciously circular" (p. vii). For example, when each of two mathematical formulas takes a value from the other formula, the relationship of the formulas is circular. In some financial statements the forecasted profit depends in part on the interest expense, which depends in part on the amount of money the company will need to borrow next year. The amount of money borrowed depends on the forecasted profit. So, profit depends on the loan balance, which depends on the profit. As with the kind of ring of statements Rubenstein laid out, there is no logical stopping or starting point. This does not, however, prove that the problem is laid out incorrectly or that the solution is to replace one of the variables. In fact, the problem is solvable despite the circularity by a process of successive approximations. Similarly, Rubenstein does not prove that our problem needs to be reframed nor that it can be resolved by replacing the statement "The existence of unconscious motives is proved by their manifestations" with the statement "The existence of unconscious motives can be proved by nonclinical evidence." What, in fact, is that nonclinical evidence? It appears to be outcome studies and neurophysiological explanation.

Each of these is alleged by Eagle to have the power that observation of the clinical situation lacks—the power to confirm the existence of unconscious processes. Outcome studies, however, do not have this power. They might have the power to prove that psychoanalysis has problem-solving effectiveness, but they do not have the power to prove its hypotheses about how minds or people work. Even if study after study argued that psychoanalysis produced higher success rates than any other form of psychotherapy, that would not confirm the existence of unconscious processes. It would only allow us to say that thinking in terms of unconscious processes and talking to patients in that language are effective ways to help people feel better and live better. This is not to say that the issue of problem-solving effectiveness is not important, only that it is not synonymous with the truth of psychoanalytic propositions.

Neurophysiology is a different matter. Eagle urges us to accept Rubenstein's argument that no psychological explanation can be correct if it contradicts what is known about the principles of neurophysiological functioning. I would argue that this has never happened. No psychological explanation has ever contradicted a proven fact about how the brain works. To begin with, by the time one has reached the level of neurophysiological discourse where one is talking about any thing or event to which a psychological explanation might be thought to refer, one is talking at the level of neurophysiological theory, not simple fact or observation. More critically, I would argue that neurophysiological theory is a language as much as psychoanalytic theory is a language. What Rubenstein says, instead, is that all psychological statements must refer to some statement made in neurophysiology or at least not contradict any statement made in that language. Having taken that position, Rubenstein (1980) then goes on to argue:

> An unconscious mental event must in some way differ neurologically from the corresponding conscious event. Thus an unconscious fantasy cannot in every respect be like a conscious fantasy, except that it is not

conscious. To think otherwise would be like saying that the same neural processes sometimes appear as conscious fantasy and sometimes not [pp. 216–217].

In other words, if psychoanalysts want to keep talking about conscious and unconscious events, they should be able to point to two corresponding types of neurophysiological events, unless they want to drop the notion of the unconscious. Rubenstein does not. He wants to keep the unconscious, and Eagle emphasizes this desire of Rubenstein to make the point that he is interested not in dismantling psychoanalytic theory, but in grounding it in what I would call the language of neural events.

So, why does he not do that, we might ask? Because, Eagle (1985) answers, "we can say little regarding the neural events underlying what we describe in the language of unconscious mental events" (p. 92). We now appear to be at a dead end. We must ground psychoanalytic language in neurophysiological language, but there is nothing we can say in this neurophysiological language about unconscious mental events. What we can do instead, and Eagle seems content with this solution, "is develop models in a neutral language."

This is quite a leap of faith. Because we must, but cannot, find a way to translate psychoanalytic language into neurophysiological language, we will, instead, develop, and believe in the value of, a third language that translates into both of them. The first requirement for this language is that it must depersonify ordinary psychoanalytic statements. Why? Because that makes them scientific, the implication clearly being that depersonified language is scientific. At the same time, this new language must also retain a sense of intentionality because, after all, it is supposed to be used to talk about human events. In essence what Rubenstein does to solve this problem is imagine how a computer would have to be designed if its very design would ensure that it worked the way psychoanalysts believe the mind works. This is a critical turn in his and Eagle's argument. Since Rubenstein believes that psychoanalysis cannot be grounded in neurophysiology (an assumption not universally shared by scholars trying to bridge the gap between the two disciplines), he suggests we ground it in the language of information processing, somewhat the way Peterfreund does.

As I read him, however, Eagle is more aware than Peterfreund of the danger of the loss of intentionality as a factor in a computer model. His reaction to this is striking. He suggests that we think of the neural events as having an intelligence of their own, not located in another place called the mind or the person. This is consistent with the position of Rubenstein and other scholars, such as Dennett (1978), that in talking about certain human mental activities it is appropriate to say that "we as persons did not do anything. Rather our brains did" (Eagle, 1985, p. 91). For someone seeking to ground psychoanalysis in a more acceptable language to end up arguing that we talk about the intelligence of neural events seems paradoxical to me, but that is where Eagle ends up. And he seems aware that he is on thin ice in doing this. After offering a few examples of what he feels can be described as self-propelled, unconscious, intelligent neural events, he concludes that "the ontological status of the processes involved in the phenomena described in these examples is difficult to pinpoint" (p. 99). There are some mental events, Eagle must admit, that are neither part of conscious experience nor connected to specifiable neural events. Yet, they appear intelligent and purposeful. So, he concludes, oddly, after having criticized Schafer for his reliance on narratives, that it is acceptable for Rubenstein to generate narratives about these mental events. This is acceptable because Rubenstein adds, as Schafer does not, that these narratives "ultimately have to answer to what is actually the case" (p. 100). Here we are back again at the argument that theories must agree with some other language-independent entities called realities even when, as in this case, the reality in question is one about which nothing can be said. As with Hanly, Eagle seems to be saying that the recognition of the need to ground psychoanalysis in things-as-they-are will have to suffice until we can actually do the grounding—in this case, grounding in "the structure of neural processes." Despite the uncertainty of our doing this, Eagle seems satisfied that the translation of "unconscious processes" into "subpersonal intelligence and intentionality" constitutes an advancement in psychoanalytic theory building. Similarly, saying that psychic reality is neural and mental clearly feels more right to him than saying it is unconscious and conscious. I do not object to his choosing the language he feels to be more useful, but I am not persuaded that this new language has added explanatory power to our discussions. The advantages are implied more by Eagle's enthusiasm for the new language than by the force of his arguments.

While I do not think Eagle's efforts to re-language and re-ground psychoanalysis are a threat or a misguided effort, I also do not think that the new "scientific" language he finds in Rubenstein's work makes sense of anything that did not make sense before. It is still not inherently true, I would argue, that we should make sure that we do not say anything in our discussions that appears to contradict something the child development researchers or the neuroscientists say in their discussions about the world—anymore than we should make sure we talk the language of Piaget, empiricism, hermeneutics, or any other school of philosophy, including Rorty's, in which I have been talking. Rorty himself points out the temptation for anyone drawn to his type of philosophy to think that it corresponds to "the ways things really are."

Language as the Only Way Around the Obstacles Created by Language

I think it is important to emphasize that refusing to think in terms of the intrinsic nature of things in favor of thinking about languages in which we talk about things is not a maneuver that must be made uniquely in behalf of psychoanalysis. Languages are how we deal with all aspects of the world that interest us. For example, as Rorty (1989) points out:

> We did not decide on the basis of some telescopic observations, or on the basis of anything else, that the earth was not the center of the universe, that macroscopic behavior could be explained on the basis of microstructural motion, and that prediction and control should be the principal aim of scientific theorizing. Rather, after a hundred years of inconclusive muddle, the Europeans found themselves speaking in a way which took these interlocked theses for granted. Cultural change of this magnitude does not result from applying criteria (or from "arbitrary decision") any more than individuals become theists or atheists, or shift from one spouse or circle of friends to another, as a result either of applying criteria or of *actes gratuits* [impulsive acts lacking motive] [p. 6].

To say this is not to give up truth. It is to give up certainty about truth. By giving up certainty we accept endlessness as the most certain thing about our discussions. In the discussion the truth emerges, submerges, and emerges again. We observe and experiment to change the way we think, and "we discover what we think by saying it" (Erwin, 1987, p. 434).

Toward a Relational Model of Inquiry, Discovery, and Truth

Just as relational psychoanalytic theory has redefined mind "from a set of predetermined structures emerging from inside an individual organism to transactional patterns and internal structures derived from an interactive, interpersonal field" (Mitchell, 1988, p. 17), so does the relational model of inquiry and discovery that I have been describing redefine truth as a rational consensus, achieved by a "dialogical community" (Bernstein, 1983) through active critical argument.

According to this definition, while the world exists independent of what we say about it, the truth is not an attribute of the world. It is an attribute of our conversations about the world, and the only way we have of determining that we are coming closer to, or moving away from, the truth in any scholarly effort is by agreement or lack of agreement with other members of the dialogical community within which the conversation has taken place. It may appear that, in some instances, an experiment has established the truth, but that is never the case. Every report of an experiment contains an invitation by the author to others in that field to talk about what he has observed or measured. It never contains only observations or measurements but always also contains a discussion in which the author can be heard to ask others: "Here is what I observed, and here is what I have made of it. Wouldn't you agree?"

If an observation or measurement could establish a truth, that truth could never become untrue. Yet this happens all the time in science. The possibility of a transition from molecular theory to string theory, mentioned earlier, is just one example of the evolution of truth through discussion. Stephen Jay Gould (1981) presents another example, in the human sciences, of how a series of seemingly scientific measurements can be taken as evidence of a particular truth and can then later be viewed as not having established the truth at all but simply as having provided material for one side—a prejudiced side—in a debate.

He traces with meticulous care the historical discussion, based first on craniometry and then standardized testing, in which the concept of intelligence became a single, reified entity. It was turned into a reflection of the quality of an individual's brain, quantifiable as a single number that supposedly accounted for how well anyone was genetically destined to do in society. So certain was everyone that any pronouncements based on experiment and measurement were the truth, that absurd ideas prevailed at all levels of the discussion about intelligence. After one researcher produced a figure of 13 as an average mental age for World War I draftees, authorities such as the chairman of Harvard's psychology department and the president of Colgate University put this figure together with Terman's claims for the Stanford-Binet test and proclaimed that about three out of four Americans were unqualified for high school and that democracy would mean chaos in such a population. Further, for many listeners to this conversation, the idea that some groups are innately inferior and deserve poverty and low social status was taken as true. That truth, too, has gone the way of all truth.

This can happen because truth resides not in the observations or measurements but in the discussion. The numbers gathered by psychometricians did not translate themselves into statements about biological determinism. The discussion of those numbers did that, and subsequent discussion translated those same numbers into something else.

Grünbaum, ironically, pursues a style of argument similar to that challenged by Gould, and in examining his doing this, we also get a rare look at what he believes is a true psychological theory. Grünbaum has taken Freud to task for trying to get away with what Grünbaum calls the tally argument. Freud (1917), according to Grünbaum, tried unsuccessfully to salvage the scientific status of psychoanalytic propositions when he wrote that the patient's "conflicts will only be successfully solved and his resistance overcome if the anticipatory ideas he is given tally with what is real in him" (p. 452). Grünbaum argued against Freud's implicit suggestion that, because of the truth of the tally argument, psychoanalysts could feel certain that their claims about the etiology of psychological disorders and their claims about the necessary role of the analyst's interpretations and reconstructions in curing them had been firmly validated. But, says Grünbaum, there might be one other way for analysts to validate such claims. If patients, after successful analyses, verified these claims, that might be sufficient to give them scientific status. Unfortunately, this last possible path to proving the validity of psychoanalytic theories of psychological problems and their resolution in the clinical situation is closed off permanently by a 1977 review article (Nisbett and Wilson, 1977) in which the authors conclude that human beings are not actually capable of accurate introspection into their mental processes. The evidence suggests, Nisbett and Wilson report, that although experimental psychologists routinely quiz their subjects about their judgments, choices, inferences, and problem-solving strategies—and although subjects routinely answer these questions—all of this evidence arguing for introspective awareness can be reexamined and reinterpreted to show that such awareness is an illusion. At best, even subjects who were able to identify the stimuli being manipulated in the experiment to get them to respond in a certain way can be understood, in retrospect, to have made correct, high-probability guesses. Even they were not actually "reading off" an account of their underlying mental processes.

Grünbaum's repeated citing of this one review article as proof positive that patients have no useful capacity to validate any etiologic or therapeutic claims their analysts might make is astonishing and disappointing—to paraphrase Grünbaum's own typical characterization of the efforts of analysts to defend themselves and their work. Nisbett and Wilson reexamined studies performed by other researchers. These other researchers had already concluded from their own studies that people are capable of introspective awareness. Nisbett and Wilson simply engaged these other researchers vicariously in a debate and took the opposite position from those researchers. So there is an argument in progress in psychology about the existence of a human capacity for introspective awareness of mental processes. Grünbaum is persuaded by the arguments of one side in that debate. His being so persuaded, however, does not close the debate. Must everyone, for example, agree with Nisbett and Wilson when they argue that, when talking about introspection into mental processes, "awareness" should not be equated with "correct verbal report," because that does not eliminate the possibility of correct guessing, but instead that "awareness" should be assumed only when the accuracy rate of the subjects in the experiment in reporting how they were manipulated by the experimenter exceeds the accuracy rate of observers who did not participate in the experiment but were provided with a general description of the stimulus and response in question? Or will everyone necessarily accept the equivalence of experiments in which the psychologist is trying to fool the subject with the psychoanalytic experiment in which the psychologist wants subjects to become aware of their mental processes? Or is it surprising that in situations where subjects have no personal stake in monitoring their mental processes—do not even know they ought to be doing this—later measurements suggest observers can reach the same conclusions without introspection? I am not claiming that these questions disprove Grünbaum, but rather I am highlighting the fact that a debate is in process and that Grünbaum, seemingly aware of the complexity of the issues in such debates throughout most of his writing, suddenly makes his sole leap out of his own discipline and into experimental psychology and asks us to accept, as case-closing proof of the impossibility of accurate introspection in psychoanalysis, a blend of experiment and argument produced by Nisbett and Wilson to negate the possibility of introspective awareness in stimulus-response studies. The discussion on introspection will not likely be closed by this one article nor by Grünbaum's citing of it at a critical juncture in his argument. Whether any of us ever knows what we are talking about or can ever report accurately why we think or feel the way we do is a question that was not resolved by Nisbett and Wilson in 1977. Talking as if we have the capacity to become aware of why we do what we do is so universal that even Grünbaum (1984) does it, for example, when he claims that Philip Holzman's "clinical experience led him to press fundamental doubts against the scientific probity of the treatment setting" (p. xii). Perhaps, we would have to say, if we accepted Nisbett and Wilson without question, as Grünbaum does, that is why Holzman was led to his doubts, and perhaps not. How would Holzman know? But as Grünbaum's acceptance of Holzman's introspective awareness suggests, it is very difficult to keep talking usefully about human life in the complete absence of any hint of introspective awareness of mental processes, even such complex ones as motivation. The sense we have of the truth or illusory status of introspective awareness rises and falls throughout a historical discussion of this critical topic of enduring human interest.

Further discussion of this and all other topics can change the truth, and this is such a fundamental property of the truth that it must be taken into account in any discussion about the truth. It redefines the truth as something not fixed and eternal but as a moment of rest in our ongoing, active, critical argument.

This redefinition allows us to understand why attempts to ground one discipline in another can so easily go wrong. Because the discussion itself is the foundation of truth, how it is conceived becomes critical. In a monadic model of inquiry and discovery, one can come looking for the authority of the correct interpretation, as Crews did. This resembles the model of psychotherapy that emerged from Freud's "monadic theory of mind" (Mitchell, 1988). In that model, the analyst gathers evidence in preparation for an interpretation. In a relational model of therapy, as in the relational model of inquiry and discovery constructed here, the truth emerges from a process of inquiry, argument, and agreement always involving at least two persons in a dialogical community.

In a relational model of inquiry, discovery, and truth, the kinds of conversations engaged in by the authors reviewed earlier in this essay are themselves viewed as problematic. They are conversations carried on as if one or the other party must, or at least might, turn out to possess the definitely authoritative mode of inquiry, the conclusive discovery, or the truth-bearing language. A conversation carried on in a dialogical community starts from the opposite assumptions. If Hanly views Grünbaum as a member of a dialogical community, he knows a priori that Grünbaum's voice is just one voice within that community, in this case a community of philosophers. If Crews sees Freud as a discussant of human nature, he can try out Freud's language, but he will not kneel before Freud's authority, and, therefore, he will never need to denounce Freud as a false god. If Sass and Woolfolk view hermeneutics as a dialogical community, they will not ask what hermeneutics really says. They will know ahead of time that hermeneutics says many things, some of which will contradict each other. If this was not the case, the hermeneutic discussion would have ended already. Its being alive, by definition, would let them make the assumption of its unresolved status.

References

Baynes, K. (1989–1990), Rational reconstruction and social criticism: Habermas's model of interpretive social science. *Phil. Forum Quart.*, 21:122–145.

Bernstein, R. (1983), *Beyond Objectivism and Relativism*. Philadelphia: University of Pennsylvania Press.

Dennett, D. C. (1978), Toward a cognitive theory of consciousness. In: *Minnesota Studies in the Philosophy of Sciences, Vol. 9: Perception and Cognition: Issues in the Foundations of Psychology*, ed. C. W. Savage. Minneapolis: University of Minnesota Press, pp. 210–228.

Eagle, M. N. (1985), Benjamin B. Rubenstein: Contributing to the structure of psychoanalytic theory. In: *Beyond Freud*, ed. J. Reppen. Hillsdale: The Analytic Press, pp. 83–108.

Erwin, R. (1987), The great language panic. *Antioch Review*, 45:421–450.

Freud, S. (1917), Introductory lectures on psychoanalysis. Part III: General theory of the neuroses. *Standard Edition*, 16:243–463. London: Hogarth Press, 1963.

Gould, S. J. (1981), *The Mismeasure of Man*. New York: Norton.

Greenberg, J. & Mitchell, S. (1983), *Object Relations in Psychoanalytic Theory*. Cambridge, MA: Harvard University Press.

Grünbaum, A. (1984), *The Foundations of Psychoanalysis*. Berkeley: University of California Press.

Hanly, C. (1988), Review of *The Foundations of Psychoanalysis* by A. Grünbaum. *J. Amer. Psychoanal. Assn.*, 36:521–528.

Hesse, M. (1980), *Revolutions and Reconstructions in the Philosophy of Science*. Bloomington: Indiana University Press.

Kelly, M. (1989–1990), Editor's introduction. *Phil. Forum*, 21.

Litz, A. W. (1979), Literary criticism. In: *Harvard Guide to Contemporary American Writing*, ed. Daniel Hoffman. Cambridge, MA: Belknap Press, pp. 51–83.

Mitchell, S. (1988), *Relational Concepts in Psychoanalysis*. Cambridge, MA: Harvard University Press.

Nisbett, R. E. & Wilson, T. E. (1977), Telling more than we can know: Verbal reports on mental processes. *Psychol. Rev.*, 84:231–259.

Rorty, R. (1979), *Philosophy and the Mirror of Nature*. Princeton, NJ: Princeton University Press.

—— (1989), *Contingency, Irony, and Solidarity*. Cambridge: Cambridge University Press.

Rubenstein, B. B. (1980), Review of *The Self and Its Brain*. *J. Amer. Psychoanal. Assn.*, 28:210–219.

—— (1983), Freud's early theories of hysteria. In: *Physics, Philosophy and Psychoanalysis*, ed. R. S. Cohen & L. Laudan. Dordrecht: D. Reidel, pp. 169–190.

Sass, L. A. & Woolfolk, R. L. (1988), Psychoanalysis and the hermeneutic turn: A critique of *Narrative Truth and Historical Truth*. *J. Amer. Psychoanal. Assn.*, 36:429–454.

Shapin, S. & Schaffer, S. (1985), *Leviathan and the Air-Pump: Hobbes, Boyle, and the Experimental Life*. Princeton, NJ: Princeton University Press.

Stern, D. (1985), *The Interpersonal World of the Infant*. New York: Basic Books.

—— (1988), Affect in the context of the infant's lived experience. *Internat. J. Psycho-Anal.*, 69:233–238.

Walzer, M. A. (1989–1990), Critique of philosophical conversation. *Phil. Forum*, 21:182–196.

Afterword

There are some things I would do differently if I were addressing now the issues I took up in this paper when I wrote it (which was about eight years ago). I am not as enamored of Rorty as I was then. I had been stimulated originally to write the paper by Grünbaum's first book and the swirl of writing that it catalyzed. It seemed to me that I would have to read philosophy to determine if Grünbaum represented a more or less uncontested consensus within philosophy or just one position. I still believe that Grünbaum was a sort of philosophical bully who moved into our neighborhood during the second half of the 1980s. He threw his weight around by telling us about a place called philosophy of science, where our primitive epistemological ways had long since been shelved along with the phlogiston theory.

When it became apparent that Grünbaum represented just one position among philosophers involved in the debates that matter to us, it was expedient for me to make my point by highlighting the opposite position I found in Rorty. Now I have read more and think neither of them is right. I didn't agree completely with Rorty even then and, especially in my response to Sass's critique of my paper, emphasized my more traditional take on the human ability to arrive at truth and maybe even Truth or at least a piece of it.

Nonetheless, I privileged Rorty quite a bit as a corrective to Grünbaum and in response to my annoyance at Grünbaum's idealization by certain analysts.

Since then, I have read more of other pragmatists, going back to C. S. Peirce. The early pragmatic tradition retains more hope for finding a little bit of the truth about mind than Rorty's pragmatism does. For Peirce, concepts were best understood in terms of their practical consequences. That seems right to my clinical self.

Now, if I were going to quote a contemporary philosopher, I would lean toward one who seemed to be trying to balance what have come to be called the modern and postmodern attitudes. For example, Gregory Bruce Smith (1996) puts it this way:

> I accept that the "hermeneutical situation" from which we start our attempts at understanding is not to be construed as an unsullied, self-grounding Cartesian detachment; but this does not imply that we are thrown blind into a situation we can in no way bracket. It is inappropriate to conceptualize the interpretive act as one of an autonomous subject completely extricated from the concrete present. But it is equally inappropriate to see it as hopelessly historical. There are many possibilities between those two poles; this is not an either/or choice [p. 7].

Along these same lines, I would not rely so much on the word conversation to capture what happens either in the analytic situation or in debates among analysts. It isn't that I think my use of the word was not a useful corrective to prevailing images of our field evolving entirely thorough hypothesis testing and weighing clinical evidence. Nonetheless, the word never escaped an image of casualness. It left the impression that I don't think there are differences that matter between clinical theories.

In addition, I would now have to take into account the reasonable concerns about and objections to the most radical deconstructionist, relativistic, and antiempirical attitudes in some postmodern, constructivist, relational, intersubjective, and hermeneutic writings about psychoanalysis. In fact, when this paper became the first chapter of a book I wrote (Spezzano, 1993), I balanced the position taken in this paper by emphasizing that, although the analyst is not a perfect instrument for observing and capturing the affective states of the analysand, nonetheless, what he observes and imperfectly captures does exist. Its existence is not automatically called into question because of the limits of either introspective or external scrutiny of it. We do want to understand accurately how the mind of the patient works, and in good analytic work such understandings do emerge. We can also show our colleagues in our writings how we formed hypotheses about a patient's unconscious psychology, offered them to the patient in interpretations, and assessed the patient's response. At the end, we can often make a valid claim to have shown that we did discover an aspect of the patient's unconscious mental activity.

Yet we must also recognize that this empirical writing is only part of our literature. The evolution of our literature has not, does not, and will not proceed simply as a report of the listening and observing analyst's forming hypotheses, testing them through interpretive interventions, and reporting the results to colleagues. Our literature will always also be, as it always has been, drama, poetry, and narrative. It will contain these elements because our clinical work contains them. The presence of these elements in our work and our writing, I wanted to make clear, brings us into contact with hermeneutics, postmodernism, and constructivism, among other trends of thought. I also wanted to make clear that no discipline is free of these elements, at least in the literatures through which we know them. Biologists, chemists, and physicists also must use metaphors to contain and communicate their thinking. The validity of these metaphors is not simply an empirical fact. Yet these metaphors often shape the direction of further thinking and research, as happens in our field as well. So, I would now make clearer the inevitable tension between the empirical and the poetic, the investigative and the constructivist, the intrapsychic being discovered and the intersubjective being created.

Another change I would make to the paper now is that I would clarify my position on the relation between psychoanalysis and other disciplines. It has been common for me to hear that my position was "other disciplines are irrelevant to us." It wasn't then and isn't now. My argument was that we should not turn to other disciplines to adjudicate thorny clinical problems. They can suggest angles of vision but cannot tell us definitively about the nature and vicissitudes of unconscious mental activity or the analytic process.

References

Smith, G. B. (1996), *Nietzsche, Heidegger, and the Transition to Postmodernity*. Chicago: University of Chicago Press.

Spezzano, C. (1993), *Affect in Psychoanalysis: A Clinical Synthesis*. Hillsdale, NJ: The Analytic Press.

The Analytic Third: Working with Intersubjective Clinical Facts

(1994)

Thomas H. Ogden

▼　▼　▼　▼　▼

Editors' Introduction

Thomas Ogden is one of the most widely read and creative contributors to contemporary psychoanalytic thought. His work reflects a unique confluence of influences and experiences: classical psychoanalytic training, intense psychoanalytic clinical experience with severely disturbed patients, immersion in both Kleinian and neo-Kleinian and also Winnicottian thought, and, most recently, a fascination with language and poetry. He has been one of the most important interpreters and synthesizers of object relations concepts, and his addition of an "autistic-contiguous" position, dialectically balanced with Klein's paranoid-schizoid and depressive positions, has been widely utilized by many subsequent writers. Ogden's introduction of the concept of the "analytic third" represents one of the richest and most intriguing perspectives on the analytic situation and the analytic process in the contemporary literature.

Ogden's notion of the "analytic third" has been particularly challenging for relationally oriented readers and clinicians. On one hand, Ogden's approach to clinical technique is quite classical in tone, emphasizing restraint, silence, and privacy for both the analysand and the analyst. In that sense, it is different from many other relational depictions of clinical work, which tend to emphasize a greater degree of mutuality in the analytic relationship and the analyst's more active and expressive participation. Ogden regards the couch as virtually indispensable for generating the state of mind necessary for analytic experience; emphasizes the differences in the roles of analysand and analyst; eschews any explicit disclosure of countertransference experience; recommends largely silent surrender to private reverie for extended periods of time; and employs countertransferential experience almost exclusively for the framing of transference interpretations.

On the other hand, Ogden offers one of the most radically intersubjective visions of the analytic situation. Whereas critics of classical restraint in traditional psychoanalytic technique tend to view that restraint as creating distance and detachment, Ogden regards the restrained, formal structure of the analytic situation as generating a profound form of unconscious connection. He portrays the minds of analysand and analyst as essentially permeable to each other, with their confluence generating a "third" subjectivity, an intersubjectivity, distinctly different from the forms of subjectivity either brings, by itself, to the analytic encounter.

Other relational authors have placed increasingly greater importance on the analyst's experience as a source of potentially useful information about the patient's dynamics. But other authors will generally divide the analyst's experience into two realms: feelings and thoughts that are responsive to and associatively linked with the patient's issues, and other feelings and thoughts that are the analyst's own issues, preoccupations, concerns and have nothing to do with this particular patient. In fact, all other relational theorists that we are aware of who have written about analytic process and use of countertransference have emphasized the importance of the analyst's responsibility to reflect on his own countertransferential experience, sorting out what is relevant to the patient and what is not.

Ogden is exploring the provocative position that, within the psychic space framed by the beginning and the end of a session (and beginnings and endings can be variably defined), all the experience of both analysand and analyst is an intersubjective mixture. Thus, all the analyst's experiences are generated, by definition, by a comingling of psychic content from two minds. This claim has enormous implications. First, Ogden is suggesting that the deepest levels of interaction between analysand and analyst are reachable not through expression and disclosure of the analyst's feelings, not through behavioral interaction and exchange, but through a kind of "being alone in the presence" of each other, which allows each to tap into unconscious, intersubjective connections emerging in private reverie. Second, Odgen is proposing a very novel approach to clinical technique: the analyst should cultivate an openness to the most seemingly irrelevant, most quotidian of his thoughts and associations—the very thoughts and associations we have all learned to block out so as to be more centered on the patient—in order to mine their potentially rich yield of access points into the patient's inner world.

Ogden has produced five highly influential books on psychoanalytic theory and clinical process: This paper was prefigured in some respects in chapters 7 and 8 of *The Primitive Edge of Experience* (1989, Aronson), in which Ogden deals with the establishment of the analytic situation in the initial interview and the complex nature of the analyst's claims to knowledge. The paper reprinted here became a key chapter in *Subjects of Analysis*, (1994, Aronson), which, along with the subsequent *Reverie and Interpretation* (1997, Aronson), explores many features of Ogden's seminal concept of the "analytic third" and contributes to his masterful rethinking of psychoanalytic theory. A review of *Subjects of Analysis* in the *Psychoanalytic Quarterly* asserted that Ogden's cumulative contribution is "among the best work that has been done since Freud" (B. Larsson, 1998, 67:157–160). Beyond its incomparable significance for psychoanalysis, Ogden's work is one of the most powerful and poetic renderings of the struggle of people at the end of the twentieth century for personal meaning and interpersonal connection.

The Analytic Third: Working with Intersubjective Clinical Facts*

▼　▼　▼　▼　▼

And he is not likely to know what is to be done unless he lives in what is not merely the present, but the present moment of the past, unless he is conscious, not of what is dead, but of what is already living (T. S. Eliot, 1919, p. 11).

---

* Originally published in *International Journal of Psycho-Analysis*, 75:3–19, 1994. Reprinted by permission.

On this occasion of the celebration of the 75th anniversary of the founding of *The International Journal of Psycho-Analysis*, I shall endeavour to address an aspect of what I understand to be 'the present moment of the past' of psychoanalysis. It is my belief that an important facet of this 'present moment' for psycho-analysis is the development of an analytic conceptualization of the nature of the interplay of subjectivity and intersubjectivity in the analytic setting and the exploration of the implications for technique that these conceptual developments hold.

In this paper, I shall present clinical material from two analyses in an effort to illustrate some of the ways in which an understanding of the interplay of subjectivity and intersubjectivity (Ogden, 1992a, b) influences the practice of psychoanalysis and the way in which clinical theory is generated. As will be seen, I consider the dialectical movement of subjectivity and intersubjectivity to be a central clinical fact of psychoanalysis, which all clinical analytic thinking attempts to describe in ever more precise and generative terms.

The conception of the analytic subject, as elaborated in the work of Klein and Winnicott, has led to an increasingly strong emphasis on the interdependence of subject and object in psychoanalysis (Ogden, 1992b). I believe that it is fair to say that contemporary psychoanalytic thinking is approaching a point where one can no longer simply speak of the analyst and the analysand as separate subjects who take one another as objects. The idea of the analyst as a neutral blank screen for the patient's projections is occupying a position of steadily diminishing importance in current conceptions of the analytic process.

Over the past fifty years, psychoanalysts have changed their view of their own method. It is now widely held that, instead of being about the patient's intrapsychic dynamics, interpretation should be made about *the interaction* of patient and analyst *at an intrapsychic level* (O'Shaughnessy, 1983, p. 281).[1]

---

1. It is beyond the scope of this paper to offer a comprehensive review of the literature concerning the development of an intersubjective understanding of the analytic process and the nature of the interplay of transference and countertransference. A partial listing of the major contributions to these aspects of the analytic dialogue includes: Atwood & Stolorow (1984), Balint (1968), Bion (1952, 1959, 1962), Blechner (1992), Bollas (1987), Boyer (1961, 1983, 1992), Coltart (1986), Ferenczi (1920), Gabbard (1991), Giovacchini (1979), Green (1975), Grinberg (1962), Grotstein (1981), Heimann (1950), Hoffman (1992), Jacobs (1991), Joseph (1982), Kernberg (1976), Khan (1974), Klein (1946, 1955), Kohut (1977), Little (1951), McDougall (1978), McLaughlin (1991), Meltzer (1966), Milner (1969), Mitchell (1988), Money-Kyrle (1956), O'Shaughnessy (1983), Racker (1952, 1968), D. Rosenfeld (1992), H. Rosenfeld (1952, 1965, 1971), Sandler (1976), Scharff (1992), Searles (1979), Segal (1981),

My own conception of analytic intersubjectivity places central emphasis on its dialectical nature (Ogden, 1979, 1982, 1985, 1986, 1988, 1989). This understanding represents an elaboration and extension of Winnicott's notion that "'There is no such thing as an infant [apart from the maternal provision]" (quoted in Winnicott, 1960, p. 39, fn.). I believe that, in an analytic context, there is no such thing as an analysand apart from the relationship with the analyst, and no such thing as an analyst apart from the relationship with the analysand. Winnicott's statement is, I believe, intentionally incomplete. He assumes that it will be understood that the idea that there is no such thing as an infant is playfully hyperbolic and represents one element of a larger paradoxical statement. From another perspective (from the point of view of the other 'pole' of the paradox), there is obviously an infant and a mother who constitute separate physical and psychological entities. The mother-infant unity coexists in dynamic tension with the mother and infant in their separateness.

Similarly, the intersubjectivity of the analyst-analysand coexists in dynamic tension with the analyst and the analysand as separate individuals with their own thoughts, feelings, sensations, corporal reality, psychological identity and so on. Neither the intersubjectivity of the mother-infant nor that of the analyst-analysand (as separate psychological entities) exists in pure form. The intersubjective and the individually subjective each create, negate and preserve the other (see Ogden, 1992b, for a discussion of the dialectic of oneness and twoness in early development and in the analytic relationship). In both the relationship of mother and infant and of analyst and analysand, the task is not to tease apart the elements constituting the relationship in an effort to determine which qualities belong to each individual participating in it; rather, from the point of view of the interdependence of subject and object, the analytic task involves an attempt to describe as fully as possible the specific nature of the experience of the interplay of individual subjectivity and intersubjectivity.

In the present paper, I shall attempt to trace in some detail the vicissitudes of the experience of being simultaneously within and outside of the intersubjectivity of the analyst-analysand, which I will refer to as 'the analytic third'. This third subjectivity, the intersubjective analytic third (Green's [1975] 'analytic object'), is a product of a unique dialectic gen-

---

Tansey & Burke (1989), Viderman (1979), and Winnicott (1947, 1951). For recent reviews of aspects of this large body of literature on transference–countertransference, see Boyer (1993) and Etchegoyen (1991).

erated by (between) the separate subjectivities of analyst and analysand within the analytic setting.[2]

I will present portions of two analyses which highlight different aspects of the dynamic interplay of subjectivities constituting the analytic third. The first fragment of an analysis focuses on the importance of the most mundane, everyday aspects of the background workings of the mind (which appear to be entirely unrelated to the patient) in the service of recognising and addressing the transference-countertransference.

The second clinical vignette provides an opportunity to consider an instance in which the analytic third was experienced by the analyst and analysand largely through the medium of somatic delusion and other forms of bodily sensations and body-related fantasies. I shall discuss the analyst's task of using verbal symbols to speak with a voice that has lived within the intersubjective analytic third, has been changed by that experience, and is able to speak *about it*, in his own voice, as analyst to the analysand (who has also been a part of the experience of the third).

Clinical Illustration: The Purloined Letter

In a recent meeting with Mr L, an analysand with whom I had been working for about three years, I found myself looking at an envelope on the table next to my chair in my consulting room. For the previous week or ten days, I had been using this envelope to jot down phone numbers retrieved from my answering machine, ideas for classes I was teaching, errands I had to attend to, and other notes to myself. Although the envelope had been in plain view for over a week, until that moment in the meeting I had not noticed that there was a series of vertical lines in the lower right-hand portion of the front of the envelope, markings which seemed to indicate that the letter had been part of a bulk mailing. I was taken aback by a distinct feeling of disappointment: the letter that had

---

2. Although, for convenience sake, I shall at times refer to the 'intersubjective analytic third' as 'the analytic third,' or simply 'the third,' this concept should not be confused with the oedipal symbolic third (the Lacanian [1953] 'name of the father'). The latter concept refers to a 'middle term' that stands between symbol and symbolised, between oneself and one's immediate lived sensory experience, thereby creating a space in which the interpreting, self-reflective, symbolising subject is generated. In early developmental terms, it is the father (or the 'father-in-the-mother,' Ogden, 1987) who intercedes between the mother and infant (or, more accurately, the mother-infant), thus creating the psychological space in which the elaboration of the depressive position and oedipal triangulation occurs.

arrived in the envelope was from a colleague in Italy, who had written to me about a matter that he felt was delicate and should be kept in strictest confidence between us.

I then looked at the stamps and for the first time noticed two further details. The stamps had not been cancelled, and one of the three stamps had words on it that to my surprise I could read. I saw the words 'Wolfgang Amadeus Mozart' and realised after a moment's delay that the words were a name with which I was familiar and were 'the same' in Italian as in English.

As I retrieved myself from this reverie, I wondered how this might be related to what was currently going on between myself and the patient. The effort to make this shift in psychological states felt like the uphill battle of attempting to 'fight repression' that I have experienced while attempting to remember a dream that is slipping away on waking. In years past, I have put aside such 'lapses of attention' and endeavoured to devote myself to making sense of what the patient was saying, since, in returning from such reveries, I am inevitably a bit behind the patient.

I realised that I was feeling suspicious about the genuineness of the intimacy that the letter had seemed to convey. My fleeting fantasy that the letter had been part of a bulk mailing reflected a feeling that I had been duped. I felt that I had been naive and gullible, ready to believe that I was being entrusted with a special secret. I had a number of fragmentary associations, which included the image of a mail sack full of letters with stamps that had not been cancelled, a spider's egg sac, *Charlotte's Web*, Charlotte's message on the cobweb, Templeton the rat, and innocent Wilbur. None of these thoughts seemed to scratch the surface of what was occurring between Mr L and myself: I felt as if I were simply going through the motions of countertransference analysis, in a way that seemed forced.

As I listened to Mr L, a 45-year-old director of a large non-profit-making agency, I was aware that he was talking in a way that was highly characteristic of him—he sounded weary and hopeless, and yet was doggedly trudging on with his production of 'free associations'. During the entire period of the analysis, Mr L had been struggling mightily to escape the confines of his extreme emotional detachment both from himself and from other people. I thought of his description of his driving up to the house in which he lives and not being able to feel it was *his* house. When he walked inside, he was greeted by 'the woman and four children who lived there', but could not feel they were *his* wife and *his* children. 'It's a sense of myself not being in the picture and yet I'm there. In that second of recognition of not fitting in, it's a feeling of being separate, which is right next to feeling lonely.'

I tried out in my own mind the idea that perhaps I felt duped by him and taken in by the apparent sincerity of his effort to talk to me; but this idea rang hollow to me. I was reminded of the frustration in Mr L's voice as he explained to me again and again that he knew that he must be feeling something, but he did not have a clue what it might be.

The patient's dreams were regularly filled with images of paralysed people, prisoners, and mutes. In a recent dream he had succeeded, after expending enormous energy, in breaking open a stone, only to find hieroglyphics carved into the interior of the stone (like a fossil). His initial joy was extinguished by his recognition that he could not understand a single element of the meaning of the hieroglyphics. In the dream, his discovery was momentarily exciting, but ultimately an empty, painfully tantalising experience that left him in deep despair. Even the feeling of despair was almost immediately obliterated upon awakening and became a lifeless set of dream images that he 'reported' to me (as opposed to telling to me). The dream had become a sterile memory and no longer felt alive as a set of feelings.

I considered the idea that my own experience in the hour might be thought of as a form of projective identification in which I was participating in the patient's experience of despair at being unable to discern and experience an inner life that seemed to lie behind an impenetrable barrier. This formulation made intellectual sense, but felt clichéd and emotionally lacking. I then drifted into a series of narcissistic, competitive thoughts concerning professional matters, which began to take on a ruminative quality. These ruminations were unpleasantly interrupted by the realisation that my car, which was in a repair shop, would have to be collected before 6:00 P.M., when the shop closed. I would have to be careful to end the last analytic hour of the day at precisely 5:50 P.M. if there were to be any chance at all of my getting to the garage before it closed. In my mind, I had a vivid image of myself standing in front of the closed garage doors with the traffic roaring behind me. I felt an intense helplessness and rage (as well as some self-pity) about the way in which the owner of the garage had shut his doors at precisely 6:00 P.M., despite the fact that I had been a regular customer for years and he knew full well that I would need my car. In this fantasied experience, there was a profound, intense feeling of desolation and isolation, as well as a palpable physical sensation of the hardness of the pavement, the smell of the stench of the exhaust fumes, and the grittiness of the dirty glass garage-door windows.

Although at the time I was not fully conscious of it, in retrospect I can better see that I was quite shaken by this series of feelings and images, which had begun with my narcissistic/competitive ruminations and had ended with the fantasies of impersonally ending the hour of my last patient of the day and then being shut out by the owner of the garage.

As I returned to listening in a more focused way to Mr L, I laboured to put together the things that he was currently discussing: his wife's immersion in her work and the exhaustion that both he and his wife felt at the end of the day; his brother-in-law's financial reversals and impending bankruptcy; an experience while jogging, in which the patient was involved in a near accident with a motorcyclist who was riding recklessly. I could have taken up any one of these images as a symbol of the themes that we had previously discussed, including the very detachment that seemed to permeate all that the patient was talking about, as well as the disconnection I felt both from him and from myself. However, I decided not to intervene, because it felt to me that if I were to try to offer an interpretation at this point I would only be repeating myself and saying something for the sake of reassuring myself that I had something to say.

The phone in my office had rung earlier in the meeting and the answering machine had clicked twice to record a message before resuming its silent vigil. At the time of the call, I had not consciously thought about who might be calling, but at this point in the hour I checked the clock to see how much longer it would be before I could retrieve the message. I felt relieved to think of the sound of a fresh voice on the answering-machine tape. It was not that I imagined finding a specific piece of good news; it was more that I yearned for a crisp, clear voice. There was a sensory component to the fantasy—I could feel a cool breeze wash across my face and enter my lungs relieving the suffocating stillness of an overheated, unventilated room. I was reminded of the fresh stamps on the envelope—clear, vibrant in their colours, unobscured by the grim, mechanical, indelible scarring of machine-made cancellation marks.

I looked again at the envelope and noticed something that I had been only subliminally aware of all along: my name and address had been typed on a manual typewriter—not a computer, not a labelling machine, not even an electric typewriter. I felt almost joyous about the personal quality with which my name had been 'spoken.' I could almost hear the idiosyncratic irregularities of each typed letter: the inexactness of the line, the way in which each 't' was missing its upper portion above the bar. This felt to me like the accent and inflection of a human voice speaking *to me*, knowing my name.

These thoughts and feelings, as well as the sensations associated with these fantasies, brought to mind (and body) something that the patient had said to me months earlier, but subsequently had not mentioned. He had told me that he felt closest to me not when I said things that seemed right, but when I made mistakes, when I got things wrong. It had taken me these months to understand in a fuller way what he had meant when he had said this to me. At that point in the meeting, I began to be able to describe for myself the feelings of desperateness that I had been feeling in my own and the patient's frantic search for something human and personal in our work together. I also began to feel that I understood something of the panic, despair and anger associated with the experience of colliding again and again with something that appears to be human, but feels mechanical and impersonal.

I was reminded of Mr L's description of his mother as 'brain dead.' The patient could not remember a single instance of her ever having shown any evidence of feeling anger or an intense feeling of any sort. She immersed herself in housework and 'completely uninspired cooking'. Emotional difficulties were consistently met with platitudes. For example, when the patient, as a 6-year-old, was terrified each night that there were creatures under his bed, his mother would tell him, 'There's nothing there to be afraid of.' This statement became a symbol in the analysis of the discord between the accuracy of the statement, on the one hand (there were, in fact, no creatures under his bed), and, on the other, the unwillingness/inability of his mother to recognise the inner life of the patient (there was something he was frightened of that she refused to acknowledge, identify with or even be curious about).

Mr L's chain of thoughts—which included the idea of feeling exhausted, his brother-in-law's impending bankruptcy, and the potentially serious or even fatal accident—now struck me as a reflection of his unconscious attempts to talk to me about his inchoate feeling that the analysis was depleted, bankrupt, and dying. He was experiencing the rudiments of a feeling that he and I were not talking to one another in a way that felt alive; rather, I seemed to him unable to be other than mechanical with him, just as he was unable to be human with me.

I told the patient that I thought that our time together must feel to him like a joyless obligatory exercise, something like a factory job where one punches in and out with a time card. I then said that I had the sense that he sometimes felt so hopelessly stifled in the hours with me that it must have felt like being suffocated in something that appears to be air, but is actually a vacuum.

Mr L's voice became louder and fuller in a way that I had not heard before as he said, 'Yes, I sleep with the windows wide open for fear of suffocating during the night. I often wake up terrified that someone is suffocating me as if they have put a plastic bag over my head.' The patient went on to say that when he walked into my consulting room, he regularly felt that the room was too warm and that the air was disturbingly still. He said that it had never once occurred to him to ask me either to turn off the heater at the foot of the couch or to open a window, in large part because he had not been fully aware until then that he had had such feelings. He said that it was terribly discouraging to realise how little he allowed himself to know about what was going on inside of him, even to the point of not knowing when a room felt too warm to him.

Mr L was silent for the remaining fifteen minutes of the session. A silence of that length had not previously occurred in the analysis. During that silence, I did not feel pressured to talk. In fact, there was a considerable feeling of repose and relief in the respite from what I now viewed as the 'anxious mentation' that had so often filled the hours. I became aware of the tremendous effort that Mr L and I regularly expended in an effort to keep the analysis from collapsing into despair: I imagined the two of us in the past frantically trying to keep a beach ball in the air, punching it from one to the other. Toward the end of the hour, I became drowsy and had to fight off sleep.

The patient began the next meeting by saying that he had been awakened by a dream early that morning. In the dream *he was underwater and could see other people, who were completely naked. He noticed that he too was naked, but he did not feel self-conscious about it. He was holding his breath and felt panicky that he would drown when he could no longer hold his breath. One of the men, who was obviously breathing underwater without diffculty, told him that it would be okay if he breathed. He very warily took a breath and found that he could breathe. The scene changed, although he was still underwater. He was crying in deep sobs and was feeling a profound sadness. A friend, whose face he could not make out, talked to him. Mr L said that he felt grateful to the friend for not trying to reassure him or cheer him up.*

The patient said that when he awoke from the dream he felt on the verge of tears. He said he had got out of bed because he just wanted to feel what he was feeling, although he did not know what he was sad about. Mr L noticed the beginnings of his familiar attempts to change the feeling of sadness into feelings of anxiety about office business or worry about how much money he had in the bank, or other matters with which he 'distracts' himself.

Discussion

The foregoing account was offered not as an example of a watershed in an analysis, but rather in an effort to convey a sense of the dialectical movement of subjectivity and intersubjectivity in the analytic setting. I have attempted to describe something of the way in which my experience as an analyst (including the barely perceptible and often extremely mundane background workings of my mind) are contextualised by the intersubjective experience created by analyst and analysand. No thought, feeling or sensation can be considered to be the same as it was or will be outside of the context of the specific (and continually shifting) intersubjectivity created by analyst and analysand.[3]

I would like to begin the discussion by saying that I am well aware that the form in which I have presented the clinical material was a bit odd, in that I give almost no information of the usual sort about Mr L until rather late in the presentation. This was done in an effort to convey a sense of the degree to which Mr L was at times quite absent from my conscious thoughts and feelings. My attention was not at all focused on Mr L during these periods of 'reverie' (I use Bion's term *reverie* to refer not only to those psychological states that clearly reflect the analyst's active receptivity to the analysand, but also to a motley collection of psychological states that seem to reflect the analyst's narcissistic self-absorption, obsessional rumination, daydreaming, sexual fantasising, and so on).

Turning to the details of the clinical material itself as it unfolded, my experience of the envelope (in the context of this analysis) began with my noticing the envelope, which, despite the fact that it had been physically present for weeks, at that moment came to life as a psychological event, a carrier of psychological meanings, that had not existed prior to that moment. I view these new meanings not simply as a reflection of a

---

3. What I have said here about the analyst's thoughts and feelings being in every instance contextualised, and therefore altered, by the experience with the patient might seem to lead to the conclusion that everything the analyst thinks and feels should be considered countertransference. However, I believe the use of the term *countertransference* to refer to everything the analyst thinks and feels and experiences sensorially, obscures the simultaneity of the dialectic of oneness and twoness, of individual subjectivity and intersubjectivity that is the foundation of the psychoanalytic relationship. To say that everything the analyst experiences is countertransference is only to make the self-evident statement that we are each trapped in our own subjectivity. For the concept of countertransference to have more meaning than this, we must continually re-ground the concept in the dialectic of the analyst as a separate entity and the analyst as a creation of the analytic intersubjectivity. Neither of these 'poles' of the dialectic exists in pure form and our task is to make increasingly full statements about the specific nature of the relationship between the experience of subject and object, between countertransference and transference at any given moment.

lifting of a repression within me; rather, I understand the event as a reflection of the fact that a new subject (the analytic third) was being generated by (between) Mr L and myself, which resulted in the creation of the envelope as an 'analytic object' (Bion, 1962; Green, 1975). When I noticed this 'new object' on my table, I was drawn to it in a way that was so completely ego-syntonic as to be an almost completely unselfconscious event for me. I was struck by the machine-made markings on the envelope, which again had not been there (for me) up to this point: I experienced these markings for the first time in the context of a matrix of meanings having to do with disappointment about the absence of a feeling of being spoken to in a way that felt personal. The uncancelled stamps were similarly 'created' and took their place in the intersubjective experience that was being elaborated. Feelings of estrangement and foreignness mounted to the point where I hardly recognised Mozart's name as a part of a 'common language'.

A detail that requires some explanation is the series of fragmentary associations having to do with *Charlotte's Web*. Although highly personal and idiosyncratic to my own life experience, these thoughts and feelings were also being created anew within the context of the experience of the analytic third. I had consciously known that *Charlotte's Web* was very important to me, but the particular significance of the book was not only repressed, but had also not yet come into being in such a way that it would exist in this hour. It was not until weeks after the meeting being described that I became aware that this book was originally (and was in the process of becoming) intimately associated with feelings of loneliness. I realised for the first time (in the following weeks) that I had read this book several times during a period of intense loneliness in my childhood, and that I had thoroughly identified with Wilbur as a misfit and outcast. I view these (largely unconscious) associations to *Charlotte's Web* not as a recollection of a memory that had been repressed, but as the creation of an experience (in and through the analytic intersubjectivity) that had not previously existed in the form that it was now taking. This conception of analytic experience is central to the current paper: the analytic experience occurs on the cusp of the past and the present, and involves a 'past' that is being created anew (for both analyst and analysand) by means of an experience generated between analyst and analysand (i.e. within the analytic third).

Each time my conscious attention shifted from the experience of 'my own' reveries to what the patient was saying and how he was saying it to me and being with me, I was not 'returning' to the same place I had left seconds or minutes earlier. In each instance, I was changed by the experience of the reverie, sometimes only in an imperceptibly small way. In the course of the reverie just described, something had occurred that is in no way to be considered magical or mystical. In fact, what occurred was so ordinary, so unobtrusively mundane, as to be almost unobservable as an analytic event.

When I refocused my attention on Mr L after the series of thoughts and feelings concerning the envelope, I was more receptive to the schizoid quality of his experience and to the hollowness of both his and my own attempts to create something together that felt real. I was more keenly aware of the feeling of arbitrariness associated with his sense of his place in his family and in the world, as well as the feeling of emptiness associated with my own efforts at being an analyst for him.

I then became involved in a second series of self-involved thoughts and feelings (following my only partially satisfactory attempt to conceptualise my own despair and that of the patient in terms of projective identification).[4] My thoughts were interrupted by anxious fantasies and sensations concerning the closing of the garage and my need to end the last analytic hour of the day 'on time'. My car had been in the garage the entire day, but it was only with Mr L at precisely that moment that the car as analytic object was created. The fantasy involving the closing of the garage was created at that moment not by me in isolation, but through my participation in the intersubjective experience with Mr L. Thoughts and feelings concerning the car and the garage did not occur in any of the other analytic hours in which I participated during that day.

In the reverie concerning the closing of the garage and my need to end the last analytic hour of the day 'on time', the experience of bumping up against immovable mechanical inhumanness in myself and others was repeated in a variety of forms. Interwoven with the fantasies were sensations of hardness (the pavement, glass and grit) and suffocation (the exhaust fumes). These fantasies generated a sense of anxiety and urgency within me that was increasingly difficult for me to ignore (although in the past I might well have dismissed these fantasies and sensations as having no significance for the analysis except as an interference to be overcome).

'Returning' to listening to Mr L, I was still feeling quite confused about what was occurring in the session and was sorely tempted to say something to dissipate my feelings of powerlessness. At this point, an

---

4. I believe that an aspect of the experience I am describing can be understood in terms of projective identification, but the way in which it was utilised, at the point when it arose, was predominantly in the service of an intellectualising defence.

event that had 'occurred' earlier in the hour (the phone call recorded by the answering machine), occurred for the first time as an analytic event (that is, as an event that held meaning within the context of the inter-subjectivity that was being elaborated). The 'voice' recorded on the answering-machine tape now held the promise of being the voice of a person who knew me and would speak to me in a personal way. The physical sensations of breathing freely and suffocating were increasingly important carriers of meaning. The envelope became a still different analytic object from the one that it had been earlier in the hour: it now held meaning as a representation of an idiosyncratic, personal voice (the hand-typed address with an imperfect 't').

The cumulative effect of these experiences within the analytic third led to the transformation of something the patient had said to me months earlier about feeling closest to me when I made mistakes. The patient's statement took on new meaning, but I think it would be more accurate to say that the (remembered) statement was now a new state-ment for me, and in this sense was being made for the first time.

At this point in the hour, I began to be able to use language to describe for myself something of the experience of confronting an aspect of another person, and of myself, that felt frighteningly and irrevocably inhuman. A number of the themes that Mr L had been talking about now took on a coherence for me that they had not held before: the themes now seemed to me to converge on the idea that Mr L was experiencing me and the discourse between us as bankrupt and dying. Again, these 'old' themes were now (for me) becoming new ana-lytic objects that I was encountering freshly. I attempted to talk to the patient about my sense of his experience of me and the analysis as mechanical and inhuman. Before I began the intervention, I did not consciously plan to use the imagery of machines (the factory and the time clock) to convey what I had in mind; I was unconsciously draw-ing on the imagery of my reveries concerning the mechanical (clock-determined) ending of an analytic hour and the closing of the garage. I view my 'choice' of imagery as a reflection of the way in which I was 'speaking from' the unconscious experience of the analytic third (the unconscious intersubjectivity being created by Mr L and myself). At the same time, I was speaking *about* the analytic third from a position (as analyst) outside of it.

I went on in an equally unplanned way to tell the patient of an image of a vacuum chamber (another machine), in which something that appeared to be life-sustaining air was, in fact, emptiness (here, I was unconsciously drawing on the sensation-images of the fantasised expe-rience of exhaust-filled air outside the garage and the breath of fresh air associated with the answering-machine fantasy).[5] Mr L's response to my intervention involved a fullness of voice that reflected a fullness of breathing (a fuller giving and taking). His own conscious and unconscious feelings of being foreclosed from the human had been experienced in the form of images and sensations of suffocation at the hands of the killing mother/analyst (the plastic bag [breast] that prevented him from being filled with life-sustaining air).

The silence at the end of the hour was in itself a new analytic event and reflected a feeling of repose that stood in marked contrast to the image of being violently suffocated in a plastic bag or of feeling disturbingly stifled by the still air in my consulting room. There were two additional aspects of my experience during this silence that held significance: the fantasy of a beach ball being frantically kept aloft by being punched between Mr L and myself, and my feeling of drowsiness. Although I felt quite soothed by the way in which Mr L and I were able to be silent together (in a combination of despair, exhaustion and hope), there was an element in the experience of the silence (in part, reflected in my somnolence) that felt like faraway thunder (which I retrospectively view as warded-off anger).

I shall only comment briefly on the dream with which Mr L opened the next hour. I understand it as simultaneously a response to the previous hour and the beginnings of a sharper delineation of an aspect of the transference-countertransference, in which Mr L's fear of the effect of his anger on me and of his homosexual feelings toward me were becoming predominant anxieties (earlier on, I had had clues about these, which I had been unable to use as analytic objects, e.g. the image and sensation of roaring traffic behind me in my garage fantasy).

In the first part of the dream, *the patient was underwater with other naked people, including a man who told him that it would be alright to breathe, despite his fear of drowning. As he breathed, he found it hard to believe he was really able to do so.* In the second part of Mr L's dream, *he was sobbing with sadness while a man, whose face he could not make out, stayed with him but did not try to cheer him up.* I view this dream as in part an expression of Mr L's feeling that in the previous hour the two of us had together experienced, and begun to better understand, something important about his unconscious ('underwater')

---

5. It was in this indirect way (i.e. in allowing myself to draw freely upon my unconscious experience with the patient in constructing my interventions) that 'I told' the patient about my own experience of the analytic third. This indirect communication of the countertransference contributes in a fundamental way to the feeling of spontaneity, aliveness and authenticity of the analytic experience.

life and that I was not afraid of being overwhelmed (drowned) by his feelings of isolation, sadness and futility, nor was I afraid for him. As a result, he dared to allow himself to be alive (to inhale) that which he formerly feared would suffocate him (the vacuum breast/analyst). In addition, there was a suggestion that the patient's experience did not feel entirely real to him in that, in the dream, he found it hard to believe he was really able to do what he was doing.

In the second portion of Mr L's dream, he represented more explicitly his enhanced ability to feel his sadness in such a way that he felt less disconnected from himself and from me. The dream seemed to me to be in part an expression of gratitude to me for not having robbed the patient of the feelings he was beginning to experience, i.e. for not interrupting the silence at the end of the previous day's meeting with an interpretation or otherwise attempting to dissipate or even transform his sadness with my words and ideas.

I felt that, in addition to the gratitude (mixed with doubt) that Mr L was experiencing in connection with these events, there were less acknowledged feelings of ambivalence toward me. I was partly alerted to this possibility by my own drowsiness at the end of the previous hour, which often reflects my own state of defendedness. The fantasy of punching the beach ball (breast) suggested that it might well be anger that was being warded off. Subsequent events in the analysis led me to feel increasingly convinced that the facelessness of the man in the second portion of the dream was in part an expression of the patient's (maternal transference) anger at me for being so elusive as to be shapeless and nondescript (as he felt himself to be). This idea was borne out in the succeeding years of analysis as Mr L's anger with me for 'being nobody in particular' was directly expressed. In addition, on a more deeply unconscious level, the patient's being invited by the naked man to breathe in the water reflected what I felt to be an intensification of Mr L's unconscious feeling that I was seducing him into being alive in the room with me in a way that often stirred homosexual anxiety (represented by the naked man's encouraging Mr L to take the shared fluid into his mouth). The sexual anxiety reflected in this dream was not interpreted until much later in the analysis.

Some Additional Comments

In the clinical sequence described above, it was not simply fortuitous that my mind 'wandered' and came to focus on a machine-made set of markings on an envelope covered by scribblings of phone numbers, notes for teaching and reminders about errands that needed to be done. The envelope itself, in addition to carrying the meanings already mentioned, also represented (what had been) my own private discourse, a private conversation not meant for anyone else; written on it were notes in which I was talking to myself about the details of my life. The workings of the analyst's mind during analytic hours in these unself-conscious, 'natural' ways are highly personal, private and embarrassingly mundane aspects of life that are rarely discussed with colleagues, much less written about in published accounts of analysis. It requires great effort to seize this aspect of the personal and the everyday from the unself-reflective area of reverie for the purpose of talking to ourselves about the way in which this aspect of experience has been transformed such that it has become a manifestation of the interplay of analytic subjects. The 'personal' (the individually subjective) is never again simply what it had been prior to its creation in the intersubjective analytic third, nor is it entirely different from what it had been.

I believe that a major dimension of the analyst's psychological life in the consulting room with the patient takes the form of reverie concerning the ordinary, everyday details of his own life (that are often of great narcissistic importance to him). In this clinical discussion, I have attempted to demonstrate that these reveries are not simply reflections of inattentiveness, narcissistic self-involvement, unresolved emotional conflict, and the like; rather, this psychological activity represents symbolic and proto-symbolic (sensation-based) forms given to the unarticulated (and often not yet felt) experience of the analysand as they are taking form in the intersubjectivity of the analytic pair (i.e. in the analytic third).

This form of psychological activity is often viewed as something that the analyst must get through, put aside, overcome, etc. in his effort to be both emotionally present with and attentive to the analysand. I am suggesting that a view of the analyst's experience that dismisses this category of clinical fact leads the analyst to diminish (or ignore) the significance of a great deal (in some instances, the majority) of his experience with the analysand. I feel that a principal factor contributing to the undervaluation of such a large portion of the analytic experience is the fact that such acknowledgement involves a disturbing form of selfconsciousness. The analysis of this aspect of the transference-countertransference requires an examination of the way we talk to ourselves and what we talk to ourselves about in a private, relatively-undefended psychological state. In this state, the dialectical interplay of consciousness and unconsciousness has been altered in ways that resemble a dream state. In becoming self-conscious in this way, we are tampering with an essential inner sanctuary of privacy, and therefore with one of the cornerstones of our sanity. We are treading on sacred ground, an area of personal isolation in which, to a large extent, we are communicating with subjective objects (Winnicott, 1963; see also Ogden, 1991). This communication (like the notes to myself on the envelope) are not meant for anyone else, not even for aspects of ourselves that lie outside of this exquisitely-private/mundane 'cul-de-sac' (Winnicott, 1963, p. 184). This realm of transference-countertransference experience is so personal, so ingrained in the character structure of the analyst, that it requires great psychological effort to enter into a discourse with ourselves in a way that is required to recognise that even this aspect of the personal has been altered by our experience in and of the analytic third. If we are to be analysts in a full sense, we must self-consciously attempt to bring even this aspect of ourselves to bear on the analytic process.

The Psyche-Soma and the Analytic Third

In the following section of this paper, I will present an account of an analytic interaction in which a somatic delusion experienced by the analyst, and a related group of bodily sensations and body-related fantasies experienced by the analysand, constituted a principal medium through which the analytic third was experienced, understood, and interpreted. As will become evident, the conduct of this phase of the analysis depended on the analyst's capacity to recognise and make use of a form of intersubjective clinical fact manifested largely through bodily sensation/fantasy.

Clinical Illustration: The Tell-Tale Heart

In this clinical discussion, I shall describe a series of events that occurred in the third year of the analysis of Mrs B, a 42-year-old, married lawyer and mother of two latency-aged children. The patient had begun analysis for reasons that were not clear to either of us; she had felt vague discontent with her life, despite the fact that she had 'a wonderful family' and was doing well in her work. She told me that she never would have guessed that she would have 'ended up in an analyst's office': 'It feels like I've stepped out of a Woody Allen film'.

The first year-and-a-half of analysis had a laboured and vaguely unsettling feeling to it. I was puzzled by why Mrs B was coming to her daily meetings and was a bit surprised each day when she appeared. The patient almost never missed a meeting, was rarely late and, in fact, arrived early enough to use the lavatory in my office suite prior to almost every meeting.

Mrs B spoke in an organised, somewhat obsessional but thoughtful way: there were always 'important' themes to discuss, including her mother's jealousy of even small amounts of attention paid to the patient by her father. Mrs B felt that this was connected with current difficulties such as her inability to learn ('take things in') from female senior partners at work. Nonetheless, there was a superficiality to this work and as time went on it seemed to require greater and greater effort for the patient to 'find things to talk about.' The patient talked about not feeling fully present in the meetings, despite her best efforts to 'be here.'

By the end of the second year of analysis, the silences had become increasingly frequent and considerably longer in duration, often lasting fifteen to twenty minutes (in the first year, there had rarely been a silence). I attempted to talk with Mrs B about what it felt like for her to be with me in a given period of silence. She would reply that she felt extremely frustrated and stuck, but was unable to elaborate. I offered my own tentative thoughts about the possible relationship between a given silence and the transference-countertransference experience that might have immediately preceded the silence or perhaps been left unresolved in the previous meeting. None of these interventions seemed to alter the situation.

Mrs B repeatedly apologised for not having more to say and worried that she was failing me. As the months passed, there was a growing feeling of exhaustion and despair associated with the silences and with the overall lifelessness of the analysis. The patient's apologies to me for this state of affairs continued, but became increasingly unspoken and were conveyed by her facial expression, gait, tone of voice, etc. In addition, at this juncture in the analysis, Mrs B also began to wring her hands throughout the analytic hours, and yet more vigorously during the silences. She pulled strenuously on the fingers of her hands and deeply kneaded her knuckles and fingers to the point that her hands became reddened in the course of the hour.

I found that my own fantasies and day-dreams were unusually sparse during this period of work. I also noticed that I experienced less of a feeling of closeness to Mrs B than I would have expected. One morning while driving to my office, I was thinking of the people I would be seeing that day and could not remember Mrs B's first name. I rationalised that I had recorded only her last name in my appointment book and never addressed her by her first name—nor did she ever mention her first name in talking about herself, as many patients do. I imagined myself as a mother unable to give her baby a name after its birth as a result of profound ambivalence concerning the birth of the baby. Mrs B had told me very little about her parents and her childhood. She said that it was terribly important to her that she tell me about her parents in a way that was both 'fair and accurate'. She said that she would tell me about them when she found the right way and the right words to do so.

During this period I developed what I felt to be a mild case of the flu, but was able to keep my appointments with all of my patients. In the weeks that followed, I noticed that I continued to feel physically unwell during my meetings with Mrs B, experiencing feelings of malaise, nausea and vertigo. I felt like a very old man and, for reasons I could not understand, I took some comfort in this image of myself, while at the same time deeply resenting it. I was not aware of similar feelings and physical sensations during any other parts of the day. I concluded that this reflected a combination of the fact that the meetings with Mrs B must have been particularly draining for me and that the long periods of silence in her meetings allowed me to be more self-conscious of my physical state than I was with other patients.

In retrospect, I am able to recognise that during this period I began to feel a diffuse anxiety during the hours with Mrs B. However, at the time I was only subliminally aware of this anxiety and was hardly able to differentiate it from the physical sensations I was experiencing. Just before my sessions with Mrs B, I would regularly find things to do, such as making phone calls, sorting papers, finding a book, etc., all of which had the effect of delaying the moment when I would have to meet the patient in the waiting room. As a result, I was occasionally a minute or so late in beginning the hours.

Mrs B seemed to look at me intently at the beginning and end of each hour. When I asked her about it, she apologised and said that she was not aware of doing so. The content of the patient's associations had a sterile, highly controlled feeling to it and centred on her difficulties at work and worries about the emotional troubles that she felt her children might be having—she brought her older child for a consultation with a child psychiatrist because of her worry that he could not concentrate well enough in school. I commented that I thought Mrs B was worried about her own value as a mother just as she was worried about her value as a patient (this interpretation was partially correct, but failed to address the central anxiety of the hour because, as I will discuss, I was unconsciously defending against recognising it).

Soon after I made the intervention concerning the patient's self-doubts concerning her value as a mother and analysand, I felt thirsty and leaned over in my chair to take a sip from a glass of water that I keep on the floor next to my chair (I had on many occasions done the same thing during Mrs B's hours, as well as with other patients). Just as I was reaching for the glass, Mrs B startled me by abruptly (and for the first time in the analysis) turning around on the couch to look at me. She had a look of panic on her face and said, 'I'm sorry, I didn't know what was happening to you.'

It was only in the intensity of this moment, in which there was a feeling of terror that something catastrophic was happening to me, that I was able to name for myself the terror that I had been carrying for some time. I became aware that the anxiety I had been feeling and the (predominantly unconscious and primitively symbolised) dread of the meetings with Mrs B (as reflected in my procrastinating behaviour) had been directly connected with an unconscious sensation/fantasy that my somatic symptoms of malaise, nausea and vertigo were caused by Mrs B, and that she was killing me. I now understood that for several weeks I had been emotionally consumed by the unconscious conviction (a 'fantasy in the body', Gaddini, 1982, p. 143) that I had a serious illness, perhaps a brain tumour, and that during that period I had been frightened that I was dying. I felt an immense sense of relief at this point in the meeting as I came to understand these thoughts, feelings and sensations as reflections of transference-countertransference events occurring in the analysis. In response to her turning to me in fright, I said to Mrs B that I thought she had been afraid that something terrible was happening to me and that I might even be dying. She said that she knew it sounded crazy, but when she heard me moving in my chair she became filled with the feeling that I was having a heart attack. She added that she had felt that I had looked ashen for some time, but she had not wanted to insult me or worry me by saying so (Mrs B's capacity to speak to me about her perceptions, feelings, and fantasies in this way reflected the fact that a significant psychological shift had already begun to take place).

While this was occurring, I realised that it was me whom Mrs B had wanted to take to see a doctor, not her older child. I recognised that the interpretation that I had given earlier in the hour about her self-doubt had been considerably off the mark, and that the anxiety about which the patient was trying to tell me was her fear that something catastrophic was occurring between us (that would kill one or both of us) and that a third person (an absent father) must be found to prevent the disaster from occurring. I had often moved in my chair during Mrs B's hours, but it was only at the moment described above that the noise of my movement became an 'analytic object' (a carrier of intersubjectively-generated analytic meaning) that had not previously existed. My own and the patient's capacity to think as separate individuals had been co-opted by the intensity of the shared unconscious fantasy/somatic delusion in which we were both enmeshed. The unconscious fantasy reflected an important, highly-conflicted set of Mrs B's unconscious internal object relationships, which were being created anew in the analysis in the form of my somatic delusion in conjunction with her delusional fears (about my body) and her own sensory experiences (e.g. her hand-wringing).

I told Mrs B that I felt that not only was she afraid that I was dying, but that she was also afraid that she was the direct and immediate cause. I said that just as she had worried that she was having a damaging effect on her son and had taken him to a doctor, so she was afraid that she was making me so ill that I would die. At this point, Mr B's hand-wringing and finger-tugging subsided. I realised then, as Mrs B began to use hand movements as an accompaniment to her verbal expression, that I could not recall ever having seen her hands operate separately (i.e. neither touching one another, nor moving in a rigid, awkward way). The patient said that what we were talking about felt true to her in an important way, but she was worried that she would forget everything that had happened in our meeting that day.

Mrs B's last comment reminded me of my own inability to remember her first name and my fantasy of being a mother unwilling to acknowledge fully the birth of her baby (by not giving it a name). I now felt that the ambivalence represented by my own act of forgetting and the associated fantasy (as well as Mrs B's ambivalence, represented in her anxiety that she would obliterate all memory of this meeting) reflected a fear, jointly held by Mrs B and myself, that allowing her 'to be born' (i.e. to become genuinely alive and present) in the analysis would pose a serious danger to both of us. I felt that we had created an unconscious fantasy (largely generated in the form of bodily experience) that her coming to life (her birth) in the analysis would make me ill and could possibly kill me. For both our sakes, it was important that we make every effort to prevent that birth (and death) from occurring.

I said to Mrs B that I thought I now understood a little better why she felt that, despite every effort on her part, she could not feel present here with me and had increasingly not been able to think of anything to say. I told her that I thought she was attempting to be invisible in her silence, as if she were not actually here and that she hoped that in so doing she would be less of a strain on me and keep me from becoming ill.

She responded that she was aware that she apologised to me continually and that at one point she had felt so fed up with herself that she felt, but did not say to me, that she was sorry that she had ever 'got into this thing' (the analysis) and wished she could 'erase it, make it never have happened.' She added that she thought that I would be better off too, and she imagined that I was sorry that I had ever agreed to work with her. She said that this was similar to a feeling that she had had for as long as she could remember. Although her mother repeatedly assured her that she had been thrilled to be pregnant with her and had looked forward to her birth, Mrs B felt convinced that she had 'been a mistake' and that her mother had not wanted to have children at all. Mrs B's mother had been in her late thirties and her father in his mid-forties when the patient was born; she was an only child and, as far as she knew, there were no other pregnancies. Mrs B told me that her parents were very 'devoted' people, and she therefore felt extremely unappreciative for saying so, but her parents' home did not feel to her to be a place for children. Her mother kept all the toys in Mrs B's room so that her father, a 'serious academic,' would not be disturbed as he read and listened to music in the evenings and on weekend afternoons.

Mrs B's behaviour in the analysis seemed to reflect an immense effort to behave 'like an adult' and not to make an emotional mess of 'my home' (the analysis) by strewing it with irrational or infantile thoughts, feelings, or behaviour. I was reminded of her comments in the opening meeting about the foreignness and sense of unrealness that she felt in my office (feeling that she had stepped out of a Woody Allen film). Mrs B had unconsciously been torn between her need to get help from me and her fear that the very act of claiming a place for herself with me (in me) would deplete or kill me. I was able to understand my fantasy (and associated sensory experiences) of having a brain tumour as a reflection of an unconscious fantasy that the patient's very existence was a kind of growth that greedily, selfishlessly and destructively took up space that it had no business occupying.

Having told me about her feelings about her parents' home, Mrs B reiterated her concern that she would present an inaccurate picture of her parents (particularly her mother), leading me to see her mother in a way that did not accurately reflect the totality of who she was. However, the patient added that saying this felt more reflexive than real this time.

During these exchanges, for the first time in the analysis, I felt that there were two people in the room talking to one another. It seemed to me that not only was Mrs B able to think and talk more fully as a living human being, but that I also felt that I was thinking, feeling, and experiencing sensations in a way that had a quality of realness and spontaneity of which I had not previously been capable in this analysis. In retrospect, my analytic work with Mrs B to this point had sometimes felt to me to involve an excessively dutiful identification with my own analyst (the 'old man'). I had not only used phrases that he had regularly used, but also at times spoke with an intonation that I associated with him. It was only after the shift in the analysis just described that I fully recognised this. My experience in the phase of analytic work being discussed had 'compelled me' to experience the unconscious fantasy that the full realisation of myself as an analyst could occur only at the cost of the death of another part of myself (the death of an internal object analyst/father). The feelings of comfort, resentment and anxiety associated with my fantasy of being an old man reflected both the safety that I felt in being like (with) my analyst/father and the wish to be free of him (in fantasy, to kill him). The latter wish carried with it the fear that I would die in the process. The experience with Mrs B, including the act of putting my thoughts, feelings and sensations into words, constituted a particular form of separation and mourning of which I had not been capable up to that point.

Concluding Comments on the Concept of the Analytic Third

In closing, I will attempt to bring together a number of ideas about the notion of the analytic third that have been developed either explicitly or implicitly in the course of the two foregoing clinical discussions.

The analytic process reflects the interplay of three subjectivities: that of the analyst, of the analysand, and of the analytic third. The analytic third is a creation of the analyst and analysand, and at the same time the analyst and analysand (*qua* analyst and analysand) are created by the analytic third (there is no analyst, no analysand, and no analysis in the absence of the third).

As the analytic third is experienced by analyst and analysand in the context of his or her own personality system, personal history, psychosomatic make-up, etc. the experience of the third (although jointly created) is not identical for each participant. Moreover, the analytic third is an asymmetrical construction because it is generated in the context of the analytic setting, which is powerfully defined by the relationship of roles of analyst and analysand. As a result, the unconscious experience of the analysand is privileged in a specific way, i.e. it is the past and present experience of the analysand that is taken by the analytic pair as the principal (although not exclusive) subject of the analytic discourse. The analyst's experience in and of the analytic third is, primarily, utilised as a vehicle for the understanding of the conscious and unconscious experience of the analysand (the analyst and analysand are not engaged in a democratic process of mutual analysis).

The concept of the analytic third provides a framework of ideas about the interdependence of subject and object, of transference–countertransference, that assists the analyst in his efforts to attend closely to, and think clearly about, the myriad of intersubjective clinical facts he encounters, whether they be the apparently self-absorbed ramblings

of his mind, bodily sensations that seemingly have nothing to do with
the analysand, or any other 'analytic object' intersubjectively generated
by the analytic pair.

References

Atwood, G. & Stolorow, R. (1984). *Structures of Subjectivity: Explorations in Psychoanalytic Phenomenology*. Hillsdale, NJ: Analytic Press.
Balint, M. (1968). *The Basic Fault*. London: Tavistock.
Bion, W. (1952). Group dynamics: a review. In *Experiences in Groups*. New York: Basic Books, 1959, pp. 141–192.
—— (1959). Attacks on linking. *Int. J. Psychoanal.*, 40:308–315.
—— (1962). *Learning from Experience*. New York: Basic Books.
Blechner, M. (1992). Working in the countertransference. *Psychoanal. Dialogues*, 2:161–179.
Bollas, C. (1987). *The Shadow of the Object: Psychoanalysis of the Unthought Known*. New York: Columbia Univ. Press.
Boyer, L. B. (1961). Provisional evaluation of psychoanalysis with few parameters in the treatment of schizophrenia. *Int. J. Psychoanal.*, 42:389–403.
—— (1983). *The Regressed Patient*. New York: Jason Aronson.
—— (1992). Roles played by music as revealed during countertransference-facilitated transference regression. *Int. J. Psychoanal.*, 73:55–70.
—— (1993). Countertransference: history and clinical issues. In *Master Clinicians on Treating the Regressed Patient, Volume 2*, ed. L. B. Boyer & P. L. Giovacchini. Northvale, NJ: Jason Aronson, pp. 1–22.
Coltart, N. (1986). 'Slouching towards Bethlehem' . . . or thinking the unthinkable in psychoanalysis. In *The British School of Psychoanalysis: The Independent Tradition*, ed. G. Kohon. New Haven: Yale Univ. Press, pp. 185–199.
Eliot, T. S. (1919). Tradition and individual talent. In *Selected Essays*. New York: Harcourt, Brace and World, 1960, pp. 3–11.
Etchegoyen, R. H. (1991). *The Fundamentals of Psychoanalytic Technique*. London: Karnac.
Ferenczi, S. (1920). The further development of an active therapy in psychoanalysis. In *Further Contributions to the Theory and Technique of Psychoanalysis*. New York: Brunner Mazel, 1980, pp. 198–217.
Gabbard, G. (1991). Technical approaches to transference hate in the analysis of borderline patients. *Int. J. Psychoanal.*, 72:625–639.
Gaddini, E. (1982). Early defensive phantasies and the psychoanalytic process. In *A Psychoanalytic Theory of Infantile Experience: Conceptual and Clinical Reflections*. London and NewYork: Routledge, 1992, pp. 142–153.
Giovacchini, P. (1979). *Treatment of Primitive Mental States*. New York: Jason Aronson.
Green, A. (1975). The analyst, symbolization and absence in the analytic setting. (On changes in analytic practice and analytic experience.) *Int. J. Psychoanal.*, 56:122.

Grinberg, L. (1962). On a specific aspect of countertransference due to the patient's projective identification. *Int. J. Psychoanal.*, 43:436–440.

Grotstein, J. (1981). *Splitting and Projective Identification*. New York: Jason Aronson.

Heimann, P. (1950). On counter-transference. *Int. J. Psychoanal.*, 31:81–84.

Hoffman, I. (1992). Some practical implications of a social-constructivist view of the psychoanalytic situation. *Psychoanal. Dialogues*, 2:287–304.

Jacobs, T. (1991). *The Use of the Self: Countertransference and Communication in the Analytic Setting*. Madison, CT: Int. Univ. Press.

Joseph, B. (1982). Addiction to near death. *Int. J. Psychoanal.*, 63:449–456.

Kernberg, O. (1976). *Object-Relations Theory and Clinical Psychoanalysis*. New York: Jason Aronson.

────── (1985). *Internal World and External Reality*. Northvale, NJ: Jason Aronson.

Khan, M. M. R. (1974). *The Privacy of the Self*. New York: Int. Univ. Press.

Klein, M. (1946). Notes on some schizoid mechanisms. In *Envy and Gratitude and Other Works, 1946–1963*. New York: Delacorte, 1975, pp. 124.

────── (1955). On identification. In *Envy and Gratitude and Other Works 1946–1963*. New York: Delacorte, 1975, pp. 141–175.

Kohut, H. (1977). *The Restoration of the Self*. New York: Int. Univ. Press.

Lacan, J. (1953). The function and field of speech and language in psychoanalysis. In *Écrits: A Selection*, trans. A. Sheridan. London: Tavistock, 1977, pp. 30–113.

Little, M. (1951). Countertransference and the patient's response to it. *Int. J. Psychoanal.*, 32:3240.

McDougall, J. (1978). Countertransference and primitive communication. In *Plea for a Measure of Abnormality*. New York: Int. Univ. Press, pp. 247–298.

McLaughlin, J. (1991). Clinical and theoretical aspects of enactment. *J. Amer. Psychoanal. Asn.*, 39:595–614.

Meltzer, D. (1966). The relation of anal masturbation to projective identification. *Int. J. Psychoanal.*, 47:335–342.

Milner, M. (1969). *The Hands of the Living God*. London: Hogarth Press.

Mitchell, S. (1988). *Relational Concepts in Psychoanalysis: An Integration*. Cambridge, MA: Harvard Univ. Press.

Money-Kyrle, R. (1956). Normal countertransference and some of its deviations. *Int. J. Psychoanal.*, 37:360–366.

Ogden, T. (1979). On projective identification. *Int. J. Psychoanal.*, 60:357–373.

────── (1982). *Projective Identification and Psychotherapeutic Technique*. New York: Jason Aronson.

────── (1985). On potential space. *Int. J. Psychoanal.*, 66:129–141.

────── (1986). *The Matrix of the Mind: Object Relations and the Psychoanalytic Dialogue*. Northvale, NJ: Jason Aronson.

────── (1987). The transitional oedipal relationship in female development. *Int. J. Psychoanal.*, 68:485–498.

────── (1988). On the dialectical structure of experience: some clinical and theoretical implications. *Contemp. Psychoanal.*, 24:17–45.

——— (1989). *The Primitive Edge of Experience*. Northvale, NJ: Jason Aronson.

——— (1991). Some theoretical comments on personal isolation. *Psychoanal. Dialogues*, 1:377–390.

——— (1992a). The dialectically constituted/decentred subject of psychoanalysis. I. The Freudian subject. *Int. J. PsychoanaL*, 73:517–526.

——— (1992b). The dialectically constituted/decentred subject of psychoanalysis. II. The contributions of Klein and Winnicott. *Int. J. Psychoanal.*, 73:613–626.

O'Shaughnessy, E. (1983). Words and working through. *Int. J. Psychoanal.*, 64:281–290.

Racker, H. (1952). Observaciones sobra la contratransferencia como instrumento clinico; communicación preliminar. *Rev. Psicoanal.*, 9:342–354.

——— (1968). *Transference and Countertransference*. New York: Int. Univ. Press.

Rosenfeld, D. (1992). *The Psychotic: Aspects of the Personality*. London: Karnac.

Rosenfeld, H. (1952). Notes on the psycho-analysis of the super-ego conflict of an acute schizophrenic patient. *Int. J. Psychoanal.*, 33:111–131.

——— (1965). *Psychotic States: A Psycho-Analytical Approach*. New York: Int. Univ. Press.

——— (1971). Contribution to the psychopathology of psychotic states: the importance of projective identification in the ego structure and the object relations of the psychotic patient. In *Problems of Psychosis*, ed. P. Doucet & C. Laurin. Amsterdam: Excerpta Medica, pp. 115–128.

Sandier, J. (1976). Countertransference and role responsiveness. *Int. Rev. Psychoanal.*, 3:43–47.

Scharff, J. (1992). *Projective and Introjective Identification and the Use of the Therapist's Self*. Northvale: NJ: Jason Aronson.

Searles, H. (1979). *Countertransference and Related Subjects*. New York: Int. Univ. Press.

Segal, H. (1981). *The Work of Hanna Segal: A Kleinian Approach to Clinical Practice*. New York: Jason Aronson.

Tansey, M. & Burke, W. (1989). *Understanding Countertransference: From Projective Identification to Empathy*. Hillsdale, NJ: Analytic Press.

Viderman, S. (1979). The analytic space: Meaning and problems. *Psychoanal. Q*, 4:257–291.

Winnicott, D. W. (1947). Hate in the countertransference. In *Through Paediatrics to Psychoanalysis*. New York: Basic Books, 1975, pp. 194–203.

——— (1951). Transitional objects and transitional phenomena. In *Playing and Reality*. New York: Basic Books, 1971, pp. 1–25.

——— (1960). The theory of the parent-infant relationship. In *The Maturational Processes and the Facilitating Environment*. New York: Int. Univ. Press, 1965, pp. 37–55

——— (1963). Communicating and not communicating leading to a study of certain opposites. In *The Maturational Processes and the Facilitating Environment*. New York: Int. Univ. Press, 1965, pp. 179–192.

Afterword

The Analytic Third: An Overview

In the five years since writing "The Analytic Third—Working with Intersubjective Clinical Facts," in large part through making clinical use of the concept, I have made some progress in becoming clearer with myself about what I mean when I use the term the intersubjective analytic third. I shall very briefly attempt to convey here a part of that enhanced understanding.

It seems to me that I use the term *analytic third* to refer to a third subject, unconsciously cocreated by analyst and analysand, which seems to take on a life of its own in the interpersonal field between them. This third subject stands in dialectical tension with the separate, individual subjectivities of analyst and analysand in such a way that the individual subjectivities and the third create, negate, and preserve one another. In an analytic relationship, the notion of individual subjectivity and the idea of a cocreated third subject are devoid of meaning except in relation to one another, just as the idea of the conscious mind is meaningless except in relation to the unconscious.

While both analyst and analysand participate in the creation and elaboration of the unconscious analytic third, they do so asymmetrically. The relationship of roles of analyst and analysand in the analytic relationship strongly privileges the exploration of the analysand's unconscious internal object world and forms of relatedness to external objects. This is a consequence of the fact that the analytic enterprise is most fundamentally a therapeutic relationship designed to facilitate the patient's efforts to make psychological changes that will enable him to live his life in a more fully human way. It is therefore the conscious and unconscious experience of the analysand that is the primary (but not exclusive) focus of analysis. The analytic third is not only asymmetrical in terms of the contributions of analyst and analysand to its creation, it is also asymmetrical in the way it is experienced by analyst and analysand: each experiences the analytic third in the context of his own separate personality system, his own particular ways of layering and linking conscious and unconscious aspects of experience, his own ways of experiencing and integrating bodily sensations, the unique history and development of his external and internal object relations, and so on. In short, the analytic third is not a single event experienced identically by two people; it is an unconscious, asymmetrical cocreation of analyst and analysand which has a powerful structuring influence on the analytic relationship.

The term analytic third, as I am using it, should not be equated with Lacan's (1977) *le nom de père* (the name of the father) which, as the representative of law, culture, and language, creates a space between mother and infant. For Lacan, with the introduction of language there is always a third: the chain of signifiers constituting the language with which we speak that mediates and gives order to the relationship of the subject to his lived sensory experience and to his relations with others. (There are, however, a great many ways in which the unconscious internal object father may play a critical role in the formation and function of the analytic third as I understand it.)

Neither am I using the term analytic third to denote a normal maturational progression in which mother and infant, analyst and patient, together create a third area of experiencing between reality and fantasy. The experience of the analytic third at times may overlap with, but is by no means synonymous with, Winnicott's (1951) notion of a generative potential space that is created between analyst and analysand when an analysis is going well.

Rather, I view the intersubjective analytic third as an ever-changing unconscious third subject (more verb than noun) that powerfully contributes to the structure of the analytic relationship. The analyst's and patient's experience in and of the analytic third spans the full range of human emotion and its attendant thoughts, fantasies, bodily sensations, and so on. The task of the analyst is to create conditions in which the unconscious intersubjective analytic third (which is always multilayered and multifaceted and continually on the move) might be experienced, attached to words and eventually spoken about with the analysand. However, this highly schematic description of the analysis of the analytic third obscures the enormous difficulty of the task. In my experience, the analyst's capacity to name and talk to himself about his experience of the analytic third almost always takes place after the fact, that is, after the analyst unwittingly (and often for a considerable period of time) has played a role in the specific experiential "shapes" reflecting the nature of the unconscious analytic third.

The possible experiential shapes (thoughts, feelings, sensations, fantasies, behaviors) generated by the influence of the analytic third on the analytic relationship are endless. For example, the influence of the analytic third might come to life in the form of acting-in or acting-out on the part of the analyst or the analysand or both; at other times, in the form of a somatic delusion on the part of the analyst (as in the second clinical example presented in my chapter); or, on still other occasions, almost entirely in the form of the analyst's reverie experiences (as in the first of the two clinical illustrations presented).

To make matters even more complex, the analytic third is at first almost entirely an unconscious phenomenon. Since the unconscious, by definition, cannot be invaded on the wings of the brute force of will, the analyst and analysand must use indirect (associational) methods to "catch the drift" (Freud, 1923, p. 239) of the unconscious cocreation. For the analyst, this means relying to a very large degree on "the foul rag-and-bone shop" (Yeats, 1936, p. 336) of his reverie experience (his mundane, everyday thoughts, feelings, ruminations, preoccupations, daydreams, bodily sensations, and so on). The analyst's use of his reverie experience requires tolerance of the experience of not knowing, of finding himself (or, perhaps more accurately, losing himself) adrift and apparently directionless. The emotional residue of a reverie experience is usually, at first, unobtrusive and inarticulate, an experience that is more a sense of dysphoric emotional disequilibrium than a sense of having arrived at an understanding. And yet the use of my reverie experience is the emotional compass on which I most heavily rely (but cannot clearly read) in my efforts to orient myself to what is happening in the analytic relationship in general and in the workings of the analytic third in particular.

The recognition and subsequent naming of one's experience in and of the analytic third involves psychological work on the part of the analyst in which he comes to sense that something is going on that both is created by analyst and analysand and simultaneously, in an important sense, is creating the analyst and analysand at that juncture in the analysis. The work of analyzing the experience of the analytic third involves gaining a sense of the nature and history of the unconscious fantasies, anxieties, defenses and object relations comprising the third cocreated "subject of analysis." While the use of my own reverie experience is an indispensable aspect of my analytic technique, when I eventually speak to the patient about what I sense is happening between us, I speak to the patient *from*, but infrequently *about*, my reverie experience (or about other forms of countertransference experience).

In analytic work conducted with a conception of the analytic third as part of one's theoretical framework, one makes one's way from experiential shapes (such as a patient's dream, the analyst's reveries, an enactment in which both patient and analyst have participated) toward an expanded sense of the fundamental nature of the third, i.e., that which renders "humanly understandable or humanly ununderstandable" (Jarrell, 1955, p. 62) the psychological purposes served by the experiential shapes that are generated and how (that is, according to what sense of self and the world) those shapes are linked with one another. Often, in my experience, the "third subject" is of a subjugating sort, which creates the effect of tyrannically limiting the range of thoughts, feelings, and bodily sensations "permissible" to both analyst and analysand. Under such circumstances, neither analyst nor analysand is able to experience himself or the other in terms outside of a very narrow band of (predominantly irrational) thoughts and feelings. At other times, the analytic third is of a perverse sort that has the effect of locking the analyst and patient into a specific, compulsively repeated perverse scenario. (See Ogden, 1997, for a discussion and clinical illustration of an analysis dominated by a perverse form of the analytic third.)

At still other times, the analytic third may be of a powerfully creative and enriching sort. Such forms of the analytic third are enlivening in the sense that "shapes" are generated in the analytic relationship (for instance, interesting, sometimes novel, forms of considering, dreaming, and fantasizing as well as richer and more fully human qualities of object relatedness marked, for example, by humor, compassion, playfulness, flirtatiousness, camaraderie, charm, love, and anger, which have "all the sense of real" [Winnicott, 1963, p. 184]).

Some forms of playing in the analytic setting involve an experience of the analytic third that might be thought of as an experience of the patient and analyst engaged in playing in the presence of the unconscious (jointly, but asymmetrically constructed) mother who facilitates the capacity of the child *to be* alone in her ("invisible," unobtrusive) presence (Winnicott, 1958). I place emphasis on the words "to be" because it is the experience of coming into being as an individual with one's own distinct and unique qualities that is of central importance in the experience of this form of the analytic third. One can see and feel and hear and smell and touch something *like* oneself in the activity of playing. This experience of playful symbol- and metaphor-making allows one to create symbols that give shapes and emotional substance (sensate "embodiments") to the self-as-object ("me") which serve as mirrors in which the self-as-subject ("I") recognizes/creates itself. Other forms of playing in the analytic relationship involve an unconscious experience of the father or the "father-in-the-mother" (Ogden, 1987), whose protectively watchful eye is felt to make safe, for example, oedipal flirtation between analyst and analysand. The creation of various forms of the analytic third which create and preserve conditions in which playing might safely occur evolves throughout the course of every analysis that is "a going concern" (to borrow Winnicott's apt phrase).

Many forms of the analytic third coexist at any moment of an analysis, some of which are pathological in the sense of limiting the range of human emotion and depth of object relatedness into which patient and analyst are able to enter. As analysis progresses, none of these pathological forms of the analytic third is "conquered" or eliminated any more than transferences are eliminated in the course of analysis (Loewald, 1960). Rather, as is the case with transferences, in the course of the analysis of a given form of pathological analytic third, the capacity of the third to timelessly hold the analytic pair hostage in a given, unchanging, unconscious form of relatedness (or unrelatedness) is gradually transmuted into forms of experience of self and other that can be preconsciously and consciously experienced, verbally symbolized, reflected on, spoken about, and incorporated into one's larger sense of self (including one's experience of and understanding of how one has come to be who one is and who one is becoming).

As I often find true, a poet, in this case A.R. Ammons, is able to convey/create in words what I can only talk about— "that stolid word *about*" (W. James, 1890, p. 246). The experience of engaging in the analysis of the analytic third is

> not so much looking for the shape
> As being available
> To any shape that may be
> Summoning itself
> Through me
> From the self not mine but ours.

> (Ammons, "Poetics," 1986)

References

Ammons, A. R. (1986), Poetics. In: *A. R. Ammons: The Selected Poems*. New York: Norton, p. 61.

Freud, S. (1923), Two encyclopaedia articles: A psycho-analysis. *Standard Edition*, 18:235–254. London: Hogarth Press, 1955.

James, W. (1890), *Principles of Psychology, Vol. 1.*, ed. P. Smith. New York: Dover, 1950.

Jarrell, R. (1955), *Poetry and the Age*. New York: Vintage.

Lacan, J. (1977), *Écrits: A Selection*, trans. A. Sheridan. New York: Norton.

Loewald, H. (1960), On the therapeutic action of psychoanalysis. In: *Papers on Psychoanalysis*. New Haven, CT: Yale University Press, 1980, pp. 221–256.

Ogden, T. (1987), The transitional oedipal relationship in female development. *Internat. J. Psycho-Anal.*, 68:485–498.

——— (1997), *Reverie and Interpretation: Sensing Something Human*. Northvale, NJ: Aronson.

Winnicott, D. W. (1951), Transitional objects and transitional phenomena. In: *Playing and Reality*. New York: Basic Books, 1971, pp. 1–25.

———— (1958), The capacity to be alone. In: *The Maturational Processes and the Facilitating Environment*. New York: International Universities Press, 1965, pp. 29–36.

———— (1963), Communicating and not communicating leading to a study of certain opposites. In: *The Maturational Processes and the Facilitating Environment*. New York: International Universities Press, 1965, pp. 170–192.

Yeats, W. B. (1936), The circus animals' desertion. In: *The Collected Poems of W. B. Yeats*. New York: Macmillan, 1966, pp. 335–336.

Index